CW01065090

THE HIDDEN ORIGINS OF THE GERMAN ENLIGHTENMENT

The early German Enlightenment is seen as a reform movement that broke free from traditional ties without falling into anti-Christian and extremist positions, on the basis of secular natural law, an antimetaphysical epistemology, and new social ethics. But how did the works which were radical and critical of religion during this period come about? And how do they relate to the dominant 'moderate' Enlightenment? Martin Mulsow offers fresh and surprising answers to these questions by reconstructing the emergence and dissemination of some of the radical writings created between 1680 and 1720. *The Hidden Origins of the German Enlightenment* explores the little-known freethinkers, persecuted authors, and secretly circulating manuscripts of the era, applying an interdisciplinary perspective to the German Enlightenment. By engaging with these cross-regional, clandestine texts, a dense and highly original picture emerges of the German early Enlightenment, with its strong links with the experience of the rest of Europe.

MARTIN MULSOW is Professor of Intellectual History at the University of Erfurt, where he is currently Director of the Gotha Research Center. An internationally renowned intellectual historian, he has been a member of the Institute for Advanced Study in Princeton and the Wissenschaftskolleg in Berlin. He is the author of more than ten monographs, winner of numerous awards, and member of several academies. His recent publications include *Enlightenment Underground: Radical Germany 1680–1720* (University of Virginia Press, 2015) and *Knowledge Lost: A New View of Early Modern Intellectual History* (Princeton University Press, 2022).

H. C. ERIK MIDELFORT, Professor Emeritus at the University of Virginia, has translated several works by noted German historians, including Bernd Moeller, Peter Blickle, and Wolfgang Behringer. Most recently he translated Martin Mulsow's book, *Knowledge Lost* (Princeton University Press, 2022).

IDEAS IN CONTEXT

Edited by DAVID ARMITAGE, RICHARD BOURKE
and JENNIFER PITTS

The books in this series will discuss the emergence of intellectual traditions and of related new disciplines. The procedures, aims, and vocabularies that were generated will be set in the context of the alternatives available within the contemporary frameworks of ideas and institutions. Through detailed studies of the evolution of such traditions, and their modification by different audiences, it is hoped that a new picture will form of the development of ideas in their concrete contexts. By this means, artificial distinctions between the history of philosophy, of the various sciences, of society and politics, and of literature may be seen to dissolve.

A full list of titles in the series can be found at: www.cambridge.org/IdeasContext

THE HIDDEN ORIGINS OF THE GERMAN ENLIGHTENMENT

MARTIN MULSOW

University of Erfurt

Translated by

H. C. ERIK MIDELFORT

University of Virginia

CAMBRIDGE
UNIVERSITY PRESS

Shaftesbury Road, Cambridge CB2 8EA, United Kingdom

One Liberty Plaza, 20th Floor, New York, NY 10006, USA

477 Williamstown Road, Port Melbourne, VIC 3207, Australia

314–321, 3rd Floor, Plot 3, Splendor Forum, Jasola District Centre, New Delhi – 110025, India

103 Penang Road, #05–06/07, Visioncrest Commercial, Singapore 238467

Cambridge University Press is part of Cambridge University Press & Assessment,
a department of the University of Cambridge.

We share the University's mission to contribute to society through the pursuit of
education, learning and research at the highest international levels of excellence.

www.cambridge.org
Information on this title: www.cambridge.org/9781009241151

DOI: 10.1017/9781009241168

© Martin Mulsow and H. C. Erik Midelfort 2023

This edition is a revised, expanded and updated translation of *Radikale Frühaufklärung in
Deutschland 1680–1720, volume 2*, published by Wallstein Verlag, Göttingen in 2018

First published 2023

A catalogue record for this publication is available from the British Library.

Library of Congress Cataloging-in-Publication Data
NAMES: Mulsow, Martin, author. | Midelfort, H. C. Erik, translator. | Mulsow, Martin. Radikale
Frühaufklärung in Deutschland 1680-1720. Band 2, Clandestine Vernunft.
TITLE: The hidden origins of the German Enlightenment / Martin Mulsow, University of Erfurt ;
translated by H.C. Erik Midelfort, University of Virginia.
OTHER TITLES: Radikale Frühaufklärung in Deutschland 1680-1720. Band 2, Clandestine
Vernunft. English
DESCRIPTION: First edition. | Cambridge, United Kingdom ; New York, NY, USA : Cambridge
University Press, 2023. | Series: Ideas in context | Includes bibliographical references and index.
IDENTIFIERS: LCCN 2022052987 (print) | LCCN 2022052988 (ebook) | ISBN 9781009241151
(Hardback) | ISBN 9781009241113 (Paperback) | ISBN 9781009241168 (epub)
SUBJECTS: LCSH: Enlightenment–Germany. | Underground literature–Europe–History and criticism.
| Philosophy, Modern–17th century. | Philosophy, Modern–18th century. | Philosophy, German. |
Europe–Intellectual life.
CLASSIFICATION: LCC B2621 .M873213 2023 (print) | LCC B2621 (ebook) | DDC 943/.044–dc23/
eng/20230421
LC record available at https://lccn.loc.gov/2022052987
LC ebook record available at https://lccn.loc.gov/2022052988

ISBN 978-1-009-24115-1 Hardback

Contents

Illustrations

Note on Translation

This is a translation of Martin Mulsow, *Radikale Frühaufklärung in Deutschland, 1680–1720*, vol. 2 (Göttingen, Wallstein Verlag, 2018), with a new introduction and conclusion. This version omits Chapter 6, which will appear later as a separate book. It also deletes most of the quotations contained in the footnotes. The items from the bibliography that are cited only in the now deleted Chapter 6 have been deleted.

Abbreviations

ADB = Allgemeine Deutsche Biographie, 56 vols., Leipzig, 1875–1912
DBA = Deutsches Biographisches Archiv, 1447 fiches, 1982–1985
HAB = Herzog August Bibliothek
TRE = Theologische Realenzyklopädie, 36 vols., 1976–2004

Introduction
A New History of the Beginnings of
the German Enlightenment

Theoretical constructions are only stable if they are based on solid knowledge of what lies underground.

Dirk Sangmeister[1]

1   The Familiar Story

We are familiar with the standard story about the origins of the Enlightenment in Germany. The Enlightenment supposedly began in the 1680s with Christian Thomasius and the University of Halle, founded in 1694, which became its first center. In Halle, Thomasius and his students developed a philosophy that was grounded in Samuel Pufendorf's ideas of natural law and drew on the sensualism of John Locke. Supported by various historical accounts, this philosophy saw itself as a Christian continuation of the achievements of the Lutheran Reformation. Radiating forth from Halle, it conquered most of the Protestant states of the Holy Roman Empire until it was superseded in the 1720s by the philosophy of Christian Wolff.

That story is not all wrong. This book, however, aims at setting a different narrative over against it, one that is polycentric, making the picture much more varied. This book therefore inquires into the individual circumstances in Germany that nourished more radical ideas than those cultivated by Thomasius and his students. Such radically Enlightened "moments" were rather rare, to be sure, and they did not prevail, at least not in the short run. But they also inform us of what sorts of things were thinkable in the late seventeenth and early eighteenth centuries, and how far, therefore, "Enlightened" thoughts might have gone. And by asking how *these* ideas arose, this book provides an account of the origins of the

---

[1] Dirk Sangmeister, *Vertrieben vom Feld der Literatur. Verbreitung und Unterdruückung der Werke von Friedrich Christian Laukhard*, Bremen, 2017, p. 16.

German Enlightenment that is totally different and more complex than the simple story centered on Halle. We will suddenly find that impulses deriving from many places and from entirely unexpected persons, from little noticed topics and hitherto neglected discussions, all played a role. In saying this, however, two things need to be emphasized.

First, the mainstream of the early Enlightenment in Halle – often described as a "moderate Enlightenment," to use the description of Jonathan Israel[2] – and the underground of the fragmented "radical Enlightenment" were mutually dependent on each other. Neither strand is really conceivable without the other. Radical Enlighteners, as we will see, often radicalized initiatives stemming from Halle; and many debates among well-established scholars were infiltrated by radical Enlighteners and "subverted." Like parasites they fed off the achievements of the great. And in contrast, moderate Enlighteners could better recognize through the efforts of radical mavericks the remarkable range of implications that lay hidden in many of their own theories, even if the scholars of Halle or elsewhere were not necessarily eager to embrace these implications. Repeatedly, even if it is often hard to recognize and to reconstruct, they reacted to these renegades. We could even go so far as to draw an analogy to the biological model of the food chain or food web, in which the cycle consists not only of the fact that eagles eat snakes, and snakes eat mice, but also of the fact that a reduction in the population of one species has mutual consequences for the population of other species, so that parasites and plants influence the balance of nature, and many other factors also play a role. Similarly the recording and circulation of "radical" ideas did not just consist of the absorption of other radical or proto-radical thoughts, for they were also embedded in a net of other writings and distributions. For example, did the "parasitic" freethinker develop his heterodox teachings by deviating from established theories, only to discover that he could not publish them or find that his book was confiscated and burned? That had the effect (or could have the effect) of branding his texts as infamous or heretical so that they were then sought after by connoisseurs of rare books and manuscripts – more for their rarity and their reputation than for their actual contents. Such texts were often preserved in the libraries of well-established collectors, but then copied out by hand and put back into

---

[2] Jonathan I. Israel, *Radical Enlightenment: Philosophy and the Making of Modernity, 1650–1750*, Oxford, 2001; Israel, *Enlightenment Contested: Philosophy, Modernity, and the Emancipation of Man, 1670–1752*, Oxford, 2006; Israel, *Democratic Enlightenment: Philosophy, Revolution, and Human Rights 1750–1790*, Oxford, 2011.

circulation again.[3] So ideas transmitted in this manner might then nourish independent minds again to draw innovative consequences from them, ideas that might well have firmer foundations than those of the original freethinker.[4]

Second, the approach chosen here displays just how thoroughly the early Enlightenment in Germany was woven into the intellectual life of Europe as a whole. It is precisely by seeing these origins in a polycentric fashion, as we will do here, that we can observe how the *concurrent* upswing of both West European and German debates, driven by both foreign and domestic authors, lent wings to the whole conversation: Pierre Bayle *and* Gottfried Arnold, Baruch Spinoza *and* Jakob Böhme, Robert Boyle *and* Johann Christoph Sturm all had an impact, but not just as individuals. German scholars found that they had to work hard to adapt foreign debates so as to produce similar but not identical initiatives domestically.

So in this sense I am pulling three hitherto relatively isolated areas of research together: (1) philosophical investigations into the history of the early Enlightenment in Germany; (2) international research into clandestine literature;[5] and (3) recent work on the European world of learning and the republic of letters. Only by combining them in this way have I been able to propose this new approach.[6]

However, the practices and forms of communication, the scholarly actors and their tactical efforts to position themselves in various contexts, also play a large role in shaping the sort of intellectual history to which this book is deeply indebted. Let me mention just three examples that have an

---

[3] To give just one example: Johann Christian Edelmann was delighted that collectors offered high prices to purchase his works because the police were hunting for them. These were regarded as books, according to Edelmann, that "God in his inscrutable wisdom has from time to time caused to be bought up for much money by their own enemies." Edelmann, *Moses mit aufgedecktem Angesicht*, s.l., 1740, pp. 33f.

[4] See Martin Mulsow, "Radikalaufklärung, moderate Aufklärung und die Dynamik der Moderne," in Jonathan I. Israel and Martin Mulsow, eds., *Radikalaufklärung*, Berlin, 2014, pp. 203–233.

[5] To give just a few references, see: Ira O. Wade, *The Clandestine Organization and Diffusion of Philosophic Ideas in France from 1700 to 1750*, Princeton, 1938; John S. Spink, *French Free-Thought from Gassendi to Voltaire*, London, 1960; Tullio Gregory et al., eds., *Ricerche su letteratura libertina e letteratura clandestina nel Seicento*, Florence, 1981; Anthony Mc Kenna and Alain Mothu, eds., *La philosophie clandestine à l'âge classique*, Oxford and Paris, 1997; Gianni Paganini, *Introduzione alle filosofie clandestine*, Bari, 2008. One word regarding terminology: "clandestine" comes from the Latin *clandestinus*, meaning secret, hidden, surreptitious. Instead of the German "*klandestin,*" I prefer "clandestine" in order to refer to the underground literature that French scholars have intensively studied as "littérature clandestine."

[6] See also the programmatic introduction to Martin Mulsow, *Enlightenment Underground: Radical Germany 1680–1720*, tr. H. C. Erik Midelfort, Charlottesville, 2015, pp. 1–28.

immediate relevance to the understanding of the early Enlightenment in
Germany. First is the thesis of Martin Gierl that it was Philipp Jakob
Spener's reform of the way in which Lutheran scholars argued (their
Streitkultur, their so-called *elenchus*) combined with changes in the book
trade that produced the new form of polemics found in Christian
Thomasius, a polemics that emphasized public openness, scholarly competition, and *historia literaria*.[7] Second is Hermann Jaumann's discovery
that the rise of the market for journals led to a "temporalization" of
scholarship (fixing it more firmly in time), which decisively changed the
structure of scholarship and gave a new meaning to criticism.[8] And third is
Ian Hunter's contention that the various philosophies of the
Enlightenment (like those of Thomasius and Wolff) embodied incom-
mensurable styles, one that emphasized a politically and socially engaged
scholarship that separated religion from politics and theology from philosophy, while the other was metaphysical and demanded the continued
unity of these areas.[9]

The many different origins of the German Enlightenment were also
connected, as this book will show, to different practices, tactics, and actors.
Radical thinkers especially had to consider how they might try to spread
their ideas. Should they weave them into literary dialogues, conceal them
in footnotes, or disguise them in forms of joking? Or should they argue
straightforwardly but then give up hopes of publishing, which would have
been forbidden anyway, and instead rely on the secret distribution of
manuscript copies? Should they use pseudonyms or stand up for themselves under their real names? And how could they discover like-minded
readers, when the authors themselves had to hide?

Here is how this book will proceed: I approach the almost overwhelm-
ingly diverse intellectual landscape of the German and European early
Enlightenment by setting several separate surveying stakes, using some
barely known freethinkers and persecuted authors, some secretly circulating manuscripts, and a few largely ignored problems that were actually
centrally important around 1700. From these markers, working as a
detective, I will cut a path through the thickets of context, following
wherever the track leads. In order to comprehend our topic, it does not

[7] Martin Gierl, *Pietismus und Aufklärung. Theologische Polemik und die Kommunikationsreform der Wissenschaft am Ende des 17. Jahrhunderts*, Göttingen, 1997.
[8] Herbert Jaumann, *Critica. Untersuchungen zur Geschichte der Literaturkritik zwischen Quintilian und Thomasius*, Leiden, 1995.
[9] Ian Hunter, *Rival Enlightenments: Civil and Metaphysical Philosophy in Early Modern Germany*, Cambridge, 2001.

matter that I must sometimes transgress disciplinary boundaries, or that German circumstances sometimes lead me into English, Dutch, French, and Italian debates, or that the context requires me to pursue a topic into classical antiquity or into the Islamic world. By ranging back and forth through the disciplines, various sorts of text, and different regions, a dense picture gradually emerges, one that has never before been visible in this manner, a new image of the early Enlightenment in Germany intertwined with the rest of European thought. This is evident not least in the fact that certain actors and themes emerge repeatedly. And at the same time intellectual centers such as Leipzig, Berlin, Halle, Hamburg, Wittenberg, Helmstedt, Frankfurt on the Oder, Jena, and Königsberg come into focus, each with its own peculiarities; and the works of others, not just of radical thinkers, but of many prominent and not-so prominent scholars also emerge with their own peculiarities.

I began this enterprise in two earlier books. In *Enlightenment Underground* (2015) and in *Knowledge Lost* (2022).[10] This book will refer to them frequently. And this book expands on some of the persons and topics already treated in *Enlightenment Underground* with many new perspectives and much new research. In *Knowledge Lost* I emphasized the fragility of many radical initiatives that we discover in the early German Enlightenment, because such initiatives were almost always precarious: they lacked the stability that institutions offered; they were fragile, easily suppressed, and revocable. That was already true of its precursors, heterodox thinkers of the sixteenth century who usually expressed their ideas for reform in religious language and whose writings were often so thoroughly suppressed that hardly any trace of them survives.[11] But by 1700 the chances of survival were a bit better, or at least the chances of rediscovering fragments of such suppressed initiatives improve. In complex and unpredictable ways, as this volume demonstrates, such works had a demonstrable impact on the larger debates of the Enlightenment. Often they laid down challenges that established scholars felt they had to respond to; we can tell from such scholars' energetic reactions that at least some provocations could not be ignored.

---

[10] Mulsow, *Enlightenment Underground* (note 6); Martin Mulsow, *Knowledge Lost: A New View of Early Modern Intellectual History*, Princeton, 2022.

[11] One especially impressive example of this sort of precarious knowledge is the *libro grande* written in 1551 by the heretical Benedictine monk, Giorgio Rioli, who was condemned and murdered in Ferrara in 1551. Not a single copy of his work has survived. But note the reconstruction by Adriano Prosperi, *L'eresia del Libro Grande. Storia di Giorgio Siculo e della sua setta*, Milan, 2000.

2 The Early Enlightenment in Halle

The early Enlightenment in Halle has been described in many monographs and collections of articles although we do need an up-to-date and comprehensive account. This is especially true for the early years of the new University of Halle, which was not intended to be an "Enlightenment university," and was really supposed to hew to a "moderate" course like that of the University of Helmstedt, but those early years still await serious reappraisal.[12] In contrast, in part because of the publication of his correspondence, research into Christian Thomasius has now worked out several basic themes that permit us to recognize the approaches and teachings at Halle in the years around 1700.[13]

Even before the University of Halle was founded in 1694, Christian Thomasius, who was then still in Leipzig, had composed his *Institutiones iurisprudentiae divinae*, his textbook on natural law, and his programmatic work on "court philosophy," the *Introductio ad philosophiam aulicam*.[14] They revealed a philosophy which, in connection with the gallant cultural movement and with the princely state, intended a fundamental reform of university education. It soon became clear that this would be more easily achieved in Brandenburg and at a newly founded university than in Saxon Leipzig, where far too many established social groups could rally to defend their turf. An alliance with the court in Berlin also seemed attractive because Brandenburg needed an educational establishment for its rapidly growing class of jurists. Thomasius established a model that freed politics more completely from theology and religion than usual and where many

---

[12] But see Marianne Taatz-Jacobi, *Erwünschte Harmonie: Die Gründung der Friedrichs-Universität Halle als Instrument Brandenburg-Preußischer Konfessionspolitik – Motive, Verfahren, Mythos (1680–1713)*, Berlin, 2014.

[13] Christian Thomasius, *Briefwechsel. Historisch-kritischen Edition*, vol. 1: *1679–1692*, ed. Frank Grunert, Matthias Hambrock, and Martin Kühnel with the collaboration of Andrea Thiele, Berlin and Boston, 2017; vol. 2: *1693–1698*, ed. Frank Grunert, Matthias Hambrock, and Martin Kühnel, Berlin and Boston, 2020. The latest volume of the encyclopedia "the New Ueberweg" provides a canonical portrait: Helmut Holzhey and Vilem Mudroch, eds., *Grundriss der Geschichte der Philosophie*, vol 5: *Heiliges Römisches Reich Deutscher Nation. Schweiz. Nord- und Osteuropa*, Basel, 2014.

[14] Christian Thomasius, *Institutiones iurisprudentiae divinae*, Leipzig, 1688; Thomasius, *Introductio ad philosophiam aulicam*, Leipzig, 1688. Here let me mention only a few of the more recent works on him: Martin Kühnel, *Das politische Denken von Christian Thomasius: Staat, Gesellschaft, Bürger*, Berlin, 2001; Klaus-Gert Lutterbeck, *Staat und Gesellschaft bei Christian Thomasius*, Stuttgart, 2002; Thomas Ahnert, *Religion and the Origins of the German Enlightenment: Faith and the Reform of Learning in the Thought of Christian Thomasius*, Rochester, 2006; Ian Hunter, *The Secularisation of the Confessional State: The Political Thought of Christian Thomasius*, Cambridge, 2007; Francesco Tomasoni, *Christian Thomasius: Geist und kulturelle Identität an der Schwelle zur europäischen Aufklärung*, Münster, 2009.

long-engrained restraints could be relaxed in order to shape a new type of political subject: one characterized by independence, freedom, and responsible thinking.

In this vision, the task of the state was to provide civic peace while a university education aimed at turning young people into independent citizens. A basis for this was provided by a modernized natural law as explained by Samuel Pufendorf, who expanded on the thinking of Hugo Grotius. To this Thomasius added a strong psychological component, which required that students learn about real human beings and gain experience in dealing with human emotions.[15] According to Thomasius, human beings were mainly characterized by their will, which needed therefore to be guided in the proper direction.

Over time, as we know, Thomasius's view of mankind became bleaker and more pessimistic. In 1705 he revised his doctrine of natural law and set forth in his *Fundamenta juris naturae et gentium* a new interpretation that viewed people as determined by their drives, for the will was always seeking pleasure, money, or power. Only for brief intervals, if no driving forces were stirred up and there were no conflicting drives, could human beings think clearly. In a few men reason came to prevail – these were "wise" men. They were the only ones who could be moved by *consilia* – that is, by convictions derived from argument; the mass of men required *imperium*, domination, the commands and prohibitions enforced by punishments.[16]

Thomasius's idea of reason was sensualist and probably derived from the Aristotelianism of his father. Our understanding is constantly in danger of being deceived by prejudices. And Thomasius saw no need for any subtle syllogisms; they were not just superfluous but actually harmful. For him hermeneutics were more important; that is, a doctrine of understanding that dealt with probabilities and an orientation toward practice. He rejected metaphysics – his education had included only a rather mystical philosophy of spirit – and replaced it with *historia literaria*, the survey of the history of philosophy and of knowledge in search of the useful, along with an eclecticism that consisted of the practice of reasoned choice.[17]

[15] Ursula Geitner, *Die Sprache der Verstellung. Studien zum rhetorischen und anthropologischen Wissen im 17. und 18. Jahrhundert*, Tübingen, 1992. On these "psychological" components, see also Chapter 3 on the doctrine of temperaments.

[16] See Friedrich Vollhardt, ed., *Christian Thomasius (1655–1728). Neue Forschungen im Kontext der Frühaufklärung*, Tübingen, 1997.

[17] See Horst Dreitzel, "Zur Entwicklung und Eigenart der eklektischen Philosophie," *Zeitschrift für historische Forschung* 18 (1991), pp. 281–343; Michael Albrecht, *Eklektik. Eine Begriffsgeschichte mit Hinweisen auf die Philosophie- und Wissenschaftsgeschichte*, Stuttgart, 1994.

At the same time Thomasius adopted the German language and the latest media, such as the expanding market for journals. He developed an essayistic and journalistic style filled with a passion for polemics as he showed in his *Monatsgespräche* ("Monthly Conversations") and in countless controversial writings. Above all the "Enlightened" intentions behind his philosophy become clear if one looks at the targets he chose: he wrote against witchcraft trials; against torture; against superstition in general; against the mania for manufacturing heretics (*Ketzermacherei*); against prejudices; against fanaticism; against any blind trust in authority, especially that of the Church; against pedantry, sectarianism, and a sclerotic university philosophy that was thickly encased in scholasticism.[18]

It is no wonder these arguments provoked a multitude of antagonists, who entangled Thomasius in bitter battles. In Copenhagen Thomasius's books were publicly burned in 1691 after court preacher Hector Masius was attacked by Thomasius, who was consequently accused of atheism and a general lack of deference. And so Thomasius was clearly regarded as "radical." In addition he helped launch into the German book market such internationally recognized Enlightenment works as Balthasar Bekker's assault on belief in witchcraft. And yet, based on his actual views, Thomasius cannot be classified as a radical Enlightener, for he deliberately separated himself from radical admirers who, like his student Theodor Ludwig Lau, interpreted his ideas in an antichristian light.

The local issues that roiled the waters of Halle show up clearly in Thomasius's work. Although in the early 1690s he was drawn to the mysticism and Pietism of his colleague August Hermann Francke, he soon distanced himself from him – indeed, it came to an open break. And with other colleagues in the faculties of medicine, law, and theology, too, we can see a complex oscillation between collaboration and opposition. Even so, Thomasius was extremely successful. His charisma certainly helps explain the fact that within a few decades Halle rose to be the leading university in the whole German Empire. Philosophers and jurists at other institutions imitated him and his teachings, and many of his students took up professorial positions at other universities. Chapters 2, 3, and 4 will go into detail about the most important of these students: Andreas Rüdiger,

---

[18] Werner Schneiders, *Aufklärung und Vorurteilskritik. Studien zur Geschichte der Vorurteilstheorie*, Stuttgart, 1983; Martin Pott, *Aufklärung und Aberglaube. Die deutsche Frühaufklärung im Spiegel ihrer Aberglaubenskritik*, Tübingen, 1992. Norbert Hinske's article is also instructive: "Die tragenden Grundideen der deutschen Aufklärung. Versuch einer Typologie," in Raffaele Ciafardone, ed., *Die Philosophie der deutschen Aufklärung. Texte und Darstellung*, Stuttgart, 1990, pp. 407–458.

Nikolaus Hieronymus Gundling, and Johann Franz Budde. Gundling extended Thomasius's line of investigation into natural law; Budde preferred to deal with the less secularized *Institutiones iurisprudentiae divinae*, which he hoped to support through a skillful blending of philosophy and theology. These chapters will, however, demonstrate that the publications of such students become especially interesting if one brings them together with developments from other places. Only then does a more complete picture emerge.

3 Other Centers, Other Origins

Obviously with Halle and the Thomasius Circle one authoritative center had been created from which inspiration flowed out to the whole Empire. But the intellectual landscape in Germany – like its political landscape – was far too diverse to allow everything to be reduced to just one center. Steffen Martus has described the Old Empire as a complex political community, a legal and constitutional community, one of information, of social regulation (*Policey*), of military and defense, and finally an economic community.[19] Each of these connections followed its own logic, which affected what it meant to be "Enlightened" in any one of them. For example the city council of Hamburg followed entirely different motives in deciding whether and how to tolerate confessionally diverse immigrants. "Catholics were tolerated because of the emperor's protection; Jews for economic reasons; Calvinists because of their expert knowledge as merchants and because of their warm relations with Brandenburg Prussia."[20] Similarly, the Empire also had intellectual connections at the university level, among religious groups, among book dealers and collectors, as well as protest movements that were all different on the local level and all followed their own inner rationale. And then in addition there were the downstream consequences of these rationales, which sometimes led in entirely unintended directions.

In *Enlightenment Underground* I described several strands that contributed to the German Enlightenment. One of these strands began in the 1630s with the burlesque talks given by Johann Balthasar Schupp, inspired by Erasmus's *Praise of Folly*. His jocular and satiric tone acted as a model

---

[19] Steffen Martus, *Aufklärung. Das deutsche 18. Jahrhundert. Ein Epochenbild*, Berlin, 2015, pp. 198–216. And more fully, Joachim Whaley, *Germany and the Holy Roman Empire 1493–1806*, 2 vols., Oxford, 2012.
[20] Martus, *Aufklärung* (note 19), p. 213.

for libertine and eclectically minded imitators, such as the author of the *Ineptus religiosus* of 1652; Schupp's work provided a model for how one might jokingly bring unorthodox thoughts into play without actually committing oneself to them. But for Orthodox theologians this provoked the boogeyman of a *religio prudentum*, a religion of the so-called wise, of worldly opportunists. Just as in a complex food web with its often unpredictable interdependencies, around 1700 this boogeyman seems to have inspired certain young, freethinking students to regard the idea of a *religio prudentum*, seen through the lens of the fashionable eclectic philosophy that was making inroads at universities, not as abhorrent but as attractive.

Another paradoxical reaction can be located in the late 1680s in such centers of Lutheran Orthodoxy as Hamburg and Wittenberg. There it was especially the sons, grandsons, or sons-in-law of prominent Orthodox theologians who had become disgusted at the excessive confessional severity and narrow-mindedness of their seniors and therefore tried furtively to break free. In Hamburg it was Johann Joachim Müller, the son of a pastor, who half-jokingly but half-seriously rebelled by composing a manuscript, *De imposturis religionum*, in which he accused the three great founders of religion, Moses, Jesus, and Mohammed, of fraud. He skillfully used the latest ideas emerging from historical Pyrrhonism, natural law, and Oriental scholarship to prove his thesis. Such thoughts direct our attention to Helmstedt, where Hermann Conring was teaching a combination of reason of state and historical criticism, but also in the direction of Altdorf and Leipzig, where one could study rabbinic sources that could easily draw one into relativizing conclusions regarding the Christian worldview.

In this book Chapter 4 features another example in the son-in-law of a Wittenberg pastor, Georg Michael Heber, whose *Symbolum sapientiae* – if the attribution is correct – was no less radical than Müller's work; here the skepticism of French libertinism mixed with ideas drawn from Hobbes and Spinoza as well as legal theories of proof to undermine the belief in divine revelation, but also in any natural law theory based on the universality of reason and sociability.

So if we are seeking the origins of a *radical* Enlightenment, we do not have to consider only the familiar "centers of the Enlightenment"; instead we need to pay closer attention to the centers of heightened Orthodoxy, where secret discontents shifted over into clandestine protests.

Aside from such examples of "shifting," many places in Germany also displayed synergies that emerged from unexpected alliances, which, as soon as they were bound together, suddenly unfurled a great intellectual reach.

Such were the alliances, for example, of Jews (or sometimes even Muslims), Socinians, and Arminians, who all regarded the central Christian doctrine of the Trinity and the divinity of Christ with skepticism. Of course there were no open coalitions among these groups, who were all in awkward minority positions and were barely tolerated. And yet we cannot help noticing mutual borrowings from among these groups, so that the force of their arguments expanded exponentially. Ultimately it was sometimes deism or atheism that happily exploited these disputes by sweeping away the last vestiges of revealed theology, even though revelation remained essential for both Jews and Socinians.

In this book the trail of such coalitions leads also to Frankfurt on the Oder, where in the gray zone between Socinianism and Arminianism, a milieu took shape where radical ideas imported from Western Europe could penetrate – blending ideas from Gassendi, Hobbes, and Spinoza. But Berlin too, with its new colony of Huguenots, fostered a similar milieu.

A totally different sort of coalition can be discovered, however, on the opposing side: the side of emphatic defenders of the Trinity. These were not necessarily traditional theologians. No, especially in spiritualist circles during the 1680s an unusual creativity arose to produce intellectual proposals that understood the Trinity in speculative fashion. That clue leads us directly to Amsterdam, which was connected to cities of the Empire through countless German immigrants and visitors. In such circles scholars tried seriously to create syntheses of Jakob Böhme with the Cambridge Platonists, the Kabbalah, and Spinoza when interpreted in a Trinitarian manner. This will be the topic of my forthcoming book *Spinozism, Arianism, and Kabbalah*. We can speak here of a sort of analogous "apperception," a simultaneous perception that awoke a need to pull different images together.[21] In the book I will argue that this perception called forth a common "thinking space" (*Denkraum*) in which the most highly diverse theorists could communicate with one another, even if they lived far from one another (e.g., on a manor in Magdeburg or in an island

---

[21] I am here using the concept that Wolfgang Proß developed using the terminology of phenomenology in his article: "'Natur,' Naturrecht und Geschichte. Zur Entwicklung der Naturwissenschaften und der sozialen Selbstinterpretation im Zeitalter des Naturrechts (1600–1800)," *Internationales Archiv für Sozialgeschichte der deutschen Literatur* 3 (1978), pp. 38–67, here at pp. 47f. and 57–60. See Martin Mulsow, *Spinozism, Arianism, and Kabbalah: Unexpected Conjunctions in German Intellectual History of the Late Seventeenth Century. With the Addition of an Unknown Attempt at Rewriting Spinoza's Ethics by Johann Georg Wachter (1704)* (forthcoming). This is an extended version of chapter VI of *Radikale Frühaufklärung in Deutschland*, vol. 2.

community on the Polish border) – far from Enlightenment centers such as Halle. But even these isolated actors of a spiritualistic bent developed "radical" proposals that over the eighteenth century had barely noticed but long-term effects.

Halle was also not the only center for the network of natural scientists who followed the lead of Descartes, Boyle, or Huygens and pursued their own discussions, which also had implications for the Enlightenment. Among them was Leibniz in Hanover, Tschirnhaus in Dresden, Sturm in Altdorf, and many others, some of whom had official positions at a princely court. The court was also where one might find cameralists and project developers, who worked tirelessly to combine science, technology, and economy effectively, even if traditional religious notions were left by the wayside.[22] Often the writings of such people exuded an air of amazing self-confidence. For example, Christian Gabriel Fischer, whom we will get to know in Chapter 2, announced a new empirical program in Königsberg and set forth a theology that fit this program. Theodor Ludwig Lau, who was also from Königsberg and who made appearances in both *Enlightenment Underground* and *Knowledge Lost*, was a reformer in the finance office but also a thinker who cultivated portions of deist philosophy. But Urban Gottfried Bucher, who stands at the center of Chapter 1 of this book, also gained the self-confidence to express his theses regarding the nonsubstantiality of the soul from the support of Tschirnhaus and other natural scientists. To be sure, with Bucher we are back in Halle but, as we will see, also in Wittenberg and Dresden, and his impact was felt in Jena and Leipzig as well. Intellectually, the German Empire was a varied patchwork.[23] For a student, the rich diversity of stimuli available as he moved about from Wittenberg to Halle, from Leipzig to Altdorf, or from Frankfurt on the Oder to Kiel, could have large implications for his thinking and writing. Here again, analogous apperception.

The case of Peter Friedrich Arpe, whom I have treated in *Knowledge Lost*, points to other strands that contributed to the Enlightenment in Germany. In Arpe we find a naturalism that extended from religion to physics and ethics – and did not shrink from even displaying sympathies for "natural magic." His naturalism was accompanied by a deep skepticism and also by a connoisseurship concerning old traditions that had been forgotten or lay under a taboo. Arpe, who came of age in Kiel, Hamburg,

---

[22] See Pamela H. Smith, *The Business of Alchemy: Science and Culture in the Holy Roman Empire*, Princeton, 1994.
[23] For an introduction, see Engelhard Weigl, *Schauplätze der deutschen Aufklärung*, Hamburg, 1997.

and Copenhagen, continued a project that Gabriel Naudé had begun in France at the time of Richelieu: a learned "libertine" form of Enlightenment inflected by stoicism and skepticism. This was an Enlightenment that did not aim for publicity but was intended for only a small circle of the learned.

I characterized my working method in *Enlightenment Underground* as a kind of "philosophical microhistory." This requires following even the smallest clues in an effort to perceive a social context that has not hitherto been studied by historians. Microhistorians have called these findings examples of the "exceptional normal": the topics and locations in these contexts may appear to be peripheral, but illuminating them allows us to see that they actually belong to a more complete image of the Enlightenment, and thus to the "normal."[24] Perfect examples of philosophical microhistory can be found in studies of the circulation of ideas that follow the spread of clandestine manuscripts. Every single copyist who obtained such a manuscript and copied it, perhaps changing it, perhaps using it for his own purposes, is interesting in his own right because he gives us access to the considerations and motives and the range of expectations and thoughts available to these actors. In *Enlightenment Underground*, for example, I reconstructed the distribution of a Jewish-Portuguese manuscript that attacked Christianity, and I detected reverberations that had a direct effect on the radical Enlightenment in Germany. In this book, too, in Chapter 7 we will deal with a clandestine work entitled *De Josepho Christi parente naturali meditatio*, in which Jesus was regarded as completely natural, with two human parents – which had major theological consequences. Here again Jewish polemics clearly played a role, as did the already mentioned mutual reinforcement from the reliance on both Jewish and Socinian arguments.

The places where we find the "exceptional normal" lie at the origins of the German Enlightenment and were extremely diverse, as we can see just from this short synopsis. Surprisingly they were often places where the Orthodox were dominant; or they were areas of contact (as in Berlin and Frankfurt on the Oder) where different confessions and currents overlapped and collided; they were small and remote islands and territories in which both the heterodox and spiritualists managed to find refuge; or princely courts where, in contrast to the universities, there was space for thinking about economics and technology; and they included foreign

---

[24] Carlo Ginzburg and Carlo Poni, "Was ist Mikrogeschichte?," *Geschichtswerkstatt* 6 (1985), pp. 48–52.

metropolises such as Amsterdam and Copenhagen, where German travelers could come in contact with foreign ideas and publications.

In any case if we let these sorts of clues to lead us into such unknown milieus, it is necessary to ignore disciplinary boundaries – they will not constrain us. Such disciplinary borders during the "polyhistorical" epoch around 1700 were much more fluid than they are today and a single scholar might be a linguist, cameralist, alchemist, and theologian, all at once. But it was also often precisely such intellectual transgressions from one area into another that brought forth new ideas and turned many a thinker into a "radical." If the natural scientist Fischer did theology, if the philosopher Rüdiger reflected on ancient Egyptian religion, if the theologian Wachter read Spinoza in a new manner, or if the historian and jurist Gundling spoke of medicine – one might regularly expect extraordinary results. Therefore this book makes an unconstrained *tour d'horizon* across the disciplines. It touches on physics, and medicine, psychology and Oriental studies, jurisprudence and historiography – and of course, constantly, philosophy and theology, those central disciplines throughout the transition from the age of the baroque to the Enlightenment.[25]

4 Jonathan Israel's *Radical Enlightenment*

The whole topic of the radical Enlightenment came to worldwide attention through the four-volume study of Jonathan Israel, which began in 2001 with *Radical Enlightenment* and then continued in 2006 with *Enlightenment Contested*. In 2011 came *Democratic Enlightenment* and in 2019 *The Enlightenment that Failed*.[26] This tetralogy was augmented by two other books on the great revolutions within the Enlightenment, *Revolutionary Ideas* (2014) on the French and *Expanding Blaze* (2017) on the American Revolution and their impact.[27] Six volumes containing almost 6,000 pages provide an impressive overview of the radical currents

---

[25] One can also understand this transition as the conceptual complement to the transformation from a society organized according to stratification to one that emphasizes social functions. See Niklas Luhmann, *Gesellschaftsstruktur und Semantik. Studien zur Wissenssoziologie der modernen Gesellschaft*, 4 vols., Frankfurt and Berlin, 1980–1999.

[26] Israel, *Radical Enlightenment* (note 2); *Enlightenment Contested: Philosophy, Modernity, and the Emancipation of Man, 1670–1752*, Oxford, 2006; *Democratic Enlightenment: Philosophy, Revolution, and Human Rights 1750–1790*, Oxford, 2011; *The Enlightenment that Failed: Ideas, Revolution, and Democratic Defeat, 1748–1830*, Oxford, 2019.

[27] Jonathan I. Israel, *Revolutionary Ideas: An Intellectual History of the French Revolution from the Rights of Man to Robespierre*, Princeton, 2014; *Expanding Blaze: How the American Revolution Ignited the World, 1775–1848*, Princeton, 2017.

in the eighteenth century and their political consequences. I regard the
main contribution of these books to be their grasp of the radical
Enlightenment as a pan-European phenomenon. Before Israel there were
mostly only descriptions restricted to individual countries and cultures: on
France, the Netherlands, England, or Germany. But Israel added a view of
countries such as Italy, Belgium, Spain, Portugal, Ireland, Greece, Russia,
and the Baltic lands, and in most of these nations Israel took on the sources
and relevant research literature in their original languages. Before Israel,
only Franco Venturi and John G. A. Pocock had provided similarly
monumental and transnational descriptions, but without the focus on
the radical fringes and not with a fully encyclopedic range of geographic
coverage.[28] Indeed, with *Democratic Enlightenment, The Expanding Blaze,*
and *The Enlightenment that Failed*, he has expanded the view to the
worldwide impact of the European Enlightenment in Spanish America,
Haiti and among the Amerindians, in Dutch Southeast Asia, India, China,
and Japan.[29]

Regardless of their undoubted merits, however, these books have something problematic about them.[30] One can see that clearly, for example, in
his treatment of the radical early Enlightenment in Germany. In *Radical
Enlightenment*, chapter 29, there is a treatment of "Germany and the
Baltic: The 'War of the Philosophers,'" which describes the controversies
surrounding Christian Wolff before Israel arrives, in chapter 34, at a fuller
discussion the German situation ("Germany: The Radical *Aufklärung*").
This description follows exactly the pattern of the basic system underlying
Israel's work. It tries to show the influence of Spinoza and of early Dutch
Spinozism on Germany because Israel's fundamental thesis is this: that the
radical Enlightenment stemmed from Spinoza and spread from the
Netherlands across all of Europe. This is how Israel treats Ehrenfried
Walther von Tschirnhaus, Friedrich Wilhelm Stosch, Johann Georg
Wachter, Theodor Ludwig Lau, Johann Lorenz Schmidt, and Johann

---

[28] Franco Venturi, *Settecento riformatore*, 6 vols., Turin, 1969–1990; John G. A. Pocock, *Barbarism and Religion*, 6 vols. so far, Cambridge, 1999–2015.

[29] On these volumes, see Martin Mulsow, "Jonathan Israel als Globalhistoriker der Aufklärung" (forthcoming).

[30] I do will not list all the critics of Israel's work here, but will confine myself to citing just a few: Siep Stuurman, "Pathways to the Enlightenment: From Paul Hazard to Jonathan Israel," *History Workshop Journal* 54 (2002), pp. 227–235; Anthony J. La Vopa, "A New Intellectual History? Jonathan Israel's Enlightenment," *The Historical Journal* 52 (2009), pp. 717–738; Antoine Lilti, *L'heritage des lumières. Ambivalences de la modernité*, Paris, 2019, pp. 223–257. For my own critique, see Mulsow, "Radikalaufklärung, moderate Aufklärung und die Dynamik der Moderne" (note 4).

Christian Edelmann. This is the customary canon of German "free-thinkers," as German research dating back to the 1960s and 1970s treated them, but for an international readership these names were mostly new, and it was a real service that they now came to much wider attention.

The problem is just that, as Winfried Schröder clearly demonstrated in 1987, it is false and misleading to follow the old theological verdicts and depict all of these thinkers simply as Spinozists.[31] For one thing, according to Schröder, when one looks more closely, Spinoza was only one influence among many because most of them eclectically pulled extremely diverse inspirations together. But second, Spinoza's system did away with absolute norms and hence created a barrier to its general reception; in Spinoza there were no normative ethical categories and no natural law in a true sense, so reformers who followed Pufendorf and Thomasius found it unappealing to draw on Spinoza. And so Schröder comes to the conclusion that, "The vanishingly small number of those who adopted any elements from the system of the *Ethics*, and the complete absence of imitative disciples let alone of any Spinozan 'school', and perhaps more importantly the fact that the central goals of the early Enlightenment were opposed to even a more or less selective reception [of Spinoza] all provoke doubts about the role often ascribed to Spinoza as a trailblazer of the Enlightenment."[32]

Schröder's conclusion set up an obstacle to Israel's approach from the very beginning, and *Radical Enlightenment* does not really succeed in coping with it at all. For that reason in *Enlightenment Contested* Israel starts over again and presents a more complex approach to the German radical Enlightenment, taking the contributions of Winfried Schröder, Ursula Goldenbaum, and me into account. This is in chapter 7, devoted to "Germany and the Baltic: Enlightenment, Society, and the Universities." This more complex approach consists of a combination of at least three aspects. First, Israel considers the writings of theologians and of the then-current academic enterprise aimed against "freethinkers" and "atheists." He finds that in this literature Spinoza was regarded as the downright ideal opponent and that one could therefore speak of an "academically constructed 'princeps' of atheism."[33] So here Spinoza himself is no longer a direct or central influence on the freethinkers (in this Israel now accommodates Schröder and me), but an imagined prototype constructed and presented by Spinoza's opponents in their analysis of the dangers that beset them. Second, Israel now describes the freethinkers,

---

[31] Winfried Schröder, *Spinoza in der deutschen Frühaufklärung*, Würzburg, 1987.
[32] Ibid., pp. 178f.   [33] Israel, *Enlightenment Contested* (note 26), p. 180.

whom he had already dealt with in *Radical Enlightenment*, in a more differentiated fashion. He now concedes a multiplicity of influences, but still remains vague about what these influences were and in general insists on the centrality of the inspiration of Spinoza. Third, he expands his earlier descriptions, for example by considering the *Symbolum sapientiae* and Gabriel Wagner, by a new evaluation of Johann Lorenz Schmidt, but also by a treatment of natural law which had been entirely absent in the first volume. Trying to understand the early German Enlightenment without the omnipresence of natural law would represent a total distortion of the situation. But Israel's treatment here is highly selective. He relegates Christian Thomasius to the sidelines and concentrates on Samuel Pufendorf, or on the way his notion of natural law "disintegrated" under the criticism of his voluntarism. In this critique the attacks from Leibniz and Wolff agreed with those of Spinoza and Bayle, according to Israel. Already by 1730 Pufendorf's natural law had become a "philosophic cripple," and the analysis by Johann Jakob Schmauss in his "New System of the Law of Nature" (*Neues Systema des Rechts der Natur*) of 1754 finally set natural law back in the place it had always occupied in Hobbes, Spinoza, and the German freethinkers.[34] A slightly delayed victory for the radical Enlightenment.

This is, however, a highly tendentious presentation of the development of natural law, not only because it ignores Thomasius's later turn to a deeply secular natural law (after 1705) but because it forces Schmauss's unique position into the center and in contrast downplays the success and impressive endurance of natural law as pursued by followers of Pufendorf and Thomasius. Above all, however, Israel's combined approach is self-contradictory. The indirect approach, which takes on the literature of theological apologists for Christianity and the academic literary historians, clashes over and over with the ever-renewed effort to demonstrate that Spinoza was, after all, the main influence on the freethinkers. The constructions created by their enemies do not actually show what was really motivating the freethinkers but rather they reveal their own perceptions of reality. Starting there, one can arrive at the thesis propounded by Alan Charles Kors (and to some extent by me as well) that the horrified rejection of atheism by theological opponents was itself responsible for radicalizing the Enlightenment; this was so because they were drawing atheistic conclusions that the sources had never contained in such explicit

---

[34] Ibid., pp. 199f. Cf. Johann Jakob Schmauss, *Neues Systema des Rechts der Natur*, Göttingen, 1754.

form.[35] But that would be a completely different line of argument from that which Israel pursues. He would like to turn the description of an "academically constructed 'princeps of atheism'" into yet another vote for the influence of Spinoza.

I would conclude that Jonathan Israel's books have marked an important advance in knowledge of the thinkers and texts of the German radical early Enlightenment especially for the English-speaking world, but his description needs correction. Despite all his efforts, the general thesis in *Enlightenment Contested* still powerfully emphasizes the decisive influence of Spinoza and thus distorts the whole picture. As opposed to this monocausal approach, my depiction stresses the multifaceted origins of the early Enlightenment in Germany, both in its radical and in its moderate variants. Stimuli did not come just from the Netherlands nor just from Halle. There were of course influences from abroad, but there were domestic developments as well, movements that took root in extremely diverse locations. Only a sort of philosophical microhistory, I believe, can cut itself free from general theses about influence and from the contemporary negative evaluations by theologians. It can do so by trying to work below the surface of such generalizations, so to speak, and reconstruct situations in some detail and thus arrive at the real motives and contexts for what I am calling radicalization. That is what the case studies in this book achieve.

---

[35] Alan Charles Kors, *Atheism in France 1650–1729*, vol. 1: *The Orthodox Sources of Disbelief*, Princeton, 1990.

CHAPTER I

The Mortal Soul
Biblicism, Materialism, and the New Science

1   Mortalist Traditions and the English Debate

When the Italian Aristotelian Cesare Cremonini died in 1631, he had
these words engraved on his tombstone: *Totus Cremonius hic iacet* ("Here
lies all of Cremonini"). At least that is what was reported by libertine
traditions, which had a penchant for inventing epitaphs.[1] The claim that
"all of Cremonini" was lying in his grave – that is, that not only his body
but also his soul – might well have been a consequence of his
Aristotelianism, which sometimes argued that Alexander of Aphrodisias
was right in considering the soul to be mortal. Pietro Pomponazzi had
revived that view with new arguments at the beginning of the sixteenth
century. But Pomponazzi had added that the mortality of the soul was only
a necessary conclusion on the level of philosophical arguments, while
theological arguments might come to a completely different conclusion.[2]

---

[1] See the report by Gisbert Voetius concerning a man from a libertine milieu: Gisbert Voetius,
Selectarum disputationum theologicarum, vol. 1, Utrecht, 1648, p. 206. See on this point, Pierre
Bayle, *Dictionnaire*, 2nd edn., Rotterdam, 1701, article on "Cremonin," Rem. C. For libertine
traditions regarding Cremonini, see the volume compiled by Antoine Lancelot, *Naudeana et
Patiniana*, Amsterdam, 1703; see Peter Friedrich Arpe's manuscript additions to his *Apologia pro
Vanino*, Ms. theol. 1222, SUB Hamburg, p. 19. See also Paul Oskar Kristeller's attack on the image
conveyed by French libertines, "The Myth of Renaissance Atheism and the French Tradition of Free
Thought," in *Studies in Renaissance Thought and Letters*, vol. 3, Rome, 1993, pp. 541–554. In
contrast, see Jean-Pierre Cavaillé, "The Italian Atheist Academics: A Myth of the French pre-
Enlightenment?" in Friedrich Vollhardt, ed., *Religiöser Nonkonformismus und frühneuzeitliche
Gelehrtenkultur*, Berlin, 2013, pp. 39–50. On Cremonini himself, see Heinrich C. Kuhn,
*Venetischer Aristotelismus im Ende der aristotelischen Welt: Aspekte der Welt und des Denkens des
Cesare Cremonini (1550–1631)*, Frankfurt and Bern, 1996. Generally for the genre of mock epitaphs,
which form part of the background here, see Italo Michele Battafarano, "Epitaphia ioco-seria.
Loredano und Hallmann," in Alberto Martino, ed., *Beiträge zur Aufnahme der italienischen und
spanischen Literatur in Deutschland im 16. und 17. Jahrhundert*, Amsterdam and Atlanta, 1990,
pp. 133–150; Battafarano, "(Scherz-)Grabschriften bei Opitz," in Barbara Becker-Cantarino und
Jörg-Ulrich Fechner, eds., *Opitz und seine Welt*, Amsterdam, 1990, pp. 21–36.

[2] Pietro Pomponazzi, *Abhandlung über die Unsterblichkeit der Seele*, Hamburg, 1990; see Bruno Nardi,
Studi su P. Pomponazzi, Florence, 1965, chapter 5; Giovanni di Napoli, *L'immortalità dell'anima nel
Rinascimento*, Turin, 1963. On the scandal triggered by Pomponazzi's book, see Etienne Gilson,

Even so, Pomponazzi's opinion had stirred up a furor and legitimated him as a hero of the libertine and "atheist" traditions of the seventeenth and eighteenth centuries. Over these centuries mortalism emerged in various contexts; natural-scientific and medical discoveries became hopelessly enmeshed with theology and biblical exegesis.[3]

Biblical scholars knew, of course, the verse from Genesis saying that God had blown his breath (*neshama*, נשמת) into Adam. That was a concept that shaped ancient Hebrew ideas of the spirit or the soul as a sort of life principle, but not in some substantial sense that implied a life after death.[4] Blood was the medium of the life force. But usage regarding these concepts was variable. Other words, such as *nefesh*, *ru'ach*, *chaya*, and *yechida* also described something like the soul. *Nefesh* (נפש, the breath or airway, but also the person) implied neither an existence before that of the body nor immortality. Indeed, *nefesh* was never used as something separate from the body, and like *neshama* and *ru'ach* they could also be used with animals; so it did not mean anything specifically human. The heart (*leb*, לב) meant the bodily organ but also the life force, the seat of one's intellectual abilities and feelings, the will and one's decisions, and in the broadest sense it meant the whole person. Whichever word one chose, the Old Testament gave no support to ideas of an immortal soul.

This interpretation could have an immediate political relevance, although not particularly in the *libertinage érudit* of French scholars who built on the tradition of Italian Renaissance naturalism; its political force is more visible in English developments during the Civil War.[5] There the belief in immortality was connected to the doctrine that the pains of hell were eternal, a controversial doctrine; in their efforts to relieve mankind of the fear of hell, some radicals took the next step and propagated the idea of the mortality of the soul. If death meant the end of the soul, they said, then the horrifying fires of hell could no longer present a threat. The debate

"Autour de Pomponazzi. Problématique de l'immortalité de l'Âme en Italie au début du XVIe siècle," *Archives d'histoire doctrinale et littéraire du moyen âge* 28 (1961), pp. 163–279.

[3] See Giuseppe Ricuperati, "Il problema della corporeità dell' anima dai libertini ai deisti," in Sergio Bertelli, ed., *Il libertinismo in Europa*, Milan and Naples, 1980, pp. 369–415; Ann Thomson, *Bodies of Thought: Science, Religion, and the Soul in the Early Enlightenment*, Oxford, 2008.

[4] Gen. 2,7. See Hans Walter Wolff, *Anthropologie des Alten Testaments*, ed. Bernd Janowski, Gütersloh, 2010; Karin Schöpflin, "Seele. II. Altes Testament," in TRE, vol. 30, Berlin, 1999, pp. 737–740.

[5] See Norman T. Burns, *Christian Mortalism from Tyndale to Milton*, Cambridge, MA, 1972; Philipp C. Almond, *Heaven and Hell in Enlightenment England*, Cambridge, 1994, esp. chapter 2; Brian Ball, *The Soul Sleepers: Christian Mortalism from Wycliffe to Priestley*, Cambridge, 2008. For the broader context, see also Daniel P. Walker, *The Decline of Hell: Seventeenth-Century Discussions of Eternal Torment*, London, 1964.

thus represented an important step toward abolishing external, ecclesiastical punishments and replacing them with a morality based on conscience.[6] Thomas Hobbes played an important role in this development; for him the notion of an immaterial soul-substance was absurd.[7] His logic demanded that even God could not be described as an immaterial substance. But this conclusion appealed to others beyond Hobbes, for whom exile in Paris had been a stimulus to his thinking. The years of Civil War in England were just as important, because the suspension or collapse of censorship enabled radical publishing of a sort that had never existed anywhere in Europe before.[8] The underground bubbled up to the surface: for example, in the Leveller Richard Overton's book, which appeared first in 1644 and had a second edition in 1655 under the title, *Man Wholly Mortal.*[9]

With these events a broad and open discussion of mortalism became possible for the first time in European history. Even so, these publications did not attain the level of a serious philosophical discussion. To attain that, religious mortalism had to be transformed into a philosophical hypothesis that took account of other discussions of the time. This was the step taken by John Locke in his *Essay Concerning Human Understanding*, in which he proposed, as an aside, the following thought experiment: it must have been possible for God in His omnipotence to have created some sort of thinking matter.[10] But that would imply that human thinking did not require a philosophical theory of an immaterial soul of the sort that Anglican theology mostly accepted.

With this argument a most peculiar kind of argument opened up. On one side stood Orthodox theologians and Platonist philosophers along with those oriented to the natural sciences, such as Richard Bentley; and

---

[6] See on this topic Heinz Dieter Kittsteiner, *Die Entstehung des modernen Gewissens*, Frankfurt, 1991.

[7] See John G. A. Pocock, "Time, History and Eschatology in the Thought of Thomas Hobbes," in John H. Elliott und Helmut G. Koenigsberger, eds., *The Diversity of History*, Ithaca, NY, 1970, pp. 149–198.

[8] See Martin Mulsow, *Enlightenment Underground: Radical Germany 1680–1720*, tr. H. C. Erik Midelfort, Charlottesville, 2015, chapter 6; and Elisabeth Eisenstein, *The Printing Press as an Agent of Change: Communications and Cultural Transformations in Early Modern Europe*, Cambridge, 1979; Christopher Hill, *The World Turned Upside Down: Radical Ideas during the English Revolution*, London, 1972.

[9] Richard Overton, *Man Wholly Mortal. Or, Treatise Wherein 'Tis proved, both Theologically and Philosophically, That as whole man sinned, so whole man died; contrary to that common distinction of Soul and Body: and that the present going of the Soul into heaven or hell, is a meer Fiction: And that at the Resurrection is the beginning of our immortality; and then actual Condemnation and Salvation, and not before*, London, 1655.

[10] John Locke, *An Essay Concerning Human Understanding*, Oxford, 1975, IV, chapter 3, sect. 6.

on the other side stood Locke along with radical freethinkers but also biblicist and fideist theologians.[11] From the very beginning the debate was a many-layered discourse, possessing philosophical components but theological elements as well. It explored the limits of human reason concerning the capacities of divine omnipotence. The paradox was that those philosophers given to sensualist and medical thinking, who claimed that thinking might be a property of cerebral structure, also appealed dogmatically to the doctrine of God's omnipotence and exegetically to biblical passages that assumed the soul's death until the resurrection. If there was no true annihilation of the soul, they claimed, there would then be no true resurrection. No one, not even the radicals, went so far as to argue openly that the soul was simply mortal. But on purely biblical grounds immortality was a promise connected to the Last Judgment and the time after the Judgment.

The difficulty for contemporaries, however, lay in deciding if such appeals to the Bible were only the self-protective gestures of crypto-mortalists, or if their fideism was genuine. There was no doubt about Locke, of course, but many of his freethinking colleagues and followers like the young Charles Gildon, John Toland, and Anthony Collins were almost certainly secret mortalists and naturalists, and maybe William Coward as well. The young Gildon had contributed a letter to Charles Blount entitled "That the Soul is Matter" to a collaborative volume on *The Oracles of Reason*.[12]

On the other side we find an alliance between Orthodox Anglican theology and modern, apologetically aligned natural science,[13] both of which hoped to reinforce with rational proofs the Christian foundations of society which also appeared to provide the moral foundation. But such proofs had to be philosophical in nature, and the proofs of the immortality of the soul assumed that the soul was an immaterial substance. This party saw itself as progressive because of their rationalism, and from our standpoint it is impossible to decide which side in the debate should be called "conservative" and which "progressive." The battle defied these categories.

[11] See the fine overview of the whole debate by David Berman, "Die Debatte über die Seele," in Jean-Pierre Schobinger, ed., *Die Philosophie des 17. Jahrhunderts 3: England*, Basel, 1988, pp. 759–781. I will not go more deeply here into the complex and paradoxical positions taken in this debate, for example, by a conservative cleric like Henry Dodwell, or especially the arguments of Pierre Jurieu in the Netherlands; see John S. Spink: *French Free-Thought from Gassendi to Voltaire*, London, 1960, p. 223.

[12] See Ugo Bonanate, *Charles Blount. Libertinismo e deismo nel Deicento inglese*, Florence, 1972.

[13] On this alliance, see Margaret C. Jacob, *The Newtonians and the English Revolution 1689–1720*, Ithaca, 1976.

Moreover, the battle had subterranean connections with other debates of the day: the controversy concerning the *anima mundi*, the soul of the world; or the debate about "plastic nature," ignited by the Cambridge Platonists; or the quarrel over the souls of animals.[14] All of these were connected to new developments in anatomy, cosmology, and physics.

Here we need to examine more closely a few works that played a leading role in English discussions about the materiality of the soul. The most provocative of all the works suspected of crypto-mortalism was William Coward's book, *Second Thoughts concerning Human Soul* (1702).[15] It was publicly burned by the hangman in 1704. That was the same year the controversy took root on German soil. Coward was a physician in Oxford, who had produced an English translation of Guillaume Lamy, an anatomist who proceeded on the atomistic principles of Gassendi.[16] Coward and more emphatically John Toland, who published his *Letters to Serena* in 1704, show the issue's complexity, for like a burning glass they brought the various problems of the soul to a focus. Both philosophers held that the doctrine of the immortality of the soul was a pagan teaching, developed first by the Egyptians before it was adopted by Jews and Christians. That cleverly tied John Spencer's theory concerning the way the Jews had accommodated the culture of ancient Egypt together with the debate about the soul. Toland and Coward used the language of Christian "selection," in which Jews and Christians were said to have selectively used pagan, idolatrous, and "dangerous" traditions for their own purposes, a trope that Gundling and Bierling had also employed. Toland had in addition absorbed such anti-idolatrous authors as Van Dale and critical naturalists like Bruno. By denouncing the doctrine of immortality as a piece of Egyptian idolatry,[17] he could use history to disavow it. This was a favorite means of combating rationalist "dogmaticians" used during the early phase of the radical Enlightenment, as we have already seen. According to Toland, immortalism was not a fundamentally philosophical thesis but was rather a secondary product, a sublimation of an "exotic" popular opinion, one that was superstitious, a mere invention, ritualistic,

---

[14] See Mulsow, *Enlightenment Underground* (note 8), chapter 5; and Friedrich Niewöhner, ed., *Die Seele der Tiere*, Wiesbaden, 2001.

[15] The full title of the second edition reads: *Second Thoughts concerning Human Soul. Demonstrating the Notion of Human Soul, As believ'd to be a Spiritual and Immaterial Substance, united to Human Body, To be an Invention of the Heathens, And not Consonant to the Principles of Philosophy, Reason, or Religion*, 2nd edn., London, 1704.

[16] See Thomson, *Bodies of Thought* (note 3), pp. 104–117.

[17] See Mulsow, *Enlightenment Underground* (note 8), chapter 2; Jean Meslier had similar thoughts; see Ricuperati, "Il problema" (note 3), p. 398.

and a misunderstanding of a "memorial practice."[18] Giuseppe Ricuperati rightly emphasizes that "with Toland, the corporeality of the soul opened up a topic with massive implications."[19]

In France the debate on the soul emerged from different traditions and contexts. But there, too, it took on a growing virulence in the late seventeenth century. As the natural sciences expanded rapidly, especially among physicians, the implication spread that the idea of an immaterial soul was no longer credible. In France it was not just the Cartesian-mechanical tradition that produced such apostates; they depended perhaps even more on the atomist and sensualist philosophy of Gassendi. That philosophy inspired the physician Abraham Gaultier, for example, in his *Réponse* of 1714, which then developed further in clandestine manuscripts.[20] Another physician, Antoine Maubec, also criticized Descartes in a book entitled *Principes physiques de la raison et des passions de l'homme* of 1709.[21] Both of these works possess strongly skeptical components that mainly address theological aspects of the problem. The basic idea is that we do not know how God did it, but obviously stimulating the vessels in the brain affects our thought processes. In the background of these rare openly published works stood a great many clandestine works of French origin. The most important of them was probably the anonymous *Âme matérielle* from the 1740s.[22] In works like these, mortalism was now completely out in the open because compromises with the censors or with the public were no longer necessary. So now the teachings of Gassendi could appear embellished with blatant quotations from Hobbes, Spinoza, or libertine texts.

---

[18] See John Toland, *Letters to Serena*, London, 1704, Letter III, p. 73. See Jan Assmann, *Tod und Jenseits im Alten Ägypten*, Munich, 2001, esp. pp. 501–525.

[19] Ricuperati, "Il problema" (note 3), p. 381. Toland developed his position against Newton's compromise and set forth a materialistic interpretation of Newton along with an interpretation of Spinoza inflected by Bruno. See Margaret Jacob, "John Toland and the Newtonian Ideology," *Journal of the Warburg and Courtauld Institutes*, 1969, pp. 307–331. Anthony Collins played his own role in this discussion. See the discussion in Mulsow, *Enlightenment Underground* (note 8), chapter 1, concerning the brilliant ideas that Collins worked out in his examination of the proof of prophecy in 1724. He intervened with equal brilliance in the debate on the soul and developed his views against those of Samuel Clarke. These works are contained in Samuel Clarke, *A Letter to Mr. Dodwell*, London, 1731.

[20] See the edition by Olivier Bloch, ed., *Parité de la vie et de la mort. La "réponse" du médicin Gaultier*, Oxford, 1993.

[21] See Spink, *French Free-Thought from Gassendi to Voltaire* (note 11), pp. 219ff.

[22] See Alain Niderst, ed., *L'âme matérielle*, Paris, 1973, but Niderst's suggested dating to 1724–1734 has been revised. See Maria Teresa Marcialis, "L'Âme matérielle tra libertinismo e clandestinité," in Tullio Gregory et al., eds., *Ricerche su letteratura libertina e letteratura clandestina nel Seicento*, Florence, 1981, pp. 353–363; Winfried Schröder, *Ursprünge des Atheismus*, Stuttgart, 1998, p. 497. For a general treatment of the topic in clandestine literature, see Thomson, *Bodies of Thought* (note 3).

Roughly speaking, that is the international profile of the debate with its many overlapping traditions, so far as we can tell in retrospect. The German reception of this debate, we must admit at the outset, took account of only fragments of this large argument, only a part of its extraordinary complexity. On the other hand, these fragments fit into a no less complex context of German academic discussions from around the year 1700. We will be able to discover precisely what sort of reception took place in the German lands, and what difference the various academic environments made in these debates.

2 An Academic Accident

At first glance the story looks like a classic case of progress and secularization: a freethinker, a materialist, who had breathed in the air of the radical ideas from the German and English early Enlightenment, a man who was thinking like a natural scientist and leaving old theological views behind.[23] He was the first one in Germany rigorously to pursue the thesis that the soul was nonsubstantial and therefore mortal. He put an empiricist physiology in the place of antiquated views regarding a "rational part of the soul" that supposedly survived and went to heaven. The name of this freethinker was Urban Gottfried Bucher.[24] In 1713, he published – anonymously – a work under the title *The Confidential Correspondence of Two Good Friends Concerning the Essence of Souls* (see Figure 1).[25] The little

---

[23] Parts of the following sections borrow from Martin Mulsow, "Säkularisierung der Seelenlehre? Biblizismus und Materialismus in Urban Gottlieb Buchers Briefwechsel vom Wesen der Seelen (1713)," in Lutz Danneberg et al., eds, *Säkularisierung der Wissenschaften seit der frühen Neuzeit*, vol. 2: *Zwischen christlicher Apologetik und methodologischem Atheismus*, Berlin, 2002, pp. 145–173.

[24] The attribution to Bucher was made by Christian Thomasius. See [Christian Thomasius], *Summarischer Nachrichten [. . .] Ein und zwanzigstes Stück*, Halle and Leipzig, 1717, pp. 774ff. Bucher was born in 1679 in Frauenhain near Meißen and died in 1724 in Dresden. His father was probably Christoph Friedrich Bucher, born in 1651, who became a deacon in Frauenhain in 1676 and lived there as pastor from 1677. In 1682 the family moved to Königshain and in 1692 to Rengersdorf, where the father served as pastor. Contrary to normal expectations, Bucher did not attend the princely school of St. Afra in Meißen but studied medicine in Wittenberg and Halle. He then became the personal physician to Anton Egon, Prince of Fürstenberg and was later given work for the prince as a geographer and engineer. He wrote a biography of Johann Joachim Becher and a book about the course of the Danube. On Bucher, see Alix Cooper, *Inventing the Indigenous. Local Knowledge and Natural History in Early Modern Europe*, Cambridge, 2007, pp. 140–151.

[25] *Zweyer Guten Freunde vertrauter Brief-Wechsel vom Wesen der Seelen / Si licet aliis quod lubet dicere, nobis quid lubeat liceat credere. / Sammt eines Anonymi lustigen Vorrede /* The Hague / printed by Peter von der Aa, Anno 1713. This little book was not really printed in The Hague, but probably in Jena. When not otherwise noted, I quote from this first edition (cited as *Briefwechsel*). A new edition that added for the first time corrections by the author appeared in 1723; in this new edition there is a "Prior Report" on pp. 3–10 and on pp. 99–104 "a Declaration of the Author of the First

book consists of a foreword and three lengthy letters. In the first one, a young man explains his ideas about the essence of the soul. He maintains that one cannot speak of the substantiality of the soul because the vegetative and sensitive parts of the soul can be explained in mechanistic and sensualist terms, and no substantial substrate is necessary for something that is just a function or capacity of the body. This letter is directed to a professor, who answers the young man's doubts in the second letter: an answer that poses a whole series of problems necessarily arising from arguments for nonsubstantiality, ranging from the juridical to the philosophical and to the exegetical problems in certain passages in the Bible. The third letter contains the young man's answer to the professor.

This work came under immediate attack, of course, from theologians, who tried unsuccessfully to identify the author, but their reaction could not prevent the work from being reprinted several times before 1723. In the broad history of Enlightenment psychology, this work was pathbreaking, making way for more secular views. In 1966 the East German Gottfried Stiehler published selections from this *Confidential Correspondence*, claiming that Bucher was a clear example of a "materialist from the age of Leibniz," the title of his anthology.[26] Secularization seemed to be the courageous achievement of individual antitheological thinkers, of martyrs for modern science.

But a second glance shows that the matter is much more complicated. So it is vital to tell the story of Bucher once more, as he appears after lengthy digging in the sources. The publication of these letters was clearly not voluntary, and it came to pass through devious means without the author's approval. In addition, the author himself was by no means a straightforward "freethinker" but a man full of doubts and genuinely seeking solutions to problems that his studies had posed for him. His location, moreover, was not at one of the "Enlightenment" universities but rather at one of the centers of Lutheran Orthodoxy, Wittenberg.

Bucher was a medical student at Wittenberg. As a 25-year-old, in his tenth semester, he was asked to serve as the official "opponent" at a disputation. On Saturday, August 23, 1704, a doctoral candidate by the

---

and Last Letter of this Correspondence on the Essence of the Soul," additions in which Bucher provided important details on the history of this book.

[26] Gottfried Stiehler, ed., *Materialisten der Leibniz-Zeit*, East Berlin, 1966. For an interpretation in this direction (along with the older work of Friedrich A. Lange, *Geschichte des Materialismus*, Iserlohn 1876, pp. 319–325), see Manfred Buhr und Otto Finger, "Zweyer guten Freunde vertrauter Brief-Wechsel vom Wesen der Seelen," in Gottfried Stiehler, ed., *Beiträge zur Geschichte des vormarxischen Materialismus*, East Berlin, 1961, pp. 124–138, a superficial analysis.

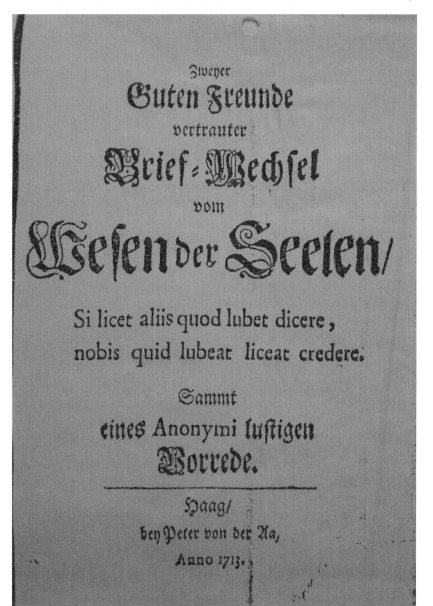

Figure 1   [Urban Gottfried Bucher], *Zweyer Guten Freunde vertrauter Brief-Wechsel vom Wesen der Seelen*, The Hague, 1713

name of Gottfried Klemm was set to defend the dissertation that his teacher Johann Gottlob Dietrich had written. This was the normal ritual: theses from the dissertation were set forth, an opponent had to defend a contrary position, and Klemm as the "respondent" then had to answer. The subject was the problem of the souls of animals, a vexed issue ever since Descartes had declared that animals were nothing more than automata.[27] Naturally, Dietrich and Klemm were careful and did not argue in opposition to Descartes that the souls of animals were immortal; fifty years earlier the physician Daniel Sennert of Wittenberg had been accused of tending in that direction, and the theological attacks on such views made it prudent to avoid suspicion. Sennert himself had been cautious, holding that animal souls were immaterial but not immortal.[28] That was the position of Dietrich and Klemm as well.

The problem, however, lay in drawing the line between animals and human beings. If one proceeded with Descartes, then humans were reasonable beings while animals were just automata; but if one accepted the traditional view that animals had souls (in the sense of an *anima sensitiva*), then it could appear than human beings were not so very different from animals. How was one to prove that the rational human soul was immortal but the animal soul was mortal? The more effectively one proved that human behavior could be explained physiologially, the less there appeared to be any difference. Then some thinkers jumped in and aggressively claimed that in that case animal souls, too, were immortal. So the thesis claiming that animal souls were immaterial but not immortal was an attempt at compromise: physiological processes required a substrate, and that was the substantial, immaterial form.

---

[27] On June 10, 1699, the young Bucher matriculated as a medical student at the University of Wittenberg. See Fritz Juntke, ed., *Album Academiae Vitebergensis*, Jüngere Reihe, Part 2 (1660–1710), Halle, 1952, p. 39. It would appear that the student had received some previous medical training because on December 11, 1700, hardly one and a half years later, Bucher and his teacher Adam Brendel presented a disputation on the topic *De catalepsi, consensu gratiosissimi medicorum ordinis*, probably to qualify Bucher as a medical licentiate. For an introduction to the souls of animals as a topic, see Leonora Cohen Rosenfield, *From Beast-Machine to Man-Machine: The Theme of Animal Soul in French Letters from Descartes to La Mettrie*, Oxford, 1940. See also *Die Seele der Tiere* (note 14). On this episode, see Mulsow, *Die unanständige Gelehrtenrepublik*, Stuttgart, 2007, pp. 202–204.

[28] See Daniel Sennert, *Hypomnemata physica*, Frankfurt, 1636, Book IV: "De generatione viventium." On Sennert, see Siegfried Wollgast, *Philosophie in Deutschland zwischen Reformation und Aufklärung 1550–1650*, 2nd edn., Berlin, 1993, pp. 439ff; Michael Stolberg, "Particles of the Soul: The Medical and Lutheran Context of Daniel Sennert's Atomism," *Medicina nei secoli* 15 (2003), pp. 177–203; William R. Newman: *Atoms and Alchemy: Chymistry and the Experimental Origins of the Scientific Revolution*, Chicago, 2006. On the Sennert controversy, see the entry in *Die Seele der Tiere* (note 14).

Thus the dissertation stated:

> We therefore conclude – so that our answer emerges more clearly – that the soul of animals is a substance, but immaterial. And don't our observations of these animals' spontaneous behaviors completely confirm this view? – their senses, imagination, memory, and similar behaviors? These behaviours do not arise from their accidents alone, per se or unmediated, because without some substantial basis the animals cannot act or behave at all. But these behaviors cannot stem from just matter because that is intrinsically crude, inert, and merely passive and therefore incapable of sense perception and animal activity regardless of how it is structured or disposed. Therefore even automata do not move themselves per se, for they are moved by some external principle, even if they behave in the same manner and carry out the same operations. But matters are much more complex in animals, who perform various actions spontaneously, not just by habit but also remembering that earlier an action produced good or bad results; they perceived and experience it as positive or negative. It is therefore clear as daylight that animals have feelings.[29]

Biblical citations followed to help make the case.

How was an advanced medical student like Bucher to compose a contrary position? He considered an argument that reversed the perspective. If one tried to explain the behavior of animals without the assumption of an immaterial soul, Bucher asked, would not one find that human behavior could also be explained without that assumption as well?[30] Of course many of the older physicians had explained the actions of animals without any immaterial soul, by referring to their blood or "spiritus," for example, or their bodily disposition. And clearly human behavior seemed to be similarly dependent on bodily dispositions. One could also invoke specific case histories of melancholy or lycanthropy, a popular medical topic in Wittenberg: the "heavy blood" of melancholics produced fixed and obsessive ideas because their brains were not mobile enough; the bite of a rabid animal could produce the delusional idea that one had become a wolf.[31]

---

[29] Johann Gottlob Dietrich [Dietericus] (praes.) / Gottfried Klemm (resp.), *Dissertatio physica de anima brutorum*, Wittenberg, 1704, fol. B3. I identified this disputation on the basis of a vague reference in the "Declaration" (note 25), p. 101.

[30] See *Briefwechsel* (note 25), pp. 16f. See "Declaration" (note 25), pp. 101f.

[31] See *Briefwechsel* (note 25), pp. 24f. For the discussion of lycanthropy in Wittenberg, see Christian Wolf, *Disputatio zoologica de lupo et lycanthropia*, Wittenberg, 1666. On the situation in Wittenberg, see, in general, Vivian Nutton, "Wittenberg Anatomy," in Peter Ole Gell and Andrew Cunningham, eds., *Medicine and Reformation*, London, 1993, pp. 11–32; Michael Stolberg, "Lykanthropie," in *Der Neue Pauly*, vol. 15(1): *Wissenschafts- und Rezeptionsgeschichte*, ed. Manfred Landfester, Stuttgart and Weimar, 2001, cols. 243–246.

And thus the conclusion: human behavior too could be explained without the assumption of an immaterial soul.[32]

An additional objection could be based on the fact that all this Aristotelian talk about "substantial forms," which lay at the basis of Dietrich's argument, had turned out to be not genuinely Aristotelian. Bucher referred to Hermann Conring, who had shown in a dissertation that this concept had no place in Aristotle and was a scholastic invention.[33]

We do not know how the candidate Klemm responded to these objections. We know only that his answer did not satisfy Bucher and that he gradually came to accept fully what he had at first defended only as the institutionally required devil's advocate.

3 Conditions and Contingencies

The fact, however, that such a development could occur, such an academic "accident," was only possible because of a whole series of preconditions and influences. Getting to know these influences is what makes the case of Bucher so interesting and instructive. This highly complex constellation of conditions helps explain why this accident was not more common and why the intellectual landscape of Germany remained essentially so moderate, nonradical, and traditional. These necessary conditions are at least five in number: (1) Bucher's argument had to fit into the "Wittenberg style" of medical argumentation. (2) There had to be exegetical models that could support his argument. (3) There had to be a receptive situation that at least offered inspiration and a standpoint different from that of a university disputation. (4) There had to be support and encouragement from a group that was not tied to the constraints of the university. (5) The argument had to be one that could be explained in another social context and in a language different from ordinary scholarly discourse.

---

[32] On the techniques of argumentation at Protestant universities, see Anita Traninger, *Disputation, Deklamation, Dialog. Medien und Gattungen europäischer Wissensverhandlungen zwischen Scholastik und Humanismus*, Stuttgart, 2012; Marion Gindhart and Ursula Kundert, eds., *Disputatio 1200–1800. Form, Funktion und Wirkung eines Leitmediums universitärer Wissenskultur*, Berlin, 2010.

[33] *Briefwechsel* (note 25), p. 35. There Bucher quoted Hermann Conring. See Conring, *De origine formarum secundum Aristotelem disputatio*, Leiden, 1630. Also printed in Conring's *Introductio in naturalem philosophiam et naturalium institutionum Liber I. Quibus praecipue vera ac Aristotelica, cum philosophandi ratio, tum doctrina de Ortu rerum ex materia, illustratur*, Helmstedt, 1638, pp. 135–150. On Conring's – rather limited – doubts about the immortality of souls, see Inge Mager, "Hermann Conring als theologischer Schriftsteller – insbesondere in seinem Verhältnis zu Georg Calixt," in Michael Stolleis, ed., *Herman Conring (1606–1681). Beiträge zu Leben und Werk*, Berlin, 1983, pp. 55–84, esp. p. 58.

These five conditions converged in Bucher. First, he made up his argument as a mixture of physiological and theological observations. In Wittenberg it was part of ordinary medical style to cite specific biblical passages that had to be compatible with natural-scientific theses – this was truer in Wittenberg than in other places. Second, there actually were biblical traditions in which the human soul was viewed as mortal. With a mortal soul, the resurrection could then appear as a real miracle. These were of course heterodox (Socinian) traditions, but they certainly gave Bucher the confidence that he was not entirely isolated in his interpretations.[34] Third, the years during which Bucher developed his views were precisely those of the high point in the above-mentioned English debate over the mortality of the soul. A superficial sort of history of philosophy would then have no trouble in pointing to the "influence" of the English mortalists on Germany. But the case of Bucher teaches us to be more cautious. Scholars in Wittenberg did know about the debate because they read about it in journals like Löscher's *Innocent Reports* (*Unschuldige Nachrichten*), an Orthodox gazette that fulminated against English thinkers such as Coward or Toland.[35] At the beginning, that was all the information anyone had. No one had access to the texts themselves. If one were lucky, and Bucher was lucky, one might obtain the works of Hobbes, who had earlier expressed mechanistic ideas and mortalism. But there was also no first-hand knowledge of the theological heresies of the Socinians, which were known only through the polemics found in Abraham Calov's *Scripta anti-Sociniana*.[36] Even so, these vague reports were enough for clever students, who were cobbling together a view that offered an alternative to traditional, tolerated theories. To correct the errors that necessarily crept into these sorts of extrapolations, students could conduct their own investigations. So, fourth, it was with thoughts like these and such half-way conjectures that Bucher ended his medical studies in Wittenberg in 1706. Already there he had associated with bright fellow-students, composing poems with them that criticized the social order. These

---

[34] See *Briefwechsel* (note 25), pp. 17f. On this, see also note 126.

[35] *Unschuldige Nachrichten von alten und neuen theologischen Sachen (1707)*, Ord. XI. See the "Declaration" (note 25), p. 103. On Löscher and his polemical role as intermediary, see Martin Greschat, *Zwischen Tradition und neuem Anfang. Valentin Ernst Löscher und der Ausgang der lutherischen Orthodoxie*, Witten, 1971.

[36] Abraham Calov, *Scripta anti-Sociniana, quibus haeresis illa pestilentissima non tantum ex ipsis Socinistarum scriptis bona fide detegitur, sed etiam e Scripturis Sacris, haud neglectis antiquitatis ecclesiasticae testimoniis, solide profligatur*, Ulm, 1684.

connections, however, provided no real support of the sort that he obtained only from his Saxon homeland, as we shall see.

And then, fifth, his supporters recommended that Bucher transfer to Halle because a fresher wind was blowing there for scholars. It seemed obvious that for medicine at the time the first port of call was in Halle with Friedrich Hoffmann, the physician who had replaced Galen with mechanism.[37] Here Bucher would have learned how to transform the doubts he had had in Wittenberg into mechanistic anatomy and physiology. But Bucher never became a real student of Hoffmann; even so, the professor allowed him to write a dissertation on chemical problems and the concept of natural law, which he was allowed to defend under Hoffmann's supervision.[38] Even so, there were secret whispers that Bucher had concocted some new heresy.[39]

It was apparently during these years, 1707 or 1708, that Bucher – though interrupted repeatedly by other activities – composed a letter to one of his former medical professors in Wittenberg. When finished it was about twenty-five pages long. In it, he tried to formulate the doubts he had expressed in 1704 in a way that would make sense of his growing medical knowledge. The letter shows that Bucher's thinking was still deeply imprinted with the "Wittenberg style" in contrast to the much more scientifically oriented texts of his fellow students in Halle. But the physiological terminology, the talk of brain fibers and mental movements, also clearly pointed to the modern Cartesian language as spoken by Friedrich Hoffmann and Ehrenfried Walther von Tschirnhaus. The Wittenberg professor to whom Bucher was writing can be identified as Johann Baptist Roeschel, a physician who had himself once toyed with the idea of the soul's mortality.[40]

4   Unorthodox Medical Students in Wittenberg: Bucher, Burghart, Hölmann

Let us linger a bit with our reconstruction of the social milieu in Wittenberg. It was not only the intellectual context of the professors and

[37] On Hoffmann, see Ingo W. Müller: *Iatromechanische Theorie und ärztliche Praxis im Vergleich zur galenistischen Medizin: Friedrich Hoffmann – Pieter van Foreest, Jan van Heurne*, Stuttgart, 1991.
[38] Friedrich Hoffmann (praes.) / Urban Gottfried Bucher (resp. et auctor), *Leges naturae in corporum productione et conservatione*, Halle, 1707.
[39] See *Briefwechsel* (note 25), pp. 15f.
[40] On Roeschel (1652–1712), see DBA 1048, pp. 197–213; for Roeschel's admission that he himself had harbored mortalist thoughts, see *Briefwechsel* (note 25), p. 43.

their debates that determined student radicalization at a university. We also need to examine the milieu among students and recent alumni, who had their own rituals, their own dynamics. When Bucher played his role as devil's advocate in 1704, he was 25 years old. Which fellow students did he associate with? What were he and his friends interested in?

In most cases, considering how long ago it was, we cannot say anything about the ephemeral contacts and projects of those students. But the culture of students was always a culture of protest, sometimes satirical, sometimes crude or bullying.[41] In the case of Bucher we are lucky to have a few traces of one such student project, even if it comes down to us encrypted. The reason for that was the enthusiasm of certain students for "gallant" lyrics. In 1704, the year of Dietrich's disputation, the fourth volume of the anthology of lyrics started by Benjamin Neukirch was published: *Choice and Hitherto Unpublished Poems by [Christian Hoffmann] von Hoffmannswaldau and other Germans.*[42] This volume, in which the authors were only identified by their initials, contained the poems of a certain "U. G. B." Owing to the sleuthing of Franz Heiduk, we now know that this cipher stood for Urban Gottfried Bucher.[43] This unexpected stroke of luck gives us a chance to learn something about the network of Bucher's friends, because several of the published lyrics came from medical students in Wittenberg.

Christian Hölmann from Breslau (Wrocław) in Silesia seems to have been the head of this group. He was the editor of this volume of poems and he may well have encouraged his friends to compose poems in the still new mode of "gallant" poetry. Hölmann had studied medicine in Wittenberg from 1699 to 1703/4. His friend Christoph Gottehr Burghart was another student from Silesia, who had begun his studies two years later, in 1701, and had taken his master's degree in medicine in 1703. The Saxon Bucher was thus associated with this little group of Silesians, and even though he was certainly not the engaged and productive man of letters that Hölmann was, he did contribute a few remarkable poems to the volume.

This interest in lyric poetry and literature more generally appears to have bound many of the sharpest students in Wittenberg together. Barthold

---

[41] See Marian Füssel, *Gelehrtenkultur als symbolische Praxis. Rang, Ritual und Konflikt an der Universität der Frühen Neuzeit*, Darmstadt, 2006.

[42] *Herrn von Hofmannswaldau und andrer Deutschen auserlesene und bißher ungedruckte Gedichte*, vol. 4, Glückstadt, 1704.

[43] See Franz Heiduk, *Die Dichter der galanten Lyrik. Studien zur Neukirchschen Sammlung*, Bern and Munich, 1971.

Feind and Michael Richey from Hamburg were also in Wittenberg at that
time – the result of the custom among many Hamburg citizens of sending
their sons there to study – and they too became literary men and critical
intellectuals.[44] And such students were quick to look beyond Wittenberg,
especially in the direction of nearby Halle. In Wittenberg, Ephraim
Gerhard was the most important German to apply the political theories
of John Locke to German conditions, but he maintained literary relations
with the early Enlightenment poets and thinkers Barthold Hinrich Brockes
and Gottlieb Stolle in Halle.[45] Another connection could be found in the
Wittenberg jurist Heber whom we got to know in connection with the
Symbolum sapientiae, and who sent his skeptical essay to Christian
Thomasius in Halle. Yet another was the character "Herr Christoph" from
Thomasius's *Monthly Conversations*, a figure who loved the burlesque style
and cultivated a passion for satire, which fueled his interest in the latest
publications.[46]

So we have to begin with an only imperfectly known web of relations
that tied critically minded medical students at Wittenberg together but
also connected them to the University of Halle, the place known for the
most provocative ideas. But what sort of impact did these sorts of relationship have on Bucher's poems? Let us examine one of them that carries
the title:

UNIVERSAL

A metaphysician and an alchemist,
Who are otherwise so different /
Do agree on many things:
One wants to get the best from everything /

---

[44] On Feind, see, above all, Ernst Fischer, "Patrioten und Ketzermacher. Zum Verhältnis von
Aufklärung und lutherischer Orthodoxie in Hamburg am Beginn des18. Jahrhunderts," in
Wolfgang Frühwald und Alberto Martino, eds., *Zwischen Aufklärung und Restauration. Sozialer
Wandel in der deutschen Literatur (1700–1848). Festschrift für Wolfgang Martens*, Tübingen, 1989,
pp. 17–47.

[45] See Heiduk (note 43), p. 71. On Gerhard, an almost unique case in Germany so far as the political
reception of Locke is concerned, see Diethelm Klippel, *Politische Freiheit und Freiheitsrechte im
deutschen Naturrecht des 18. Jahrhunderts*, Paderborn, 1976, pp. 88–91. In 1718 an anonymous
translation of the Second Treatise appeared under the title, *Le Gouvernement Civil, Oder die Kunst
Wohl zu Regieren Durch den berühmten Engelländer Jean Lock Beschrieben*. The translation was based
on the French translation that had appeared in 1691 and was probably by David Mazel. The
German text gives only the abbreviated "G" as a hint at the translator, but I suspect that this was
none other than Ephraim Gerhard.

[46] For Heber, see Mulsow, *Enlightenment Underground* (note 8), chapter 4; for "Herr Christoph," see
Christian Thomasius: *Lustiger und Ernsthaffter Monats-Gespräche Erster Theil: in sich begreifend Die
sechs ersten Monate des 1688*, Saalfeld, 1688. It continued until 1690.

> The other wants to combine everything.
> Both of their brains must have a broad compass /
> So it takes a lot of bracing /
> To hold itself together.
> Whatever else they think and see in large numbers /
> They try to bundle it all into one thing /
> This is their one action and effort /
> So they speak of nothing but the Universal.[47]

The poem obviously denounces the metaphysician by comparing him to the discredited profession of alchemist. Both detested the sciences – or what they saw as pseudosciences – but agreed (according to the author) that they should forcibly combine what does not belong together. They aimed at the "Universal" instead of at individual things and experiences. But Bucher clearly sympathized with the latter and therefore with the empirical sciences without charlatanism.

When Burghart obtained his master's degree in medicine in 1703, Bucher composed a satirical poem for him as a gift:

> Salin has now become a doctor /
> And had now decked himself out /
> So that everyone can judge his high rank
> From just one glance at him /
> And then his wig with queue
> Right doctorally decorating his head.[48]

Both Heber and Mayer had complained about the nasty and envious social environment of Wittenberg,[49] which offers us a glimpse of the many rituals and ceremonies and also the exaggerated respect for authority found in academia. These poems were therefore an exercise aimed at creating some critical distance from these rituals. The refrain of all the later verses generally runs:

> And so one must get used to the taste
> of Spirit of Salmiac.

---

[47] *Hernn von Hoffmanswaldaus [...] Gedichte* (note 42), p. 266. See also the *Briefwechsel* (note 25), p. 76. On potable gold as an elixir, see Johann Rudolf Glauber, *De auri tictura sive auro potabile vero*, Amsterdam, 1646; Ernst Darmstaedter, "Zur Geschichte des Aurum potabile," *Chemiker-Zeitung* 48 (1924), pp. 653–655 and 678–680.

[48] *Hernn von Hoffmanswaldaus [...] Gedichte* (note 42), p. 355.

[49] Earlier in Mulsow, *Enlightenment Underground* (note 8), chapter 4. See also Martin Mulsow, "Views of the Berlin Refuge: Scholarly Projects, Literary Interests, Marginal Fields," in Sandra Pott, Lutz Danneberg, and Martin Mulsow, eds., *The Berlin Refuge 1680–1780: Learning and Science in European Context*, Leiden, 2003, pp. 25–46, esp. pp. 39–43 on Heber; as well as Chapter 4.

Here was a laughing reference to the mordant panacea (sal ammoniac), which a physician regularly prescribed if he had run out of other ideas. The poem was a satire aimed at the social order of physicians and a self-distancing by students from the rituals and accoutrements of their art. In another connection Peter Burke has spoken of a "crisis of representation" in the late seventeenth century.[50] But this crisis is evident here too. For our purposes these poems give us a vivid impression of the contentious spirit with which Bucher played his opponent's role in the disputation of August 23, 1704. His was not merely a theoretical opposition; it was a provocative challenge to the guild that displayed a self-confidence filled with the spirit of a new, pragmatic science.

And yet the criticisms expressed by the three young physicians opposing alchemy and its universal claims later dissipated. Almost twenty years later Bucher reviewed the work of the cameralist and alchemist Johann Joachim Becher and drew an outline of him – along the lines of Gassendi's portrait of Peiresc – emphasizing his career as the very model of a "useful" life in service to the state.[51] As a further sign of his declining irritation with alchemy, there are clues that Bucher asked his friend Christian Hölmann in Breslau (Wrocław) to check around for the papers of the Polish alchemist Sendivogius.[52] Hölmann was able to find one manuscript, which Bucher then passed on Friedrich Roth-Scholz in Nuremberg, a man who had settled in Breslau. Roth-Scholz then had it printed in his collection of alchemical texts entitled *Theatrum Chemicum*.[53]

5 Innovations Surrounding Tschirnhaus and at the Electoral Saxon Court

Before we turn to the correspondence between Bucher and Roeschel, we have to pursue one more clue that the dedication to Bucher's Halle dissertation hands us. Unlike the poem it does not lead us to Silesia but

---

[50] Peter Burke, *The Fabrication of Louis XIV*, New Haven, 1992.
[51] Urban Gottfried Bucher, *Das Muster eines nützlichen Gelehrten in der Person Herrn Dr. J. J. Bechers*, Nuremberg, 1722. On usefulness, see Pamela H. Smith, *The Business of Alchemy: Science and Culture in the Holy Roman Empire*, Princeton, 1994; Vera Keller, *Knowledge and the Public Interest, 1575–1725*, Cambridge, 2015.
[52] Roman Bugaj, *Michał Sędziwój (1566–1636): Życie i Pisma*, Wrocław, 1968; Zbigniew Szydlo, *Water which Does Not Wet Hands: The Alchemy of Michael Sendivogius*, London and Warsaw, 1994.
[53] Friedrich Roth-Scholz, ed., *Deutsches Theatrum Chemicum*, Part 1, Nuremberg, 1728, Foreword, pp. 22f., with thanks to Hermann Stockinger for the reference. On the trade in manuscripts in the social circle around Roth-Scholz, see Daniel Bellingradt and Bernd-Christian Otto, *Magical Manuscripts in Early Modern Europe: The Clandestine Trade in Illegal Book Collections*, Basingstoke, 2017.

rather to the Saxon homeland of Bucher. His dissertation was dedicated to Ehrenfried Walther von Tschirnhaus, who was one of the few outstanding scholars in Germany who had international range and influence.[54] The dedication reads:

> Perillustri Domino
> Dr. Walthero Ehrenfrido a Tzirnhausen
> equiti lusato
> Domino clientelarum Kieslingswaldae et
> Stolzenbergae
> Sereniss. Regis et Princip.
> electoris saxoniae
> consiliario:
> Domino suo perquam gratioso[55]

> [To the most illustrious lord
> Dr. Walther Ehrenfried von Tschirnhaus
> Knight of Lusatia
> Lord of the Dependents of Kieslingswald and
> Stolzenberg
> Councillor to the King and Prince
> of Electoral Saxony:
> To his most gracious lord]

From the dedication to Tschirnhaus we can suddenly recognize the sort of force that could have reinforced Bucher's courage, encouraging him to bring the new science into harmony with the Wittenberg style. And it also reveals the later network in which Bucher found himself and that provided him with both patronage and a position after his graduation. We know that there were connections between Tschirnhaus and the princes of Fürstenberg, Friedrich Hoffmann, and Christian Wolff. So we should look more closely at this network.

<hr />

[54] On Tschirnhaus, see Eduard Winter, *Frühaufklärung. Der Kampf gegen den Konfessionalismus in Mittel- und Osteuropa und die deutsch-slawische Begegnung*, Berlin, 1966; Winter, E. W. *Tschirnhaus und die Frühaufklärung in Mittel- und Osteuropa*, Berlin, 1960; Peter Plassmeyer and Sabine Siebel, eds., *Experimente mit dem Sonnenfeuer – Ehrenfried Walther von Tschirnhaus*, Dresden, 2001; Dagmar Hülsenberg, ed., *Kolloquium aus Anlass des 350. Geburtstags von Tschirnhaus am 10.4.2001 in Dresden*, Leipzig, 2003; Omero Proietti und Giovanni Licata, eds., *Il carteggio Van Gent-Tschirnhaus (1679–1690): Storia, cronistoria, contesto del "editio posthuma" spinoziana*, Macerata, 2013. Unfortunately the project of publishing a complete collection of his works collapsed after just a few volumes.

[55] Friedrich Hoffmann (praes.) / Urban Gottfried Bucher (resp. et auctor), *Leges naturae* (note 38), Dedikation.

From 1698 on Tschirnhaus enjoyed the full confidence of Anton Egon von Fürstenberg, whom Elector August II installed as governor in the Electorate of Saxony.[56] Bucher could have met him after 1702, because at that time Tschirnhaus finally returned from his long sojourn in Paris. He settled into his estate in Kislingswalde, east of Görlitz (today Sławnikowice in Poland), which was not all that far from Bucher's hometown of Meißen. During those years, until his death in 1708 in Kieslingswalde, Tschirnhaus was working intensively with chemistry and mineralogy, investigations that led directly to the invention of porcelain. When Johann Friedrich Büttger was brought to Saxony to make gold – once again we find the topic of alchemy – his work shifted under the influence of Tschirnhaus after 1705 until he finally figured out how to manufacture porcelain.[57]

These are all well-known facts; they are relevant to our story only if we can situate Bucher in that constellation. We note that after initial studies of medicine in his dissertation, Bucher proved himself an expert in basic questions of natural science and chemistry, which makes it seem likely that even during his days as a student he might have changed his focus to chemical research based on contacts he already had in his homeland of Meißen. The dedication to Tschirnhaus in his dissertation might therefore have been a result of his new interest but also a sign of his hopes for involvement in the Saxon research. The contact with Tschirnhaus, however, also gives us a clue about who may have been Bucher's colleagues in Halle. We know that from 1705 on Tschirnhaus had contacts with the young genius Christian Wolff, whom Tschirnhaus as well as Leibniz had recommended for the University of Halle.[58] At the end of 1706 Wolff therefore came to Halle to teach mathematics; from the beginning he was a member of the circle of Friedrich Hoffmann. As early as 1709 Hoffmann allowed Wolff to take his place in lecturing on experimental physics. These men were all bound together through their dedication to mechanistic ideas, and it seems plausible that Wolff became one of the intellectual contacts for the convinced mechanist Bucher. Moreover, when Wolff was in Breslau (Wrocław), he had been a fellow student with Bucher's friend Hölmann,[59] so that connection provided another way that they could have gotten to know each other.

[56] See Winter, *Frühaufklärung* (note 54).
[57] Klaus Hoffmann, *Johann Friedrich Böttger: Vom Alchemistengold zum weißen Porzellan*, Berlin, 1985.
[58] See *Christian Wolffs eigene Lebensbeschreibung*, ed. (with an essay on Wolff) Heinrich Wuttke, Leipzig, 1841, p. 125.
[59] See Heiduk, *Die Dichter der galanten Lyrik* (note 43), p. 70.

At first it was by no means clear that Bucher's dedication to Tschirnhaus had gained him anything. On October 11, 1708 Tschirnhaus died. The matriculation books of the University of Halle show that this was the very day that Bucher left the university.[60] I do not think that that is just an accident. Tschirnhaus may well have been financing Bucher's stay in Halle so that Bucher could pursue his research there for a year after he obtained his medical degree. Reports of the death or the near-death of his patron obviously called Bucher at once to Meißen or Kieslingswalde. We do not know if he lent Tschirnhaus's close associate Steinbrück a hand in dealing with the literary estate of the great scholar.[61] At that time there was some excitement about that estate because Tschirnhaus had been on the brink of the major breakthrough in research into manufacturing porcelain, which was a hot topic; porcelain was such an economically important material that the Saxon government immediately seized the Tschirnhaus papers and declared them to be state secrets.

This was also connected to the fact that the "freethinker" Tschirnhaus had been unfairly attacked as an "atheist" in 1688 – by no less a man than Christian Thomasius![62] – and now in Kieslingswalde he had come under unrelenting attack from a Pietist named Johann W. Kellner. Tschirnhaus's last few years after October of 1704 were darkened by Kellner's aggressive sermons and the conflicts they ignited. Kellner was an extension of the Pietists in Halle, and through him the Pietists expanded their fight against the newer philosophy into the Saxon hinterland. Kellner directed this question at Tschirnhaus: "What should I think of your notion of a self-cultivation beyond the infinite soul? . . . Where is Scripture, where is God's will, where growing and becoming strong in the good?"[63] Here again the contest involved the soul, even if only marginally, because for the scholar Tschirnhaus it was just one example out of many of the necessity of eradicating *praejudicia auctoritatis* (prejudices based on respect for authority).

In any event after Tschirnhaus's death, his goods were auctioned off to pay his creditors (he had gone deeply into debt to support his research), his

---

[60] *Matrikel der Martin-Luther-Universität Halle-Wittenberg*, vol. 1: *1690–1730*, ed. Fritz Juntke, Halle, 1960, p. 56.

[61] The city archive of Kieslingswalde is now contained within the city library of Wrocław.

[62] See Günter Gawlick, "Thomasius und die Denkfreiheit," in Werner Schneiders, ed., *Christian Thomasius*, Hamburg, 1989, pp. 256–273.

[63] Kellner to Tschirnhaus, Oct. 1704, SLHA Dresden, Loc. 9571, concerning the pastor J. W. Kellner [. . .]; see also the collection of documents on this controversy in the Archive of the Francke Foundations in Halle. Quoted from Winter, *Tschirnhaus* (note 54), p. 65.

literary estate was put under seal, and his significance for the discovery of porcelain was downplayed. So, for those persons who had been protected by Tschirnhaus, the situation was by no means simple. The great man could no longer support his protégés, and at first Bucher had to make his way alone.[64]

6   Discussion with Roeschel and Publication

In this situation Bucher wrote, perhaps from Halle, or maybe from Saxony,[65] to his old teacher Roeschel. He received a reply but wrote a second letter, strengthening his doubts about the substantiality of the soul. And yet down to this point everything had remained in the realm of private correspondence. The five above-mentioned conditions had enabled Bucher to solidify and fully embrace his own doubts and formulate them as a theory. Still, other contingent factors had to come into alignment before the correspondence with Roeschel could become a book, indeed a well-known pamphlet of the "early Enlightenment."

After some hesitation and a delay of about two years, Roeschel finally answered Bucher's first long letter, perhaps around 1710. He accepted the

---

[64] And yet his contacts within the network to which he belonged were good enough that Bucher obtained a position with Prince Anton Egon. He became his personal physician, but he may have performed smaller duties before that. When Roeschel died in 1712, Anton Egon, acting as the official governor for the Saxon University of Wittenberg, tried to install Christian Wolff as Roeschel's successor in 1714. It would have been a sort of belated vindication of Bucher against Roeschel. But the appointment fell through because of the opposition of the university. At the Electoral Saxon court plans were being made during those years for a Saxon Academy of Sciences, and there were energetic efforts toward innovation in politics and economics. Bucher was sent by Anton Egon, before his death in 1716, to the territories of the Fürstenbergs, which lay far to the south in Donaueschingen at the foot of the Black Forest. There, in the Landgraviate of Baar, he had the task of inspecting the economy and of improving it if possible. When his lord died, Bucher was immediately dismissed from his post, on February 17, 1717. So then Bucher had to see how he might serve his new lord in Dresden. He stayed a while in the Black Forest and began making geographical investigations into the Danube. At the beginning of 1717 he had completed a book on the Danube. It appeared in 1720, long after Bucher had returned to Dresden, under the title "The Source of the Danube in the Landgraviate of Fürstenberg." In 1718 Bucher journeyed back to Dresden with the book manuscript in his luggage. When he arrived there, he obtained a post with Anton Egon's successor, Joseph Ernst, Prince of Fürstenberg. The range of his qualifications now spanned medicine, natural science, geography, geology, and economics. Johann Joachim Becher was one of the pioneers in combining natural science, technology, and economics. Bucher wrote the above-mentioned biography describing him as a model for future learned state servants, *Das Muster eines Nützlich-Gelehrten in der Person Herrn Doctor Johann Joachim Bechers*. See notes 24 and 51. In 1722 Bucher published another natural-scientific and geographical book: *Sachsen-Landes Natur Historie*. On July 23, 1724 Bucher died at the age of 45. For a more extended account of his biography, see my introduction of the reprint edition of Bucher's *Brief-Wechsel*, Stuttgart, 2021, pp. 9–172.

[65] See *Briefwechsel* (note 25), p. 15.

challenge, and understood also that out of caution Bucher could not identify himself but would deliver his writing anonymously through a friendly intermediary. Roeschel made an effort at refutation and in his reply patiently went through Bucher's tract point by point and at equal length. Amazingly, at the end of his reply he declared that he would agree to publish his answer along with Bucher's letter.[66] In many Wittenberg intellectual circles scholars were thoroughly prepared to allow the free discussion of explosive topics so long as they were accompanied by a refutation.

Bucher, however, was not yet ready. He replied to Roeschel and tried to refute his objections. He was certainly not prepared to publish his reflections: he had always described his thoughts as *dubia* (doubts), that might be expressed *problematice* (as problems), so that he might personally learn something.[67]

So then why were these letters published? Roeschel died in 1712, and in his literary estate were Bucher's two letters and a copy of his reply. Roeschel's literary executor – probably his colleague Planer[68] – must have allowed the letters to be read by others; perhaps someone made copies. In any event these texts fell into the hands of a cunning early Enlightener.[69] He at once seized the opportunity of making Bucher's statements public to further his movement by publishing provocative pieces, even if he did not always agree with the views expressed. In the foreword to the *Correspondence* this anonymous editor claimed that these three letters had come into his hands by chance, that he had prepared them for the printer, and under pressure of a friend had hastily composed a foreword.

I am calling the unknown composer of this foreword an "early Enlightener" because he speaks unmistakably in the tones of a Gundling or a Thomasius.[70] He described his foreword as "witty" (*lustig*) because of the burlesque and conversational tone that Thomasius had introduced in

---

[66] See ibid., p. 67.

[67] On the genre of *dubia*, see Mulsowm, *Die unanständige Gelehrtenrepublik* (note 27), pp. 200f.

[68] Planer wrote the "Vita Roeschelii" and the printed library catalog of his teacher, *Catalogus bibliothecae J. B. Roeschelii*, Wittenberg, 1713. There see the (unpaginated) p. 24* of the "Vita" with a rendition of Roeschel's views on the soul. Planer himself dealt with the problems of traducianism: Johann Andreas Planer (Praes.) / M. E. Wendius (Resp.), *Novam de animae humanae propagatione sententiam [. . .] publice tuebitur [. . .]*, Wittenberg, 1712. On the basis of this work he was attacked for Socinian tendencies. See note 127. On Roeschel and Planer, see also Walter Friedensburg, *Geschichte der Universität Wittenberg*, Halle, 1917, p. 513.

[69] See the "lustige Vorrede" by a certain "Anonymi," in *Briefwechsel* (note 25), p. 13

[70] See, e.g., the "Foreword," in *Briefwechsel* (note 25), pp. 7f. The author of the foreword also gives a short, humorous survey of the "Quarrel between the Ancients and the Moderns" in the realm of logic and natural philosophy, p. 5.

his *Monthly Conversations*; he blasted away at logic and metaphysics and alluded to the *Querelle des anciens et des modernes*, obviously sympathizing with the moderns. Thus against his will and without his knowledge, Bucher was assimilated into the Early Enlightenment of Halle, to which he did not belong at all.

In 1713 the little book appeared, obviously printed in Jena because that is where the first responses to it can be found. Several professors reacted harshly to the new theses; one announced that he would lecture against the work.[71] But to this day we do not know who the Early Enlightener was who published this text, for his name was unmentioned just as were the names of Bucher and Roeschel.[72]

7 False Trails

At first when the work was published it was suspected that the author of the first and third letters was Johann Georg Hocheisen.[73] The reason for this suspicion, voiced by Gottlieb Stolle,[74] was that in the correspondence there were references to the debates in Wittenberg, and Roeschel as well as his student and later colleague Hocheisen were both teachers at the University of Wittenberg. In addition certain insinuations do seem to point directly at them both, not least the fact that both teachers had been trained in theology as well as natural science.

A different suspicion pointed to the physician Johann Caspar Westphal of Delitzsch, for Westphal was one of the few persons named in the letters. Westphal was also known as a pugnacious early Enlightenment scientist, who had not shied away from confronting the Orthodox of Wittenberg.[75] At the end of his first letter Bucher says

---

[71] See section 13, esp. note 193. Today in library catalogs the publisher Meyer from Jena is often listed as a publisher who during these years published, among other things, the natural law jurist Ephraim Gerhard. Johann Jakob Syrbius did give a lecture in 1713–1714 in Jena that considered the "Correspondence" in a critical light; Johann Franz Budde also occupied himself with topics from the "Correspondence" in his *Programma de Arabicorum haeresi*, Jena, 1713. In 1714 various works opposing it were published in Leipzig. The Thüringische Universitäts- und Landesbibliothek Jena possesses three copies: 8 Ph. VII, 123, 8; Theol. XXXI, 40(2), 8; Theol. XXXII, 5(2).

[72] On the possible authors, see note 189.

[73] On Hocheisen (1677–1712), see ADB, vol. 12, p. 520.

[74] Gottlieb Stolle, *Anleitung zur Historie der Gelahrheit*, Jena, 1736, p. 530.

[75] On Westphal (1649–1722), Manfred Wilde, "Korrespondenten von G. W. Leibniz. Johann Caspar Westphal, geb. 28. November 1649 in Rügenwalde/Pommern – gest. 24. März 1722 in Delitzsch/ Sachsen," *Studia Leibnitiana* 38/39 (2008), pp. 219–234.

that those who posit three parts to the human being, body, soul, and spirit come the closest to my view, if they understand "spirit" as the instruction received by word or through hearing, whose effect the human then expresses partially through inner words [*per λόγον internum*] or thoughts, and partially through external words and actions. And by the soul they understand the aptitude of all the members of our body [*Aptitudinem omnium membrorum corporis nostri*], but especially the fibers of the brain, in other words the mental "faculty." But these, especially the soul, they attribute to animals too, and they say that they perish with the body. Here one could consult D. Westphal's *Pathologia Daemonica.*[76]

Because of this passage some scholars believed that all of the letters in question – or perhaps just the letter in response – were written by Westphal. That was, to be sure, a rough kneejerk reaction. But what connected Bucher with Westphal? Was Westphal one of the early Enlighteners? This question opens up the tricky problem of what we mean by the Early Enlightenment and whether there was more than one style of "Early Enlightenment." When we examine the physician from Delitzsch we learn that Westphal belonged to a movement of "*curious*" natural scientists around 1700, who got together in small societies to discuss natural phenomena.[77]

On closer inspection Westphal's *Pathologia daemoniaca* of 1707 turns out to be a strange mixture, typical for the time, of theosophy and progress. He encouraged a physics based on the Bible, and enshrined the idea of the "wisdom of the ancients," but with the purpose of demytho-logizing and naturalizing supposed miracles. Let us recall the critical function of "naturalism" in Arpe, Kayser, or Bierling, a naturalism that could definitely take on hermetic elements but could also debunk idolatry and miracles. Westphal's talk of a "spirit" standing above the soul points to the tradition inspired by theosophy and Platonism, which instead of the duality of body and soul favored a triple division: *Mens, Anima* (in the sense of spirit), and *Corpus*. This tripartition almost automatically exag-gerated the traditional notion of the soul as connected to the divine; but it also brought a demotion of the "simple" parts of the soul to purely bodily functions. This was clearly the interpretation that Bucher found attractive.

---

[76] *Briefwechsel* (note 25), p. 39.
[77] On "curious" natural science, see Christoph Daxelmüller, *Disputationes curiosae. Zum "volkskundlichen" Polyhistorismus an den Universitäten des 17. und 18. Jahrhunderts*, Würzburg, 1979; Fabian Krämer, *Ein Zentaur in London. Lektüre und Beobachtung in der frühneuzeitlichen Naturforschung*, Affalterbach, 2014.

We can wonder, however. How could a young man, impressed by Hobbes and modern medicine and oriented toward the Early Enlightenment of Halle, also use a tripartite division that smacked of theosophy? Actually, we have already seen repeatedly that traditional concepts of "Early Enlightenment" do not always work. Here we must allow that perhaps there was a movement we should call the "theosophic Early Enlightenment." One argument in favor of that is the fact that many radical Pietists integrated theosophy into their views. But another argument would emphasize that Christian Thomasius himself took a spiritualist position on the question of the soul, especially in his book *On the Nature of the Spirit* (1699).[78]

Occasionally there was staunch opposition to the theosophical efforts of the Enlighteners. Gabriel Wagner was probably the most vociferous of them. He had originally been a follower of Christian Thomasius, but under the pseudonym "Realis de Vienna" he excoriated his teacher on grounds that were sober, logical, and empirical. Seventy years before Kant and his *Dreams of a Spirit-Seer*, his treatise attacking Swedenborg, Wagner aimed his *Ghostmaker* against Thomasius:

> A Thomasian ghostmaker is worse than a Scaligerian geometer. For surely a ghostmaker is more dangerous than a new Messiah because the latter sets a limit to the government, while the former allows it freedom, because it regards its teachings as indifferent or worthless; similarly through ghost-making people are robbed of their five senses and are brought to unreason and superstition, and this suppresses philosophy ... [79]

Because Thomasius's "Ghost essay ... turns the air, stones, cabbage, and turnips into spirits,"[80] Wagner warned against pressing the concept of spirit too hard. The shot of the Enlightener (Thomasius) could all too easily backfire.

Such concerns united radical Enlighteners and Orthodox theologians. As mentioned earlier, the other person suggested as a possible author of the *Correspondence* also had to cope with such concerns. Perhaps Hocheisen was suspected because he had engaged with numerous recent heterodox tendencies. For example, in 1709 Hocheisen had composed a theological

---

[78] Christian Thomasius, *Versuch vom Wesen des Geistes*, Halle, 1699; see Wilhelm Schmidt-Biggemann, "Pietismus, Platonismus und Aufklärung. Christian Thomasius, *Versuch vom Wesen des Geistes*," in Frank Grunert and Friedrich Vollhardt, eds., *Aufklärung als praktische Philosophie. Werner Schneiders zum 65. Geburtstag*, Tübingen, 1998, pp. 83–98.
[79] Realis de Vienna [G. Wagner], *Prüfung des Versuchs Vom Wesen des Geistes / den Christian Thomas / Prof. in Halle / 1699. An Tag Gegeben*, s.l. 1707, "Foreword."
[80] Ibid., p. 80.

disputation and defended it under Johann Georg Neumann. It was entitled "On Deism Detected in Theosophy" (*De Deismo in theosophia deprehensum*) and seemed intended to refute the "innovator," Westphal.[81]
Hocheisen probably hoped that this disputation would assist him in his
desired academic career, which was now supposed to lead from the
philosophical faculty, where he as teaching as an adjunct, to a theological
professorship. But nothing came of it; in the same year (1709) Hocheisen
assumed a position as a teacher at the Elisabeth-gymnasium in Breslau
(Wrocław).

Gottlieb Stolle must have thought that Hocheisen's refutation of
Westphal was insincere and that it concealed a secret fascination with
theosophy. And indeed Hocheisen did confirm many of Westphal's
merits, admitting that if he had not insulted the honor of the
Wittenberg theologians he would deserve full praise.[82] Valentin Ernst
Löscher, the standard bearer of Lutheran Orthodoxy in the early eighteenth century,[83] had felt especially wounded by Westphal's insult, and so
Hocheisen now formed an accusation that exactly imitated Löscher's own
thinking. Just one year earlier Löscher had discovered an implicit "deism"
lurking in the theories of the "fanatic" theosophs,[84] and now Hocheisen
leveled the same sort of charge against Westphal. By "deism" Löscher had
understood theories that misunderstood both nature and the workings of
God.[85] If this sort of deism could include "fanatics," for Löscher it was
because they allowed their fantasy to delude them with completely false
visions. He focused on those Platonic and spiritualist underpinnings that
did indeed play a role in Westphal's thinking.

There is another work of Hocheisen's, however, that is even more
interesting for us than his refutation of Westphal, because it yields a deep
insight into the scope of Hocheisen's educational purposes. In 1705, one
year after the Dietrich disputation on the souls of animals, when Bucher
was prompted to consider the matter, Hocheisen wrote the first of two

---

[81] Johann G. Neumann (Praes.) / Johann G. Hocheisen (Resp. et auctor), *Disputatio theologica qua Deismum in theosophia deprehensum [. . .] publice sistit [. . .]*, Wittenberg, March 8, 1709.

[82] Ibid., p. 6.

[83] On Löscher (1673–1749), see Greschat, *Zwischen Tradition und neuem Anfang. Valentin Ernst Löscher und der Ausgang der lutherischen Orthodoxie* (note 35).

[84] Valentin E. Loescher (Praes.) / G. E. Habbius (Resp.), *Deismus fanaticorum aliquot praenotationibus theologicis expensus*, Wittenberg, February 1, 1708.

[85] See ibid., as well as Loescher (Praes.) / Habbius (Resp.), *Praenotationes theologicae contra naturalistarum et fanaticorum omne genus [. . .] custodiendae*, Wittenberg 1708, p. 37. See Greschat, *Zwischen Tradition und neuem Anfang* (note 83), p. 227.

treatises on the *Comte de Gabalis*.[86] At first glance this was a weirdly remote topic for it dealt with a novel, indeed a Rosicrucian novel. *Gab* in Old French meant a "witty tale," but of course "Gabalis" also evokes the Kabbalah, the Jewish tradition of secret wisdom. The novel had appeared first in 1670, published anonymously by its author, the Abbé de Villars, Nicolas de Montfaucon.[87] The *Comte de Gabalis* was one of those texts about which it is not easy to say if they were meant seriously. Bayle and many others thought that it dismantled occultism and that its author "wanted above all to play games, or, as he gives us to understand, to have fun at the expense of fools."[88]

In Wittenberg, however, they took everything more seriously. The novel was a best seller, a favorite among students, and there were concerns that it was surreptitiously spreading "fanatic" or even "deist" thoughts. Above all – and that is our concern here – the *Comte de Gabalis* was cryptically connected to the debate on the souls of animals.[89] After all, the spirits of nature that make up the center of the novel were also responsible for the souls of animals: elves were the life principle for birds; water nymphs (*undines*) for fish; gnomes for land animals; and salamanders for just this amphibian.[90] Paracelsus had written about such beings, and from Paracelsism they had migrated into many spiritualist theories.

Hocheisen's treatise turned out to be a further proof of the vehemence of the Wittenberg debates about the souls of animals, spirits, and thinking matter during the years just after 1700. From this perspective the Dietrich disputation – so important for Bucher – shared a background in the common student reading culture, which had prepared the ground for debate with its enthusiasm for the *Gabalis* novel. Hocheisen's text attained a high level: he was able to quote from rare and forbidden books, from Vanini to Koerbagh, from Cardano to Spinoza, from Stosch and Hobbes to Beverland.[91] The two dissertations were doubtless also the fruits of Hocheisen's sojourn in Hamburg from 1702 to 1705, where, during his

---

[86] Johann Georg Hocheisen, *Dissertationum physicarum quibus elementicolae Comte de Gabalis examinantur, dissertatio prior und dissertatio posterior*, Wittenberg, 1705.

[87] [Nicolas-P. Villars de Montfaucon], *Le Comte de Gabalis, ou entretiens sur les sciences secretes*, Amsterdam, 1670 and editions thereafter. On this, Erika Treske, *Der Rosenkreuzerroman Le Comte de Gabalis und die geistigen Strömungen des 17. und 18. Jahrhunderts*, Greifswald, 1933.

[88] Quoted from Treske, *Der Rosenkreuzerroman* (note 87), p. 24.

[89] Leonora Cohen Rosenfield saw that: *From Beast-Machine to Man-Machine. Animal Soul in French Letters from Descartes to La Mettrie* (note 27), pp. 93–97.

[90] On such creatures, see Bernd Roling, *Drachen und Sirenen. Die Rationalisierung und Abwicklung der Mythologie an den europäischen Universitäten*, Leiden, 2010. On the Comte de Gabalis, see pp. 78f.

[91] Hocheisen, *Dissertationum* (note 86). See in *Dissertatio I*, e.g., fol. A2r on Maimonides and Spinoza; fol. A2v on Vanini, Bodin, Spinoza, Koerbagh, and Hobbes; fol. B2v on Cardano; and fol. B3r on

years as a private tutor, he obtained access to scholarly connoisseurs such as Johann Albert Fabricius and Johann Christoph Wolf, who harbored such books in their cabinets.[92] In Hamburg, above all, he could expand his knowledge of Oriental studies, for the *Gabalis* novel had also touched on the Kabbalah, and so he had the opportunity to combine his awareness of the Wittenberg attacks on "enthusiasm" and "Spinozism" with a more complex understanding of Neoplatonic and Kabbalistic currents that Fabricius could impart. One of the main sources of confusion for Hocheisen and Wolf around 1700 was Franciscus Mercurius van Helmont, the propagator of the Lurian Kabbalah, which Lutherans regarded as a corrupted late-antique form of Kabbalah. In one of his letters to Wolf, Hocheisen wrote: "And even if Helmont may" seduce through his writings "those who display their erudition through such a character, truly astute people are not converted to him, for Helmont with his many vulgar principles" makes himself a laughing stock "among philosophers and chemists."[93]

With all this in mind, it was not absurd to connect Hocheisen's name with Bucher's *Correspondence on the Nature of Souls*. But the letters also showed that Hocheisen was no mere dissimulator; he was actually pressing forward a campaign against "fanatic Deists" with great seriousness. So Stolle was being misled by an idle rumor when he suggested that Hocheisen was the author of the mortalist *Correspondence*.

8 Bucher's Physiology of the Soul

Before Thomasius outed Bucher as the author in 1717, all the names that had surfaced in earlier discussions turned out to be false leads, but they illuminate the sensitivities that enflamed Wittenberg in the early

---

Beverland; in *Dissertation II*, fol. B1r on Bekker and Hobbes; fol. B1v on Spinoza, Koerbagh, and Stosch; and fol. B2r on F. M. van Helmont.

[92] On Fabricius, see Erik Petersen, *Johann Albert Fabricius. En Humanist i Europa*, 2 vols., Copenhagen, 1998; Ralph Häfner, *Götter im Exil. Frühneuzeitliches Dichtungsverständnis im Spannungsfeld christlicher Apologetik und philologischer Kritik (ca. 1590–1736)*, Tübingen, 2003, pp. 425–566 and passim; on Wolf, see Martin Mulsow, "Johann Christoph Wolf (1683–1739) und die Geschichte der verbotenen Bücher in Hamburg," in Johann Anselm Steiger, ed., *500 Jahre Theologie in Hamburg. Hamburg als Zentrum christlicher Theologie und Kultur zwischen Tradition und Zukunft*, Berlin, 2005, pp. 81–112. For Fabriciius's encounter with Neoplatonism and Kabbalah, see Mulsow, *Enlightenment Underground* (note 8), chapter 5.

[93] Hocheisen to Wolf, 1703, SUB Hamburg, Supellex Ep. 117, 181. See Franciscus van Helmont, *Seder olam sive Ordo saeculorum, historia enarratio doctrinae*, s.l. 1693. On van Helmont, see Allison P. Coudert, *The Impact of the Kabbalah in the Seventeenth Century: The Life and Thought of Francis Mercury van Helmont (1614–1698)*, Leiden, 1999.

eighteenth century concerning "naturalism," whether such tendencies came from theosophy or mechanical philosophy. But it is now finally time to turn to Bucher's actual argument. First we must sketch his understanding of cerebral physiology, which formed the basis of his theory of the soul. For him there were two faculties that could be ascribed to the soul: intellect and will. Both were "based on sensation"[94] – that is, on perception or sensory experience. For the intellect that meant that the sensory organs (especially those of sight and hearing) in the process of perception caused a movement in the fibers of the brain, through which an idea was formed. Bucher's medical mish-mash of German and Latin sounded like this:

> Such a movement *in cerebro* [in the brain]) comes together with whatever is *radii ab objectis protensi* [projected like rays from objects] in various ways onto the *Album* [blank page] in the *Camera obscura* [darkened room, optical box] and form a certain idea of one kind, but this idea is not really on the *albo* [blank page], but originates *pro varia dimotione fibrillarum tunicae retinae in oculo* [in various displacements of the tiny fibers of the retinal coat in the eye].[95]

The combination of ideas – in the form of movements of the fibers – produces thoughts.[96] But not all thoughts and ideas came from the process of perception because some were inborn, they were *ideae innatae* (innate ideas), which ultimately derived from Adam, whom God had equipped with perfect wisdom.[97]

The will was defined as "the stronger adhesion of a concept."[98] In saying this Bucher meant a disposition to certain movements, whether from a natural readiness or from some "prescribed law, . . . which constantly floats in the mind."[99] Here again he referred to Adam, for all of Adam's bodily members "were pleasing to God."[100] The law and his personal inclination

---

[94] *Briefwechsel* (note 25), p. 19.   [95] Ibid.   [96] Ibid.

[97] The doctrine of innate ideas had long been common among theologians, but it attained a new relevance with the reception of Descartes in the second half of the seventeenth century because theologians were trying to protect their own conceptions from Cartesianism. Internally they argued over whether the human soul possessed an inborn *habitus* (or better, "quasi habitus" as Calov said) for the perception of God, or only an "inner disposition" for such perceptions (as in Musaeus). We need to understand Bucher's use of the term "disposition" in this context. See Siegmund Jacob Baumgarten, *Untersuchung theologischer Streitigkeiten [. . .]*, vol. 1., ed. Johann Salomo Semler, Halle, 1762, pp. 418ff; Anselm Schubert, *Das Ende der Sünde. Studien zur lutherischen Anthropologie zwischen Reformation und Aufklärung*, Göttingen, 2002, pp. 140ff. For the connection of *ideae innatae* to Melanchthon, see below.

[98] See the corresponding mechanistic theory of Tschirnhaus or Hoffmann.

[99] *Briefwechsel* (note 25), p. 19.   [100] Ibid., p. 20.

were in accord – just as when ideas corresponded to the nature of things. It was the fall into sin that separated the two.

Here we can sense the presence of the Wittenberg theory of traducianism (which had medical as well as theological aspects), according to which the souls of the first human beings contained all the souls of their successors.[101] But the Wittenberg theory was desubstantialized and bound up with ideas of the fall into sin.[102]

If one tries to determine more exactly what Bucher meant by the two dispositions of the will, which he also called its "instincts,"[103] they were, on the one hand, the emotions and, on the other hand, the law, in the sense of the rules of reason, but also of public regulations. For "us Christians," according to Bucher, there was a third as well, the "instinct" of the Holy Ghost, which impels the faithful. What interested him above all, however were the affects or emotions, which predominated in normal actions (*in denen Civil-actionibus*). They were understood as motions that "either injured or delighted the structure of the body," a theory that thus follows the schema of pain or pleasure; in this way the heart is set in its motion, and the motion of the heart makes the blood thick or thin.[104]

All in all, this was not an unusual psychology or doctrine of the affects, but it was certainly notable in its reductive tendencies. The philosophical conclusion from this psychology was that the soul is not a substance but an attribute (*accidens*) of the body.[105] This was better than saying that there was no soul at all, but it implied that there was no separable part in the

---

[101] The theory of traducianism was one of the three current theories on the origin of the soul in the early modern period: The theory of preexistence asserted a one-time creation of all souls on the sixth day of creation; creationism (common among Calvinists) claimed that souls were created on the fortieth day of pregnancy; traducianism (mostly among Lutherans) assumed a mediating passing on of embrionic souls from parents at the moment of procreation. See Markus Friedrich, "Das Verhältnis von Leib und Seele als theologisch-philosophisches Grenzproblem vor Descartes. Lutherische Einwände gegen eine dualistische Anthropologie," in Martin Mulsow, ed., *Spätrenaissance-Philosophie in Deutschland 1570–1650*, Tübingen, 2009, pp. 211–249. For contemporary works, see Theodor Thumm (praes.) / Bernhard Wildersin (resp.), *Controversia de traduce sive De ortu animae rationalis*, Tübingen, 1622; Jacob Thomasius (praes.) / Johann Vake (resp.), *Disputatio physica de origine animae humanae*, Leipzig, 1669.

[102] See *Briefwechsel* (note 25), p. 43, on the theological advantages that Bucher claimed for his ideas.

[103] Ibid., p. 22.

[104] On the problem of the motion of the heart: Thomas Fuchs, *Die Mechanisierung des Herzens. Harvey und Descartes – Der vitale und der mechanistische Aspekt des Kreislaufs*, Frankfurt, 1992.

[105] See *Briefwechsel* (note 25), p. 78: "Ich halte die Seele vor nichts anders / als vor die Potentias, die Gott dem Leibe imprimiret hat / oder vor den Trieb / dergleichen Operationes zu verrichten / die ihn von anderen Geschöpffen distinguiren." And these *potentias* were deduced from matter. Johann Hermann von Elswich spoke in his analysis of the soul as accident in Bucher's thinking: *Recentiores de anima controversae*, Wittenberg, 1717, p. 5.

human being that automatically survived death and ascended to heaven.
That was a theologically risky doctrine.

9 The Wittenberg Style

All the same, Bucher did not shrink from trying to reformulate this theory
in the Wittenberg style of his teachers by making it compatible with the
Bible. We have to make a sharp distinction between the Wittenberg style
and the two better-known styles of Halle (that of Stahl and that of
Hoffmann).[106] We recognize the Wittenberg style even at a distance from
the quantity of references to biblical prooftexts. First purely medical
arguments would be presented, but then came a discussion of the relevant
passages from Holy Scripture. In Bucher's first letter to Roeschel there
were nine pages of medical text in contrast to fifteen pages of biblical
exegesis. Nine to fifteen? That was a rather common ratio for Wittenberg.
And someone would misunderstand these texts completely who regarded
the fifteen pages of biblical exegesis as gratuitous, nothing more than a fig
leaf added after the fact.

From the great mass of medically relevant biblical exegeses, let me
choose just a few examples. That man was the "image of God" (*imago
Dei*), was a common argument for the immortality and immateriality of
the soul: God was immaterial and immortal, and so must his image be also.
Bucher tried to avoid this conclusion by asking what was an "image," or
any likeness. An image was only the immaterial copy of something material
and was only real to the viewer. So there was a contrast. God was
immaterial, and we are not divine beings but only "images,"[107] so we
must be the contrast or opposite, and hence material. And because God
was a unitary being, his image could not consist of two things (material
and immaterial), and so man must be only material.[108]

This was a round-about and far-fetched argument, which was typical of
Bucher's sort of adventurous theologizing. He did the same thing with
passages from the New Testament. With the Old Testament Bucher had

---

[106] On the concept of style in the historiography of science, see Alastair C. Crombie, *Styles of Scientific Thinking in the European Tradition*, London, 1994; Ian Hacking, "Styles of Scientific Reasoning," in John Raijchmann and Cornel West, eds., *Post-Analytic Philosophy*, New York, 1985, pp. 145–165.

[107] This thought agreed with a teaching in Wittenberg, represented by Johann Stigel, *De anima, commentarii clarissimi atque doctissimi viri, D. Philippi Melanchthonis, explicata*, Wittenberg, 1581, p. 173.

[108] *Briefwechsel* (note 25), pp. 27f.

very few real difficulties because, as we have mentioned, the ancient Hebrews had not believed in immortality, and so their scriptures contained many passages in which the soul or life was said to reside in the blood. Taken literally the Hebrew of the Old Testament had no actual word for the "soul," as we have seen. But what was one to make of Jesus's words that seem so unequivocal? For example in the Gospel of Matthew, "And fear not them which kill the body, but are not able to kill the soul" (Matthew 10:28), and in Luke with reference to Lazarus (Luke 16:22), that "the beggar died, and was carried by the angels into Abraham's bosom"; or with regard to the thief on the cross next to Christ (Luke 23:43): "Today shalt thou be with me in paradise." Bucher labored to interpret all of these verses so that they pointed to his interpretation, including references to the Greek text, to Luther's method of translation, and to Lutheran Orthodox interpretations directed against the followers of Valentin Weigel.[109]

In addition, what I am calling the Wittenberg style required not only compatibility with Holy Scripture, but also included a series of other topoi, deriving often from Melanchthon, that found expression in dissertation titles and specific arguments. Thus, with regard to the fall into sin and the resulting ignorance of mankind: the human soul itself does not know what the soul actually is.[110] This was connected to the classification of medical doctrines under the rubric "self-knowledge." Bucher treated this matter, but he used it aggressively to defend the possibility of knowing oneself; even if pure reflexivity was not possible, one might at a pinch imagine the condition of others. And God would not have created men to be rational if he then could not even know himself.[111]

By the standards of Wittenberg, these were rather self-confident tones, totally different from the tone of Roeschel and his colleagues, and they reveal the spirit of the Tschirnhaus circle. But on the other hand Bucher, who certainly did not deny the Fall and its darkening effects, took seriously the contemporary metaphysics found in the philosophy of *Medicina mentis* (medicine of the mind)[112] and combined it summarily with a "vulgar Averroism". Human ignorance could be dispelled only with "education"

---

[109] Ibid., p. 29.

[110] See the appropriate books by van Helmont, Spener, Reimmann, and others. For a summary, see Samuel Christian Hollmann (praes.) / Adrian Gottlieb Söhner (resp.), *Dissertatio prior de stupendo mysterio anima humana sibi ipsi ignota*, Greifswald 1722, printed in expanded form in Wittenberg, 1724, and reprinted in Göttingen, 1750.

[111] *Briefwechsel* (note 25), p. 36.

[112] See, e.g., Ehrenfried Walther von Tschirnhaus, *Medicina mentis*, Leipzig, 1695.

and "learning" (*Doctrin*),[113] and this "learning" was in actual fact the human soul, "which makes him into a reasonable creature." Bucher should really have been speaking here of "spirit," because he was referring to the *intellectus agens* (active intellect) of Averroes, which was separated from the individual;[114] and just a few pages later he actually did speak of "spirit" as the "instruction received through word or hearing," which he places next to body and soul – soul here understood as the "faculty" or "aptitude" for movement of the bodily members.[115] So here we find Enlightenment Averroism serving as a partner to reductionist psychology.[116]

Another element of the "Wittenberg style" was the emphasis on the difference between pagans and Christians. We have seen one example of that already in the idea of the "instinct" of the Holy Ghost. As far as pagans were concerned, Bucher's doctrine of *notitiae innatae* (innate ideas) could function in an entirely traditional manner, for pagans did have traces of the knowledge of God, but they possessed them only confusedly; even for Jews and Christians the Ten Commandments and constant preaching were necessary to make true doctrine effective. Bucher went so far as to assert that he could even support Orthodox apologetics with his theory.[117] One might think this was a joke, a piece of insolence and provocation, for how could a "materialist" like Bucher pretend to bring pagans to Christianity? Yet he was not joking.

10   Melanchthon and the Soul

It was no joke because traditionally at the University of Wittenberg scholars had already discovered the use of certain materialist traditions. Unlike Halle, Wittenberg had not been infiltrated by modern Cartesian

---

[113] *Briefwechsel* (note 25), p. 25.

[114] Note the mentions of Averroes and Themistius, ibid., p. 35. On Averroes, see Dominique Urvoy, *Ibn Rushd*, London, 1991.

[115] *Briefwechsel* (note 25), p. 39.

[116] Bucher made a small excursus (p. 36f.) to examine the problem of inventions and discoveries. Such innovations could not be learned through (Averroistic) doctrine, but because of Adam's fall into sin they could no longer be directly remembered. Therefore, men employ the method of "analogism." By conceiving of analogism as a mixture of novelty and reminiscence, Bucher was here referring to books like that of Georg Pasch, *De novis inventis*, Leipzig, 1700; so all inventions were ultimately restorations of a lost knowledge. But invention was thus often connected to the suppression of impressions from the external senses so that one could reflect on oneself and in this way "remember" in the Platonic sense. Men had to free themselves from "der äusserlichen actionum ... , damit sie die *ideas innatas* evolvieren, oder besser zu reden, den *motum* und *tremorem fibrarum nervearum*, der von denen äusserlichen obiectis gemacht worden suppremiren können, damit sie zu ihrer natürlichen Constitution kommen mögen."

[117] *Briefwechsel* (note 25), pp. 37f.

and mechanistic ways of thinking, but had remained pretty conservative and Aristotelian and, at most, oriented toward eclecticism. Aristotelianism did harbor a latent notion of the soul's mortality, as we saw at the outset with Pietro Pomponazzi and Cesare Cremonini. Of course, Pomponazzi was not celebrated in Wittenberg, but in his place was Melanchthon, who was actually in agreement with Pomponazzi on one important point: he conceived of the soul as strongly influenced by the body. His work "On the Soul" (*De anima*) contains anatomical and medical portions and was commented on and expanded as a medical treatise by Johannes Magirus in Marburg and by Johann Stigel in Wittenberg.[118] One sign that Melanchthon saw great importance in the bodily dispositions was that he had taken sides with those who spelled the Aristotelian word "entelechy" with a "d" as "endelechy." The reason for this rested on a misunderstanding of Cicero, who, perhaps because he misunderstood the ancient Attic dialect, turned the "principle" which contained its own end or goal (entelechy) into merely continuous motion. As an entelechy, the soul was the organizing principle of the body; as an "endelechy" it was merely a condition of the body, to wit, its inner movement. In the late fifteenth century the editors of Themistius and Simplicius, Ermelao Barbaro, and Angelo Poliziano stressed this difference, but Barbaro was so distraught about the question of which description was the right one that he went so far as to pray to the devil to solve the riddle for him. Unfortunately the answer given by the devil was so softly spoken that he could not understand it.[119]

In any event, Melanchthon chose the variant with "d." The idea behind the choice was naturally that dualistically the soul had to be contrasted all the more sharply against the body, preserving the purely spiritual impact of a transcendent God on the world, without supplying a teleological principle that would exert its own shaping influence.[120] But if one ignored the theological parts of Melanchthon, an astonishing materialistic doctrine remained. Bucher referred also not only to the "entelechy" but also to Melanchthon's expression of "form" as an *axaedificatio rei* (a completion of

---

[118] Johannes Magirus, *Anthropologia*, Frankfurt, 1603; Stigel, *De anima* (note 107).

[119] See Pietro Crinto, *De honesta disciplina libri XXV*, Florence, 1504, VI, XI. On the concept of entelechy, see Cicero, *Tusculanae disputationes* I, 22.

[120] See Gideon Stiening, "Deus vult aliquas esse certas noticias. Philipp Melanchthon, Rudolph Goclenius und das Konzept der notitiae naturales in der Psychologie des 16. Jahrhunderts," in Barbara Bauer, ed., *Melanchthon und die Marburger Professoren (1527–1627)*, vol. 2, Marburg, 1999, pp. 757–787.

something), the development of something from its matter.[121] And his argument with Conring against the medieval and scholastic idea of "substantial forms" fitted well with this framework.[122]

If Bucher adopted only the nontheological half of Melanchthon, why did he take on his idea of the *notitiae innatae* or *notitiae naturales* – inborn ideas? In Melanchthon these *notitiae* were the influences of God within the human apparatus of perception.[123] Bucher was not interpreting against Melanchthon's meaning when he wrote that the *notitiae innatae* were inherited from generation to generation, in a manner that was strictly analogous to the common Wittenberg (and actually the generally Lutheran) doctrine of the transmission of souls. Thus there was divine intervention only at the very beginning, in the act of creating the first human being. Because Melanchthon got rid of the rational soul from his theory, this distancing of God became virtually absolute. The theological structure that Melanchthon built had survived, but it was partially disabled.

When he defended himself against the accusation of inventing a new heresy, it is astonishing how boldly Bucher reacted by citing Socinian exegesis. He noted that his views were those of "the ancient Sadducees and

---

[121] *Briefwechsel* (note 25), p. 17. See Philipp Melanchthon, *Liber de anima*, in *Opera quae supersunt omnia*, ed. Karl Gottlieb Bretschneider, vol. 13, Halle, 1846, p. 12. See Johannes Rump, *Melanchthons Psychologie in ihrer Abhängigkeit von Aristoteles und Galen*, Dissertation, Jena, 1897; Jürgen Helm, "Zwischen Aristotelismus, Protestantismus und zeitgenössischer Medizin. Philipp Melanchthons Lehrbuch De anima," in Jürgen Leonhardt, ed., *Melanchthon und das Lehrbuch des 16. Jahrhunderts*, Rostock, 1997, pp. 175–194; Helm, "Die Galenrezeption in Philipp Melanchthons De anima (1540–1552)," *Medizinhistorisches Journal* 31 (1996), pp. 298–321; Günter Frank, "Philipp Melanchthons Liber de anima und die Etablierung der frühnuzeitlichen Anthropologie," in Michael Beyer and Günther Wartenberg, eds., *Humanismus und Wittenberger Reformation*, Leipzig, 1996, pp. 313–327; Frank, *Die theologische Philosophie Philipp Melanchthons*, Hildesheim, 1995; Stephan Rhein, ed., *Melanchthon und die Naturwissenschaften*, Pforzheim, 1997; Sachiko Kusukawa, *The Transformation of Natural Philosophy: The Case of Philipp Melanchthon*, Cambridge, 1995; on his impact, see Hans-Theodor Koch, "Bartholomäus Schönborn (1530–1585)." Melanchthons *De anima* als medizinisches Lehrbuch," in Heinz Scheible, ed., *Melanchthon in seinen Schülern*, Wiesbaden, 1997, pp. 323–340. On the general context, see Katherine Park, "The Organic Soul," in Charles B. Schmitt et al., eds., *The Cambridge History of Renaissance Philosophy*, Cambridge, 1992, pp. 464–484.

[122] *Briefwechsel* (note 25), p. 35.

[123] Stiening, "Deus vult" (note 120), p. 775. See Sascha Salatowsky, *De anima. Die Rezeption der aristotelischen Psychologie im 16. und 17. Jahrhundert*, Amsterdam, 2006, pp. 119ff. Ursula Goldenbaum also interprets Bucher as a "rational" materialist because he accepted innate ideas; see "A Materialistic Rationalist? Urban Gottfried Bucher's Defense of Innate Ideas and Mechanism, added by his Denial of Free Will," *Quaestio. Journal of the History of Metaphysics* 16 (2016), pp. 47–73.

today's Socinians (who should not be regarded as stupid)."[124] Obviously aligning himself with this mortally hated and persecuted sect was better so far as he was concerned than having a reputation as an "innovator" or avant garde "neoteric." That tells us something: not that Bucher was indeed a Socinian, but that he was a thorough-going conservative. In his first letter to Roeschel, too, he took sides in the *Querelle des anciens et des modernes*, decisively defending the ancients, the "consensus of the old philosophers."[125]

There is no doubt that the question of the soul was a theological minefield. It was easy to stumble into a dangerous neighborhood. Thus the mixtures of Melanchthon and Sennert, which were so popular in seventeenth-century Wittenberg, brought direct contact with Socinianism, as happened in the case of the Socinian Christoph Sand, who published in 1671 a book, *De origine animae* ("On the Origin of the Soul"), an interpretation of the Church Fathers that explicated the "sleep of the soul" – that is, the condition of the soul after death but before the resurrection of the dead.[126]

We can see how closely this came to Orthodox Lutheranism in the fact that Roeschel's student and biographer, Johann Andreas Planer, found himself accused of Socinianism in 1712, just a year before the publication of Bucher's *Correspondence*. In a publication he had held that the soul of a living being existed earlier in its parents and ancestors and was transmitted by semen: *Latet anima in semine genitali* ("The soul lies hidden in the genital seed").[127] The crucial point was that for Planer the soul was not just potentially but, as in Sand, actually preexistent in the parents. As a theologian, Sand had claimed that his view was in full accord with Holy Scripture. Even if the physicians of Wittenberg did not wish to concede the point, we can assume that they would have had considerable interest in certain aspects of Socinian exegesis.

---

[124] *Briefwechsel* (note 25), p. 17. On the philosophy and especially on the materialism of the Socinians, see Sascha Salatowsky, *Die Philosophie der Sozinianer. Transformationen zwischen Renaissance-Aristotelismus und Frühaufklärung*, Stuttgart, 2015.

[125] *Briefwechsel* (note 25), p. 17.

[126] Christoph Sand, *Tractatus de origine animae*, "Cosmopoli," 1671. On Sand, see Sascha Salatowsky, "Debatten um den Ursprung der Seele. Der Arianer Christoph Sand und sein lutherischer Kritiker Balthasar Bebel," *Morgen-Glantz* 24 (2014), pp. 111–132. On this problem, see Baumgarten (note 97), vol. 3, Halle, 1764, pp. 453ff. This was a view close to that of Stoicism, which the early Church Fathers also shared. But Sand had accepted their view, and therefore his view was close to Melanchthon, who probably absorbed Stoic thinking from Vives and integrated it with his Aristotelianism.

[127] Planer, *Novam de animae humanae propagatione sententiam [...] publice tuebitur [...]* (note 68). On this, see von Elswich, *Recentioribus de anima controversae* (note 105), pp. 51ff

The traducian theory of the soul, which we have suggested as the background for Bucher's derivation of "innate ideas" from ancestors all the way back to Adam, was a complex area, often so tricky that those involved with it could find it impenetrable. With animals it was relatively unproblematic, but if one followed Sennert in regarding the rational soul as preexistent in one's ancestors, one could fall into considerable difficulties. Bucher seems to have been led by traducian theory into claiming that all "divine" parts of the soul (i.e., all parts that could not be explained physiologically) had existed in the distant past of Creation itself.

11   The Problem of Body and Soul: A Collision with Halle's Teachings on the Moral Temperaments

Bucher could not have developed his ideas in Wittenberg alone. For that, as we have seen, he had to connect with the physicians of Halle. We cannot imagine the explosiveness of emphasizing the bodily properties of the soul if we look only at the theological and natural-scientific debates in Wittenberg or the theosophical and early-Enlightenment efforts of what we have called "curious" physics. It was no accident that, once in Halle, Bucher chose Hoffmann to be his teacher. At that time in Halle there was great interest in the climatological and psychological connections between law and morals. For this purpose a kind of "Hippocratism" was brought up to date, because the Hippocratic doctrine of temperaments offered a psychological foundation for the newly important disciplines of natural law and literary history.[128] Like his colleague Stahl, Hoffmann had been working since 1705 on the temperaments.[129] From the philosophical, historical, and juridical side they were joined by their colleague Nikolaus Hieronymus Gundling, whom we will take up in Chapter 3.[130]

Gundling argued for a tight connection between the soul and the body, which served as its "house." In 1705–1706 he too wrote works dealing with the temperaments. In his characteristically aggressive way, and in

---

[128] See, e.g., the relevance of the doctrine of temperaments in thinking about melancholy. See the classic study by Raymond Klibansky, Erwin Panofsky, and Fritz Saxl, *Saturn and Melancholy: Studies in the History of Natural Philosophy, Religion and Art*, New York, 1964.

[129] Friedrich Hoffmann (praes.) / Thomas Kennedy (resp.), *Dissertatio inauguralis physico-moralis de temperamento fundamento morum et morborum in gentibus*, Halle, 1705; somewhat later, Georg Ernst Stahl (praes.) / Johann Andreas Wendt (resp.), *De mutatione temperamenti*, Halle, 1712.

[130] See Mulsow, *Enlightenment Underground* (note 8), chapter 6; and Chapter 3, esp. sections 1–4.

order to anticipate and parry the expected and obvious accusations, Gundling made the allegation of mortalism his topic:

> Don't be so gross as to make me out to be a Pomponazzian, for I do not claim that the soul is something corporeal; others, however, have defended [such a claim] not only long ago but even today. The pagans sometimes made [the soul] into a celestial body, or into a sort of subtle air, or an indivisible particle (atom). But does its supposed corporeality mean that it cannot be immortal? That is a different question. I believe that one cannot draw such a conclusion, but I do hold that it would make better sense if the soul is distinguished from matter, for then its immortality could be thought probable according to reason.[131]

Thus Gundling cloaked himself in the vagueness of probability and in the skeptical claim that he did not know.[132] What had been a sort of pure skepticism for libertines was now a matter of graduated reflection. But Bucher was different. Even though his switch from Wittenberg to Halle confronted him with an intellectual environment that was full of subtle thoughts about the relationships between the temperaments and the moral and behavioral dispositions, he aimed more decisively and clearly at categorical materialism. His dissertation under Friedrich Hoffmann was very different from what other students of Hoffmann defended at that time. Whereas Hoffmann composed texts for those students that almost exclusively dealt with concrete medical problems, Bucher wrote a short treatise on the principles underlying the physical-chemical foundations of medicine. He entitled it *Leges naturae* ("The Laws of Nature"), because he was interested in the linkage between the bodily processes relevant to medicine and more general physical processes. Of course, as Bucher said, one could not expect a complete explanation of all such bodily processes. So he referred to Morhof's fable of the fox and the porridge that pointed to the unknowability of things in themselves, which illustrates the wide impact that it was having in German universities. Bucher claimed that

---

[131] Nikolaus Hieronymus Gundling, "Von dem Temperament der Spanier," in *Otia*, 1st edn. (= Part 1), Halle, 1706, pp. 1–80; here at p. 12.

[132] See Luigi Cataldi Madonna, "Wissenschafts- und Wahrscheinlichkeitsauffassung bei Thomasius," in Werner Schneiders, ed., *Christian Thomasius*, Hamburg, 1989, pp. 115–136. For England, Barbara J. Shapiro has investigated the connections in *Probability and Certainty in Seventeenth-Century England: A Study of the Relationships between Natural Science, Religion, History, Law and Literature*, Princeton, 1983. See the remark of David Wootton, "If we are looking for an epistemological caesura separating the world of faith from the world of unbelief, probability, not Cartesianism, is our best candidate." Wootton, "New Histories of Atheism," in Michael Hunter and David Wootton, eds., *Atheism from the Reformation to the Enlightenment*, Oxford, 1992, pp. 13–53; here at pp. 51f.

the body must have an extremely subtle mechanism that cannot be compared to gross mechanical models.[133]

The result was a practical anti-essentialism like that developed in the contemporary experimental physics of Boyle and Sturm. They formulated hypotheses in order to explain phenomena but they no longer believed that doing so finally laid bare the underlying structure of nature.[134] We have already seen that this anti-essentialism was expressed in Bucher's rejection of the soul's substantiality. And indeed in his dissertation Bucher quoted both Sturm and Boyle.[135] But his theories were actually closer to the physics of that "most ingenious philosopher" (*ingeniosissimus philosophus*), Johann Joachim Becher, an experimentalist who rigorously argued in empirical terms.[136] Later, in 1722, Bucher transformed his admiration for Becher into a biography of the multifaceted scholar.[137]

In his dissertation presented in 1707, Bucher saw Becher as a representative of the atomist tradition, which forbade all reference to occult forces and explained the birth and death of things through the *synkrisis* (coming together) and *diakrisis* (separation) of atoms or particles. Following the conventions of the history he had absorbed, Bucher thought this tradition had arisen in the legendary Moschus the Phoenician, and been passed along from Hippocrates to Gassendi.[138] This was precisely the atomism – but a better term would be corpuscularism – that Bucher had come to know in Wittenberg through the medical thinking of Daniel Sennert. Recently William R. Newman has reclaimed Sennert as an important chemical inspiration for the Scientific Revolution.[139] His notion of "atoms" conceived of elements that could not be further reduced, and thus he introduced a criterion that for too long was ignored and

---

[133] See Mulsow, *Enlightenment Underground* (note 8), chapter 4; and Bucher, *Leges naturae* (note 38), p. 6.

[134] See e.g., Johann Christoph Sturm, *Physica electiva, hoc est, exercitationes academicae*, Altdorf, 1685; Robert Boyle, *A Free Enquiry into the Vulgarly Received Notion of Nature*, Cambridge, 1996. On this, Barbara Bauer, "Der Fortschritt in der deutschen Physik. Jakob Friedrich Reimmann, ein Vorläufer der Hypothese von Frances Yates," in Martin Mulsow und Helmut Zedelmaier, eds., *Skepsis, Providenz, Polyhistorie. Jakob Friedrich Reimmann (1668–1743)*, Tübingen, 1998, pp. 148–174, esp. 154–158; further Michael Albrecht, *Eklektik*, Stuttgart, 1994, pp. 309–360.

[135] *Leges naturae* (note 38), p. 11 (on Sturm), p. 14 (on Boyle).

[136] See *Leges naturae* (note 38), p. 12. See Johann Joachim Becher, *Actorum laboratorii chymici Monacensis seu physicae subterraneae libri duo*, Frankfurt, 1681. In 1663 Becher edited a selection of Sennert's aphorisms, *Aphorismi ex institutionibus medicis Sennerti*, Frankfurt, 1663.

[137] Urban Gottfried Bucher, *Das Muster eines nützlichen Gelehrten in der Person Herrn Doctor Johann Joachim Bechers*, Nuremberg, 1722.

[138] See Ralph Cudworth, *The True Intellectual System of the Universe*, London, 1678.

[139] William R. Newman, *Atoms and Alchemy. Chymistry and the Experimental Origins of the Scientific Revolution*, Chicago, 2006.

underestimated as "merely alchemical." Boyle, moreover, could not have developed his corpuscular theory without the prior work of Sennert; and so now we can understand Bucher's "chemical" version of physiological phenomena as deriving from Sennert and Becher and hence as part of this central strand of the history of science.

Around 1707, before he left the university, Bucher must have tried to discuss his ideas about the soul with one of the major luminaries in the area. In coded terms he spoke of "a highly learned man," whom he had always upheld as an authority in physical-theological matters. With these words he could have meant Hoffmann, whose works such as *De atheo convincendo* ("On Persuading the Atheist")[140] insisted on the theological relevance of his medical investigations. We will come back to that in Chapter 3. But Bucher stressed that he was not one of the actual students of the man – which our examination of his dissertation confirms – and that he could not claim the right to consult the professor on such a dangerous question. His fellow students may well have been gossiping and intriguing against Bucher, giving him another reason to avoid such discussions. He had entered the circle of this great man too late, "for I was already preparing my exit from the academy."[141]

And so Bucher retreated and confined himself to discussing these matters with only a few of the private students of this luminary in exchanges that helped him to clarify his ideas.[142] Yet this was not enough for him. He wanted a confrontation with one of the leading scholars. That was the reason that he finally fell back on his old connections with Wittenberg and decided to write to Roeschel. But there, too, he had to overcome some resistance because he was not really a student of Roeschel either, and knew him only from public disputations at the university.[143] But one of Hoffmann's students evidently offered to transmit Bucher's letter to Roeschel for him and thus vouch for Bucher's honor, defending him against nasty rumors. After all, it was far from common to question the substantiality of the soul, and so some sort of help from an intermediary seemed necessary.

It is worth noticing the precautions Bucher used to fend off "all evil imaginings" (*allen üblen Concept*), as he put it. We can glimpse the gulf between a professor and a mere student, the dangers of being a reputed materialist and "atheist," and his deep need for personal recommendations. This was all part of the "social history of truth" that Stephen Shapin has

---

[140] Friedrich Hoffmann, *De atheo convincendo*, Halle, 1705.   [141] *Briefwechsel* (note 25), p. 68.
[142] Ibid.   [143] Ibid.

described, a respect for the communicative relationships without which theoretical formulations and assertions were flatly impossible.[144]

What rumors were spreading in Halle and Wittenberg to prompt such anxiety in Bucher? He provided this hint: "For they are talking about me as if I were deliberately launching a new heresy and had already misled many youths, who could not be brought to think otherwise."[145] A new heresy – that can only have been a reference to Bucher's opposition to the immateriality of the soul. After all, in 1704 Bucher had publicly expressed such thoughts in the context of the disputation by Klemm, and he had perhaps repeated them on other occasions; groups of students and professors near him knew what thoughts he was harboring. The fact that Bucher had also composed antimetaphysical verses only strengthens the impression he gave as a rebellious student. Perhaps the novelties he had found in the English debates over mortalism led some to see Bucher's thinking as a "new heresy," but maybe the source was just the mechanical and physicalist explanations common among students. In any case he was worried that a bad reputation would do him harm. We have already gotten to know the case of the Halle student Johann Friedrich Kayser in *Enlightenment Underground*, about whom rumors were also circulating that he was a "rationalist" or even an "atheist," so that his adviser, Böhmer, openly refused to preside at his doctoral disputation. Kayser and Bucher must have had similar problems in trusting their professors.

In addition, one of those with whom Bucher had spoken in Halle[146] – perhaps the Hoffmann student who put him in touch with Roeschel – told the young physician outright that Bucher had plagiarized his views directly from a printed text.[147] He was referring doubtless to William Coward, whom Bucher obviously did not yet know. In 1707 he did read about the controversy over Coward in the journal *Unschuldige Nachrichten* (*Innocent Reports*, edited in Wittenberg by Valentin Ernst Löscher), and also about John Locke's *Essay Concerning Human Understanding*, as he said later.[148] And this reference to the time corresponds well with our suspicion that it was his conversations with Hoffmann's students in Halle that had brought

---

[144] Stephen Shapin, *A Social History of Truth. Civility and Science in Seventeenth-Century England*, Chicago, 1994.

[145] *Briefwechsel* (note 25), p. 15.

[146] Christian Wolff may have been one of these people. From the end of 1706 Wolff was a young professor of mathematics in Halle who had befriended Friedrich Hoffmann, recognizing in him an intellectual partner. In 1709 Hoffmann allowed Wolff to take over his lectures on experimental physics. See Martin Pott, *Aufklärung und Aberglaube*, Tübingen, 1992, pp. 373f.

[147] *Briefwechsel* (note 25), p. 69.   [148] "Declaration" (note 25), p. 103.

Bucher up to speed with international discussions. But even so it was then only secondhand, through reading about these debates in a journal edited in Wittenberg.

This unexpected agreement with a scholar who had explicitly defended the nonsubstantiality of the soul, had strengthened Bucher in his views.[149] He "let fly with this doubt," he said in his retrospective of 1723, and after 1710 he said in his answer to Roeschel's refutation, "Therefore I became completely resolved to think no more of this matter and certainly not to discuss it anymore or to write about it before I had read them [i.e., those authors] properly."[150] In other words, Bucher had decided to immerse himself in studying Locke and Coward before he again gave full-throated vent to his heretical views among other students. And yet, as an exception, he did want to compose a response to Roeschel.

12 Publicity and Marketing

Roeschel took his encounter with Bucher extremely seriously; indeed, he proposed to publish their correspondence. He would be prepared, he said at the end of his letter of refutation, "to make my piece known to impartial spirits, or even to have it published alongside your own."[151] That was a bigger step than Bucher had intended. He defended himself energetically, "I protest above all against divulging my shoddy and stormily composed writing, which is not of any real importance, and against publishing it in print."[152]

We should bear these circumstances clearly in mind: Against all the stereotypes regarding offensive and radical freethinkers, it was the professor who wanted to publish, not the representative of extreme views. Bucher repeatedly emphasized that the status of his assertions was technically "problematic"; his doubts were hypothetical and did not represent a firm conclusion.[153] He had appeared so outspoken and decisive with his argument only because he had developed it in the context of a Wittenberg disputation:

---

[149] Another agreement that Bucher retrospectively discovered was with an opponent of a book by Johann Ludolf Thilo, *Gedanken über die Frage, ob die Seelen in der triumphierenden Kirche auch besonders für die hinterlassenen Angehörigen beten*, Gotha, 1714. On that, see note 183, and Bucher, "Declaration" (note 25), p. 103.

[150] *Briefwechsel* (note 25), p. 69.   [151] Ibid., p. 67.   [152] Ibid., p. 68.

[153] On this, see also Martin Mulsow, *Knowledge Lost: A New View on Early Modern Intellectual History*, Princeton, 2022, Introduction.

I showed a greater *parrhesia* [freedom or openness of speech] because it is not a doubt that I made up myself, as usually happens in [the role of] opposing [theses in a disputation]; rather it was a [doubt] into which I'd been tempted by the "Opinion concerning The Immaterial Soul of Animals" [i.e., Dietrich and Klemm's *Dissertatio physica de anima brutorum*].

But Bucher maintained that he could not imagine that "anyone against whom I thought up something on the nullity of the soul's substance would have seized this opinion and championed it so obstinately."[154]

His fellow students at the disputation were, he thought, far from accepting this extreme line of argument, which he had drawn from Klemm's position.

Bucher concluded that he would not pursue his correspondence in such an open manner, issuing new and more extensive theses to Roeschel, but would instead merely react defensively to his objections.[155] The professor's announcement that he wanted to publish their correspondence had deeply shocked him.

Later on, Bucher depicted Roeschel's urging of publication as if Roeschel had taken to heart the principle that with heretics one did not necessarily have to keep one's promises – including the assurance he gave at the start that he would respect confidentiality. But maybe there Bucher's fear of public humiliation prompted him to view Roeschel's intentions in too sinister a light. In any event it is a fact that Bucher became heated and threatened public sanctions to deter Roeschel from publishing.[156]

The death of the Wittenberg professor brought this indecisive conflict to an end. And yet it is not too surprising that the very year of Roeschel's death brought the publication Bucher had so feared. There must have been people in Roeschel's camp – one might think of the executor of Roeschel's literary estate, Johann Andreas Planer, for example – who no longer felt restrained from divulging the correspondence.[157] One could think of the manuscript extracts that circulated in Wittenberg. Anyway, that was the scenario that the unnamed editor offered. He said that he wrote his foreword "at the behest of an honored friend"[158] as if the text had first come into the hands of this friend (and perhaps into the hands of others as well). Yet that could have been just a self-protective assertion. The manuscripts may well have been leaked directly to the publisher. Whatever the case, the text that served as the basis for the publication of 1713 was

---

[154] *Briefwechsel* (note 25), p. 69.   [155] Ibid., p. 69.   [156] "Declaration" (note 25), p. 100.
[157] See note 127.   [158] *Briefwechsel* (note 25), p. 12.

corrupt. One page was missing (or even both sides of a page), and some words were misconstrued. That may have happened during the printing process, but it increases the probability that the printer was printing from one of the badly copied transcripts that were circulating. So here we may have an example of the microform clandestine literature that was passed around within a small circle and not much beyond the small region where the text had arisen. This microform was characteristic of the university ambience with its niches and informal discussion groups, and it should be regarded as distinct from the macroform of clandestine literature that unfolded along much more extensive networks. We have seen in the case of Müller's *De imposturis religionum,* however, how quickly the microcirculation could spin out of control and be transformed into a macroform that had its own dynamic. This was just the sort of transformation that resulted when contextually limited ironies and allusions were decontextualized and took on a different tone: usually a tone of rigor and decisiveness that was never the author's intention.

So too in this case. The letters wound up with a publisher, who printed them and added a tendentious introduction, making only minor changes in the text. Thus the editor doubtless recognized from the salutation to the first and third letters or from the signature beneath the second letter that Roeschel was the professor, who was trying to confute the student. For that reason he obviously slightly modified a passage in the third letter – namely, in Bucher's reply to Roeschel's "Response" (*Überlegung*). The direct address of Bucher to Roeschel must have sounded like this: "Several times I heard Your Magnificence recount the stories of Peiresc and the nymphs,"[159] in which Bucher was referring to Roeschel's lectures. In the printed text, however, we read, "Several times I heard Your Magnificence, the late Herr Doctor Röschel, recount the stories of Peiresc and the nymphs," This was a risky move by the editor, allowing the name of Roeschel to slip in here, but evidently it seemed innocuous and defensible.

We do not know if the publisher and the author of the foreword were the same person. We know only that he did not come from Bucher's close circle – otherwise Bucher would have been able to prevent the printing or at least the corrupt version – and that it represented a different intellectual milieu. The editor was obviously a follower of Christian Thomasius, a typical representative of the popular and "galant" tone of the early Enlightenment. That much is perfectly clear.

---

[159] Ibid., p. 82.

In contrast to Bucher, however, the editor was not a natural scientist but someone more attuned to literary and philosophical themes. "Messieurs," he began, "in the more polished world it is now a recognized fact that the much needed sun of philosophical Truth has for too long been obscured by the thickest and darkest clouds in a gloomy sky."[160] It was time for the sun to break through these clouds, an image that alluded to the emblems we see in frontispieces of early Enlightenment books: a sun with the motto "*Dispellam*" (i.e., I scatter) as it breaks through the clouds of prejudice and superstition, and drives them away.[161]

The editor presented his foreword as fully in accord with this emblem, with a historical sketch of the recent advances in logic and physics:

> The obstacles that plagued an innocent physics were like the plagues of Job and lasted almost until the beginning of the seventeenth century when Francis Bacon (the Baron of Verulam) came to the aid of this half-dead and gruesomely tortured person.[162]

The witty foreword thus places the correspondence into the context of the "Quarrel of the Ancients and the Moderns," which was undergoing a fervent reception in Germany in just these years.[163] Swift's *Battle of the Books* became an especially well-loved source of metaphors for the controversies between the old and the new.[164] The editor evidently loved it too:

> And after an enraged logic was driven into such heated battle that the bewildered sentinels got so close to each other that they could look each other in the eye and fumigate each other with their smoking tobacco pipes, the learned world renewed its hopes, and not in vain, because the horrid Mathematical grenadiers with their learned allies played so fiercely with the eight kinds of Platonic bodies among the enemy troops that the enemy's right wing – where the horrible "Barbara Celarent" along with her "Darii Ferioque Baroco" etc. were deployed – was brought into utter confusion (before they were even aware of it) and obliged to abandon their lines.[165]

[160] Ibid., p. 3.
[161] It was, however, two years later, in 1715, that the first volume of *Gundlingiana* appeared, which used this emblem on its title page. Werner Schneiders, *Hoffnung auf Vernunft. Aufklärungsphilosophie in Deutschland*, Hamburg, 1990, p. 83.
[162] *Briefwechsel* (note 25), p. 3.
[163] See Peter K. Kapitza, *Ein bürgerlicher Krieg in der gelehrten Welt. Zur Geschichte der Querelle des Anciens et des Modernes in Deutschland*, Munich, 1981.
[164] Jonathan Swift, *A Tale of a Tub and Other Works*, ed. Marcus Walsh, Cambridge, 2010. See Joseph M. Levine, *The Battle of the Books: History and Literature in the Augustan Age*, Ithaca, 1991.
[165] *Briefwechsel* (note 25), p. 5. Despite Peter Kapitza's admirable diligence in collecting documents on the reception of the "Quarrel," this passage escaped him. [Translator's note: These terms ("Barbara Celarent" etc.) were customary names for valid Aristotelian syllogisms.]

The battle of the books was here connected to the reform of logic, and according to the words of the foreword "a bright light soon projected the improved doctrine of reason," obviously in the person of Thomasius.[166]

The fight for the new philosophy was understood – like the early Enlightenment in Halle as a whole – as a fight against various prejudices, and especially the blind respect for authority.[167] Starting there the author came to the doctrine of the soul:

> But stop amending it! [*Manum de tabula!*] It's enough that in all our actions we harbor an ugly and even slavish deference [*Praejudicia*] toward authority. Just take one instance from a thousand, that of our Soul. What vicissitudes this poor creature has already undergone – wandering all through the human body? How many amazing ideas about its nature have been spread throughout the world? One person places it in the brain, and has a multitude of followers. Another sets it in the pineal gland, and more than a few agree. Still others regard this abode as too small, and rightly. It cannot just be as if one were just playing the card game of piquet over a pot of coffee. So they place it totally in some part of the body, or totally in the whole body; and even though reason easily understands that there must be as many souls in a person as there are points within him, yet there are many apes ready to follow . . . Others again place the soul in the heart and make it swim around in the blood, while for others it has to creep into the ventriculum. Another even makes it a merciful gatekeeper for the anxious captain's deck, as a glance at these books fully demonstrates.[168]

This was a witty sketch of the various philosophical doctrines regarding the soul in which the author imitated the style of Gundling or Thomasius. The result of his ironic distance from the scholarly debate seems to be a strong skepticism:

> I confess that my youthful innocence is not yet capable of digging out the remaining essences of the soul from the cordial elixir [found in] these fat folios bound in pig leather, who should actually plunge into the sea along with the other Gadarene swine.[169]

The anti-academic but academically well-trained author also poured out his scorn on the method of extracting definitions from biblical quotations.

---

[166] Ibid., p. 6. Christian Thomasius, *Einleitung zur Vernunftlehre*, Halle, 1691; Thomasius, *Ausübung der Vernunftlehre*, Halle, 1691.

[167] On the critique of prejudice in the early Enlightenment, see Werner Schneiders, *Aufklärung und Vorurteilskritik. Studien zur Geschichte der Vorurteilstheorie*, Stuttgart, 1983.

[168] *Briefwechsel* (note 25), pp. 7f. See the English translation in Friedrich Albert Lange, *History of Materialism and Criticism of its Present Importance*, tr. Ernest Chester Thomas, vol. 2, London, 1892, pp. 40–41.

[169] *Briefwechsel* (note 25), p. 10.

To do so he uses Luke 24:39: "for a spirit hath not flesh and bones."[170] The author pretends to complain that as a layman he was obliged to believe that – except that he was in fact so enlightened that he understood Bible verses in the modern manner, in their context instead of randomly citing them as fixed arguments, as had been customary earlier:

> I believe that we can no longer be so broad with our definitions because instead of spirits we could be talking about pancakes, wheelbarrows, the shadow of an ass [i.e., all trifling matters], the wool of a goat [another image of arguing over trifles], chicken baskets, and a thousand other somethings [*Quelqueschoserien*] that have as little to do with flesh and bone as with their spirits.[171]

The author was here playing with the techniques of substituting one thing for another as we find in comic poems and paradoxical encomia that praised "nothing" or the hair of a goat, as practiced by Schupp and many others.[172] The point was that pancakes, too, have no flesh or bones, and so the definition of spirit under discussion was far too broad.

Because thinking of the soul as an immaterial spirit was so inadequate, however, the author of the foreword claimed that some thinkers hit upon the idea of the soul as a subtle material substance. That became a fashionable claim, as we may recall from the Wittenberg theologians' fears of theosophy:

> Many embraced it as something new because they heard that its authors had been called heretics and atheists and because these days atheism – or rather just the name of atheist – according to their perverted way of thinking, was an essential part of "galant" German learning. Like the earlier "freethinkers" [*forts esprits*] in France, they sought a reputation as dangerous and heretical; because they could not otherwise seem enlightened, they introduced their perverted theses on the soul into polite company, seeking "Gloriolam in Mustacco," as the old adage has it: as if against their will they were made to look like heretics. But with a little reflection anyone could see if this claim was true or false.[173]

Like Gabriel Wagner, who had earlier lambasted such theses on spirits, the ironical author blasted them as neither really new nor convincing,

---

[170] Ibid.   [171] Ibid.

[172] Martin Mulsow, *Die unanständige Gelehrtenrepublik. Wissen, Libertinage und Kommunikation in der Frühen Neuzeit*, Stuttgart, 2007, chapter 4.

[173] *Briefwechsel* (note 25), p. 11. [Translator's note: seeking "Gloriolam in Mustacco," was a misquotation from Cicero: *Ad Atticum* 5:20 "coepit laureolam in mustaceo quaerere," i.e., "to seek a bay leaf in a wedding cake," a proverbially easy task, because wedding cakes were baked on bay leaves.]

advanced by young people who were merely attracted by the thrill of the forbidden.

He saw a bit of that spirit in Bucher too: "The honorable reader will find some of that garbage here because various theses have been assembled in a clever and scholarly system."[174] That was certainly not fair because we have seen that Bucher was not just following some intellectual fashion and that with his corpuscular theory he was clearly distinguishing his ideas from theosophical ideas of spirits. That had also occurred to the editor of the manuscript, for he himself seemed dissatisfied with current theories of the soul and spirits, and was looking for a chance to engage with them. So when he came upon the manuscript, he published it. He noted that he had followed the Wittenberg case of Planer and was stimulated by it to consider other and more recent theories of the soul that differed from imagining a "subtle spirit."[175]

The Planer affair thus provides a key to the publication of the correspondence. Planer's *Nova de animae humane propagatione sententia*[176] ("A New Thesis on the Propagation of the Human Soul") was provocative because it renewed the tradition of Sennert and assumed that nature consisted of tiny particles (atoms). With that as a start, he validated neither the creationists nor the traducianists, but a new idea: "The soul is propagated through its unity."[177] Planer was another who argued in the Wittenberg style with just as many citations of the Church Fathers as we find in such adherents of the Sennert school as Sperling or Magirus. At the end of this tradition we then find major modern scientific innovators such as Leeuwenhoek and Swammerdam, whose microscopic observations led them to assume the existence of tiny seminal animals.[178]

We know little about the scandal provoked by this work, but obviously the theologians of Wittenberg had complained about its conclusions. Because Planer was just then preoccupied with the organization of his teacher Roeschel's literary estate and had come across Bucher's letters and

---

[174] Ibid.   [175] Ibid., p. 13.
[176] J. A. Planer (Praes.) / M. E. Wendius (Resp.), *Novam de animae humanae propagatione sententiam [. . .] publice tuebitur [. . .]*, Wittenberg, 1712. For a proper treatment of the Planer scandal, one would need to consult the letters from Planer to Valentin Ernst Löscher held in the SUB Hamburg, Sup. Ep. 76, 251–302. There are four letters from 1709–1711, but then fifteen letters from 1712/23, when the scandal broke.
[177] Ibid., p. 36: "Anima propagatur unione."
[178] Ibid., pp. 57 and 59. On these authors, see Lesley Robertson et al., eds., *Antoni van Leeuwenhoek: Master of the Minuscule*, Leiden, 2016; Edward G. Ruestow, *The Microscope in the Dutch Republic: The Shaping of Discovery*, New York, 1996; Eric Jorink, *Reading the Book of Nature in the Dutch Golden Age, 1575–1715*, Leiden, 2010.

Roeschel's response, he had a motive for passing these texts on to others. Doing so allowed him to shift responsibility away from himself, for it would divert attention from his own "heterodoxies," or it could lend him support in his concerns about notions of the soul that were more in accord recent ideas than the old conceptions dictated by Orthodoxy.

Interestingly, Planer and Bucher may have known each other from their common Saxon hometown, Frauenhain. Planer's father had been a pastor there until 1676 and his son (born in 1665) grew up there; while Bucher's father served as deacon under Planer's father and rose to be the pastor after Planer's death in 1667.[179] But because Bucher himself had been born in 1679 into a family that moved away in 1682, the lives of these two men, who were separated by fourteen years, overlapped only during Bucher's infancy. Even so, once they were both in Wittenberg, their common birthplace may have drawn them together into the circle of Roeschel's followers. When Bucher began his studies in 1699, Planer was already an adjunct in the philosophy faculty, and in 1702 he assumed a professorship in mathematics as a colleague of his teacher Roeschel.

Did Planer realize this when he came across the letters between Roeschel and Bucher? They had been composed anonymously, of course, and Bucher did not reveal his identity to Roeschel. But both Roeschel and later Planer may have guessed who the feisty student was who had concocted these thoughts. Planer, however, found an ally in the publisher, who was obviously an experienced publicist and an anti-academic who knew every trick in the book, a man who was eager to toss a bomb at both the Orthodox Lutherans and the theosophically inspired "visionaries."[180] And his bomb exploded.

Who was this publisher or editor, the writer of the "witty" foreword? Who could he have been? We can develop a sort of "suspect profile." The editor claimed to be young (referring to "my innocent youth") and insisted that his work had been prompted by the desires of a patron ("produced in great haste and at the pleasure of a distinguished patron").[181] Of course, both of these statements could have been defensive and deceptive gestures. Whatever the case, however, he must have been someone who had some contact with the early Enlightenment in Halle but who also had connections with Jena, where the text was probably published. He had a broad

[179] On the father Andreas Planer, see Reinhold Grünberg, *Sächsisches Pfarrerbuch*, vol. 2, Freiberg 1939/40, p. 690.
[180] At the same time the publisher did not wish to have the author regarded as a heretic, even if he was taking that risk by publishing him. *Briefwechsel* (note 25), p. 14.
[181] Ibid., pp. 11f.; but on p. 12 he said only: "auf Geheiß eines geehrten Freundes."

scholarly education, was well versed in writing German, and had both scholarly and literary interests. He had read about the *Querelle des anciens et des modernes* and cultivated a mocking style targeting academic culture.

One indication of his identity could be the parallels in a text that Bucher himself had noticed without knowing who the author was. He claimed that he had drawn comfort from more or less the same Bible passages confirming the mortality of the soul as those used by an anonymous author in 1714, who had objected to an edifying tract by a pastor from Polleben (a village near Eisleben), Johann Ludolf Thilo.[182] Thilo's Orthodox work was entitled *Thoughts on the Question whether Souls in the Triumphant Church* [i.e., in heaven] *also Pray Especially for the Members of the Church whom they have Left Behind*.[183] The anonymous author doubted that the Bible had really implied that souls lived on after death. He wondered "whether Christ had not actually denied that God was also a GOD of the dead."[184] One could and should view these souls as dead and, therefore, as beings who would rise again only on the day of the Last Judgment.

The place in which these objections were published was the periodical *The Secretary, Concerned with Matters relating to Politics, Peace, War, the Court, Literature, Religion, and also Private Affairs*. This was one of the many reviews that flourished during the surge of new journals in the early eighteenth century.[185] It appeared anonymously, as if published in "Freyburg" (i.e., Free City), but it was actually published in Leipzig as we know today, under the editorship of Andreas Stübel. As a generalist, Stübel wrote reviews of new works from all sorts of disciplines.[186] He was a private scholar who had had unfortunate experiences with the Church: after earning a master's degree in philosophy in 1676 and a bachelor's in theology in 1687, he provoked the ire of the Orthodox because of his

---

[182] *Briefwechsel* (note 25), p. 103. These references cited Ecclesiastes 12:7, Wisdom 3:1, Luke 16, Luke 22:43, and Matthew 22:32.

[183] Johann Ludolf Thilo, *Gedanken über die Frage, ob die Seelen in der triumphierenden Kirche auch besonders für die hinterlassenen Angehörigen beten*, Gotha, 1714.

[184] *Der mit allerhand Staats- Friedens-, Kriegs, Hof-, Literatur- und Religions- wie auch Privat-Affairen beschäfftigte Secretarius, 22. Expedition* [this was the name of the part], "Freyburg," 1714, pp. 891–904, here at p. 897.

[185] On this market, see Olaf Simons, "Von der Respublica Literaria zum Literaturstaat? Überlegungen zur Konstitution des Literarischen," *Aufklärung* 26 (2014), pp. 291–330.

[186] On Stübel (1653–1725), see Friedrich Koleway, "Stübel," in ADB, vol. 36, pp. 702–704; Johannes Arndt, *Herrschaftskontrolle durch Öffentlichkeit. Die publizistische Darstellung politischer Konflikte im Heiligen Römischen Reich (1648–1750)*, Göttingen, 2013, pp. 119f. Stübel, who taught at the School of St. Thomas in Leipzig, has played an intermittent role in the literature on Johann Sebastian Bach. See Hans-Joachim Schulze, "Texte und Textdichter," in *Die Welt der Bach-Kantaten*, vol. 3, ed. Christoph Wolff, Stuttgart, 1998/1999, chapter 6.

Pietist inclinations and chiliast convictions. For that reason he lost his position as a school teacher and his permission to lecture on theology at the University of Leipzig. So he then sought his fortune in journalism and in 1699 began editing a series of journals.[187]

The date of Stübel's review of Thilo's work was September 5, 1714. At that point the correspondence with Bucher had appeared more than a year earlier, and so Stübel could have found the biblical passages – the ones that were the obvious passages that mentioned the soul – from reading the published *Correspondence* if he had not already compiled the list of them on his own. We do not need to assume that he knew of them through the manuscript. But the argumentation opposing the soul's survival of the death of the body was far from commonplace, and so Bucher took note of the review.

Stübel was then no longer a young man who could speak of his "innocent youth," for he was 60 years old when the *Correspondence* appeared in print. But the tone that he struck in his journals definitely had something of the conversational tone that we also hear in the foreword to the *Correspondence*. Stübel's reviews in his journal always begin with the salutation, "Mein Herr," or sometimes "Monsieur" or something similar, just as the foreword to the *Correspondence* began with "Messieurs." In his years as a journalist Stübel had taken up the spirit of the early Enlightenment in Halle, and in the very same volume that contained his review of Thilo's work (in "Expedition" no. 22) he also reviewed a new book by Nikolaus Hieronymus Gundling, whom he respectfully described as the "excellent professor."[188] In this way Stübel, with his desire to get back at the Orthodox professors of Wittenberg, perfectly fits the profile we have imagined for the unknown editor of the *Correspondence*. These few indicators do not suffice, however, to conclude that Stübel was that editor. They only point to where the search should continue.[189]

---

[187]   1699–1703: *Aufgefangene Brieffe, welche zwischen etzlichen curieusen Personen über den jetzigen Zustand der Staats- und gelehrten Welt gewechselt worden*; 1704–1709: *Der neubestellte Agent von Haus aus, mit allerhand curieusen Missiven, Brieffen, Memoralien, Staffeten, Correspondencen und Commissionen, nach Erforderung der heutigen Staats- und gelehrten Welt*; 1710–1719: *Der mit allerhand Staats- Friedens- Kriegs- Hof- Literatur- und Religions- wie auch Privat-Affairen beschäfftigte Secretarius und dessen der heutigen curiösen Welt zur galanten Wissenschafft ertheilete ... Expedition.*

[188]   *Der mit allerhand Staats- Friedens-, Kriegs, Hof-, Literatur- und Religions- wie auch Privat-Affairen beschäfftigte Secretarius*, 22. *Expedition* (note 184), p. 844. There follows a review of Heumann's *Politische[r] Philosophus*, Frankfurt and Leipzig, 1714.

[189]   Other possibilities include Johann Gottlieb Krause, the editor of the *Neue Zeitungen von Gelehrten Sachen* in Leipzig, who was 29 years old in 1713. In his journal he was a sharp observer of the "Quarrel between the Ancients and the Moderns"; in 1715 he published a translation of a French

13   Reactions to the *Correspondence*

As Bucher had feared, the reception of his *Correspondence* almost inevitably denounced the anonymous author as a heretic. The work had appeared at the beginning of February, 1713, as we can tell from the fact that Johann Franz Budde reacted to it on February 5 from Jena, writing that it had been in circulation for a few days. Budde was the editor of a manifesto entitled *Programma de Arabicorum haeresi* ("A Proclamation on the Heresy of the Arabs").[190] Those knowledgeable in the history of theology would have recognized at once that this was a reference to the synod convened to deal with Beryl of Bostra, where an Arab sect of Christians had defended the mortality of the soul (and its later resurrection), but had been brought back to the truth by Origen. With this description, Budde was following his historical line of interpretation, which was constantly concerned to pursue heresies back to their historical origins and to name them accordingly. Naming them was thought sufficient to condemn them because history (he thought) had long since passed them by.

During the summer semester of that year a lecture was delivered in Jena on the *Correspondence*. That represents a surprisingly quick reaction to a recently published work, indicating that the book had probably been printed in Jena or at least had been delivered and distributed among students there. The professor who undertook to discuss the book *ex cathedra* was Johann Jakob Syrbius, who had been a professor in the philosophical faculty from 1707, where he was responsible for the teaching of logic and metaphysics.[191] Syrbius had first intended to discuss this

---

satire on the battles of the books: *Beschreibung des Landes der Alten und Neuen*, attached to the *Neue Zeitungen* of 1715. Krause wrote a "Foreword" for it. So if Krause was the editor of the *Correspondence*, then the "patron" who stood behind him would be none other than Johann Burckhard Menke, who published the *Neue Zeitungen*. One might also consider the young Gottlieb Stolle, but he was already 40 years old in 1713. In that year Stolle was an adjunct in the philosopical faculty of the University of Jena. Stolle possessed a satirical and publicistic bent and he was an opponent of Syrbius, who had held an entire lecture attacking the *Correspondence*; he had absorbed the "Quarrel" (citing it, e.g., in his treatise on Homer from 1712: Stolle (praes.) / Laurentius Hagemann (resp.), *Quaestio historico-philosophica, an Homerus fuerit philosophus moralis*) and had experience with anonymous publications; in addition he was the first who mentioned possible names of the authors of the *Correspondence*.

[190] For Budde as a "conservative Enlightener," see Mulsow, *Enlightenment Underground* (note 8), chapter 6. On the Arabs, see Johann Franz Budde, *De Arabicorum haeresi commentatio*, Jena, 1713, which was a pamphlet of a few pages introducing the lecture. See fol. A4v which refers directly to the newly published *Correspondence*.

[191] On Syrbius, see ADB, vol. 37, pp. 290f. See the announcement of lectures for the summer semester of 1713 in Jena (under the aegis of Prorector Wilhelm Hieronymus Bruckner), dated May 7, 1713, in the collections of the University Library of Jena.

current topic just at the beginning of the semester and then to give the rest of his normal lectures on philosophy, but he ended up giving over the whole semester to the *Correspondence*.[192]

Obviously in Jena they had the impression that the English controversy over mortalism was threatening to invade Germany, and the Orthodox reacted forcefully to stem this threat. But if the *Correspondence* really was printed in Jena, who was its editor? Löscher's *Innocent Reports*, which also discussed the *Correspondence* in 1713, suspected who the printer was and threatened to expose him.[193] This may have been an empty threat, however, because it did not apparently lead to anything.

In the next year such reactions continued, and now Leipzig got involved. August Friedrich Cämmerer published a theologically motivated *Investigation into the Soul*,[194] and Gottfried Polycarp Müller published a philosophical work entitled *Dissertatio pro loco gemina de mente substantia, a corpore essentialiter diversa* ("Double-Dissertation on the Origin of the Mind's Substance, as Essentially Different from the Body").[195] Many other works over the following years took up the controversy, which had spread and become generally well-known.[196] The editor of the *Correspondence* must have rubbed his hands with glee because the controversy was very good for business. He published three editions of it. If Stübel really was the editor, the trail pointed correctly to Leipzig, but then Stübel must have begun selling the book in Jena to cover his tracks, and only then expanded to his own hometown.

[192] In the announcement of lectures for the winter semester of 1713/14 (under the aegis of Prorector Johann Adolph Wedel) and dated October 8, it stated that the lecture dealing with the soul had just been completed.

[193] *Unschuldige Nachrichten von alten und neuen theologischen Sachen, Büchern, Uhrkunden, Controversien, Anmerckungen und Vorschlägen* (1713), Ord. 1, nos. 23, 155 and passim.

[194] August Friedrich Cämmerer, *Untersuchung über die Seele*, Leipzig, 1714. On the *Correspondence*, see pp. 10–28. On Cämmerer, a physician in Zörling, see DBA.

[195] Gottfried Polycarp Müller, *Dissertatio pro loco gemina de mente substantia, a corpore essentialiter diversa*, Leipzig, 1714. On Müller, see Reinhard Breymayer, "Pietistische Rhetorik als eloquentia nov-antiqua. Mit besonderer Berücksichtigung Gottfried Polycarp Müllers (1684–1747), in Berd Jaspert and Rudolf Mohr, eds., *Traditio – Krisis – Renovatio aus theologischer Sicht*, Marburg, 1976, pp. 258–272.

[196] Georg Nitsche, *Beantwortung der Frage: Ob die heilige Schrifft GOtt sey?*, Gotha, 1714, p. 70. Further: Johann Melchior Verdries, *De aequilibrio mentis et corporis commentatio*, Frankfurt, 1726, p. 4; Christian Gottfried Engelschall (Electoral Saxon Court Preacher), *De praejudiciis vitae*, Dresden, 1724, pp. 237 and 263; Polycarp Gottlieb Schacher, *Dissertatio de consideratione animae rationalis medica*, resp. R. A. Behrens, Leipzig, 1720, p. 6; Johann Heinrich Bocrisius (Steinfurt), "Apologetica pro subsistentia, immaterialitate et immortalitate animae rationalis," in *Miscellanea Lipsiensia*, vol. 8, Leipzig, 1719; Israel Gottlieb Canz, *Meditationes philosophiae*, Tübingen, 1750, I, I, 2.

The most competent survey of the increasingly labyrinthine discussions of the soul came from a Wittenberg insider, Johann Hermann von Elswich. In 1717 he published an extensive *Disputatio de recentioribus de anima controversiis* ("Disputation on the More Recent Controversies Concerning the Soul").[197] Elswich was five years younger than Bucher and had studied philosophy and theology in Wittenberg at about the same time. In 1703 he had earned his master's degree and by 1712 he was an adjunct in the philosophy faculty.[198] As an adjunct he first wrote a survey in 1716 of the recent debates on atheism, debates involving Gundling, Budde, Wolf, Hase, and others, in which the central point of contention was which traditions were "atheist," and which not.[199] Elswich demonstrated that he was completely familiar with "dangerous" literature – for example, he possessed a copy of Stosch's *Concordia rationis et fidei*[200] – but also that he was a stern opponent of the early Enlighteners in Halle.

And yet Elswich was not a blind fanatic. His book on debates about the soul, which appeared in the same year as he took up a pastoral position in Stade, shows us better than any other work the many strands of this discussion. Already on page 5 Elswich mentions Spinoza and Stosch and then the treatise that interests us here; he claimed that the anonymous author of the two letters in the *Correspondence* was philosophizing like Stosch:

> He holds that the soul is just an accident; or the abilities [*facultatibus*] and powers that the body has from God; or an instinct that allows a human being to accomplish those things that distinguish a human from other beings. From that it follows that the soul is not real but just "formally different," as they say at the university, from the body, and that it perishes with the body at last; for when the body is destroyed, the powers or abilities [*facultates*] that are in it cannot remain or be preserved. This is why it is crucial that he shows how the human being can [produce acts of] thinking and willing without a principle distinct from the body. It all comes down to this: that understanding [*intellectum*] consists of a trembling [*tremore*], which arises when things that are outside us are passed by our senses to

---

[197] Johann Hermann von Elswich, *Disputatio de recentioribus de anima controversiis*, Wittenberg, 1717.

[198] On Elswich (1684–1721), see Mulsow, *Enlightenment Underground* (note 8), chapter 5; and ADB, vol. 6, p. 73.

[199] Johann Hermann von Elswich (praes.) / Johann Sigismund Buchwald (resp.), *Controversiae de atheismo recentiores*, Wittenberg, 1716. As we saw in Mulsow, *Enlightenment Underground* (note 8), chapter 6, Elswich had directly attacked Gundling for defending Hobbes and had demanded the death penalty for atheism.

[200] See Detlef Döring, *Frühaufklärung und obrigkeitliche Zensur in Brandenburg. Friedrich Wilhelm Stosch und das Verfahren gegen sein Buch "Concordia rationis et fidei,"* Berlin, 1995.

the fibers of the brain, which are connected to those very sense organs. And the will is supposed to be nothing other than the tension of that trembling when it is excited in the fibers, through which a person who clings to an idea is then further excited from whatever ability was either implanted in it by nature or given by law, and always heeding its memory. The cardinal error that led this man to such a view lies in the affinity that he sees between the actions of men and animals, in whom he denies the [existence of] an immaterial soul.[201]

The actual importance of Elswich's work lies less in the arguments he marshaled against Bucher than in the fact that he embedded Bucher's *Correspondence* in the whole debate. Elswich dealt thoroughly with Andreas Rüdiger, whom we will come to later; he incorporated the Planer affair in his exposition; he treated mystics like Poiret and the Platonists, along with Westphal and the tradition of Melanchthon, Sennert, Sperling, and many others.[202]

14   The Late Bucher: Definitions of God with Vanini and Simoni

The published version of Bucher's *Correspondence*, which had appeared without his knowledge, was reprinted twice in 1723.[203] In the meantime Bucher had been unmasked by Thomasius as the author. We do not know if this revelation did him any harm, but at least his career at the court of Dresden seems to have been undisturbed. By 1723 in any event, Bucher was firmly established in Dresden and had published several recognized books, and it now appeared to matter to him that the unauthorized version of the *Correspondence* of 1713 should be replaced with a correct version. So he established contact with a publisher and provided him with the original manuscripts. We do not know if this was the original printer in Jena or perhaps Bucher's current publishers in Nuremberg or Dresden. Bucher still preferred to remain anonymous despite his exposure by Thomasius, and this new version also appeared with a fictitious place of publication:

---

[201] Elswich, *Disputatio de recentioribus de anima controversiis* (note 197), p. 5.

[202] Ibid., pp. 24ff. and frequently on Rüdiger; p. 51 on Planer; p. 75 on Manichäism and metempsychose, esp. in van Helmont's *Seder Olam*; p. 77 on Poiret; pp. 61ff. on the Platonists, z. B. Stepanus Theupolos (d. i. Francesco Piccolomini); pp. 48 and 62 on Westphal; p. 47 on Stigel's Melanchthon Commentary; p. 53 on Sennert and Sperling, etc.

[203] *Zweyer Guten Freunde vertrauter Brief-Wechsel vom Wesen der Seele. Sammt des Editoris Vorrede und des Autoris näheren Erklärung, wie auch anderweitigen Untersuchung des Wesens der Seele u. des Geistes*, Amsterdam, 1723, p. 3. An edition from 1721 is held by the SB Berlin, bound with Gotthard Guenther, *Schediasma historico dogmaticum de anima*, Leipzig, ca. 1706; it can also be found in Heidelberg, Greifswald, Jena, Munich, Bamberg, and Erlangen among other places.

but this time not "In The Hague" but "In Amsterdam." As an epigraph Bucher inserted two sentences that were supposed to provide cover, one under the name of Cicero (*Qui fit, ut optime cogitata saepe pessime cadant* – "How comes it that the best intentions often produce bad results?") and the other supposedly by Lactantius (*Sunt plurima, quae nec ignoranti nocent, nec scientem juvant* – "Many things neither harm the ignorant nor help those who know").[204] These were far different slogans from the provocative ones that the first editor had chosen.[205]

Bucher decided not to revise the text but to leave it in its original form and merely correct the many typographical errors. As we have noted, in the original text a whole page of the manuscript had gone missing, which had led to a deformed version. This page was now supplied. Bucher even allowed the original editor's "witty foreword" to survive in his new edition.

The new publisher wrote a short preface, which obviously relied on exact instructions from Bucher. The editor, who we assume was holding Bucher's master copy in his hands, kept so scrupulously to the master text that at one point he neglected to replace Bucher's "to me" with the appropriate "to him" in the third person.[206] So in this preface we can actually speak of a text by Bucher himself. And the preface expresses the amazement that Bucher obviously felt that his little book from 1713 had not been confiscated by the censors, and sales had not been forbidden even though the printer was well-known.[207] It carefully added a list of the refutations that had appeared in the meantime. Bucher agreed that at least some of them had been written "in a gentle spirit and without prejudice."[208]

The new preface appears to have been deeply skeptical about recent "fashionable" mechanistic philosophies and affirmed the value of many

---

[204] The first sentence was a general saying, "Why do good intentions so often produce bad results?" that can also be found in Cicero; it was a reflection on the unintended effects of Bucher's *Dubia*. The second saying, "There are many things that neither harm the ignorant nor help those who know," came not from Lactantius but from Seneca, *Epistula* XLV, and reclaimed a region of epistemic adiaphora, where Bucher thought his meditations belonged.

[205] There it said: "Si licet aliis quod lubet dicere, nobis quid lubeat liceat credere." Gundling had begun his *Otia*, vol. 1, Frankfurt and Leipzig 1706, in similar manner: "So wenig es dir verboten ist, etwas zu schreiben, so wenig ist es mir auch verboten."

[206] *Brief-Wechsel vom Wesen der Seele*, 1723 (note 203), p. 8: "Aristoteles, der bey mir mehr gilt, als des Cartes."

[207] Foreword, p. 3. Indeed, Agatha Kobuch in her investigation of censorship cases in Electoral Saxony says nothing about Bucher; see her *Zensur und Aufklärung in Kursachsen. Ideologische Strömungen und politische Meinungen zur Zeit der sächsisch-polnischen Union (1697–1763)*, Weimar, 1988. But there is no comparable study of censorship for Jena and the duchy of Saxony Weimar.

[208] *Brief-Wechsel vom Wesen der Seele*, 1723 (note 203), pp. 9f.

Aristotelian observations on the soul. He had provided many a "tough nut to crack," for Aristotle could not be easily explained away in mechanical terms. And he referred to the old idea that Paracelsus had also supported, that the imagination of a pregnant woman could have an influence on the developing fetus:

> The fact that a pregnant woman can imprint something corporeal and real upon the fruit of her womb forces modish philosophers to ask if the axiom, "The spirit cannot act upon the body," will serve to protect and preserve themselves against the attacks of the devil?[209]

The "modish philosophers" he had in mind were the followers of Balthasar Bekker, who tried to base a sort of Enlightenment on mechanistic principles.[210] But according to Bucher things were not so simple. Even though he did use mechanistic arguments in the *Correspondence*, he was not ready to join the Cartesian mechanists wholeheartedly because he was impressed by the many phenomena that could not simply be reduced to their principles.[211] Certain phenomena, such as magnetism, were flatly beyond human ability to explain, and so the intellect had to restrict itself to describing effects without providing any first causes.[212]

From a basis in moderate skepticism, however, Bucher also warned the theologians not to celebrate their triumph too quickly as if they imagined they "could see farther with the eye of faith" than others could with the eye of reason.[213] He accused the countless theological treatises that attacked the dreaded "atheism" of the naturalists of actually prompting the "desire" of many freethinkers to become atheists.[214] That claim led Bucher to consider a few of these so-called atheists, who he tried to show had not really been (or should not have been called) atheists.

Here Bucher was treading on thin ice, for he revealed what he had been reading, and these sources did not firmly testify to his Orthodoxy, as he had hoped. He thought he could openly adopt the idea of God as

---

[209] *Brief-Wechsel vom Wesen der Seele*, 1723 (note 203), p. 6.

[210] Balthasar Bekker, *Die Bezauberte Welt: Oder Eine gründliche Untersuchung Des Allgemeinen Aberglaubens / Betreffend / die Arth und das Vermögen / Gewalt und Wirckung Des Satans und der bösen Geister über den Menschen / Und was diese durch derselben Krafft und Gemeinschafft thun*, Amsterdam, 1693. See Annemarie Nooijen, *"Unserm grossen Bekker ein Denkmal"? Balthasar Bekkers "Betoverde Weereld" in den deutschen Landen zwischen Orthodoxie und Aufklärung*, Münster, 2009.

[211] See *Brief-Wechsel vom Wesen der Seele*, 1723 (note 203), p. 8: "Aristoteles, der bey mir mehr gilt, als Des Cartes."

[212] Ibid., p. 7.   [213] Ibid.

[214] This comports well with the thesis of Alan Charles Kors, discussed above in the Introduction, on the "orthodox sources" of atheism.

expressed by two philosophers who had been condemned as notorious arch-atheists: Lucilio Vanini and Simone Simoni. Admittedly, he did so in the context of other recent attempts to "rescue" those accused of atheism:

> How many have been turned into atheists who never ever were so? Just read the *Apology* for Giulio Cesare [i.e., Lucilio] Vanini. Has there ever been a better description of God that that of this unlucky scholar? And that is the judgment of a great theologian in Württemberg. But if you want to know what brought him to the stake, just read the *Apology*.[215]

Like many other radical representatives of the early Enlightenment,[216] Bucher had obviously read Arpe's *Apologia pro Vanino* of 1712 and been encouraged by it to avoid demonizing all naturalistic approaches to God as atheism.

Vanini's works themselves were surely unavailable to Bucher. In Arpe he could read, however, that Vanini had depicted God as the Principle and End of Himself, even though He had neither one because he had no need of them, seeing that he was the creator and generator of them both.[217] Vanini described his God with paradoxical predicates so that, as Arpe said, he might approximate the divine majesty at least allegorically. For himself, Arpe said that he liked best the definition of God given by the "Hermetics" – namely, that He was a sphere whose center was everywhere but whose circumference was nowhere.[218]

The other "atheist" mentioned by Bucher was Simone Simoni (1532–1602), the Italian physician who lived in exile – in Geneva, and then in Paris, Germany, Poland, and finally Moravia. The anti-atheist literature of the early modern period often claimed that in 1588 he wrote a blasphemous book under the title *Simonis Religio* ("The Religion of Simoni").[219] But that book was really a satirical attack on Simoni launched by his opponent Marcello Squarcialupi, in which the naturalist views of the

[215] *Brief-Wechsel vom Wesen der Seele*, 1723 (note 203), pp. 7f.

[216] See the Introduction to this book; on Arpe and his anonymous *Apologia pro Vanino*, see Mulsow, *Knowledge Lost* (note 153), chapter 4.

[217] Arpe, *Apologia pro Vanino*, "Cosmopoli," 1712, pp. 41f. See Vanini, *Amphitheatrum aeternae providentiae*, Lyon, 1615, Exercitatio 11.

[218] This is the definition of the pseudo-Hermetic *Liber XXIV philosophorum*. See Martin Mulsow, "Ignorabat Deum. Scetticismo, libertinsmo ed ermetismo nell'interpretazione arpiana del concetto vaniniano di Dio," in Francesco Paolo Raimondi, ed., *Giulio Cesare Vanini e il libertinismo. Atti del convegno si studi Taurisano 28–30 ottobre 1999*, Galatina (Lecce), 2000, pp. 171–182.

[219] *Simonis Simonii Lucensis, primum Romani, tum Calviniani, deinde Lutherani, denuo Romani, semper autem Athei summa religio*, Kraków, 1588. In Bucher's day this work was only known through rumors. See József Simon, *Die Religionsphilosophie Christian Franckens (1522–1610?): Atheismus und radikale Reformation im frühneuzeitlichen Ostmitteleuropa*, Wiesbaden, 2008, pp. 39f. On Simoni's actual views, see pp. 53–61.

antitrinitarian physician were construed as atheism. His apparently blasphemous confession of faith was famous and could be read in Voetius, Spizel, or Bayle: "I believe in the Three: heaven, earth, and the form of heaven; in heaven as the Father and Creator of everything; in the earth as the Mother and Nourisher of everything; and in the form of heaven as that which feels and understands everything."[220] Bucher quotes that sentence but adjusts it by saying, "So the author meant to conclude, blasphemously, that there is no God; but then where did heaven and earth come from? For even if one derived them from Eternity, how could a form arise without something that forms it?"[221] Thus Bucher agreed with Aristotle in emphasizing a first cause, the effective cause behind everything else. He interpreted it, however, as if Aristotle had intended the cause to be "the *Ens Entium*, the being of all beings, in whom we live and move and have our being." The quotation from St. Paul (Acts 17:28) barely disguised the fact that Bucher understood his first cause as a principle different from nature, to be sure, but one that worked everywhere in nature and could be perceived only in nature. That explains his interest in the quotation from Simoni.[222]

15   The Treatise, *De natura mentis et spiritus*

Bucher used this indirect confession of God in order to transition to a work that he attached to the reprint of the *Correspondence*. This short text was entitled *De natura mentis et spiritus* ("On the Nature of the Mind and Spirit"). It was a work that treated the problem of the soul again but with its Latin it was deliberately aimed at an academic readership, in order to offer no further provocation to critics.[223] This twelve-page text must come from a time after 1714, for it refers to Gottfried Polycarp Müller's *Mens substantia* ("Mind Substance"). Probably Bucher wrote it specially for the publication of 1723. It was his last word – a sort of forced confession of faith[224] – in the debate on the soul, and it may have been a concession to the censorship authorities or to his patrons as an agreed precondition to getting this new edition published. Concerning this text Bucher now says in the preface to the new edition of the *Correspondence*:

---

[220] *Brief-Wechsel vom Wesen der Seele*, 1723 (note 203), p. 8. On Simoni, see also Mariano Verdigi, *Simone Simoni. Filosofo e medico del'500*, Lucca, 1997.

[221] Ibid.

[222] In the *Simonis [. . .] summa religio* (note 219), *calor*, the warmth of heaven formed the connection between heaven and earth.

[223] *Brief-Wechsel vom Wesen der Seele*, 1723 (note 203), pp. 105–118.   [224] Ibid., p. 4.

If one had from the start argued against our author's doubts concerning the substance of the soul with the logical *canon* [rule] that God, divine matters ... , and other things of the sort must be excluded from the philosophical categories, he would have immediately retreated, as he says in the last investigation [i.e., in his final letter].[225]

That sentence is hard to interpret. First one has to remember that Bucher (like Arpe) was reading Vanini and Simoni as skeptics, as theorists who acknowledged their lack of knowledge from the start but then tried to define God using paradoxical statements. Vanini had said explicitly:

> If I knew what God is, then I would actually be God; for no one knows God and knows what he is except for God Himself. As with a little sunlight shining through a cloud, however, we can glimpse a little of what He is through His works.[226]

So if Bucher now spoke of the "exclusion" of topics like the divine, he was pointing to this border between the human and the divine. Thus he wanted to say that if someone had earlier pointed out that statements about what humans can understand needed to be kept strictly separate from statements about God, he would have accepted that.

Thus later in life Bucher was showing a growing uncertainty in his views. He also said in considering the "logical Canon [rule]":

> If I were asked about its position in the body, its transplantation, and such matters, I trust that I'd be allowed to answer with the logical rule that Predicates must be such as are permitted by their subjects. So if the soul is a spirit, it would be better to keep such questions in their place rather than applying to them the idea of a bodily thing ... .[227]

Predicates could only be what their subjects permitted, according to a scholastic logic that preserved the separation of philosophy from theology.[228] In 1713 Bucher had obviously ventured onto theological terrain when he described the powers of the soul as divine attributes that expressed themselves in human beings:

> I regard the soul as the faculties [*potentias*] that God has imprinted on the body, or as the drive to accomplish the sorts of operations that distinguish man from other creatures. So with these powers how does the human resemble GOD without being GOD himself? I hold that these [powers]

---

[225] Ibid., p. 8.   [226] See the reference in note 217.

[227] *Brief-Wechsel vom Wesen der Seele,* 1723 (note 203), p. 104.

[228] See Luisa Valente, "Le principe de l'approche contextuelle et sa genèse," in Joel Biard und Irène Rosier-Catach, eds., *La tradition médiévale des catégories (XIIe–XVe siècles),* Louvain, 2003, pp. 288–311. See also the *Briefwechsel,* 1713 (note 25), p. 76.

are the divine attributes through which the likeness to GOD is expressed, but I cannot form a concept of the highest GOD at all, except according to human attributes even if they are given to Him in a higher or in the highest degree; and yet I must never confuse these two opposing beings, namely the material and the immaterial.[229]

It is certainly not true that Bucher was thinking of Spinoza when he wrote about the "expression" of the divine attributes.[230] His language emphasizing the difference between the material and the immaterial could hardly be reconciled with Spinoza, who eliminated that contrast.[231] Rather, this form of thinking about "expressing" belonged to the theological doctrine concerned with the image of God, as we find for example in the Wittenberg theologian Johann Andreas Quenstedt, who in 1685 formulated his understanding of a "certain general conformity between God and Man" this way:

> One must distinguish between the image of God, (1) in the improper and indirect sense, as the substance of the rational soul itself, its essential faculties (reason and will), and thus a general congruence and analogy according to which the human soul expresses something divine (and in this sense we concede that the image of God has survived in the descendants of Adam down to today) – and (2) the image of God in the proper sense, that is the perfections and capacities of the soul or of the faculties of the soul, i.e., a substantial ["concrete"] righteousness and piety, an integrity and rightness of all its powers. In this last sense it [the image of God] has been completely destroyed.[232]

He was saying that the human being in possessing reason and will reflected a very general analogy to the being of God. But original sin has disturbed the right functioning of these faculties. We will return to this doctrine of the image of God, which we have earlier treated with respect to Bucher's idea of "image" because its great importance becomes especially evident here in *De natura mentis et spiritus*.

In any case, by 1723 Bucher treated the separation from theology with the greatest caution. Was he retracting his radical assertion of 1708? He

---

[229] *Briefwechsel*, 1713 (note 25), p. 83.

[230] Spinoza, *Ethik* I. Def. VI: "Per Deum intelligo ens absolute infinitum, hoc est, substantiam constantem infinitis attributis, quorum unumquodque aeternam, et infinitam essentiam exprimit."

[231] See in general Wolfgang Bartuschat, *Spinozas Theorie des Menschen*, Hamburg, 1995.

[232] Johann Andreas Quenstedt, *Theologia didactico-polemica, sive Systema theologicum in duas sectiones didacticam et polemicam divisum*, Leipzig, 1715 (the first edition was in Wittenberg, 1685), Part II, p. 901. I am quoting essentially the text and translation according to Schubert, *Das Ende der Sünde. Anthropologie und Erbsünde zwischen Reformation und Aufklärung*, Göttingen, 2002, p. 120.

begins by again quoting a sentence from Cicero: "It would have been better … to admit you didn't know what you didn't know instead of sickening and disgusting yourself by babbling as you did."[233] That seems like a confession made by the mature Bucher: that in his youth he should not have asserted such stupid things. In any case this motto expresses the desire for restraint in theological matters. The point that was now subjected to a reappraisal concerned what I have earlier called "vulgar Averroism": Bucher's characterization of what makes a human being "into a rational creature." Back then Bucher called it "doctrine" because he was strongly averse to talking about "spirit."[234] But now (in 1723) it was different.

Bucher now had to concede that

> there is, however, something in the human that can suppress or excite actions, whether they are a property of the intellect or the judgment, or of the will: the former of which refers to the so-called theoretical, namely the true and the false, while the latter refers to the practical, namely the just and the unjust. No one will deny that this faculty of choice or free will is a capacity or a force or an ability, which is clearly something different from being the essence of a body; and it is not necessary that it have its origin in the principle through which bodily or animal actions arise, because it conflicts with the actions and affects of the body. For two contradictories cannot exist in one subject.[235]

The freedom and morality of human beings do not have to be thought of as physiological functions, Bucher says, but can be understood as actually opposed to them, because they sometimes contradict one's feelings.

But then what are the qualities and attributes of this capacity for free will? Bucher rejected the answer that Müller proposed in his discussion of the *Correspondence,* namely that there were three criteria. Müller had first mentioned the "penetrability" of the mind – in contrast to the impenetrability of the body; Bucher argued against that view.[236] Müller also emphasized the quality of "indivisibility,"[237] but Bucher was unpersuaded. And finally, the quality of "activity," but Bucher insisted that that was a quality possessed also by the body – just think of the movement of the

[233] *Brief-Wechsel vom Wesen der Seele,* 1723 (note 203), p. 106. See Cicero, *De natura deorum,* Lib. 1, 84; translation modified from Brian A. Krostenko, *Cicero, Catullus, and the Language of Social Performance,* Chicago, 2001, p. 112, n. 71.
[234] See note 113.   [235] *Brief-Wechsel vom Wesen der Seele,* 1723 (note 203), p. 111.
[236] Gottfried Polycarp Müller, *Dissertatio pro loco gemina de mente substantia* (note 195), p. 24.
[237] Ibid., p. 28.

heart, which cannot be stopped deliberately.[238] Instead, Bucher defined the mind (*mens*) in this manner:

> It is the principle of the incorporeal which judges [the difference between] the true and the false as understood by the intellect; and which determines what to do and what not to do; it is a supplement to the human body and mostly opposes the body's motions.[239]

This was a definition that was well calculated to curb those critics who charged Bucher with crude materialism. He stressed that he had derived this definition precisely from the difference between body and mind. While animals are not directed by such an immaterial principle, but rather by their bodily structure or by their innate capacities, human beings are specifically different in that they do follow such a principle. And what is it? We can recognize what it is, according to Bucher, if we see how it is nourished and what it draws its strength from. "The mind however sustains itself from the divine Word; therefore it is necessary that it is spirit [i.e., divine spirit], for otherwise it would be incapable of appropriating it; and no one perceives what God is, excepting only the spirit of God."[240]

The theological reversal in the later Bucher is thoroughly astonishing. We should not invoke here the Kantian idea that man is a citizen of two worlds, the phenomenal and the noumenal, because that would be anachronistic. But Bucher's distinction does have a bit of this flavor, although it comes from the contemporary Orthodox Lutheran doctrine regarding the image of God. So when Bucher spoke of the divine Word, he was not just referring to the biblical or revealed Word. Rather he was thinking of the *lumen naturae* (the light of nature), the inner Word, the inner Christ. That sheds light on what Bucher in the *Correspondence* was still calling "doctrine." He was Christianizing his vulgar Averroism. And the term *Christus internus*[241] (the inner Christ) makes us sit up and take notice, for that was a key notion for Quakers and for many Pietists. Even Lutherans such as Andreas Osiander had spoken of it, when they were concerned about the unity of the human being. But was not the "inner Christ" just a guideline for the born-again man, for the baptized and believing Christian? Could one employ this concept generally for man and his free will or mind?

In the *Correspondence* Bucher had noted St. Paul's claim that the pagans had the Law written on their hearts, but this involved only a recognition or

[238] Ibid., pp. 29f., but in contrast, see Bucher, *Brief-Wechsel vom Wesen der Seele*, 1723 (note 203), p. 112.
[239] *Brief-Wechsel vom Wesen der Seele*, 1723 (note 203), p. 112.   [240] Ibid., p. 113.   [241] Ibid.

veneration of the creator, not anything dealing with the salvation or future of man.[242] Did that justify speaking as if all men had an "inner Christ"? Actually, no; but Bucher deemphasized such theological niceties.

Yet what were the actions that were typical for the mind? They were *immanent*, like perception and reflection (Bucher did not shy away from adopting the distinction drawn by John Locke, which had infiltrated the early German Enlightenment[243]) or *transient*, such as utterance or judgment, but also *moderamen*, the direction of actions.[244] The mind, after all, displays itself precisely there where it either suppresses impulses from the sensitive soul, such as phantasy and feelings, or receives and strengthens them. But Bucher held that one should not fall into the error of thinking that the body was merely passive while only the mind was active; the body had its own resistances and repugnances.

Thus Bucher understood the mind as more than cognitive, for it was anticorporeal in the sense of being free and morally conscious. This led him to distinguish between free will (*arbitrium*) in the sense of choice (*electio*) and the actions or those powers that come into play in an action. Along with St. Paul he recognized that one may sometimes will something but be unable to accomplish it,[245] and he agreed with Pierre Chauvin, Bayle's collaborator and a liberal Calvinist, who had said (in *De naturali religione*), "If you destroy free will [*liberum arbitrium*], you also destroy reason [*rationem*], along with virtue's rewards and the punishment of wickedness."[246] The fall into sin took away human powers to act but not human free will, Bucher said.[247] What helps us to accomplish good nonetheless, however, was divine grace, which assists us and dwells within us.[248]

Here we find ourselves again in the middle of theological anthropology, in the tangle of *imago Dei*, original sin, grace, and free will. Bucher's distinctions between our postlapsarian weakness in actions and our genuine freedom reflects again the difficult position in which Lutheranism found itself after Matthias Flacius's sharp interpretation of Luther's

---

[242] *Briefwechsel,* 1713 (note 25), p. 77.

[243] John Locke, *An Essay Concerning Human Understanding,* London, 1690, Book II.

[244] *Brief-Wechsel vom Wesen der Seele,* 1723 (note 203), p. 114.

[245] Ibid., p. 115. Bucher refers to Romans 7:18ff.

[246] Ibid. Cf. Pierre Chauvin, *De naturali religione liber, in tres partes divisus. Ubi falsa candidè refelluntur, vera probantur vel deteguntur, ac Orthodoxarum Ecclesiarum fratres ad concordiam vocantur,* Rotterdam, 1693.

[247] This was Bucher's attempt to weaken Orthodox Lutheran and Calvinist positions, according to which human freedom had been impaired by original sin.

[248] *Brief-Wechsel vom Wesen der Seele,* 1723 (note 203), p. 115. See also p. 116.

position – according to which original sin had destroyed the image of God
in mankind; but since that image constituted man's substance this meant
that the substance of man had been destroyed.[249] Lutheran Orthodoxy
spent the whole seventeenth century struggling to create distinctions
between a general and a special sort of "image of God" so that these
disastrous Flacian consequences could be avoided. If, for example, original
sin had become the actual substance of man, then that would mean that
God was the origin of sin or it would ascribe to the devil genuine powers of
creation. But of course they rejected these conclusions, too.

We have already seen that Bucher aligned himself with the description
of the relationship between God and man implicit in the terminology that
Quenstedt had used, emphasizing the "general" agreement of man with
the image of God. Here too we can recognize the effort to make distinctions about the effects of original sin: the *imago Dei* in its essence had been
lost, and therefore man's ability to act had been weakened, but in a general
sense the *imago Dei* was still present, and so in principle the freedom to act
had survived. Bucher did not wish to deny all freedom and rationality to
man; and yet he conceded that men were dependent on God, and indeed
he made this insight the cornerstone of his understanding of the mind. In
this sense he was "more conservative" than most radical Enlighteners and
showed again that his many biblical and exegetical reflections along the
lines of the "Wittenberg style" were not just camouflage. They were
earnest reflections on the Christian worldview.

After all, the Christian notion of grace depended on how one understood the human condition, on "anthropology": the grace of God was the
auxilium (aid) that helped man overcome his weakness and do good.[250]
But once again Bucher smoothed over some of the distinctions: for him
the grace of God came only to those who truly believed, who were "born-
again"; he did not think it was available to all.[251]

But Bucher hastened to add that one should by no means confuse the
soul (*anima*) itself with this "being" which assists the soul. He rejected all
contemporary tendencies that understood the soul as a distinct substance

---

[249] Schubert, *Das Ende der Sünde* (note 232), pp. 36–41.
[250] The doctrine of *auxilium* came from Spanish late scholasticism (Molina and others) and was later
absorbed in Lutheranism, and especially by the Pietists, who strongly emphasized human freedom.
[251] At this point one can ask whether the late Bucher, who was living in Dresden from 1718 on, met
with Nicolaus Ludwig von Zinzendorf, who was a judicial and court official in Dresden from
1721 and who had founded his commune in Herrnhut (about 55 miles east of Dresden), where the
refugee Bohemian Brethren had settled. Gottfried Polycarp Müller, with whose *De mente
substantia* Bucher disagreed, became school rector in Zittau in 1723, and gradually came closer
and closer to the Herrnhuters until he finally took on a leading position among them.

(*hypostasis*) as Helmont had with his *archeus*, or as Leibniz did with his monads.[252] If one followed them, one might arrive at a *spiritus* doctrine of the inborn divine in man, which had indeed become popular by 1700. But how many parts did man then have? Three: namely body, soul, and spirit? Or two? Or was he a unity? Bucher chose not to decide the matter. He composed the last passages of his tract so as to have a double meaning that permitted both a naturalistic and a Christian interpretation:

> While the spirit is sometimes seen as an inborn force, something that drives the body into action, something that acts voluntarily, but sometimes as something that assists the soul as the principle of voluntary actions, there seems to be agreement in this: that both versions influence the parts of the body and both are impermanent, and therefore cannot be regarded as essential parts [of man].

This was the only important point for his argument: the "divine" in us, which helps us to act freely and in a morally responsible manner against many of our inner impulses, is not permanent; it acts only occasionally. "The first Spirit proceeds from the general impulse of desire, which we call the world soul [*Anima mundi*] or universal Spirit; but the second proceeds from the divine essence."[253] Those were the two possibilities under discussion, between which Bucher refused to decide: the more pagan or the more pronouncedly Christian.

Bucher added, however, that if one posed the question of the spirit from a specifically philosophic point of view, then it would have to be: "Is this spirit a substance or an accident?" That had been the topic of the *Correspondence,* and he concluded that the soul was accidental. Bucher laid out the consequences clearly: "If one assumes the first, that the spirit was a substance, the binarity of the human parts becomes a trinity, which appeals to the fanatic."[254] The so-called fanatics (i.e., the spiritualists) were happy to assume a trinity of spirit, soul, and body.[255] Even Andreas Rüdiger, who was not a fully fledged "fanatic," did take a step toward

---

[252] *Brief-Wechsel vom Wesen der Seele,* 1723 (note 203), pp. 115f. For more on this, see Chapter 3. Thus Bucher turned against every attempt to "divinize" nature. Among his opponents he listed Henry More, Johann Baptist van Helmont, Johann Doläus, Leibniz, and James Stair.

[253] Ibid., p. 117.   [254] Ibid.

[255] Johann Gerhard, for example, "repeatedly emphasized in his work that the human consists only of the two parts, 'body' and 'soul.' He explicitly criticized Paracelsists, Schwenckfeldians, and 'enthusiasts' who referred to Lk 1: 46–47, 1 Thess 5:23, and Hebr 4:12, which attributed a three-part structure to the human being." See Salatowsky, *Die Philosophie der Sozinianer* (note 124), p. 375, but also p. 424. See also the article "Seelenbeschaffenheit" in Johann Georg Walch's *Philosophisches Lexicon,* Leipzig, 1726, esp. cols. 786f., concerning those who follow "Platonist ways," "which is where the fanatics belong."

the spiritualists by sympathizing with Helmont's notion of the *archeus*; he assumed three parts: the body; a suprapersonal mind; and an *anima*, which was similar to the Aristotelian *intellectus possibilis* but which, like the *archeus*, possessed an ability to discriminate the true from the false.[256] From the high ramparts of Lutheran Orthodoxy with its fight against the "fanatics," Bucher said that this sort of trinity looked deeply suspect.

But opting for seeing the soul as an accident also had a drawback:

> If you mean the latter, that would rob it of its effectiveness, for who would wish to ascribe operative force to a [mere] accident? It's not enough to settle this dispute by citing the logical rule that exempts God and divine things from having predicates because of their excellence; here the logical rule got lost, and for that reason one wants to measure divine and bodily things using the same measuring stick.[257]

The situation was aporetic. A merely accidental grace (because it was not permanent) in the form of an indwelling spirit could not be persuasive because it could not really be effective as the source of actions. Bucher the skeptic pushed this aporia into the mixture of natural-scientific questions with theological topics, which surpassed human understanding. In the end he could only comment:

> Yet in its pitfalls this controversy seems to me to be just like the one launched by the Flacians over the substantiality of sin. Paul himself says in [his letter to the Romans], at verse 20, that committing a sin is something one does not will; thus just as an action can be imputed [to sin], so too the action of the born again can be ascribed to divine power.

According to the theological anthropology of Flacius, original sin had become the substance of man, and so original sin gave the final push to an action – this was Bucher's somewhat amateurish analogy[258] – and so it was sin to which the action could be attributed. The corollary was that, for the believing Christian, God's grace gave the last shove. And so their actions could be attributed to grace. "They unite the spiritual forces of the mind or soul, which they call the 'spiritual man,' in order that the animal [parts] might obey and the instruments of wickedness might become the armor of the spirit."[259] The spirit, understood as the helping

---

[256] Andreas Rüdiger, *Philosophia synthetica methodo mathematicae aemula comprehensa*, Leipzig, 1707. On Rüdiger, see Chapter 2.
[257] *Brief-Wechsel vom Wesen der Seele*, 1723 (note 203), p. 117.
[258] In the "manichaean" theology of Flacius (as his opponents called it), it was the devil rather than sin to which the act could be imputed.
[259] *Brief-Wechsel vom Wesen der Seele*, 1723 (note 203), p. 118.

grace of God, changes the capacities of man, which are not in themselves morally oriented, so that they could perform good deeds. "Our reason does not perceive how this union takes place because it is a matter of faith, which we cannot dispute but must take on faith, as Holy Scripture teaches ... ."[260] So he finishes with a confession of not knowing. Somehow divine power makes man into a unitary being, but we have no way of knowing how.

Bucher's theologically articulated position from 1723 can be summarized this way: It was founded in an Aristotelianism that had been augmented with mechanistic principles. The nonsubstantialist *anima sensitiva* (sensitive soul) could be understood in a manner that also included the capacities of the *anima rationalis* (rational soul), because both intellect and will could be explained largely through the workings of the cerebral fibers in connection with the stimulations of the senses – at least in principle. Even so, there was a sort of inner principle that gave human beings a sense of truth and falsehood, and that also helped to support righteous actions against the inclinations of the senses. This was what distinguished men from animals. This "spirit" was not, however, to be regarded as something substantial for it was probably only accidental, even if that was hard to judge. The model for this inner principle and its role as helper was the grace that came from God to born-again, believing Christians. That meant, however, that for Bucher in a sense non-Christians were not human. They had reason and will, to be sure, but they lacked the essential property (of humans).

Bucher did not fully discuss this counterintuitive and exaggerated conclusion. He was almost suggesting that Christians were so radically different from others that the essential features of Christianity were eviscerated, a thought that would not have pleased Bucher's theological critics. Was he here trying to Christianize his "Averroism" or at least offer a Christian explanation for it? That seems possible, and yet from the very beginning the context of the discussion of the *imago Dei* and the problem of original sin flowed so completely into Bucher's theory that here we are more likely seeing the shortcomings of an amateur theology than some hidden heterodoxy.

---

[260] Ibid. In Bucher's view, this page of the *Correspondence* (1713 edition) was in conformity with the Bible.

16   Secularization?

We have reconstructed the case of Bucher in such detail because only in this way can we see that belief in the mortality of the soul during the early Enlightenment was not a simple case of secular reason and intentional modernization. For one thing, several actors with entirely different intentions and mental horizons had to collaborate so that the *Correspondence* could be published as a book.[261] They were not freethinkers at all, but respectable Wittenberg professors, liberal natural scientists, shrewd publicists – and one student who was plagued with doubts. If today we sometimes speak of "relational authorship," in order to describe the fact that a book is the product of a whole series of persons working together,[262] then the *Correspondence* is a prototypical product of relational authorship. Moreover, Bucher's philosophy – and especially his late philosophy – was not simply secular, but permeated through and through with theological anthropology. Bucher fended off charges that his materialism should be subsumed under the label of "Spinozism"; he defended himself against Cartesian mechanists, and even against Enlighteners such as Balthasar Bekker.

If what occurred in the case of *The Confidential Correspondence of Two Good Friends Concerning the Essence of Souls* is secularization, then what do we mean by secularization? Obviously it is not a category that can be applied across the board in undifferentiated fashion. The only reason for using the category at all is to dissolve it into a series of distinctions. Recent research has begun to do that already, as we now distinguish more carefully between de-Christianization, estrangement from the Church, and desacralization. Beyond that we clearly must deny that it describes any global, single-track path to the present day. For example, instead of disengagement from the Church, one can also describe an opposing process of respiritualization.[263] But we should not get stuck here, and instead – as the case of Bucher shows – outline at least four further distinctions.

---

[261] In my essay, "Radikalaufklärung, moderate Aufklärung und die Dynamik der Moderne," in Jonathan Israel and Martin Mulsow, eds., *Radikalaufklärung*, Berlin, 2014, pp. 203–233, I argue in analogy with ecology that "radical" texts of the Enlightenment emerge from a whole food chain or nutrient web, in which outsiders are connected to established scholars; ideas come from one person, but are then taken up by others, then are collected and passed on by third persons, and may then be adopted by a fourth layer.

[262] See, e.g., the announcement of a conference in Berlin on "Works in a Network: Relational Authorship in the Eighteenth Century," org. by Carlos Spoerhase and Erika Thomalla, May 11–12 and November 16–18, 2017.

[263] On these differentiations, see Hartmut Lehmann, ed., *Säkularisierung, Dechristianisierung, Rechristianisierung im neuzeitlichen Europa*, Göttingen, 1997.

First it appears that we must distinguish between secularization as intention and as result. With Friedrich Hoffmann in Halle, secularization was an intended and well-considered effort to differentiate between the realms of medicine and theology while maintaining an orthodox Christian worldview and while using modern medicine as an example of Christianity seen as a mode of ethics.[264] In contrast to Hoffmann, Bucher's secularization was completely one of effect, and an effect that was unintentional and magnified by the uncontrolled publication of his correspondence – a result that emerged from the deep confusions in an intensely theological milieu. Bucher's text worked as a pioneer for a secular and reductionist psychology in areas where scholars had ignored theological or biblical ideas that could (surprisingly) support the natural sciences.[265]

Second, there is something like regional types of secularization just as there were what I have called different "styles" at certain universities or within certain faculties. Corresponding to a given style one can then distinguish between places that upheld the traditional style and achieved a form of secularization within that style – as Bucher did – and those places where the style itself became secularized.[266] But it is crucial to notice in detail which parts of a theory became "secular" (for example, in Bucher one might point to his ideas of cerebral physiology, or perhaps his vulgar Averroism, and his erasure of the differences between pagans and Christians), and which parts remained "sacral," along with how the two parts stayed in balance. From that standpoint one can then consider the internal dynamics of the theory: Where was theological thinking cut off so that there might be room for something else?

Third, there is a need for a further, very difficult fine determination of just what and how much was left to the truth of revelation. Often, and indeed partially in Bucher, we find an insistence on the exact text of the Bible, which became the basis for an apparently "secular" position, as we find in the case of mortalism. In this way it could happen that theologically "orthodox" thinkers became mortalists precisely in order to combat the optimism about reason found among "Enlighteners" or "deists," who believed that they could rationally prove the immortality of the soul.

[264] On Hoffmann, see notes 37 and 140, as well as Chapter 3.

[265] On the further developments of the Enlightenment understanding of the soul, see the article "Seele" in Johann Heinrich Zedler, ed., *Grosses vollständiges Universal-Lexicon aller Wissenschaften und Künste*, 68 vols., Halle and Leipzig, 1732–1754.

[266] Here one should note the difference between preserving a theological model as a model, even if "secularizing" processes take place within the model, and replacing that model with another, entirely different secular model.

One example came from England, where around 1700 the discussion was at least as confusing as it was in Germany. But there at least the discussion was carried out rather openly, so that the different positions appeared more clearly. Indeed, in England we can study the tactics and dissimulations of various participants, so that "it is possible that . . . the theory of conditional immortalism served to conceal an unconditional mortalism,"[267] – a point that I will not discuss here.

Fourth and finally, such processes of secularization were not fundamentally processes of a *longue durée*; they could rather be intermediate processes of medium duration. To take an extreme example, Wittenberg was an intellectual milieu that had become thoroughly confessionalized from the sixteenth century onward. Although medicine before the Reformation and especially in Padua and Bologna had always been a fairly secular enterprise, that changed during the confessional era. We know that Melanchthon modified the Aristotelian idea of the soul, rejecting Christian-scholastic doctrines and establishing a new theological domination over Renaissance Aristotelianism and Renaissance Galenism; this is a very good example of how a process of theological domination could become a movement of medium-term duration, but then was "resecularized" by thinkers like Bucher. Such resecularizations then can seem almost like academic accidents.

---

[267] See David Berman, "Die Debatte über die Seele," in *Grundriss der Geschichte der Philosophie ('Neuer Überweg'). Die Philosophie des 17. Jahrhunderts*, vol. 3: *England*, ed. Jean-Pierre Schobinger, second half volume, pp. 759–781, here at p. 778.

CHAPTER 2

Nature and Idolatry
The Ambivalence of the Natural from Henry Stubbe to Christian Gabriel Fischer

1 The Activity of Nature

The debates about idolatry in the seventeenth century exercised a powerful influence, and not just in theology and in religious controversies.[1] Because these debates have fallen into oblivion, however, their influence on other disciplines has remained invisible and underestimated for too long. Even though their explicit focus was on ancient Israel and ancient Egypt it is obvious that they structured a nascent ethnology, the study of the religions of the New World and of exotic cultures.[2] But they had an impact upon discussions of politics as well, as we saw, for example, in the critique of absolutism as "political idolatry." On the surface this was about the deification of rulers in antiquity, but beneath the surface it concerned the semireligious veneration of King Louis XIV. And these debates

---

[1] For a sketch of the debates on idolatry, see chapters 3 and 4 of Martin Mulsow, *Enlightenment Underground: Radical Germany 1680–1720*, tr. H. C. Erik Midelfort, Charlottesville, 2015. This present chapter draws on three modified and expanded essays of mine, which have appeared in English before, at least in part: "Henry Stubbe, Robert Boyle and the Idolatry of Nature," in Sarah Mortimer and John Robertson, eds., *The Intellectual Consequences of Religious Heterodoxy 1600–1750*, Leiden, 2012, pp. 121–134; "Idolatry and Science: Against Nature Worship from Boyle to Rüdiger, 1680–1720," *Journal of the History of Ideas* 67 (2006), pp. 697–711; "Der Wolffianer Christian Gabriel Fischer und seine Vernünftigen Gedanken über die Natur," in Jürgen Stolzenberg and Oliver-Pierre Rudolph, eds., *Christian Wolff und die europäische Aufklärung*, Part 5, Hildesheim, 2010, pp. 145–162. [Translator's note: I have gratefully used parts of the two English translations in translating this chapter.]

[2] See Francis Schmidt, "La discussion sur l'origine de l'idolatrie aux XVIIe et XVIIIe siècles," in *L'idolatrie. Rencontres de l'École du Louvre*, Paris, 1990, pp. 53–68; Guy G. Stroumsa: *A New Science: The Discovery of Religion in the Age of Reason*, Cambridge, MA, 2010; Martin Mulsow, "John Seldens *De diis Syris*: Idolatriekritik und vergleichende Religionsgeschichte im 17. Jahrhundert," *Archiv für Religionsgeschichte* 3 (2001), pp. 1–24; Peter N. Miller, "Taking Paganism Seriously: Anthropology and Antiquarianism in Early Seventeenth-Century Histories of Religion," *Archiv für Religionsgeschichte* 3 (2001), pp. 183–209; Jonathan Sheehan, "The Altars of the Idols: Religion, Sacrifice, and the Early Modern Polity," *Journal of the History of Ideas* 67 (2006), pp. 648–674; Joan-Pau Rubiés, "Theology, Ethnography, and the Historicization of Idolatry," *Journal of the History of Ideas* 67 (2006), pp. 571–596.

prepared the materials from which Vico and Lafitau created anthropology and the history of philosophy.[3] Where would a Vico have been without the prior speculations on the genesis of heathen beliefs in the gods? Where would a Lafitau have been without the parallels to idolatrous Greece?[4] And, finally, where would the radical religious critique or Hazard's *crise de la conscience européene* have been without the "confrontation with the gods" as Frank Manuel described it?[5] Despite these well-recognized impacts, there is one area in which the influence of the idolatry debates has not even been suspected: the natural sciences, or more specifically physics. We have already seen in the case of Bucher that natural-scientific and medical questions were closely bound up with theology, and that one can hardly speak of a completely secular radical Enlightenment. But did physics in the age of the Scientific Revolution also have theological undertones? Did it have anything to do with the problem of idolatry? In this chapter we will see that it did indeed.

In 1686, in his work, *A Free Inquiry into the Vulgarly Received Notion of Nature*, Robert Boyle observed: "Many atheists ascribe so much to nature that they think it needless to have recourse to a deity for the giving an account of the phenomena of the universe."[6] That was the basic problem: all of the activities that were traditionally ascribed to God as the First Cause were more and more ascribed to nature, starting with the naturalizing tendencies of Renaissance philosophy. Concepts like *natura universalis* (universal nature), the *anima mundi* (the soul of the world), and the notion of *naturae agentes* (active separate natures), emerged to explain immanent activities. We observed this tendency in the previous chapter

[3] Giambattista Vico, *La Scienza Nuova*, ed. Fausto Nicolini, Bari, 1913. On Vico I will here recommend only Nicola Badaloni, *Introduzione a Vico*, Bari, 1999; Giuseppe Mazzotta, *The New Map of the World: The Poetic Philosophy of Giambattista Vico*, Princeton, 1999.

[4] Joseph François Lafitau, *Moeurs des sauvages américains comparées aux moeurs des premiers temps*, Paris, 1724; see Andreas Motsch, *Lafitau et l'émergence du discours ethnographique*, Sillery, 2001; Carl F. Starkloff, *Common Testimony: Ethnology and Theology in the "Customs" of Joseph Lafitau*, St. Louis, 2002; Martin Mulsow, "Joseph-François Lafitau und die Entdeckung der Religions- und Kulturvergleiche," in Maria Effinger, Ulrich Pfisterer, and Cornelia Logemann, eds., *Götterbilder und Götzendiener in der Frühen Neuzeit*, Heidelberg, 2012, pp. 37–48.

[5] Frank E. Manuel: *The Eighteenth Century Confronts the Gods*, Cambridge, MA, 1959.

[6] Robert Boyle, *A Free Enquiry into the Vulgarly Received Notion of Nature*, ed. Edward B. Davis and Michael Hunter, Cambridge, 1996, p. 3. See John McGuire, "Boyle's Conception of Nature," *Journal of the History of Ideas* 33 (1972), pp. 523–542; Michael Hunter and Edward B. Davis, "The Making of Robert Boyle's Free Enquiry into the Vulgarly Received Notion of Nature (1686)," *Early Science and Medicine* 1 (1996), pp. 204–271; Rose-Mary Sargent, *The Diffident Naturalist: Robert Boyle and the Philosophy of Experiment*, Chicago, 1995; Keith Hutchinson, "Supernaturalism and the Mechanical Philosophy," *History of Science* 21 (1983), pp. 297–333.

when Bucher, in his 1723 *Naturae mentis et spiritus disquisitio*, failed to answer the question whether one should see the human spirit as originating in the *anima mundi* or in God. But such a shift, according to Boyle's diagnosis, was ultimately nothing but idolatry: the veneration of creation instead of the creator.[7] To be precise it was the veneration of an ersatz deity instead of the true God. Indeed, one can find this sort of adoration among truly committed naturalists and "atheists" such as Giulio Cesare Vanini, who directed his adulation toward *Natura Dea*, the "Goddess Nature."[8]

During the seventeenth century, natural philosophers, and particularly those associated with the occult tradition, often invoked "Goddess Nature." Hermeticists, Paracelsists, and alchemists of the early modern period were quick to indulge in metaphors of nature worship, and philosophers from Descartes to Malebranche and Boyle developed deep concerns about this tendency and demanded a wholly different notion of nature.[9] Moreover, the iconology involving the "traces of nature" or of the "veil of nature," as used, for example, by Michael Maier, went well beyond the remit of "normal" scientists of the Scientific Revolution.[10] Take a look at the title illustration of Gerhard Blasius's *Anatome animalium* of 1681 (see Figure 2) or at the somewhat later work of Leeuwenhoek in his *Arcana naturae detecta* (see Figure 3), in which Diana of Ephesus is unveiled as Isis.[11]

To depict the recent discovery of physical truths allegorically as the unveiling of a goddess implicitly supported the tendency to hypostasize or reify nature. And the iconographic problems that resulted from seeing nature as Isis or as Diana of Ephesus or from mixing the two cults together

[7] Boyle, *A Free Enquiry* (note 6), p. 41.

[8] Just look at the title of Vanini's book: *De admirandis naturae reginae deaeque mortalium arcanis, libri quatuor*, Paris, 1616. On the problems of determining Vanini's true views, see Cesare Vasoli, "Riflessioni sul 'problema' Vanini," in Sergio Bertelli, ed., *Il libertinismo in Europa*, Milan and Naples, 1980, pp. 125–168.

[9] See generally Thomas Leinkauf and Karin Hartbecke, eds., *Der Naturbegriff in der Frühen Neuzeit, Semantische Perspektiven zwischen 1500 und 1700*, Tübingen, 2005.

[10] Michael Maier, *Atalanta fugiens, hoc est, emblemata nova de secretis naturae chymica*, Oppenheim, 1618. On Maier, see Hereward Tilton, *The Quest for the Phoenix: Spiritual Alchemy and Rosicrucianism in the Work of Count Michael Maier (1569–1622)*, Berlin, 2003.

[11] Gerard Blasius, *Anatome animalium*, Amsterdam, 1681; Antonius van Leeuwenhoek, *Arcana naturae detecta*, Delft, 1695. See Pierre Hadot, *La voile d'Isis*, Paris, 2004; on the *arcana naturae*, see also William Eamon, *Science and the Secrets of Nature*, Princeton, 1994; Martin Mulsow, "Arcana naturae. Verborgene Eigenschaften und universelle Methode von Fernel bis Gemma und Bodin," in *Der Naturbegriff in der Frühen Neuzeit* (note 9), pp. 31–68.

Figure 2   Gerard Blasius, *Anatome animalium*, Amsterdam 1681

led inexorably into the maze of the history of ancient religions, with all its
superimpositions of cults from the most diverse Mediterranean traditions.[12] In the end this meant finding connections between idolatry and
naturalism, astrology, and the cult of the stars.

[12] On the complicated history of "syncretistic" ancient religions, see Glen W. Bowersock, *Hellenism in
Late Antiquity*, Ann Arbor, 1990; Frank R. Trombley, *Hellenic Religion and Christianization
c. 370–529*, 2 vols., Leiden, 1993 and 1994, as well as the series *Religions in the Graeco-Roman
World* in general; on the problems of early modern representations of such syncretisms, see Martin
Mulsow, "Antiquarianism and Idolatry: On the 'Historia' of Religions in Early Modern Europe," in
Gianna Pomata and Nancy Siraisi, eds., *Historia: Empiricism and Erudition in Early Modern Europe*,
Cambridge, MA, 2005, pp. 181–210.

Figure 3   Antonius van Leeuwenhoek, *Arcana naturae detecta*, Delft 1695

2   Henry Stubbe and the Odor of Sanctity

We may begin our religious history of natural science with an episode from the history of smell.[13] When Valentine Greatrakes, the famous Irish

---

[13] On the history of smell, see Alain Corbin, *The Foul and the Fragrant. Odor and the French Social Imagination*, tr. Miriam Kochan, Roy Porter, and Christopher Prendergast, Cambridge, MA, 1986.

miracle healer of the 1660s, entered Viscount Edward Conway's house hoping to cure the viscount's wife's headaches, he exuded a surprisingly good smell. Conway noticed "a smell strangely pleasant, as if it had been of sundry flowers."[14] He was amazed and examined Greatrakes's hand, his chest, and found that a pleasing fragrance streamed forth from everywhere even though the healer had not, apparently, used any perfume. Upon examination the healer's urine, amazingly, also smelled of violets.

Why were they so especially attentive to his odor? There was at the time a notion that the wonder healer produced his effects through his bodily emanations, his effluvia, which accounted for his being much in demand. After all, ever since ancient Greece, gods and semi-divine beings signaled their presence by emitting a pleasant smell.[15] How should one interpret the healings worked by a man who possessed such a "divine" fragrance? To understand this, we need to turn to the writing of Henry Stubbe, the physician, natural philosopher, and former republican, who was physically present on that occasion at the Conway estate in Ragley, Warwickshire. Far from denying the "miracles" of Greatrakes, he tried to explain then in natural scientific terms.

The pleasant smell gave him a first major clue. In his work, *The Miraculous Conformist*, published in 1666, Stubbe used the prevailing theory of effluvia set out by Thomas Willis to explain what had happened. According to him the noxious effluvia of the patient were eliminated by the healer's good effluvia, and the desired process of fermentation and chemical processes in the blood were restored. Stubbe thought the pleasing odor of Greatrakes testified to his excellent bodily constitution and to the high quality of his effluvia, which emanated from him and which he could infuse into another person through stroking or lightly striking the body.[16]

James R. Jacob has seen this *Miraculous Conformist* as a subversive treatise, in which the naturalizing explanations are not so innocent as they might appear; indeed, Jacob argues, Stubbe's explanations implied that there were no actual miracles in the sense of supernatural interventions and that what was apparently supernatural could not be distinguished from the

---

[14] Henry Stubbe, *The Miraculous Conformist*, Oxford, 1666, p. 11. On Greatrakes, see Leonard Pitt, *A Small Moment of Great Illumination: Searching for Valentine Greatrakes, the Master Healer*, Washington, DC, 2006; A. Bryan Laver, "Miracles No Wonder! The Mesmeric Phenomena and Organic Cures of Valentine Greatrakes," *Journal of the History of Medicine and Allied Sciences* 33/1 (1978), pp. 35–46. There is a brief encounter with Stubbe in Mulsow, *Enlightenment Underground* (note 1), chapter 3.

[15] See Ernst Lohmeyer, "Vom göttlichen Wohlgeruch," *Sitzungsberichte der Heidelberger Akademie der Wissenschaften. Philologisch-historische Klasse* 9 (1919).

[16] Stubbe, *The Miraculous Conformist* (note 14).

natural. I think Jacob's thesis is correct, and here I want to amplify the historic and religious background for the *Miraculous Conformist*.[17] This will help to show why some of Stubbe's early readers also came to the same conclusion.

The wondrous healings of men like Greatrakes were problematic both religiously and politically. At his restoration in 1660, Charles II had revived the old ceremony in which the king "touched" for the king's evil, scrofula.[18] This supposedly royal power of healing helped sustain the divine authority of the monarchy. If someone like this "Irish Stroker" Greatrakes could cure the scrofulous as well as the king, then the border-line between upper and lower was no longer secure, between royalty and the common man. About half a century earlier when the French king had reclaimed the royal touch for himself, the Paris theologian, Jean Filesac, had protested quietly and indirectly in a treatise on "political idolatry," published in 1615. Political idolatry was understood as worshiping the king instead of God, because of falsely identifying kingship with the divine.[19] To a theologian this was blasphemous. Earlier, in 1609, Filesac had composed a tract with a similar title: *De idololatria magica*. With his notion of magical idolatry, he aimed at the witchcraft of his times, supporting his claim with numerous references to Tertullian. But he was also targeting the Paracelsians of Paris, such as Joseph du Chesne.[20] Magic was a sort of idolatry, Filesac argued, because magic attributed supernatural powers to created beings or it invoked such powers – here meaning not kings but witches – that really belonged to the creator alone.

This indirect connection between magical and political idolatry should make us to sit up and take notice, for it casts light on the comparable problem that emerged fifty years later in Restoration England. The case of Greatrakes provoked David Lloyd to charge that the famous wonder

[17] James R. Jacob, *Henry Stubbe, Radical Protestantism and the Early Enlightenment*, Cambridge, 1983, pp. 50–63 and 165–173. But see the critique of Jacob by Nicholas H. Steneck, "Greatrakes the Stroker: The Interpretations of Historians," *Isis* 73 (1982), pp. 161–177.

[18] See Marc Bloch, *The Royal Touch: Sacred Monarchy and Scrofula in England and France*, tr. J. E. Anderson, London, 1973.

[19] For political idolatry, see Mulsow, *Enlightenment Underground* (note 1), chapter 4; Jean Filesac, *De idololatra politica, et legitimo principis cultu commentaries*, Paris, 1615.

[20] Jean Filesac, *De idolatria magica, dissertatio*, Paris, 1609. On Joseph du Chesne, see Didier Kahn, *Alchimie et Paracelsisme en France (1567–1625)*, Geneva, 2007. Agreeing with Tertullian, Filesac held practical magic to be a veneration of the devil, p. 18: "Cum iam Christi fides in dies magis ac magis propageretur, daemonumque potentia passim à Christianis traduceretur, tum vix daemones palam et publice se deos praedicabant, at in Magia in quam ut tutissimam arcem sese receperant, audacter Deos se profitebantur, quemadmodum refert Tertullianus libro de Anima: . . . ." See also pp. 22ff. for Filesac's polemic against hermetic and magical medicine.

worker was guilty of a dangerous fraud, rightly comparing Stubbe's effort
to explain Greatrakes's cures to those mentioned in Renaissance treatises
on natural magic.[21] Indeed, even if Stubbe was apparently only giving a
scientific explanation of the "miracles," the implications of his argument
inescapably had a subversive effect. If Greatrakes was healing others by
virtue of his optimal temperament, his almost divine nature, then this
could have been the case with Christ, too. But if so, that relativized and
undermined Christ's miracles: they were no longer signs by which God
intervened in the world; they would have been merely natural – even if
extraordinary – phenomena. It is hard to say whether Stubbe was deliberately using libertine tactics of indirect argument and whether his real goal
was to polemicize against Christ and his miracles, or whether he was just
willing to accept that possible implication.[22]

In any event he used the Galenic theory of an "ideal temperament"
(*optima temperies*) to support his naturalistic explanation.[23] His approach
was similar to that of Pietro Pomponazzi in his book *De incantationibus*
("On the Causes of Marvelous Natural Effects or On Incantations") where
the Italian philosopher remarked that at times certain human beings
"through the influence of the gods or the stars cause miracles and obtain
[special knowledge of the stars, of omens, dreams, and other matters]
without any effort and practice."[24] Such special persons had ideal bodily
constitutions, and they had become what they were through the influence
of heavenly bodies. The anti-Christian effect of Pomponazzi's work was
the same as those implied by Stubbe, and provided the reason that
Pomponazzi had prudently refrained from publishing his thoughts during
his lifetime.[25]

Jacob suggested that Stubbe wrote his *Miraculous Conformist* mainly to
advocate a naturalistic exposition of corpuscular theory and to oppose
reconciling the new natural sciences with theist Christianity. In contrast,

---

[21] [David Lloyd], *Wonders No Miracles*, London, 1666.
[22] On libertine strategies, see Jean-Pierre Cavaillé, *Dis/simulations. Jules-César Vanini, François La Mothe le Vayer, Gabriel Naudé, Louis Machon et Torquato Accetto. Religion, morale et politique au XVIe siècle*, Paris, 2002.
[23] See Martin Mulsow, "Der vollkommene Mensch. Zur Prähistorie des Posthumanen," *Deutsche Zeitschrift für Philosophie* 51(5) (2003), pp. 739–760; Mulsow, "Das Vollkommene als Faszinosum des Sozialimaginären," in Aleida Assmann and Jan Assmann, eds., *Vollkommenheit. Archäologie der literarischen Kommunikation*, no. X, Munich, 2010, pp. 185–200.
[24] Pietro Pomponazzi, *De naturalium effectuum causis, sive De incantationibus*, Basel, 1567.
[25] See Giancalo Zanier, *Ricerche sulla diffusione e fortuna del De incantationisbus di Pomponazzi*, Florence, 1975; Paola Zambelli, "Pietro Pomponazzi's *De immortalitate* and His Clandestine *De incantationibus*: Aristotelianism, Eclecticism or Libertinism?," *Bochumer Philosophisches Jahrbuch für Antike und Mittelalter* 6 (2001), pp. 87–115.

Lloyd saw Stubbe's explanation as a regression to sympathetic magic of the sort associated with Cardano or the Paracelsians and would have agreed with Filesac in condemning political and magical idolatry both for its fraudulent or subversive leanings, as well as for its naturalism.

3 Stubbe and Boyle

Stubbe wrote his *Miraculous Conformist* in the format of a letter to Robert Boyle, who had been a patron of his during these years. Boyle supported Stubbe because he viewed him as a former radical, who could be re-educated in the spirit of the Royal Society and won over to the alliance of experimental philosophy and latitudinarian Anglicanism that Boyle hoped to promote. But what Stubbe had written in his *Miraculous Conformist* went too far for his correspondent. After Boyle had received the book from Stubbe, he replied on March 9, 1666, denouncing

> those enemies to Christianity ... that granting the truth of the historical part of the New Testament (which relates to the miracles) have gone about to give an account of it by celestial influences or natural (though peculiar) complexions or such conceits, which have quite lost them, in my thoughts, the title of knowing naturalists.[26]

Boyle had apparently identified two strategies of the "enemies of Christianity": an astrological and a complexional explanation of the miracles of Christ. But both were really just one strategy: namely, the one based on historical astrology along the lines of Abū Maʿšar, which claimed that during times of so-called great conjunctions of Jupiter and Saturn the influence of the stars produces human beings who are prophets and who create new religions.[27] Around the year 1300, the Italian Pietro d'Abano combined this theory with the Galenic doctrine of the *optima temperies* in his *Conciliator*.[28] According to d'Abano, the influence of the stars produces human beings who have a perfect mixture of bodily fluids, and this enables them to prophesy and work miracles. Men such as Moses, Jesus, or Mohammad were *homines perfecti*. This theory prompted the Church to disinter Pietro's body and burn it, because, if it was possible to cast a

---

[26] *The Works of the Honourable Robert Boyle*, 6 vols., vol. 1, ed. Thomas Birch, London, 1772, p. lxxix; see Jacob, *Stubbe* (note 17), p. 56.

[27] *Abū Maʿšar on Historical Astrology: The Book of Religions and Dynasties (On the Great Conjunctions)*, ed. and tr. Keji Yamamoto and Charles Burnett, 2 vols., Leiden, 2000; see David Pingree, *The Thousands of Abū Maʿshar*, London, 1968.

[28] Pietro d'Abano, *Conciliator controversiarum, quae inter philosophos et medicos versantur*, Venice, 1565. See Eugenia Paschetto, *Pietro d'Abano, medico e filosofo*, Florence, 1984.

"horoscope of religions" such as Christianity, then this determinism would contradict the divine nature of Christ and the Christian religion would become just one cultural phenomenon among many others. This is why Boyle viewed historical astrologers in the tradition of Pietro d'Abano as "enemies of Christianity." D'Abano was not alone in his beliefs, however, and his writings inspired and influenced such illustrious figures as Pietro Pomponazzi, Girolamo Cardano, and Giordano Bruno.[29] Although Stubbe never talked about astrology in his *Miraculous Conformist*, Boyle nonetheless knew that the *homo-perfectus* naturalism, on which Stubbe's theory was based, had an astrological side to it.

This heterodox tradition of astrology may have been in Boyle's mind when he composed his digression about the history of idolatry in the *Free Enquiry into the Vulgarly Received Notion of Nature*. By drawing attention to it, I hope to shed light on a connection between idolatry and astrology, which James Jacob left rather unclear. In his digression, Boyle, basing himself on Maimonides, explains that the oldest form of idolatry was practiced by the Sabaeans in their worship of the stars.[30]

How did the scientist Boyle know about all of these connections from the field of the history of religions? During the later 1640s Boyle was deeply impressed by the Irish archbishop and chronologist James Ussher, and he had studied biblical philology, ancient languages, and the history of religions. In the course of his travels in the Netherlands in 1648, he met and talked with Menasseh ben Israel.[31] Through the work by Menasseh entitled *De creatione*, he learned of the theories of Moses Maimonides, who taught that the most ancient paganism, against which the Laws of Moses were aimed, had been the astral worship of the ancient Sabaeans.[32] A draft from that period, Boyle's *Essay of the Holy Scriptures*, took up the history of religion.[33] When Boyle read Johann Heinrich Hottinger's

---

[29] See Eugenio Garin, *Astrology in the Renaissance: The Zodiac of Life*, tr. Carolyn Jackson and June Allen, revised Clare Robertson, London and Boston, 1983.

[30] See note 26.

[31] See Boyle, *A Free Enquiry* (note 6), p. 46 ("with whom I have conversed at Amsterdam"). Boyle quotes Menasseh ben Israel, *De creatione problemata XXX*, Amsterdam, 1635. On Menasseh, see Cecil Roth, "The Mystery of the Resettlement," in *Essays and Portraits*, Philadelphia, 1962, pp. 86–107 and 306–308, and Sina Rauschenbach, *Judentum für Christen. Vermittlung und Selbstbehauptung Menasseh ben Israels in den gelehrten Debatten des 17. Jahrhunderts*, Berlin, 2012.

[32] Moses Maimonides, *Guide for the Perplexed*, tr. M. Friedländer, 4th edn., New York and London, 1904, Part III, chapters 29 and 30 and passim. On the Sabaeans, see Daniel W. Chwolson, *Die Szabier und der Szabismus*, St. Petersburg, 1856; repr. Cambridge, 2011; Michel Tardieu, "Sâbiens coraniques et 'sâbiens' de Harrân," *Journal Asiatique* 274 (1986), pp. 1–44.

[33] See Hunter and Davis, "The Making of Robert Boyle's *Free Enquiry into the Vulgarly Received Notion of Nature* (1686)" (note 6).

Historia orientalis after 1650, he learned more about the legendary Sabaeans in section VIII of that book, and his studies of the works of Selden and Vossius complemented this perspective.[34]

In the mid-1660s, at just the time of the Greatrakes controversy, Boyle wrote a first draft of his *Free Enquiry*, which combines both the history of religion and natural philosophy. Its main thesis was that if too much power were assigned to the inner forces of nature, one turned nature into an idol and deprived God of the honor of being the sole influence on all natural activities. "Nature" for Boyle was not active substance; it was something passive and lacked its own forces. Everybody who talked about a *natura universalis* or an *anima mundi* or nature's innate power to preserve and regenerate, dishonored God and became, at least implicitly, an atheist.[35]

Some of the basic principles of Hippocratic and Galenic medicine come in for Boyle's particular criticism. He focuses on maxims which suggest that nature is an independent, active force: maxims like *natura est morborum medicatrix* (nature is the healer of diseases), *natura nihil facit frustra* (nature does nothing in vain), or *omnis natura est conservatrix sui* (all nature preserves itself).[36] From Boyle's religious-historical perspective these ideas appeared as pagan remnants that had persisted into his own time. In the same way, he felt that the deification of nature, which he associated with Orphism, was still exercising too much influence in contemporary Aristotelianism. On Boyle's reasoning, such deifications of nature or of the stars had to be rejected not only from a Christian point of view but – and here we hear the voice of the natural scientist – because they contradicted the evidence men could gather from modern scientific instruments. For Boyle, his contemporaries had no excuse: "For whereas the Zabians [i.e., the Sabaeans] and Chaldeans considered and adored the planets as the chief gods, our telescopes discover to us that ... they shine but by a borrowed light."[37]

---

[34] For the reference to Hottinger, see Boyle, *A Free Enquiry* (note 6), p. 42. See Johann Heinrich Hottinger, *Historia orientalis quae ex variis orientalium monumentis collecta*, Zurich, 1651. On Hottinger, see Jan Loop, "Johann Heinrich Hottinger (1620–1667) and the Historia Orientalis," *Church History and Religious Culture* 88 (2008), pp. 169–203; Loop, *Johann Heinrich Hottinger: Arabic and Islamic Studies in the Seventeenth Century*, Oxford, 2013. See further John Selden, *De diis Syris syntagma*, London, 1617; Gerhard Johannes Vossius, *De theologia gentili et physiologia christiana, sive De origine et progressu idololatriae*, Amsterdam, 1641; complete edn., Amsterdam, 1668. On Vossius, see C. S. M. Rademaker, *Gerardus Joannes Vossius*, Zwolle, 1967; Ralph Häfner, *Götter im Exil. Frühneuzeitliches Dichtungsverständnis im Spannungsfeld christlicher Apologetik und philologischer Kritik (ca. 1590–1736)*, Tübingen, 2003, esp. pp. 224–248. On Selden, see Gerald Toomer, *John Selden: A Life in Scholarship*, Oxford, 2009.

[35] Boyle, *A Free Enquiry* (note 6), section IV.   [36] Ibid., pp. 31ff.   [37] Ibid., pp. 55f.

Based on a study of the original manuscript, which allowed for a distinction between early drafts of the *Enquiry* and later additions to it, Michael Hunter has disagreed with Jacob's interpretation that Boyle was responding specifically to Stubbe.[38] Yet even if Hunter is right and Boyle was referring to Galenic-Aristotelian naturalism in general, as well as to Paracelsians and philosophers such as Francis Glisson or Ralph Cudworth with their theories of an "energetical" or "plastic" nature, Hunter nonetheless talks about Boyle's experience of a crisis, an experience of what could be called an "anxiety of influence."[39] Boyle's crisis was prompted by his fear of naturalism, whose genealogy he explained by placing it in its religious-historical context and tracing it all the way back to ancient Sabaean star worship.

4 The Battle over Nature

Robert Boyle was worried about the whole complex of implicit and iconological idolatry. He saw himself as a truly Christian scientist whose program of an anti-idolatrous science rested on the principle of denying Nature any activity. According to Boyle, attributions of activity expressed in the traditional aphorisms cited earlier should be scientifically refuted. Nonetheless, Boyle insisted that such idolatrous attributions be refuted not just in physical terms but also on the basis of the history of religions. Hence in section IV of his *Enquiry*, Boyle made a historical digression, explaining what he considered to be the origins of idolatry:

> The most ancient idolatry (taking the word in its laxer sense), or at least one of the earliest, seems to have been the worship of the celestial lights, especially the sun and the moon: that kind of *aboda zara* (as the Jewish writers call strange or false worshiping), being the most natural, as having for its objects glorious bodies, immortal, always regularly moved and very beneficial for man.[40]

His source here was Moses Maimonides, whose commentary on the Talmudic treatise *Avoda Zara* in his *Mishneh Torah* had been translated

---

[38] Hunter and Davis, "The Making of Robert Boyle's *Free Enquiry into the Vulgarly Received Notion of Nature* (1686)" (note 6); see also Michael Hunter, *Robert Boyle (1627–91): Scrupulosity and Science*, Woodbridge, 2000, as well as Hunter, *Boyle: Between God and Science*, New Haven, 2009. On Francis Glisson, see Karin Hartbecke, *Metaphysik und Naturphilosophie im 17. Jahrhundert: Francis Glissons Substanztheorie in ihrem ideengeschichtlichen Kontext*, Tübingen, 2006.

[39] I am using a modified form of the concept introduced by the literary theorist Harold Bloom, *The Anxiety of Influence: A Theory of Poetry*, New York, 1973.

[40] Boyle, *A Free Enquiry* (note 6), p. 41.

in 1641 by Dionysius Vossius as *De idololatria*.[41] It seems possible that Boyle had also been reading John Spencer's book, *De legibus Hebraeorum earumque rationibus*.[42] This work, was published in the same year as Boyle's *Enquiry* and contained a whole chapter on the so-called Zabians or Sabaeans, the legendary people who had purportedly established idolatry in ancient times. Boyle, too, spoke of the Sabaeans and emphasized their belief in celestial gods, as heavenly bodies endowed with a soul.[43] The idea of "animation" led him straight to the ancient Greeks – for example, to Hippocrates's *thermon* or *calidum innatum* (i.e., the notion of vital heat, still fundamental to medicine down to Boyle's time).[44] However, Boyle held that notions like these were relics of an earlier idolatry (ultimately, from the Sabaeans) invoking an animated nature that was unacceptable. Platonic and Stoic ideas of a world soul or the Aristotelian celestial intelligences all belonged, in the words of Lactantius, to the history of error, the history of false religion, not of true faith.[45] Hence the "social history of truth," a history in which Boyle plays a large role in the story told by Stephen Shapin and Simon Schaffer, also impinges on what could be called a "religious history of truth."[46]

In the scientific controversies of the age, Boyle's work was perceived primarily as a statement in the struggle between Aristotelianism and Cartesianism. Particularly in Germany the debate had focused on this polarization. The dispute between Günter Christoph Schelhammer, a

---

[41] Moses Maimonides, *De idololatria*, Amsterdam, 1641, often printed as an appendix to the book by Gerhard Johannes Vossius, *De theologia gentili*; see also Maimonides, *More nebuchim, sive Liber doctor perplexorum*, Basel, 1629; see Aaron L. Katchen, *Christian Hebraists and Dutch Rabbis*, Cambridge, MA, 1984. Gerhard Johannes Vossius was Dionysius's father.

[42] John Spencer, *De legibus Hebraeorum earumque rationibus*, Cambridge, 1685. On this work, see Mulsow, *Enlightenment Underground* (note 1), chapter 2. On Maimonides and Spencer, see Jan Assmann, *Moses the Egyptian: The Memory of Egypt in Western Monotheism*, Cambridge, MA, 1988, pp. 55–80.

[43] Boyle, *A Free Enquiry* (note 6), pp. 41f.

[44] Ibid., p. 43, On the idea of life heat, see Jacques Jouanna, *Hippocrates*, Baltimore and London, 1999; Everett Mendelsohn, *Heat and Life: The Development of the Theory of Animal Heat*, Cambridge, MA, 1964. On the role of this idea in early modern medicine and natural philosophy, see Martin Mulsow, *Frühneuzeitliche Selbsterhaltung. Telesio und die Naturphilosophie der Renaissance*, Tübingen, 1998; Rudolph M. Bell, *How to Do It: Guides to Good Living for Renaissance Italians*, Chicago and London, 1999. See also Chapter 3.

[45] Lactantius Firmianus, "De origine erroris," in *Opera*, ed. Servatius Gallaeus, Leiden, 1660, pp. 136–230, as Book II of the *Divinae institutiones*.

[46] Stephen Shapin, *A Social History of Truth. Civility and Science in Seventeenth-Century England*, Chicago, 1994. On the cultural history of truth, see Martin Mulsow, *Knowledge Lost: A New View of Early Modern Intellectual History*, Princeton, 2022, chapter 6. On the doctrine of the world soul, see Boyle, *A Free Enquiry* (note 6), p. 50: "But I shall give a further answer to the above proposed objection, if I can show how sacrilegiously they abused the being we are speaking of, as well under the very name of 'nature,' as under that of the 'soul of the world.'"

professor at Kiel, and the Altdorf experimental physicist and Boyle correspondent, Johann Christoph Sturm, who published his *Idolum naturae* in
1692, is well-known.[47] Schelhammer represented the position of the
anciens or Aristotelians who still acknowledged the usefulness of
Aristotle's active substances in nature and considered such a physics to
be indispensable, particularly in medicine. Sturm, on the other hand,
belonged to the *modernes* and supported Boyle's attempt to conceive of a
notion of nature as completely passive and devoid of innate powers. In his
answers to Sturm, Schelhammer dealt explicitly with the religious-
historical context of nature worship and rejected any parallel between
idolatry and the acceptance of natural activity.[48] This dispute has been
repeatedly studied because Leibniz involved himself in it and tried to work
out a compromise position in his 1695 treatise *De ipsa natura*.[49] Leibniz
did not deal with the problem of idolatry; rather he concentrated on
satisfying both sides with his notion of the organism as an infinitely subtle
mechanism.[50]

5   Andreas Rüdiger and the Egyptians

It is far less well-known, however, that Boyle's idolatry diagnosis was very
soon superseded by another, that of Pierre Bayle, which also had a bearing
upon natural science. Bayle's thesis in the 1683 *Pensées diverses sur la
comète* claimed that the danger of idolatry was at least as bad as the danger
of atheism.[51] Seeing the two in parallel was enormously influential. For

---

[47] Johann Christoph Sturm (praes.) / Leonhard Christoph Riederer (resp.), *De ipsa natura*, Altdorf,
      1682; Sturm (praes.) / Riederer (resp.), *Idolum naturae, similiumque nominum vanorum ex hominum
      Christianorum animis deturbandi conatus philosophicus sive De naturae agentis, tum universalis, tum
      particularis aliorumque cognatorum quasi numinum superstitiosis erronicisque conceptibus dissertatio*,
      Altdorf, 1692; Günter Christoph Schellhammer, *Natura sibi et medicis vindicata sive De natura liber
      bipartitus*, Kiel, 1697; Schellhammer, *De natura libri tres*, Kiel, 1697; Schellhammer, *Naturae
      vindicatae vindicatio*, Kiel, 1702; see Georg Baku, "Der Streit um den Naturbegriff am Ende des
      17. Jahrhunderts," *Zeitschrift für Philosophie und philosophische Kritik* 98 (1891), pp. 162–190.
[48] See the description in the *Journal de Savans*, Paris, 1703, pp. 569–574, here at pp. 572f.
[49] Gottfried Wilhelm Leibniz, "De ipsa natura," in *Die philosophischen Schriften*, ed. Carl Gerhardt,
      vol. 4, Berlin, 1875–1890, pp. 504–516. The work appeared in 1698 in the *Acta eruditorum*. See
      Heribert M. Nobis, "Die Bedeutung der Leibnizschrift 'De ipsa natura' im Lichte ihrer
      begriffsgeschichtlichen Voraussetzungen," *Zeitschrift für philosophische Forschung* 20 (1966),
      pp. 525–538; Catherine Wilson, "De ipsa natura: Leibniz on Substance, Force and Activity,"
      Studia Leibnitiana 19 (1987), pp. 148–172; Guido Giglioni, "Automata Compared: Boyle, Leibniz,
      and the Debate on the Notion of Life and Mind," *British Journal for the History of Philosophy* 3
      (1995), pp. 249–278; Christia Mercer, *Leibniz's Metaphysics: Its Origins and Development*,
      Cambridge, 2001.
[50] Leibniz, "De ipsa natura" (note 49), p. 511.
[51] Pierre Bayle, *Pensées diverses sur la comète*, Rotterdam, 1683.

example, John Toland spoke of the opposing Scylla and Charybdis, which were equally to be avoided,[52] and he exemplified the search for a middle course between the two, a search that became especially common in Germany. In 1716, this model was used theologically by Johann Franz Budde in his *Theses theologicae de atheismo et superstitione*, and Andreas Rüdiger used it in physics in his controversial *Physica divina, recta via, eademque inter superstitionem et atheismum media* that same year.[53] Although Rüdiger was an old acquaintance of Budde's – both were among the earliest students of Christian Thomasius – it is unlikely that he borrowed the idea from Budde. Although Rüdiger had completed his book in 1714, because of censorship in Leipzig, it only appeared two years later, in Frankfurt.[54] But the idea of seeking the middle way could easily have come from the old Aristotelian model of the golden mean, which remained popular in Germany. Christian Thomasius had already used it as an illustration for his *Philosophia aulica*.[55] In Germany, the concept of "idolatrie," which Bayle had balanced against "superstition," was now bundled together under the term *superstitio*, because in the polemic against magic and witchcraft as well as against the ceremonies of Catholicism, it appeared more important than the concept of idolatry, which loomed larger as a target among Calvinists.[56]

Rüdiger wrote the *Physics* that Christian Thomasius might well have written, had he been versed in physics. Rüdiger's thesis was that Cartesian-

---

[52] John Toland, *Letters to Serena*, London 1704, Letter III. On Toland, see Justin Champion, *Republican Learning: John Toland and the Crisis of Christian Culture, 1696–1722*, Manchester, 2003. But naturally one should also consult Plutarch's *De superstitione* as the ancient model for this distinction.

[53] Johann Franz Budde, *Theses theologicae de atheismo et superstitione*, Jena, 1716; Andreas Rüdiger, *Physica divina, recta via, eademque inter superstitionem et atheismum media ad utramque hominis felicitatem, naturalem atque moralem ducens*, Frankfurt, 1716. On Budde's book, see Martin Pott, *Aufklärung und Aberglaube. Die deutsche Frühaufklärung im Spiegel ihrer Aberglaubenskritik*, Tübingen, 1992, pp. 171–182. On Rüdiger, see Heinrich Schepers, *Andreas Rüdigers Methodologie und ihre Voraussetzungen. Ein Beitrag zur deutschen Schulphilosophie im 18. Jahrhundert*, Cologne,1959; Riccarda Suitner, "Jus naturae und natura humana in August Friedrich Müllers handschriftlichem Kommentar zu Andreas Rüdigers Institutiones eruditionis," *Aufklärung* 25 (2013), pp. 113–132.

[54] On such publication problems, see Agatha Kobuch, *Zensur und Aufklärung in Kursachsen. Ideologische Strömungen und politische Meinungen zur Zeit der sächsisch- polnischen Union (1697–1763)*, Weimar, 1988, pp. 53f. See as well Detlef Döring, *Die Philosophie Gottfried Wilhelm Leibniz' und die Leipziger Aufklärung in der ersten Hälfte des 18. Jahrhunderts*, Stuttgart, 1999.

[55] Christian Thomasius, *Introductio ad philosophiam aulicam*, Leipzig, 1688.

[56] See, e.g., Friedrich Wilhelm Bierling, *De superstitione adhibita tanquam arcano dominationis*, Rinteln, 1701. On that work, see Pott, *Aufklärung und Aberglaube* (note 53), and Mulsow, *Enlightenment Underground* (note 1), chapter 4.

mathematical physics led to atheism because the mathematics ventured well beyond its proper limits. He contended that mathematics could only deal with quantities, but that physics had a more divine object because it concentrated on nature and the essence of things. A physics, however, that credited natural things with more divinity than was appropriate, was superstitious. Hence, the right physics supplied a decisive antidote to superstition and atheism. This view was in total agreement with Gerhard Johannes Vossius, who entitled his work on idolatry *De theologia gentili et physiologia christiana* ("On Gentile Theology and Christian Physiology") in order to convey that only a correct and "Christian physics" could dispel the phantasms of "heathen theology."[57]

In just this manner Rüdiger also tried to find a middle ground between mechanism and vitalism, but in a different way from that of Leibniz.[58] Borrowing from Henry More, Rüdiger considered the notion of space and the spatial nature of the spiritual as central. With More and Van Helmont in the background, and with the help of Gassendi's corpuscular theory, Rüdiger developed a physics of "bubbles" (*bullulae*) that moved from the periphery to the center; their elasticity, vibrations, and oscillations seemed to resolve physical problems.[59] Thomasius pursued a similar approach in his own physical theory, in his *Versuch vom Wesen des Geistes*, but he got lost in generalities. Like Rüdiger, Budde had preferred Henry More as physicist, and adopted More's and Cudworth's thesis that the true physical-theological teachings of the ancient Hebrews had later been corrupted.[60]

We find Rüdiger on a similar historical-philosophical path. Like Boyle, in his book on physics he inserted a historical digression about the origin of idolatry. Idolatry was the kind of superstition which mistook an effect for a cause.[61] Rüdiger was not the sort of person who quoted much, especially not from contemporary authors. He was too cautious to do that. He nevertheless hinted at two important sources for his historical outlook:

[57] Vossius (note 34), esp. introduction. On Vossius, see C. S. M. Rademaker, *Gerardus Joannes Vossius*, Zwolle, 1967; Häfner, *Götter im Exil* (note 34), esp. pp. 224–48.

[58] Rüdiger, *Physica divina* (note 53), Praefatio, pp. 2f.

[59] Ibid., p. 4 and passim; on More's physics, see Serge Hutin, *Henry More. Essai sur les doctrines théosophiques chez les Platoniciens de Cambridge*, Hildesheim, 1966; Roberto Bondi, *L'onnipresenza di Dio. Saggio su Henry More*, Soveria Mannelli, 2001; on his relationship with Boyle, see Robert A. Greene, "Henry More and Robert Boyle on the Spirit of Nature," *Journal of the History of Ideas* 23 (1962), pp. 451–474.

[60] Christian Thomasius, *Versuch vom Wesen des Geistes*, Halle, 1699; Johann Franz Budde, *Introductio ad historiam philosophiae Ebraeorum. Accedit dissertatio de haeresi Valentiniana*, Halle, 1702. On Budde and More, see Mulsow, *Enlightenment Underground* (note 1), chapter 6.

[61] Rüdiger, *Physica divina* (note 53), p. 48.

Olaus Borrichius's 1674 *Hermetis Aegyptiorum et chemicorum sapientia* and Edmund Dickinson's 1702 *Physica vetus et vera*.[62] Both books regarded Egyptian culture as the most ancient, followed by the Phoenician. Moses had been educated in both cultures, Rüdiger agreed, and viewed the concepts Moses employed in the beginning of Genesis as technical terms associated with Egyptian-Phoenician culture. Since physical truth was "subtle" (Rüdiger was here possibly alluding to Cardano's *subtilitas*), a higher, "more secret," acroamatic (i.e., esoteric) physics was necessary, which could bring out the world's divine principles.[63]

Rüdiger could not, however, support the widely held view that an autochthonous animal cult was the origin of idolatry. It seemed impossible that common people could have been so stupid. They must have followed their sages, and their sages, with their hieroglyphic writing, were to blame for idolatry:

> The Egyptians realized that higher truths could not be explained without abstract concepts, but the common people, immersed in their senses, could not grasp that. And yet a knowledge of divine things seemed necessary because the cult of the highest deity had to be observed with utmost spiritual devotion. Therefore, they tried with images to shape the thinking and stimulate the worship of the common people – to the extent simple people could understand. ... Thus because they thought that various attributes of the divine being were an excellent stimulant to people's piety, they tried to express those with the most adequate hieroglyphs. So they imprinted in people's minds God's omnipresence with the symbol of the sun, his omniscience with an eagle, his omnipotence with a lion, and his wrath with a wolf or a crocodile.[64]

It is apparent here that without mentioning him, Rüdiger was drawing on Athanasius Kircher and his *Oedipus Aegyptiacus* (1652–1654), which had

---

[62] Olaus Borrichius, *Hermetis Aegyptiorum et chemicorum sapientia*, Copenhagen, 1674, quoted in Rüdiger, *Physica divina* (note 53), p. 5; Edmund Dickinson, *Physica vetus et vera, sive Tractatus de naturali veritate hexaemeri Mosaici*, London, 1702, quoted in Rüdiger (note 53), p. 2. On Dickinson's work, see also Chapters 3 and 6.

[63] Rüdiger, *Physica divina* (note 53), pp. 61f. Rüdiger was referring implicitly to Daniel Georg Morhof's treatise "De eo, quod in disciplinis divinum est" in his *Polyhistor*, vol. 1, Lübeck, 1708, chapter I, p. 12. These views were criticized by Rüdiger's censors. See *Physica divina*, pp. 779ff. ("Monita der Zensoren"). For a comparable discussion of the problems of the divine and the secret in nature, see the treatise (examined in Mulsow, *Enlightenment Underground* (note 1), chapter 4) by Johann Friedrich Kayser, *De eo, quod theion est in disciplinis*, Halle, 1715.

[64] Rüdiger, *Physica divina* (note 53), pp. 53f., § 129. See the later discussion of Egyptian writing in Johann Georg Wachter, *Naturae et scripturae concordia: commentario de literis ac numeris primaevis, aliisque rebus memorabilibus cum ortu literarum*, Leipzig and Copenhagen, 1752. See generally Aleida Assmann and Jan Assmann, eds., *Hieroglyphen*, Munich, 2003.

interpreted the hieroglyphs represented an arcane theology.[65] In contrast
to Kircher, however, Rüdiger was aware of the dangers of this method.
Rüdiger was – not least because of his readings of Locke – a sensualist, who
did not believe in the existence of innate ideas; he considered the process of
abstraction on the basis of sense perception to be essential. Even though
abstraction was for him one of the most significant steps forward in the
history of mankind, abstraction also had its dangers. Already in his 1702
master's thesis Rüdiger had written about the "use and abuse of technical
terms" and criticized the abuse of artificial expressions.[66] This semiotic
consciousness also guided him in his assessment of the origins of idolatry.
Their success in encouraging piety, Rüdiger held, had seduced the Egyptian
sages. They invented more and more hieroglyphs, no longer prompted by
theological necessities, because they rejoiced to discover that this method
encouraged religious worship better than mere concepts. But in this way the
cult of images became independent and soon people attributed to such
images, the simulacra, a divinity that should have been reserved for the
highest principles. This was the origin of worshiping animals:

> The worship of a unique supreme being originated in the souls of the
> onlookers through their observation of animals and plants, and thus
> humans were much better and more aroused in their faith than ever before
> when wise men conveyed the sacred [merely] through ideas; the first
> creators of hieroglyphics therefore became so enthusiastic about their
> success that they strove to increase piety among the masses even further
> by adding more and more hieroglyphic symbols. So they furnished public
> temples as well as private buildings with these images. Although this was
> not actually reprehensible, nonetheless partly because of the ignorance of
> the people partly because of the negligence of the priests, the systematic
> devotion stirred up through these images became over time so profoundly
> linked to the images that most of the people assigned divinity to the images
> themselves. Although there were those who opposed this error and who
> rightly emphasized that such behavior was by no means in accordance with
> their ancestors' intentions, the common people, who never accept correc-
> tion, sided with the more superstitious among the scholars and priests; with
> hatred and terror they strangled the words of the more sensible. So it
> occurred that all of Egypt was flooded like the Nile with disgraceful

[65] Athanasius Kircher, *Oedipus Aegyptiacus*, Rome, 1652–1654. On Kircher, see Thomas Leinkauf, *Mundus combinatus*, Berlin, 1993; Paula Findlen, ed., *Athanasius Kircher: The Last Man Who Knew Everything*, New York, 2004; Wilhelm Schmidt-Biggemann, "Hermes Trismegistos, Isis und Osiris in Athanasius Kirchers Oedipus Aegyptiacus," *Archiv für Religionsgeschichte* 3 (2001), pp. 67–88; Daniel Stolzenberg, *Egyptian Oedipus: Athanasius Kircher and the Secrets of Antiquity*, Chicago, 2013.
[66] Andreas Rüdiger, *De usu et abusu terminorum technicorum in philosophia*, Leipzig, 1700.

superstition. And since, according to Tacitus, the Greeks received their alphabet from the Egyptians and then the Romans from the Greeks, it is obvious why Egyptian superstition but also that of the Greeks and Romans, seems to contradict our previously mentioned theory.[67]

Thus for Rüdiger idolatry was the price paid for separating esoteric from exoteric culture, dividing the rationalism of the elite from the superstition of the masses.[68] The attempt to involve the common people by means of accommodation and to teach them the subtle truths of theology had failed, because such accommodation developed a dangerous dynamic of its own. It is possible to read this analysis as a criticism of theological orthodoxy in general, even the Lutheran Orthodoxy of Rüdiger's day: priests still tended to separate their artificial liturgies and dogmas from reality. Rüdiger apparently thought that this failed accommodation, the unachieved transmission of abstraction, was the cost of modernity. Idolatry, once on the scene, spread like a virus. In the process of the transmission of written culture to the Greeks and Romans, idolatry was disseminated in various forms. It was an inverted form of *translatio sapientiae*, as a *translatio idololatriae*, so that in Protestant cultures (and especially within Calvinism) the history of mankind was understood above all as the transmission of idolatry.[69] According to Rüdiger, only a reformation, one that was both epistemological and semiotic, could halt the spread of the idolatry virus.

To summarize: It seems clear that the use of the idolatry diagnosis had nearly diametrically opposed effects in Germany and England. While Boyle argued precisely against theoreticians like Francis Glisson or Henry More, the diagnosis in Germany aimed at supporting a physics whose principal model was Henry More. In the end, spiritualism was strengthened, even if it was of a "reasonable," enlightened sort. It comes as no surprise, then, that it was a thinker like the young Emanuel Swedenborg who adapted Rüdiger's ideas, further developing them.[70] On the other hand, Rüdiger's ideas – that mathematics must respect its own limits because unchecked it invited an atheist ontology, but also that

---

[67] Rüdiger, *Physica divina* (note 53), pp. 53–54, §§ 131f. See the similar argument concerning a transmission of superstitions (or, more precisely, of demonology) from the Greeks to Asia, Egypt, and Italy, and indeed through the transmission of language in Thomas Hobbes, *Leviathan*, ed. C. B. Macpherson, London, 1968, chapter 45, p. 659.

[68] On such separations, see Jan Assmann, *Religio duplex. Ägyptische Mysterien und europäische Aufklärung*, Berlin, 2010.

[69] See, e.g., Abraham Heidanus, *De origine erroris libri VIII*, Amsterdam, 1678.

[70] See Ernst Benz, *Emanuel Swedenborg: Naturforscher und Seher*, Munich, 1948; 2nd edn., Zurich, 1969.

one must not confuse effects for causes because such a confusion led to an idolatrous ontology – indirectly influenced Immanuel Kant, through Rüdiger's pupil Crusius.[71] Kant was also looking for a middle course – between skepticism and dogmatism. The point was now that reason must respect its own limits. What was atheism for Rüdiger became skepticism for Kant. What was idolatry for Rüdiger, however, was dogmatism for Kant: the hypostasization of ideas into real entities.

6 Christian Gabriel Fischer and Wolffianism

Rüdiger was not the only one during the 1680s and 1690s to find the starting point for his ideas in the debate over the nature of idolatry. There were more radical thinkers for whom this problem provided a sort of launch pad. One of them was Christian Gabriel Fischer, who had studied in Königsberg, Rostock, and Jena and had finished his master's degree in Jena in 1710, at a time when Johann Franz Budde was teaching there.[72] As we will see, he used his time as a student to take careful notice of the controversy involving Boyle, Sturm, Schelhammer, and Leibniz. Until 1695 Schelhammer was a professor in Jena, a fact that prompted many in that city to follow the argument with special attention. Fischer, however, drew from it conclusions different from those of Rüdiger.

After his master's examination Fischer had returned to his hometown, Königsberg, where he was appointed associate professor (*außerordentlicher Professor*) of physics. A decade later the University of Königsberg became embroiled in a series of harsh conflicts between the philosophical followers of Christian Wolff on one side and the theologians – mainly Pietists – on the other. In these rivalries, the theologians Heinrich Lysius and his son-

---

[71] On Crusius and Kant, see Anton Marquardt, *Kant und Crusius*, Kiel, 1885; Manfred Kühn, *Kant. Eine Biographie*, Munich, 2003.

[72] Fischer was born in 1683 (1686?), the son of a merchant in Königsberg. He died there in 1751. On him, see Carl Günther Ludovici, *Ausführlicher Entwurf einer vollständigen Historie der Wolffischen Philosophie*, Part I, Leipzig, 1737, § 467; Part III, Leipzig, 1738, § 112, pp. 91–97; *Acta historico-ecclestiastica* 9 (1745), pp. 286–298; Friedrich Wilhelm Kraft, *Nachrichten von den neuesten theologischen Büchern*, vol. 3, Leipzig, 1743, pp. 665–695; Georg Ernst Sigmund Hennig, "Leben des Professors Fischer in Königsberg," *Preußisches Archiv* 1 (1790), pp. 312–333; August Kurz, *Über Christian Gabriel Fischers Vernünftige Gedanken von der Natur*, Halle, 1908; Paul Konschel, "Christian Gabriel Fischer, ein Gesinnungs- und Leidensgenosse Christian Wolffs in Königsberg," *Altpreußische Monatsschrift* 53 (1916), pp. 416–444; Albert Predeek, "Ein vergessener Freund Gottscheds," *Mitteilungen der deutschen Gesellschaft für vaterländische Sprache und Alterthümer* 12 (1937), pp. 109–123. On the reform program at the university, see Albert Predeek, "Ein verschollener Reorganisationsplan für die Universität Königsberg," *Altpreußische Forschungen* 4(2) (1927).

in-law Christoph Langhansen, along with their followers, again and again held the stronger position. Things became especially difficult for the Wolffians in Königsberg after the Pietists defeated Wolff in Halle and after he was deprived of his professorship there on November 8, 1723. But it was in just those years that Fischer, who had a mind of his own, declared his allegiance to the Wolffian program of reform. He had been persuaded by Wolff's *German Metaphysics* of 1720, which Fischer described as a "golden book" (*librum aureum*), and the *German Physics* of 1723. In the winter semester of 1722/1723 he confronted his students with a manifesto declaring that the natural sciences should rightly have a foundation only in mathematics, experiment, empirical observation, and in connections with modern philosophy. It was only to be expected that he came under immediate fire from the theologians. Their shots found their target as we can see even in the foreword to Fischer's disputation, *An spiritus sint in loco* ("Whether spirits have location").[73] There he said:

> It was proposed that his present thoughts be defended from an official university lectern [i.e., in a disputation]. But because fate called the "respondent" [i.e., the student-candidate] ... down from the university before the noted little dispute over the manifold forms of censorship was concluded, I wanted to publish these few pages in this form, which would not have been so easily wrested from the hands of the printers, ... rather than burden the respondent with another trip and requiring him to repeat himself ... .[74]

What he here downplayed as a "little dispute" over prior censorship was by no means uncommon in the Königsberg of those years. The former freethinker Theodor Ludwig Lau, who had more recently developed sympathies for the philosophy of Leibniz and Wolff, had to endure this kind of censorship in 1727 from the juridical faculty; there too the theologians again prevented a planned disputation.[75] As for Fischer, he shared Wolff's fate in 1725, when he was banished by the Prussian king, told to leave Prussia "within 48 hours." He fled to Danzig (Gdansk).[76]

[73] *Quaestio philosophica, an spiritus sint in loco? Ex principiis rationis scientificae resoluta*, Königsberg, 1723; repr. Königsberg, 1740.

[74] Ibid., Foreword.

[75] On Lau, see Mulsow, *Enlightenment Underground* (note 1), chapters 5 and 7; Hanspeter Marti, "Grenzen der Denkfreiheit in Dissertationen des frühen 18. Jahrhunderts. Theodor Ludwig Laus Scheitern an der juristischen Fakultät der Universität Königsberg," in Helmut Zedelmaier and Martin Mulsow, eds., *Die Praktiken der Gelehrsamkeit in der Frühen Neuzeit*, Tübingen, 2001, pp. 295–306. On Lau, see also Mulsow, *Knowledge Lost* (note 46), chapters 1–3.

[76] The final trigger was a memorandum of Fischer's on university reform. See Predeek, "Ein vergessener Freund" (note 72), p. 111, as well as Predeek, "Ein verschollener

The life he led thereafter was precarious, without regular employment.[77] From his travel diaries he kept over the next years (diaries that I rediscovered in Danzig), we can partially follow him as he worked as a tutor, accompanying young noblemen on their overseas educational tours.[78] (See Figure 4.) The diaries show him acting as an ambassador for Wolffian philosophy in France and Holland, but they also reveal that he was repeatedly in Leipzig, where he maintained close contact with his friend Johann Christoph Gottsched. What interests us here, however, is Fischer's philosophical development from being a Wolffian natural scientist and philosopher into a much more independent thinker, who in 1743 returned to Königsberg as a private individual where he set forth his own system. He called it *Reasonable Thoughts on Nature*, which survives now in very few copies. It is a fat volume of 746 pages, published anonymously and listing no place of publication.[79] It begins with thorough examinations of the concepts of cause, effect, and force (*Kraft*), and then proceeds through the fields of cosmology, botany, and zoology until it comes to human beings and human nature.

Fischer's philosophy baffled his earliest listeners and readers. Right after his volume appeared, the Königsberg theologians wrote an anxious memorandum, and soon the *Reasonable Thoughts* was also accused of Spinozism.[80] For the 20-year-old Immanuel Kant this scandal was one of

---

Reorganisationsplan" (note 72). Fischer's forced confession of faith from 1726 is printed in *Fortgesetzte Sammlung von alten und neuen theologischen Sachen* (1731), pp. 927–933, and reprinted in Ludovici, *Ausführlicher Entwurf* (note 72), Part III, pp. 91–97.

[77] In 1726 he took two semesters of botany, anatomy, and differential calculus in Leiden, and in the following years he occupied himself as a private tutor on educational journeys with patrician clients to England, the Netherlands, France, Italy, and Germany, with lengthy stays in Leipzig (1727, 1731, 1732/33) in the orbit around Gottsched. In 1736 he was permitted to return to Königsberg, but only as a private citizen.

[78] *Herrn Nathanael Jacob Gerlachs [. . .] Reise [. . .] in einem akkuraten Journal beschrieben [. . .] durch Christian Gabriel Fischern aus Königsberg. Anno 1727–1731*, 12 vols. (3533 pp.), in folio. The manuscript was earlier in the possession of the "Naturforschende Gesellschaft" in Danzig. Today, only vols., 1, 2, 4, 5, 8, 9, 10, and 12 survive in the main library of the der Danzig Technical University. In 2009 one volume was auctioned by the auction house Peter Kiefer: *Auktion 66*, Nr. 289.

[79] Anon., *Vernünftige Gedanken von der Natur, was sie sey: daß sie ohne Gott und seine allweise Beschränkung unmächtig sey, und wie die einige unmittelbare göttliche kraft in und durch die Mittelursachen, nach dem Maaß ihrer verliehenen Wirkbarkeit oder Tüchtigkeit, hie in der Welt alles allein thätig wirke [. . .]; herausgegeben von einem Christlichen* [i.e., Christian] *Gottes* [i.e., Gabriel] *Freunde* [i.e., Fischer], s.l., 1743.

[80] Reactions to his "Vernünftigen Gedanken" can be found in *Fortgesetzte Sammlung von alten und neuen theologischen Sachen*, Leipzig, 1745, pp. 700–721; *Hamburgische freye Urtheile*, 1744, Issues 4 and 5. Archival materials on the censorship activities of the University of Königsberg can be found in the Archive of Olszyn (Poland), Signature XXVIII/1 and XXVIII/2; a query about whether Fischer could be found among the censorship proceedings was answered in the negative (letter to the author dated June 2, 2004).

Figure 4   Christian Gabriel Fischer's travel diary: Herrn Nathaniel Jacob Gerlachs [...]
Reise, vol. 1, p. 25

the important experiences of his youth.[81] To be sure, all of these reactions
to Fischer's book remained vague and inexact. The work could not be

---

[81] See Kühn, *Kant. Eine Biographie* (note 71), pp. 102–104. See also Erich Riedesel, *Pietismus und Orthodoxie in Ostpreußen*, Königsberg, 1937, p. 142.

easily placed in one of the usual pigeonholes; its originality and empirically rich contents exploded all the conventional categories. It seems sensible, therefore, to try in several steps to reconstruct Fischer's basic thought process and to situate it in the debates of his time. When we do so, we will find that we are dealing once again with the central problem of nature and idolatry.

But first a word about Fischer's terminology. His book belongs to the history of attempts to develop philosophical concepts in German, a history that begins with the medieval mystics, passes through Jakob Böhme and Erhard Weigel, and on to Gabriel Wagner until it reaches Fischer – but was then taken up again by Heidegger. Thus we hear Fischer speak of "stufflike things," "world stuff," "basic thing," and "world particles" (*zeughafte Sachen, Weltzeug, Grundsache, Weltschrötlein*), and it took a long time before these concepts could be interpreted using more traditional terms.

7   The Four Fundamental Motifs

Fischer's philosophy has four fundamental motifs: anti-idolatrous natural science; monism; the avoidance of immanence; and freedom. These were motifs that were connected to extremely different philosophical systems, and the interpreter has to be patient in making their connections understandable.

Let us begin with the motif of anti-idolatry, which takes pride of place in this chapter. For Boyle, nature had to be completely powerless and mechanical because the basis of all activity had been displaced to a voluntaristic God. Fischer sounded the same tones. Already in his *Reasonable Thoughts* he made it clear that his philosophy took its starting point with the battle over *de ipsa* (i.e., whether nature could act on its own). He begins:

> It is well-known what gross errors, endless fights, as well as thoughtless and exasperating talk have flowed over and flooded the world from the misuse of the word "nature." I have sailed these wild waters for forty years now [i.e., ever since the beginning of his student years] and have searched for the proper source of healthy perception.[82]

---

[82] *Vernünftige Gedanken* (note 79), fol. *2r. On p. 34, Fischer refers to an anonymous essay on the controversy over nature and idolatry that took a position against the Aristotelians: "Aristotelis error circa definitionem naturae," *Observationes selectae* 3 (1701), Obs. VII. The author of this essay was Georg Ernst Stahl.

And now comes the central thesis concerning the extraterrestrial nature of what Fischer called "the force" instead of calling it God:

> The force which Spinoza sought in the world; and the ancient pagans sought in the light; and the most recent philosophers [*Weltweisen*] seek in "world stuff" [*Weltzeuge*], imagining it as a divisible outflowing [a discharge, an emanation]; this I find outside the world, beyond all world stuff, only and exclusively in the immaterial spirit, which perfects the world structure according to its most wise decree, and has occupied it with immaterial creatures, that is, with souls.[83]

If translated into traditional terminology, he meant to say: It is an extraterrestrial, immaterial spirit that has created the world – that is, has created immaterial souls and is the continuing ground for all activity in the world. The "intermediary causes" (*causae secundae*) in contrast are to be seen as completely dependent and must not be given an independent existence.[84] In claiming this, Fischer came close to the occasionalism of Malebranche, but without sharing his Augustinian foundations.

He accused the pagans of imagining intermediary causes as independent entities – when they sought the basis of the force in light – and more recent materialists made the same mistake. Fischer was here firing a heavy cannon: where Boyle had quoted Selden, he now named Tobias Pfanner's *Systema theologiae gentilis* ("The System of Pagan Theology") in order to condemn the idolatry of secondary causes.[85] The gist of his argument seemed to run in a theological direction, but in reality it criticized a certain sort of "backward" natural philosophy and to that extent understood itself as "enlightened."[86] The formulation that spirit created souls – or let us just say it: "monads" – reminds us of Leibniz and Wolff. And indeed we find that the above-mentioned dissertation, *An spiritus sint in loco* of 1723, permits us to see how Fischer made Leibniz and Wolff's God into his starting point. In that work, which examines the problem of an "extended spirit" along the lines of Henry More, Fischer developed a series of thoughts that allowed him to proceed from our own spirit (*spiritus*) to another spirit of a different and higher sort, which had to be unique. God

---

[83] *Vernünftige Gedanken* (note 79), fol. *2v.   [84] Ibid., p. 25.

[85] Tobias Pfanner, *Systema theologiae gentilis*, Basel, 1679. *Vernünftige Gedanken* (note 79), p. 24; see *An spiritus sint in loco* (note 73), p. 24. On Pfanner, see Martin Mulsow, "Impartiality, Individualisation, and the Historiography of Religion: Tobias Pfanner on the Rituals of the Ancient Church," in Bernd-Christian Otto, Susanne Rau, and Jörg Rüpke, eds., *History and Religion: Narrating a Religious Past*, Berlin, 2015, pp. 257–268.

[86] See, e.g., *Vernünftige Gedanken* (note 79), p. 18, attacking talismanic or mathematical magic: "Ohne Kraft ist demnach keine würkende Ursach im Stande etwas auszurichten. . . . Deswegen sind Worte, Züge, Zahlen, und Gedanken, aus der Zahl derer würkenden Ursachen ausgeschloßen . . . ."

had not, he suggested, created other spirits, such as demons, the devil, etc.[87] But we do not understand how our own spirit subsists.[88] In this way Fischer stands in a tradition that defended the paradox of subjectivity (to press the discussion into a more modern form), a condition that does not know its own basis – this was a tradition that continued on into German idealism.[89] The being of the highest spirit, however, can still be inferred by extrapolating from our own spiritual characteristics, and Fischer does so with Wolff's definition: "God is a simple subsistent who represents to himself all possibilities at once and most distinctly, without body."[90]

In his mature work of 1743 this God is nothing more than force. There is no more talk of representation, and that is Fischer's decisive reduction. He admitted that Spinoza had declared in his *Tractatus* the capacity of nature to be nothing other than God's power and force so that together they constituted the divine being. Thus, Spinoza stood behind his reduction. He also borrowed from Spinoza the idea that God was (monistically) the only being that exists for itself. And yet, crucially, Fischer did not see himself as a Spinozist because he did not identify God with nature.[91] Indeed, he accused Spinoza of provoking this identification by using the concept of substance ambiguously. He argued that one must distinguish rigorously between first substance (*res subsistens* or, for Fischer, "basic thing" – *Grundsache*) and substance as "stock" or "inventory" (*Bestand*), which could include second substances. But because Spinoza described God as substance and not as *res subsistens* (as Wolff had done), he threw open the door to seeing God as immanent and not separate from the world.[92]

According to Fischer, a *Grundsache* (*res subsistens*, or "basic thing") is a substance in relation to which other things can be perceived.[93] "Force" is

---

[87] *An spiritus sint in loco* (note 73), p. 24.   [88] Ibid., p. 25.

[89] See, e.g., [Jakob Friedrich Reimmann], "Nescire animalia rationalia quid sit anima rationalis," in *Observationes selectae*, Additimentum (1705), Obvs. XIV, pp. 354–389; on that, see Martin Mulsow, "Asophia philosophorum. Skeptizismus und Frühaufklärung in Deutschland," in Transactions of the 9th International Congress on the Enlightenment *(Studies on Voltaire and the Eighteenth Century)*, vol. 346, Oxford, 1996, pp. 203–207; see also Samuel Christian Hollmann (praes.) / Adrian Gottlieb Söhner (resp.), *Dissertatio prior de stupendo mysterio anima humana sibi ipsi ignota*, Greifswald, 1722, printed in augmented form in Wittenberg, 1724, and reprinted again in Göttingen, 1750. For the discussion of the problem of the soul, see generally Chapter 1. On German idealism, see Dieter Henrich, *Fichtes ursprüngliche Einsicht*, Frankfurt, 1967; Henrich, *Grundlegung aus dem Ich*, 2 vols., Frankfurt, 2004.

[90] *An spiritus sint in loco* (note 73), p. 25. Fischer gives as his source Wolff, *Specimen physicum ad theologiam naturalem applicatum*, Halle 1717; see Wolff, *Deutsche Metaphysik*, Frankfurt and Leipzig, 1719, § 1067. See also *Vernünftige Gedanken* (note 79), p. 32.

[91] *Vernünftige Gedanken* (note 79), p. 32. See note 90.   [92] Ibid., p. 9.   [93] Ibid., p. 12.

then the "indispensable element in the cause through which basic things come into being, exist, and are made fit and active for making other things."[94] But nature in contrast is only "workable" – in other words, a passive disposition to achieve things with the help of divine force. It was "in itself a dead thing," a view that agreed completely with the anti-idolatry of Boyle and Sturm.[95]

We can sense the direction this metaphysics is leading us when we get to the later parts of Fischer's book that dealt with zoology and botany.[96] There he defended a theory of epigenesis, which, instead of assuming some collection of preformed beings, invoked the always-working, extraterrestrial *res subsistens* as an explanation: "deriving the multiplication of plants from the divine force collaborating with the appropriate matter, through the influence an original plant [*Stammgewächs*]."[97] Fischer did not shrink from evoking the sort of collaboration buttressing the scholastic theory of *concursus*[98] and he quoted the pseudo-Aristotelian *Liber de causis.*[99] The effect was eclectic but I do not think that this carefully constructed work was just an eclectic collection. He even pointed the way forward in biology by introducing the term *Bildungstrieb* (formative drive, *mechansimus plasticus, nisus formativus*) well before Johann Blumenbach popularized the term in the life sciences.[100]

8 Distancing Spinoza

The problem that Fischer created for himself by copiously exploiting the theories of Spinoza is obvious: How could he argue that despite this exploitation he had managed to avoid the dreaded "naturalism" or "atheism" of Spinoza? Fischer did explicitly reject the philosophy of immanence,[101]

---

[94] Ibid., p. 16.

[95] Ibid., p. 36. Fischer discusses the difference between *natura naturans* and *natura naturata* on p. 37, calling them the "original" and the "derived" nature.

[96] Fischer was a thorough-going empiricist. He was famous for his extensive collection of physical instruments and exhibits.

[97] *Vernünftige Gedanken* (note 79), p. 412.   [98] Ibid., p. 223.   [99] Ibid., pp. 217f.

[100] Ibid., p. 423. See Johann F. Blumenbach, "Über den Bildungs- Trieb und das Zeugungsgeschäft," *Göttinger Magazin* 1(5) (1780); Blumenbach speaks of a *nisus formativus*. Both Reimarus and Herder regarded the formative drive as very important. See Ernst Lichtenstein, Article on "Bildung"/5 in *Historisches Wörterbuch der Philosophie*, vol. 1, Basel, 1971, cols. 923–925. Fischer is not mentioned there.

[101] *Vernünftige Gedanken* (note 79), p. 29. On the pantheism of the Ranters, see Christopher Hill, *The World Turned Upside Down: Radical Ideas During the English Revolution*, London, 1975. For Apollonius, Fischer referred to Johann Chr. Herzog, *Sciagraphia philosophiae practicae Apollonii Thyanei*, Leipzig, 1709.

and also theories of emanation.[102] But was that no more than a rhetorical formula, a *façon de parler*? Or did it represent a serious insight? At the very least a real debate stood in the background. From the 1660s onward, for Jacob Thomasius the primary mark of Lutheran Orthodox philosophy and theology had been the separation of the creator from his creation; it had been Thomasius's central thesis. As a thesis it exerted an almost uniquely large influence even during the early Enlightenment.[103] Most notably Johann Franz Budde, one of Fischer's teachers in Jena, had dealt with what he called "Spinozism before Spinoza," in several treatises that took off from Thomasius and described a long series of ancient materialist streams of thought (such as Stoicism) that had not made this crucial distinction clearly enough.[104] It was not only naturalism but also ideas of emanation that assumed the preexistence of matter even before the creation; these schools also assumed that the world was eternal. Both of these ideas stood in sharp contradiction to Christian dogma.

In this connection let me repeat Fischer's central thesis: "The force which Spinoza sought in the world; and the ancient pagans sought in the light; and the most recent worldly wise seek in 'world stuff [*Weltzeuge*], imagining it as a divisible discharge; this I find outside the world . . . ." The "divisible discharge" referred to the idea of "emanation," the shift from divine force, to the extent that it was divine, to intermediate causes: "This was the ancient error," Fischer claimed, "which started in Babel and infected the entire East; and then from there to Egypt; from there it pushed into Greece and the Europeans; and finally it's now been warmed up again by Spinoza."[105] With such questions in the history of philosophy, Fischer built not just on Budde but also on Thomas Stanley's history of "oriental" philosophy even if Stanley was dealing with "the origin of false ideas of spirits."[106]

---

[102] *Vernünftige Gedanken* (note 79), p. 30.

[103] On the separation of creator from creation, see Mulsow, *Enlightenment Underground* (note 1), chapter 5. Jacob Thomasius, *Schediasma historicum*, Leipzig, 1665. See Ralph Häfner, "Jacob Thomasius und die Geschichte der Häresien," in Friedrich Vollhardt, ed., *Christian Thomasius 1655–1728. Neue Forschungen im Kontext der Frühaufklärung*, Tübingen, 1997, pp. 141–164.

[104] See Johann Franz Budde, *De Spinozismo ante Spinozam*, Halle, 1701. See also *Vernünftige Gedanken* (note 79), p. 71.

[105] *Vernünftige Gedanken* (note 79), pp. 30f.

[106] Thomas Stanley, *Historia philosophiae orientalis*, Leipzig, 1711. See on this Michael Stausberg, *Faszination Zarathushtra. Zoroaster und die Europäische Religionsgeschichte der Frühen Neuzeit*, vol. 2, Berlin, 1998, pp. 604–612.

"The basis of all error on this path," Fischer explained,

> is the false concept of the "essence of a spirit," – that it's imagined as a fluid light or dark thing, according to whether it's supposedly good or evil; ... that one can derive the whole structure of the world (along with all the things and changes in it) from fire or light, as if from some loose stuff that has no nature or force [of its own].[107]

This was exactly the Zoroastrian-Pythagorean philosophy of light in which not only Brockes and Fabricius had interested themselves,[108] for at just this time another ex-Wolffian, Siegmund Ferdinand Weißmüller, also discovered it for himself. He too thought of God as essentially force, but as a collection of lines that produced movement in the form of a "first-born light."[109] But here the paths diverged around 1740 if one wanted to push on from Wolff to a more extensive natural theology. The problem was not so much one of pure immanence or pure transcendence, but the notorious middle position of a light metaphysics and its model of emanation. Which side was the light metaphysics on? For Fischer the destructive potential of a belief in demons and spirits, which lay here concealed like a bomb, was too great for him to accept this sort of thinking. But other naturalizing ex-Wolffians such as Weißmüller and Schade were attracted to the possibilities that a "Zoroastrian" belief in spirits might allow them to extract a natural moral theory of spirits who either improved or corrupted themselves, even if it required the doctrine of metempsychosis.[110]

The controversy over emanation became much sharper after Wachter made it seem to many that Spinoza himself was a part of the tradition of

---

[107] *Vernünftige Gedanken* (note 79), pp. 139f. See Francesco Patrizi, *Zoroaster et eius CCCXX oracula chaldaica*, Ferrara, 1591 (published separately in Patrizi's *Nova de universis philosophia*, Ferrara, 1591). Fischer interpreted the biblical passages concerning spirits using the theory of accommodation, so that they could really mean something moral, p. 155.

[108] See Häfner, *Götter im Exil* (note 34), Part Three.

[109] See Martin Mulsow, "Pythagoreer und Wolffianer: Zu den Formationsbedingungen von vernünftiger Hermetik und gelehrter 'Esoterik' im Deutschland des 18. Jahrhunderts," in Anne-Charlott Trepp and Hartmut Lehmann, eds., *Antike Weisheit und kulturelle Praxis. Hermetismus in der Frühen Neuzeit*, Göttingen, 2001, pp. 337–396, esp. pp. 376ff; Mulsow, "Esoterik versus Aufklärung? Vermessung des intellektuellen Feldes anhand einer Kabale zwischen Weißmüller, den Gottscheds und Ludovici," in Monika Neugebauer-Wölk, ed., *Aufklärung und Esoterik. Rezeption – Integration – Konfrontation*, Berlin, 2009, pp. 331–376; Mulsow, "Eine unwahrscheinliche Begegnung. Siegmund Ferdinand Weißmüller trifft Christian Wolff in Marburg," in Monika Neugebauer-Wölk et al., eds., *Aufklärung und Esoterik. Wege in die Moderne*, Berlin, 2013, pp. 183–207.

[110] See Martin Mulsow, *Monadenlehre, Hermetik und Deismus. Georg Schades geheime Aufklärungsgesellschaft 1747–1760*, Hamburg, 1998; Mulsow, "Vernünftige Metempsychosis. Über Monadenlehre, Esoterik und geheime Aufklärungsgesellschaften," in Monika Neugebauer-Wölk, ed., *Aufklärung und Esoterik*, Hamburg, 1999, pp. 211–273. See also Mulsow, *Enlightenment Underground* (note 1), chapter 7.

emanation.[111] That made it necessary to determine if emanation necessarily boiled down to seeing God as immanent in the world. Budde had employed several fine distinctions, which Fischer also used, in which he could speak, for example, of "essential emanation."[112] Fischer explained:

> We do not say that the invisible, inconceivable, and indivisible Being of God can be found in his creatures; nor that it is distributed in them – for both of these are impossible; but that the divine force, which we can observe of God from the outside, does not only remain effective in him, but that through it his working activity in the world is evident all around and shows itself to be busy and active.[113]

There was a second point on which Fischer wanted nothing to do with Spinoza. Freedom was very important for him. Along with Leibniz he distinguished two kinds of spirits: those that are no more than tools and obey the laws of necessity; and those who perform the "service" of "observing the government of the world."[114] But in contrast to Leibniz's notion, souls for Fischer were only modes of being, possessing no power of their own; they are "just an activity and a freedom that allows space for the working of divine power."[115] Fischer was performing a balancing act between Spinoza and Leibniz: souls were only modes but they did possess freedom:

> If the choice of movements in one's mind does not comport with the divine purposes in one's soul, then the divine power operates according the choice of souls in the world, not the way one's soul might wish it but in the manner that God finds useful in the world and conducive to His holy purposes.[116]

Then there follows a grief in the soul, which is experienced as if one's body is completely alien. So here again: a Spinozistic doctrine of the affections

---

[111] See Johann Georg Wachter, *Der Spinozismus im Jüdenthumb*, Amsterdam, 1699; Wachter, Elucidarius Cabalisticus, "Rom," 1706. See Martin Mulsow, "A German Spinozistic Reader of Cudworth, Bull and Spencer: Johann Georg Wachter and his Theologia Martyrum (1712)," in Christopher Ligota and Jean- Louis Quantin, eds., *History of Scholarship*, Oxford, 2006, pp. 357–383, as well as Martin Mulsow, *Spinozism, Arianism, and Kabbalah: Unexpected Conjunctions in German Intellectual History of the Late Seventeenth Century. With the Addition of an Unknown Attempt at Rewriting Spinoza's Ethics by Johann Georg Wachter (1704)* (forthcoming).

[112] *Vernünftige Gedanken* (note 79), p. 31; see the reference in note 35 and the addendum: "Causam externam, creantem, sistentem, assistentem, non essentialiter influentem"; Budde, *De Spinozismo ante Spinozam* (note 104); Budde, *Introductio ad historiam philosophiae Ebraeorum*, note 60; see Wilhelm Schmidt-Biggemann, "Die Historisierung der Philosophia Hebraeorum im frühen 18. Jahrhundert. Eine philosophisch-philologische Demontage," *Aporemata. Kritische Studien zur Philologiegeschichte* 5 (2001), pp. 103–128.

[113] *Vernünftige Gedanken* (note 79), p. 29.

[114] Ibid., fol. *3r; also fol. *4r. See Leibniz, *Monadologie*, §§ 84 and 86 (in *Philosophische Schriften*, vol 6, Berlin, 1885).

[115] *Vernünftige Gedanken* (note 79),   [116] Ibid., fol. *3vf.

but formulated under a Leibnizian cloak. Fischer rejected determinism – but he was also not entirely in tune with Leibniz's prestabilized Harmony. His criticism of that notion – which is of some real interest – maintains, on the one hand, that if the soul proceeds in step with its body, it is not clear to what extent it could have an advantage over the body. The order of its tasks was already completely established – and so it allowed for too little freedom.[117] On the other hand, many psycho-physical "tasks" of the soul would be superfluous, such as assimilating food or caring for the effective functioning of one's organs. Fischer did not, however, simply accept the "influxus" theory, and he constructed his own solution to the body–soul problem. He explains it in a simile:

> Thus the body behaves in the Hand of God and under His common direction like a music box in the hand of its inventor. Just as it responds to the choice of a lover about what song is chosen and should be played, so too God allows the soul to choose for the body which inclinations should continue and should express themselves in movements of the body. As in the music box, so in the body everything is ready and prepared; it is just waiting for the nod from the soul, like that of a lover, so that what the soul desires is fulfilled in the body, like the chosen song in the music box. Here is no force or necessity.[118]

Barrel organs or hurdy-gurdies were common music boxes in Germany in the first third of the eighteenth century and thus provided a charming metaphor for the problems he was dealing with here. God gives the soul its full freedom, allowing it to give a "nod" to the body, prompting it to play one of the many melodies that God arranged for the body. The soul chooses; God makes it possible with His power that the body should play whatever it wants, even if it is a bad piece. But as he admitted, if a false melody is chosen, the result is deep sorrow (*Seelenbetrübnis*).

It is astonishing to witness how resolutely Fischer insisted on this element of freedom even if he understood human souls to be no more than modes and only as instrumental beings of divine power. But this too may have been the result of an early Enlightenment debate. Among the followers of Christian Thomasius, the acceptance of Spinoza's thinking almost always hit a wall of rejection when the topics of freedom and the foundations of natural law were broached. For then they felt that

---

[117] Ibid., p. 716.
[118] Ibid., pp. 712f. On the body–soul discussion, see Eric Watkins, "The Development of Physical Influx in Early Eighteenth-Century Germany: Gottsched, Knutzen, and Crusius," *The Review of Metaphysics* 49 (1995), pp. 295–340.

determinism and leveling norms and reality were undermining their
Enlightenment agenda.[119] Moreover, Fischer with his doctrine of
Seelenbetrübnis was coming close to those theorists of monads or "spirits"
who (expanding on Leibniz and Wolff) invented a natural theory of moral
sanctions that operated through enlarging the "pleasures" or "displeasures"
associated with actions of one sort or another.[120]

How should we evaluate this peculiar mixture of Boyle, Spinoza,
Leibniz, and Wolff? The theologians in Königsberg first accused Fischer
of "frivolity" for his treatment of theological matters, probably because he
brazenly applied his theory to suggest interpretations of transubstantiation,
the two natures of Christ, or the human fall into sin.[121] And then Fischer
behaved much as Urban Gottfried Bucher or other obstinate thinkers had.
But then came the obvious but not very meaningful accusation of
Spinozism. After what we have said about Fischer's motives, we could
describe his position using our current terminology this way: Fischer was
trying to adopt the discourse of the conservative Enlightenment, an
Enlightenment that insisted firmly on a strict distinction between God
and the world, but within that tradition to formulate a monism of
substance. Of course the theologians rightly recognized Fischer's attempt
as a Trojan horse. He was and remained a hybrid. Categories like "left-
wing Wolffianism"[122] or "deism" do not really help our understanding
much – especially because Fischer did not call the existence of revelation
into question.[123] I would, however, not go so far as August Kurz, who
tried to find in Fischer a dissimulating "political" style as if he was
intentionally laying down red herrings and was ready to reveal his true
Hobbesian-Spinozistic position only to readers who pierced the veil of his
intentional contradictions.[124] I think that Fischer's anti-idolatrous motive

---

[119] Winfried Schröder, *Spinoza in der deutschen Frühaufklärung*, Würzburg, 1987.

[120] See Mulsow, *Monadenlehre, Hermetik und Deismus* (note 110), pp. 112–127.

[121] See the remarks on transubstantiation (*Vernünftige Gedanken* (note 79), p. 114: "zwar eine
Vereinigung zweyer sachen, aber nich zweyer würkender Ursachen"), on the doctrine of the two
natures of Christ (pp. 178ff) and on the fall into sin (p. 732).

[122] See Günter Mühlpfordt. "Radikaler Wolffianismus. Zur Differenzierung und Wirkung der
Wolffschen Schule ab 1735," in Werner Schneiders, ed., *Christian Wolff*, 2nd edn., Hamburg,
1986, pp. 237–253.

[123] Fischer was no deist: he acknowledged both reason and revelation as sources (*Vernünftige Gedanken*
(note 79), p. 48); but for him the way of natural cognition was sufficient: "Was die Werke
gnugsam bezeugen, dazu sind keine Wort vonnöthen." The centrality of natural research as a
complement to natural theology reminds us of Reimarus, but Fischer lacked Reimarus's destructive
abilities, founded on philological biblical criticism.

[124] Kurz, *Über Christian Gabriel Fischers Vernünftige Gedanken von der Natur* (note 72), pp. 26ff. He
was describing the technique that Leo Strauss later described in *Persecution and the Art of Writing*,
Glencoe, 1952. Kurz combined this thesis with the claim that Fischer's book contained the

was genuine and to some extent it necessarily pushed him into a coalition with certain "conservative" theorists. This was how his peculiar thought construction came about.

9 Conclusion: Between the Radical and Conservative Enlightenments

Rüdiger and Fischer have provided two examples of philosophical self-confidence and strong-minded stubbornness in the early eighteenth century.[125] In Rüdiger's case it is hard to draw the line between the Thomasian early Enlightenment and Pietist spiritualism; but in Fischer's it is no longer easy to distinguish between the "radical" and the "conservative" Enlightenment. Although one might call Boyle a conservative Enlightener, a perfect example of what James and Margaret Jacob called the "Newtonian Enlightenment," precisely because his anxiety over being influenced by early religious misconceptions of nature (as active or worthy of veneration) was so great, with Fischer such borders were erased. He was consciously trying to position himself as a conservative Enlightener, and as the representative of an anti-idolatrous natural philosophy; but he took this framework as an opportunity to preserve as much of Spinoza in this philosophy as possible.

We find these tactics over and over again. Stubbe himself claimed to be a defender of Greatrakes the miracle healer, precisely in order to use his defense to stimulate reflection about the implicitly naturalistic consequences. The use of tactics and only implicit positions means that it is not always easy to separate "radical Enlightenment" views from those of the "conservative Enlightenment," and to avoid the error of practicing a sort of pure *Konsequenzenmacherei* (i.e., the drawing of forced, unintended, and unfair conclusions from what are presumed to be – usually implicit – assumptions), as was often practiced by the theologians of that age.[126] It seems to me important that we should clearly distinguish clearly between the descriptions given by others and by the authors themselves.

---

unfinished developmental history of his thinking, so that "an autobiography was formulated as theses in the style of a dogmatic work" (at p. 30).

[125] On the concepts here, see Oskar Negt, *Geschichte und Eigensinn*, Frankfurt, 1993; Norbert Schindler, *Widerspenstige Leute. Studien zur Volkskultur in der Frühen Neuzeit*, Frankfurt, 1992; English tr. Pamela Selwyn: *Rebellion, Community and Custom in Early Modern Germany*, Cambridge, 2002.

[126] See the critique of Israel from this point of view in Martin Mulsow, "Radikalaufklärung, moderate Aufklärung und die Dynamik der Moderne," in Jonathan Israel and Martin Mulsow, eds., *Radikalaufklärung*, Berlin, 2014, pp. 203-233.

The danger of idolatry was certainly descried from the ramparts of Christian philosophy along with what I have called "the anxiety of influence" – the fear of being influenced by star worship and astrology. And from that, over time, there arose a governing rhetoric in the controversy between the *modernes* and the *anciens* in the natural sciences – that is, between mechanists and Aristotelians.

And yet the rhetoric against idolatry could also reveal other sides, as we have seen in this chapter. If we just think of the criticism leveled at the priesthood by thinkers from Herbert of Cherbury to Charles Blount and John Toland, we can see how easily it could be turned into the language of idolatry. So then we get works like Blount's *Great is Diana of the Ephesians, or the Original of Idolatry* from 1680, with its biting genealogies claiming that modern priestcraft arose out of ancient abuses of sacrificial cults and the worship of idols.[127] In this way, used as a weapon in religious politics, the accusation of idolatry – and with it the charge of religious heterodoxy – could be employed on the side of the radical Enlightenment against Orthodoxy. The hermeneutics of idolatry was therefore a two-edged sword. It was always a weapon with which one described others, never oneself,[128] but it could be deployed by both sides, by the naturalists just as much as by the conservative Enlighteners and the Orthodox. And both parties were drawing on a historical background that was rooted in the Orientalist compendia of Kircher, Vossius, and Spencer.

Notoriously, men like Rüdiger and Fischer tried to maintain awkward positions between the fronts. Like many other early Enlighteners, Rüdiger did not want an "idolatrous" physics, but he did want to avoid a "godless" physics, and so he made suggestions of compromise that went in the direction of spiritualism. In contrast, Fischer stood firmly on a foundation of "modern," Wolffian natural science, but he shrank back from a pure philosophy of immanence because he sensed within it the doctrine of emanation, and with it a gateway for the invasion of pagan astrology and star worship. But deciding where the actual danger of idolatry lay was a matter of interpretation. The constant for almost all contemporaries was the recognition that together nature and idolatry created a problem.

---

[127] Justin Champion, *"The Pillars of Priestcraft Shaken": The Church of England and its Enemies, 1660–1730*, Cambridge, 1992.
[128] See also Voltaire, "Idolatrie," in *Dictionnaire philosophique*, Geneva, 1764.

CHAPTER 3

The Doctrine of Temperaments, Medicine, and the Problem of Atheism

1 The "German Bayle" as a Reader of La Mothe le Vayer

"Godless physics" was not the only boogeyman to threaten Germany in the decades around 1700 because a fear of "godless" psychology developed as well. This was not just the sort of mortalism that we got to know with Bucher in Chapter 1 of this book. We also saw that in Halle a doctrine of the affects or passions arose that combined the common interests between the medical and the philosophical faculties. We need to devote more attention to this combined interest because some external observers thought it harbored a sort of implicit atheism.

Take the observer Christoph Heinrich Oelven, for example. He was a small fish, a *demi-savant*, a conservative philosophical dilettante.[1] When he started publishing a journal in Berlin under the fashionable title, *Curious Monthly Letter for Nature, Art, State Matters, and Morals*, he used his organ to polemicize against liberal scholars of his day. He warned readers, for example, against the works of Nikolaus Hieronymus Gundling,[2] and especially against the volume of his essays entitled *Otia* from 1706–1707; he described Gundling as the successor to Bayle. Oelven asked

---

[1] On Oelven, see Anne Goldgar, *Impolite Learning: Community and Conduct in the Republic of Letters 1680–1750*, New Haven, 1995, pp. 168–171; Sebastian Kühn, *Wissen, Arbeit, Freundschaft – Ökonomien und soziale Beziehungen an den Akademien in London, Paris and Berlin, ca. 1700*, Göttingen, 2011, pp. 191–206.

[2] For literature on Gundling, see chapters 5 and 6 of Martin Mulsow, *Enlightenment Underground: Radical Germany 1680–1720*, tr. H. C. Erik Midelfort, Charlottesville, 2015. The central source for his biography and for the controversies surrounding him is still the work of Christian Friedrich Hempel in vol. 5 of Gundling's *Vollständige Geschichte der Gelahrtheit*, Frankfurt and Leipzig, 1736, entitled "Umständliches Leben und Schrifften, Collegia, Studia, Inventa und eigene Meinungen." The most recent literature can be found in Martin Mulsow, "Nikolaus Hieronymus Gundling," in Helmut Holzhey and Vilem Mudroch, eds., *Grundriss der Geschichte der Philosophie – Die Philosophie des 18. Jahrhunderts*, vol. 5/1, Basel, 2014, pp. 67–71.

whether the manner that has sneaked in through the writings of the now recently deceased Bayle can be approved and imitated in good conscience by good Christians and true scholars? For he was a scholar infamous throughout the world as a libertine, a skeptic, and even an atheist – it was especially his huge *Dictionnaire Critique* that broke the ice.[3]

Trying to cosy up to the magistrates at the Berlin court, Oelven continued with a denunciation of the professor at the Prussian university at Halle, which had the official duty to raise up future servants of the state:

> Under the pretext of a supposed critique they make bold to doubt God and his Word, to reject healthy principles, to introduce a monster that's called *bel esprit*, to corrupt morals, to set aside historic faith in favor of their blind and vulgar "videtur" ["it seems"], and in a word to enwrap the world with their apparently learned writings in such a blue haze that if they page through them long enough, they fall into a damnable skepticism and then, logically, into atheism.

Such teachings would surely corrupt the youth at the universities. The *bel esprit* that Oelven impugned was the "healthy human understanding" that had become a rallying cry in Halle – a reversal of previous practice, a turn that could be described, using the phrase of Charles Taylor, as the "affirmation of ordinary life."[4] Setting aside "historical faith" in favor of "it seems" meant having no confidence in traditional stories and values anymore, and attaching "it would seem" to everything called all tradition into question. In chapters 3 and 4 of *Enlightenment Underground* we were able to observe the destructive consequences that could flow from this skepticism in connection with political and religious critiques. Oelven was therefore an attentive observer, even if ultra-conservative.

Oelven labeled Gundling "the German Bayle," meaning it as a rebuke and a warning even if today it might sound like praise. Oelven was by no means Gundling's only opponent, for he was only telling the court in Berlin what they were also saying in Wittenberg, Rostock, or Leipzig.[5]

---

[3] [Christoph Heinrich Oelven], *Monatliche Curieuse Natur- Kunst- Staats- und Sitten- Praesenten*, Berlin, 1708, Issue 2, pp. 34ff. See Gerhard Sauder, "Bayle-Rezeption in der deutschen Aufklärung (Mit einem Anhang: In Deutschland verlegte französische Bayle-Ausgaben und deutsche Übersetzungen Baylescher Werke)," *Deutsche Vierteljahresschrift für Literaturwissenschaft und Geistesgeschichte* 49 (1975), Sonderheft, pp. 83*–104*; here at pp. 93*f.

[4] Charles Taylor, *Sources of the Self: The Making of the Modern Identity*, Cambridge, MA, 1989.

[5] Thus the Rostock theologian Johann Fecht described Gundling as a libertine; see Hempel, *Umständliches Leben* (note 2), pp. 7678ff. There Hempel listed still other opponents of Gundling. On Thomasius as the "German Bayle," see Sandra Pott (today: Sandra Richter), "'Le Bayle de l'Allemagne.' Christian Thomasius und die europäische Refuge. Konfessionstoleranz in der wechselseitigen Rezeption für ein kritisches Bawahren von Tradition(en)," in Manfred Beetz and Herbert Jaumann, eds., *Thomasius im literarischen Feld*, Tübingen, 2003, pp. 131–158.

But the court in Berlin never dropped its support for Gundling or for his teacher and colleague Thomasius.

As we have seen, Gundling belonged to the first of many generations of German intellectuals who grew up with Bayle's *Dictionnaire*. When the *Dictionnaire* was published in 1697, Gundling was 26 years old and had already completed his theological studies at the universities of Jena, Leipzig, and Altdorf. He used Bayle's volumes as a sort of collection of *loci communes*,[6] common topics, a treasury of historical, biographical, and philosophical themes that could be used for many purposes. And so it is understandable that we do find a thoroughgoing acceptance of Bayle in his work, beginning with his adopting such formal matters as Bayle's footnoting technique, as well as his satirical and lively manner of writing, but even following Bayle's historical and critical intentions on certain topics. In his *Otia*, which enraged Oelven and others, Gundling had followed Bayle's manner in doubting the chastity of Saint Kunigunde,[7] for example, or in his opinions concerning the question of whether Nice belonged to Savoy, Anjou, or to others.[8] An anonymous pamphlet that was published in 1706 and immediately showed up in a Leipzig bookseller's shop, set forth a list of complaints about the *Otia* that reads just like the better-known complaints about the works of Bayle.[9]

Of course, Bayle's *Dictionnaire* was not the only work that Gundling exploited as a collection of *loci communes*. Along with it, and probably even earlier, Gundling was using in a similar manner the so-called lexicon of Suidas and also the works of François de La Mothe le Vayer, the "potential Bayle,"[10] whom Gundling himself had compared

---

[6] See Hempel's annotations in Gundling, *Vollständige Geschichte der Gelahrtheit* (note 2), pp. 2940 and 7031.

[7] Gundling, *Otia*, vol. 3, Halle 1707, pp. 151–213.

[8] Gundling, *Otia*, vol. 1, Halle 1706, pp. 93–158.

[9] *Erbauliche Gedancken über D. Nicol. Hieron. Gundlings Otia / So Von einem Liebhaber der Warheit wohlmeinend Dem Leser und sonderlich dem Herrn Doctori hiermit eröffnet werden*, Nuremberg, 1706. This pamphlet of forty-eight pages presents itself on the title page in its type font and in the opening passages almost as a copy of the original. In 1709 another work appeared (with no place of publication listed), *Weitere Fortsetzung der Erbaulichen Gedancken über D. Nicol. Hieron. Gundlings Otia / Worinne desselben seltsame Aufführung und schlechte Beantwortung der Einwürffe / so wider den 1. Theil der Otiorum gemachet worden / denen Liebhabern der Wahrheit aufrichtig gezeiget werden.*

[10] On the relationship between Bayle and La Mothe le Vayer, see Ruth Whelan, "The Wisdom of Simonides: Bayle and La Mothe le Vayer," in. Richard H. Popkin and Arjo Vanderjagt, eds., *Scepticism and Irreligion in the Seventeenth and Eighteenth Centuries*, Leiden, 1993, pp. 230–253; Isabelle Moreau, "Pierre Bayle et La Mothe le Vayer: de la liberté de conscience à l'indifférence des religions," in Philippe Fréchet, ed., *Pierre Bayle et la liberté de conscience*, Toulouse, 2012, pp. 135–150.

to Bayle.[11] He obtained, as he admitted, his first "substantial ideas in the history of philosophy" from Le Vayer's "The Virtue of the Pagans": "That is my handbook. Because there I can find a series of ancient and new things. For it is like half a library, and if I want something, I run to it, as if to *loci communes*. It contains the quintessence of the ancient writers."[12] It was, however, a most idiosyncratic "handbook." La Mothe le Vayer's work on the "virtue of the pagans" was a treatise that set forth the author's understanding of the teachings and virtues of ancient philosophers before a specific background, that is in a polemic against the extreme Augustinianism of Jansenius. But he did not attack Jansenism directly, in his doctrines concerning original sin or grace; instead, he attacked indirectly, in a reaction to the supposed depravity of the pagans – no matter how virtuous they may have been. He also engaged in a discussion of "philosophical sin," a violation of the natural order but not one that could be regarded as an insult to God, because, for example, a pagan from pre-Christian antiquity could not know God.[13] But according to St. Augustine, even the virtues of the pagans were sinful because they did not know God, and the Jansensists followed him in this. La Mothe le Vayer then proposed that Augustine should be read differently, so that one might agree with Bellarmine that God had purged such vices – if that was what they were – because it would be absurd otherwise. Other Church Fathers despite their respect for Augustine had actually valued the virtues of the pagans. And had not Augustine himself spoken well of the virtues of

[11] See Hempel, *Umständliches Leben* (note 2), p. 7031. On La Mothe le Vayer, see, e.g., Jean-Pierre Cavaillé, *Dis/simulations. Jules-César Vanini, François de La Mothe le Vayer, Gabriel Naudé, Louis Machon et Torquato Accetto. Religion, morale et politique au XVIIe siècle*, Paris, 2002; Isabelle Moreau, *"Guérir du sot." Les stratégies d'écriture des libertins à l'âge classique*, Paris, 2007; Pietro Capitani, *Erudizione e scetticismo in François de La Mothe le Vayer*, Florence, 2009.

[12] Gundling, *Vollständige Geschichte der Gelahrtheit* (note 2), p. 5048. See his *Ausführlicher Discours über den jetzigen Zustand der europäischen Staaten*, Frankfurt and Leipzig, 1733, p. 107, on La Mothe's *Oeuvres*. Hempel tried on p. 7031 to make up a list of these books based on Gundling's mentioning them in his lectures; it included, e.g., Hieronymus Wolf and Coelius Rhodiginus, and for more specialized topics John Spencer, Locke's *Letter on Toleration*, Henry Dodwell, Hugo Donellus and Johann Friedrich Hombergk zu Vach.

[13] I owe my knowledge of these discussions to Jacob Schmutz, who referred to them in a lecture in Gotha. See, e.g., the anonymous work (by Dominique Bouhours) entitled *Sentiment des Jesuites touchant le peché philosophique*, Paris, 1690. On the more specific context of the "Quarrel" concerning the virtues of the pagans, see a few further texts that appeared between 1641 and 1647: Antoine Sirmond, *La deffense de la vertu*, Paris, 1641; Antoine Arnauld, *Extract de quelques erreurs et impiétez contenues dans un livre intitulé: "La deffence de la vertu," par le Père Antoine Sirmond, de la Compagnie de Jésus*, s.l., 1641; Jean-Pierre Camus, *Animadversions sur la preface d'un livre intitulé, Deffence de la vertu*, Paris, 1642; François de La Mothe le Vayer, *De la vertu des payens*, 2nd edn. augmented, Paris, 1647.

Caesar and Cato?[14] The text that followed his polemical foreword served ultimately as a proof of the anti-Jansenist thesis that the pre-Christian Greeks and Romans had not been damned and had possessed true virtues. To that extent *The Virtue of the Pagans* was an unconventional history of ancient philosophy – including its various "sects" – from the standpoint of their morality and immorality.[15]

From studying Gundling's reading of La Mothe le Vayer we can discover many things about his early work, and especially about his *History of Moral Philosophy* from 1706, which, like the Frenchman's book, took up the separate sects of Greek philosophy and evaluated them according to their moral contents. Gundling, however, published only the first part, which did not advance far enough to place "barbaric" philosophy in a historical and critical framework.[16] In a certain sense his essays on the atheism of Plato, of Parmenides, of Hippocrates, and others can be regarded as a substitute for the never-completed second part, for they offered a discussion of the various philosophical schools of antiquity.

The central problem here was not the problem of ancient moral skepticism, which will be our topic in the next chapter. Gundling was content for the moment to leave this problem in the background when he discussed La Mothe; his skepticism had been just a pedagogical provocation aimed at making the reader think:

> And yet La Mothe le Vayer shows that the skeptics did not doubt absolutely everything; they had been unwilling to affirm anything for certain, and were content to leave it open whether something was shameful or decent, right or wrong. Seriously, anyone who always doubts must be a useless person. You just cannot deal with someone who says "perhaps" all the time. How could I argue with such a person. Arguing does not cure any patients. The fever of fools will fade away by itself. You just have to let it go. . . . So if the skeptics are now commonly disparaged, the above-mentioned Le Vayer answered that the skeptics were, after all, entrusted with the highest offices, but they had only acted foolishly to make fun of the "dogmatists" while refusing to affirm anything. These *Opera* of Le Vayer are available in 15 volumes in

---

[14] François de La Mothe le Vayer, *De la vertu des païens*, Paris, 1642. I am citing the modern edition in Jacques Prévot, ed., *Libertins du XVIIe siècle*, vol. 2, Paris, 2004, pp. 1–215, here at pp. 7ff. Le Vayer also worked through the scholastics, e.g., p. 6.

[15] See April Shelford, "François de La Mothe le Vayer and the Defence of Pagan Virtue," *The Seventeenth Century* 15 (2000), pp. 67–89; Michael Moriarty, *Disguised Vices: Theories of Virtue in Early Modern French Thought*, Oxford, 2011, pp. 175–210. See also Louis Capéran, *Le problème du salut des Infidèles. Essai historique*, Paris, 1912.

[16] See Mulsow, *Enlightenment Underground* (note 2), chapter 6; as well as Helmut Zedelmaier, *Der Anfang der Geschichte. Studien zur Ursprungsdebatte im 18. Jahrhundert*, Hamburg, 2003, pp. 84–96.

duodecimo format. He had been the tutor of the old Duke of Orleans, but because he especially defended the skeptics in his *Problème sceptique*, he was not trusted to teach the [young] King Louis XIV, for fear that he might turn him into an atheist.[17]

Gundling was clearly aware of just how controversial La Mothe le Vayer had been: "I know," he said in an open letter to Heumann, "that this Frenchman (who has been in his grave for some time now) will either be turned into an atheist or into at least a Socinian, so that his cursed manner of speech can be disarmed and thus harm no one."[18] And yet Gundling cared little about that.

This interpretation does reveal something of Gundling's self-understanding. He too maintained skeptical positions, and he too was labeled an atheist. And Gundling, too, had only wanted to unsettle and provoke the "dogmatists." In *Enlightenment Underground* I called one kind of Enlightenment "skeptical-liberal," and it arose out just these sorts of provocation. According to his students, Gundling erupted with laughter, sending forth "from his eyes a joy, an understanding, and a jovial essence," loving jokes as much as he did conflicts.[19] His actions cannot be understood just from their theoretical content because they need to be evaluated for their pragmatic character; they were speech acts. With such figures in mind, Ian Hunter has focused on the "persona" of the philosopher and not just on the texts alone, and that proves to be extremely helpful for understanding the early German Enlightenment.[20]

[17] Gundling, *Der Philosophischen Discourse anderer und dritter als letzter Theil*, Frankfurt and Leipzig, 1740, Part III, p. 29. In the early eighteenth century, the skeptics and Bayle as well were often read as fideists whose simple Christian piety restrained them. That was true for Ludwig Martin Kahle, the editor of La Mothe and follower of Gundling in Halle. See La Mothe le Vayer, *Cinq dialogues faits a limitation des Anciens*, ed. Ludwig Martin Kahle, Berlin, 1747. At this time Kahle was a professor of law in Halle. This interpretation was later supported by Richard H. Popkin, *The History of Scepticism from Erasmus to Spinoza*, Berkeley, 1979.

[18] Gundling, "Brief an … Heumann," in *Satyrische Schriften*, Jena and Leipzig, 1738, p. 505.

[19] For different kinds of Enlightenment, see Mulsow, *Enlightenment Underground* (note 2), chapter 6. Johann Michael von Loen, "Ausbildung des Professor G.," in *Gesammlete kleine Schriften*, Part 1, 4th edn., Frankfurt and Leipzig, 1753, p. 218.

[20] Ian Hunter, "The History of Philosophy and the Persona of the Philosopher," in *Modern Intellectual History* (2007), 4(3), pp. 571–600. See also my *Knowledge Lost: A New View of Early Modern Intellectual History*, Princeton, 2022, chapter 4, where I argue that the "knowledge precariat" of the early eighteenth century favored tolerating unheard-of and paradoxical views, plurality, and libertine opinions; a tolerance that demanded virtues such as restraint and calmness to prevent a fall into the *logomachia eruditorum*.

2 Friendship and Conflict

To make such an unsettling provocation, Gundling crafted a theory of conflict as embracing, so to speak, a theory of friendship. Where Thomasius saw friendship and reasonable love as the cornerstones of his understanding of natural law, Gundling used this topos as the precondition for dissent and criticism:

> If someone does not like my ideas, I can easily tolerate that. We have no need on that account to break the bond of general or even of special friendship. For [disagreements] are only thoughts, and friendship does not depend on thoughts . . . .[21]

Gundling was saying that friendship belonged to the practical side of life, which had to be kept separate from the theoretical. Sebastian Kühn has pointed out that friendship played a central even if an ambivalent role in the Republic of Letters.[22] Especially in the third volume of his *Otia*, in which Gundling reacted to the attacks on earlier volumes of his book, most especially the anonymous *Erbauliche Gedancken* ("Edifying Thoughts"), Gundling spontaneously developed a theory of controversy as a theory of friendship.[23] With it he hoped to move beyond the constant reinforcing of hostile sectarian boundaries in which only conformity mattered. After all, if one properly understood the separation of theory and practice, one would no longer be so concerned to create social unity by insisting on identical opinions, a unity "which endures as long as one is a member of their sect and pray the same Our Father and the same Hail Mary . . . ."[24] True friendship consisted, as Gundling said in his treatise on the will, in the community of virtue. That opened up a free space for a theory in which dissent of all sorts was possible. All the provocative theses that Gundling defended over the coming years – including the assertion that Plato and Hippocrates had been atheists – were ultimately tests of this wide-open free space.

Gundling pursued this enterprise with great enthusiasm and with a burlesque tone that was typical for him: "If anyone hates me for this or becomes my enemy, he should know that I do not deserve his enmity for I am ready, with all imaginable friendliness to heap fiery coals on his

---

[21] *Otia*, vol. 3 (note 7), pp. 149f.   [22] Kühn, *Wissen, Arbeit, Freundschaft* (note 1).
[23] On the culture of dispute, see Carlos Spoerhase and Kai Bremer, eds., *Gelehrte Polemik: Intellektuelle Konfliktverschärfungen um 1700*, Frankfurt, 2011; Spoerhase and Bremer, eds., *"Theologisch-polemisch-poetische Sachen." Gelehrte Polemik im 18. Jahrhundert*, Frankfurt, 2015.
[24] *Otia*, vol. 3 (note 7), p. 151.

head [. . .]"^{25} Or again, "He should not imagine that I would wish to tussle with him just to amuse others. He is great while I am small; he is evil but I am pious; he is furious and I am calm; he's full of fire while I'm full of phlegm."^{26} He was practicing a sort of cheerful, peaceful belligerence which remained constantly aware of how easily his offensive tactics could overstep their proper limits. For example, when Johann Hermann von Elswich accused him of atheism,^{27} one sees how Gundling's defenses of authors like Anthony Collins and Thomas Hobbes could have brought him into real danger. But he insisted, "I don't want to be – and would not relish being – a martyr."^{28}

This was what made him different from the German freethinkers. While they might seek out confrontations, Gundling sought to embrace his opponents. And while they might dogmatically assert the corporeality of the soul or the identity of God with nature, he reserved a little Orthodoxy for himself, just in the name of probability; and he denied that one should necessarily put theoretical conclusions into practice. In this he was following the same path as Pierre Bayle before him,^{29} but also Richard Simon, who provided an example of how one could critique of the Bible while remaining a member of the Order of Oratorians.^{30}

"Just as you are not forbidden to write something, so I am not forbidden either." With this laconic syllogism Gundling began his *Otia* of 1706. He was echoing Thomasius, and he echoed him repeatedly in later writings. The statement epitomizes the freedom of thought claimed by the early German Enlightenment. Gundling continued: "We live in a republic, where people have a free vote. As the times change, and the opinions of scholars also change." The word of the people "who have a free vote" was a reference to Juvenal's phrase, "libera si dentur populo suffragia" ("if a free vote were given to the people...")^{31} He was referring of course to the Republic of Letters, but by not mentioning political freedom, he made his dictum all the more self-confident and provocative. Behind his self-confidence stood his clear sense of progress, as the preface to his *Gundlingiana* shows: "The world is certainly wiser in some respects than

^{25} Ibid. ^{26} *Otia*, vol. 2, Halle, 1706, "Foreword."
^{27} Johann Hermann von Elswich (praes.) / Johann Sigismund Buchwald (resp.), *Controversiae de atheismo recentiores*, Wittenberg, 1716.
^{28} *Otia*, vol. 3 (note 7), "Foreword."
^{29} Michael Czelinski-Uesbeck, *Der tugendhafte Atheist. Studien zur Vorgeschichte der Spinoza-Renaissance*, Würzburg, 2007.
^{30} See Hempel, *Umständliches Leben* (note 2), p. 7036
^{31} Juvenal, *Satires*, no. 8, v. 211. Generally, on the freedom of thought, see Kay Zenker, *Denkfreiheit. Libertas philosophandi in der deutschen Aufklärung*, Hamburg, 2012.

a century ago."[32] This awareness fed his patience and ability to withstand slanders, for the truth would ultimately prevail.

3   The Critique of Bayle and the Recognition of National Character

On this basis Gundling unfolded a program in his *Otia* that rehabilitated the doctrine of temperaments and also clarified the relationship of the understanding to the will; but he also made such complete use of his freedom to theorize that it seemed not to matter that he could accuse Hippocrates of atheism even as he valued him medically for his doctrine of the temperaments.

It is striking that the first two essays in *Otia* from 1706 dealt with La Mothe le Vayer and Bayle. The first essay was entitled "On the Temperament of the Spaniards,"[33] while the second, which followed directly after it, was called "On the Antipathy of the Spanish to the French, against Msr. Bayle."[34] He was measuring himself against Bayle, as if the French savant were his bigger brother, whom he might like to beat just once. But even though Gundling may have taken his bearings from Bayle, there were also differences between the two. His critique focused on one small point from the work of the Rotterdam Huguenot, an observation mentioned on just a few pages, and yet that point was symptomatic, it seems to me, and the critique revealed larger consequences. Gundling had read Bayle's *Response to the Questions of a Provincial*, published two years earlier, and had stumbled over chapter 14, which dealt with the antipathy between the Spanish and the French:

> Indeed, Monsieur Bayle thinks that it's a foolish chimaera that gets planted in the heads of some, who then imagine that it's the difference in their temperaments that explains why the French and the Spanish cannot stand one another. He says, set aside the differences in customs and mores between neighboring nations, remove their jealousy and their sense of equality or of superiority, but arrange it so that they have the same political interests, and you'll see them sympathize with each other in short order and get along very well.[35]

But Gundling was reluctant to dismiss too quickly the doctrine concerning differences in temperaments.

---

[32] *Gundlingiana*, vol. 1, Halle, 1715, "Foreword," fol. 4v.   [33] *Otia*, vol. 1, Halle 1706, pp. 1–80.
[34] Ibid., pp. 81–93.
[35] Ibid., pp. 81f., with reference to Bayle's *Réponse au questions d'un provincial*, vol. 1, Rotterdam, 1704, p. 102. Bayle's chapter 14 comprises pp. 94–103.

Earlier Thomasius had also used the legendary enmity between the Spanish and the French to attempt to work out an arithmetic of the affections with variations of degree.[36] The topic was, therefore, well-known in Halle. The interesting feature, however, is that in criticizing Bayle, Gundling went back to La Mothe le Vayer. He cited his *Discourse on the Difference in Humors Shown by Certain Nations* (1636), which Bayle had criticized, but Gundling now strove to rehabilitate Le Vayer against Bayle's critique.[37] Along with Bayle, Gundling added that La Mothe le Vayer may have been inspired by Carlos Garcia, whose book *La Antipatia de los Franceses y Españoles* (Paris, 1617) had recently been translated into German.[38] Combining Garcia and La Mothe le Vayer, Gundling maintained against Bayle that there was and indeed had long been a real antipathy between Spaniards and Frenchmen. Okay, but why did the early German Enlightenment choose to differ with Bayle over this issue? To answer that question it will be necessary to pursue the chain of reception from Garcia to La Mothe le Vayer and on to Bayle and to examine a bit more closely the different ways the topos of hereditary Spanish–French enmity was used.

Garcia composed his treatise on the occasion of the wedding between Louis XIII and the Spanish infanta (1615), and so he understandably minimized the oppositions between the two nations. It was, however, a time in which European countries were beginning to see themselves as separate nations and to formulate their emerging profiles and the European constellation of peoples using whatever means they had at their disposal.[39]

---

[36] Christian Thomasius, *Weitere Erleuterung durch unterschiedene Exempel [. . .] das Wesen aus der Menschen Gemüther zu erkennen*, Halle, 1692; see also Thomasius, *Außübung der Sitten-Lehre*, Halle, 1696; on that, see Karl Borinski, *Balthasar Gracian und die Hofliteratur in Deutschland*, Halle, 1894, pp. 88ff.

[37] La Mothe le Vayer, *Discours de la contrarieté d'humeurs qui se trouve entre de certaines nations, et singulierement entre la Francoise et l'Espagnole: traduit de l'Italien de Fabricio Campolini Veronois*, Paris, 1636. On the theory of cultural differences in La Mothe, see Joseph Beaude, "Amplifier le dixième trope, ou la difference culturelle comme argument sceptique," *Recherches sur le XVIIe siècle* 5 (1982), pp. 21–29. See generally René Pintard, *Le libertinage érudit dans la premiere moitié du XVIIe siecle*, Paris, 1943.

[38] Gundling was referring to *Anthipathia Gallorum et Hispanorum, Das ist Angebohrne Wider-Artigkeit der Frantzosen und Spannier gegen einander. Nachsinnig beschrieben in Spannischer Sprach von Herrn Dr. Carlo Garzia. In das Italienische versetzt von Clodio Vilopoggio. Auß disem der eyferigen Teutschen Nation zur Nachricht so lustig als nützlich zulesen ins Teutsch gantz neu verfertigt und gedruckt*, Regensburg, 1701. According to Jöcher's *Gelehrten-Lexicon* this translation was first published in Regensburg in 1676. For a critical edition of the original, see Michel Bareau, ed., *Carlos Garcia, La oposición y conjunción de los dos grandes luminares de la tierra; O la Antipatia de los Franceses y los Españoles (1617)*, Edmonton, Alberta, 1979.

[39] See Winfried Schulze, "Die Entstehung des nationalen Vorurteils. Zur Kultur der Wahrnehmung fremder Nationen in der europäischen Frühen Neuzeit," in Wolfgang Schmale, ed., *Menschen und*

For that purpose Garcia used Renaissance occult ideas about "sympathy," which he mixed with Aristotelian and Galenic ingredients, even though he took care to reject natural magic and preferred to speak of the influence of the devil.[40] In contrast, La Mothe le Vayer, who exploited Garcia in many ways, was writing from the French side against the Spanish but was also eager to use the topic to smuggle his libertine views into the text.[41] A half century later Bayle regarded a debate that invoked occult qualities as no longer credible, and so in his *Dictionnaire* he undertook to deconstruct the discourse over temperaments.[42] Magical formulations, he thought, were an *asylum ignorantiae*, used only by the historically ill-informed. Bayle had been sensitized to these issues by Adrien Baillet,[43] and he tried to bring the debate down from the speculative level of eternal antipathies, produced either by God or other forces, to the level of constantly changing historic constellations that depended on shifting interests and political factors. The reasons for national antipathies were real historical tensions, especially the many wars that the Spanish and the French had fought with each other.[44]

In principle Gundling agreed with such deconstructions, but in the case of the temperaments he felt that the baby was being thrown out with the bath water; for him, the doctrine of the temperaments did not have to involve "occult qualities" at all. They were too valuable and useful to be rejected entirely. It was true that the many sorts of determinants were confusing:

> So many people, so many new categories on which you can test your understanding and your skill. Indeed, we have become aware of so many peoples, so many new observations; and so many unique [qualities] among all nations; so many deviations and varying temperaments. ... that one might almost consider the idea of national temperaments, nature, and

Grenzen in der Frühen Neuzeit, Berlin, 1998, pp. 23–49. See also Ruth Florack, *Tiefsinnige Deutsche, frivole Franzosen. Nationale Stereotype in deutscher und französischer Literatur*, Stuttgart, 2001; Manfred Beller, *Eingebildete Nationalcharaktere*, Göttingen, 2006.

[40] Garcia, *Anthipathia Gallorum et Hispanorum* (note 38), chapter IX, in the German edition, pp. 137ff. For example, pp. 139f., where the astrological and demonological context in Garcia is clear. Or p. 143 (wrongly paginated as p. 135), where it becomes clear that the analogy applies to those examples from the contemporary literature on *magia naturalis*. On *magia naturalis*, see Paola Zambelli, *White Magic, Black Magic in the European Renaissance*, Leiden, 2007.

[41] Ioana Manea, "L'Espagne chez La Mothe le Vayer ou comment utiliser les stéréotypes de la littérature politique pour exprimer des opinions libertines," *Loxias* 26, placed online on September 15, 2009.

[42] Pierre Bayle, *Dictionnaire historique et critique*, 2nd edn., Rotterdam, 1702, Article on "Louis XI," rem. X.

[43] Adrien Baillet, *Jugement des savants sur les principaux ouvrages des auteurs*, Paris, 1685–1686.

[44] See Gundling, *Ausführlicher Discours* (note 12), p. 107. See Gundling, *Philosophische Discourse* (note 17), p. 640.

properties to be useless, as if it produces no certain conclusions; that [John] Barclay was wasting his time in finishing his *Icon animorum* ["Mirror of Minds," 1614] or that [Juan] Huarte de San Juan lucubrated uselessly over his *Scrutinium ingeniorum* ["The Examination of Men's Wits," 1575]; or that Pufendorf and other political writers burned the midnight oil for no good reason in describing the various mighty nations.[45]

But, even so, Gundling thought the doctrine should be preserved.

4 Gundling and the Doctrine of Temperaments

Gundling drew this conclusion for very different reasons. First, around 1700 the "Quarrel of the Ancients and the Moderns" was reaching a high point, and with it such companion pieces as the squabble over the derogatory observations that Dominique Bouhours, S.J., had made concerning Germany.[46] These works made constant use of national stereotypes in their arguments. Second, there was the tradition of climate theory, which had been interwoven with political theory and ideas of natural law ever since Jean Bodin.[47] But treating politics and law together historically and in detail was a central goal of the early Enlightenment in Halle. And with the reinterpretation of natural law produced by Christian Thomasius in 1705 with his *Fundamenta juris naturae et gentium* ("The Foundations of the Law of Nature and of Nations"), which set forth a more realistic and more pessimistic image of human nature and society,[48] the evaluation of how human behavior depended on affects and temperaments became all the more important.

Gundling defended his own version of temperaments, which in contrast to Thomasius acknowledged only three temperaments instead of four: the sanguine, choleric, and melancholic. The phlegmatic was missing, and without it the physiological basis for Thomasius's "reasonable love" disappeared.[49] In Gundling's terminology, based on Harvey, the Spanish typified the model of the choleric – theorists had agreed on that ever since

---

[45] Gundling, *Philosophische Discourse* (note 17), p. 511.

[46] See the comprehensive documentation in Peter Kapitza, *Ein bürgerlicher Krieg in der gelehrten Welt. Zur Geschichte der Querelle des anciens et des modernes in Deutschland*, Munich, 1981.

[47] On climate theory, see Waldemar Zacharasiewics, *Die Klimatheorie in der englischen Literatur und Literaturkritik: Von der Mitte des 16. bis zum frühen 18. Jahrhundert*, Vienna, 1977.

[48] Thomasius, *Fundamenta juris naturae et gentium*, Halle, 1705. On the *Fundamenta*, see Peter Schröder, *Christian Thomasius*, Hamburg, 1999, pp. 80–98.

[49] See Gundling, *Via ad veritatem*, vol. 2, Halle, 1713; Gundling, *Philosophische Discourse* (note 17), pp. 447–650; on that work, see Martin Pott, *Aufklärung und Aberglaube. Die deutsche Frühaufklärung im Spiegel ihrer Aberglaubenskritik*, Tübingen, 1990, pp. 304–309.

Garcia. They had a high concentration of sulfur in their blood and therefore exceptionally high heat and prominent characteristics such as ambition.[50] A description of the Spanish mentality could start with the Spanish climate and geography and then proceed to Spanish food. The point of the whole exercise was to produce a *unified* explanation of mentality that would be begin with nature and connect that to historical behavior all the way to intellectual activity. So the doctrine of temperaments was a sort of argumentative bracket used as a tool by early Enlighteners to aid in the task of classifying and criticizing. How did this work for Gundling? Spaniards had boldness and courage, ate very little, and were restless.[51] Starting with these preconditions, one could then explain political or historical phenomena such as the turbulent conquest of South and Central America. The Spaniard was given to thought, and so his country suffered from a lack of trades and crafts;[52] he was often taciturn – and that had consequences for foreign policy because he frequently concealed his intentions.[53] It also produced cognitive strength in their powers of discernment or judgment, and so the land had subtle scholars but it had produced little poetry (which was more typical of the sanguine) or history (which emerged from the greed that was characteristic of the melancholic).[54] Gundling's schema was actually a bit less simple-minded than it seems at first. He thought there was also an "accompanying" influence, an "ascendent" so to speak, and it was melancholy because of earthy components in the blood. That had the primary effect of stimulating caution and fear, but secondarily greed;[55] and also cruelty – that explained the Spanish behavior against the Indians[56] – a "sinking into malevolence" based on the mixing of pride and greed.[57] The results were simulation, dissimulation, cunning, and malice, with further consequences for political dealings. In addition, the mixture of meditative brooding with greed, Gundling thought, led Spaniards into torpidity and excessive caution, which had further results for politics as well as for military conflicts.[58]

Today we may well be astonished at the naïvety with which, at the beginning of the eighteenth century, Enlightened minds like Gundling produced schematic simplifications like these. And yet it is true that they often practiced their Enlightening work by critically scanning and reorganizing large masses of material and then deploying argumentative brackets like these. Thus Gundling says programmatically at the end of his essay, "If

---

[50] Gundling, "Von dem Temperament der Spanier" in *Otia*, vol. 1 (note 8).   [51] Ibid., pp. 26–29.
[52] Ibid., p. 41.   [53] Ibid., p. 44.   [54] Ibid., p. 47.   [55] Ibid., p. 55.   [56] Ibid., p. 60.
[57] Ibid., p. 67   [58] Ibid., p. 70.

this method pleases you, go ahead and take the time to describe the English, Swedes, Dutch, and the French in the same manner."[59] And indeed Gundling did pursue this "method" further in his lectures, which were published as "A Thorough Discourse on the Current Condition of the European States," but he was not dogmatic; he merely suggested it as a sort of vague foundation.[60] The specific "euphoria" that spread throughout Halle in the first decade of the eighteenth century under the influence of the physicians Hoffmann and Stahl (and which we will examine in more detail below) was having results. In 1706, at any rate, Gundling's view of the then much beloved "statistics" (the systematic collection of information about sovereign states)[61] was suffused with this euphoria.[62] The temperaments seemed to offer a universal interpretive tool. If for example one wished to analyze in a literary manner the stubbornness with which the Aristotelian tradition held on in Spain, one only had to refer to the temperament of the Spanish.[63] If as a student of "mentalities," one wished to explain their love of mysticism, one might seize on the Spanish tendency to melancholy and the "enthusiasm" that resulted from it.[64]

To be sure, Gundling hedged his bets in the end by guarding against the possible accusation of "temperamental determinism":

> Pay attention, however, that you do not rashly ascribe these affects to all individuals or conclude that no virtuous Spaniards can exist. [It's true that] customs follow temperament in a natural manner, but virtue does not allow itself to be ruled by temperament, and higher spiritual states [*Genade*] even less so.[65]

All of this was miles away from Bayle. To be sure, Gundling criticized Garcia: "I most dislike that he so often ascribes all this enmity to the devil, which I do not so much doubt but that I might prefer to see a more proximate cause."[66] Thus he distanced himself from Garcia's broadest

---

[59] Ibid., pp. 77f.

[60] Gundling, *Ausführlicher Discours* (note 12), vol. 1, for the Spanish and French, see pp. 99ff; vol. 2, Frankfurt and Leipzig, 1734. See Hempel, *Umständliches Leben* (note 2), pp. 7274ff.

[61] See, e.g., Arno Seifert, "Staatenkunde. Eine neue Disziplin und ihr wissenschaftstheoretischer Ort," in Mohammed Rassem and Justin Stagl, eds., *Statistik und Staatsbeschreibung in der Neuzeit, vornehmlich im 16.–18. Jahrhundert*, Paderborn, 1980, pp. 217–248.

[62] On Gundling's self-confidence in dealing with the doctrine of temperaments, see an announcement of lectures from 1710: *Philosophische Discourse* (note 17), editor's foreword, fol. a4 r.

[63] In his lectures Gundling applied the doctrine of temperaments to intellectual history and the history of philosophy emphasizing especially the example of the Spanish. See *Philosophische Discourse* (note 17), pp. 612–646, here at p. 621.

[64] Ibid., p. 627.

[65] Gundling, "Von dem Temperament der Spanier," in *Otia*, vol. 1 (note 8), p. 78.

[66] Ibid., p. 85.

demonological speculations. And yet he held onto that naturalizing element. If Bayle held that one had only to remove jealousy from the relations of the French and Spanish and then everything would regulate itself, that was, for Gundling, an illusion. "Should the Spaniards change? That's as if I were to say that a stone should soften; or that iron should change into wood."[67] Nature could not be forced onto different tracks.

So how did Gundling combine his ideas about temperaments with all of his more critical views? We see that most clearly from his *Historia philosophiae moralis* ("History of Moral Philosophy"), published in 1706, the same year as his critique of Bayle. The book provided a fast-paced mixture of materials that raised the early German Enlightenment to a European level: a combination of Hobbes, Locke, Pufendorf, Bayle, Spencer, together with Thomasius's teachings on the emotions along with historical-philological criticism. First the text was organized along the lines of Bayle: a rather sparse text to which copious footnotes were added like chains of pearls – and it was only in the footnotes that real discussion took place. Next came the Hobbesian principle of self-preservation, which provided a foundation; all human doctrines were ultimately shaped by the drive for survival and the desire to preserve one's current status. There was room here for Bayle's condemnation of the prejudice that atheists could produce nothing but wicked philosophy and could only lead vicious lives. For, according to Gundling, whether one were a pagan or a God-fearing person, everyone possessed a drive for self-preservation. That showed the advantage that an indifferentist natural law perspective had over theological-apologetic reservations. The natural law perspective came equipped to deal with geographical and national-psychological differences, as we have seen in the case of the Spanish and the French. Here Gundling calls this the "coloration" of different peoples. In order to free this viewpoint from all the historical ballast of fables, Gundling soaked such traditions in a stringent historical criticism – a reminder of Bayle and La Mothe le Vayer but more generally by using the historical critique deployed ever since Casaubon and Conring. To prevent the skepticism from becoming too destructive, he plugged in Locke's speculation that at least certain hypothetical statements might have a sort of relative operational validity, such as the claim, "Where there is no property, there is no injustice." With that much secured, and with his theory of friendship that encompassed conflict, he could feel free to destroy ancient and

[67] Ibid., pp. 86f.

foundational origin-myths, starting with the allegedly "Christian spirit" of ancient thinkers.

5   Hippocrates an Atheist?

Therefore, let us turn to Gundling's short essay entitled *Hippocrates* ἄθηεος ("Hippocrates an Atheist"),[68] which appeared in the second volume of *Otia* in 1706. Did Gundling regard Hippocrates as a "virtuous pagan"? Did his essay depend indirectly on the example set by La Mothe le Vayer? At first it may well appear that that is the case because, as with so many topics, his treatment of Hippocrates had a predecessor in Christian Thomasius, who had published in 1693 an essay on Hippocrates and Democritus as moral philosophers in his short-lived journal *The History of Wisdom and Folly*.[69] Obviously we find here an early interest in the moral history of antiquity. That essay, however, dealt only with an edition of the supposed correspondence between the two ancients, letters that turned out to be fictions. That fact soon gave some philologists pause.

Perhaps that is also the reason Gundling began his own investigations into Hippocrates. Because the Hippocratic theory of temperaments had become the basis of an "information economy" that informed his understanding of politics and history, the "pagan" character of the theory could not remain a matter of indifference for him. But Gundling was also happy to deploy his texts as alluring hooks. When he said that Hippocrates had been an atheist, he was well aware of how provocative that was, and all the more because this was only the first of a whole series of similar provocations that he scattered in various disciplines over the following years. With his "Plato an Atheist" of 1713 he aimed at provoking all who hoped to lend the early Enlightenment a Platonic or Neoplatonic shape; with his "Thoughts on the Philosophy of Parmenides" of 1717 he continued his series on the atheism of ancient thinkers.[70] These seemed to be works along the lines of Jacob Thomasius's effort to devalue those ancient traditions that could not provide a model for any modern Christian philosophy or like Johann Franz Budde's treatise on *De Spinozismo ante*

---

[68] Gundling, "*Hippocrates* ἄθηεος," in *Otia*, vol. 2 (note 26), chapter 3, pp. 73–140. See also Mulsow, *Enlightenment Underground* (note 2), chapter 6.

[69] Christian Thomasius, "Democritus Abderita et Hippocrates Medicus Philosophi Morales ad invidiam Philosophorum Pseudo-Christianorum," in *Historia sapientiae et stultitiae*, Part II, Halle, 1693, pp. 1–112.

[70] Gundling, "Plato atheos," *Neue Bibliothec* 31 (1713), pp. 1–31; Gundling, "Gedancken über Parmenidis Philosophie," in *Gundlingiana*, vol. 14, 1717, pp. 372ff

Spinozam ("Spinozism before Spinoza") of 1701, in which ancient Stoic and materialist thought was condemned as pre-Spinozan.[71] Gundling, however, was deliberately misleading his readers. As the favorite student of Christian Thomasius, he was known as someone who was especially liberal and who, like his teacher, complained that the rampant "manufacture of heretics" (*Ketzermacherei*) from earlier years had now become a rampant "manufacture of atheists."[72] Orthodox theologians now smelled atheists under every bed.

How could one explain all this? Had a liberal Thomasian become himself one of the fiercest atheist hunters? Just that suspicion may have irritated scholars in Halle and beyond. But it just shows that Gundling's provocation had not been rightly understood. To see more clearly, it will be necessary to pay close attention to the actual argumentation in these texts and to their engagement with current debates. So let us first read *Hippocrates ἄθεος* and pay special attention to what he was doing in the footnotes. Gundling had learned a lot from Pierre Bayle's *Dictionnaire* and unrestrainedly used footnotes at this time as the true but secret heroes of his texts – and which often easily overwhelmed the main text in length.[73] Thus in the Hippocrates essay in the *Otia*, the reader stumbles over the first footnote after just seven lines, a note that then fills the next two and a half pages. "We live in a century," Gundling says there, "in which this 'extreme' [claim] occurs more than too often."[74] The "extreme claim" was the accusation of atheism, and Gundling, to the surprise of his readers, immediately explores such a claim about someone, "although I usually disregard such accusations."[75] After all, the accusation resulted in social ostracism, as had been the case for heretics as well. "Here such a hapless person might stand out like a wild elephant in Africa, whose rage was supposed to drive everyone away."[76] But such accusations, according to Gundling, could now be leveled against men who were long dead and who

<hr/>

[71] See Ralph Häfner, "Jacob Thomasius und die Geschichte der Häresien," in Friedrich Vollhardt, ed., *Christian Thomasius. Neue Forschungen im Kontext der Frühaufklärung*, Tübingen, 1997, pp. 142–164; Sicco Lehmann-Brauns, *Weisheit in der Weltgeschichte – Philosophiegeschichte zwischen Barock und Aufklärung*, Tübingen, 2004, as well as Mulsow, *Enlightenment Underground* (note 2), chapter 5.

[72] On the discourse concerning the "manufacture of heretics," see Martin Gierl, *Pietismus und Aufklärung. Theologische Polemik und die Kommunikationsreform der Wissenschaft am Ende des 17. Jahrhunderts*, Göttingen, 1997, pp. 292–341. On the zealous identification of "atheist" views in theology, see Hans-Martin Barth, *Atheismus und Orthodoxie. Analysen und Modelle christlicher Apologetik im 17. Jahrhundert*, Göttingen, 1971.

[73] He did this as early as 1706 in his *Historia philosophiae moralis*. Later the share of footnotes compared to the whole text became much diminished.

[74] *Hippocrates ἄθεος* (note 68), p. 74.   [75] Ibid., p. 73.   [76] Ibid., p. 74.

would no longer have to suffer from them. In such cases the ethical or social considerations evaporated and the way was clear for an entirely different agenda. But what was his agenda exactly?

Hippocrates ἄθεος was Gundling's first trial balloon in the direction of this different agenda, and it can prove instructive to follow it and its consequences more closely. This sort of "speech act" (to use Quentin Skinner's phrase) was surely aimed first and foremost at physicians, and especially at the medical faculty at Halle. So in the following investigation I will interpret Gundling's provocation mainly within the context of the epistemic situation of medicine at Halle. There were two full professors of medicine there, Georg Ernst Stahl (starting in 1694) and Friedrich Hoffmann (starting in 1693), both of whom were students of Georg Wolfgang Wedel in Jena. Stahl is known as a vitalist with close connections to Pietism, while Hoffmann is known as a mechanist and a secularizer of medicine. Of course those are just clichés that do more to conceal than reveal the finer differences and nuances.[77] Especially with respect to the relations of medicine and religion, both professors had highly sophisticated ideas. For example in 1693, right at the beginning of his tenure in Halle, Hoffmann gave a lecture entitled "On Convincing an Atheist on the Basis of the Most Ingenious Structure of the Human Machine"; it was the physico-theological pleading of a passionate researcher.[78] He did not speak of theology at all but spent his time instead on the amazing structures and functionings of the human body, from which one could supposedly recognize God's handiwork. In 1702 Hoffmann gave another lecture, "On the Duties of a Good Theologian and the Idea of a Good Physician."[79] There again Hoffmann touched on the Christian religion as he worked out parallels between the harmony of the virtues in a truly Christian life and the harmony of the bodily mechanism in good health. But it was evident that he was also abandoning theology in the sense of a dogmatic discipline. Medicine and "practical Christianity" (as Spener saw it, for example) were structurally analogous, but that did not mean that theology was directly relevant for a physician.

---

[77] See Francesco Paolo de Ceglia, "Hoffmann and Stahl: Documents and Reflections on the Dispute," *History of Universities* (22) 2007, pp. 115–168; Johanna Geyer-Kordesch, *Pietismus, Medizin und Aufklärung in Preußen im 18. Jahrhundert. Das Leben und Werk Georg Ernst Stahls*, Tübingen, 2000.

[78] Friedrich Hoffmann, *Oratio de Atheo convincendo ex artificiosissima machinae humanae structura*, Halle, 1705. The first edition appeared in 1693.

[79] Friedrich Hoffmann, *De officio boni theologi ex idea boni medici*, Halle, 1702. See Sandra Pott (today: Sandra Richter), *Medizin, Medizinethik und schöne Literatur*, Berlin, 2002 (*Säkularisierung in den Wissenschaften seit der Frühen Neuzeit*, vol. 1), pp. 52–60.

Hoffmann pursued a complex strategy over against his colleagues from the theology faculty at Halle. He taught a mechanistic medicine that was strictly secular both institutionally and in its content, even though he sought topics that approached Christian teachings, especially of a simple, practical Christianity. We will see that this double strategy was not really so far removed from the complex positioning of Gundling, but Gundling was eleven years younger than Hoffmann and thus knew and valued him not just as a colleague but also as a teacher whose lectures he had heard during the time he was completing his studies in Halle.[80]

Could one say that in his *Hippocrates ἄθηεος* Gundling was reacting to the medical situation in Halle by carrying Hoffmann's intentions further? We are not yet in a position to answer but must first make sure we have understood his argument, and then observe his conflicts with physicians, and especially with one of Hoffmann's students.

6 The Argument

So how did Gundling draw the conclusion that Hippocrates was an atheist? In view of Budde's treatise *On Spinozism before Spinoza* and in view of Hoffmann's canny secularizing, perhaps the basic idea of *Hippocrates ἄθηεος* was this thought: Hippocrates was an atheist because he was a proto-Spinozist, but actually that was not so bad because a physician did not have to be a Christian in order to do good work. Only if we understand that he was expounding a double thesis, a pointed *junctim* ("a linked argument" in which each part is true only if the other is also), will we able to judge Gundling's decades-long fascination with this problematic.

Gundling surely felt strengthened in his position by Pierre Bayle, whose *Continuation des pensées diverses* ("Continuation of the Diverse Thoughts on the Occasion of a Comet that appeared in [...] 1680") had just appeared in 1704 and was a constant presence in Gundling's text.[81] One could even call it one of the foundational texts in the Halle physician's process of shaping his own point of view. Bayle had often mentioned his conviction that ancient thinking was *in toto* atheistic because at its basis it could not comprehend Christian revelation – but that that was far from tragic because practicing a profession capably had nothing to do with

---

[80] See Hempel, *Umständliches Leben und Schrifften* (note 2), p. 7029.
[81] Pierre Bayle, *Continuation des pensées diverses écrites à un docteur de Sorbonne, à l'occasion de la comete qui parut au mois de Decembre 1680 [...]*, Rotterdam, 1704.

revelation.[82] Perhaps for that reason Gundling chose as his first example a representative of a practical art – medicine – for his campaign, because with Hippocrates he could better explain his paradox than with Plato or Parmenides. Thus, even an atheistical Hippocrates could and should be an authority for modern physicians.

Any concept of atheism that was stretched to cover more or less all of antiquity was obviously extremely broad, and we may well wonder how Gundling managed that. Today we have become very careful if we speak of atheists in the ancient world at all, and we tend to concentrate on just a few individual cases such as Diagoras of Melos or Theodorus of Cyrene, although even with them it is not always clear whether these descriptions depend on the tendentious classifications of later opponents. People had been compiling denunciatory lists of atheists ever since Epicurus.[83] Criticism of Gundling started right here, accusing him of exaggerating his critique beyond all measure and of dragging the completely innocent Hippocrates before the tribunal of history.

Gundling used many of the introductory pages of his essay to clarify the fundamental point under discussion. Basing himself on Jacob Thomasius, he set forth a clear criterion for atheism: the confusion of God and the world. If God was not unambiguously understood as the creator of the world (*ex nihilo*), one could not speak of "God" in the full sense.[84] For then everything would turn into a kind of pantheism or Spinozism, and contemporary discussion of Spinoza had shown how dangerous that was.[85] On this point Gundling was completely lucid and uncompromising; it remains to be seen why he was unwilling to abandon a clear-cut and traditional notion of God. "Most pagan philosophers," said Gundling, "are lying sick in this hospital [i.e., Spinozism]: the Ionian and Eleatic sect, the Stoic and Aristotelian, and many scholastic teachers are also not free of this impiety."[86] That was the status quo of the controversy as discussed by

---

[82] Ibid.

[83] See Jan N. Bremmer, "Atheism in Antiquity," in Michael Martin, ed., *The Cambridge Companion to Atheism*, Cambridge, 2006, pp. 11–26, esp. pp. 19f. On denunciations, see Marek Winiarczyk, "Der erste Atheistenkatalog des Kleitomachos," *Philologus* 120 (1976), pp. 32–46.

[84] *Hippocrates* ἄθεος (note 68), pp. 82f. See Jacob Thomasius (praes.) / J. F. Hekel (resp.), *Theses philosophicae, quas de quaestione: An Deus sit materia prima?*, Leipzig, 1672, and Mulsow, *Enlightenment Underground* (note 2), chapter 5.

[85] On these debates, see Jonathan Israel, *Radical Enlightenment. Philosophy and the Making of Modernity 1650–1750*, Oxford, 2001; Israel, *Enlightenment Contested: Philosophy, Modernity, and the Emancipation of Man 1670-1752*, Oxford, 2006.

[86] *Hippocrates* ἄθεος (note 68), p. 83.

Jacob Thomasius and Budde. And now Gundling added: "To this list I will now add Hippocrates as well."[87]

His argument intended to show that Hippocrates mixed up God and the world, doing so by connecting Hippocrates to one of the identified pre-Socratic traditions. That is just what Gundling did. In a precise sense, only the last twenty-five pages of his seventy-page essay were devoted to Hippocrates. Everything else was a chatty discussion of atheism accusations in general and specifically in antiquity.

7 Innate Heat in Hippocrates

Hippocrates – who was still thought of as a single person, rather than a body of writings – was known for his doctrine of ἔμφυτον θερμόν, of implanted or innate heat.[88] He was describing the "warmth of life," which distinguishes a living organism from a dead one, but which also was thought to have a healing power.[89] It was maintained by food that was cooked in the stomach and then distributed throughout the whole body; it steered the body's inner workings and helped it with sicknesses. Where did Hippocrates get such an idea? Today no researcher would pose this question so naïvely, for the *Corpus Hippocraticum* has long been attributed to a host of different potential authors, who wrote under the influence of various sources. Gundling, who was still untouched by such subtleties, argued strenuously for one specific influence: Heraclitus, the Ionian natural philosopher. With his philosophy of fire as the original element, the dark thinker from Ephesus supposedly had set forth a kind of cosmic warmth that expressed its primordial properties in living bodies. Before Gundling came upon such ideas, Daniel Le Clerc had expressed similar thoughts in his *Histoire de la médicine* of 1696,[90] and Gundling adopted them while strengthening the thesis further by joining them to Jacob Thomasius's condemnation of the pre-Socratics.

[87] Ibid., pp. 83f.

[88] On him, see Jacques Jouanna, *Hippocrates*, Baltimore, 1999; Werner Golder, *Hippokrates und das Corpus Hippocraticum. Eine Einführung für Philologen und Mediziner*, Würzburg, 2007. For the literature of the sixteenth to the eighteenth centuries on Hippocrates, see Johann Ludwig Choulant, *Bibliotheca medico-historica*, Leipzig, 1842, pp. 40–46.

[89] On this topic, see Everett Mendelsohn, *Heat and Life: The Development of the Theory of Animal Heat*, Cambridge, MA, 1964; Michael Stolberg, "Die Lehre vom 'calor innatus' im lateinischen Canon medicinae des Avicenna," *Sudhoffs Archiv* 77 (1993), pp. 33–53; Martin Mulsow, *Frühneuzeitliche Selbsterhaltung: Telesio und die Naturphilosophie der Renaissance*, Tübingen, 1998, pp. 201–250.

[90] *Hippocrates* ἄθηεος (note 68), p. 109. See Daniel Le Clerc, *Histoire de la médecine*, Geneva, 1696.

What Hippocrates understood as "nature," according to Gundling, could at first seem to be God, because he ascribed to it the power that sustains all living beings, along with omniscience and righteousness. But this could not be God for it was clear "that this nature was nothing more than an undying fire or heat, which understood everything, saw everything, and knew everything, both in the present and also in the future."[91] The primary work by Hippocrates that Gundling was referring to was Περί σάρκων ("On Fleshes"), a work that is today classified as pseudo-Hippocratic[92] and that probably was attached to the schools of medicine on Cos and Cnidus. It is a good question whether the author of Περί σάρκων was actually even a physician in the narrow sense or whether he should be regarded instead as a pre-Socratic philosopher. Gundling was, therefore, placing a work from the *Corpus Hippocraticum* in the center of his discussion, a work that because of its philosophical interests was really peripheral to the *Corpus*. Nowadays scholars are less likely to see a connection with Heraclitus, and emphasize instead the possible relations with Empedocles or Diogenes of Apollonia.[93] In the cosmogony of this "Hippocratic" work, heat was the αἴθηρ of "the ancients" while αἴθηρ for Empedocles was air; but otherwise there were large structural similarities, including the circumstance that organic matter was conceived as a combination of the three elements mentioned in the cosmogony: fire, earth, and air. According to Gundling:

> It is irrelevant that Hippocrates mentions the names of so many gods and that the sun, Jupiter, Minerva, Apollo, Hercules, and Neptune are mentioned on almost every page. For these were *"Dii producti"* [manufactured gods], sometimes imagined by the pagans as more perfect than human beings.[94]

To make this unusual view plausible, he cited the *Ars critica* of Jean Le Clerc.[95] That Genevan theologian and journalist had referred to authors such as Hesiod in his *Theogony* in order to make clear that in the language used by the ancients the gods represented only beings who were always

---

[91] Ibid., p. 114.

[92] On the problem of dating it, see the review by Anargyros Anastassiou of the edition by Robert Joly, *Hippocrate*, vol. 13, Paris, 1978, *Gnomon* 52 (1980), pp. 309–311.

[93] Diels-Kranz, *Die Fragmente der Vorsokratiker* (DK) 31 A 74 (Empedokles); DK 64 B 5 (Diogenes). Werner Golder, *Hippokrates und das Corpus Hippocraticum* (note 88), pp. 89f. Oliver Primavesi, "Medicine between Natural Philosophy and Physician's Practice: A Debate around 400 BC," in Susanna Elm and Stefan Willich, eds., *Quo Vadis Medical Healing: Past Concepts and New Approaches*, Berlin, 2009, pp. 29–40.

[94] *Hippocrates ἄθεος* (note 68), p. 123.

[95] Ibid., p. 124; see Jean Le Clerc, *Ars critica*, Amsterdam, 1697, II, I, 3.

there, or natures that did not have to be regarded as independent beings at all. So, according to Gundling, they did not at all have to be thought of as external causes. "From the θερμόν of Hippocrates arose not only Jupiter, the greatest of the gods, but also Saturn, his father, along with heaven, his grandfather, and aether, his great-grandfather."[96] Thus heat needed to be thought of as resembling the Chaos of Hesiod[97] or the air of Anaximenes: primal matter, that was then differentiated further. Such matter could be understood as like the subtle matter of the Stoics: eternal, to be sure, and made of very fine matter, but still material and this-worldly. Finally Gundling carried his rather freewheeling associations with ancient teachings so far that he brought heat close to the Stoics' "fate" because "that is no different from a strict and unchanging law according to which heat operates."[98] The fundamental point remained the same: θερμόν was an immanent cause in this world, not some transcendent creator like God.

All of this was mainly an interpretation on the basis of the cosmology of Περι σάρκων, enriched by passages from other works, and as such it is extremely problematic by modern standards. But from a different point of view, Gundling had pointed correctly to an attitude that we would not today call "atheism," but perhaps identify as the so-called rationalism found in many of the Hippocratic authors of the Periclean period. This rationalism appeared, for example, in the denial that the "sacred disease" of epilepsy was especially sacred, because all diseases were equally divine or natural,[99] or when, as in the treatise *On Airs, Waters, and Places*, the discussion turns to the question of whether the impotence of many rich Scythians was caused by the gods. The Hippocratic authors argued that that was impossible because a divine curse would more likely affect the poor, and not the rich who could honor the gods with the construction of temples. Instead, impotence was thought to be entirely natural, caused by riding horseback, which only the rich could afford.[100] This passage prompted a lively discussion in the early modern French-speaking world. The physician Guillaume Lamy had emphasized its implicit godlessness,

---

[96] *Hippocrates* ἄθηεος (note 68), pp. 129f.

[97] On Hesiod and Hippokrates, see Hermann Fränkel, *Dichtung und Philosophie des frühen Griechentums*, Munich, 1962, pp. 131 and 589; Friedrich Kudlien, *Der Beginn des medizinischen Denkens bei den Griechen von Homer bis Hippokrates*, Zurich, 1967.

[98] *Hippocrates* ἄθηεος (note 68), p. 131

[99] Jacques Jouanna, *Hippocrates* (note 88), pp. 181–209; Philip van der Eijk, "The Theology of the Hippocratic Treatise *On the Sacred Disease*," in *Medicine and Philosophy in Classical Antiquity: Doctors and Philosophers on Nature, Soul, Health and Disease*, Cambridge, 2005, pp. 45–73.

[100] "De aeris," in *Hippocrates* (Loeb Classical Library), vol. 1, Cambridge, MA, 1984, p. 120. See Jouanna, *Hippocrates* (note 88), pp. 188–190.

because religion was here reduced to the external ceremonies of wealthy people, and Bayle along with others had eagerly emphasized that.[101] Gundling was only updating these debates when he compared Hippocrates to the *ésprits forts* of his day, who were willing to tolerate the piety of common people even though they themselves had at least inwardly long since rejected piety.[102]

But seeing Hippocrates as a free spirit or an atheist? For many readers that was too much, including even Budde whose *Spinozismus ante Spinozam* had served Gundling as a model. In his *Theses theologicae de atheismo et superstitione* of 1717, Budde remarked that Gundling here had been misled by his zeal to become famous through the use of paradoxes (*studio per paradoxa inclarescendi ductus*) – that is, by announcing unusual and counterintuitive views, such as in this case his attempt to defame "the good old man," Hippocrates (*optimum senem . . . infamare*). Budde pointed out that no one else had ever before called Hippocrates an atheist, even in antiquity.[103]

8   The Connection with Natural Law

Thus Gundling's argument was by no means persuasive, even for other scholars who were also pursuing the atheists of the ancient world. So how did he structure it, and why did Budde not agree? The easiest way to understand the situation is perhaps to look at an entirely different field, that of jurisprudence or the philosophy of natural law. In our earlier discussion of Gundling's version of the temperaments, we saw that natural law was playing a role in the background. Now we can reinforce that point. In the study of natural law, Gundling was following Pufendorf; one might even call him a "left-Pufendorfian." What would that mean? Samuel Pufendorf based his understanding of natural law on voluntarism, with an emphasis on God as creator. This creator God created all the *entia moralia* (moral beings) – that is, moral-social phenomena, or more specifically natural law itself. By making this theological voluntarism so strong,

---

[101] Guillaume Lamy, *Discours anatomiques de M. Lamy [. . .] Avec des Reflexions sur les Objections qu'on luy a faites contre la maniere de raisonner de la nature de l'Homme & de l'usage des parties qui le composent, et cinq Lettres du mesme Autheur, sur le sujet de son Livre*, Rouen, 1675; Bayle, *Continuation* (note 81), p. 233; *Hippocrates ἄθηεος* (note 68), pp. 135f. Gundling took up the discussion again in his "Andere Reflexion über Herrn D. Trillers Hippocratum atheismi accusatum," *Gundlingiana*, vol. 23, Halle, 1719, pp. 187–286, here at pp. 273–275.

[102] *Hippocrates ἄθηεος* (note 68), p. 136.

[103] Johann Franz Budde, *Theses theologicae de atheismo et superstitione*, Jena, 1717, I, § 20.

however, he was also able (on the other hand) to adopt an extreme form of conventionalist moral doctrine: for him men did not have some inborn sociality or ties to society as Grotius had thought; instead sociality was itself a commandment of natural law. Therefore, human beings were, so to speak, cut off from all divine intentions; God merely lay in the background, as the effective precondition for everything.[104]

Pufendorf was often interpreted in a less conventionalistic manner, even or perhaps especially by Gundling's contemporaries, and indeed Budde was clearly a theologian who favored a concept of God that was much more substantive in its content. In the next chapter we will see that more clearly. We can also see it in Budde's alliances with Platonizing authors such as Henry More and Ralph Cudworth, for whom God influenced events in this world.[105] Gundling, however, based his thinking on Thomasius's pessimistic abandonment (in his *Fundamenta*) of sociality as the foundation of human life. For him, the validity of natural law was limited to the domain of enforceable social behavior.[106] For Budde, what remained as the foundation of natural law was thus Hobbes's principle of self-preservation.

For that reason we can speak of him as a left-Pufendorfian, so to speak, just as today Pufendorf has been once again acknowledged as a "disciple of Hobbes," whose radical conventionalism has now been recognized.[107] In addition to the accusation of Hippocrates in his *Otia*, Gundling composed at the same time (1707) a defense of Hobbes in his *Observationes selectae*: a work entitled *Hobbesius ab Atheismo liberatus* ("Hobbes Freed from [the Charge of] Atheism").[108] In view of the fact that from Gundling's point of

---

[104] Knud Haakonssen is the main scholar who has worked the radicalism of this claim: "Morality without Dignity. Samuel Pufendorf's Concept of Personhood" (forthcoming). I am grateful to Knud Haakonssen for sharing his manuscript with me.

[105] See Mulsow, *Enlightenment Underground* (note 2), chapter 6.

[106] Hinrich Rüping, *Die Naturrechtslehre des Christian Thomasius und ihre Fortbildung in der Thomasius-Schule*, Bonn, 1968. For more recent works on Gundling as a jurist, see also Alexander Aichele, "Von der Fiktion zur Abstraktion. Nikolaus Hieronymus Gundling über mögliche Urteilssubjekte anhand seiner Auseinandersetzung mit Dadino Alteserras Begriff der persona ficta," *Archiv für Rechts- und Sozialphilosophie* 96 (2010), pp. 516–541; Aichele, "Was kann die Philosophie für die Jurisprudenz tun? Eine Antwort am Beispiel des Problems der Zurechnungs- und Schuldfähigkeit von Gesellschaften zwischen Immanuel Kant, Nikolaus Hieronymus Gundling und Samuel Stryk," in Kristian Kühl, ed., *Zur Kompetenz der Rechtsphilosophie in Rechtsfragen. Akten der IVR-Tagung 2008*, Wiesbaden, 2010 (*Archiv für Rechts- und Sozialphilosophie*, Beiheft 126), pp. 31–51.

[107] Fiametta Palladini, *Samuel Pufendorf discepolo di Hobbes: per una reinterpretazione del giusnaturalismo moderno*, Bologna, 1990.

[108] Gundling, "Hobbesius ab Atheismo liberatus," in *Observationum selectarum ad rem litterariam spectantium*, vol. 1, Halle 1707, pp. 37–77. See Noel Malcolm, *Aspects of Hobbes*, Oxford, 2002,

view one could not ascribe any attributes to God, we may find in this constellation of natural law philosophy and the defense of Hobbes an explanation for why Gundling, in his literary-historical writings on the supposed atheism of ancient thinkers, focused so intently on the ahistorical criterion of God as creator. At the end of his essay on Hippocrates, he claimed almost triumphantly:

> We as Christians, enlightened by [God's] eternal and powerful Word, know all of this much more profoundly from the purest source, a Creator Who is fundamentally separate from the world. Lord, preserve us in Your truth, for your Word is Truth. Amen.[109]

It seems that Gundling was happy to agree here with Lutheran Orthodoxy and to withdraw to a divine revelation that guaranteed voluntarism.

9 Opposition to Gundling

After a period of latency that lasted seven years, works opposing Gundling began to appear. The first was entitled *Hippocrates ab atheismi crimine nuper ipsi imputato absolvitur* ("Hippocrates Absolved from the Crime of Atheism that Has Been Recently Imputed to Him") and came from the pen of Andreas Ottomar Goelicke.[110] By 1713 arguments accusing authors of atheism or defending them from such accusations were in full spate: Wolf, Hase, Reimmann, Zimmermann, and dozens of others were involved in the business.[111] Goelicke was a young physician who had also studied briefly in Halle. But he had given this talk at the University of Duisburg, where he had just been hired as a professor. Even though the title page claimed that "Halle" was the place of publication, he could not have delivered this lecture there because associate professors

---

pp. 533f. On the indescribability of God for Christian Thomasius, see Gierl, *Pietismus und Aufklärung* (note 72), p. 450.

[109] *Hippocrates ἄθεος* (note 68), p. 140.

[110] Andreas Ottomar Goelicke, *Hippocrates ab atheismi crimine nuper ipsi imputato absolvitur*, Halle, 1713.

[111] Johann Christoph Wolf (praes.) / Peter Adolph Boysen (resp.), *De atheismi falso suspectis*, Wittenberg, 1717; Theodor Hase (praes.) / Rudolph W. Boclo (resp.), *De gentilium philosophis atheism falso suspectis*, Bremen, 1716; Jakob Friedrich Reimmann, *Historia universalis atheismi*, Hildesheim, 1725; Johann Jakob Zimmermann, *Apologia virorum illustrium falso atheismi suspectorum*, 7 manuscript vols., Ms. F. 200–206, Zentralbibliothek Zurich. On the latter, see Dagmar von Wille, "Apologie häretischen Denkens. Johann Jakob Zimmermanns Rehabilitierung der 'Atheisten' Pomponazzi und Vanini," in Friedrich Niewöhner and Olaf Pluta, eds., *Atheismus im Mittelalter und in der Renaissance*, Wiesbaden, 1999, pp. 29–44. On Hase, Wolf, and others, see Alan Charles Kors, *Atheism in France*, vol. 1, Princeton, 1990, pp. 232f. On the business of classifying apologetic efforts, see also Mulsow, *Knowledge Lost* (note 20), chapter 4.

(*Professores extraordinarii*) were forbidden in Halle to speak openly against the full professors (*Professores ordinarii*).[112] With his feeble work Goelicke was joining a long series of traditional early modern physicians, who went on the offensive, speaking of the "theology of Hippocrates," as Giovanni Stefani (Stephanus Belluensis) had done in 1638, and Johann Andreas Schmidt, the polyhistor of Jena, in 1691. Stefani's book carried the subtitle *Placita Christianae religioni consentanea exponuntur* ("Their Doctrines Are Delineated as Compatible with the Christian Religion"). That is just what Gundling intended to finish off: the almost automatic reflex of physicians or other scholars to legitimate the teachings of their heroes as if they must have agreed with the Christian religion.

Gundling replied immediately, in Issue No. 29 of his New Library (*Neue Bibliothec*), with a "Declaration of His Judgment Concerning the Atheism of Hippocrates."[113] But Goelicke did not yield and now wrote a "Defense of Divinely Inspired Hippocrates in Opposition to the Judgment Concerning the Atheism of Hippocrates Recently Undertaken by Nicolas Hieronymus Gundling," published in 1714 in Duisburg.[114] But by then Gundling had no desire to reply again.

Instead, a new opponent entered the ranks a few years later, this time a highly gifted young man from Erfurt named Daniel Wilhelm Triller.[115] Full of literary ambition, he composed poems, completed a master's thesis on the sorceress Circe in Homer, in 1716, and then obtained his medical degree under Friedrich Hoffmann in Halle in 1718, with a thesis on obesity and excessive sugar in the body.[116] Just one year after his doctoral exam this young man dared to oppose the great Gundling. "The greater your enemy, the greater the honor." He called his polemic "Hippocrates Falsely Accused of Atheism, [written] against the Great Man Dr. Nicolas

---

[112] See Gundling, "Erste Reflexion über Herrn D. Trillers Hippocratum atheismi accusatum," *Gundlingiana*, vol. 22, Halle, 1719, pp. 87–186, here at p. 91.

[113] "Declaratio suae de atheismo Hippocratis sententiae," *Neue Bibliothec* 29 (1713), pp. 802–818.

[114] Andreas Ottomar Goelicke, *Defensio pro Hippocrate entheo opposite declaratione sententiae de atheismo Hippocratis Nic. Hier. Gundling denuo suscepta*, Duisburg, 1714. See also the fifth volume of his *Historia medicinae universalis*, Frankfurt, 1719, which treats the "universa Hippocartes Coi medicina" and is aimed against the "Censurae Hallensium."

[115] Rüdiger Lorentzen, *Daniel Wilhelm Triller und seine "wahrhaft hippokratischen" Freunde*, typewritten Dissertation, Göttingen, 1964. A thorough (laudataory) biography of Triller can be found in Johann Christoph Strodtmann, *Beiträge zur Historie der Gelahrtheit*, vol. 1, Hamburg, 1748, pp. 142–181. For more on Triller as a literary figure, Hans-Georg Kemper, *Deutsche Lyrik der frühen Neuzeit: Frühaufklärung*, vol. 5(2), Tübingen, 1991, pp. 33–37; Uwe Steiner, *Poetische Theodizee. Philosophie und Poesie in der lehrhaften Dichtung im achtzehnten Jahrhundert*, Munich, 2000.

[116] *Diss. inaug. med.* (praes. Fr. Hoffmanno), *de pinguedine seu succo nutritio superfluo*, Halle, 1718.

Hieronymus Gundling." It was published anonymously, with the author listed merely as D.W.T. D. (which stood for Daniel Wilhelm Triller Doctor), and at a safe distance from Halle, in Rudolstadt (about 80 miles south of Halle).[117] That was not far enough – as in most cases like this, Gundling found out almost at once who was hiding behind the abbreviation.

Triller had actually written his invective in 1716, when he was still a student in Halle, and obviously he made use of it in the disputation he took part in as an element of the process of obtaining his doctorate. Gundling said that if he had known that in that disputation he was being criticized, he would have attended and would have made things more difficult for the candidate.[118] It was of course awkward that Gundling's critic was Triller, a student of Friedrich Hoffmann's. Did that imply that Gundling and his colleague were not in fundamental agreement with each other? That was not necessarily so for Gundling bluntly criticized Triller, claiming that he had not really understood the teachings of his adviser:

> In the meanwhile I know this much for sure, that if the author had known his doctoral adviser (the current pro-rector of the university) for any length of time, he would have heard him say that because the pagan philosophers (and Hippocrates in this case) did not know the philosophy of Moses and of the Christians, according to whom the world was created from nothing, they went mad and fell into gross error in their understanding of God and His Being.[119]

The dedication of Triller's work also made things awkward for Gundling. It was dedicated to Johann Albert Fabricius, which was a clever move by the young nobody because he hoped in this way to assure himself of the authority and protection of the great Hamburg scholar, who had, like Budde, criticized Gundling concerning Hippocrates. Fabricius's words carried great weight, even if he had only briefly discussed Hippocrates in his *Bibliotheca graeca*, when he noted that the ancient physician "had been attacked with arguments that are much less certain and persuasive than they should be for such a serious charge."[120] That amounted to a firm rebuke.

---

[117] *Hippocrates atheismi falso accusatus contra virum ampl. D. Nicol. Hieron. Gundlingium*, Rudolstadt, 1719. Reprinted in Triller, *Opuscula medica ac medico philologica*, vol. 2, Frankfurt and Leipzig, 1766, with a text opposing Le Clerc's position on the controversy in the *Bibliothèque ancienne et moderne* 15(2) (1721).

[118] "Erste Reflexion über Herrn D. Trillers Hippocratum" (note 112), pp. 87f.   [119] Ibid., p. 95.

[120] Johann Albert Fabricius, *Bibliotheca graeca*, vol. 1, 2nd edn., Hamburg, 1708, cap. 24, p. 843.

And yet Gundling was not to be intimidated. He did not hesitate a moment before replying. He quickly published two *Reflections Concerning Herr Dr. Triller's "Hippocrates Accused of Atheism."* Whereas Triller had written 112 pages, Gundling's reply took up about 200 pages.[121] And thus the dispute over Hippocrates lasted about as long as that of Gundling's *Plato an Atheist* controversy, which had begun in 1713, went through a middle stretch in 1724, and found its crowning conclusion in a 200-page, two-part treatise directed against Zimmermann and entitled *Velitatio de atheismo Platonis* ("Wrangling Over the Atheism of Plato") published in 1729, the year of Gundling's death.[122]

What Gundling really disliked in Triller was his zeal. The man clearly loved his Hippocrates – later he dedicated himself to editing him, and he simply could not allow his hero to be defamed as an atheist. So right at the beginning Gundling stated

> that between me and the author there is this significant difference: namely
> that he has taken up his pen with ludicrous passion; but for me it's a matter
> of indifference whether Hippocrates, like almost all the ancient sages, had
> or did not have an atheistical system.[123]

Here again someone had failed to grasp that Gundling was practicing what I have elsewhere called "the art of deflation" or of de-escalation. He thought one should abandon the theological over-burdening of all topics.[124] He calmly countered the dedication to Fabricius by using a tactic that he often used: He explicitly identified the game that was being played – claiming openly that an ambitious degree candidate was trying to attach his name to that of a major figure. He then showed, offhandedly, that Herr Fabricius of Hamburg, with whom he had a good understanding, would surely not be pleased to see the weak arguments offered by Triller.[125]

Gundling, moreover, did not retreat one bit from his general argument regarding the atheism of Hippocrates. He took up Triller's objections point for point, and indulged himself in several digressions, but stuck mainly to the fundamental passages that he had earlier cited. In his later lectures from the 1720s, published as *Philosophical Discourses*, Gundling

---

[121] Gundling, "Erste Reflexion über Herrn D. Trillers Hippocratum" (note 112); Gundling, "Andere Reflexion über Herrn D. Trillers Hippocratum atheismi accusatum" (note 101), pp. 187–286.
[122] "Velitatio de atheismo Platonis," in *Gundlingiana*, vol. 43, Halle, 1729, pp. 187–280; *Gundlingiana*, vol. 44, Halle, 1729, pp. 281–360.
[123] "Erste Reflexion über Herrn D. Trillers Hippocratum" (note 112), p. 89.
[124] Mulsow, *Knowledge Lost* (note 20), chapter 4.
[125] "Erste Reflexion über Herrn D. Trillers Hippocratum" (note 112), pp. 97f.

took pride in the fact that he had yielded nothing to his opponent.[126] To the end he defended his provocation.

That did not mean, of course, that everyone accepted his deflationary attack. In Halle itself in addition to the followers of Hoffmann there were followers of Stahl, who had long distanced themselves from Hoffmann's modest secularizing. Just look briefly at a dissertation from 1722 that emerged from Stahl's mostly Pietist milieu, for we quickly see that among the followers of Stahl medicine was still regarded as a pious discipline. Joachim Lange's brother-in-law, Michael Alberti, presided with Friedrich Brösike as respondent, over a dissertation entitled *De religione medici*, a work that of course alluded to Thomas Browne's famous treatise.[127] Among other things, the dissertation treated the relationship of pagans (*ethnici*) to medicine.[128] Hippocrates was regarded as godless to be sure, just as Gundling would have thought: he did not recognize God as the creator, but these Pietists held that such a position was far from harmless because this flaw spelled trouble on ethical questions, such as abortion:

> Therefore we do not concur with the philosophy of Aristotle and the medicine of Hippocrates, who approve of performing an abortion. These pagans here deviate from the true religion and have lent their faulty trust to this dangerous practice.[129]

For these physicians it was not a matter of indifference whether in science or medical practice one drew on a Christian or an atheist author or adopted doctrines from him. Religion and medicine were tightly bound together for them, especially in the *habitus* and attitudes of a physician.

10 Subsequent Incomprehension

Looking back at these controversies, the great historian of medicine of Halle, Kurt Sprengel (1766–1833),[130] suggested that the quarrels involving Gundling, Le Clerc, Goelicke, and Triller were often ridiculous, but in the first decades after 1700 questions of authorship were still completely

---

[126] Gundling, *Philosophische Discourse* (note 17), p. 238.
[127] Michael Alberti (praes.) / Friedrich Brösike (resp.), *De religione medici*, Halle, 1722. Thomas Browne, *Religio medici*, London, 1643.
[128] See Pott, *Medizin, Medizinethik und schöne Literatur* (note 79), pp. 80f.
[129] Albert (praes.) / Brösike (resp.), *De religione medici* (note 127), p. 38.
[130] On Sprengel, see Hans-Uwe Lammel, *Klio und Hippokrates: Eine Liaison littéraire des 18. Jahrhunderts und die Folgen für die Wissenschaftskultur bis 1850 in Deutschland*, Stuttgart, 2005, chapter 4.1, "Sprengel, Hippokrates und die knidische Frage," pp. 178–195, within a discussion of medical history as a part of *historia literaria*.

unsettled. He added that, "In all of this, anyone can recognize Gundling's willful shallowness when he adduces passages in support of his view that Hippocrates was an atheist when they could more easily prove almost anything else."[131] Triller too had shown weaknesses, while Goelicke had been extremely feeble. Sprengel, a thoroughly pious Christian, tried to make a new start in the late eighteenth century with his *Apology for Hippocrates*. By placing the ancient physician from Cos into historical context, he removed him from the line of fire of debates that were suffused with epistemic and religious questions: the Hippocratic works were a scattered corpus, but even so they constituted the beginnings of medicine as the Rousseauian incarnation of medical-ethical values.[132] Even though Sprengel was trying to place Hippocrates into a historical context, he still maintained the thesis of Leclerc and Gundling claiming that Hippocratic doctrines were derived from Heraclitus.

Recently Hans-Uwe Lammel has given renewed attention to Sprengel,[133] but unfortunately he begins his study of the relations between literary history and the history of medicine no earlier than the middle of the eighteenth century, and so the earlier history of this relationship escapes him, and with it the huge importance that the exaggerated fear of atheism had for the construction of a secularized medicine. This paradox – that one could complain about atheism precisely in order to free medicine from the burden of this accusation – had obviously dissi-pated over the intervening years. It belonged to one of the specific forms of discourse from the early eighteenth century and to a constellation of problems that had more to do with the participants in the debate and with other philosophical problems or power struggles than with the actual historical objects that were supposedly the core of the quarrel. By the later phases of the Enlightenment this was no longer even understandable. And the more the figure of Hippocrates morphed into a complex collection of Hippocratic writings, the less it made sense to describe him as personally godless.

In the end we must see that we need to keep the claims of all four university faculties (theology, medicine, jurisprudence, and philosophy) in mind in order to understand a polemical campaign like that of Gundling's concerning Hippocrates. Medically, the essay on *Hippocrates an Atheist* was

[131] Kurt Sprengel, *Apologie des Hippokrates und seiner Grundsätze*, Leipzig, 1789, p. 112.
[132] Hans-Uwe Lammel, "Kurt Sprengel und die deutschsprachige Medizingeschichtsschreibung," in Andreas Frewer and Volker Roelke, eds., *Die Institutionalisierung der Medizinhistoriographie*, Stuttgart, 2001, pp. 27–38.
[133] Lammel, *Klio und Hippokrates* (note 130).

relevant, I think, because it supported Friedrich Hoffmann's efforts to keep theology at arm's length by simultaneously rendering a clear statement of his belief in God as creator. Gundling hoped to end once and for all the tendency of physicians and other practitioners to credit their ancestors with (proto-Christian) theologies so that they could then legitimately refer to them. So his essay was also an example of "boundary work" directed against the theological faculty, to use Thomas Gieryn's useful term.[134] Theology needed to restrain itself from infringing with its dogmas on other areas. That was of course not just a problem for many Orthodox Lutherans, but perhaps especially for the Pietists, who, let us recall, just a few years after Gundling's last reply had driven Christian Wolff out of Halle; as a young teacher in Halle, Wolff had profited from his connection to Friedrich Hoffmann.[135] In the deeper background we have also identified La Mothe le Vayer as an author to whom Gundling appealed for orientation in ancient philosophy and intellectual history; moreover, the theological context of the debate over the *vertu des payens* (i.e., the virtues of those who could not have known the Christian revelation) seemed to prompt Gundling to ask whether the supposed "atheism" of Hippocrates implied that his teachings had to be condemned as well. I suspect that jurisprudence also helps explain why Gundling so clearly favored a voluntaristic creator God over all immanentist or emanationist ideas. It appears that he needed such a God to guarantee his idea of natural law, precisely because he retained such a minimalist and conventionalist version of natural law. And then the philosophical faculty? Gundling's text pertained directly to those colleagues because it was an example of *historia literaria*. One might say it was "only" a literary-historical essay pertaining to this fourth part of university learning. But it did come from a time when *historia literaria* occupied the intellectual core, the burning center of the university. And Hippocrates had become so important for *historia literaria*

---

[134] Thomas F. Gieryn, "Boundary-work and the Demarcation of Science from Nonscience: Strains and Interests in Professional Ideologies of Scientists," *American Sociological Review* 48(6) (1983), pp. 781–795; Gieryn, *Cultural Boundaries of Science: Credibility on the Line*, Chicago, 1999. See Martin Mulsow and Frank Rexrodt, eds., *Was als wissenschaftlich gelten darf. Praktiken der grenzziehung in Gelehrtenmilieus der Vormoderne*, Frankfurt, 2014.

[135] See Albrecht Beutel, "Causa Wolffiana. Die Vertreibung Christian Wolffs aus Preußen 1723 als Kulminationspunkt des theologisch-politischen Konflikts zwischen Pietismus und Aufklärungsphilosophie," in Ulrich Köpf, ed., *Wissenschaftliche Theologie und Kirchenleitung*, Tübingen, 2001, pp. 159–202; on Hoffmann and Wolff, see Martin Mulsow, "Säkularisierung der Seelenlehre? Biblizismus und Materialismus in Urban Gottlieb Buchers Briefwechsel vom Wesen der Seelen (1713)," in Lutz Danneberg et al., eds., *Säkularisierung der Wissenschaften seit der frühen Neuzeit*, vol. 2: *Zwischen christlicher Apologetik und methodologischem Atheismus*, Berlin, 2002, pp. 145–173, or Chapter 1; Pott, *Aufklärung und Aberglaube* (note 49), p. 377.

because his doctrine of the temperaments became a tool with which to group together all sorts of psychological, moral, political, historical, and intellectual analyses. And because literary history had become such a core discipline, Gundling's essay acted like a magnifying glass – as did many other texts by Gundling – to focus the concerns of all the approaches that were part of literary history. Its importance lay there, rather than in any lasting contribution to scholarly research on Hippocrates. Classical philology, when it treats ancient medical texts, has steadily abandoned this whole set of problems. But we should not do so, for we can recognize these quarrels as the "cockfights" of the early Enlightenment, to use the image that the anthropologist Clifford Geertz deployed when he studied Balinese cockfighting as a means of understanding that whole society.

CHAPTER 4

Natural Law, Religion, and Moral Skepticism

1 "Modern" Natural Law

Samuel Pufendorf's version of natural law formed one of the foundations for the early Enlightenment in Germany, something we have noted in several of the chapters of this book, but the actual problems of law have not yet received their own chapter. Here I do not intend to summarize or comment on the many excellent contributions to this topic.[1] To do so would not make much sense and, besides, the task could not be completed in the tight space of one chapter. Instead I would like to treat a few neglected authors, currents, and connections and pay special attention to radicalizing impulses.

In 1987 Richard Tuck pointed out for the first time that the genesis of modernity in the realm of natural law has long been presented from the perspective of the nineteenth century, dominated by philosophical and historical notions that derived from Kant.[2] But that is not very helpful in this area. Rather, natural law had its own developmental logic, and it was

---

[1] I will mention only a few works: Frank Grunert, *Normbegründung und politische Legitimität: Zur Rechts- und Staatsphilosophie der deutschen Frühaufklärung*, Tübingen, 2000; Friedrich Vollhardt, *Selbstliebe und Geselligkeit. Untersuchungen zum Verhältnis von naturrechtlichem Denken und moraldidaktischer Literatur im 17. Und 18. Jahrhundert*, Tübingen, 2001; Ian Hunter, *Rival Enlightenments: Civil and Metaphysical Philosophy in Early Modern Germany*, Cambridge, 2001; Merio Scattola, *Dalla virtù alla Scienza. La fondazione e la trasformazione della disciplina politica nell'età moderna*, Milan, 2003; Tim Hochstrasser and Peter Schröder, eds., *Early Modern Natural Law Theories: Context and Strategies in the Early Enlightenment*, Dordrecht, 2003; Ian Hunter, *The Secularisation of the Confessional State: The Political Thought of Christian Thomasius*, Cambridge, 2007; Knud Haakonssen, ed., *Grotius, Pufendorf and Modern Natural Law*, Aldershot, 1999; Dieter Hüning, *Naturrecht und Staatstheorie bei Samuel Pufendorf*, Baden Baden, 2009; Vanda Fiorillo and Frank Grunert, eds., *Das Naturrecht der Geselligkeit. Anthropologie, Recht und Politik im 18. Jahrhundert*, Berlin, 2009.

[2] Richard Tuck, "The Modern Theory of Natural Law," in Anthony Pagden, ed., *The Languages of Political Theory in Early Modern Europe*, Cambridge, 1988, pp. 235–263; further, Tuck, "Grotius, Carneades, and Hobbes," *Grotiana* n.s. 4 (1983), pp. 43–62; Tuck, *Hobbes*, Oxford, 1989. For Tuck's earlier views, see his book *Natural Right Theories*, Cambridge, 1979. But see also the critique of Tuck by Robert Shaver, "Grotius on Scepticism and Self-Interest," *Archiv für Geschichte der*

narrated very differently in the eighteenth century as a process that had begun with Montaigne and Charron and had reached its decisive phase with Grotius. Why Montaigne? Why Grotius? The early eighteenth century regarded the modern period through eclectic and skeptical lenses. From the point of view of Gundling, Budde, Heumann, or Brucker, eclecticism had conquered the sectarian thinking that dominated well into the sixteenth century and had set up its own historically Enlightened analysis in opposition. But the modern period also had to cope with the challenge of skepticism, which had resurfaced in the form of neo-Pyrrhonism.[3] So, according to Tuck, that is where the history of natural law has to start. Indeed, the foreword to Grotius's *De jure belli ac pacis* of 1625 includes an argument against the very possibility of a natural law that seemed to focus on the Hellenistic philosopher Carneades of Cyrene (the Academic skeptic) but was actually aimed at the neo-Pyrrhonists.[4] Strictly speaking, Grotius was basing his natural law in these antiskeptical arguments.

Following Samuel Pufendorf it became established practice from the 1680s onward to recount this genealogy;[5] however, according to Tuck, it was the Huguenot Jean Barbeyrac who first clearly depicted the crucial role of moral skepticism in that genealogy. In 1706 he published his French translation of Pufendorf's *De jure naturae et gentium* and attached to it a hugely influential foreword of almost 100 pages, a foreword that was later given the title *Histoire critique et scientifique de la science des moeurs*.[6]

Philosophie 78 (1996), pp. 27–47; Perez Zagorin, "Hobbes without Grotius," *History of Political Thought* 21 (2000), pp. 16–40; Benjamin Straumann, *Roman Law in the State of Nature: The Classical Foundations of Hugo Grotius' Natural Law*, Cambridge, 2015; Knud Haakonssen, "The Moral Conservatism of Natural Rights," in Ian Hunter and David Saunders, eds., *Natural Law and Civil Sovereignty*, New York, 2002, pp. 27–42.

[3] Richard Popkin is the one who has brought this aspect back to renewed prominence: *The History of Scepticism from Savonarola to Bayle*, Oxford, 2003.

[4] Hugo Grotius, *De jure belli ac pacis*, Paris, 1625, Prolegomena, §§ 5–18. See also Benjamin Straumann, *Hugo Grotius und die Antike*, Baden-Baden, 2007, pp. 96–110, 129–139. On Carneades of Cyrene, see Woldemar Görler, "Karneades," in Hellmut Flashar, ed., *Grundriss der Geschichte der Philosophie. Die Philosophie der Antike*, vol. 4(2): *Die hellenistische Philosophie*, Basel, 1994, pp. 849–897; Suzanne Obdrzalek, "Living in Doubt: Carneades' *Pithanon* Reconsidered," in *Oxford Studies in Ancient Philosophy* 31 (2006), pp. 243–279.

[5] Taking off from Tuck, Tim Hochstrasser has given a rather thorough picture of the production of the history of philosophy within the study of natural law: *Natural Law Theories in the Early Enlightenment*, Cambridge, 2000.

[6] Jean Barbeyrac, "Preface du Traducteur," in Samuel Pufendorf, *Le droit de la nature et des gens*, Amsterdam, 1706, pp. i–xcii. On Barbeyrac, see Sieglinde C. Othmer, *Berlin und die Verbreitung des Naturrechts in Europa*, Berlin, 1970; Simone Zurbuchen, *Naturrecht und natürliche Religion. Zur Geschichte des Toleranzbegriffs von Samuel Pufendorf bis Jean-Jacques Rousseau*, Würzburg, 1991; Horst Dreitzel, "A Strange Marriage: Pufendorf's Natural Jurisprudence and Protestant Moral

Barbeyrac was a follower of Pierre Bayle and therefore saw natural law through the lens of skepticism. And so, according to Tuck, he was able to see something that no one had earlier seen so clearly: that Grotius's achievement consisted chiefly in providing an answer to the skeptics. And Barbeyrac hoped to reinforce that answer.

But was Barbeyrac really the first to place moral skepticism at the center of the debate over natural law? And was not the history of combating skepticism actually richer and more complex? Here I would like to recount this history differently and set forth a new agenda. First we need to look at a neglected aspect of the development of natural law, namely the reception of John Selden and his effort to create a universalistic law that was disconnected from the Bible. Why? Because what Selden focused on is often a good indicator for his dissatisfactions with natural law as understood by Grotius. These dissatisfactions, however, seem to me to provide a key for understanding radicalizing moves that led toward naturalizing, but also the contrary efforts to outdo Grotius in emphasizing the Will of God as the basis of natural law. We will see that the traditions that ran parallel to or even against Grotius were important here.

Doing so will also give us an opportunity to place the debate over natural law in relation to the contemporary development of clandestine literature, especially concerning moral skepticism. Would it be possible to understand the founding of natural law not just in Grotius – as Tuck has shown – but also as a reaction to clandestine skeptical arguments in the period around 1700, just before Barbeyrac's publications?

We will find a key witness for what I am suggesting in the young Johann Franz Budde, who combined his reception of Selden with his discussion of skepticism and an emphasis on the divine foundation of natural law. We will also see if the moral skepticism he opposed flowed directly from his reading of radical manuscripts or perhaps from a fictive and "constructed" radicalism imagined by the conservative side. Either way the result is the same: the foundation of "modern" natural law as a theory that could withstand skepticism.

Philosophy in Early Enlightenment," a lecture given in Scotland on October 19, 1996; I am grateful to Horst Dreitzel for showing me his text. Ross Hutchison, *Locke in France 1688–1734*, Oxford, 1991, chapter 2: "Jean Barbeyrac, John Locke and Jurisprudence," pp. 42–85; Sandra Pott, *Reformierte Morallehren und deutsche Literatur von Jean Barbeyrac bis Christoph Martin Wieland*, Tübingen, 2003; Fabrizio Lomonaco, *Jean Barbeyrac editor of Gerard Noodt*, Berlin, 2012; Fiammetta Palladini, *Die Berliner Hugenotten und der Fall Barbeyrac. Orthodoxe und "Sozinianer" im Refuge (1685–1720)*, Leiden, 2011.

Gundling's lectures from the 1720s show us how this whole problematic looked in retrospect to the scholars of Halle. A copy of them was printed in 1740. Gundling first summarized the challenge to which Grotius had felt he needed to respond:

> the true opinion [of Carneades] was that "there is nothing just, there is nothing honorable, but everything must be measured by the standard of its utility." He wanted to dismiss everything both honorable and dishonorable, and he said, "Only that is just which is useful." So when the Romans prattled on about justice, he just laughed. . . . But if Carneades' principle were true, we would possess no moral truth. Like beasts we would just behave according to what is useful. Of course Spinoza too thought that this should be the principle for human beings, that one should do just what one wished. And thus many other *politici* also think that the only thing that matters in human life is whatever each individual regards as useful. Indeed, many men truly do behave like this. But it's quite another question whether that's right.[7]

It is interesting that Gundling brought Spinoza into play here, for Spinoza was no skeptic. And yet he had begun with an argument from Hobbes and had presented an idea of morality and law based on the human drive for self-preservation.[8] So there was certainly some similarity between the threat to natural law posed by Spinoza's metaphysics and that posed by skepticism. Gundling went on:

> Using the voice of "Carneades," Bayle has therefore asked whether Cicero really refuted Carneades. It was Grotius in his *Prolegomena on the Law of War and Peace* § 5 who did the best job of doing that, and indeed he appeals to me above all others.

Gundling then revealed his source: "Budde mentioned something of that in the above-cited *Dissertation on Moral Scepticism*." We will pursue that clue later.

> And Bayle did no less in his *Dictionnaire Historique et Critique*, citing much of this material, but he did not decide the question, and merely stated that

---

[7] Nikolaus Hieroymus Gundling, *Philosophischer Discourse anderer und dritter als letzter Theil, oder Academische Vorlesungen über seine Viam ad Veritatem moralem und Kulpisii Collegium Grotianum nebst nöthigen kurzen Anmerckungen und zulänglichen Registern*, Frankfurt and Leipzig, 1740, pp. 30f.

[8] See Don Garrett, "Spinoza's Ethical Theory," in Don Garrett, ed., *The Cambridge Companion to Spinoza*, Cambridge, 1996, pp. 267–314; Thomas Kisser, *Selbstbewußtsein und Interaktion. Spinozas Theorie der Individualität*, Würzburg, 1998; Aaron Garrett, "Spinoza as Natural Lawyer," *Cardozo Law Review* 25 (2003–2004), pp. 627–642.

the refutation of Carneades by Lactantius was only twaddle and that it possessed no "conclusive force" [*vim concludendi*].[9]

Gundling is a good example of the impact of Bayle and of his manner of proceeding. By casually noting that the existing refutations of moral skepticism were inadequate, he created a gap in the argument that prompted his readers to think more strenuously. Was it really impossible to set natural law on a firm foundation?[10]

2   Grotius and Skepticism

Strictly speaking, in his "Prolegomena" to *De jure belli ac pacis*, in arguing against the Academic skeptic Carneades, Grotius was opposing a whole range of views deriving from Epicureanism, skepticism, and reason-of-state theories. He attacked those who founded law on nothing more than utility but also those who denied even the possibility of a universal law because the variability of climates and temperaments produced various forms of legal system.[11] In addition to Epicurus and the skeptics, he had in mind Montaigne, Charron, and those who derived a relativity of manners from the Galenic treatise, *Quod animi mores corporis temperamentum sequantur* ["That the Qualities of the Mind Depend upon the Temperament of the Body."][12]

Thus relativism or legal minimalism were also targets of Grotius's critique. And yet the mere claim that communal action promised greater utility than individual actions did not provide an adequate basis for legal theory. What was needed in addition was the force of contract that arose from that calculation. Surprisingly the ancient Epicureans themselves had

---

[9] Gundling, *Philosophischer Discourse* (note 7), p. 31.

[10] And Gundling even sharpened the irritation by saying, ibid.: "Es ist auch sonst wohl kein Doctor Juris naturae, der nicht etwas von dem Carneade beygebracht habe; wiewohl die wenigsten das rechte Ziel getroffen. Selbst Boecler zu Strasburg, der doch sonst ein gutes *jugement* gehabt, hat besagte controvers in seinen Notis, oder *Commentario ad Grotium*, Lib. II, cap. 7. nicht sonderlich entschieden."

[11] Grotius, *De jure belli ac pacis* (note 4), Prolegomena, § 5 (in the Amsterdam edition, 1702, ed. Johann F. Gronovius, p. iv). A possible source for Grotius's critique of Carneades is Alberico Gentili's *De armis Romanis* (1599). See David Lupher, "The *De armis Romanis* and the Exemplum of Roman Imperialism," in Benedict Kingsbury and Benjamin Straumann, eds., *The Roman Foundations of the Law of Nations: Alberico Gentili and the Justice of Empire*, Oxford, 2010, pp. 85–100.

[12] See Galen, "Quod animi mores corporis temperamentum sequantur," in *Opera omnia*, vol. 4, ed. Karl Gottlob Kühn, Leipzig, 1821–1833, pp. 767–822; concerning that, see Martin Mulsow, *Frühneuzeitliche Selbsterhaltung. Telesio und die Naturphilosophie der Renaissance*, Tübingen, 1998, pp. 296–305.

emphasized this point and thus from early on had shown how to escape the disastrous consequences of full-fledged moral skepticism, even if one was arguing on the basis of utility. In his *Ratae sententiae* ["Fundamental Propositions"] XXXIff., which later formed the starting point for Gassendi's political Epicureanism,[13] Epicurus had formulated this argument clearly: "Natural law is a covenant of what is useful, leading men to avoid injuring one another and being injured."[14] The first evidence we have of the revival of this sort of thinking can be found in the Italian naturalists of the late sixteenth century. Bernardino Telesio did not use the word "covenant" (σύμβολον) (with its implication of reciprocity); instead he used the verb *statuere*, (i.e., "to set up") which testifies to some insight (*intellegens*) or to some excellence (*virtus*):

> Therefore intelligence is a virtue that is called justice: it has determined that no person should be treated unjustly or injuriously, for every one should be content with what they have provided for themselves; and also that those who want to seize the property of others must be condemned and punished if possible.[15]

The capacity for justice sets forth the rules of property.

That was a minimalist theory of law, resting only on considerations of utility. From the point of view of Grotius, it was too minimal. He argued in a neo-Stoic manner against the whole syndrome of thinking that law lacked adequate foundations:

> For man is not just a living being but the highest of living beings; and the difference from all other living beings is much greater that the differences among all the other genera. This is proved by the many specific properties

---

[13] Gassendi, "Ethica," in *Opera omnia*, vol. 5, Lyon, 1658. See Gianni Paganini, "Épicurisme et Philosophie au XVIIe siècle. Convention, utilité et droit selon Gassendi," *Studi filosofici* 12/13 (1989–90), pp. 5–45; Paganini, "Hobbes, Gassendi et le De cive," in Miguel Benítez et al., eds., *Materia actuosa. Antiquité. Age Classique. Lumières. Mélanges en l'honneur d'Olivier Bloch*, Paris, 2000, pp. 183–206.

[14] Epicurus, Rat. Sent. XXXI [Translator's note: the translation here from *Lives of the Eminent Philosophers*, Book X, by Diogenes Laertius, is that of Robert Drew Hicks, Cambridge, MA, 1925, nos. 31ff. (a.k.a. no. 150). On the context, see Reimar Müller, *Die epikureische Gesellschaftstheorie*, Berlin, 1972; Victor Goldschmidt, *La doctrine d'Epicure et le droit*, Paris 1977 (see English tr. C. D. Yonge, Diogenes Laërtius, *Lives of Eminent Philosophers*, London, 1905, p. 478).

[15] Bernardino Telesio, *De rerum natura iuxta propria principia*, Rome,1586, liber IX; I am quoting from the critical edition by Luigi de Franco: *De rerum natura libri VII-VIII-IX*, Florence, 1976, p. 384. See Martin Mulsow and Claudia Schmitz, "Eigennutz, Statuserhaltung und Naturzustand. Tradierungen des ethisch-politischen Epikureismus vom 15. bis zum 17. Jahrhundert," in Gianni Paganini and Edoardo Tortarolo, eds., *Der Garten und die Moderne. Epikureiche Moral und Politik vom Humanismus bis zur Aufklärung*, Stuttgart, 2004, pp. 47–86. I am taking some passages in the following paragraph from that essay.

that belong only to the human race, such as the social drive to have a peaceful community with his fellows according to the measure of his insight – which the Stoics called οἰκείωσις.[16]

Grotius did not appeal here to a natural law with theological foundations, as had been common, but maintained a certain minimalism, one that was rather different from that of the Epicureans. For his antiskeptical strategy, "insight" or reason was the crucial quality that marked human beings as different from the beasts. Borrowing from Cicero he distinguished between a "primary" and a "secondary nature" in human beings:

> According to [Cicero] the primary natural law is what any living being possesses the moment it is born, so that it feels an attachment to itself and an impulse to preserve itself and its constitution, and a desire for whatever can preserve that constitution; on the other hand it conceives an antipathy to destruction and to those things that appear to threaten destruction.[17]

This was the drive to self-preservation, which even the Epicurean minimalists took as their basis. And Ulpian, the Roman jurist, also understood this natural foundation of law: "Natural law is what nature teaches all living creatures."[18]

Grotius, however, added Cicero's "second nature," which only human beings had. This superior, "secondary" natural law established the rule of "right reason" (recta ratio), and corresponded to the drive for community. And that provided the real source of law. It corresponds to human nature by pursuing the rule "that human insight [intellectus] should follow whatever is recognized as right and thus avoid being led astray by fear or by the temptations of some present pleasure and also avoid being transported by passionate excitements. Whatever opposed these commands was contrary to the law of nature, i.e., of the human."[19]

Grotius's disagreed with the Epicurean foundations of law not by emphasizing reason and using long-term calculations, which could avoid the appeals of tempting pleasures, but only in his stress on the independence of a reason oriented to community. Grotius's "socialitas" made all

---

[16] Grotius, *De jure belli ac pacis* (note 4), Prolegomena, § 6 (p. v in the 1702 edition).

[17] Grotius, *De jure belli ac pacis* (note 4), Lib. I., cap. II, 1 (p. 25 in the edition of 1702). See Cicero, *De finibus* III, 5. The English translation borrows from Harris Rackham, tr., *Cicero, De finibus bonorum et malorum*, London, 1914.

[18] *Corpus juris civilis*, D. I, 1, tit. 1 (Ulpian), "Jus naturale est, quod natura omnia animalia docuit." For a comment, see Robert A. Greene, "Instinct of Nature: Natural Law, Synderesis, and the Moral Sense," *Journal of the History of Ideas* 58 (1997), pp. 173–198.

[19] Grotius, *De jure belli ac pacis* (note 4), Prolegomena, § 9 (p. viii in the 1702 edition).

the difference.[20] And it was this "communality" that proved so controversial when later skeptics came to criticize Grotius.[21]

3   Dissatisfaction with Grotius

In Germany Grotius met with strong approval; the reception was both multifarious and productive.[22] And yet, for some, his theory of natural law was too weakly connected to Christian principles, and so some scholars tried to integrate Grotius more firmly with religion. A litmus test for these sorts of dissatisfaction with Grotius was the somewhat later German reception of Grotius's adversary, John Selden.[23] With that in mind we will find it rewarding to pursue this neglected clue more closely.

On the one hand, the fact that Selden's works were often reprinted in Germany, and probably in sizable print-runs, shows that there was great interest in the works of the English jurist, historian, and student of religion: works that included Selden's *De diis Syris*, *De jure naturali*, *Uxor Hebraica*, *De successionibus in bona defuncti*, and *De successione in pontificium*. On the other hand, one searches in vain for German scholars who actually adopted his idiosyncratic blend of natural law and rabbinic tradition. Instead, it appears that Selden acted as a powerful impetus, but one that some thinkers modified to suit German conditions; other scholars merely exploited him as a gigantic quarry. The key period for the reception

[20]   See Hans Blom, "Sociability and Hugo Grotius," *History of European Ideas* 41 (2015), pp. 589–604; Marcelo de Araujo, "Hugo Grotius, Moral Scepticism and the Use of Arguments in Utramque Partem," *Veritas: Revista de Filosofia da PUCRS* 56 (2011), pp. 145–166; Hans Blom and Laurens Winkel, eds., *Grotius and the Stoa*, Assen, 2004; Benjamin Straumann, *Roman Law and the State of Nature* (note 2); Christopher Brooke, *Philosophic Pride: Stoicism and Political Thought from Lipsius to Rousseau*, Princeton, 2012, chapter 2. On the biographical context, see Henk Nellen, *Hugo Grotius: A Lifelong Struggle for Peace in Church and State, 1583–1645*, Leiden, 2014.

[21]   Translator's note: Parts of the translation of the sections which follow this borrow gratefully from the translation by Andrew McKenzie-McHarg of Mulsow, "John Selden in Germany: Religion and Natural Law from Boecler to Buddeus (1665–1695)," in Ann Blair and Anja-Silvia Goeing, eds., *For the Sake of Learning: Essays in Honor of Anthony Grafton*, 2 vols., Leiden, 2016, pp. 286–308.

[22]   Hans-Peter Schneider, *Justitia universalis. Quellenstudien zur Geschichte des "christlichen Naturrechts" bei Gottfried Wilhelm Leibniz*, Frankfurt, 1967.

[23]   On Selden, see David Sandler Berkowitz, *John Selden's Formative Years: Politics and Society in Early Seventeenth-Century England*, London, 1988; Jason P. Rosenblatt, *Renaissance England's Chief Rabbi: John Selden*, Oxford, 2006; Gerald J. Toomer, *John Selden: A Life in Scholarship*, Oxford, 2009. For the German reception, until now there were only pp. 908–913 in the book by Sergio Caruso, *La miglior legge di regno. Consuetudine, diritto naturale e contratto nel pensiero e nell'epoca di John Selden (1584–1654)*, 2 vols., Milan, 2001. These few pages deal only with Pufendorf, Prasch, Leibniz, and Barbeyrac. In the following sections I have adopted some of what I published in an article that appeared in English, "John Selden in Germany: Religion and Natural Law from Boecler to Buddeus (1665–1695)," in Ann Blair and Anja-Silvia Goeing, eds., *For the Sake of Learning: Essays in Honor of Anthony Grafton*, Leiden, 2016, pp. 286–308.

of Selden, as the dates of the German editions show, was the 1660s, but scholarly attention to Selden remained high during the following decades as well.

The first clue to the German reception may be found in the fact that Selden's *De jure naturali* ("On Natural Law") was published in 1665 by Johann Heinrich Boecler in Strasbourg, twenty-five years after its first edition and eleven years after Selden's death.[24] Boecler was a professor of history at the University of Strasbourg and one of Germany's leading historians, political scientists, and commentators on Grotius. His edition was the culmination of an intensive engagement with Selden in a whole circle of Grotius experts, who constituted something of a scholarly "constellation" in the 1660s: a tight network of theorists who were searching for an adequate form of natural law.[25] One of the leaders of this group was Johann Christian von Boineburg, who served as the first minister of Archbishop and Elector Johann Philipp von Schönborn between 1653 and 1664 and helped shape the foreign policy of the Electorate of Mainz; but he was also a scholar of European stature, who had "discovered" Leibniz and supported his career.[26] Boineburg had converted to Catholicism and worked to restore religious unity to Germany.[27] He also saw to it that his friend Boecler received an appointment as a councilor to the elector of Mainz. Both of them maintained regular correspondence

[24] John Selden, *De jure naturali et gentium*, Strasbourg, 1665. On Boecler (1611–1672), see Fiametta Palladini, "Un nemico di Samuel Pufendorf, Johann Heinrich Boecler," *Jus Commune* 24 (1997), pp. 133–152; Wilhelm Kühlmann, "Geschichte als Gegenwart. Formen der politischen Reflexion im deutschen 'Tacitismus' des 17. Jahrhunderts," in Wilhelm Kühlmann and Walter E. Schäfer, eds., *Literatur im Elsaß von Fischart bis Moscherosch*, Tübingen, 2001, pp. 41–60; Wolfgang Weber, *Prudentia Gubernatoria. Studien zur Herrschaftslehre in der deutschen politischen Wissenschaft des 17. Jahrhunderts*, Tübingen, 1992, pp. 232–267. Boecler was among the sixty French and foreign scholars in 1662 to whom the French king, Louis XIV, paid a royal pension. See the letter of dedication from Boecler to Jean Chapelain; at the conclusion of his dedication Boecler connected Selden's book to King Louis in a manner that emphasized that Louis, as a most Christian king, acted according to justice: instead of waging war, he favored peace and friendship among princes. This may have been an early sign of the Strasbourger's worry about Louis's expansionist plans, and indeed sixteen years later Louis abandoned peace and conquered Strasbourg, incorporating the city into the French state.

[25] See Schneider, *Justitia universalis* (note 22), pp. 122–158; Michael Stolleis, *Geschichte des öffentlichen Rechts in Deutschland*, vol. 1: *Reichspublizistik und Policeywissenschaft 1600–1800*, Munich, 1988, pp. 195ff. On the concept of constellations, see Martin Mulsow and Marcelo Stamm, eds., *Konstellationsforschung*, Frankfurt, 2005.

[26] On Boineburg (1622–1672), see Kathrin Paasch, *Die Bibliothek des Johann Christian von Boineburg (1622–1672): ein Beitrag zur Bibliotheksgeschichte des Polyhistorismus*, Berlin, 2005.

[27] On religious conversions, see Ricarda Matheus, "Zwischen Rom und Mainz. Konversionsagenten und soziale Netze in der Mitte des 17. Jahrhunderts," in Daniel Bauerfeld and Lukas Clemens, eds., *Gesellschaftliche Umbrüche und religiöse Netzwerke. Analysen von der Antike bis zur Gegenwart*, Bielefeld, 2014, pp. 227–252.

with Hermann Conring in Helmstedt,[28] along with Conring's student Samuel Rachel, a professor in Kiel, with Caspar Ziegler, a professor of church law in Wittenberg, and with Johann Joachim Zentgraf, Boecler's theological colleague in Strasbourg.[29]

One letter from Boineburg to Samuel Rachel serves to illustrate the importance of this constellation. Rachel had said:

> At the mention of Selden, I recall the very illustrious Johann Christian von Boineburg . . . When writing to me in his exceptionally cultured vein about many other matters, he would sometimes also express his desire to follow in Selden's footsteps with a Commentary of the Law of Nature from a Christian point of view.[30]

This letter may have been written in the late 1660s. A little group that included Boineburg, Boecler (eleven years older than Boineburg), and Conring (sixteen years older than Boecler) had for some time been thinking about the application of Selden's theories to German conditions. The fact that Boineburg had encouraged Rachel to write a natural law "from the standpoint of Christianity" rather than "according to the theory of the Hebrews" as Selden had done, reveals that he was shifting the emphasis in two ways. Whereas Selden had emulated Grotius[31] by embedding natural law in a *philosophia perennis*, according to which knowledge of the laws of nature had started in ancient Israel but then spread out to all peoples, now the German admirers of Grotius wanted to use Selden to imitate his theory and to bring it into harmony with Lutheran principles. They adopted Selden's critique of Grotius, in other words, claiming that natural law had to be understood as God's legislation, but they had little use for Selden's Hebraism and developed a Christian natural law instead.

There were German precedents for that project. Over 100 years earlier, Philipp Melanchthon had formulated a "theonomous natural law" (i.e., a natural law that was equivalent to rule by God), in which the Ten

---

[28] See the correspondence between Conring and Boineburg in Daniel Gruber, ed., *Commercii epistolici Leibnitiani prodromus*, 2 vols., Hanover and Göttingen, 1745. And further, Albrecht von Arnswaldt, *De Vicariatus controversia. Beiträge Hermann Conrings in der Diskussion um die Reichsverfassung des 17. Jahrhunderts*, Berlin, 2004, pp. 32–70.

[29] See Johann Joachim Zentgrav, *De origine, veritate et immutabili rectitudine juris naturalis secundum disciplinam Christianorum*, Strasbourg, 1678.

[30] Samuel Rachel, *De jure naturae at gentium dissertationes*, Kiel, 1676, diss. I, § 101, p. 99. See Schneider, *Justitia universalis* (note 22), p. 220. For an English translation of Rachel, see Samuel Rachel, *De jure naturae et gentium dissertationes*, Ludwig von Bar, ed., tr. John Pawley Bate, 2 vols., Washington, D.C., 1916, vol. 2, here at p. 67.

[31] According to Boecler in the foreword to his edition of *De jure naturali* (note 24).

Commandments were regarded as natural law.[32] Starting with Melanchthon, therefore, the intellectual climate in Germany included assumptions that affected the reception of both Grotius and Selden. In Rachel we can see clearly how he read Grotius's *De jure belli et pacis* as a further development of Cicero's *De officiis*, which he understood in turn through the lens of Melanchthon's Christian humanism.[33]

But how did Boineburg read Selden? The answer may be found in his personal copy of Selden, which today resides in the University library of Erfurt. Boineburg was an energetic reader, who read with pencil in hand. We can see how he worked through a book from his copy of Grotius's *De jure belli ac pacis*. Page after page is littered with underlinings and summary marginal notes. Selden's *De jure naturali*, however, had nothing like the same importance for Boineburg. He donated his first copy of it to the Jesuit college in Cologne because in 1654 Elector Karl Ludwig of the Palatinate gave him a copy of the 1640 folio edition.[34] Despite this, he generally read Selden's work cursorily, concentrating almost exclusively on the essential Book I, strewing these pages with his characteristically quick, almost hasty pencil underlinings, which he used in most of the books he read. But he read certain chapters more intensively and underlined in ink certain passages in them. If we look more closely at what sections interested Boineburg the most, we discover two patterns.

The first emphasized the universality of Selden's reconstructed natural law and resulted from Boineburg's notion of true "catholicity." Thus for example he wrote NB in the margin of page 29 where he noted Selden's pronounced hope of depicting a genuine and simple moral and legal philosophy that preceded any division into various sects. And he added the remark: "The philosophy of eternal law, of both ecumenical and catholic duty, and the wisdom [*prudentia*] of behaving morally and simply."[35] This was exactly what interested Boineburg: a doctrine that transcended sects and had an ecumenical and catholic validity when translated

---

[32] Merio Scattola, *Das Naturrecht vor dem Naturrecht. Zur Geschichte des "ius naturae" im 16. Jahrhundert*, Tübingen, 1999; Horst Dreitzel, "Von Melanchthon zu Pufendorf: Versuch über Typen und Entwicklung der philosophischen Ethik im protestantischen Deutschland zwischen Reformation und Aufklärung," in Martin Mulsow, ed., *Spätrenaissance-Philosophie in Deutschland 1570–1650. Entwürfe zwischen Humanismus und Konfessionalisierung, okkulten Traditionen und Schulmetaphysik*, Tübingen, 2009, pp. 321–398, esp. pp. 360–369.

[33] Dreitzel, "Von Melanchthon zu Pufendorf" (note 32), p. 383, concerning Samuel Rachel's *In universam Aristotelis philosophiam moralem introductio*, Helmstedt, 1660.

[34] See Paasch, *Die Bibliothek des Johann Christian von Boineburg* (note 26), pp. 83f.

[35] Selden, *De jure naturali* (note 24), UB Erfurt 03 – R. 4O 01455g, p. 29.

into practical behavior.[36] That fitted well with his efforts in favor of a union of all churches and parties in the badly splintered Germany after the Thirty Years' War.[37] Somewhat later Boineburg took note of the words *gentes seu Populi omnes* ("the nations or all the people") and added in the margin, "*Nota bene.*"[38]

The second pattern in Boineburg's reading was more specific. It manifested his lively interest in the nature of obligation, of *obligatio*.[39] This problem was fundamental for any theory of natural law: What kind of burden do the fundamental laws place on us? Where does their peculiar force come from, even if there are no powers to compel obedience? In this connection Selden had spoken of a natural duty, *naturalis obligatio*. But in traditional Roman law, natural obligation was not actionable and provided no grounds for punishment. For Selden, who followed the later scholastics of Spain, however, *obligatio naturalis* had the deeper meaning of a *nexum conscientiae* (a "bond of conscience") that was not enforceable in civil law but did oblige one to follow God's commandments.

The German commentators on Grotius seized on this point because they could not accept Grotius's thesis that natural law could be valid even in the absence of divine laws. That conclusion did not seem Christian enough, but it was also unconvincing. And so they made natural obligation to God into the foundation of their teaching on the necessary connection between natural law and natural religion.[40] In 1664 in his commentary on Grotius, Boecler pointed out that not even Hobbes contested the binding force of natural law on conscience – though he did exclude the rule of God from his understanding of the state of nature.[41] Two years later Caspar Ziegler, in his commentary, criticized Grotius on the grounds that a human action directed toward the good and toward an obligation to

---

[36] On Selden's sort of "eclecticism," see Michael Albrecht, *Eklektik. Eine Begriffsgeschichte mit Hinweisen auf die Philosophie- und Wissenschaftsgeschichte*, Stuttgart, 1994, pp. 189–196.

[37] On the final endpaper of his intensively used copy of Grotius (Amsterdam, 1692, held in UB Erfurt 03 – R. 8° 01543bk [01]), he wrote these words: "De usu pio Christianarum justifica ... fidei in catholica ac orthodoxa sanctoris communione, si quando conscientia ... luctu ... affectiones et calamitates in nos virumpunt ac ingluunt" – unless this remark was written earlier by Johann Georg Egrer from Dresden in the book that he gave to Boineburg in 1641.

[38] Selden, *De jure naturali* (note 24), UB Erfurt 03 – R. 8° 00221ac, p. 78.

[39] See Gerald Hartung, "Gesetz und Obligation. Die Spätscholastische Gesetzestheologie und ihr Einfluß auf die Naturrechtsdebatte der Frühen Neuzeit," in Frank Grunert, ed., *Die Ordnung der Praxis: Neue Studien zur spanischen Spätscholastik*, Tübingen, 2001, pp. 381–402; Hartung, *Die Naturrechtsdebatte. Geschichte der Obligatio vom 17. bis 20. Jahrhundert*, Freiburg, 1998.

[40] Hartung, "Gesetz und Obligation" (note 39), p. 392.

[41] Johann Heinrich Boecler, *In Hugonis Grotii Juris belli ac pacis ad illustrissimum Baronem Boineburgium commentatio*, Strasbourg, 1664.

observe moral conduct was only conceivable by positing a divine ruler whose powers were constrained by the pangs of conscience.[42] Even Pufendorf later adopted the concept of "natural obligation" although he was less interested in the origin of this obligation than in its effect.[43]

To be sure, in contrast to Selden, commentators on Grotius placed even greater importance on natural obligation. While the Englishman allowed natural and civil obligation to stand alongside each other, for Boecler, Ziegler, and Boineburg the notion of natural obligation was the fundamental basis that permitted men to enter into further relationships of obligation.

All of this is reflected also in Boineburg's underlinings and marginal annotations to Selden's *De jure naturali* (see Figure 5). Thus on page 85, just before the end of chapter 6 of Book I, he underlined a lengthy passage in which Selden tried to show that one could not base natural law on some imagined *consensus gentium* because national customs and traditions were too variable:

> If no other basis for an obligation can be found than the mutual customs and ordinances [of the nations], what is to prevent it happening that any old original law, after some initial agreement on customs and ordinances might cease to play any role? Such instances might include demands for compensation or reprisals, declarations of war, or other intervening events from the laws of war and of fighting, which as we know change over the course of time.[44]

The norms of law were historical, Selden said; they had changed, even if at first there may have been consensus. Boineburg may well have been reminded here of his own experiences with different traditions – including those originating in confessional differences. But historically conditioned traditions needed to retreat and defer to one single and universal law that was binding on everyone. On page 105 in Book I.8 he underlined Selden's statement that "the efficient cause of a binding law is natural insofar as it is described as natural in the Holy Scripture."[45]

Another contemporary reader of Selden, the Giessen professor Johann Conrad Arnoldi, commented on *De jure naturali* I.4, where Selden

---

[42] Caspar Ziegler, *In Hugonis Grotii De jure belli ac pacis libros, quibus naturae et gentium jus explicavit, notae et animadversiones subitariae,* Wittenberg, 1666.

[43] Samuel Pufendorf, *Elementorum jurisprudentiae universalis libri II,* Cambridge, 1672. See Hartung, "Gesetz und Obligation" (note 39), p. 399.

[44] Selden, *De jure naturali* (note 24), p. 85 shortly before the end of chapter I, para. 6, where obligation is considered.

[45] Ibid., p. 105.

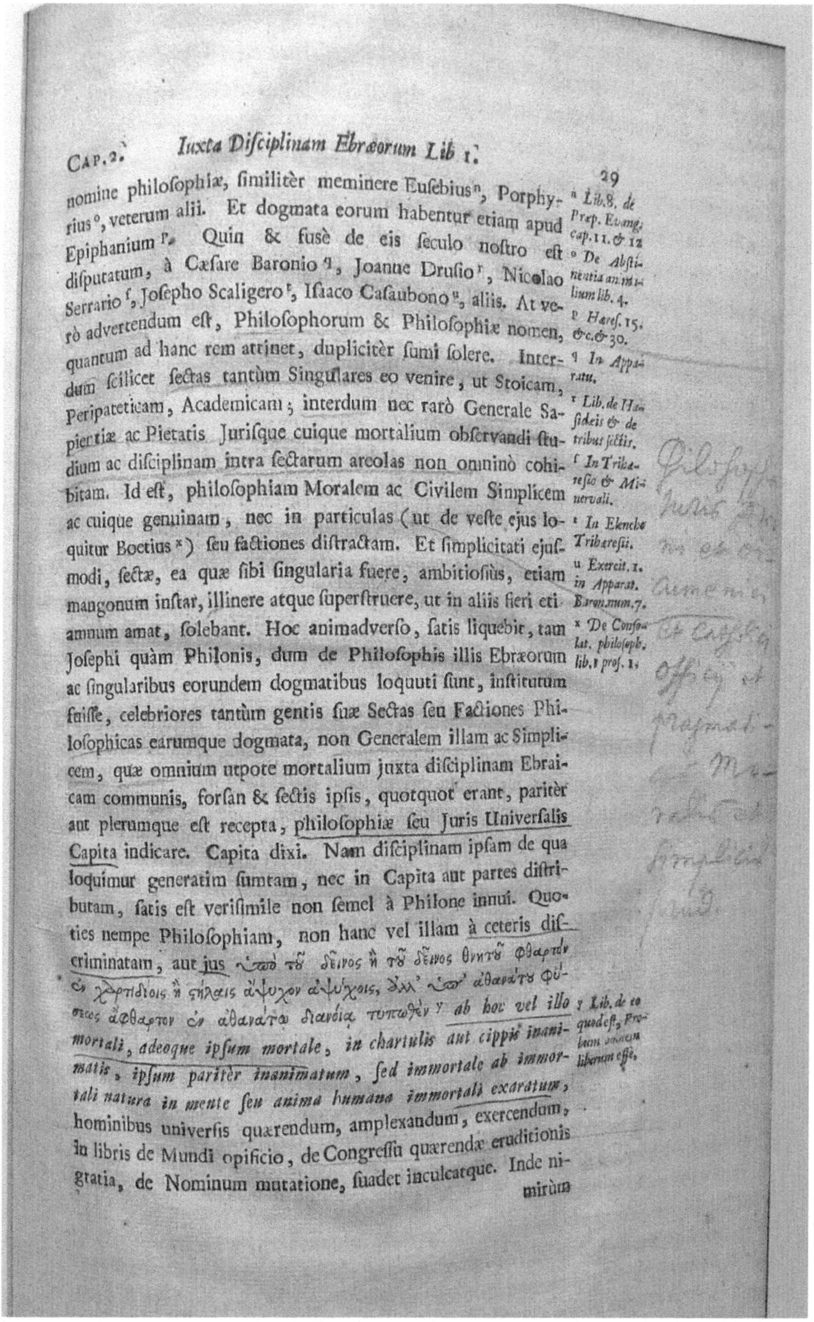

CAP. 2. *Iuxta Disciplinam Ebræorum Lib* 1.

29

nomine philosophiæ, similiter meminere Eusebius[n], Porphy-
rius[o], veterum alii. Et dogmata eorum habentur etiam apud
Epiphanium[p]. Quin & fusè de eis seculo nostro est
disputatum, à Cæsare Baronio[q], Joanne Drusio[r], Nicolao
Serrario[s], Josepho Scaligero[t], Isaco Casaubono[u], aliis. At ve-
rò advertendum est, Philosophorum & Philosophiæ nomen,
quantum ad hanc rem attinet, dupliciter sumi solere. Interdum scilicet sectas tantùm Singulares eo venire, ut Stoicam,
Peripateticam, Academicam; interdum nec rarò Generale Sa-
pientiæ ac Pietatis Jurisque cuique mortalium observandi stu-
dium ac disciplinam intra sectarum areolas non omninò cohi-
bitam. Id est, philosophiam Moralem ac Civilem Simplicem
ac cuique genuinam, nec in particulas (ut de veste ejus lo-
quitur Boetius[x]) seu factiones distractam. Et simplicitati ejus-
modi, sectæ, ea quæ sibi singularia fuere, ambitiosiùs, etiam
mangonum instar, illinere atque superstruere, ut in aliis fieri eti-
amnum amat, solebant. Hoc animadverso, satis liquebit, tam
Josephi quàm Philonis, dum de Philosophis illis Ebræorum
ac singularibus eorundem dogmatibus loquuti sunt, institutum
fuisse, celebriores tantùm gentis suæ Sectas seu Factiones Phi-
losophicas earumque dogmata, non Generalem illam ac Simplicem, quæ omnium utpote mortalium juxta disciplinam Ebrai-
cam communis, forsan & sectis ipsis, quotquot erant, pariter
aut plerumque est recepta, philosophiæ seu Juris Universalis
Capita indicare. Capita dixi. Nam disciplinam ipsam de qua
loquimur generatim sumtam, nec in Capita aut partes distri-
butam, satis est verisimile non semel à Philone innui. Quo-
ties nempe Philosophiam, non hanc vel illam à ceteris dis-
criminatam, aut jus ἀπὸ τοῦ δεῖνος ἢ τῷ δεῖνος θνητῷ φθαρτῷ
ἐν χαρτιδίοις ἢ στήλαις ἀψύχοις ἀψύχοις, ἀλλ᾽ ἀπὸ ἀθανάτου φύ-
σεως ἀφθαρτον ἐν ἀθανάτῳ διανοίᾳ τυπωθὲν[y] ab hoc vel illo
*mortali, adeoque ipsum mortale, in chartulis aut cippie inani-
matis, ipsum pariter inanimatum, sed immortale ab immortali natura in mente seu anima humana immortali exaratum*,
hominibus universis quærendum, amplexandum, exercendum,
in libris de Mundi opificio, de Congressu quærendæ eruditionis
gratia, de Nominum mutatione, suadet inculcatque. Inde ni-
mirùm

[n] Lib. 8. de Præp. Evang. cap. 11. & 12
[o] De Absti-nentia anima-lium lib. 4.
[p] Hæres. 15. &c. & 30.
[q] In Appa-ratu.
[r] Lib. de Ham fideis & de tribus sectis.
[s] In Triha-resio & Mi-nervali.
[t] In Elencho Trihæresii.
[u] Exercit. 1. in Apparat. Exron. mm. 7.
[x] De Consou-lat. philosoph. lib. 1 prof. 1.
[z] Lib. de eo quod est, Pro-bum omnium liberum esse.

Figure 5 Johann Christian Boineburg's annotated copy of John Selden, *De jure naturali*, London 1640, p. 29

introduces *obligatio*; he reacted forcefully to Selden's claim that obligations are normally guaranteed by the threat of punishment:[46] "Hah! As if no one is bound by his love of virtue?"[47] That illustrates the tension between the concept of law and the ethics of love, of a *charitas ordinata*, a reasonable love, which was typical of German discussions of the late seventeenth century and which suffused their discussions of *obligatio*.[48]

4   The Law of Noah and the Early History of Mankind

The question of natural law was not, however, discussed only in purely systematic terms. The German discussion also tried to connect Selden's reconstruction of Noachian natural law to a theory of human history.[49] Indeed, the passages Boineburg underlined about the changes in norms and laws after an initial period of agreement point to this connection. If Noachian natural law was also the very first law of all, how had it been embedded in the earliest social conditions? As early as 1660 the polyhistor Georg Kaspar Kirchmaier of Wittenberg devoted close attention to the question of how politics, the state, and legal relations were organized even in the period before Noah.[50] This space had already been occupied for a few years by the pre-Adamite theory of Isaac La Peyrère, with his thesis that there had been human beings before Adam, in an epoch he called *sub natura*, a time when states could have developed along with various forms of rule.[51] Kirchmaier was an unusually multifaceted scholar, whose interests ranged from mining technology and chemistry to zoology, history, the study of Latin, but also encompassing Jewish, Germanic, and Roman

---

[46] Ibid., p. 47.

[47] A marginal comment on Selden, *De jure naturali* (note 24), inscribed in the exemplar owned by the author, p. 47: "quasi! ergo nemo virtutis amore suae satisfaciet obligari?"

[48] See Werner Schneiders, *Naturrecht und Liebesethik. Zur Geschichte der praktischen Philosophie im Hinblick auf Christian Thomasius*, Hildesheim, 1971.

[49] Concerning the commandments of Noah, see Klaus Müller, *Tora für die Völker. Die noachidischen Gebote und Ansätze zu ihrer Rezeption im Christentum*, Berlin, 1998.

[50] Georg Kaspar Kirchmaier, *De imperio antediluvianorum*, Wittenberg, 1660. See Sicco Lehmann-Brauns, "Die Sintflut als Zäsur der politischen Institutionengeschichte," in Martin Mulsow and Jan Assmann, eds., *Sintflut und Gedächtnis. Erinnern und Vergesen des Ursprungs*, Munich, 2006, pp. 265–287. Even earlier, Wittenberg had scholars who received Selden as a philologist. See esp. Johann Ernst Gerhard (praes.) / Johann Vogelhaupt (resp), *Ritus foederum gentis Ebreae*, Wittenberg, 1650.

[51] Isaac La Peyrère, *Praeadamitae*, Amsterdam, 1655. See Richard H. Popkin, *Isaac La Peyrère (1596–1676): His Life, Work and Influence*, Leiden, 1987; Andreas Pietsch, *Isaac La Peyrère. Bibelkritik, Philosemitismus und Patronage in der Gelehrtenrepublik des 17. Jahrhunderts*, Berlin, 2012; Martin Mulsow, "Vor Adam. Ideengeschichte jenseits der Eurozentrik," *Zeitschrift für Ideengeschichte* 1 (2015), pp. 47–66.

antiquities as well as civil law, theology, and rhetoric. That he could pose such speculative questions may stem from his general curiosity about what the most ancient times were like.

According to Kirchmaier, before the Flood there was no political rule, but only the direct rule of God over mankind.[52] Like his Wittenberg colleague Ziegler, Kirchmaier argued against the tendency to emphasize sociality as the very essence of man. In Ziegler, this claim was directed against Grotius, but Kirchmaier directed it against political Aristotelianism with its propensity to speculate about the social formations found in the earliest period of human history.[53] The natural law that God had established had not yet been written down, but it constituted the only norm for human behavior. Therefore God had to intervene directly again and again in order to establish his rules. When Kirchmaier imagined the antediluvian forms of human interaction, he blithely adopted Caesar's reports on the Celts and Tacitus's description of the Germans and projected them onto the contemporaries of Cain and Abel. In trying to describe the antediluvian epoch, he applied the concept of theocracy, as discussed by Grotius, Cunaeus, and others, instead of imagining some Jewish form of government of the sort that had prevailed from Moses to the establishment of the Jewish monarchy.[54] In this light, the theocracy of that period appeared as the direct rule of God not just over the Jews but over all human beings. "Kirchmaier thus expanded ... the historical area of validity for the concept of theocracy backward into the antediluvian epoch, where it could serve to describe God's experiment with fallen mankind as a whole."[55] And that made Selden relevant, for in his *De jure naturali* he had offered a model for God's earliest legal instructions for all of mankind. Boineburg underlined such historical claims in his copy of Selden, where the text referred to "Enoch and Noah, who lived under natural law."[56]

Before the Flood, Selden thought, at least certain persons had been granted insight into the laws of God through direct revelation from the

[52] Kirchmaier, *De imperio antediluvianorum* (note 50), § 12.

[53] Lehmann-Brauns, "Die Sintflut als Zäsur" (note 50), p. 278. On political Aristotelianism, see Horst Dreitzel, *Politischer Aristotelismus und absoluter Staat. Die "Politica" des Henning Arnisaeus*, Wiesbaden, 1970; on theories of early human history, see Helmut Zedelmaier, *Der Anfang der Geschichte. Studien zur Ursprungsdebatte im 18. Jahrhundert*, Hamburg, 2003.

[54] Petrus Cunaeus, *De republica Hebraeorum libri III*, Leiden, 1617; see Adam Sutcliffe, *Judaism and Enlightenment*, Cambridge, 2003; Jonathan R. Ziskind, "Petrus Cunaeus on Theocracy, Jubilee and the Latifundia," *The Jewish Quarterly Review*, New Ser. 68 (1978), pp. 235–254; Eric Nelson, *The Hebrew Republic: Jewish Sources and the Transformation of European Political Thought*, Cambridge, MA, 2010.

[55] Lehmann-Brauns, "Die Sintflut als Zäsur" (note 50), p. 284.

[56] Selden, *De jure naturali* (note 24), UB Erfurt 03 – R. 8° 00221ac, p. 104.

intellectus agens ("active mind").[57] His borrowing of this idea from a Platonizing Aristotelianism that had been filtered through the Aristotelianism and Averroism of medieval Arab and Jewish scholars, was peculiar to Selden and was also occasionally criticized by those who were influenced by him. In Germany, however, this was more of a plus, for here a late humanist reader could find his footing again; such readers often understood Selden's universalism through the lens of a Platonizing *philosophia perennis* like that of Agostino Steuco (1497–1548) or Athanasius Kircher (1602–1680). A symptomatic reaction can be found in a passage in Daniel Georg Morhof, the Rostock (later Kiel) scholar and literary historian.[58] As we saw, in 1661 the young Morhof wrote a *Theologia gentium politica* ("The Political Theology of the Nations"), which clearly was an imitation of Gerhard Vossius and of Boecler's treatise *De auspicio regio* ("On Royal Augury") – a work that had been inspired by Vossius even if that work had had more of a political purpose. In his little treatise Morhof cited Selden when discussing the possibility of inspiration and of participation in the divine:

> Such views have remained lively among the Arabs and the Jews, and the incomparable John Selden has collected their famous and divine traditions in his book on the natural law of the Hebrews . . . . He has extracted from that the philosophy of all the philosophers of all the nations, including even the barbarian [i.e., the Hebrews], from whom the secrets of all wisdom have been disseminated.[59]

The fact that the most ancient philosophers as well as the ancient jurists understood themselves as servants of God gave Selden reason to suppose that natural law was God's law, and Morhof saw in that claim the possibility of defending ideas of the "divine" in politics.

5 *De diis Syris* and Oriental Studies in Leipzig

The debate over natural law was, however, by no means the only context in which Selden's books were read and discussed in Germany. Another central context was the connection between the history of religions and

---

[57] Ibid., Section I, 9; Toomer, *John Selden* (note 23), pp. 503f. See also Martin Mulsow, *Enlightenment Underground: Radical Germany, 1680–1720*, tr. H. C. Erik Midelfort, Charlottesville, 2015, chapter 4.

[58] On Morhof, see Françoise Waquet, ed., *Mapping the World of Learning: The "Polyhistor" of Daniel Georg Morhof*, Wiesbaden, 2000. See also Mulsow, *Enlightenment Underground* (note 57), chapter 4.

[59] Daniel Georg Morhof, *Theologia gentium politica*, Rostock, 1661, pp. 116f.

apologetic Christian theology. Let us recall that the early efforts at a history of ancient religion in the seventeenth century were all written as attempts to reconstruct pagan "idolatry," as we saw in Chapter 2 above.[60] To accomplish that it was necessary to describe the gods of the Canaanites and the Egyptians as they were known from the Bible and other sources and then to explain how worship of these animal and celestial divinities had come about. Early on, and inspired by Scaliger, Selden had written a pioneering work, *De diis Syris* ("On the Syrian Gods"), remarkable and influential especially for using Orientalist scholarship within a framework provided by Maimonides. We know that Selden's book decisively shaped Gerhard Johannes Vossius's *De theologia gentili* ("On Pagan Theology"), and following on from Vossius, after the translation into Latin of Maimonides's *De idololatria* (1641), a form of early comparative religious scholarship began to develop, which engaged the energy of many German scholars, especially theologians.[61] For that reason we find references to Selden all over the German works of this sort. Starting with Elias Schede's *De diis Germanis* ("On the German Gods") of 1648 to Johann Saubert's *De sacrificiis veterum* ("On the Sacrifices of the Ancients") of 1661, they all borrowed from Selden's *De diis Syris* and his *Marmora arundelliana*, even when those works did not actually provide models for their own works.[62]

Among all these works, however, one had a more direct connection to Selden than the others. This was the *Additamenta* ("The Additions") that

---

[60] See Jonathan Sheehan, "The Altars of the Idols: Religion, Sacrifice, and the Early Modern Polity," *Journal of the History of Ideas* 67 (2006), pp. 648–674; Guy G. Stroumsa, *A New Science: The Discovery of Religion in the Age of Reason*, Cambridge, MA, 2010. See also Mulsow, *Enlightenment Underground* (note 57), chapter 4.

[61] Martin Mulsow, "John Seldens *De diis Syris*: Idolatriekrik und vergleichende Religionsgeschichte im 17. Jahrhundert," *Archiv für Religionsgeschichte* 3 (2001), pp. 1–24; Mulsow, "Antiquarianism and Idolatry: The 'Historia' of Religions in the Seventeenth Century," in Gianna Pomata and Nancy G. Siraisi, eds., *Historia: Empiricism and Erudition in Early Modern Europe*, Cambridge, MA, 2005, pp. 181–210; Peter N. Miller, "Taking Paganism Seriously: Anthropology and Antiquarianism in Early Seventeenth-Century Histories of Religion," *Archiv für Religionsgeschichte* 3 (2001), pp. 183–209; Toomer, *John Selden* (note 23), pp. 211–256; Asaph Ben-Tov, "Pagan Gods in Late Seventeenth- and Eighteenth-Century German Universities: A Sketch," in Asaph Ben-Tov, Yaakov Deutsch, and Tamar Herzig, eds., *Knowledge and Religion in Early Modern Europe: Studies in Honor of Michael Heyd*, Leiden, 2012, pp. 153–178.

[62] Elias Schede, *De Diis Germanis, sive Veteri Germanorum, Gallorum, Britannorum, Vandalorum religione, syngrammata quatuor*, Amsterdam, 1648; Johann Saubert, *De sacrificiis veterum*, Jena, 1659. On Saubert, see Martin Mulsow, "Tempel, Münzen und der Transfer von Bildern: Zur Rolle der numismatischen Illustration im religionsgeschichtlichen Antiquarianismus," in Sabine Frommel and Eckhard Leuschner, eds., *Architektur- und Ornamentgraphik der Frühen Neuzeit: Migrationsprozesse in Europa / Gravures d'architecture et d'ornement au début de l'époque moderne: processus de migration en Europe*, Rome, 2014, pp. 295–312. On the reception of Selden especially in Jena, see e.g., Johannes Hoffmann, *Deorum gentilium praecipuorum origines [. . .]*, Jena, 1674, chapter I; Christoph Cellarius, *Sciagraphia philologiae sacrae*, Jena, 1678, p. 44.

Andreas Beyer attached to Selden's work on the Syrian gods as an appendix to the edition of the book published in in 1668 in Leipzig. This Leipzig edition of *De diis Syris* had its origins with an ingenious book dealer, Lorenz Sigmund Körner, who found out that Beyer, a theologian with whom he was friends, had assembled exhaustive indexes in his copy of *De diis Syris*.[63] At the time Beyer was in his middle twenties; he had finished his university studies and was later to become co-rector of the gymnasium in Freiberg (Saxony) and senior pastor of the Church of St. Nicholas there.[64] In 1667 he wrote a little antiquarian work on the shekel, the ancient coin of Israel, *Siclus sacer et regius* ("The Sacred and Royal Shekel").[65] Beyer obviously belonged to the generation of Leipzig theological students who read ancient Near Eastern texts from different traditions and languages and who had been influenced by enterprises such as Walton's London polyglot Bible and by Gerhard Vossius and John Marsham.[66] Leipzig began to be a center for those with such interests. In 1663 Johann Adam Scherzer, for example, published his *Trifolium orientale* ("Oriental Trefoil") with commentaries by Isaak Abravanel, Jarchi (i.e., Shlomo Yitzchaki, a.k.a. Rashi), and Moses Maimonides, well before the establishment of a professorship in Oriental Studies, to which Johann Benedict Carpzov was appointed in 1669, and before the impact of August Pfeiffer and Andreas Acoluthus could raise Oriental Studies to levels of greatness in Leipzig.[67]

Lorenz Körner saw that Beyer was collecting masses of notes on Selden, in just the way that many other contemporaries bound books of special interest to them with interleaved pages that then filled up with their learned additions.[68] So he encouraged Beyer to carry on, and finally took

---

[63] See Beyer's Foreword to the "Additamenta," in John Selden, *De diis Syris syntagmata II: Adversaria nempe de Numinibus commentitiis in veteri instrumento memoratis; Accedunt fer. quae sun reliqua Syrorum, Prisca porr. Arabum, Aegyptiorum, Persarum, Afrorum, Europarorum item theologia, subinde illustratur*, Leipzig, 1672.

[64] On Beyer, see Christian Gottlieb Jöcher, *Allgemeines Gelehrten-Lexicon*, vol. 1, Leipzig, 1750, cols. 1065f.

[65] Andreas Beyer, *Siclus sacer et regius*, Leipzig, 1667.

[66] Peter N. Miller, "The 'Antiquarianization' of Biblical Scholarship and the London Polyglot Bible (1653–57)," *Journal of the History of Ideas* 62 (2001), pp. 463–482.

[67] See the exhibition catalog, *Die Erleuchtung der Welt. Sachsen und der Beginn der modernen Wissenschaften*, 2 vols., Dresden 2009; the essays by Boris Liebrenz both entitled "Orientalistik," in vol. 1 (the essay volume), esp. pp. 202–209, and in vol. 2 (the catalog volume), esp. pp. 127–139. For primary sources, see esp. Johann Adam Scherzer, *Trifolium orientale: continens commentarios R. Abarbenelis in Haggaeum, R. Sal. Jarchi in Parsch. I. Geneseos, et R. mos. Majemonidae theologiam [...]*, Leipzig, 1663.

[68] See Martin Mulsow, "Mikrogramme des Orients," in *Prekäres Wissen. Eine andere Ideengeschichte der Frühen Neuzeit*, Berlin, 2012, pp. 367–398 (*Knowledge Lost. A New View of Early Modern Intellectual History*, Princeton, 2022, chapter 14).

his copy and published his notes as an appendix to the new edition of *De diis Syris*, which he had organized.[69] To that extent Beyer's *Additamenta*, which took up almost as much space as Selden's original text, can stand as a monument to the adaptation of Selden by German Orientalists – mainly those of Leipzig. Beyer's additions brought Selden's research up to date, expanding it with what had been discovered in the interim. And that was not a small achievement, because from 1617 onward antiquarian religious research and knowledge of ancient languages had dramatically exploded. So it is no wonder that Körner's edition was reprinted as early as 1672 and that in 1680 another edition appeared in Amsterdam with even more of Beyer's additions.[70]

6 Johann Christoph Becmann between Natural Law and the Talmud

As we have seen, in the debate over natural law, Selden's dependence on the Jewish-rabbinic tradition never really took root in Germany. From the beginning scholars diverted his suggestion of a God-given natural law into a *disciplina Christianorum* ("Christian Instruction") instead. But by the second half of the seventeenth century there were other movements too. Increasingly Talmudic studies and rabbinic commentaries were deemed worthy of consultation to help understand biblical texts.[71] Among Lutherans this tendency was sponsored by men such as Johann Gerhard, Johann Matthias Dilherr, Salomon Glassius, and Johann Hülsemann; among the Reformed the leaders were Johannes Buxtorf (father and son), Johann Heinrich Hottinger, and Johann Heinrich Heidegger. Beyer too was influenced by this development. This branch of research made such progress that by 1697–1699 Christian and Jewish scholars could produce a new edition of the whole Babylonian Talmud in

---

[69] See Beyer's foreword to the "Additamenta" (note 63).

[70] John Selden, *De diis Syris syntagmata II*, Amsterdam, 1680.

[71] See Johann Anselm Steiger, "Die Rezeption der rabbinischen Tradition im Luthertum (Johann Gerhard, Salomo Glassius u. a.) und im Theologiestudium des 17. Jahrhunderts. Mit einer Edition des universitären Studienplanes von Glassius und einer Bibliographie der von ihm konzipierten Studentenbibliothek," in Christiane Caemmerer et al., eds., *Das Berliner Modell der Mittleren Deutschen Literatur. Beiträge zur Tagung Kloster Zinna 29.9.–01.10.1997* (= *Chloe* 33), Amsterdam, 2000, pp. 191–252. For Christian Hebraism generally, Stephen G. Burnett, *From Christian Hebraism to Jewish Studies: Johannes Buxtorf (1564–1629) and Hebrew Learning in the Seventeenth Century*, Leiden, 1996; Anthony Grafton and Joanna Weinberg, *"I have always loved the Holy Tongue": Isaac Casaubon, the Jews, and a Forgotten Chapter in Renaissance Scholarship*, Cambridge, MA, 2011.

Frankfurt on the Oder.[72] The Frankfurt theology professor Johann Christoph Becmann and Michael Gottschalk were responsible for this large enterprise.

As a Reformed Christian, Becmann had studied in the Netherlands and while there had also received instruction in rabbinic Hebrew from Jacob Abendana.[73] He was, therefore somewhat predisposed to publish Jewish texts, but Becmann was also a follower of Thomas Hobbes and hence in the vanguard of the early Enlightenment in Germany.[74] Before he took up duties as a theologian he had been active for a long time as a historian and political philosopher. And so we can wonder if absorbing Selden somehow supported these other interests. We note that Becmann was the moving force behind a new edition of Selden's *Uxor Ebraica* in Frankfurt on the Oder in 1673, printed by Jeremias Schrey and including a very short foreword by Becmann.[75] But two other works by Selden were also republished at the same time: *De successionibus ad leges Ebraeorum in bona functorum* and the *De successione in pontificatum*. So through these publications a sizable body of expert knowledge concerning rabbinic law was now available.[76] Why? Why in Frankfurt on the Oder?

The explanation for these editions may have been similar to that of the Talmud edition of 1698–1699 – a thoroughly external explanation. Becmann had taken over the printing privilege of the university printing bureau on June 1, 1673, and he soon "realized that there were not just customers for Hebrew books among the local theologians but that a much larger Jewish customer base existed in Poland, not far from Frankfurt/ Oder."[77] From the mid-seventeenth century onward, the Jewish

[72] See Marvin J. Heller, *Printing the Talmud: A History of the Individual Treatises Printed from 1700 to 1750*, Leiden, 1999, pp. 179ff. Generally, see Anthony Grafton, "The Jewish Book in Christian Europe: Material Texts and Religious Encounters," in Andrea Sterk and Nina Caputo, eds., *Faithful Narratives. Historians, Religion, and the Challenge of Objectivity*, Ithaca, 2014, pp. 96–114.

[73] On Becmann, see Jöcher, *Allgemeines Gelehrten-Lexicon* (note 64), vol. 1, cols. 904f.; Jürgen Splett, "Becmann," in Lothar Noack and Jürgen Splett, eds., *Bio-Bibliographien Brandenburgischer Gelehrter der Frühen Neuzeit. Mark Brandenburg 1640–1713*, vol. 3, Berlin, 2001, pp. 36–60; as well as Chapter 5.

[74] Johann Christoph Becmann, *Meditationes politicae XXIV*, Frankfurt a.O., 1679. See Horst Dreitzel, "Hobbes-Rezeptionen. Zur politischen Philosophie der frühen Aufklärung in Deutschland," in Hans-Erich Bödeker, ed., *Strukturen der deutschen Frühaufklärung 1680–1720*, Göttingen, 2008, pp. 263–307.

[75] John Selden, *Uxor Ebraica*, Frankfurt a.O., 1673; new edns. 1695 and Wittenberg, 1712.

[76] John Selden, *De successionibus ad leges Ebraeorum in bona functorum*, Frankfurt a.O., 1673; John Selden, *De successione in pontificatum*, Frankfurt a.O., 1673.

[77] Reimund Leicht, "Daniel Ernst Jablonski und die Drucklegungen des Babylonischen Talmud in Frankfurt a.O. and Berlin," in Joachim Bahlcke and Werner Korthaase, eds., *Daniel Ernst Jablonski. Religion, Wissenschaft und Politik um 1700*, Stuttgart, 2008, pp. 491–516, here at p. 499.

communities in Poland were suffering both from rebellions among the Cossacks and from the depredations of the Swedish–Polish war, and therefore a massive migration toward the west had begun. In 1671 with the permission of Elector Friedrich Wilhelm of Brandenburg, ten Austrian Jewish families found a new home in Frankfurt; in 1678 the first Jewish students were admitted to the university. So the new editions of Selden's works and the new Hebrew publications can be seen within the context of this new settlement policy and as an effort to serve a market that was aimed first and foremost at Poland and Eastern Central Europe. Selden's works on rabbinic law, therefore, would have been aimed at least in part at learned Jews. In 1695, shortly before the new edition of the Talmud, Becmann published a new edition of Selden's *De jure naturali* (printed by Schrey), and in 1712 another reprint appeared in Wittenberg (printed by Zimmermann).[78]

Had Becmann also taken Selden as a guide for his own political-juridical-historical works? I do not think so. His *Meditationes politicae* of 1679 and the historical-political dissertations that he sponsored contain no reference to Selden or to rabbinic roots. In this area Becmann started from the assumption of self-preservation as a primary category and then tried to develop an entire social doctrine on that basis.[79] In the next chapter we will see that the early Becmann was indeed among those in Germany who developed in a radical direction and did not shrink from establishing contact with Socinians or from incorporating the ideas of Thomas Hobbes in their own books. But that had little to do with any of the later editions of Selden.

7   The Young Johann Franz Budde

Although Becmann did not integrate his interest in the Talmud into his theories of natural law, and instead pursued them in different contexts and with different persons, things were different in Halle. There in 1694 a new university was founded in which natural law along the lines of Pufendorf was a leading discipline from the very beginning. Christian Thomasius but also Samuel Stryck and others provided instruction along these lines.[80] At

[78] John Selden, *De jure naturali*, Frankfurt a.O., 1695; repr. Wittenberg, 1712.
[79] See Dreitzel, "Hobbes-Rezeptionen" (note 74); Merio Scattola, *Dalla virtu alla scienza* (note 1), pp. 454–461. Becmann, *Meditationes politicae* (note 74); Becmann, *Dissertationum academicarum [. . .] volumen unum*, Frankfurt a.O., 1684.
[80] Hunter, *Rival Enlightenments* (note 1); Detlef Döring, *Pufendorf-Studien*, Berlin, 1992; Hochstrasser, *Natural Law Theories in the Early Enlightenment* (note 5); Notker Hammerstein,

first it might appear that there was no place for Selden in such a program. Although the early career of their younger colleague Johann Franz Budde has attracted almost no scholarly attention, that scholar had started out with a special interest in the Hebrew-Jewish tradition.[81] This culminated in 1702 in his *Introductio ad historiam philosophiae Ebraeorum* ("Introduction to the History of the Philosophy of the Hebrews"), but his interest went back to his student years, at the latest in Jena between 1689 and 1692, and then continued during his short time at the gymnasium in Coburg.[82] In the foreword to his argument with Isaak Abravanel's *Dissertatio de principatu Abimelechi* ("Dissertation on the Rulership of Abimelech") of 1693 (which was an excerpt from Abravanel's biblical commentary, *Perush al nev'im rishonim*), Budde clearly stated that he was delighted to "introduce a Jew to a broader public," but of course not some superstitious or mumbling mystagogue, some supporter of a devious cult, but rather a connoisseur of the political arts.[83] It was of course unusual to redeploy a Hebrew political work from the fifteenth century to the context of late seventeenth-century political theory, but it made some sense in connection with current discussions about the *respublica Hebraeorum*, the republic of the Hebrews.[84] Abravanel had defended God's guidance of history, to be sure, but he had also praised republican constitutions and had emphasized the importance of human wisdom. And he criticized kings when they tried to exercise an unrestrained power.[85] The case of Abimelech, the king of Schechem, from the ninth chapter of the book of Judges, offered Budde a good opportunity to discuss the problems of

Jus und Historie. Ein Beitrag zur Geschichte des historischen Denkens an deutschen Universitäten im späten 17. und 18. Jahrhundert, Göttingen, 1972.

[81] On Budde generally, see Arnold F. Stolzenburg, *Die Theologie des Jo. Franc. Buddeus und des Chr. Matth. Pfaff. Ein Beitrag zur Geschichte der Aufklärung in Deutschland*, Berlin, 1927; Friederike Nüssel, *Bund und Versöhnung. Zur Begründung der Dogmatik bei Johann Franz Buddeus. Forschungen zur systematischen und ökumenischen Theologie*, Göttingen, 1996, as well as Mulsow, *Enlightenment Underground* (note 57), chapter 6.

[82] Johann Franz Budde, *Introductio ad historiam philosophiae Ebraeorum. Accedit dissertatio de haeresi Valentiniana*, Halle, 1702.

[83] Johann Franz Budde, *Prudentiae civilis rabbinicae specimen sive R. Isaaci Abarbanelis dissertatio de principatu Abimelechi observationibus illustrate*, Jena, 1693, fol. A2v sq.: "Hebraeum in scenam prodire jubeo ... ." The book is 310 pp. in octavo. The foreword dedicated the book to Duke Albert of Saxony, Coburg's lord, where Budde at this time was still teaching at the gymnasium before he left for Halle. On Abravanel's printing history in Germany, see Marvin J. Heller, "A Tale of Two Cities: Leipzig, Hamburg, and Don Isaac Abrabanel," in *Further Studies in the Making of the early Hebrew Book*, Leiden, 2013, pp. 153–168. On Abravanel (1437–1508), Benzion Netanyahu, *Don Isaac Abravanel, Statesman & Philosopher*, Philadelphia, 1953.

[84] See Sutcliffe, *Judaism and Enlightenment* (note 54).

[85] Netanyahu, *Abravanel* (note 83), pp. 150 and 186.

monarchy, abuse of power, political prophecies, rebellion, and the fear of God.

Budde pursued this program with determination over the following years. After he was named a professor of moral philosophy at the age of 26 at the newly founded University of Halle in 1693, he composed short treatises such as *Pineas Zelotes sive De iure Zelotarum in gente Hebraea* ("Phinehas the Zealous, or On the Law of the Zealots among the Hebrew People") (1694) and *De eo, quod abominabilis Deo est, ceu charactere legis moralis* ("On That Which Is Abominable to God, or On the Character of the Moral Law") (also 1694).[86] He was trying to blend his interest in the Hebrews with his new duty in Halle to teach natural law as understood by Grotius and Pufendorf. That necessarily brought him into a scholarly area in which John Selden was the dominant guide. Of course Budde did not say so explicitly and continued to cite mainly Grotius, but his choice of the case of the zealot Phinehas (or Pinchas), who killed the Israelite Zimri and his Midianite lover and was rewarded with the immediate approval of God, points directly to the influence of Selden. Grotius had mentioned the problem briefly, to be sure, but Selden was the first to discuss the case thoroughly – in three separate works, *De jure naturali*, *De successione in pontificatum*, and *De Synedriis*.[87] The main purpose of Budde's treatise was to explain why in the case of Phinehas a killing was approved that ran afoul of the prohibition on murder in natural law. Budde cut off any escape that might claim the case had occurred in a state of nature before a state existed; and he criticized Grotius's use of the case to illustrate the deterrent effect of a punishment that supposedly reflected the primitive conditions of an early age. Instead, following Pufendorf, he emphasized the way that human actions were always crucially embedded in the relations of rulership within a society. Whoever was the ruler could also decide that private individuals might be given a special right to kill.[88] But ordinarily no one would do this, and it was clear, according to Budde, that in general it was best that one not introduce such a right. To support this view he cited various cautious statements from rabbinic literature. With respect to the atrocities

---

[86] Johann Franz Budde, *Pineas Zelotes sive De iure Zelotarum in gente Hebraea*, Halle, 1694; Budde, *De eo, quod abominabilis Deo est, ceu charactere legis moralis*, Halle, 1694.

[87] On the biblical Phinheas, see Martin Hengel, *Die Zeloten*, 2nd edn., Leiden, 1976, pp. 153–181. See Toomer, *John Selden* (note 23), pp. 529f.; Jason Rosenblatt, *Renaissance England's Chief Rabbi* (note 23), pp. 112–134.

[88] Budde, *Pineas Zelotes* (note 86), fol. D1r.

committed by religious fanatics, including those of recent times,[89] Budde held that the state was right to forbid such actions. Here Budde was following the basic thrust of Selden, who had also implicitly distanced himself from any "Law of the Zealots." Even if Christ had taken advantage of the *Jus Zelotarum* when he drove the money changers out of the Temple, Budde claimed that that was only because as God he already possessed absolute power over all mankind; in view of that fact, he had actually let them off easily. The real beneficiaries of a zealots' law were the Pharisees, the enemies of Christ. In a word, anyone living in a republic that officially forbade such offenses would be guilty in the highest degree if he acted out of zeal to injure another. Even if he acted from good intentions or was directed by passion, that did not mean that he had acted without guilt.[90] And even though the Jesuits, such as Lessius, Hurtado, Molina, Caramuel, or Baunius, were inclined to construct exceptions to the rules with their casuistic moral teachings, that was not permissible. Here Budde referred to a certain Ludovicus Montaltius, who (though Budde could not yet know this) was none other than Blaise Pascal, whose *Lettres provinciales* had blasted this sort of casuistry.[91] This shows that Budde's treatise, among other things, had a polemical theological point: the law sanctioned by the state was generally and strictly valid and was not to be diluted through casuistry; it did not abolish biblical law but it regulated and moderated it.

In his work "On That Which Is Abominable to God," Budde mainly treated the views of the "scholars among the Hebrews" – most especially Maimonides – concerning moral laws.[92] Whatever was disgraceful or abhorrent to God was forbidden in the strictest sense. That touched on an area of laws that were directly connected to the divine author of the laws. As we have seen in the case of the *Jus Zelotarum*, here the question arose again of how this Jewish – or biblical – tradition might be reconciled with the precepts of natural law.

Budde referred to the Hebrew expression for "abomination" (תועבה), and reminded readers of those passages from Exodus that described the

---

[89] Budde refers on fol. D1v to France and cites de Thou (the beginning of book XL and book XLV of his *Historia sui temporis*, whose first edition had appeared in 1620).

[90] Budde, *Pineas Zelotes* (note 86), fol. D2r.

[91] Ibid., fol. D2r. Budde refers to Epist. VII. pag. 183 sqq. On Pascal's book, see Gérard Ferreyrolles, *Les Provinciales de Pascal*, Paris, 1984; Pierre Cariou, *Pascal et la casuistique*, Paris 1993; Olivier Jouslin, *La campagne des Provinciales de Pascal: étude d'un dialogue polémique*, Clermont-Ferrand, 2007. On casuistry, see also Stefania Tutino, *Shadows of Doubt: Language and Truth in Post-Reformation Catholic Culture*, Oxford, 2014.

[92] Budde, *De eo* (note 86), p. 4.

rejection of Egyptian ideas and rites. John Spencer had adopted Maimonides's interpretation of the ceremonial laws as normative inversions of pagan customs and saw them especially as inversions of Egyptian rules.[93] How could this conclusion be reconciled with the natural knowledge of religion that Grotius (in *De jure belli ac pacis*, Book II, chapter 20, para. 45ff.) conceded to all peoples? Grotius had argued that nations like the Jews would very likely regard "idolaters" as worthy of death. But he thought this conclusion should be softened: punishments should be meted out only to the leaders, and even they should not be punished immediately but only if they committed further offenses.[94] Budde did not regard these mitigations as persuasive, referring here to the critique of Grotius by Caspar Ziegler, whom he may well have heard during his student days in Wittenberg.[95] Starting with Ziegler, therefore, a thin line can be drawn backward to the circle around Boecler, among whom the relations between natural law and religion were first discussed.

Budde's *Pineas Zelotes* objected to Grotius on the grounds that one should not see the Jewish right to kill an idolater as a primitive remnant of legal notions from an age before the state existed; instead he argued that the problem was one of rulership. In following Ziegler's critique of Grotius's "desire for society" (*appetitus societatis*) and "the dictates of right reason" (*dictamen recte rationis*), Budde again set the accents rather differently. Ziegler had insisted – just as Selden had – that *jus naturale* did not arise from human nature but from a foundation in "divine rulership."[96] There was in God both an eternal law and a natural law, which preceded every voluntary action and according to which God could not wish anything that contradicted this law.

This all approximated the fundamental character of Selden's thinking. Budde's colleague in Halle, Christian Thomasius, did not share Budde's interest in Selden even though he did value Ziegler's critique of Grotius. Instead he supported Pufendorf's position, who had indeed adopted

---

[93] John Spencer, *De legibus Hebraeorum ritualibus, et eorum rationibus*, Cambridge, 1685; on Spencer, see Jan Assmann, *Moses the Egyptian: The Memory of Egypt in Western Monotheism*, Cambridge, MA, 1988; Dimitri Levitin "John Spencer's *De Legibus Hebraeorum* (1683–85) and 'Enlightened' Sacred History: A New Interpretation," *Journal of the Warburg and Courtauld Institutes* 76 (2013), pp. 49–92. See also Mulsow, *Enlightenment Underground* (note 57), chapter 2.

[94] Hugo Grotius, *De jure belli ac pacis* (note 4), II, 20, §§ 45 and 47.

[95] Budde, *De eo* (note 86), p. 15. See Caspar Ziegler, *Notae et animadversiones subitariae [...] in Hugonis Grotii De jure belli ac pacis* (note 42).

[96] Schneider, *Justitia universalis* (note 22), p. 146; Friedrich Vollhardt, "Die Grundregel des Naturrechts. Definitionen und Konzepte in der Unterrichts- und Kommentarliteratur der deutschen Aufklärung," in Frank Grunert and Friedrich Vollhardt, eds., *Aufklärung als praktische Philosophie. Werner Schneiders zum 65. Geburtstag*, Tübingen, 1998, pp. 129–147.

Selden's concept of natural obligation, one that rested on a universally valid law, and required a divine legislator – God.[97] But he accused Selden of having failed to test whether the commandments of the Hebrews necessarily agreed with human nature and whether the judgments of the rabbis agreed with common sense.[98] To that extent, as early as 1688 in his *Institutiones jurisprudentiae divinae* ("Instruction in Divine Jurisprudence") – which aimed at separating law from theology – Thomasius had already claimed that Selden's theory did not really belong to natural law, but it did not belong to divine law either, because Selden had reported only the traditions of the rabbis; in contrast, Thomasius (along with Ziegler) urged that one should depend directly on the Bible.[99]

One can understand Budde's early dissertations in Halle as arguments within this range of problems. While Pufendorf thought that Selden had not tested whether the commandments of the Hebrews corresponded properly to human nature, Budde appeared to draw inspiration from this accusation as well as from Ziegler's critique of Grotius, undertaking a project to study those cases in which the Bible explicitly invoked *imperium divinum*. To what extent did they agree with a natural law that was supposed to depend on reason? On the one hand, he was concerned to defend the rigor of biblical law over against Catholic casuistry, but on the other hand to embed that law in the processes of reasonable deliberation that were found among other peoples as well.

This was also true of *De eo, quod abominabilis Deo est* ("On That Which Is Abominable to God"). Laws such as the prohibition of idolatry, magic, pederasty, concubinage, and adultery were, according to Budde, implicitly moral, but even such laws as were not within the narrow range of Noachite laws, such as the prohibition against eating certain animals; or against remarriage for a divorced woman if she had in the meantime been with another man; or against exchanging the clothing of men and women. All of these apparently "positive" laws could be found to some extent among other nations and had, therefore, a claim to being at least partially in accord with natural law. Budde decisively opposed those who rejected the

---

[97] Samuel Pufendorf, *Elementorum jurisprudentiae universalis libri II*, Cambridge,1672, Lib. I, def. 12, § 17. See Hartung, "Gesetz und Obligation" (note 38), p. 399. See also Pufendorf's letter to Boineburg from January 13, 1663, in which he criticizes Selden: Pufendorf, *Briefwechsel*, ed. Detlef Döring (*Gesammelte Werke* vol. 1), Berlin, 1996, p. 27.

[98] Pufendorf, *Specimen controversiarum circa ius naturale ipsi nuper notarum*, Uppsala, 1677. See Albrecht, *Eklektik* (note 36), p. 191.

[99] Christian Thomasius, *Institutiones jurisprudentiae divinae*, Halle and Leipzig, 1688; see Albrecht, *Eklektik* (note 36), p. 192.

laws of the Jewish tradition as if they were merely ceremonial regulations with no moral relevance:

> I conclude from all that has been adduced so far that no Scriptural passage can be found that might prove that a formula of abomination was applied to such sins as violated only the laws that pertained to the Hebrews and contained nothing moral about them.

To the contrary, he now said,

> that therefore the force [of this Hebrew formula of abomination] consists in this: that if someone is charged with a crime, we recognize he has violated a moral law, unless it can be clearly proved that the infraction had never been condemned by the original law of the Jewish people.[100]

The Jewish formula condemning abominations with horror opened up for Budde precisely the problem of *obligatio* that had so vexed the theorists of natural law. It lent credence to the moral relevance of infractions; it was evidence of "divine rule." While Grotius had tried to reduce the relationship between natural law and religion to a sort of rationally minimal religion, Budde in contrast – and in good Lutheran form, but following the idea of *Hebraica veritas*, "Hebrew truth" – defended the continuing relevance of Jewish law.[101]

With that Budde had opened an offensive against his colleagues in Halle and their Selden-influenced version of natural law. When in 1695 Zeitler published a new edition of Vitrarius's textbook on natural law, which was heavily indebted to Grotius, Budde contributed two small pieces as appendices, which could be read as a supplement to Vitrarius: a thirty-page *Historia juris naturalis* ("History of natural law") along with a brief, hundred-page *Synopsis juris naturalis et gentium juxta disciplina Ebraeorum* ("A General View of the Law of Nature and of Nations along with the Teaching of the Hebrews").[102] His *Synopsis* of Selden's work was intended to serve the same purpose as what he had announced in his earlier case histories: a complement and corrective to Grotius's too-minimal connection between religion and law.[103] It made complete sense that,

---

[100] Budde, *De eo* (note 86), § 37.

[101] See ibid., p. 32. On *Hebraica veritas* see Allison Coudert and Jeffrey S. Shoulsen, eds., *Hebraica Veritas? Christian Hebraists and the Study of Judaism in Early Modern Europe*, Philadelphia, 2004.

[102] Johann Franz Budde, *Historia juris naturalis* and *Synopsis juris naturalis et gentium juxta disciplina ebraeorum* – both in Philipp Reinhard Vitriarius, *Institutiones juris naturae et gentium*, Halle, 1695

[103] Ibid., Foreword, p. 3: He said that Selden had provided an excellent survey of the natural law of the Jews; even his digressions were of great importance. Especially because of his language abilities, his work was simply essential: "Quare operae pretium me facturum arbitratus sum, si quae prolixius a Viro summo scripta sunt, in compendium mitterem, et citra ambages, sine cultu,

while Boineburg had only absorbed the foundations presented in Book I of *De jure naturali*, Budde began his overview with Book II, describing only the concrete applications of Jewish natural law.

In his annotations Budde presented Selden's theories in the context of more recent Hebraic studies, and especially in comparison with John Spencer's *De legibus Hebraeorum ritualibus* ("On the Ritual Laws of the Hebrews"), but also with Vossius, Marsham, Pufendorf, Grotius, Ziegler, and others. Thus he was doing something similar to what Beyer had done with Selden's *De diis Syris*, bringing Selden's legal work up to date and placing it in the context of contemporary research. Budde's relationship to Selden became completely clear in his short history of natural law. There he took up the Englishman's thinking when the topic turned to the relationship of natural law to specific traditions:

> Therefore the laws of nature are accordingly clothed and encased, as they say, in the wrappings of the positive laws, and even if they have been obscured and scattered by the ignorance of legislators, they have been dispersed and diffused throughout all communities. At the same time, of course, civil laws and natural laws have been mixed and muddled together, so that it would be the most difficult and even hopeless task to separate them again. That's something recognized by none other than John Selden, the immortal ornament of Britain.[104]

Earlier Samuel Rachel, whom Budde quoted here, had also seen this complex relationship and highlighted it in his commentary on Cicero's *De officiis*. Natural law and positive law could not really be separated; but since the biblical tradition was the decisive one here, the "wrapping" of moral laws found there was especially important, even if one always had to compare them to the traditions of other peoples.[105]

This notion that the laws established by God had been "obscured" and "scattered" ran exactly parallel to late seventeenth-century theories that influenced the history of theology. It was Pierre-Daniel Huet, first and foremost, who influentially asserted that the mythologies of pagan peoples were nothing other than obscure and secondary versions of the original

---

sine ornatu, moralem Hebraeorum doctrinam eruditorum oculis subjicerem, et, ipsius utplurimum Seldeni verbis, exponerem."

[104] Budde, *Historia juris naturalis* (note 102), pp. 7f.

[105] Samuel Rachel, "Prolegomena, in M. Tullii Ciceronis De officiis libros tres, quibus natura honesti, aliaque ad jus natura," in Cicero, *De officiis libri III*, Frankfurt and Kiel, 1668.

Mosaic truth. What jurists were calling the positive laws of nonbiblical peoples were what Huet called the theologies of the pagans.[106]

8 Juridical Skepticism: Georg Michael Heber

But was there any connection between this program of Budde's and actual moral skepticism? If Budde was making up for the harmonizations of natural law with revealed law that Pufendorf had criticized as missing, did that derive partly from the problems Grotius supposedly had with justifying laws and obligations? At first glance, surely not. But as Budde worked away at his self-imposed task, he got caught up in a skepticism that called the whole foundation of law into question. In 1697 Pierre Bayle's *Dictionnaire* appeared, and it contained not only the notorious article on "Pyrrho," which revived epistemological skepticism, but also an article on "Carneades," in which (as we saw earlier with respect to Gundling) Bayle presented all too feebly the refutations of moral skepticism voiced by that ancient Greek.[107] In that article, however, Bayle had not directly attacked the idea of natural law.

Yet of course it was not only Bayle who could write so audaciously. Some provocateurs came from much closer to home. In the first years of the University of Halle, which had existed as a noble academy before it was officially founded as a university on July 12, 1694, Budde's esteemed colleague Christian Thomasius had published a monthly journal during 1693 under the title *Historia sapientiae et stultitiae* ("History of Wisdom and Folly").[108] There he assembled examples of what one might call a "negative history of scholarship" and highlighted highly unusual opinions.[109] Among other things, he sympathized with a generally skeptical attitude because only such a stance could free his contemporaries from their cherished false opinions.[110] For example, his *Historia* published a remarkable little text entitled *Scepticismus juridicus Wittebergensis*

---

[106] See Martin Mulsow, "The Seventeenth-Century Confronts the Gods: Bishop Huet, Moses, and the Pagans," in Martin Mulsow and Asaph Ben-Tov, eds., *Knowledge and Profanation: Transgressing the Boundaries of Religion in Premodern Scholarship*, Leiden, 2019, 159–196; Ralph Häfner, *Götter im Exil. Frühneuzeitliches Dichtungsverständnis im Spannungsfeld christlicher Apologetik und philologischer Kritik (ca. 1590–1736)*, Tübingen, 2003.

[107] Pierre Bayle, *Dictionnaire historique et critique*, Rotterdam, 1697, article on "Carneades."

[108] Christian Thomasius, *Historia sapientiae et stultitiae*, 2 parts, Halle, 1693.

[109] See on this enterprise Merio Scattola, "Geschichte aus dem Negativen. Christian Thomasius und die Historiographie des Fehlers und Vorurteils," in Martin Espenhorst, ed., *Unwissen und Missverständnisse im vormodernen Friedensprozeß*, Gottingen, 2013, pp. 145–166, esp. pp. 161ff.

[110] So too Francesco Tomasoni, *Christian Thomasius. Geist und kulturelle Identität an der Schwelle zur europäischen Aufklärung*, Münster, 2009, p. 83.

("Juridical Skepticism in Wittenberg"). Its author was the Wittenberg jurist Georg Michael Heber.[111] Thomasius introduced Heber's announcement for a course of juridical lectures with these words:

> To this day we have regarded the Pyrrhonists as the most foolish of all. At least that's what our teachers taught – until even this sect found a defender in that most erudite Frenchman, La Mothe le Vayer, who showed that this sect, like the other pagan philosophies, did indeed have its bad aspects, but also its good aspects; and that the Pyrrhonists were extremely astute in that they defended their sect against all others and not without success; and that they were very clever in that their followers often held respected positions in the governments of their polities.[112]

In the previous chapter we have already noted the importance of La Mothe le Vayer for the early Enlightenment in Halle. Thomasius then appended to his expressed admiration for the Frenchman his condemnation of academic estimates of skepticism ever since the Middle Ages:

> And I confess that the common sophism is not only completely inhuman but lacking in serious force as well; for they say that one can dispute with skeptics only with cudgels in order to convict them of being wrong. For then he would either have to admit that he'd been beaten, and thus that indeed something *was true*; or else expose himself to vulgar laughter of everyone by trying to get his attacker punished because it *merely seemed* that he had been beaten.[113]

For Thomasius that was a brutal and uncivilized assessment, one that treated the subtlety of ancient skepticism unfairly:

> For what if the skeptic insisted on his hypothesis and formulated his accusation this way: That it *seems* to him that Titius had beaten him, and it *appeared* that way to other witnesses too, and therefore that a judge should arrange things so that it might *appear* to him as well that the defendant was beaten, e.g., with a stick.[114]

Of course he said that with heavy irony. Thomasius was indicating, however, that there were indeed strategies by which one might circumvent the supposedly practical self-contradictions into which skeptics might be driven – and especially if one expanded the scenario and brought in witnesses. And yet Thomasius did not wish to insist too strenuously.

---

[111] Georg Michael Heber, "Scepticismus juridicus Wittebergensis," in Christian Thomasius, ed., *Historia sapientiae et stultitiae* (note 108), part 2, pp. 124–134; here at p. 126: "His, qui amant bonam mentem."

[112] Thomasius, "Foreword," ibid., p. 124.   [113] Ibid., p. 124.   [114] Ibid., pp. 124f.

He was not committed to the public role of a skeptic; his aim was something different:

> But even if I do not present myself here or anywhere else as belonging to the party of skepticism, there are nonetheless disciplines in which one cannot hope for anything certain, anything beyond the merely probable, and in which we are often forced to admit that the conclusion we seek is not clear. In my view, this is especially the case in jurisprudence, both in Roman Law and in ours. I have given ample reasons for that in my book, *Makeln der Jurisprudenz* ["The Blemishes of Jurisprudence"], which should be published, God willing, at the next book fair.[115]

That was why he felt so close to agreeing with Heber's theses: it was their awareness of the problem. In a profession such as jurisprudence, how does one proceed when there can be no absolute determination of truth or falsehood? Such questions were not welcome because they verged on a prohibited skepticism and exposed one to the suspicion of moral relativism. Thomasius was happy to discover in Heber an ally:

> But because my view does not appear to fit the taste of our times, I cannot refrain from inserting in this journal a recently published notice written by a supporter and friend from Wittenberg, who has avowed the same heresy [i.e., someone who like Thomasius had embraced a degree of skepticism]; and I confess openly that I now hope that in the famous University of Wittenberg liberty is also growing, and that traditional teachings are in retreat; and that that university is starting to cast off the yoke of a more than tyrannical slavery, under which until now it – along with the other universities of Germany – has been groaning. May God grant that the proposal offered by this most expert author should succeed, so that he is not added to the catalog of heretics, in which Wittenberg has already listed so many, [a list which] others create in order to disguise their most impotent passions under the cloak of an ungodly zeal.[116]

Thomasius clearly hoped that Heber would take a leading role in making Wittenberg a reforming university, just as he intended for Halle. Heber's skepticism, he thought, could break through the encrusted structures there. It would take strong measures to escape the "yoke of slavery," as Thomasius dramatically put it.

---

[115] Ibid., p. 125; the book finally appeared in 1695. Christian Thomasius, *De naevis jurisprudentiae Romanae antijustinianiae libri duo*, Halle 1695. See Hammerstein, *Jus und Historie* (note 80), p. 90. Concerning Thomasius's juridical skepticism see also Maximilian Herberger, *Dogmatik. Zur Geschichte von Begriff und Methode in Medizin und Jurisprudenz*, Frankfurt, 1981, pp. 322–327, esp. p. 322f.

[116] Thomasius, "Foreword," in Thomasius, ed., *Historia sapientiae et stultitiae* (note 108), pp. 125f.

Thomasius was making common cause with a radical who used words just as dramatically as his friend in Halle. At the beginning of Heber's programmatic text stood a confession:

> Just as from my earliest days I have followed my nature – I know not under what leadership – and have always shunned the vice of credulity and have not permitted the eyes of my mind to be closed, as if only others should have the glory of seeing and understanding, so now after some use and some confirmation of my views have come to me with the passing years, I have come to a profound understanding that the strength and power of wisdom lies in this: "non temere credere," *to believe nothing blindly.*[117] This makes it necessary that especially in all matters that are far from perception and are constructed in the understanding and judgment, I should not be persuaded by the authority of any man concerning what is true, unless my reason, which I feel within me, should persuade me also . . . .[118]

These were words that could have been spoken just as well by Gabriel Wagner or Theodor Ludwig Lau, radicals in other words, who were fed up with compromises.[119] Heber continued: "and thus my mind cannot accept anything that would provoke in me a sacred horror, such as the pages on which authors of nonsense today are often glorified and praised as 'famous and the most highly famous.' I am so lacking in sympathy for them that I would be grieved to receive the praise of naïve men who are born for slavery."[120] To speak in this manner, saying that all his contemporaries who used the salutation ("most famous") in their letters had been "born for slavery," betrays how deeply discontented he was, how impatient with the conventions of seventeenth-century court society:[121]

> And because I know that men keep most things hidden and buried in darkness so that they cannot be penetrated for any purpose, and that it's not true that they can understand the nature of things with respect to their hidden inner causes,[122] I have concluded that the best way to philosophize

---

[117] The *non temere credere* of Epicharmus, to which Heber was here alluding, was often a slogan of those who criticized prejudice and religion in the early Enlightenment. On Epicharmus, see Lucia Rodríguez-Noriega Guillén, ed., *Epicarmo de Siracusa. Testimonios y Fragmentos,* Oviedo, 1996.

[118] Heber, "Scepticismus juridicus" (note 111), pp. 126f.

[119] On Wagner and Lau, see Mulsow, *Enlightenment Underground* (note 57), passim; Mulsow, *Knowledge Lost* (note 68), chapters 1–3.

[120] Heber, "Scepticismus juridicus" (note 111), p. 127.

[121] See also the letter from Heber to Johann Friedrich Mayer, Wittenberg May 9, 1692, Staats- und Universitätsbibliothek Hamburg, Sup. ep. 82, fol. 32r. See Martin Mulsow, "Literarisches und Philosophisches Feld im Thomasius-Kreis. Einsätze, Umbesetzungen, Strategien," in Manfred Beetz and Herbert Jaumann, eds., *Thomasius im literarischen Feld,* Tübingen, 2003, p. 113.

[122] An allusion to the "qualitates occultas" the hidden causes of nature. On that, see, e.g., August Buck, ed., *Die okkulten Wissenschaften in der Renaissance,* Wiesbaden, 1992.

is that of the Academics and especially that of the Pyrrhonists, who confront every argument with an equally weighty counter-argument, or who also believe that they can find arguments of equal weights on both sides of an issue.[123]

While many men were "born for slavery," according to Heber, others – those who ruled over them – kept "most things hidden." In other words, they dissimulated[124] and invoked the *arcana imperii* ("the secrets of sovereign rule"), by which they justified cunning and deceit over against common people. Here was a man who deeply distrusted the authorities. It is amazing that Heber was not, as Thomasius feared, called to account or punished by university leaders, at least after the publication of his essay. Heber was obviously so much a part of Wittenberg society (although he secretly loathed it) that nothing happened to him. Indeed, in 1692 he was named a syndic of the city, and then mayor, and then in 1695 he became university rector again.[125] His father-in-law had been the recently deceased Johann Andreas Quenstedt, one of the central authorities within Lutheran Orthodoxy.[126] Probably no one dared denigrate such a professor by calling him a freethinker.

Of course, for Heber the price was that he himself had to dissimulate. Reading between the lines of his manifesto, we can sense his huge frustration: "often the vain and profitless professorial chair made me discontent."[127] His choice of words reveal how disgusted he was with his colleagues, who showed off their lofty titles, names, and positions: "It seems that you'd like to overwhelm me by citing your authorities, while I want to be persuaded by reason; no matter what authorities these parasites bring to you, I will not give in to your [authorities,] and it's not fitting that I should give in to them."[128] But beyond such short outbursts of discontent, Heber was restrained. He did not accept the role

---

[123] Heber, "Scepticismus juridicus" (note 111), p. 127.

[124] On the "political" behavior of simulation and dissimulation in the seventeenth century, see, e.g., Ursula Geitner, *Die Sprache der Verstellung. Studien zum rhetorischen und anthropologischen Wissen im 17. und 18. Jahrhundert*, Tübingen, 1992.

[125] See Johann Heinrich Zedler, *Grosses vollständiges Universal-Lexicon*, 68 vols., Halle and Leipzig, 1732–1754, vol. 12, cols. 1024f.

[126] On Quenstedt see Jörg Baur, *Die Vernunft zwischen Ontologie und Evangelium. Eine Untersuchung zur Theologie Johann Andreas Quenstedts*, Gütersloh, 1962; Michael Coors, *Scriptura efficax. Die biblisch-dogmatische Grundlegung des theologischen Systems bei Johann Andreas Quenstedt. Ein dogmatischer Beitrag zu Theorie und Auslegung des biblischen Kanons als Heiliger Schrift*, Göttingen, 2009.

[127] Heber, "Scepticismus juridicus" (note 111), pp. 127f. Heber was also quoting Juvenal, Sat. VII, 202.

[128] Heber, "Scepticismus juridicus" (note 111), p. 130.

urged upon him by Christian Thomasius: that he should become the
reformer and early Enlightener of the University of Wittenberg. It was
rumored, however, that he was indeed busying himself not just with
juridical matters but increasingly with theological issues,[129] though he
published none of these thoughts. He was clearly writing just for his
desk drawer.

And what lay concealed in that drawer? I have earlier voiced the
suspicion that Heber may have written the *Symbolum sapientiae*, in which
an extreme skepticism was deployed first against religion but then against
natural law as well.[130] I quoted this last part of the work under its title, *De
origine mali* ("On the Origin of Evil"). Down to today, however, no
documents or letters have surfaced that might prove this suspicion, and
so it remains speculative. And yet the profile of Heber as we can see from
his *Scepticismus juridicus Wittebergensis* would comport very well with what
we would expect of the author of the *Symbolum*: a German jurist around
1690, who got into theological topics but trusted only in his reason; a
Pyrrhonist, who analyzed society coolly in terms of its power relationships
and its superstitions, who understood such complex juridical constructions
as the "proof of presumptions" (i.e., legal proof of what seems merely
probable), and who had adopted a life of dissimulation. If so, we would
then have another case in which an atheistical clandestine work had its
origins in the very center of Lutheran Orthodoxy. In Hamburg it was the
Latin treatise *De tribus impostoribus*, which emerged from the circle around
the family of Pastor Müller (see chapter 3 of *Enlightenment Underground*);
here it would be the *Symbolum sapientiae*, which might have emerged from
the circle of the Wittenberg family of Pastor Quenstedt.

In any case, the antipedantry, critique of authority, and skepticism were
the very same qualities that brought Heber into contact with the young
Christian Thomasius. In his *Scepticismus juridicus Wittebergensis*, Heber
also revealed the influence of the arguments surrounding the *nouveaux
pyrrhoniens* from France. Heber, after all, was interested in the hermeneutic problem of ambiguity and uncertainty in legal rules,[131] but especially in

---

[129] Johann Samuel Ersch and Johann Gottfried Gruber, *Allgemeine Encyclopädie der Wissenschaften
und Künste*, Leipzig, 1850, Sect. II, Part 3, p. 302.

[130] See Mulsow, *Enlightenment Underground* (note 57), chapter 4; and Winfried Schröder, "Il contesto
storico, la datazione, gli autori e l'influenza su pensiero dell' epoca," in *Cymbalum mundi sive
Symbolum sapientiae*, critical edition, ed. Guido Canziani, Winfried Schröder and Francisco Socas,
Milan, 2000, pp. 9–35, here at pp. 26f.

[131] See Georg Michael Heber, *In ambiguarum legum interpretatione criterium veritatis non dari*,
Wittenberg, 1700.

the irreducible subjectivity of opposing parties who disagree about a legal text.[132] His answer was a plea for withholding judgment in such cases because – here was Heber's basic idea – they were to be treated like the *isotheneia* of the skeptics, for whom one argument was always met with an opposite of equal weight. But he always distanced himself from the radical skepticism about reason that we find in the Jesuit François Veron and balanced against it the moderate skepticism of the Huguenot Jean Daillé, who had emphasized that logical conclusions were not really the problem; more difficult was the choice of where to begin.[133] Starting points were always subjective and determined by personal preferences and temperaments,[134] because in epistemology Heber was a follower of Gassendi.[135] Subjective views, for him, rested finally on decisions, and the unflinching confusion of irrational decisions with the authority of truth was what Heber called "enthusiasm," drawing an analogy to the favorite problem of contemporary Wittenberg Lutheran theology:[136]

> Here I would wish that you were sure of your case, and that you decided it on the basis of the weightier evidence, [which is] your "movement," your inclination, the propensity of your mind, or in a word, Enthusiasm; that is, the naked fact for which you can give no reason. This criterion is of course uncertain and therefore easily avoided by someone else who is not stimulated by the enthusiasm that moves you. But if you continue to maintain that you still, nevertheless, no matter what you do, simply have to agree with this side more than the other – then I accuse your ignorance and the wicked habit in which you have acknowledged your own guilt. And just as you may accustom your intellect to this acceptance of unknown and obscure matters, in order to give someone assurance of your agreement, you should also suspend your judgment in unexamined matters, even though now you regularly collapse as soon as something happens that

[132] Heber, "Scepticismus juridicus" (note 111), p. 132: "cum pleraque erunt dicta, quae utrinque afferri possunt . . . ."

[133] Ibid., pp. 128f. See Jean Daillé, *La Foy fondée sur les Saintes Escritures: contre les nouvelles methodistes*, 2nd cdn., Charenton, 1661; on that Richard H. Popkin, *The History of Scepticism from Erasmus to Spinoza*, Berkeley, 1979, p. 74. Barbeyrac's conception of morally criticizing the Church Fathers flowed from Daillé's description of the subjectivist dogmatic views of the Church Fathers, which derived from their moral disposition.

[134] Decisive here for Heber was clearly the debate that arose after the reception of Galen's *Quod animi mores temperamentum corporis sequuntur* (i.e., Huarte, Bodin, La Mothe le Vayer among others). See also note 12.

[135] Heber, "Scepticismus juridicus" (note 111), pp. 129f. See Pierre Gassendi, *Exercitationes paradoxicae adversus Aristoteleos*, Grenoble 1624. See also Olivier Bloch, *La philosophie de Gassendi*, The Hague, 1971; Tullio Gregory, *Scetticismo ed empirismo. Studio su Gassendi*, Bari, 1961; Popkin, *The History of Scepticism* (note 134), pp. 99ff

[136] For the Wittenberg attitude toward the problem of enthusiasm, see, e.g., Valentin Ernst Löscher, *Praenotiones theologicae*, Wittenberg, 1713.

moves your intellect through some appearance of truth, not by reason but from a blind force.[137]

Enthusiasm was for Heber – as it was for the theologians, with whom he here tried to ally himself – an irrational impulse that came from within and could have damaging effects. One had to restrain it, just as the Wittenberg theologians hoped to restrain all sorts of spiritualist currents that led believers to claim that they were communicating directly with God.

Heber tried to fend off the possibility of practical indifferentism, however, by holding that the maxims urging people to withhold judgment in these cases were valid only for judges, and not for a statesmen who had to act quickly and could not pause to split hairs.[138]

Here was a fairly radical skepticism, which, as I have said, seems to have been derived from the skeptical-libertine traditions of France. How can we explain that? Let us look a bit more closely at Heber's biography. He had been born in Wittenberg in 1652 and studied both there and in Leipzig. Then in the late 1670s and early 1680s[139] Heber was in Paris, where he associated with the social circle around Henri Justel and Gilles Menage. Justel was a Calvinist, a jurist and historian, who formed a famous group around himself in these years, one that Leibniz also frequented in 1673.[140] David Ancillon, who became a preacher near the end of his life in the Berlin "Refuge" for Huguenot exiles, was at that time one of Justel's best friends and young assistants. Heber's second Parisian "teacher," the literary figure and historian of language, Menage, was a Catholic, to be sure, but he was an heir to the *libertinage érudit* of the first half of that century, and a transmitter of the skeptical ideas of La Mothe le Vayer and Gassendi.[141] In 1664, Menage had written an amusing work, *Amoenitates juris civilis* ("Delights of the Civil Law"), and so, like Justel, he was, for the young

---

[137] Heber, "Scepticismus juridicus" (note 111), p. 131.   [138] Ibid., pp. 132f.

[139] These estimates of timing result from the fact that Heber was born in 1652 and therefore took his peregrinatio at about 25 years of age (i.e., starting around 1677). Tradition suggests that he had a "long" stay with Menage and Justel, and also sojourned in Holland and England. He must have returned no later than 1683, when Heber began to publish as a professor in Wittenberg.

[140] On Justel see Harcourt Brown, "Un cosmopolite du grand siècle: Henri Justel," *Bulletin de la Société de l'histoire du protestantisme français: études, documents, chronique littéraire* (1933), pp. 187–201.

[141] Concerning Menage, see Elvire Samfiresco, *Ménage polémiste, philologue, poète*, Paris, 1902; further, Lea Caminiti Pennarola, "La correspondance Ménage–Huet, un dialogue à distance," in Suzanne Guellouz, ed., *Pierre Daniel Huet (1630–1721). Actes du colloque de Caen (12–13 nov. 1993)*, Seattle and Tübingen, PFSCL 94 (= Biblio 17, n° 83), pp. 141–154. See esp. *Menagiana, ou les bons mots, les pensées critiques, historiques, morales et d'Erudition de Monsieur Ménage, recueillies par ses amies*, 4 vols., Paris, 1715.

civil lawyer Heber, a model for a literary and learned but unpedantic style of jurisprudence.[142]

If we take Heber's biography into account, his intellectual origins, it is completely reasonable to notice the parallels between the *Scepticismus juridicus* and the skeptical-libertine *Symbolum sapientiae*. Even if the question of authorship is still unsettled, we ought to recognize the parallels. For if we read Heber's Wittenberg text in the light of the *Symbolum*, then his phrase about the "sinews and power of the truth"[143] sounds like a reference to that *sapientia* which delivers its confession in the *Symbolum sapientiae*. And then one reads with some astonishment in the *Scepticismus juridicus* a confession of a sort of "atheism of the wise (or of the prudent)" (*Atheismum prudentum*). In a long and complicated sentence Heber expressed a hope:

> Because of the vices of our age things have gotten so bad that those who have a "strong mind" in comparison with others and believe that they therefore overflow [with wisdom] now offer convoluted and ridiculous conclusions and an abundance of words (which actually make their case weaker) and have learned to drive GOD and God's providence out of the world; thus they have been led through an *Atheism of Fools* into denying GOD and have become corrupt in the judgment of the Holy Spirit – [but] dear fellow scholars, may the entrance to an *Atheism of the Prudent* be opened to you.[144]

Here the Wittenberg professor distanced himself from would-be *esprits forts*, and he rejected their stupid (i.e., dogmatic) atheism. That put him in complete agreement with the Wittenberg consensus. But his sentence goes on: Heber hoped that students would find their way to an *atheismum prudentum*. That was of course an unusual and, at first glance, indeed a radical statement. What was an *atheismus prudentum* if it stood in contrast to an *atheism stultorum* (an "atheism of fools")? Was it not a reference to the *religio prudentum*, the boogeyman that circulated virally among Orthodox Lutherans? Would "atheismus prudentum" therefore represent the lack of faith among skeptics? At this point he merely alluded to this provocative idea, one that only a few readers may have understood. And then he quickly steered back into safer waters and offered a harmless interpretation of the concept: "This is an injunction not to venerate garlic

---

[142] Gilles Menage, *Amoenitates juris civilis*, Frankfurt and Leipzig, 1680 (first published in 1668).
[143] See note 118: "nervos atque artus sapientiae."
[144] Heber, "Scepticismus juridicus" (note 111), pp. 133f.

and onion as gods, meaning your professors, whether they wish to be called Dogmatics or Axiomatics, and not to regard the disgusting inventions of their minds as sacred teachings and oracles . . . ."[145] Thus the wise "denial of God" was now supposedly nothing more than a rejection of juridical authorities for claiming to be equal to God. Heber was playing again, as in the case of "enthusiasm," on the keyboard of Wittenberg semantics. And yet for a neutral reader the real point here could not be that such opposition to university authorities was a sort of "atheism." That would only make sense if Heber were here referring in a positive manner to a skeptical as opposed to a dogmatic atheism of the sort we find in the *Symbolum sapientiae* – an atheism that he identified as a *religio prudentum*. He continued his sentence this way:

> [students should] rather to accustom themselves to withholding their agreement from what they have not deeply investigated, concerning which the poet has spoken so truly:
>
> > *If you try to conquer the Uncertain*
> > *With reason, you do nothing more*
> > *Than if you spend your energy going mad with reason.*[146]
>
> I have surely proved that the [real] *doctores* are not those who are decorated with laurels or who wear a doctor's hat (for children can have this badge in common with adults, and fools with the wise), but all those who think reasonably and who can fully use that faculty that everyone is inwardly aware of possessing, and that is called reason, – ultimately they are the ones who deserve the name [of *doctores*].[147]

Thus Heber rescued himself with a general encouragement to his students that they should use their reason and not judge prematurely if they were not certain. And yet if that is all that the *Scepticus juridicus* was aiming at, he could surely have chosen a simpler way to say it.

[145] Ibid. For *religio prudentum* see Mulsow, *Enlightenment Underground* (note 57), chapter 7.

[146] Terence, *Eunuchus* I, I, 14, quoted by Cicero in his *Tusculan Disputations* IV, (35) 76: "Ratione certa facere, nihilo plus agas, / Quam si des operam, ut cum ratione insanias" ("if you expect to render these things, *naturally* uncertain, certain by dint of reason, you wouldn't effect it a bit the more than if you were to use your endeavors to be mad with reason"]. From *The Comedies of Terence*, "The Eunuch," tr. Henry Thomas Riley, New York, 1896, Act I, scene 1, l. 71. See Cicero, *Tusculan Disputations*, IV, 35: "The man who seeks to fix / These restless feelings, and to subjugate / Them to some regular law, is just as wise / As one who'd try to lay down rules by which/ Men should go mad." Excerpt from Marcus Tullius Cicero, *Cicero's Tusculan Disputations / Also, Treatises On The Nature Of The Gods, And On The Commonwealth*, tr. C. D. Yonge, New York, 1877.

[147] Heber, "Scepticismus juridicus" (note 111), p. 134.

9   The Critique of Grotius by Gassendi and Hobbes

Let us push the search for parallels further, looking especially at the foundations of law. When Heber in his manifesto asks: "In matters of justice and injustice, if we want to disregard the authority and will of the legislator, what do we actually have that we can securely hold onto and rely on with certainty?"[148] One could answer this from the *Symbolum* that there simply is no foundation of any sort for a universal law that would hold for all mankind. Let us read the text of Heber's manifesto again; he complains that the texts of laws contain absolutely no sentences that could be asserted sensibly because the concepts contained in them are unclear and fuzzy:

> What follows, I think, is not that I regard reason as a fallible teacher for mankind or that I believe that reason always fails because it sometimes fails, as the Pyrrhonists think, and whom I here oppose; but that I regard the principles that are drawn from reason alone as never so undeniable, evident, and so clearly and distinctly perceived that they cannot have their terrifying opposite as a constant companion.[149]

By referring to the "terrifying opposite" Heber could only have meant that the law of nature and of reason could perhaps have no justification at all. Reason made "a mistake in trying to establish the principle and the foundation [of natural law]."[150] The "principle" of natural law – the reader probably has to add – such as "sociality" or the "care of society," was founded on error. In 1634 Jean Daillé had accused the "new fanatics of method" of trying to support the structure of the Christian faith with a fallible reason; and that is just what Heber was implicitly criticizing in his juridical colleagues in Wittenberg, such as Caspar Ziegler:

> One reason, which might appear to one person to be of no weight at all can appear to another to play an important role with the full appearance of truth; but also, in contrast, what might seem to be of great importance to one person may seem to someone else as no more than a whim. Therefore men prove and like contradictory things; and therefore instead of seeing the variation of minds, we think the shapes of things vary; and even the fundamentals and principles on which everything else rests, as if on columns – no matter how shaky or rotten – are taken in this manner or that manner according to the property of the minds, so that the most one can say is that they seem good and just to one person, but not what is truly so according to its own nature ....[151]

---

[148] Ibid., p. 130.   [149] Ibid., pp. 128f.   [150] Ibid., p. 129.   [151] Ibid., pp. 129f.

This was a rather different line of argument from that followed by the *Symbolum*. There it was not so much the sensualist finding that different human starting points for theorizing led to different theoretical constructions, but a direct denial of natural law of the sort that Grotius had designed. The reason for the difference may lie in the fact that the *Scepticus juridicus Wittebergensis* was pursuing the somewhat less shocking purpose of teaching students to be cautious in their judgments. It did not intend a fundamental and thoroughly argued destruction of natural law.

But that intention was exactly what the *Symbolum sapientiae* contained, in a manner that followed Gassendi and Hobbes. In Gassendi, to be sure, one finds only a concealed dismissal of Grotius, concealed in that Gassendi did not actually quote Grotius.[152] For the "Epicurean" efforts to base law on individualist and utilitarian principles in the seventeenth century, it was crucial to argue against Grotius and to deny the idea of a "second nature" – as we explained earlier – and to dispense with it. And yet Gassendi worked with the concepts of a first and second nature and folded it into the model of *natura pura* ("pure nature"). Thus his thinking was complex and not easily categorized. When he examined the Hermarchos fragments that Porphyry had handed down,[153] which described the origins of legal rules among early human beings, Gassendi explicitly used the terminology of "the state of pure nature" (*status naturae purae*) so that, if one considered it, one could detect the foundations of the "first law of nature" (*ius naturae primarium*).[154] Here there was as yet no mention of the "desire for sociality." Human beings at first simply pursued their needs and had the wisdom – as Telesio described it – to see that cooperating with one another would make it easier to fulfill their needs.[155] Yet Gassendi quickly downgraded this hypothetical construction by conceding that society, as it actually was, had known both cooperation or even conventionality from the beginning:

> So whatever one makes of the assumption or fiction of a state [of nature], in which Epicurus or others suppose that the first men lived: The society of men as such appears actually to have been like its origin, i.e., ancient; and not only like that in which animals are communal among themselves but also in the manner in which human beings, to the extent that they are intelligent and possessed of reason, recognize that there can be no secure

---

[152] See Paganini, "Épicurisme et philosophie" (note 13), pp. 26ff

[153] Porphyrios, *De abstinentia* 1.71–9.4 and 1.10.1–12.7; German tr. in Arthur A. Long and David N. Sedley, *Die hellenistischen Philosophen: Texte und Kommentare*, Stuttgart, 2000, pp. 150–154.

[154] Gassendi, "Ethica" (note 13), pp. 794f.   [155] See ibid., p. 795a.

society among themselves if they are not stabilized by conventions and mutual contracts.[156]

So even the earliest men lived in societies. They always recognized the utility of mutual support and combined in contractual communities. Gassendi disagreed with Hobbes's description in *De cive* of a constitutive act undertaken by isolated and aggressive early men, in which they founded a state.[157] Although Gassendi was obviously both attracted to and repelled by this vision, he emphasized instead that sociality had existed from the very beginnings of history. It was only hypothetically that one might reconstruct the foundations of law from mere considerations of utility. And yet as opposed to Grotius, Gassendi did insist on the utilitarian roots of law. Even the *ius naturae secondarium* ("the secondary law of nature") was nothing really new:

> Because in addition from these same contracts and from the origin of society, this newly granted capacity takes hold as soon as it feels secure against the force of others, the law – to the extent it depends on contracts – can be called secondary . . . It can, however, be called natural law even if it's secondary because it too is from nature and in conformity with [nature's] intention. And it demands no other nature than that by which everything uses what it needs and what is useful to it, according to the possibilities presented to it. And that cannot succeed if contracts are not entered into.[158]

That was his critique of Grotius: there was no additional "second nature" when the step toward a secondary natural law was taken. Gassendi did not assume some drive for sociability or any independent reason that would support such a drive; instead, he merely extended the calculation of utility belonging to the "first nature," using contracts to arrive at the upper area of the "secondary."

The minimalism of Thomas Hobbes was blunter and simpler than that of Gassendi. Whereas the latter preserved at least the terminology of a higher region of ethics, Hobbes championed the *natura pura* construct as a simple, logical and gradual set of different stages beginning with isolated and hostile beings, on the one hand, to social subjects of the law, on the other. So a secondary law of nature was no longer necessary.

---

[156] Ibid. (directly following the previous quotation).

[157] Thomas Hobbes, *Elementorum Philosophiae sectio tertia, De cive*, Paris, 1642; in the second edition of *De cive*, Hobbes was reacting in part to Gassendi's reaccentuations. See Paganini, "Hobbes, Gassendi, e le De cive" (note 13); Bernd Ludwig, *Die Wiederentdeckung des Epikureischen Naturrechts: Zu Thomas Hobbes" philosophischer Entwicklung von De cive zum Leviathan im Pariser Exil 1640–1651*, Frankfurt, 1998.

[158] Gassendi, "Ethica" (note 13), p. 795a.

Self-preservation (*conservatio sui*) was a sufficient principle to account for the portion of ethics and law that were relevant to the state.

10   The Critique of Grotius in the *Symbolum sapientiae*

Whoever he was, the author of the *Symbolum sapientiae* knew the works of Gassendi and Hobbes. But he also had an education in the literature of juridical classics, which he reinterpreted for a radically minimalist understanding of law. One could say that his "Epicureanism" originated in a radicalizing inversion of the principles of Ulpian against Grotius.[159] The principle encapsulated in the statement, "Natural law is what nature has taught all the beasts," had been recognized ever since the sixteenth century[160] as a weakening of the idea of law, because it applied to beasts as well as men. If that was natural law, one could no longer talk about a law of reason, for beasts have no laws.[161] The only natural sociality, according to the *Symbolum*, was the domestic, which mankind shared with beasts.

On this basis, the author attacked Grotius's argument in his "Prolegomena" to *De jure belli ac pacis*, saying: "Grotius asserted that the drive for sociality, which dwells in the human species, necessarily implies a law, because no society can survive without law. Therefore he thinks that nature forbids everything that would lead to the destruction of human society."

But against that one could register various objections:

> First, one certainly cannot find among mankind a drive to cultivate a community that would include the whole human species without favoring smaller communities, such as polities or cities. There's no way to prove such a thing. Secondly, nature clearly knows only the domestic community consisting of the married partners (who constitute it) and their children until they reach the age of maturity, which makes it clear that human beings as well as beasts have the same sort of universal drive for community.

Any striving for community therefore, for men as well as beasts, was confined to the narrowest circle.

---

[159] See note 18. See also Martin Mulsow, Review of Merio Scattola, "Das Naturrecht vor dem Naturrecht," *Ius Commune. Zeitschrift für Europäische Rechtsgeschichte* 28 (2001), pp. 440–444. I am grateful to Horst Dreitzel for pointing to the possible importance of Ulpian for this text.

[160] See Merio Scattola, *Das Naturrecht vor dem Naturrecht. Zur Geschichte des "ius naturae" im 16. Jahrhundert*, Tübingen, 1999, pp. 153f. and 160ff.

[161] For the following I am citing Section IV of the *Symbolum sapientiae* (note 130), entitled "De origine boni et mali ex doctrina Hobbesii, ubi de origine societatum," § 15, p. 276.

But, thirdly, no law derives from this community, and from it flows no special capacity restricted only to men, for after all animals also care for their community and yet they have no laws. But if, fourthly, mankind had maintained themselves in this state of nature and had remained in this natural community, content with their fate and only its fruits, if they had not striven for possessions and dominion over things, they would have had no need for laws, but would have been able to cultivate their domestic society in the same peace as beasts have always done and continue to do.

Striving for possessions and dominion is here interpreted as the fall into sin, as it was later in Rousseau, a fall that had led men out of the restricted society of the natural condition. Laws became necessary only because of this nascent inequality, which the laws sustained. So in this view laws maintain dominion. "But when, fifthly, men overstepped the bounds of their domestic community, excluding outsiders from the common possession of things seeking to rule over their neighbors, they began to murder, quarrel, and wage wars. This caused many from the same family or the same clan to come together and in the end to develop into nationalities and peoples." Inequality, the text suggests, produced war, and from war came the formation of larger communities, which by banding together could feel safer – as Hobbes also argued, but not with the purpose of avoiding a war of all against all, but with a view to avoiding an external war against some other community. "Therefore, sixthly, this society derives not from nature but from contract and from fear; the laws established to protect a community came not from the will of God but from agreement and they apply not to all men but only to that state (*rempublicam*), or more specifically to that partner to the contract." Of course one might argue that this contractual community could still develop into an all-encompassing world community. But the author cut off this move:

> From all this, eighthly,[162] it is clear that there is no common or universal community among these various societies and citizenries. Not by nature because aside from the domestic society [i.e., the family] there is no other [society] known to nature; and not contractually because there is no such agreement among peoples. And therefore, ninthly, there is by nature no general law among nations, for where a society ends, there too ends any reason for such an engagement. All men, however, live without law, trusting in their natural instinct, which does not permit anyone to injure his own kind, so that animals of the same kind are safe amongst themselves.[163]

---

[162] Number seven was intentionally skipped.   [163] "De origine" (note 161), § 10, pp. 271ff.

That was a soberingly pessimistic assessment, a total denial of any sort of law of nature or of nations. Thus the skeptical Carneades, whom Grotius had chosen as his opponent, had arisen again in the 1690s in the author of the *Symbolum sapientiae.*

11   Budde Strikes Back: *Dissertatio de scepticismo morali*

These circumstances prompt many questions. If we assume that the author of the *Symbolum* really was Wittenberg's Professor Heber, had Christian Thomasius read his clandestine treatise? Did their friendship go so far that Heber explained his hidden references in his *Scepticus juridicus Wittebergensis* and inform him of his atheistical and morally skeptical views? We do not know. It is not probable because Thomasius, who did value healthy provocations, would have thought that such views went much too far. His later treatment of Theodor Ludwig Lau shows clearly where his limits lay – limits that, as an early Enlightener from Halle, he did not wish to transgress.[164] But we cannot overlook an irony: that the *Symbolum* for its part clearly was working through specific proposals of Thomasius, especially from his *Introductio ad philosophiam aulicam* of 1688.[165]

Did Budde know the *Symbolum sapientiae*? Nothing is known about that, and yet in 1698 in a dissertation he did take on the problem of moral skepticism directly.[166] We can do little more than guess about how intensively such a skepticism was discussed among students, whether it was stimulated by Bayle, Le Mothe le Vayer, Hobbes, or even by unpublished theses along the lines of the *Symbolum.* Whatever the stimulus, clearly the resulting uncertainty was strong enough that Professor Budde felt he had to take a stand on this topic. Budde had already established himself as an expert in moral philosophy, and in the preceding year, in 1697, he published a first sketch of his own practical philosophy, under the title of *Elementa philosophiae practicae.*[167] That gave him a firm base from which to confront the skeptical challenge. Budde began with the statement:

[164] Günter Gawlick, "Thomasius und die Denkfreiheit," in Werner Schneiders, ed., *Christian Thomasius 1655–1728*, Hamburg, 1989, pp. 256–274.
[165] *Symbolum sapentiae* (note 130), "Introduzione," p. 25.
[166] Johann Franz Budde (praes.) / Joachim Heinrich Engelbrecht (resp.), *Exercitatio historico-critica de scepticismo morali*, Halle, 1698.
[167] Johann Franz Budde, *Elementa philosophiae practicae*, Halle, 1697.

> There is, however, no more difficult and more prominent opponent than
> the skeptics, devious and slippery men who aim to undermine every
> certainty and every sort of knowledge and to tear down and demolish all
> the foundations on which divine and human wisdom rests.[168]

He built his treatise in scholastic manner, beginning with the various sorts
of skepticism that needed to be distinguished (§ 2), turning then to the
ancients (§ 3), and reaching the modern period with figures such as
Pyrrhonists like La Mothe le Vayer (§ 4), but then treating also the
controversial philosophers Hobbes and Spinoza (§ 5). According to
Budde, skepticism could be found in the area of natural philosophy if
one thought of figures such as Claude Berigard or Sebastien Basson (§ 6),
but then also of course in moral philosophy. As in natural philosophy so
too moral skepticism could appear in different forms, some open but
others surreptitious (§ 7). The main topic was the so-called ἐποχή, that
withholding of judgment that placed one's mind in a condition of equa-
nimity seen as crucial to true felicity (§ 8). That brought Budde to his
central point (§ 9): that according to Pyrrho (as Diogenes Laertius
reported) in nature there was no justice. "He denied that anything was
honourable or dishonourable, just or unjust. And so, universally, he held
that nothing really exists, but that custom and convention govern human
action ... ."[169] Budde also cited Carneades – following Lactantius, who
ascribed these words to him:

> For utility men established laws that varied according to customs, and
> thereafter they changed them often. There was no natural law. Both men
> and all other living beings, had by nature only the drive for what was useful.
> And so there is either no justice or, if there is such a thing, it is the highest
> folly because concern for the advantage of others only hurts oneself.[170]

These were words that Grotius too had quoted in his "Prolegomena."

Budde continued with Epicurus whose teachings he introduced with a
quotation from the Epicurean Horace (§ 10), and the followers of
Epicurus such as Gassendi, who had softened (*emollire*) his doctrine of
utility as the foundation of law but did manage to preserve it in the end
(§ 11). An important sideline of the debate over skepticism was the
question of whether in the realm of morality there were actual proofs or
only probabilities. One star witness on this question was none other than

---

[168] Budde (praes.) / Engelbrecht (resp.), *De scepticismo morali* (note 166), § 1.
[169] Diogenes Laertius IX 61; the translation adapts R. D. Hicks, *Lives of Eminent Philosophers*, New
York, 1925, IX, 61 (p. 474).
[170] Budde, *De scepticismo morali* (note 166), § 9. Cf. Lactantius, *Divinae institutiones* V, 15.

Aristotle, and Budde pointed out that even Grotius had followed Aristotle, when he said in Book II of *De jure belli ac pacis*:

> What Aristotle wrote is perfectly true, that certainty is not to be found in moral questions to the same degree as in mathematical science. This comes from the fact that mathematical science completely separates forms from substance, and that the forms themselves are generally such that between two of them there is no intermediate form, just as there is no mean between a straight and a curved line.[171]

Budde's dissertation thus ran increasingly toward the problems that Grotius himself had raised – but with sharp criticisms aimed at Grotius too. Budde hoped to defend certitude in morality and law, but he accused the opponents of the skeptics, such as Grotius, of choosing a path that would itself ultimately lead to moral skepticism, especially if they argued on the basis of *consensus gentium* ("the agreement of all nations").[172] We have already seen that in 1694, when Budde was writing his dissertation, *Pineas Zelotes sive De iure Zelotarum*, he was already relying on "Ludovicus Montaltus" (i.e., Pascal in his *Lettres Provinciales*) in order to attack moral thought that depended on probabilities. He relied on him again here.[173] He warned against the dangerous consequences of probabilism in Thomism, which he thought undermined morality. This was a point where Budde could join in the battle of his colleague Thomasius against "scholasticism."

There were, according to Budde, also positive counter-examples. He named John Selden and other "most excellent men" (*praestantissimi viri*), who had proposed principles, but their principles all brought along their own uncertainties. He especially feared that emphasizing the natural instinct of self-preservation made the distinction between man and animal so fuzzy that a naturalistic position was almost unavoidable.[174] On the other hand Budde did not want to go over to the other side, namely to those who ascribed everything to the will of God. We will consider that in a moment, for this disagreement constituted a central part of Budde's concern. Here he referred just briefly and approvingly to Pierre de Villemandy, who the previous year had published a work entitled *Scepticismus debellatus* ("Skepticism Conquered").[175] But Budde also

---

[171] Budde, *De scepticismo morali* (note 166), § 12; Grotius, *De jure belli ac pacis* (note 4), II, XXIII, § 1. [Translator's note: the translation uses the translation by Francis W. Kelsey et al., Oxford, 1925; updated edn., Lonang Institute, 2005.]

[172] Budde, *De scepticismo morali* (note 166), § 13.   [173] Ibid., § 14.   [174] Ibid., § 15.

[175] Pierre de Villemandy, *Scepticismus debellatus seu humanae cognitionis ratio: ab imis redicibus explicata; eiusdem certitudo adversus Scepticos quosque veteres ac novos invicte asserta; facilis ac tuta*

wanted to avoid endorsing the claim that the highest justification for law
lay in the human conscience, either because it was supposedly infallible or
because one was obliged to follow even an erroneous conscience.[176] "None
of these can be totally acquitted of skepticism as we will soon see."[177]

It slowly becomes clear that Budde was pursuing an extreme strategy.
He was looking for implicitly skeptical consequences in many different
philosophical positions, even in those which did not see themselves as
skeptical at all but were concerned to justify morality. In doing so he was
imitating those Lutheran Orthodox "manufacturers of heresy"
(*Ketzermacher*) who sniffed out the implicit atheism in every sort of
theological position. Under these conditions where could one find firm
ground? Before Budde addressed that, he discussed an "even more hidden"
form of skepticism that lay beyond theory. Even if people seemed to hold
opinions that were far from skepticism, they could still exhibit it in their
behavior, in daily life. Such persons included, for example, the ambitious
who were always seeking something new, always seeking to argue, and
showing a desire for the obscure and the uncertain.[178] According to
Budde, they became easily entangled in error. Authors like Gassendi,
Mersenne, Schook, and many others had written against them (§ 18).
And even when skeptics seemed to doubt everything, Budde maintained
that they nonetheless usually held onto one firm moral ideal, their goal of
ἀταραξία. For him that represented a self-contradiction: they might have a
highest goal, but they wanted to preserve a state of *epoché*, according to
which one could make no judgments at all (§ 20). The diversity of
common opinions about mankind's highest goal did not constitute for
Budde a real argument for skepticism. Moreover it just was not true that
one could attain peace of mind only through *epoché*: ataraxia was not the
highest felicity according to Budde; it was just a result; mystics were
forever claiming that ataraxia was part of the process of uniting with
God. Moreover, any true epoché was never truly attainable.[179]

And finally, in § 23 Budde arrives as the center of his argument against
Carneades:

> Those who deny the morality of human actions [*actionum humanarum*]
> actually have no more firm foundation themselves. If we consider the

certitudinis jujus obtinendae methodus praemonstrata, Leiden, 1697. On Villemandy see Carlo
Borghero, "Scepticism and Analysis: Villemandy as a Critic of Descartes," in Gianni Paganini,
ed., *The Return of Scepticism: From Hobbes and Descartes to Bayle*, Dordrecht, 2003, pp. 213–229.
[176] Budde, *De scepticismo morali* (note 166), § 15.   [177] Ibid.   [178] Ibid., § 17.
[179] Ibid., § 22.

nature of man, we assume that he was created by God and was not thrown blindly into this world, but was part of a wise plan; in addition we assume that an honorable person is only allowed to behave and arrange himself according to certain specific laws; that God, finally, can only wish the man, whom he has created, to be good and understanding; that above all His will must be regarded as the law. One is inclined therefore to conclude that it is a holy law, given and established for man, one that he must piously follow.[180]

As a theologian Budde, unlike Grotius, was clearly proceeding from the assumption of a highest and best being. From the plan of creation it followed automatically that the world has rules according to which mankind must act:

What I am here assuming can easily be confirmed by assuming that it would be complete madness to dare denying any part of it. If God's law is established, the automatic result is the morality of human actions if they are in accord with it, but partly also the immorality [*turpitudo*] if they are opposed to it. And that is sufficient to refute the error of Carneades. And yet he scandalously thought that because all men and other living things are led by their nature to pursue their own utility, that fact proves that there is either no justice at all or that the very idea is close to the highest folly. But instead one must hold together what nature itself has connected with the tightest bond, and by no means allow [these two elements] to be separated: Namely, whatever is moral is *eo ipso* useful. How could it be otherwise?[181]

That was Budde's main argument. He maintained that there was a complex connection between morality and utility, which was grounded in the fact of divine creation – for normativity served to support humanity. Budde thus took one step toward the skeptics in that he accepted *utilitas* as a central principle of morality; but at the same time he tied this *utilitas* to the already reasonable plan for the world. As early as 1697 in his *Elementa philosophiae practicae* Budde had developed a sketch of this position.[182] "The highest godhead has ordained its laws in order that they should contribute to the welfare and sustenance of humankind." Of course Budde now had to explain the cases in which naked calculations of utility and morally good behavior diverged. He claimed that any amoral calculation of utility was only apparently useful because, seen from the higher vantage point of creation, it was not useful at all:

Naturally it happens that something can seem useful even if it is not moral. That is most dangerous: men seduced by error may regard something as

---

[180] Ibid., § 23.   [181] Ibid.   [182] Budde, *Elementa philosophiae practicae* (note 167), pp. 236ff

useful. But men are not foolish if they pursue righteousness. In and of itself they are doing the right thing. The most foolish and least understanding among mortals, however, are those who zealously pursue the convenient [*commodo*] – or at least what they think is convenient – and do not realize that they are casting themselves into something much more inconvenient, if indeed they don't bring destruction down upon themselves.[183]

From the viewpoint of theology, the identity of moral behavior and true utility, not least in view of punishments and rewards after death, made Carneades's denial of morality absurd.

Budde's position, even if it represented the consensus of a large portion of society in the time around 1700, does not appear at all original or interesting from today's viewpoint, for we take for granted the development of a secular law of nature. But its significance looks very different if one takes its contexts into account: from the motives of using Selden against Grotius, or of complementing Pufendorf with biblical references, or to – as we will now see – a move to push Grotius over into the "pagan" camp.

12   Heinrich von Cocceji, Budde, and the Will of God

"This argument," Budde continued, "leaves prostrate all the fancies of Epicurus."[184] Indeed, Epicurus had developed a theory of law, but one that was also based on nature and utility. Even if he separated the "honorable" from the "useful," Budde held that that had no basis and was of no help. "But those who with Hugo Grotius and others draw the laws of nature from a concern to protect community as their first principle, as they call it, in order to avoid relying only on utility, cannot for any reason be charged with Epicureanism, from which they are far removed, or indeed with Skepticism."

That is just what one would expect. But then came an addition that cast a shadow over Grotius: "But they would actually be guilty of that if they were to assume only utility as the foundation of natural law."[185] From Budde's point of view, this was exactly the view that "a certain learned man

---

[183] Budde (praes.) / Engelbrecht (resp.), *De scepticismo morali* (note 166), § 23.

[184] Ibid., § 24: "Hoc ipso vero et Epicuri commenta prostrata iacent."

[185] Ibid.: "Ast qui cum Hugone Grotio, aliisque ex societatis custodia, ceu primo, ut vocant, principio, leges naturae derivant, ut neutiquam ad solam utilitatem respiciunt, ita ab Epicuri mente, quam longissime absunt, nec Scepticismi ulla ratione accusari possunt. Cuius profecto essent manifesti, si nihil aliud quam utilitatem, fundamenti loco iuri naturae substernerent."

has attributed" to them.[186] He was referring to an interpretation of Grotius that accused the Dutch legal theorist of not really being much different from the Epicureans and Skeptics – that is, of relying only on "utility."

Let us examine the highly refined argument that Budde was quoting from an unidentified commentator, for the question involves nothing less than the foundations of "modern" natural law. Was Grotius's antiskepticism successful or not? The author had said:

> But even the principle of protecting the community cannot be regarded as firm and stable. For if some utility, on which a community depends, were to be the basis of natural law, it would then follow that natural law was within the power of men, for anyone could renounce his own utility – Book I, Chapter on Treaties – and then live without natural law, which was supposedly founded in the utility of the community.[187]

The point of this objection was that any reliance on the community was itself a calculation of utility. But one is free to waive one's own utility, according to this argument, just as one can withdraw from a contract. And if that is true, then this calculated reliance produces no secure result:

> Moreover, this principle is exceedingly uncertain because the community is supported by many different or even contrary methods. So if natural law should result from this principle, it would follow that the principle could be endlessly modified. What is useful in supporting the community today might be damaging at some other time.[188]

Calculations of utility were dependent on many conditions and could arrive at different results. And then the author adduced an additional problem:

> It would, moreover, erase the differences that exist between natural law, the law of nations, and the civil law: the latter two equally aim at mere utility if there is no certain obligation [to obey] this law; because a law established for utility can be changed. And from that it would follow that such a law could be modified at will.[189]

---

[186] Ibid., "Quam sententiam vir quidam doctus illis tribuit."

[187] Ibid.: "Neque etiam principium de societatis custodia, pro firmo ac stabili habendum. Si enim utilitas aliqua, ex qua societas constat, fons iuris naturalis esset, sequeretur ius naturae in potestate hominum esse, cum quilibet utilitati suae renunciare possit, l. p. C. de pact. et sine naturali iure quod fundatum esset in communi utilitate, vivere."

[188] Ibid.: "Deinde, hoc principium valde indefinitum est, nam societas multis et variis, imo contrariis modis promovetur. Quin si ius naturae ex hoc principio flueret, sequeretur illud ius in infinitum posse mutari. Nam quod hodie utile est ad societatem colendam, alio tempore noxium esse potest."

[189] Ibid.: "Tolleretur insuper differentia ista, quae inter ius naturae, gentium, et civile est: quorum duo postrema utilitatem aeque intendunt: quin nulla certa huius iuris obligatio foret: quod enim ob

If even the law of nature follows some calculation of usefulness that depends on changeable conditions, then it is no different in kind from the law of nations and the civil law. "Add to that that this principle would not oblige the most powerful princes and the ones most distant from us because they (if they are satisfied with their lands) would not care about other peoples, because they would not be bound by any other law."[190]

The argument that Budde was describing was so dangerous and took up the center of Budde's dissertation because this interpretation of Grotius would destroy the foundations for those who hoped to build their further considerations of natural law on his approach. Grotius would then have opposed Carneades in vain. He would not have advanced one inch beyond his views. These were points that did not really agree with the criticisms of Grotius in the *Symbolum sapientiae*, whose central thrust lay in its attack on the idea of a universal community that would extend beyond the domestic community that it shared with all animals. In contrast, the unknown author whom Budde was summarizing threw the certainty of Grotius's proposed calculation into doubt.

Who could have come up with such a destructive interpretation? Was it a student of Budde's, who had formulated this *dubium*, a potential contrary view? Or was it perhaps some radical author, who was proceeding on a different track from the *Symbolum* but one that was no less dangerous? Did Budde suppress his name because the work from which he quoted was clandestine?

No, that is not the case. We can show that the quoted arguments had been developed by a man who had been a colleague of Budde's, a professor of law at the Electoral Brandenburg University of Frankfurt on the Oder. His name: Heinrich von Cocceji.[191] Cocceji had studied in Leiden and in 1670 had gone to England, where his uncle Henry Oldenburg lived. He earned a doctorate at Oxford, and in 1677 was appointed to a professorship in the law of nature and of nations, as the successor to Pufendorf in Heidelberg. In 1689 he moved to Utrecht and then in 1690 to Frankfurt. At the time of Budde's dissertation he had not yet published his objections

---

utilitatem statuitur ius, mutari potest l.12.13ff. d. LL. Inde sequeretur hoc ius pro lubitu mutari posse."

[190] Ibid.: "Accedit et illud, quod principium hoc potentissimos et a nobis remotos Principes haud obligaret, cum enim hi suis terris contenti nullos alios populos curent, nullo alio iure obstricti essent."

[191] With thanks to Knud Haakonssen for the proof. On Cocceji (1644–1719) see Schneider, *Justitia universalis* (note 22), pp. 223–240; Knud Haakonssen, *Natural Law and Moral Philosophy: From Grotius to the Scottish Enlightenment*, Cambridge, 1996, pp. 135–145.

to Grotius, and so Budde could only refer vaguely to a "learned man." But those objections were available, perhaps as lecture notes that students brought along from Frankfurt to Halle, or perhaps as manuscripts that wound up in Budde's hands; or maybe even in letters from Cocceji to Budde. Most of his writings, and especially those dealing with Grotius and natural law, were only published posthumously in the eighteenth century by his son Samuel, who revised and expanded them and then defended them against critics such as Leibniz and Ludovici. That makes it difficult sometimes to identify the actual, original theses of the father. And yet the son did not alter in any way the general thrust that his father had laid down; and so the published texts do reflect the basic statements of Heinrich von Cocceji. They were published most abundantly in his *Grotius illustratus*, which appeared in four volumes between 1744 and 1752, accompanied by an *Introductio* in which the fundamental questions of the "Prolegomena" were discussed.[192] Here was what Budde was referring to, the attempt to show that Grotius's basis for natural law was Epicurean. Among his contemporaries, this focus on the "concern for community" was relatively uncommon, and so we can be relatively certain that this was the author to whom Budde was referring.

Cocceji asserted that from the premises that Grotius provided, "there is no universal community among mankind.[193] Men who find themselves in a state of nature," he said, echoing Hobbes and the author of the *Symbolum*, "care only about their domestic community, i.e., about the union of man and wife, and about the procreation of children and about protecting themselves and their own [families]."[194] They did not find it necessary to enter into any larger community.[195] Beyond that, "care for society" could not be assumed as a principle of natural law that would function even if there were no God. And here Cocceji gave reasons that were similar to those reported by Budde: Without God, any natural law would reside in the hands of men and could be changed or even

---

[192] Samuel Cocceji, *Introductio ad Henrici De Cocceji Grotivm illustratum: continens dissertationes proeminales XII in quibus principia Grotiana circa jus naturae per totum opus dispersa, ad justam methodum revocantur [. . .]*, Halle, 1748. One finds a list of the early works of Heinrich von Cocceji that could have influenced Budde in *Vita viri perillustris [. . .] Henrici de Cocceji in qua fata ejusdem succinte enarrantur, motae controversiae ordine recensentur, singulaque scripta exacta enumerantur*, Quedlinburg, 1721.

[193] Cocceji, *Introductio ad Henrici De Cocceji Grotivm illustratum*, p. 11a (a denotes left column and b the right column): "nullaque inter homines existat universalis conjunctio."

[194] Ibid., p. 8a: "Homines enim in statu naturae positi feruntur ad solam domesticam societatem, nimirum, ad conjunctionem maris et foeminae, ad procreationem sobolis, et ad sui, suorumque defensionem . . . ."

[195] Ibid.

renounced.[196] Moreover, the concern for community could vary from place to place and from time to time.[197]

Was Cocceji trying to destroy natural law? No, he was only painting the disastrous consequences of assuming a law that was not based finally on God.[198] Earlier, in Chapter 2, we saw that important parts of natural science in the late seventeenth century positioned themselves emphatically as an anti-idolatrous and nonpagan science. Here we find a kind of jurisprudence that also hoped to position itself emphatically as nonpagan. Cocceji accused Grotius of having derived his principle of sociality too directly from Greco-Roman forms of thought,[199] making his whole legal construction "pagan."[200] Even the abominable name of Spinoza came up in this context, for in his attempt to identify the pagan principles that Grotius was using as a basis for his *societas universalis*, Cocceji was reminded of the Stoic notion of the common materiality of all things, an idea that Spinoza's monism of substance seemed to have inherited.[201] In this way we see another example of what Alan Charles Kors showed in his discussion of atheism: from the mere effort to avoid being pagan or atheistical, a position for one's opponent was imagined or constructed that artificially turned him into a radical.[202] Thus radical positions were created that either did not exist in reality at all or that one had not really seen, because, as in the case of the *Symbolum sapientiae*, they circulated only in manuscript and among very small groups. So it is not remarkable that we first thought of the author whom Budde was quoting as a clandestine naturalist. But it turned out that this was "only" the artificial creation of Cocceji:

> Because it is thus certain that the emphasis on human community drew its
> origin from the false principles of pagan philosophy, it would appear safer to

[196] Ibid., p. 12a: "Posito hoc principio illud absurdum sequeretur, quod societas humana, eaque divisa singulae Respublicae, juri naturae renunciare, eoque mutare legem naturae possent; cum e contrario Deo jura, quae ex socialitate sequuntur, nec mutare, nec tollere liceret."

[197] Ibid., p. 12b: "negari nequit, quod uti cujusque civitatis, ita et totius humanae societatis, commoda, et utilitates temporibus variare, et alio seculo alia esse possint. Sic igitur jus naturae; quod ad rationes societatis humanae exigitur, non esset jus constans, aeternum, et immutabile, sed pro temporibus, et ratione utilitatum varium, et mutabile. Neque tantum hac ratione temporibus, sed et locis variaret jus naturae. Cum enim eodem tempore, alia quoque in orbis parte, aliae rationes sint et esse possint societatis humanae, non minus singulis applicandum esset proprium jus naturae, ac singulis civitatibus jus civile."

[198] Erich Döhring, "Cocceji, Heinrich Freiherr von," *Neue Deutsche Biographie* 3 (1957), pp. 300f.

[199] Cocceji, *Introductio ad Henrici De Cocceji Grotivm illustratum* (note 192), p. 2.

[200] Ibid., p. 6a.   [201] Ibid., p. 6b.

[202] See Mulsow, *Enlightenment Underground* (note 57), chapter 1, as well as Alan Charles Kors, *Atheism in France. 1650–1729*, vol. 1: *The Orthodox Sources of Disbelief*, Princeton, 1990.

avert our gaze; for it is certain that a community in this sense cannot be permitted without impiety or accepted as the most sacred source of law.[203]

What was Cocceji driving at ultimately? The position he developed as an antidote to the Stoic-Epicurean-Skeptical Grotius was a grounding of natural law in the will of God. He was aiming not at another theonomous natural law in the tradition of Melanchthon, which was what most Christian theorists of natural law in Germany held, but at a theo-voluntarist natural law. This was a voluntarism different from what Pufendorf relied on for his law of nature, for he relied on the will of God to capture the binding quality of natural law, but in other respects he assumed the principle of "sociality"; in contrast Cocceji based his entirely on the divine will.[204]

Budde, however, did not regard Cocceji's critique of Grotius as decisive: "Even if those who upheld 'community protection as the basic principle of natural law [as in Grotius] actually agreed with Epicurus and Carneades in basing all law on utility alone, the efficacy of their arguments adduced would not be entirely destroyed."[205] It was therefore not absolutely necessary to react like Cocceji and drop Grotius completely. "But if they who defend this view were to avow that 'protecting the community' was infused [into human beings] by God, and that the law of nature did not rest on utility alone but rather on the will of God, which is visible in the social nature of man, they would still in my opinion achieve nothing."[206] Thus Budde rejected Cocceji's escape, as he had already signaled in § 15 when he had referred to Villemandy:

> Because it is said that every person could then renounce at will his own utility, he is, I admit it, not obliged to obey the command of one who gives orders. Protecting the community seems convenient to us, but it is God above all who has prescribed it and infused it into us. And therefore it is not within our remit to terminate it.[207]

The words that Budde used, *nuntium mittere*, were a technical legal term found in Ulpian, one that described the cancellation of a contract.[208] As a Calvinist, Cocceji was close to Federal theology, as Knud Haakonssen

---

[203] Cocceji, *Introductio ad Henrici De Cocceji Grotivm illustratum* (note 192), p. 7b.
[204] Thus Cocceji ultimately had an impact even on the moral theory of Adam Smith because the divine will relates to the individual person. His influence extended also to Kant. See Haakonssen, *Natural Law* (note 189), p. 144.
[205] Budde, *De scepticismo morali* (note 166), § 25.   [206] Ibid.   [207] Ibid.
[208] Immanuel Scheller, *Lateinisch-Deutsches Wörterbuch*, 3rd edn., Leipzig, 1804, vol. 5, col. 6902, s. v. "nuntius."

suspects, and therefore he understood man's relationship with God in terms of a contract.[209] But it appears that Budde did not think one could terminate a law if the law ultimately came from God.

> In addition God has not determined what care goes into protecting the community so exactly that it could not be changed according to varying circumstances. But that was not even necessary – because the law itself is stable and the principle of cognition is firm, even if its objects vary. No matter what one chooses as the principle of natural law, if this argument had any probative force, the principle would collapse for this reason.[210]

That would be absurd. Budde here insisted that the law of nature was stable and immune to skepticism, but that its shapes varied – as he had already shown in his *Historia juris naturalis*. And so Cocceji's argument had no probative force. "Nevertheless, the efficient cause of the law, which some call its foundation must not be confused with its 'principle of cognition' – as they love to call it at the university."[211] Cocceji had drawn special attention to this distinction or at least to the difference between *principium essendi* and *principium cognoscendi*.[212] "Protecting the community" was not the efficient cause of natural law, he argued, but the principle of cognition could not provide that cause either. Budde disagreed: "The will of God is incontrovertibly the cause of natural law; but if one discusses from whence this most clear understanding comes, especially with regard to the duties of men to others, it is rightly said, that this can be understood no where better than from the social nature of mankind."[213] So here too Budde insisted on the gain in understanding that the principle of sociality provided. And he insisted as well on the differences among the kinds of law:

> The distinctions, however, between civil law, the law of nations, and the law of nature are not destroyed by this. At least with the law of nations, its difference from the law of nature has already been described by wiser men than I. But civil law and the law of nature differ both in their lawgivers and in their highest goal, for the latter applies to the entire human race, while the former is directed to the welfare of a specific society.[214]

---

[209] Haakonssen, *Natural Law* (note 189), p. 140. On Johannes Coccejus see Gottlob Schrenk, *Gottesreich und Bund im älteren Protestantismus vornehmlich bei Johannes Coccejus: Ein Beitrag zur Geschichte des Pietismus und der heilsgeschichtlichen Theologie*, Gütersloh, 1923; Willem Asselt, *The Federal Theology of Johannes Coccejus (1603–1669)*, Leiden, 2001.
[210] Budde, *De scepticismo morali* (note 166), § 25.   [211] Ibid.
[212] Cocceji, *Introductio ad Henrici De Cocceji Grotivm illustratum* (note 190), p. 18.
[213] Budde, *De scepticismo morali* (note 166), § 25.   [214] Ibid.

This brought Budde very close to his goal; he had countered most of the objections of Cocceji. The law of nature was stable. In summary, he said, "From this it follows of itself and is rightly emphasized by everyone that it cannot be changed at the nod or pleasure of men."[215] But if that is the case, then the last threat that Cocceji feared also collapsed, a scenario that the *Symbolum sapientiae* had also depicted vividly: that there could be no transnational obligations.

> In the end kings and princes, no matter how far distant they are from one another, are bound by the law of nature because they are members of that larger society in which they participate, one that extends over everyone; they are subject to God's lordship, in the same manner as any number of others; so that if they think to break these commandments, God has ordained that they should be given the harshest punishments for their crimes.[216]

Budde was maintaining the Halle interpretation that agreed with Grotius and Pufendorf about the basis of law, even though his view was also more clearly based in natural theology. He rejected a voluntarism that he thought was exaggerated. Villemandy, who had opposed Malebranche's voluntarism, had made it clear that the pendulum of relying on God's will must not be allowed to swing too far to one side or the other. The rest of Budde's treatise ran along the lines that Villemany had sketched: a balancing act between Descartes on one side and Poiret on the other.

13   The End of *lex divina positiva universalis*

It has been necessary to reconstruct with some care the clandestine debate between Budde and Cocceji concerning the validity of Grotius's understanding of the foundations of natural law, because that was what set the course over the next years toward what became known as the Halle doctrine of natural law. For one thing, it resulted in the program in the history of philosophy that Budde pursued in the years around 1700, a program that aimed to provide historical underpinnings for the close connection of philosophy and theology that he needed in order to secure his moral foundations. But these were also the years in which Thomasius abandoned the ideas of natural law found in his *Institutiones* of 1688 and developed a new, more secular and more pessimistic position. Thus he made more room for skeptical objections that might have appealed to his colleague Budde.

---

[215] Ibid.   [216] Ibid.

Let us start with this second development. Thomasius abandoned the part of law called the *Lex divina positiva universalis* (universal positive divine law). This was precisely the field that Budde had earlier developed by wrestling with John Selden – namely, the idea that God's laws were ordained for all mankind, not just for the Jews, as a complement to or an extension of the pure law of nature. "The general, divine, positive Law," said Budde, "is a decree of the Divinity, which it issued of its own free will for the welfare and use of men, and which it revealed to those who represent the whole human race, thereby obliging all men to do or to avoid doing something."[217] Originally the name for this kind of universal law came from the Arminian minister and translator, Étienne de Courcelles, who regularly cited Selden in this connection.[218] The extraordinary thing about this type of universal law was that it did not have to be grounded in reason. It sufficed to assume that God had ordained it by employing his superior wisdom. In 1688 Thomasius in his *Jurisprudentia divina* had accepted the possibility of a universal law and had incorporated it into his construct.[219] In one way it was an offering to the theologians, for Thomasius was assembling biblical passages that spoke of justice and law, but they were not examples of natural law. The doctrine here was not unproblematic because a supposedly universal law depended on whether a revelation given only to certain people had really penetrated to all of mankind. It was the young Nikolaus Hieronymus Gundling, in his personal discussion group, who posed the probing questions that finally prompted Thomasius to drop the doctrine. "When he defended his prior opinion, I opposed him once very sharply, so that he even admitted in a lecture that he had himself long had doubts about this, but would now renounce this opinion as soon as possible, and that also happened."[220] That must have been in 1702 when Gundling did not yet even have his licentiate in law, because Thomasius begins his *Fundamenta juris naturae et gentium* ("The Foundations of the Law of Nature and of Nations") with an autobiographical account of how he

---

[217] Budde, *Elementa philosophiae practicae* (note 167), p. 239.

[218] Gundling gives a brief sketch of the history of this doctrine in *Ausführlicher Discours über das Natur- und Völkerrecht*, Frankfurt and Leipzig, 1747, pp. 37–40. Étienne de Courcelles, *Diatriba de esu sanguinis inter Christianos*, Amsterdam, 1659. Appeals to Selden on pp. 34ff. and passim. See also the full discussion in Andreas Adam Hochstetter, *Collegium Puffendorfianum super libris duobus de officio hominis et civis*, Tübingen, 1710.

[219] Christian Thomasius, *Institutiones jurisprudentiae divinae*, Frankfurt and Leipzig, 1688.

[220] Gundling, *Ausführlicher Discours über das Natur- und Völkerrecht* (note 218), pp. 38f.

came to abandon this doctrine, a development he dated to that year.[221] Now, Thomasius concluded that all universal laws were also natural laws. The residue from Selden was now gone.

And how did Budde regard this shift in foundations from that time? He had moved so far in the direction of the moral skeptics that he had adopted their concept of utility, even though he never tired of stressing that "utility" had to be interpreted from the perspective of God and as part of his reasonably constructed creation.[222] By doing so he had in a sense retheologized the secular natural law of Pufendorf, but in a nonconfessional form that did not particularly please the Orthodox Lutherans.[223] The difference reflects the distance between the late Thomasius and Gundling on one side and Budde on the other.[224] With his theologizing, Budde was pursuing a program that reconstructed the sorts of philosophical histories that were useful for supporting his general views.

---

[221] Thomasius, *Fundamenta Juris naturae et gentium*, Halle, 1705. I have used the edition Halle and Leipzig, 1718, chapter 1, "Caput prooeminale ratio instituti."

[222] This openness to utility had an echo among Budde's students. It is visible for example in Christoph August Heumann, who studied with Budde when he moved to Jena in 1705. Budde's *Elementa philosophiae practicae* became for Heumann the standard for his thinking on moral philosophy and natural law. When he took up a teaching position in Eisenach in 1713 and held his own lectures on natural law, he searched (like Budde, p. 236) for the "norma actionis" (i.e., the specific rule for human conduct). This internal norm was to be described as self-love. I am quoting from the manuscript of his lecture, which Dieter Kassing made available to me and which now resides on loan in the Leibniz-Library in Hanover. (With thanks to Gideon Stiening, who brought this passage to my attention when he reported on it at the Conference on Heumann held in Gotha on November 8, 2017.) On p. 151 he remarked: "Etliche sagen, amor sui wäre das primum principium Juris naturae, das kommt mit meinem überein, nur daß es differirt mit Worten." Indeed, in his *Elementa philosophiae practicae* (note 167), pp. 250ff., Budde had referred to "conservatio" as a fundamental norm and had derived from it the duties of honoring God, and living both moderately and sociably. This was an independent continuation of Budde's intentions, for he had indeed proceeded from the idea that God wanted human beings to be happy. And thus Heumann arrives at a self-criticism on p. 156. Of course Heumann rejects this objection and speaks prudently of an "amor nostri tenerrimus," a most tender love, in order to turn aside all gross connotations of egoism. And still his thought was undeniably close to Epicureanism. As an introduction to Heumann's set of lectures, see Martin Mulsow, "Heumanns Eisenacher Naturrechts-Kolleg von 1713. Eine vorläufige Skizze," in Martin Mulsow, Kasper Risbjerg Eskildsen, and Helmut Zedelmaier, eds., *Christoph August Heumann (1681–1764). Gelehrte Praxis zwischen christlichem Humanismus und Aufklärung*, Stuttgart, 2017, pp. 127–137.

[223] See the debates that broke out in 1697 around Budde's *Elementa philosophiae practicae* described in Marianne Taatz-Jacobi, *Erwünschte Harmonie. Die Gründung der Friedrichs-Universität Halle als Instrument Brandenburg-Preußischer Konfessionspolitik – Motive, Verfahren, Mythos (1680–1713)*, Berlin, 2014, p. 232.

[224] I described this difference in *Enlightenment Underground* (note 57), chapter 6. Simon Grote has recently qualified my distinction by pointing, correctly, to aspects on which Budde and Gundling agreed, while Gundling differed with the later Thomasius in some of their views. That brings Gundling more into opposition to Christian Wolff. See Simon Grote, *The Emergence of Modern Aesthetic Theory: Religion and Morality in Enlightenment Germany and Scotland*, Cambridge, 2017, pp. 47–64.

At first he conducted a series of disputations which examined ancient Greek lawgivers and philosophers;[225] but then, in the journal *Observationes selectae*[226] he anonymously opened up investigations of a series of authors from the Hermetic-Neoplatonic-Kabbalistic tradition, such as Guillaume Postel, Giorgio Veneto, but even Pythagoras, the "Orphic" tradition, and the Kabbalah itself. These were all philosophers who favored a philosophical-theological understanding of God along the lines of a *prisca theologia* ("ancient or earliest theology") or a *philosophia perennis* ("perennial philosophy"), a doctrine concerning God from which insights into the purpose of creation could be obtained.[227] In other essays Budde revealed that he was interested in the thought patterns of syncretism, i.e., the combination of philosophy and theology that all of these authors were engaged in.[228] A further line of studies were devoted to the "third force" of the Reformation: irenic figures such as Erasmus, Dudith, and Aconcio, men who were also theological thinkers.[229]

14   The End of the Pythagoras Narrative

Was this antiskeptical strategy the beginning of "modern" reflection on the history of natural law? Initially, at the start of this chapter, we looked at

---

[225] See, e.g., Johann Franz Budde (praes.) / Carl Gottlob Goldstein (resp.), *Leges Solonis cum Mosaicis dissertatione morali conferent atque contendent [. . .]*, Halle, 1699; Johann Franz Budde (praes.) / Clamor Johannes Busch (resp.), *Ethicam Solonis Salaminii [. . .]*, Halle, 1699; Budde (praes.) / Philipp Wilhelm Busch (resp.), *Ethicam Cleoboli Lindii [. . .]*, Halle, 1699; Budde, *Sapientia Veterum, hoc est dicta illustriora septem Graeciae Sapientum*, Halle, 1699; Budde (praes.) / Carl Gottlob Goldstein (resp.), *Ethicam Thaletis Milesii [. . .]*, Halle, 1699; Budde (praes.) / Clamor Johannes Busch (resp.), *Ethicam Chilonis Lacedaemonii*, Halle, 1699; Budde (praes. / Philipp Wilhelm Busch (resp.), *Ethicam Pittaci Mitylenaei*, Halle, 1699; Budde (praes.) / Johann Ludwig Stösser (resp.), *Ethicam Periandri Corinthii [. . .]*, Halle, 1699.

[226] See Martin Mulsow, "Ein kontroverses Journal der Frühaufklärung: Die *Observationes selectae*, Halle 1700–1705," *Aufklärung* 17 (2005), pp. 79–99.

[227] *Observationes selectae*, vol. 1, Halle, 1700: "Defensio Cabbalae Ebraeorum contra Auctores quosdam modernos," pp. 207–230; "De Guilelmo Postello," pp. 323–369; vol. 2, Halle, 1700: "Apologia Pythagorae praesertim contra Episcopum Worcestriensem," pp. 199–230; "Francesci Georgii Veneti Harmonia mundi," pp. 338–399; vol. 4, Halle 1701: "Continuatio observationis XX. Tomi I. de Guilielmo Postello," pp. 231–264; vol. 6 (1701): "De philosophia Orphica," pp. 307–331. The essay about defending the Kabbalah unleashed a controversy with Wachter which I will treat in *Spinozism, Arianism, and Kabbalah: Unexpected Conjunctions in German Intellectual History of the Late Seventeenth Century. With the Addition of an Unknown Attempt at Rewriting Spinoza's Ethics by Johann Georg Wachter (1704)* (forthcoming).

[228] *Observationes selectae*, vol. 3, Halle, 1701: "De Syncretismo philosophico generatim," pp. 218–229; "De conciliatione philosophorum cum scriptura sacra," pp. 230–257; "De conciliatione philosophorum inter se," pp. 258–279. On the problem of syncretism, see Michael Albrecht, *Eklektik. Eine Begriffsgeschichte mit Hinweisen auf die Philosophie- und Wissenschaftsgeschichte*, Stuttgart, 1994.

[229] For this turn of phrase and current of thought, see Friedrich Heer, *Die dritte Kraft. Der europäische Humanismus zwischen den Fronten des konfessionellen Zeitalters*, Frankfurt, 1959.

Barbeyrac, the key figure for Richard Tuck's "reconstruction," with its emphasis on skepticism in the history of law; notably Barbeyrac used Budde's treatise *De scepticismo morali* for his own purposes. Repeatedly in the footnotes to his long foreword to Pufendorf, Barbeyrac quoted Budde's treatise ("which is worth reading"[230]), and especially to § 26, which was the paragraph that followed immediately after Budde's dispute with Cocceji's interpretation of Grotius. In this paragraph the topic was whether or how moral conclusions could be proved; to be sure, Budde regarded this problem as less acute than the one he had just tried to settle. "Those who allow no proofs in moral teachings, however, give us fewer problems. I do not see how they can escape being suspected of skepticism."[231] And he explained what he meant by proof – that is, a conclusion drawn from clear and evident premises, that is from ultimate principles. "Therefore moral teaching, in my opinion, proves most if not all its claims in this way."[232] The variability and uncertainty of human actions did not cause him any worries in this regard: so long as the foundations of morality were recognizable, the basis for everything else was secure.

Barbeyrac found it necessary to expand Pufendorf's understanding of natural law by adding a history of morals, and we have seen that not only he, but also Budde, Gundling, and others – both before and after Barbeyrac – also felt this need. A history of morals could on the one hand provide a critical examination of the whole tradition, focusing on virtues and vices, as La Mothe le Vayer and Bayle had offered. We saw this in Chapter 3. In so doing one of the important goals was to focus on the divergence of theory and practice, and sometimes to discredit a theory by its bad practice. A good example was Mosheim's history of the morals that dealt with those Church Fathers who had accepted gnostic ideas.[233] And according to the early Enlighteners of Halle – especially according to Thomasius's *Fundamenta* of 1705 – if it was the will's corrupt nature that held men back from doing what reason correctly told them to do, then historically speaking it was most interesting to see in different times what effects a corrupt will and corrupt morals had had. A history of morals and

---

[230] Barbeyrac, "Preface" (note 6), p. 27: "Voyez ... la Dissertation de Mr. Buddeus, de Scepticismi Morali § 26. Que j'ai déjà citée, et qui d'ailleurs mérite d'être lue."

[231] Budde, *De scepticismo morali* (note 166), § 26: "Qui vero demonstrationibus in morali disciplina locum concedere nolunt, minus quidem negotii nobis facessunt. Sane quo pacto Scepticismi effugere suspicionem queant, non video."

[232] Ibid.: "Moralem itaque doctrinam ita comparatam esse autumo, ut non quidem omnia, pleraque tamen asserta sua hac ratione demonstret."

[233] See Mulsow, *Enlightenment Underground* (note 57), chapter 6.

of moral consciousness appeared therefore to be worth pursuing. This research goal was all the more understandable because these scholars rejected the view that Christianity was a collection of "scholastic" dogmas and instead valued its teaching of simple morals – even though they were not ready to agree with Deists and Socinians that Jesus was primarily a teacher of morality. Thus the history of morality could appear more interesting than just a pure history of dogma or theology. Yet even the doctrinal history of morals itself could be useful, especially if it was the history of the antiskeptical "modernization" of morals and law.

Jerome B. Schneewind has pointed out, however, that in addition to the "normal" history of morals, one that begins with Socrates and can be told as an antiskeptical history of moral foundations, there was a second narrative, which we should not neglect. He calls this "the Pythagoras Story."[234] He means by this a history that connects ethics to more ancient origins, preferably to its earliest origins with Noah, Moses, and the philosophy of the Hebrews. Pythagoras came into play not only because he was, according to Aristotle, the first Greek moral philosopher, but because he supposedly drew his teachings from the Hebrews. That at least was the legend that was widely accepted in the early modern period; so it is not surprising that none other than John Selden applied and defended it extensively in his *De jure naturali*.[235] For him, one of his dearest goals was combining morals and law with *historia sacra* ("sacred history"), and he saw the law of nature as part of a *philosophia perennis*.[236]

We have seen in the case of Johann Franz Budde that this second tradition was still playing an important role around 1700, and indeed that it interfered with the skeptical tradition that Tuck emphasized. What does that tell us about the genesis of modernity during the period of the early Enlightenment? At the very least it makes the image that we construct for ourselves of the development of ethics more complex. Precisely the debate with moral skepticism, whether led by the opponents of Grotius or by others in clandestine treatises, was carried out by authors who were pursuing a specific program of philosophical theology.

[234] Jerome B. Schneewind, "No Discipline, No History: The Case of Moral Philosophy," in Donald R. Kelley, ed., *History and the Disciplines: The Reclassification of Knowledge in Early Modern Europe*, Rochester, 1997, pp. 127–142; Schneewind, *The Invention of Autonomy: A History of Modern Moral Philosophy*, Cambridge, 1998, pp. 536–548.

[235] Selden, *De jure naturali* (note 24), Lib. I, cap. 2, p. 14. See Schneewind, *The Invention of Autonomy* (note 234), p. 539.

[236] Concerning the *philosophia perennis*, see Wilhelm Schmidt-Biggemann, *Philosophia perennis. Historische Umrisse abendländischer Spiritualität in Antike, Mittelalter und Früher Neuzeit*, Frankfurt, 1998.

The early German Enlightenment was ambivalent in this area. As we have repeatedly seen, it contained a rather conservative wing and another, rather skeptical and liberal. Of course, over time at least, in the field of natural law the latter prevailed. John Selden, who had seen himself as a universalist, was marginalized as a "Hebraizing particularist" by Pufendorf and finally even by Thomasius; they dropped the *lex divina positiva universalis*. The reason was that the early Enlighteners, with their historical skepticism, often worked to destroy the notion of a *philosophia perennis* that had supposedly grown out of the biblical tradition. Although theses of diffusion, perhaps beginning with Scaliger, had undergirded historical narratives of religious and human history from Selden to Huet, they crumbled in the 1680s and 1690s under the pressure of historical criticism but also because of new empirical theories of knowledge, which rejected notions of inborn ideas. Under such conditions Adam no longer possessed all the knowledge of mankind within himself, and the Hebrews were no longer the perfect nation, and instead were only a particular tradition[237] – now the "Pythagoras Story" was no longer acceptable.[238]

Morhof had once been inspired by the quest for traces of the divine to be found in the earliest wisdom of the human race, but now that quest was barely imaginable. Gundling no longer followed the young Budde in valuing John Spencer as support for Selden's basic ideas but now saw him rather as a destructive agent undermining the primacy of the Hebrew tradition; he now regarded the Mosaic ritual laws as deriving from the degradation and transformation of the earlier Egyptian cults, a process that reduced the Mosaic laws historically to secondary importance. That also meant that the Hebrews were no longer a people possessed of an original wisdom.[239] Gundling's early major work in the history of philosophy, his *Historia philosophiae moralis*, must therefore be placed right next to Barbeyrac's *Preface* to Pufendorf of the same year if we want to see more clearly how the history of morals affected the form in which modern natural law emerged.

---

[237] See Mulsow, *Enlightenment Underground* (note 57), chapters 5 and 6; and Helmut Zedelmaier, *Der Anfang der Geschichte* (note 53).

[238] Schneewind, *The Invention of Autonomy* (note 234), pp. 542f., pushes the end of the "Pythagoras story" to the late eighteenth century – with Stäudlin – but I think that puts it too late.

[239] For this point, see Mulsow, *Enlightenment Underground* (note 57), chapter 6.

CHAPTER 5

From Becmann to Stosch
The Socinian Contexts of the *Concordia rationis et fidei* (1692)

1 The *Concordia rationis et fidei*

In the previous chapter we watched Johann Christoph Becmann react to the immigration of Jews to Frankfurt on the Oder by supporting an edition of the Talmud. In 1695 he also published a new edition of Selden's *De jure naturali*, which must have been of interest to Jewish scholars as well. In these years, however, he had to grapple with a controversial case that was triggered by a book that had been secretly published in 1692 by the printer Runge in Berlin and was being sold by the book dealer Jeremias Schrey from Frankfurt on the Oder.[1] The book was entitled *Concordia rationis et fidei* ("The Harmony of Reason and Faith") and bore no author's name while claiming to have been published in Amsterdam. In reality, as was soon discovered, the author was Friedrich Wilhelm Stosch, a privy counsellor at the Brandenburg court.[2] The work pretended to unite faith and reason, but actually it took the side of reason. In about 100 octavo pages it offered a homemade attempt at intellectual orientation of the sort that several others had attempted in the decades before 1700. Such attempts were often the result of more-or-less inadequate compilations and were hardly real syntheses because they were amateur philosophies rather than professional works.

---

[1] See the detailed reconstruction of the printing and distribution history in Detlef Döring, *Frühaufklärung und obrigkeitliche Zensur in Brandenburg: Friedrich Wilhelm Stosch und das Verfahren gegen sein Buch "Concordia rationis et fidei,"* Berlin, 1995, pp. 28–31 and 75–81.

[2] [Friedrich Wilhelm Stosch], *Concordia rationis et fidei, sive Harmonia philosophiae moralis & religionis Christianae,* "Amstelodami," 1692; repr. ed. Winfried Schröder, Stuttgart, 1992. For more on Stosch's book, see Gottfried Stiehler, *Beiträge zur Geschichte des vormarxistischen Materialismus,* East Berlin, 1961, pp. 139–163; Winfried Schröder, *Spinoza in der deutschen Frühaufklärung,* Würzburg, 1987, pp. 32–58; Martin Pott, *Aufklärung und Aberglaube. Die deutsche Frühaufklärung im Spiegel ihrer Aberglaubenskritik,* Tübingen, 1992, pp. 295–303; as well as Ernst Feil, *Religio. Die Geschichte eines neuzeitlichen Grundbegriffs im 18. und 19. Jahrhundert,* vol. 4, Göttingen, 2007, pp. 124–128.

In this case it was a compilation mainly from the atomism and Epicureanism of Gassendi and Descartes, along with Spinoza's one-substance and ethics; but there were also elements from Jean Le Clerc's theory of cognition and mind, and thus indirectly from John Locke. The work begins by stating:

> The first thing a student of philosophy can clearly establish is the following: He thinks, therefore he is. He is not of himself but from another and in another. He exists not for himself alone but is a part of the whole, an appendage of heaven and earth. He is attached to the earth, with air flowing around him, without which he cannot breathe even a moment. He cannot exist without food, clothing, shelter, and protection against the inclemency of the weather, nor without the society of his own kind and many other things. In a word: He is a finite being who thinks, has extension, and is ordained to live and to act in a certain manner.[3]

We are hearing the voice of a person with a feeling for life who has been paying attention to the new scientific worldview. But the new philosophy of natural law taught by Pufendorf also presupposed a scenario of an entirely dependent human being.[4] For Stosch this changed view of man was central, a man who no longer stood in the center of the world as the crowning glory of creation, the image of God. From this new viewpoint he aimed at a philosophy that culminated in a new moral teaching.

In those places where he gave details, Stosch was digesting the results of the medical work of Theodor van Craanen – who had been practicing at the court of Brandenburg from 1687 onward – but also the thoughts of Isaac La Peyrère, Gabriel Wagner, Arnold Geulincx, Thomas Hobbes, and Nicolas Malebranche. After the first printing of his book, Stosch added at the end of his compilation the results of his further reading, which he called *additamenta* in a second printing from the fall of 1693 – references, for example, to Balthasar Bekker, Matthew Hale, Johann Christoph Sturm, and the edition of Horace prepared by Anne Daciers. At the end of the main body of text came a section on ethics and the philosophy of law, corresponding to his title, according to which he was offering a *Harmony of Moral Philosophy and the Christian Religion*. Was that really what this was? Or was it a subterfuge?

---

[3] Stosch, *Concordia* (note 2), p. 1. [Translator's note: In the text, Mulsow adopted the German translation from Gottfried Stiehler, ed., *Materialisten der Leibniz-Zeit*, East Berlin, 1966, p. 39, a translation that forms the basis (along with the Latin) for what is translated into English here.]

[4] See esp. Simone de Angelis, *Anthropologien. Genese und Konfiguration einer "Wissenschaft vom Menschen" in der Frühen Neuzeit*, Berlin, 2010.

Perhaps we need to ask more precisely which Christian religion Stosch was talking about. His *additamenta* provide a clue. They dealt with the soul, the problem of eternal punishment in hell, and with Christianity in general: *Chapter X: Appendix de Anima, Chapter XI: Appendix de Poenis Divinis,* and *Chapter XII: Fundamentum et Elementa Religionis Christianae.*[5] At the very end, and disconnected from Stosch's Latin treatise, came a German work printed in Gothic type entitled: "On Eternal Death, and on the Eternity of the Punishments of the Wicked." It was, as the text says, a translation from the French, perhaps a work by Etienne de Courcelles or by Dirk Rafaelsz Camphuysen.[6] But it is also possible that the text was by Stosch himself. These paratexts, which dealt with apparently marginal issues, perhaps represented in a sense the original core of Stosch's concerns. Mortalism in the doctrine of the soul, after all, and the denial of eternal hellfire, were characteristic of Socinian philosophy.[7]

The immediate reaction of those surrounding Stosch when his treatise appeared was predictable, and shortly after an investigation was opened against the author. At the end of 1693 Stosch was identified as the author, and on January 9, 1694, his book was forbidden, and all the copies that could be found were burned. The distinguished investigative commission was made up of high-ranking officials, Ezechiel van Spanheim, Paul von Fuchs, Daniel Ernst Jablonski, Philipp Jakob Spener, Samuel von Pufendorf, and Benjamin Ursinus; they accused Stosch of ignoring the authority of the Bible and demanded that he renounce his work.[8] Detlef Döring has pointed out that this exceptional commission was itself very liberal, but it had to deal harshly with the book in order to pacify Orthodox critics. He rightly emphasizes the reasons why the court with its referees reacted in such a nuanced manner to Stosch's book: His intentions were painfully close to their own program of fostering a

[5] Stosch, *Concordia* (note 2), pp. 71–124.

[6] In the reprint of Stosch, *Concordia* (note 2) on pp. 213–235, unpaginated in the original. Concerning de Courcelles, see Corinna L. Vermeulen, "Strategies and Slander in the Protestant Part of the Republic of Letters: Image, Friendship and Patronage in Etienne de Courcelles' Correspondence," in Toon van Haal et al., eds., *Self-Presentation and Social Identification: The Rhetoric and Pragmatics of Letter Writing in Early Modern Times,* Leuven, 2002, pp. 247–280. See also Schröder, *Spinoza* (note 2), p. 36. On Camphuysen's letter opposing the eternity of punishment in hell, see Daniel P. Walker, *The Decline of Hell: Seventeenth-Century Discussions of Eternal Torment,* London, 1964, pp. 86–92.

[7] See Sascha Salatowsky, *Die Philosophie der Sozinianer. Transformationen zwischen Renaissance-Aristotelismus und Frühaufklärung,* Stuttgart, 2015.

[8] The text of the accusation, first published by Oelrichs, was reprinted in Döring, *Frühaufklärung und obrigkeitliche Zensur in Brandenburg* (note 1), pp. 88–90.

collaboration of faith and reason – that made the whole case extremely delicate. Stosch had set forth this program in so radical a fashion that it undercut the efforts of the high-ranking officials rather than supporting them.[9] But because they felt they could not leave themselves open to attacks from the hardliners among the Frankfurt theologians, they used the Stosch scandal to strengthen their own troubled collaboration internally by joining in a common dismissal of an "atheist" radical;[10] and so they acted swiftly to demand a recantation. Stosch was, however, so well connected to the court preachers that the commission did not fully publicize the scandal and then, once Stosch recanted, he was restored to his official position.

With what larger purpose had Stosch rejected the court's program of fostering a "harmony of reason and faith"? Was he in favor of Socinianism? On the surface, apart from a few statements, Stosch's book is not explicitly Socinian. Indeed, Winfried Schröder speaks of "an extremely selective reception of Socinianism, whose doctrines he adopted only if they could be used to criticize religion in general . . . ."[11] For Schröder these borrowings were functionally dependent upon a more fundamental critique of religion. He interprets all of Stosch's verbal avowals of Christianity as mere camouflage, like the whole idea of combining faith and reason. But in the light of his contextualization of the case, Döring insists that what Stosch really wanted was to clear away the scholastic obstacles standing in the way of a simple, reasonable, but biblically justified Christianity. Stosch was operating as an awkward amateur in philosophy, but he did not wish to make a radical break with the Church.[12]

Can we resolve this interpretative conflict? Was Stosch a disguised atheist or a rather weird supporter of a simplified Christianity? I am not sure that I can reconcile this conflict satisfactorily, but in the following I would like to pursue the Socinian background of Stosch's intellectual development in order to make clear how muddy this whole intellectual field was where Stosch was operating: theologically a field between Reformed and Socinian views, geographically a field between Dutch and Brandenburg theorists, and temporally a field between the early radical and later Orthodox views of certain participants.[13] So the real question should be: In this "field" could a "Socinian" become an "atheist"? And: What did

---

[9] Ibid., p. 72   [10] Ibid., p. 46.

[11] Schröder, *Spinoza in der deutschen Frühaufklärung* (note 2), p. 42.

[12] Döring, *Frühaufklärung und obrigkeitliche Zensur in Brandenburg* (note 1), p. 74.

[13] On the sociological theory of intellectual fields, see Pierre Bourdieu, *Homo academicus*, tr. Peter Collier, Stanford, 1988. See also Marian Füssel, "Intellektuelle Felder. Zu den Differenzen zwischen

these terms mean in different contexts? Were the "Socinians" of 1620 the same as the "Socinians" of 1690?

2 A New Document

Recently as part of her archival research into the internal conflicts within the Berlin Refuge, Fiametta Palladini has uncovered some new details. A document from Sylvester Jakob Danckelmann (Junior), the president of the Consistory and the Chamber Court, a record she has published, reveals that it was the information service connected to the office of taxation that set the investigation in motion. The piece was dated January 22, 1694, and dealt with a denunciation dating from the middle or end of December: "At the end of the last year, Tax Prosecutor Strimesius brought a charge that a treatise filled with many serious errors appeared under the title, *Concordia Rationis et Fidei*, printed here [in Berlin], even though the title page would have one believe that it was printed in Holland." Down to this point the document referred only to Stosch, but then it mentioned other cases that provide an interesting context for the affair:

> At the start of this new year, a year which may, God willing, prove a genuine blessing to Your Electoral Highness both in body and soul, the *Adjunctus Fisci* [The Assistant Tax Prosecutor] complained that a citizen of Cölln [an ancient central district of Berlin] named Schaum had asserted that there is no devil and no hell and has thus directly contradicted Holy Scripture. No sooner had we therefore interrogated him on that account than the above-mentioned *Adjunctus Fisci* Duhram complained that another person had spoken lightly of Holy Scripture, especially insulting the Books of Moses, saying that they should be considered no different from the *Metamorphoses* of Ovid. We would be remiss to omit that in accord with our solemn duty we investigated both of them more closely. But these sorts of blasphemies are now becoming so common, especially through the drawing of equivalences between Scripture and the fables of Ovid, defiling God's honor, and thus overturning the only means ordained through which adults may be converted and brought to blessedness, and without which no potentate can remain sure of his rule because we are bound to obey the godly and biblically revealed will of the magistrates. In addition there's a certain woman from Dorotheenstadt [another section of central Berlin] who over the most recent holidays brought to Your Highness's ministers in the cathedral an extremely wicked book filled with the most dangerous opinions; she claimed that [the book] was discussed in

Pierre Bourdieus Wissenssoziologie und der Konstellationsforschung," in Martin Mulsow and Marcello Stamm, eds., *Konstellationsforschung*, Frankfurt, 2005, pp. 188–206.

secret *conventicula* [conventicles or gatherings] at her house; because this brotherhood appears to be growing and spreading, we have seen it as our duty to report all of this to Your Electoral Highness . . . .[14]

This was a sort of status report, which the president of the Consistory forwarded to the Elector from spies employed by the tax authorities. Stosch's book got tossed together in the same pot as two blasphemies against the Bible along with a "wicked book," which had been discussed by secret assemblies. The first of the sacrilegious opinions, "that there is no devil and no hell," was the sort of typical mixture of skepticism about the hell-and-brimstone sermons of the clergy along with provocative blasphemy[15] common in the early modern period; the other sacrilege – with its comparison of the Bible to Ovid – was guilty of profanity but its aim was more subtle than the first, suggesting that many statements in the Bible were intended merely allegorically. The third case was of a different nature: here a landlady or neighbor presented her pastor with a *corpus delicti*, a book that was regularly discussed by a small circle of people. It was by no means clear that the book was an example of "atheist" literature; indeed, it is more likely that this was a religious group Pietists or perhaps radical Pietists whom this woman suspected.

Stosch was outraged that a "false report" and the "slander" from a "tax official with a history of fighting and manslaughter" had unleashed an avalanche against him – obviously Strimesius was a locally known thug (not to be confused with the Frankfurt professor of theology with the same name).[16] Including his case with these other rumors and denunciations, however, shows us that we need to look more carefully at the indistinctly defined field in which Stosch was moving. Blasphemers and secret conventicles did not belong to his favored associates; in his own self-estimation he was hoping to open up topics for discussion with his serious but unpopular arguments. If we understand that, we can then perhaps follow how, within a group of Brandenburg Calvinists who were close to Socinianism, a group open to various influences from the most recent

[14] Berlin, Geheimes Staatsarchiv Preußischer Kulturbesitz, I, HA, Rep. 47, Tit 20a, (Blasphemien Sache, 1497–1802), Paket 15725; quoted in Fiametta Palladini, *Die Berliner Hugenotten und der Fall Barbeyrac. Orthodoxe und "Sozinianer" im Refuge (1685–1720)*, Leiden, 2011, p. 86.
[15] See on this, Gerd Schwerhoff, *Zungen wie Schwerter. Blasphemie in alteuropäischen Gesellschaften 1200–1650*, Konstanz, 2005; Francisca Loetz, *Mit Gott handeln. Von den Zürcher Gotteslästerern der Frühen Neuzeit zu einer Kulturgeschichte des Religiösen*, Göttingen, 2002.
[16] Letter from Stosch to Eberhard von Danckelmann (?) from January 1, 1694, in Döring, *Frühaufklärung und obrigkeitliche Zensur in Brandenburg* (note 1), p. 85.

philosophers, a process of radicalization had transported the young Stosch beyond Socinianism.

3   A Fluid Situation

In earlier chapters we have already noticed how powerfully Socinianism and Arianism collaborated to allow materialist and rationalist thoughts to crystallize. Interestingly Stosch's accusers spoke of a "new Socinianism." The expression can perhaps be used to understand the radicalism that emerged from a Socinian milieu and metamorphosed into an eclectic Spinozism. Stosch's accusers used the word when they mentioned a work "by one of the new Socinians, the publication in folio of Samuel 'Przipocov' from the year 1692."[17] They meant the edition of Przypkowski's works, edited by Philipp van Limborch, with its combining of moderate Socinianism with Arminianism.[18] We might at first think that the "new" referred only to the time (i.e., to the younger generation of Socinians). But when Stosch defended himself against this designation, it seems he had something deeper in mind: "What they mean by the distinction between old and new Socinians I do not know ... ."[19] He clearly perceived a differentiation between the original Socinians of the early seventeenth century and the authors of the 1670s and 1680s, who differed in both profile and in teachings. But he hoped that they were not claiming that all who professed a *docta ignorantia* (learned ignorance) with respect to doctrines like the Trinity should be regarded as "new" Socinians.[20] For then he would indeed be one of them. If the Frankfurt theologians were thinking like that, then a decisive mark of the "new" Socinianism would be a skeptical withholding of judgment (*epoché*) regarding traditional theology and not an aggressive denial of it.

Elsewhere Stosch appealed to Conrad Bergius, Jr., and to the *Liberius de Sancto Amore* ("Liberius' Letters on Holy Love") – that is, the

---

[17] Draft of a letter from the University of Frankfurt a.O. to Elector Friedrich III, December 18, 1693, printed in Döring, *Frühaufklärung und obrigkeitliche Zensur in Brandenburg* (note 1), pp. 96–100, here at p. 100. For the following I will use a few passages from an essay of mine in English: "The 'New Socinians.' Intertextuality and Cultural Exchange in Late Socinianism," in Martin Mulsow and Jan Rohls, eds., *Socinianism and Arminianism*, Leiden, 2005, pp. 49–78.

[18] Samuel Przypkowski, *Cogitationes sacrae ad initium Evangelii Matthaei et omnes epistolas apostolicas*, *"Eleutheropolis"* [Amsterdam], 1692. On him, see Fiorella De Michelis Pintacuda, *Socinianesimo e tolleranza nell'età del razionalismo*, Florence, 1975. There is more literature cited below.

[19] Submission by Stosch on February 13, 1694, in *Acta Stoschiana*, in *Fortgesetzte Sammlung von Alten und Neuen theologischen Sachen* (1749), p. 686; reprinted in Stosch, *Concordia* (note 2), p. 292.

[20] Ibid.

pseudonymous early work of Jean Le Clerc, with which Le Clerc had begun his writing career.[21] We will return to both of these authors later. In the *Liberius*, the fictive editor emphasized in his introduction that the author was fully aware of human fragility, the human capacity for error, and that this was clear in each of the letters.[22] That explained his *docta ignorantia*. Conrad Bergius had been a professor of theology in Frankfurt on the Oder from 1629 to 1628 and then a professor in the academic gymnasium in Bremen from 1629 until his death in 1642.[23] He was the brother of Johann Bergius, who had also taught theology in Frankfurt University before he took up duties as Brandenburg court preacher in 1623 and became a confidant of Elector Friedrich Wilhelm. Both had originally been Lutherans but had become Reformed while in the Netherlands; both supported a policy of irenic affinity if not one of genuine union between the two Protestant confessions. Johann Bergius composed an "Apostolic Rule" in 1641, which became a constant reference point in the debates over these issues. It was a proposal for how to deal with the differences between Calvinists and Socinians that had erupted in sharp controversies during the first decades of the seventeenth century. In 1695, one year after the scandal surrounding Stosch, the text of the Rule seemed once again so timely that it was republished:

> If they [the Socinians and Arians] deal with such high and imponderable mysteries by sticking unperturbedly and unrestrainedly to the words of Scripture, but without rancor and anger, and do not add their own interpretations or the conclusions of their reason, which go beyond or against the articles of faith, we would have no cause to condemn them if they do not accept or use all of our interpretations or our [merely] human forms of speech.[24]

The Rule proposed that the official Church tolerate the Socinians so long as they did not agitate polemically and did not make their rationalist interpretations of Scripture too explicit. By referring to dogmas such as the Trinity as "imponderable mysteries," Bergius was implying that no rational discussion of them was possible in any event, and that therefore

---

[21] Ibid., p. 670. I will explore this passage further below.

[22] Liberius de Sancto Amore [= Jean Le Clerc], *Epistolae theologicae, in quibus Varii Scholasticorum errores castigantur*, s.l., 1679, Praefatio.

[23] The work that Stosch quotes is: *Praxis catholica divini canonis contra quasvis haereses et schismata*, Bremen, 1639.

[24] *Apostolische Regul / Wie man in Religions-Sachen recht Richten solle / Erkläret durch D. Johannem Bergium, Weiland Churfürstl. Brandenburg. Consistorial-Raht und Hoff-Prediger*, Cölln an der Spree, 1695.

they should not prompt dogmatic fighting.[25] So here too we find an invocation of *docta ignorantia*.

In the later seventeenth century this sort of restraint was overlaid with more complex forms of skeptical self-reflection and written forms of *epoché*. And yet the appeal to "learned ignorance" in questions of theological speculation and biblical interpretation was certainly not the only characteristic of Socinians in the late seventeenth century. It is not easy to pin down this "new" type of antitrinitarian, especially if one hopes to say exactly what they believed. There were certainly Socinians who had taken on Cartesian ideas; others followed Locke's theories of cognition, others agreed with Denis Petau's historical arguments about the development of dogma; and still others had connections to Spinoza, for example among the Dutch Collegiants.[26] It may therefore be simplest to identify the "new Socinians" as the products of a cultural transfer, the results the migration of Socinians from Poland to the West and their complex intermixing in a completely different intellectual world.

We do have to insist, however, that these products of transfer were not just the results of the various philosophical and theological currents they encountered, for at the same time a variety of other "modern" views crystallized around their antitrinitarian beliefs. The new Socinians did not develop just a mixed identity; they were also marked by the growth of a new unity and commonality. The reason for this lay in their regular appeal to reason in questions of biblical exegesis, and then, connected to that, an appeal to the believer's individual conscience. When the concept of reason was uniformly and consistently understood (which certainly did not always occur – just think of the differences among Descartes, Locke, and Spinoza), the groups of new Socinians were also united. They provided the seedbed for many later deists and so-called early Enlighteners.[27]

The concept of cultural transfer seems useful in this case because Socinianism was unusually marked by migration and the transfer of cultures: its origins lay in the Protestant movement of sixteenth-century Italy; the Socinians then emigrated to Poland, Moravia, and Transylvania

[25] For the controversy over toleration, see also Sascha Salatowsky and Winfried Schröder, eds., *Duldung religiöser Vielfalt – Sorge um die wahre Religion. Toleranzdebatten in der Frühen Neuzeit*, Stuttgart, 2015.

[26] See Andrew Fix, *Prophecy and Reason: The Dutch Collegiants in the Early Enlightenment*, Princeton, 1991; Emanuela Scribano, *Da Descartes a Spinoza. Percorsi della teologia razionale nel Seicento*, Milan, 1988.

[27] See Paul Wrzecionko, ed., *Reformation und Frühaufklärung in Polen. Studien über den Sozinianismus und seinen Einfluß auf das westeuropäische Denken im 17. Jahrhundert*, Göttingen, 1977.

from the 1560s and 1570s onward; and finally, after the 1640s and 1650s, the succeeding waves of expulsions from Eastern Europe pushed them in large numbers to Brandenburg-Prussia, England, and the Netherlands.[28] In research into cultural transfers scholars have too often overlooked Socinianism even though it provides an almost uniquely excellent example.[29] It has probably been neglected because the idea of transfer was first developed for the history of national states from the eighteenth century onward. And yet the general idea (with some modifications) can be useful for the early modern period as well.[30]

The whole point of focusing on transfers has been to avoid simplistic notions of "influence." Transfer implies rather the decontextualization and then recontextualization of a cultural object, a separation from the culture of origin and an adaptation to a new destination culture, with all the resulting questions of what really happened to it and whether that cultural object retains an identity "in itself." Therefore we can ask if Socinianism stayed the same when it was transferred from Poland to the Netherlands. Was it not important that many antitrinitarians after 1650 stopped calling themselves Socinians and took on new names, such as "Arians," "Unitarians," or "Artemonians"? What does it mean that even though Huguenots and Arminians doubted the Trinity, Christology, or the doctrine of the atonement, they still did not wish to be counted as Socinian sectarians? Starting at least in the 1670s with the spread of Socinian doctrines, a spread dramatically visible in the many folio volumes in the *Bibliotheca fratrum Polonorum* (Library of the Polish Brethren) – in which we find the works of Przypkowski under the sponsorship of Huguenots and Dutch Calvinists – but then especially after the Catholic biblical criticism of Richard Simon, intellectual borders became highly permeable. The result was a remarkable fluidity of "new" thinking, with mixed forms made up more or less of Cartesian philosophy and historical-critical theology.

---

[28] For a comprehensive study of these migratory movements, see Earl Morse Wilbur, *A History of Unitarianism: Socinianism and Its Antecedents*, Cambridge, MA, 1945; Wilbur, *A History of Unitarianism in Transylvania, England, and America to 1900*, Cambridge, MA, 1952. See also Martin Mulsow, "Exil, Kulturkontakt und Ideenmigration in der Frühen Neuzeit," in Herbert Jaumann, ed., *Diskurse der Frühen Neuzeit*, Berlin, 2010, pp. 441–464.

[29] See also Martin Mulsow, "Transnational Dissidence: Samuel Crell's Socinian Exile," in Yosef Kaplan, ed., *Early Modern Ethnic and Religious Communities in Exile*, Cambridge, 2017, pp. 94–116.

[30] See, e.g., Wolfgang Schmale, *Kulturtransfer. Kulturelle Praxis im 16. Jahrhundert*, Vienna, 2003; Andreas Höfele and Werner von Koppenfels, eds., *Renaissance Go-Betweens: Cultural Exchange in Early Modern Europe*, Berlin, 2005. Peter Burke provides a good overview in *Kultureller Austausch*, Frankfurt, 2000.

4 Jean Le Clerc's Pseudonymous *Epistolae theologicae*

The most creative scholars such as Jean Le Clerc reacted to this new situation by producing equally ambiguous sorts of texts – subtle, dialogically constructed treatises. To understand this development we have to go more deeply into the life and work of Le Clerc. His *Epistolae theologicae* ("Theological Letters"), which he published in 1681 (but which he dated to 1679) were supposedly written by a certain "Liberius de Sancto Amore"; they were the product of his student years in Geneva and Saumur, a series of treatises on the Trinity, original sin, or Christology, all artfully arranged in letters.[31] We need to look more closely at this composition, especially when we recall the significance that such arrangements later could have for an author like Kierkegaard. For Le Clerc too, the work as a whole was bracketed by a technique of distancing based on the fact that his pseudonymous Liberius was not even the supposed editor of these letters. Instead, that was a fictitious editor, a "friend" of Liberius, a theologian in "Eleutheropolis," a "Free City," a place like the one in which Johann Crell's *Vindiciae* were printed.[32] The editor tells us that the texts of Liberius had their origins in *adversaria* ("memoranda"), thoughts jotted down while reading, but then expanded into letters. Many of the views expressed had an experimental sense, as if they were attempts to capture personal conversations (*saepe se expertum in familiaribus confabulationibus*).[33]

The "letters" published this way were all written by "Liberius," but they were sent to different recipients. The first letter, dating from August 1679, was written to a "Firminius Parrhasius" and dealt with his topic under the assumption that Christ was God, co-eternal with the Father. He developed a theory of the hypostatic union of the two natures of Christ, using Cartesian concepts. Then comes the second letter, which promptly undermines these assumptions. It was supposedly written on New Year's Eve 1678 and was addressed to a certain "Ambrosius Theographus," but it distanced itself even further from the author by being the supposed report

---

[31] *Epistolae theologicae* (note 22). On Le Clerc see Cristina Maria Pitassi, *Entre croir et savoir. Le problème de la méthode critique chez Jean Le Clerc*, Leiden, 1987.

[32] See the fictitious notice of the place of publication, "bei Junius Brutus Polonus" [= Johann Crell], *Vindiciae pro religionis libertate*. Eleutheropolis [= Amsterdam], 1637; it seems possible that Le Clerc, in assigning this place to the publisher, was thinking of his friend Jacques Lenfant, who described himself in a letter of July 15, 1684, as an *Eleutheropolitanus* (a citizen of "Free City"). See Annie Barnes, *Jean Le Clerc (1657–1736) et la république des lettres*, Paris, 1968, p. 60.

[33] *Epistolae theologicae* (note 22), Praefatio.

of "Ludovicus Solinus," a friend of the uncle of Theographus, who
recounts a discussion or argument (*collatio*) that he had had with two
nephews to whom he had posed certain questions. This "Solinus" is
introduced as someone who has had to leave his country and seek a new
home.[34] It is unclear whether we should imagine him as one of the
Socinians recently driven out of Poland, but in any event a sort of cultural
transfer is built into the framework of the letter; the scene surely reflects
real conditions in Saumur. The discussion of Solinus with his nephews
describes a living theological experiment: he has educated the two young
men in Hebrew, Greek, and Latin but without the accompanying theological debates, and then he has allowed them to read the Bible without
any commentary. For three years they have studied in isolation from each
other. And the question was now: What conclusion would they reach with
respect to the Trinity? One of them had arrived at the Reformed position,
the other at the Socinian. But the debate between the two brought no
resolution; and three friends, when drawn in, did not succeed in declaring
a victor. The moral of the story was thus: if Holy Scripture is so equivocal
and unclear in this matter, it must mean that one simply had to tolerate
various opinions, including the views of Socinians. The common basis
they had on other questions – that God possessed all possible perfections,
that He wanted to save mankind, and that Christ died for that purpose –
should, along with identical moral teachings, suffice for mutual acceptance. Thus the conditions set forth by Johann Crell's *Vindiciae pro
religionis libertatis* ("Defense of Liberty of Religion"), which had appeared
in 1637 and was later published in a clandestine French version, were in
this way fulfilled.[35]

The third letter was directed to "Coelius Optatianus" and had supposedly been composed a bit later, in February 1679. This Coelius had read
Liberius's first two letters while visiting a certain "friend" (in Crell's
fiction), and had requested a "full explanation of the three modes of
thought in the Godhead." But now, as opposed to his first letter,
Liberius had to concede that his starting position had changed: "Before

[34] Ibid., pp. 14f.
[35] Polonus [= Johann Crell], *Vindiciae pro religionis libertate* (note 32); French in [Charles Le Cène],
*Conversations sur diverses matières de religion, où l'on fait voir la Tolerance que les Chrétiens de differens
sentimens doivent avoir les uns pour les autres, [et] où l'on explique ce que l'Ecriture Sainte nous dit des
Alliances de Dieu, de la Justification, [et] de la Certitude du Salus. Avec un traité de la liberté de
conscience. Dedié au Roi de France [et] à son Conseil*, "Philadelphia," 1687. See Pintacuda de
Michelis, *Socinianesimo* (note 18), pp. 68–94; Jerome Vercruysse, "Crellius, Le Cène, Naigeon
ou les chemins de la tolérance socinienne," *Tijdschrift voor de Studie van de Verlichting* 1 (1973),
pp. 244–320; Mulsow, "The 'New Socinians'" (note 17), pp. 53–55.

I read the discussion I took the view that the mystery of the Holy Trinity (supposing that it could be proved from Scripture) could be explicated in the same way, and I thought that it was therefore not needful to write on this matter to my [friend] Solinus ... ."[36] But now if the Scriptural authenticity of the Trinity was suddenly no longer guaranteed, the rational reconstruction of the Trinity that followed had only a hypothetical character.

I cannot analyze the content of Liberius's theory here, but I should note that this hypothetical interpretation represents a sort of psychological doctrine of the Trinity: "Even though [God] is one, He can produce numerous different sequences of thought simultaneously, and therefore the Persons in Him can also be different. God is called Father according to a certain manner of thinking, Son according to another, and the Holy Spirit in yet another."[37] Thus it all comes down to the *modi cognoscendi* ("modes of knowledge") in the *series cogitationum* ("series of thoughts"): the "mode" of the judge (Father), of the Intermediary (Son), and of the Consoler (Holy Spirit). The language of "modus" and "series" seems like a firm reference to Spinoza or Malebranche.

Liberius extols this theory because it seemed to escape the charge of Sabellianism (since in this modalistic view the three Persons come one after the other, not next to each other), and to that extent it was an alternative to Socinianism: the stance was "just as probable as the Socinian" and it agreed "with right reason."[38] In this way it was in accord with the uncertainty of revelation, which Stosch had viewed as a precondition for the "new" Socinianism.

The further progress of the *Epistolae theologicae* continued this complex construction and in this way the letters formulated ideas concerning original sin, the creation of man, and the problem of miracles. It seems true, however, that with these letters the author had created an ingenious and ambiguous dialogical situation, with letters that partially neutralized one another. How had he managed that? As Annie Barnes recognized in the 1960s, Le Clerc's model was the Saumur philologist Tanneguy Lefebvre with his *Epistolae* of 1665/1674.[39] It was Lefebvre who had introduced gallant French conversational culture into philology, and had formulated his philological observations on the ancient classics and the Bible in fictitious letters to friends in a loose and unforced tone. He was

---

[36] *Epistolae theologicae* (note 22), p. 95.   [37] Ibid., p. 103.   [38] Ibid., p. 107.
[39] *Tanaquilli Fabri epistolae*, Saumur, 1665; 2nd edn., 1674. See Barnes, *Jean Le Clerc (1657–1736) et la république des lettres* (note 32).

part of the libertine-philological culture of France and the Netherlands, a culture to which Patin, Ménage, and even Scaliger to an extent also belonged, and whose table-talk Lefebvre published.[40] He was presenting philology in the form of an epistolary novel, so to speak, and that is what Le Clerc hoped to provide for theology. For him it was a fitting form of expression for the uncertain epistemological situation regarding the revealed text of Scripture: the use of dialogue presupposed the hypothetical suspension of distinctions between true and false, and the acknowledgment of plurality.[41]

5   The Socinians, Stosch, and Spener's Sermons of 1691–1693

Thus Jean Le Clerc created a textual form in which he could represent the instability of current theology in all its multiplicity and uncertainty. His university studies in Saumur in the late 1670s had exposed him to more-or-less secret discussions of just the sort that he described. And how were things in Brandenburg? It was there that Friedrich Wilhelm Stosch read the *Epistolae theologicae* as an expression of a *docta ignorantia* – perhaps without even knowing that Jean Le Clerc was the author. In Brandenburg too Socinians and Reformed rubbed shoulders, and similar questions arose there about how one should react to problems of coexistence, toleration, and the challenges posed by recent philology.

The small communities of tolerated Socinians had some extremely active members, and at the court of Brandenburg some officials obviously sympathized with these radical Protestants. Among the more publicity minded members of the Socinians we should count especially Johann Preuß and Samuel Crell. That is not just because of the manuscripts they wrote and had circulated, but also because they were trying to sell to booksellers the books that they had printed anonymously in Guben, the little backwater town in the area where Brandenburg, Silesia, Poland, and

---

[40] *Prima Scaligeriana, nusquam antehac edita, cum praefatione T. Fabri,* Utrecht, 1670.

[41] According to Mikhail Bakhtin, dialogicity really means the ambiguity of words or utterances, an ambiguity that arises from the interference of two kinds of speaking or "voices." What he means is not some external dialogue formed between two speech partners but, as it were, an internal aspect of an utterance, as can be expressed in novels. But Klaus W. Hempfer has attempted to apply the concept for actual dialogues as well: "Lektüren von Dialogen," in Klaus W. Hempfer, ed., *Möglichkeiten des Dialogs. Struktur und Funktion einer literarischen Gattung zwischen Mittelalter und Renaissance in Italien,* Stuttgart, 2002, pp. 1–38. In my view, Le Clerc transferred this "dialogical" form of dialogues to theology. For the recognition of plurality, see also Martin Mulsow, *Die unanständige Gelehrtenrepublik. Wissen, Libertinage und Kommunikation in der Frühen Neuzeit,* Stuttgart, 2007.

Lusatia came together. Ever since 1635, Guben had belonged to the jurisdiction of the Wettin dynasty (Electoral Saxony), who also ruled as margraves of Lusatia. In 1689 Preuß and Crell had tried to sell some unitarian books to publisher and bookdealer, Jeremias Schrey, in Frankfurt (on the Oder), but they ran into bad luck. Schrey was cautious and pressed charges at the university, which issued a stiff reprimand.[42] The echoes of this affair were still audible in the case of Stosch in 1694. Schrey was again the bookdealer, whom Stosch had identified as a contact who could help distribute his book; and this time Schrey agreed to sell the book – at least until the case of Stosch was investigated and the work was forbidden.[43]

In the course of the investigations, however, various parallels were drawn between the sale of the Stosch book and that of the not-yet-forgotten affair involving Preuß and Crell. This letter from the University of Frankfurt on the Oder to the Elector of Brandenburg illustrates the problem:

> Because the oft-mentioned book [meaning Stosch's *Concordia*] is full of the grossest Socinian errors, from which the earlier noted [?] blasphemous doctrines proceed, may your Electoral Highness understand that the named Socinians Preuß and Crell along with others have not ceased spreading their teachings, both secretly and openly, orally and in writing. These kinds of godless books and others like them will continue to turn up in Your Electoral Highness's lands so long as you and your peers give the impression that smuggling them in is tolerated. So we cannot avoid adding this: that in the edition of one of the New Socinians, Samuel Przypkowski, in his works published in folio in 1692, the title page invokes his official status as a "Counsellor of the Elector of Brandenburg."[44]

The author of this letter, whether Becmann or one of his colleagues, was trying to use the prosecution of Stosch in order to repeat a warning against what he saw as dangerous Socinian influences. The author was well-informed when he denounced the new edition of Przypkowski by connecting it to the elector of Brandenburg and his policy of toleration.[45] After all, the publication had been edited by Philipp van Limborch,

---

[42] See Theodor Wotschke, "Die unitarische Gemeinde in Meseritz-Bobelwitz," *Zeitschrift der Historischen Gesellschaft für die Provinz Posen* 26 (1911), pp. 161–223. See further Wotschke, "Zur Geschichte der Unitarier in der Mark," *Jahrbuch für brandenburgische Kirchengeschichte* 7/8 (1911), pp. 227–242.

[43] See Döring, *Frühaufklärung und obrigkeitliche Zensur in Brandenburg* (note 1), pp. 75ff.

[44] Draft of a letter from the University of Frankfurt a.O. to Elector Friedrich III, December 18, 1693, printed in Döring, *Frühaufklärung und obrigkeitliche Zensur in Brandenburg* (note 1), pp. 96–100, here at p. 100. See also note 17.

[45] See Martin Lackner, *Die Kirchenpolitik des Großen Kurfürsten*, Witten, 1973.

Samuel Crell's friend.[46] As we saw earlier, Limborch had willingly con-
sorted with Socinians, and in the writings of the Socinian theorist Samuel
Przypkowski, and especially in his *Dissertatio de pace et concordia ecclesiae* as
well as in *De jure Christiani magistratus*, he found an approach to toleration
virtually identical to his own. In Amsterdam he used his connections with
several young Socinians, such as Andreas Wiszowatys's son Benedictus, to
gather information about Przypkowski and then to obtain his manuscripts,
which he then published.[47]

These were the activities of the Socinians and Arminians, which they
shared with their allies and sympathizers in Brandenburg. But Stosch
developed from a Socinian into an extremist who deployed Spinoza,
Hobbes, and Gassendi for what had originally been Socinian goals; and
the Socinians were disconcerted by this development. From their standpoint Stosch had gone much too far and was virtually denying the
importance of Holy Scripture. Asked for a formal evaluation, Johann
Preuß was quick to distance himself from Stosch: "The book *Concordia
rationis & fidei* is in truth the friend of reason but the enemy of revelation
or faith. I find a dissonance in this supposed harmony." Theologians had
of course often argued that Holy Scripture and philosophy, rightly understood, could not contradict each other:

> But how is it that this new philosophy allows so little to be healthy in Holy
> Scripture, and gives to faith or revelation not even half a voice, but claims
> only that it deceives simple and believing Christians, regarding their devo-
> tions as smoke and mirrors, as one can also see in Spinoza as well as his
> forerunners and disciples.[48]

Let us grant that Preuß was reacting defensively. As a Socinian he was
sufficiently suspect that he did not wish to implicate himself in the scandal
surrounding the rationalist Stosch. Regardless, the new court preacher
Philipp Jakob Spener chose the day after the Christmas holidays,
December 27, 1693, to deliver a sermon in the Church of St. Nicholas
in Berlin, entitled "The Eternal Birth of the Son from the Being of the

---

[46] Samuel Przypkowski, *Cogitationes sacrae ad initium Evangelii Mathaei et omnes epistolas apostolicas nec non tractatus varii argumenti praecipue de iure Christiani Magistratus [. . .]*, "Eleutheropoli" [Amsterdam], 1692.

[47] See Luisa Simonutti, *Arminianesimo e tolleranza nel Seicento olandese. Il carteggio Ph. Van Limborch – J. Le Clerc*, Florence, 1984, pp. 30–36; Simonutti, "Resistance, Obedience and Toleration: Przypkowski and Limborch," in Martin Mulsow and Jan Rohls, eds., *Socinianism and Arminianism*, Leiden, 2005, pp. 187–206. See Przypkowski, *Cogitationes sacrae* (note 46), p. 689. See Limborch, *Theologia christiana ad praxin pietatis ac promotionem pacis Christianae unice directa*, Amsterdam, 1686, Book VII, cap. XX, §§ 37f.

[48] Johann Preuß concerning Stosch, in *Acta Stoschiana* (note 19), p. 695.

Father," in which he attacked the Brandenburg Socinians.[49] For his part, Stosch in his defense referred to this sermon and tried to depict Spener's anti-Socinianism as an example of the misunderstandings to which he had been exposed in Frankfurt:

> If our first and best teachers and the public Confessions now be heresies, may God forgive those who have not taught us better, including Herr Doctor Spener in his recent sermon on the eternal and double birth of the Son of God, translating the verse in Acts 13:33 badly, so that instead of the word *erwecket* [inspired, aroused, awakened], he has placed *auferweckt* [revived, resurrected]. And thus he has misled people who do not know the original language, or has left them in error.[50]

In contrast, Preuß and Crell felt pushed by Spener's sermon onto the defensive. Earlier, in 1691, Spener had already held two anti-Socinian sermons on "the eternal divinity of Christ."[51] The Socinians then gave thought to how they should react to the challenge of the superior court preacher. One of them, Stephan Gutturph, composed a text with the title "Observations on Herr Doctor Philipp Jacob Spener's Sermon on the eternal Divinity of Christ ... delivered in 1691" and had it circulated in manuscript, anonymously of course, in Berlin. Then in 1700 it appeared in print, possibly printed in Amsterdam.[52]

It is interesting to see how Spener also reacted. He took the attack of Gutturph as a "divine challenge," to explain the divinity of Christ in total clarity, and in his last years, until 1705, he spent a great deal of energy composing 800 quarto pages on the subject.[53] He does not seem to have

---

[49] See Johannes Wallmann, "Pietismus und Sozinianismus. Zu Philipp Jakob Speners antisozinianischen Schriften," in *Theologie und Frömmigkeit im Zeitalter des Barock. Gesammelte Aufsätze*, Tübingen, 1995, pp. 282–294. Spener's sermon was printed in 1694; Stosch wrote his defense on February 13, 16944; so either he had heard the sermon six weeks earlier, or he had a printed copy of it.

[50] Stosch to the elector, in *Acta Stoschiana* (note 19), pp. 673f. [Translator's note: Luther had also used the word *auferweckte*: his translation of Acts 13:32–33 reads: "Und wir verkündigen euch die Verheißung, die zu unseren Vätern geschehen ist, daß sie Gott uns, ihren Kindern, erfüllt hat in dem, daß er Jesum auferweckte; wie denn im zweiten Psalm geschrieben steht: "Du bist mein Sohn, heute habe ich dich gezeuget.")

[51] Wallmann, "Pietismus und Sozinianismus" (note 49).

[52] In a later essay Wallmann showed that the text was not by Crell as was assumed at first: "Philipp Jakob Spener und György Enyedi," in *Pietismus und Orthodoxie. Gesammelte Aufsätze III*, Tübingen, 2010, pp. 277–290, here at p. 279 n. 10.

[53] Jakob Philipp Spener, *Vertheidigung des Zeugnisses von der Ewigen Gottheit Unsers HErrn JESU CHRISTI, als des Eingebohrnen Sohns vom Vater [...] Sowohl Gegen den Angriff seiner hievon gehaltenen Predigten / welche hier mit beygedruckt sind / als auch am meisten gegen Enjedinum, Freyherrn von Wollzogen / Jer. Felbinger / Jo. Preussen / u. a. In den letzten Jahren seines Lebens verfasset und kurtz vor seinem seel. Ende geschlossen / so nun an das öffentliche Licht gestellet wird / Sampt einer Vorrede Pauli Antonii*, Frankfurt a.M., 1706.

known that his anonymous opponent was the relatively unknown Gutturph; perhaps he had thought he was Samuel Crell, whose anonymously published *Cogitationes novae de primo et secundo Adamo* ("New Thoughts on the First and the Second Adam")[54] had so provoked him, for he knew Crell and had conversed with him. When Gottlieb Stolle visited Spener in 1704, he noted what Spener told him:

> He was working on a book, *Contra Socinianos* ["Against the Socinians"] whenever he could, and was dictating to a servant for a couple of hours daily. There was no reason to think that the Socinians had given him doubts, but a few years earlier in Holland a work (consisting of three letters in German) had been published in quarto, including a few observations concerning Herr Doctor Spener's sermon from 1698. against the so-called Socinians These letters do not seem to be by one author; indeed, one seems to have been written by a woman. But they did not attack him [Spener] very effectively, and he intended to answer them briefly in the last chapter of the work he was writing.

> Crell himself confessed to him that he was the author of the book *De primo et secundo Adamo*. He had been with him two years earlier. In this book he accepted the concept of "satisfaction" [i.e., Christ's atonement for sin] although he disapproved of that word because it was not Scriptural.[55]

Crell had a specific person in mind, therefore, as he wrote his refutation. But in addition to the treatises of Crell and Gutturph, he was also arguing against the works of Preuß and Felbinger. Johannes Wallmann has shown that the late Spener understood that the "new Socinianism" was no longer a simple sect that was reviving the old Photinian heresy – as Abraham Calov had thought – but was instead trying to transform Christianity into a set of secular and humanist ethical teachings.[56] That is what made the rather opaque controversy of Gutturph, Crell, and Spener so significant for the intellectual situation in Germany at the beginning of the eighteenth century, and for the light it sheds on the case of Friedrich Wilhelm Stosch.

The strategy that Spener used against Crell and his comrades in arms was to isolate them. He quoted Jacques Abbadie, the Huguenot who had lived in Berlin and later in London, and he quoted the Huguenot-Anglican

---

[54] [Samuel Crell], *Cogitationes novae de primo et secundo Adamo*, s.l. 1700. See on this, Martin Mulsow, "Samuel Crell: An Intellectual Profile," in Lech Szczucki, ed., *Faustus Socinus and his Heritage*, Kraków, 2005, pp. 477–494.

[55] Stolle, *Reisejournal 1703/4*, Cod. IV. oct 49 in the University Library of Wrocław, p. 1188. See the edition by Martin Mulsow, ed., *Eine Reise durch die Gelehrtenrepublik. Gottlieb Stolles Journal der Jahre 1703/4*, Wiesbaden, 2018.

[56] Wallmann, "Pietismus und Sozinianismus" (note 49), p. 294. For the later process, Jonathan Sheehan, *The Enlightenment Bible: Translation, Scholarship, Culture*, Princeton, 2005.

theologian Pierre Allix, in order to present an apparently united front of Protestants against the Socinians.[57] But this tactic also illuminates the proceedings against Stosch. The explosiveness of his position, as I have explained, consisted in this: that the idea of a harmony between faith and reason was matter of great interest to large portions of the elite at the court in Berlin.[58] So Stosch, too, had to be isolated, even if not in the glaring manner demanded by the Frankfurt theologians. When Spener dealt with a religious rationalist like Abbadie, who had tried to prove the truths of faith "in a geometric manner,"[59] and when he enlisted him as part of his attack on the Socinians, he was being rather broad-minded.[60] As for his reliance on Allix, we can see how tightly connected the discussions in Germany were with the Trinitarian controversy in England and Holland – not just on the Socinian side but also that of their opponents. For example, in just these years Spener's friend Christoph Matthäus Seidel translated Allix's book into German, and that German translation should be regarded as a gesture precisely parallel to Spener's book against the Socinians.[61] Allix's book played Jews and Socinians off against each other, placing great weight on the value of oral traditions that mediated between the Old and New Testaments, namely mystical traditions like the Kabbalah that provided secret evidence of the Trinity. That was why even Gottfried Arnold had provided a foreword to the German translation. Allix was a defender of George Bull and provided welcome support against Crell's criticisms of Bull.[62] In this way Allix was to a certain extent – poignantly – a Socinian apostate. It seems that at least in the beginning he had belonged to the crypto-Socinian circle around Jacques Souverain and then only later, in

[57] See Wallmann, "Pietismus und Sozinianismus" (note 49), pp. 292f. For the positionings among the Huguenot communities, see Palladini, *Die Berliner Hugenotten* (note 14).
[58] Döring, *Frühaufklärung und obrigkeitliche Zensur in Brandenburg* (note 1), p. 58.
[59] See, e.g., Jacques Abbadie, *La vérité de la religion chrétienne*, Rotterdam, 1684.
[60] But one could also think of the generosity of Isaac Jaquelot - another member of the rationalist wing of the Huguenots – in the transmission of the Judaeus Lusitanus, which we observed in Martin Mulsow, *Enlightenment Underground: Radical Germany, 1680–1720*, tr. H. C. Erik Midelfort, Charlottesville, 2015, chapter 1.
[61] Christoph Matthäus Seidel, *Ausspruch der alten jüdischen Kirche wider die Unitarier, in dem Streite von der Dreyeinigkeit und Gottheit unsers Erlösers*, Berlin, 1707. See also Mulsow, *Enlightenment Underground* (note 60), chapter 2.
[62] Allix wrote his book against the work of an unknown Socinian, who like Crell had criticized Bull: *The Judgment of the Fathers Touching the Doctrine of the Trinity*, London, 1695. See Walter Glawe, *Die Hellenisierung des Christentums*, Berlin, 1912, pp. 66f. On Bull see Mulsow, *Enlightenment Underground* (note 60), chapter 5; and Mulsow, *Spinozism, Arianism, and Kabbalah: Unexpected Conjunctions in German Intellectual History of the Late Seventeenth Century. With the edition of an unknown attempt at rewriting Spinoza's Ethics by Johann Georg Wachter (1704)* (forthcoming).

England, turned decisively against the Socinians.[63] We can see here how incredibly complicated the alliances and appropriations were in these efforts to dismiss some thinkers or to set oneself apart from others. We need the concept of "intellectual field" in order to do even partial justice to such complexity. In the next chapter we will see, for example, that Johann Georg Wachter took up his position on the Trinitarian side, the side of Bull and Allix; along with the Unionists of Brandenburg [Translator's note: Unionists hoped to unite the Lutheran and Reformed churches] he also sympathized with Anglicanism, even though (like Stosch) he was also fascinated by Spinoza. We need to develop an alert "social sense" for such positional maneuvering if we hope to navigate these turbulent waters.

6 Samuel Crell and the Court Preachers of Brandenburg

Let us now return to Friedrich Wilhelm Stosch and his own self-description. The second name next to that of Le Clerc that Stosch mentioned in explaining his idea of *docta ignorantia* in dogmatic questions, the approach to which he was so attracted, was the name of Conrad Bergius. The Bergius family had many branches, comprising one of the central dynasties of theologians and court preachers in Brandenburg. In the late seventeenth and early eighteenth century, Brandenburg was a world which – like the Dutch – was characterized by the cohabitation of Calvinists and Socinians. The ruling house of Brandenburg had been Calvinist ever since 1613, and it worked steadily to establish a Calvinist elite in their largely Lutheran territory.[64] But Brandenburg had not signed the final resolutions of the Synod of Dort from 1618–1619, which had condemned the Arminians. Above all, Conrad Bergius's brother, the court

---

[63] Concerning Allix's work against Jews and Socinians, see Matt Goldish, "The Battle for 'True' Jewish Christianity: Peter Allix's Polemics against the Unitarians and Millenarians," in James E. Force and David S. Katz, eds., *Everything Connects: In Conference with Richard H. Popkin*, Leiden, 1998, pp. 143–162. On the circle around Souverain, see Martin Mulsow, "Jacques Souverain, Samuel Crell et les crypto-sociniens de Londres," in Jacques Souverain *Lettre à Mr. *** touchant l'apostasie*, ed. Sylvain Matton and Elisabeth Labrousse with a study by Martin Mulsow, Paris and Milan, 2000, pp. 49–63.

[64] Rudolf von Thadden, *Die brandenburgisch-preussischen Hofprediger im 17. Und 18. Jahrhundert. Ein Beitrag zur Geschichte der absolutistischen Staatsgesellschaft in Brandenburg-Preußen*, Berlin, 1959; Bodo Nischan, *Prince, People, and Confession: The Second Reformation in Brandenburg*, Philadelphia, 1994; Jürgen Luh, "Zur Konfessionspolitik der Kurfürsten von Brandenburg und Könige in Preußen 1640 bis 1740," in Horst Lademacher et al., eds., *Ablehnung, Duldung, Anerkennung. Toleranz in den Niederlanden und in Deutschland. Ein historischer und aktueller Vergleich*, Münster et al., 2004, pp. 306–324. See the more recent biograpical work of Lothar Noack and Jürgen Splett, *Bio-Bibliographien. Brandenburgische Gelehrte der Frühen Neuzeit. Berlin-Cölln 1640–1688*, Berlin, 1997.

preacher and professor at the University of Frankfurt on the Oder, Johann Bergius, had rejected these resolutions. He was himself later suspected of antitrinitarianism. His son, Georg Conrad Bergius, also became court preacher in 1664 and in 1696 followed Bartholomäus Stosch, the father of Friedrich Wilhelm Stosch, as a member of the Consistory. The families of Bergius and Stosch were so tightly intermeshed that Georg Conrad Bergius gave his daughter Eleonore as wife to the son of Bartholomäus Stosch, Friedrich Wilhelm. Both of these families, the Bergiuses and the Stoschs, favored not only peace among Protestants, but also supported contacts with Socinians and even showed a certain openness to their cause.

There was a pattern in all of this: almost all of these Brandenburg theologians had spent some of their time as students in the Netherlands. That was the place where the avant garde of the Reformed Church were living and spreading their influence. The same was true for the Socinians of Brandenburg, who also cultivated close connections with the Netherlands. We obtain a glimpse of this transnational milieu if we pursue the letters that went back and forth between Brandenburg and Holland, for example between the Socinian Samuel Crell and his fatherly friend Philipp van Limborch.

Crell wrote on January 14, 1701 to Limborch:[65] "Not so long ago a minister sent me the biography of [Simon] Episcopius [Translator's note: i.e., the leading Dutch Remonstrant, 1583–1643] that you recently published." The book had just appeared, probably at the end of 1700, but with the year 1701 on the title page.[66] "I devoured it hungrily, but it did not include the supplement aimed against Bull, which if I'm not mistaken the distinguished Herr Le Clerc was going to add."[67] In this matter Crell was well-informed about the activities of the publisher; in 1699–1700 he had been in Amsterdam and had published books there among the followers of Le Clerc, including works opposing George Bull, the defender of the

---

[65] Samuel Crell to Philipp van Limborch, Universiteitsbibliotheek Amsterdam, Ms. J 21 a. Concerning Limborch, see Mulsow, *Enlightenment Underground* (note 60), chapters 1 and 2; as well as Simonutti, *Arminianesimo* (note 47).

[66] *Historia vitae Simonis Episcopii scripta a Philippo a Limborch e Belgico in Latinum sermonem versa, et ab auctore aliquot in locis aucta*, Amsterdam, 1701. On Episcopius, see Kestutis Daugirdas, *Die Anfänge des Sozinianismus. Genese und Eindringen des historisch-ethischen Religionsmodells in den universitären Diskurs der Evangelischen in Europa*, Göttingen, 2016, pp. 439–487; Mark A. Ellis, *Simon Episcopius' Doctrine of Original Sin*, New York, 2005.

[67] Crell to Limborch (note 65): "Vir Doctissime atque Celeberrime. Communicavit mecum non ita pridem doctus quidem Ecclesiastes Historiam Vitae Dn. Episcopii nuper a Te editam, quam avidissime perlegi, sed appendicem contra D. Bullum, quam ni fallor Clariss. Dn.us Clericus additurus erat, desiderui."

Trinity.[68] I have earlier shown that Bull played a formidable role in these discussions. In the current enterprise Le Clerc had the task of writing a polemic against Bull intended as an appendix to Limborch's work. But evidently there had been opposition, which made it seem reasonable to Limborch that he should omit this polemic. Crell added, "I do hope, however, that whatever was not included for certain reasons in this biography will not be omitted from some other book on another occasion."[69]

Then he turned to another topic:

> Moreover, when I recently indicated to a certain professor of theology, a very good man, that the letter from J[ohann] Bergius concerning the Resolutions of the Synod of Dort was included in this book, he praised it with great pleasure and exuberance and said that he would have to purchase the book for that reason alone, even though it also included many observations on the life of Episcopius.[70]

Who was this man with whom Crell had been conversing? Because he was a professor, he must have been a member of the University of Frankfurt on the Oder, for that was the only university within Crell's range. And indeed the university did have a professor who was open-minded about the Socinians and who might well have been interested in the biography of the leader of the Remonstrants at the Synod of Dort in 1619: Samuel Strimesius. Indeed, in 1687 Strimesius was accused by his colleague Johann Christoph Becmann of harboring Socinian views.[71] Such an accusation commonly arose whenever anyone spoke in favor of openly tolerating the antitrinitarians, who were suffered only tacitly in Brandenburg. Strimesius, who was pushing for Unionist policies and was close to the Dutch Remonstrants, favored peace among the churches, a peace that would include the Socinians.

The letter from Bergius that Limborch published was addressed to his father-in-law, the court preacher Martin Füssel, who was therefore a deeply

---

[68] See also note 83. As early as 1697 Crell had written against Bull, using the pseudonym "Lucas Mellier," *Fides primorum Christianorum ex Barnaba, Herma et Clemente Romano illustrata*, London, 1697. See also the anonymous *Tractatus tres; quorum qui prior Ante-Nicenismus dicitur; is exhibet testimonia patrum Ante-Nicenorum: In quibus elucet sensus Ecclesiae Primaevo-catholicae, quoad articulum de Trinitate. In secundo brevis responsio ordinatur, ad D. G. Bulli defensionem Synodi Niccenae. Auctore Gilberto Clerke, Anglo. Argumentum postremi: Vera et antiqua fides de divinitate Christi, explicata et asserta, contra D. Bulli Iudicium Ecclesiae Catholicae etc.*, s.l., 1695.

[69] For Bull's role, see Mulsow, *Enlightenment Underground* (note 60), chapter 5. Crell to Limborch (note 65).

[70] Crell to Limborch (note 65).

[71] See the reconstruction of the case by Palladini, *Die Berliner Hugenotten* (note 14), pp. 20–40.

trusted fellow-combatant. Bergius complained to him about the Synod of Dort, which he had left in a state of disgust, appalled at the unfair suppression of Remonstrant arguments.[72] Bergius, who was then a professor at Frankfurt on the Oder and somewhat later, in 1623, a court preacher in Berlin, and then a counsellor to Elector Friedrich Wilhelm, had originally been a Lutheran, but in Leiden he had been educated as a Calvinist. Theologically he was near to the Remonstrants because he rejected the doctrine of double predestination.[73] After Elector Johann Sigismund of Brandenburg converted to Calvinism in 1613, relations between the Reformed elite and the Lutheran population were a constant issue in his territory. Bergius was the first one to come out in favor of official toleration in the electorate.

As Crell and Strimesius conversed about Bergius, Strimesius confided something to his Socinian interlocutor that must have been of great interest to him: "On this occasion," Crell reported to Limborch, "he showed me an excerpt from the writings of this Doctor Bergius." There he obviously found evidence for Bergius's liberal views, views that perhaps even hinted at Socinian tendencies. "I asked him whether there was an autograph copy somewhere that could prove even to a stiff-necked opponent that these were the actual words of Bergius, and that they had not been merely attributed to him by someone else."[74] Why was he so interested in this? In 1700 Crell had anonymously published a work that demanded open and not merely tacit toleration for the Socinians of Brandenburg.[75] That was risky because if the antitrinitarians expressed themselves in public or caused any kind of public disturbance, the court in Berlin was sure to cancel their de facto toleration. And indeed in this case an investigative commission was formed to examine the background of the publication; Crell got lucky because his authorship was kept secret.[76]

---

[72] Johannes Berg to Martin Füssel [probably 1619], in Limborch, *Historia vitae Simonis Episcopii* (note 66), pp. 210f.

[73] Bodo Nischan, "John Bergius: Irenicism and the Beginnings of Official Religious Toleration in Brandenburg-Prussia," *Church History* 51 (1982), pp. 389–406. Generally, see Rudolf von Thadden, *Die brandenburgisch-preußischen Hofprediger im 17. u. 18. Jahrhundert. Ein Beitrag zur Geschichte der absolutistischen Staatsgesellschaft in Brandenburg-Preußen*, Berlin, 1959.

[74] Crell to Limborch (note 65).

[75] [Samuel Crell], *Kurtze und einfältige Untersuchung, ob und warum die Reformierte Evangelische Kirche die also genannten Sozinianer mit gutem Gewissen dulden oder auch in ihre Gemeinschaft aufnehmen könne oder solle*, s.l., 1700. (Available in Halle, Franckesche Stiftungen and in Thüringer Universitäts und Landesbibliothek Jena.)

[76] The records are deposited in the Geheimes Staatsarchiv Preußischer Kulturbesitz Berlin, I. HA, Rep. 13, Nr. 24, Fasz. 22: "Gutachten der Hofprediger." See Palladini, *Die Berliner Hugenotten* (note 14), p. 18.

The court preachers were ordered to refute the work, but they refused, claiming that in doing so, the arguments as formulated by Crell would only reach a broader readership. Instead, they recommended that a foreign anti-Socinian work should be translated into German or that a Frankfurt professor should write a dissertation on it.[77]

In his work Crell had cited Johann Bergius among other authorities.[78] That produced a special state of alarm at court because they did not want to see Bergius, who had died in 1658, fall under suspicion of being too close to the Socinians.[79] And yet that was exactly why Crell and Strimesius were corresponding about Johann Bergius, for Strimesius was actually one of the Frankfurt professors who had been suggested as someone who might write against the "anonymous author." So if Crell and Strimesius were now exchanging unknown texts by Bergius, the issue was nothing less than the posthumous reputation of a theologian whom the Berlin court regarded as authoritative. Could it be proved that he was indeed close to the Socinians? There were rumors. In 1693 the Reformed preacher Andreas Malcom had reported to the court preacher Daniel Ernst Jablonski about Socinian activities over near the Polish border, and he added, "Item: Herr Bergius the court preacher was said to belong to their sect as well."[80] But Malcom tried to hush that rumor up and threatened to arrest the informer, Michel Escher, if he were to spread such talk further.[81] Bergius's son Georg Conrad was probably implicated in this rumor, but that indicated only all too clearly that the whole Bergius family was scandalously liberal.

As for obtaining autograph copies of Bergius's letters, Crell reported that Strimesius was pessimistic: "He doubted that this could be done, especially because Bartholomäus Stosch, the renowned courtier, preacher, and consistory councilor, who had provided him the excerpt, was no longer living."[82] The elder Stosch, who had died in 1686, had himself always had an open ear for the Socinians. Bergius's son Georg Conrad had followed Stosch in office as court preacher and consistory councilor. He had, as mentioned, married off his daughter to Stosch's son, Friedrich Wilhelm, whose career as a freethinker will occupy us further, and the marriage deepened the connections between the two families. And yet, ever since Bartholomäus Stosch had died, the source had dried up from

[77] Geheimes Staatsarchiv Preußischer Kulturbesitz Berlin (note 76).

[78] Thus for example on p. 4 Johann Berg was quoted with his Apostolic Rule.

[79] They did not want Crell to refer to Berg, for that would support his "truly heretical opinions" which "could thereby easily cast a shadow on the church here and its teachers." Quoted by Palladini, *Die Berliner Hugenotten* (note 14), p. 19.

[80] Ibid., p. 13.   [81] Ibid., pp. 13f.   [82] Crell to Limborch (note 65).

which one could obtain liberal documents from Brandenburg on the early history of toleration around 1700.

7 Bartholomäus Stosch and Socinianism

For this topic, however, I have found an unexpected clue to the sort of text Crell may have been hoping to find printed as an appendix to Limborch's life of Episcopius. For when he was in Amsterdam in 1700, he was occupied with printing a series of books, among them his own *Cogitationes de primo et secundo Adamo*, but also Jacques Souverain's *Platonisme dévoilé* as we have seen. Jean Le Clerc was in Amsterdam the whole time and he knew the arguments that men like Crell and Souverain were using against Bull. He would obviously have drawn on them for material to continue the attack on Bull, arguments that he could contribute as an appendix to Limborch's life of Episcopius. And yet he had so much to do that he did not get around to writing it.[83]

Back then – at least a year earlier – Crell had worked as a copy editor, probably with Charles Le Cène, a Huguenot, Arminian, and crypto-Socinian. He was most likely the man whom Crell criticized as "too close a friend of Le Clerc," because he had smoothed over Souverain's critique of Le Clerc in his book before it was published.[84]

Le Cène was also a translator who saw himself as a distributor of Socinian texts in Latin to a broader French-speaking public.[85] He was unable to publish many of his translations, however, for that would have been too dangerous. And so they probably circulated only in manuscript among like-minded people, first in Amsterdam and then from 1703 on in London, where Le Cène had relocated. Today a great many of these texts can be found in the Library of the Huguenot Society in London.[86] Among Le Cène's translations is the treatise entitled *Deux Considérations sur les termes et sur les façons de parler que des théologiens*

---

[83] We know this from a sentence in a draft letter from Limborch to Crell, November 26, 1701, Universiteitsbibliotheek Amsterdam, III, D 17, fol. 166r: "Appendicem contra Bullum D. Clericus, aliis majoris momentis lucubrationibus impeditus, hactenus non scripsit."

[84] [Samuel Crell], *Cogitationum novarum de Primo & Secundo Adamo*, s.l., 1700; [Jacques Souverain], *Le platonisme dévoilé ou Essai touchant le verbe platonicien*, "Cologne," 1700. See Mulsow, "Transnational Dissidence" (note 29), pp. 111f.

[85] See Hubert Vandenbosche and Jeroom Vercruysse, "Charles Le Cène: un Traducteur peu commun," in Andreas Wissowatius, *Religio rationalis*, ed. Zbigniew Ogonowski, Wiesbaden, 1982, pp. 63–66.

[86] See Eric R. Briggs, "Les manuscrits de Charles Le Cène (1647?–1703) dans la Bibliothèque de la Huguenot Society of London," *Tijdschrift voor de studie van de verlichting* 5 (1977), pp. 358–378.

employent pour expliquer la doctrine de la Trinité ("Two Considerations of
the Terms and Phrases which Theologians Use in Explaining the
Doctrine of the Trinity"). This was a French version of the work, *Duae
considerationes vocum, terminorum ac phrasium*, which was probably
published by Johann Preuß in 1684 in Guben (in Electoral
Brandenburg), but perhaps in Amsterdam as well.[87]

The work contains two texts: first the *Considerations* itself, which may
have been written by Preuß; but also the treatise, *Progressus in studio
cognitionis Dei*, which Le Cène translated as *Progrez dans la Connoissance
de Dieu* ("Progress in the Knowledge of God"). In the *Considerations*, the
various Socinian warnings (*Cautiones*) are subjected to an external examination because the treatment of Trinitarian "persons" and "substances"
appears to be so confusing and unclear that a reader was expected to shrink
from the whole doctrine. We can assume that it was Preuß's friend
Bartholomäus Stosch who composed this generally sympathetic evaluation. Le Cène strongly implied as much in a note added to his translation.[88] At the very end of the published volume came two additional
letters, which were clearly Preuß's replies to the criticisms of Stosch.[89]
Together with those letters the work represents a sort of *amica collatio*, or
friendly discussion, between the Reformed and Socinians in Brandenburg,
a tolerant disagreement like the one a year earlier between Philipp van
Limborch and the Jew Orobio da Castro,[90] which we saw in the early work
of Le Clerc that we discussed earlier.

Around 1700 Crell could have passed on the news (or was it just a
rumor?) of Bartholomäus Stosch's authorship to Le Cène when the two of
them were working on the edition of Souverain's book. Stosch had in fact
once before fallen under suspicion of being a Socinian or at least of making
common cause with the Socinians. That must have been before 1661 when
Johann Ludwig von Wolzogen was still alive – the Reformed Austrian

---

[87] *Duae considerationes vocum, terminorum ac phrasium, quae in doctrinà trinitatis a theologis
usurpantur, & quà ratione lis circa doctrinam de trinitate mitigari possit ac debeat. conscripta a
veritatis et pacis studioso, ut doctoribus occasio detur planiora et pleniora in eandem sententiam
commentandi,* "Cosmopolis," s.d., in the handwritten translation by Le Cène, fols. 315–345.

[88] Briggs, "Les manuscrits de Charles Le Cène" (note 85).

[89] Another text translated by Le Cène was entitled: *La Foy des premiers Chrétiens, martyrs et Ancient
Pères.* At the end the name of Jonas Schlichting is given, but it would be a mistake to attribute this
text to Schlichting. In reality it was a translation of seven pages from the work, *Fides primorum
Christianorum,* which appeared in 1697 pseudonymously under the name of Lucas Mellier. Its
author was none other than Preuß's son-in-law, Samuel Crell. So here we again find
Brandenburg Socinianism.

[90] Printed as Philipp van Limborch, *De veritate religionis christianae amica collatio cum erudito Judaeo,*
Gouda, 1686.

nobleman and theologian, who became a Socinian. Actually, we can be more precise about the time, for it must have been in 1646 because Wolzogen was then living in the Netherlands. Stosch had just been appointed a Brandenburg court preacher. Daniel Heinrich Hering reported:

> Through an unlucky accident this contact [between Stosch and the Socinians] was exposed: In order to learn his opinion the well-known Socinian Wolzogen in Holland had sent Stosch his work, 'Christian Instruction on how to Understand those Passages of Scripture, which today's Christians generally abuse to Claim the Three-Personhood of the One and Only True God'[91] Stosch had responded with his approval. But the postal service failed; the [postal] knapsack[92] fell into some water and stayed there for a time, but was then retrieved with all the wet letters, whereupon Stosch's letter was also discovered and opened. The Privy Councilor von Meinders, who was dealing with the matter, suppressed the news of the discovery but then revealed parts of it, whereupon the whole matter came to light.[93]

Naturally, this was a disagreeable scandal, for the Reformed elite of Brandenburg regularly had to distance themselves from the detested Socinians in order to avoid endangering their position. And therefore Stosch too in those years had to take all the more care that during his further contacts with the Socinians nothing of his secret views should reach a wider public.

And yet, with the work entitled *Progressus in studio cognitionis Dei* we find a similar pattern to that involving the contact with Wolzogen. A Socinian sends Stosch a treatise hoping for a favorable reaction, and Stosch gives his evaluation of it, which was partial agreement but with some sharp criticisms as well. From the diary of Daniel Ernst Jablonski, Hering concluded[94] that Limborch had

> written glosses on his copy of the *Duae Considerationes*, and on the title page [he set down] a sentence from Episcopius ... claiming that: "He would only too gladly peer into the hearts of such men who know the truth

[91] Johann Ludwig von Wolzogen, *Christliche Unterweisung, wie diejenige Oerter der Schrift, welche die heutigen Christen insgemein zu Behauptung der Drey-Persöhnlichkeit des einigen und allein wahren Gottes mißbrauchen, schriftmäßig zu verstehen seyn*, s.l., 1684.
[92] The term was *Felleisen*: an iron-clad postal box or knapsack.
[93] Daniel Heinrich Hering, *Beiträge zur Geschichte der Evangelisch-Reformierten Kirche in den Preußisch-Brandenburgischen Ländern*, vol. 2, Wrocław, 1785, p. 93.
[94] The diaries in which Jablonski took his notes on the Socinians of Brandenburg no longer survive. See Palladini, *Die Berliner Hugenotten* (note 14), p. 12.

and who cannot restrain themselves from now and then confessing it, but later do not wish to inform others of it."[95]

How had Jablonski come upon this copy? His diary entry came from 1693. Had Limborch sent it to Stosch? Had Jablonski then seen it after the death of Bartholomäus Stosch at the house of his son, Friedrich Wilhelm Stosch, perhaps after he was arrested in the middle of December because of his *Concordia*? The note concerning Limborch's glosses is a bit unclear, but the meaning probably was that Limborch had chosen a quotation from Episcopius in order to signify to Stosch, by writing in his book, that he knew that Stosch was an enthusiastic Remonstrant (or perhaps even a Socinian), even though he could not openly admit it because of his official position at the Berlin court. But also that he knew that Bartholomäus Stosch was the author of part of the *Deux Considérations*.

If the book had been printed in Amsterdam, then that was surely known to those close to Limborch, so it would be no surprise if Limborch sent off a copy. Bartholomäus Stosch was at the time in very poor health – he had been weak from the late 1660s on and had only occasionally felt up to being transported to church or to meetings of the Consistory.

8   The Search for Bergius's Autograph Manuscript

By 1702 this was all past history. Bartholomäus Stosch was dead and could no longer help. So how could one now get hold of works by Bergius that had been suppressed? Crell proposed to Limborch:

> But maybe you yourself, good sir, could obtain the autographs of this *amoebaea* [i.e., this correspondence][96] from the same source that apparently provided you with the autograph of this Bergius letter, as you indicate on p. 211 of your biography of Episcopius, unless I'm mistaken. For you testify that a few years ago you received from Germany not a copy of a letter but a letter.[97] But whoever was able to provide you with an autograph letter of Bergius could perhaps provide you also with the autograph of this excerpt.[98]

---

[95] Hering, *Beiträge zur Geschichte der Evangelisch-Reformierten Kirche* (note 93), p. 94.

[96] The word "amoebaeus" can be found among late Latin grammarians as a made-up word for a "dialogue song" between two singers in equal verses. See Johann Philipp Krebs, *Antibarbarus der lateinischen Sprache*, Frankfurt, 1843, p. 155. Here it probably meant the back and forth of a two-sided correspondence.

[97] Limborch had written: "Praetermittere non potui, quin Apographum hujus Epistolae, quam ex Germania paucos ante annos nactus sum, hic insererem." *Historia vitae Simonis Episcopii* (note 66), p. 211.

[98] Crell to Limborch (note 65).

That was a sensible proposal. Limborch clearly had a correspondent in Germany, who had been in a position – at least that was Crell's guess – to provide an authentic letter from Bergius.

Crell continued, "I have meanwhile implored a famous man in Berlin either to send me these letters, if they still exist, or to pass them on to the Remonstrants, whom they mainly concern, or to send them directly to you, my good sir."[99] Crell had connections to men at court, and especially to Field Marshall Count Heino Heinrich von Flemming.[100] He could have asked him, unless Flemming had already retired to Schloß Buckow in the "Märkische Schweiz"(the hill country about 30 miles east of Berlin). Continuing his line of questions to Limborch, Crell asked

> if the authentic letter from Bergius to Füssel was perhaps being kept hidden by his heirs, seeing that the words in your biography of Episcopius do not sufficiently clarify whether you yourself possess it as an authentic autograph [letter]. This famous man has not deprived me of all hope of recovering it, and he's promised me many times that he would try his best in the matter.[101]

Six weeks later Limborch answered, on November 26: "Your friend Daniel Stadnitz brought me the excerpt of the letter from Johann Bergius that was included with your letter, and I read it with great pleasure."[102] (See Figure 6.) So we can tell that in his letter to Limborch Crell had enclosed a copy of the excerpt that Strimesius had given him; the Socinian Daniel Stadnitz (Stadnik, Stadnicki) had carried Crell's letter with him on his way from Berlin or Frankfurt on the Oder to Amsterdam. That was safer than sending it by post. "I would wish," Limborch continued, "that this letter as a whole and many others from this man were in our hands. But it appears that it's not an excerpt of a letter from Bergius to Spanheim, but rather to a third person, for he does not address Spanheim in the second person and refers to Spanheim in the third person."[103] He was alluding to Friedrich Spanheim the Elder, the Orthodox Calvinist theologian and professor in Geneva and after 1642 in Leiden, the father of Ezechiel Spanheim.[104]

---

[99] Ibid.   [100] Palladini, *Die Berliner Hugenotten* (note 14), p. 40.

[101] Crell to Limborch (note 65).

[102] Draft of a letter from Limborch to Crell, November 26, 1701 (note 83).

[103] Ibid.: "Vellem hanc epistolam integram, aliasque illius Viri plures in manibus nostris esse. Verum esse non videtur excerptum ex epistola Bergii ad Spanhemium, sed ad tertium quaedam scripta: quia Spanhemium non alloquitur in secunda persona, sed de Spanhemio in tertia persona disserit."

[104] Concerning Friedrich Spanheim senior (1600–1649), see Dorothea Nolde, *Grenzüberschreitende Familienbeziehungen: Akteure und Medien des Kulturtransfers in der frühen Neuzeit*, Cologne, Weimar, and Vienna, 2008, pp. 140f.

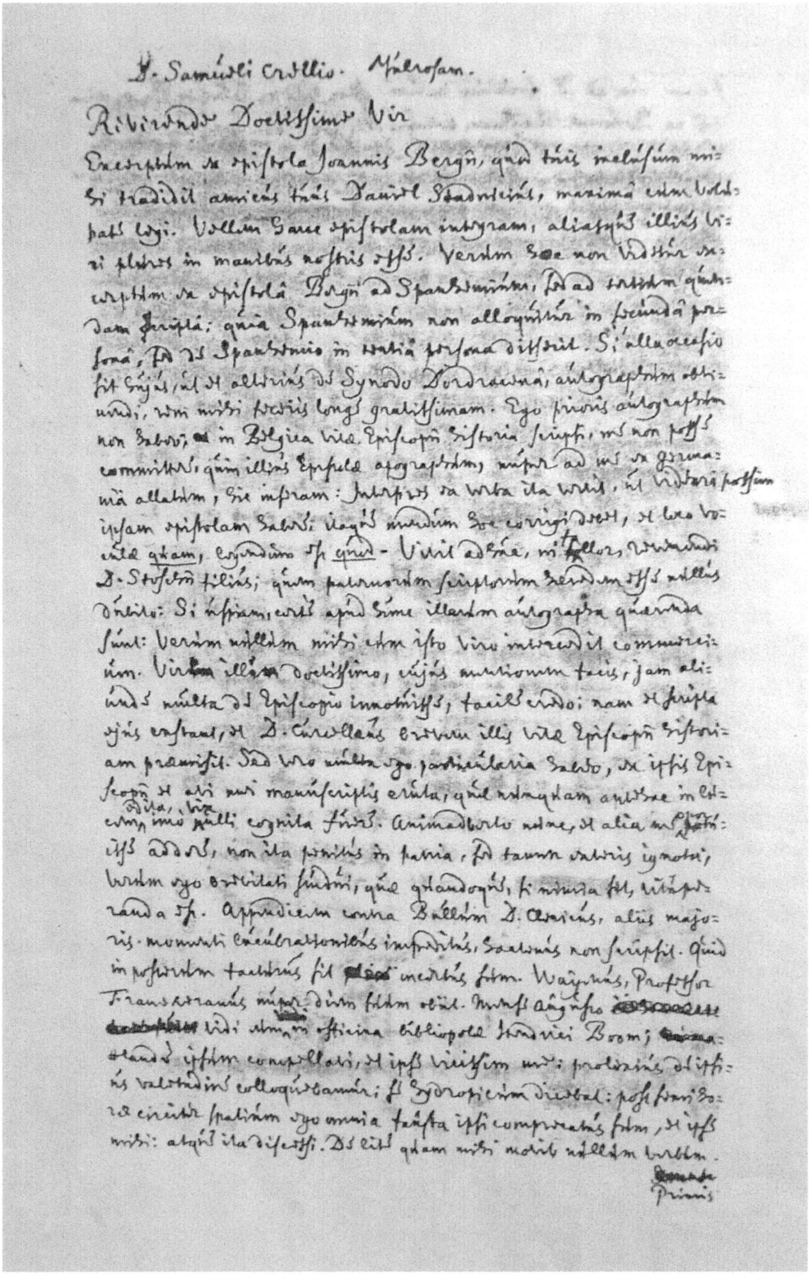

Figure 6   Philipp van Limborch: letter to Samuel Crell, November 26, 1701, University
Library Amsterdam, Ms. III, D 17, fol. 166r

If there's another opportunity to obtain this autograph letter as well as other letters concerning the Synod of Dort, I would be much obliged to you. I myself do not have the autograph of the first letter; in the Dutch version of the Life of Episcopius I wrote that I could not refrain from inserting the copy of this letter that recently arrived for me from Germany. From these words you concluded that it appeared that I might possess this letter, and so I must now correct the impression, and instead of the word *quam* one should read *quid*.[105]

Limborch realized that his first formulation had been ambiguous, but he made it clear that he had never had the autograph.

He continued: "If I'm not mistaken, however, Herr Stosch Junior, the son, is still living who doubtless is the heir of his father's writings. If they are anywhere, then they should surely be sought there. But I have no connection with that man."[106] Thus the task for Crell became clear. He had to establish contact and visit the heir to ask him for the texts. We still do not know, however, if the Stosch in question was Friedrich Wilhelm or one of his brothers.[107]

Did Crell do this? We do not know. We know only his answer to Limborch dated February 6, 1702. In it he expressed thanks first for the copy of the Bergius excerpt that Limborch had included with his reply:

I am delighted that you sent me that excerpt of the letter from Bergius, for which I would not wish to seem ungrateful. And I will certainly not rest until I have tried everything to obtain a copy of the whole letter, if not indeed the autograph of the one or of the other [letter] concerning the Synod of Dort. If only Pastor Stosch were still alive, with his humanity and the pious favor that he showed for the cause of the Remonstrants, even if he could not support their cause. Especially because he undertook on his own to have a copy of that letter on the Synod of Dort – [a letter of which] no one of us had even heard rumors – sent to me who was then living in Holland; for he had noticed that I was attending their lectures.[108]

---

[105] Draft of a letter from Limborch to Crell, November 26, 1701 (note 83): "Si alia occasio sit hujus, ut de alterius de Synodo Dordracena, autographum obtinendi, rem mihi feceris longe gratissimam. Ego prioris autographum non habeo; in Belgica vita Episcopii historia scripti, me non posse committere, quin illius Epistola apographum, nuper ad me ex Germania allatum, hic inseram: Interfieris ex verba ita . . . , ut videri . . . ipsam epistolam haberi; itaque interdum hoc corrigi debet, et loco voculae quam, legendum est quid."

[106] Ibid.: "Vivit adhuc, ni fallor, venerandi D. Stoschii filius, quem paternorum scriptorum haeredem esse nullus dubito: Si uspiam, certe apud hunc illarum autographa quaerenda sunt: Verum nullum mihi cum isto viro intercedit commercium."

[107] In addition to Friedrich Wilhelm Stosch, his brother Heinrich might have been meant.

[108] Samuel Crell to Philipp van Limborch, February 6, 1702 (note 65).

Indeed, Crell was in Amsterdam in the 1680s in order to study with Limborch.

> Not much later he [Bartholomäus Stosch] was removed from human affairs [i.e., he died], so when I returned from Holland I could no longer talk with him. Much was doubtless buried with him that would have been worth knowing, that could indeed have been made more widely known if he had not himself already revealed or communicated it. In any event he so admired Johann Bergius that he often said, if Bergius were still alive, I would sit at the feet of this Gamaliel so that he might instruct me. He valued the apostolic practice of his brother Conrad Bergius as second only to Holy Scripture. He had given this book to Martin Ruar, submitting it thereby to a prior censorship, as is apparent from his letters to Ruar. That excerpt is not from the letter to Spanheim but was written about Spanheim to others; that was apparent to me at the start; and I pointed that out to the learned excellent man from whom I received it. But since there are examples of learned men who speak in the third person concerning those from whom they have received letters when they write in response; and the honorable Herr Stosch doubtless had the autographs in his hand; he presented that excerpt with a notice attached that testified that the excerpt really did come from the letters of Bergius to Spanheim. Without better evidence, in any event, I know of nothing with which to justify a doubt, even if there may still be reason for doubt.[109]

The question of authenticity gave them no peace; proof of its decisive authority was too important.

On September 24 Limborch replied to Crell:

> I have no doubt that much went to the grave with Herr Stosch, material which if he were still alive could have been published to the great benefit of the Christian church. That man was working very hard for Christian peace. He did not at all approve the harshness of others against [the Remonstrants]. And whatever was useful to him for this pious purpose he seems to have collected with great care and enormous zeal. We do often see that the collections of great men are scattered after their deaths. I am hopeful for a better outcome with these writings, however, because the son, who inherited all his writings, has experienced the immoderate rigor of the clergy directed against himself, and perhaps groans under its weight even today.[110]

So here we have a crucial clue: the heir to the works of Bartholomäus Stosch was indeed most likely his son Friedrich Wilhelm. Limborch had

[109] Ibid.
[110] Draft of a letter from Limborch to Crell, September 24, 1702, Universiteitsbibliotheek Amsterdam, III, D 17, fol. 167r.

learned of his condemnation on account of the *Concordia,* and was referring to the scandal from which Stosch continued to suffer. He extracted a bit of hope from this: "Such [people] often preserve whatever might help heal or compensate for such tyrannical rigor."[111] Limborch was assuming, therefore, that Friedrich Wilhelm Stosch would have preserved the papers of his father, probably well hidden and protected against searches of his house, in order to have a bargaining chip in case he were subjected to even harsher repression, something he could use against the court. We do not know if this suspicion was justified,[112] but Limborch was already rubbing his hands at the prospect: "If you were able to obtain something from this highly learned man that might be published with profit, I will take care that it sees the light of day in a secure manner."[113] In a secure manner? That meant publishing in Amsterdam, without mentioning the editor or the publisher. We can sense how excited Crell must have been as he prepared to get in touch with Stosch.[114]

9 Friedrich Wilhelm Stosch and His Contacts

What did Friedrich Wilhelm Stosch do in 1702 when Crell sought to contact him? He had tried to return to honor for years after his trial and the condemnation of his book. His recantation in 1694 had not been sufficient. Yes, his salary was now being paid again, but he had to wait seven years for it and had had to repress any desire to express his opinions, until finally, in 1701, he returned to favor. On January 18 he participated in the festive coronation ceremony held in Königsberg and was named Prussian Privy Chamberlain and raised to the ranks of the nobility.[115] That was the day that Elector Frederick III became King Frederick I of Prussia, a rise in title and status that he had long and systematically pursued.[116] This was the occasion on which to rehabilitate Stosch, the son of the court

[111] Ibid.
[112] Even so, Peter Friedrich Arpe reported on the accusation leveled at Stosch: "ipsum patrem suum theologum de studio in Socino asseclas, reddere suspectum." Accordingly he apparently made his father seem guilty of sympathizing with Socinians. Arpe, *Feriae aestivales,* Hamburg, 1726, p. 127.
[113] Draft of a letter from Limborch to Crell, September 24, 1702 (note 110).
[114] This is the end of the surviving portion of the correspondence between Crell and Limborch. There is only one more draft letter from Limborch to Crell, dating from May 6, 1704, which no longer mentions this matter.
[115] See generally Melchior Friedrich von Stosch, *Genealogia des Hoch-Gräflich Freyherrlich- und Hoch-Adelichen Geschlechts derer von Stosch,* Leipzig and Breslau, 1736.
[116] See Steffen Martus, *Aufklärung: Das deutsche 18. Jahrhundert – ein Epochenbild,* Hamburg, 2015, pp. 23–44. [Translator's note: In 1701 Elector Frederick III became "King in Prussia"; his son Frederick II (reg. 1740–1786) was the first to be styled "King of Prussia."]

preacher, who had finally sufficiently proved that he would behave peacefully.

Stosch would have been crazy to risk a rehabilitation that had been gained only through much effort by complying with Crell's request and turning over the explosive material contained among his father's papers. Ten years earlier Crell's chances would have been better, for at that time he had taken the risk of receiving the radical philosopher Gabriel Wagner into his home (just as later Hermann Samuel Reimarus took in the radical biblical translator Johann Lorenz Schmidt as a tutor for his household[117]) – if it was indeed Wagner who was employed by Friedrich Wilhelm Stosch from 1693 to 1696. We know only that Wagner had a post with "Privy Secretary Stosch."[118] That could have been Friedrich Wilhelm Stosch, but also his brother Wilhelm Heinrich. As an intellectual, however, Friedrich Wilhelm would have had the far greater interest in conversing with Wagner and in supporting him financially. At that time Wagner had just published a work of almost 300 pages attacking Christian Thomasius, under the pseudonym "Realis de Vienna";[119] Stosch knew that book and cited it in his *Concordia*.[120] Scholars have paid very little attention to what this possible connection between Stosch and Wagner might have meant at the time of the trial against Stosch. Mostly, of course, clandestine authors remained opaque to one another; that is, they did not know each other personally even if they all read one another's anonymous or pseudonymous writings.[121] But there were rare exceptions and even close collaborations, of the sort that we may have here. In the records of Stosch's trial Wagner's name does not once appear; at that time his pseudonym had not yet been unmasked, and so his role as Stosch's accomplice appears to have remained undiscovered. But we may recall the denunciation mentioned at the start, in which a landlady or neighbor complained of "secret conventicles" and of "a wicked book," whereupon the government immediately sent a platoon of troops to Stosch's house.[122] But we should hesitate before concluding

[117] Paul Spalding, "Der rätselhafte Tutor bei Hermann Samuel Reimarus. Begegnung zweier radikaler Aufklärer in Hamburg," *Zeitschrift des Vereins für Hamburgische Geschichte* 87 (2001), pp. 49–64.

[118] See Siegfried Wollgast, "Einleitung," in Gabriel Wagner, *Ausgewählte Schriften und Dokumente*, ed. Siegfried Wollgast, Stuttgart, 1997, pp. 11f., without naming his source.

[119] Realis de Vienna [= Gabriel Wagner], *Discursus et dubia in Christiani Thomasii introductionem ad philosophiam aulicam*, Regensburg, 1691. On Wagner see also Arnaud Pelletier, "Substances défendues: l'accès à la substance selon Christian Thomasius et l'enjeu métaphysique des échanges entre Leibniz et Gabriel Wagner," in Herbert Breger and Sven Erdner, eds., *Natur und Subjekt, IX. Internationaler Leibniz-Kongress*, vol. 3, Hanover, 2011, pp. 821–830.

[120] Stosch, *Concordia* (note 2), p. 6.

[121] See Mulsow, *Die unanständige Gelehrtenrepublik* (note 41), p. 234.

[122] Palladini, *Die Berliner Hugenotten* (note 14), p. 87.

that this was how Stosch and Wagner collaborated. Instead they would have been extremely cautious in their dealings with each other because they had to worry about possible reciprocal denunciations.

When Samuel Crell knocked on Stosch's door in 1702, would he have appealed to their common connections, because he was the son-in-law of Johann Preuß, and Preuß and Bartholmäus Stosch – along with his son – were known to be friends?[123] It could not have been that simple for in that case Crell would have used his correspondence with Limborch long before to discuss this possible way of obtaining the letters of Johann Bergius. Ever since the publication of the *Concordia* (if not earlier), Preuß had broken off his friendship with Friedrich Wilhelm Stosch; in the proceedings against Stosch he had spoken clearly against the book. Between the genuine Socinians and Stosch there were no longer any close connections. It was therefore more likely that he would have appealed to their friendship during Stosch's student years when he was living in Frankfurt on the Oder.

So we must turn to those student years and go back to the 1660s in order to understand Stosch's social connections better. Several Socinian congregations were living near Frankfurt. Often, in the first half of the seventeenth century, Socinian "island" communities came to light in Poland very near the border with Brandenburg or near Silesia; for example, in the villages of Schmiegel or Meseritz.[124] That is because the reach of the central authorities was even weaker there than elsewhere.[125] When the Socinians were expelled from Poland in 1658, their settlements removed themselves just a few dozen miles to the west to be inside the borders of the Holy Roman Empire.[126] If there were many German immigrants to these

---

[123] On the relations between Preuß and Bartholomäus Stosch, see again the *Duae considerationes vocum, terminorum ac phrasium, quae in doctrinâ trinitatis a theologis usurpantur* (note 87). Concerning the friendship between Friedrich Wilhelm Stosch and Preuß see Georg Gottfried Küster, *Marchiae litteratae specimen tertium*, Berlin, 1743, p. 4.

[124] I have profited here from a proposed research project (not yet approved) by Lukasz Bieniasz on the island communities. See Bieniasz, "Über Schmiegelisten. Schmiegel und Meseritz als Wirkungsorte polnischer und deutscher Antitrinitarier am westlichen Rande der Adelsrepublik Polen-Litauen im 16. und 17. Jahrhundert," in Martin Mulsow, ed., *Kriminelle – Freidenker – Alchemisten. Räume des Untergrunds in der Frühen Neuzeit*, Cologne, 2014, pp. 61–80; Hans-Jürgen Bömelburg, "Konfession und Migration zwischen Brandenburg-Preußen und Polen-Litauen 1640–1722. Eine Neubewertung," in Joachim Bahlcke, ed., *Glaubensflüchtlinge. Ursachen, Formen und Auswirkungen frühneuzeitlicher Konfessionsmigranten in Europa*, Berlin, 2008, pp. 119–144.

[125] Maciej Ptaszyński, "Das Ringen um Sicherheit der Protestanten in Polen-Litauen im 17. Jahrhundert," in Christoph Kampmann and Ulrich Niggemann, eds., *Sicherheit in der Frühen Neuzeit*, Cologne, 2013, pp. 57–75.

[126] On migration for religious reasons generally, see Alexander Schunka, "Konfession und Migrationsregime in der Frühen Neuzeit," in Ute Frevert and Jochen Oltmer, eds., *Europäische Migrationsregime* (*Geschichte und Gesellschaft*, 35(1) (2009)), Göttingen, 2009, pp. 28–63.

western Polish island communities before 1658, afterward there were Polish immigrants to the Silesian and eastern Brandenburg villages.[127] For example, in Brandenburg there were the villages of Königswalde (today Lubniewice), Selchow (today Żelechów), and Griesel (today Gryżyna in Bytnica, German Beutnitz), all just a few miles apart from each other. When Jablonski asked Pastor Malcom for a report on the Socinians in Brandenburg in 1693, he learned from him, "There are some [Socinians] along the border in great numbers . . . . They help one another with money and buy up many farms for themselves."[128] Crell's family lived in Königswalde, the Preuß family in Selchow. Malcom reported that Preuß was the spiritual leader of the Socinians, while Paul Schlichting, the son of Johan Schlichting was their political head. Johann Preuß was living from the mid-1660s as a preacher in Selchow, and he must have traveled often – like many Socinian students[129] – to nearby Frankfurt on the Oder. That is where Friedrich Wilhelm Stosch went to study in 1666.

It seems obvious, therefore, that as a young man Stosch would have gained a close acquaintance with Socinian ideas, even if, as he insisted during his trial, he never read any Socinian writings. That is not the point. Rather, a mixture of Socinianism and Arianism appeared to have been just part of the spiritual air that the young Stosch learned to breathe. No wonder Frankfurt University in its accusation against him quickly hit upon the charge of Socinianism. Samuel Pufendorf reported:

> The crazy book, *De condordia rationis et fidei*, is causing great terrors here. The author is an Electoral secretary named Stosch, whose father was a court preacher here, but was rumored to be a secret Socinian. He may have spread some of that same poison in these villages, and otherwise done our churches great harm. But now God appears to be punishing the sins of the fathers [by taking it out] on their children.[130]

Stosch vehemently rejected these suspicions. He had to do so, of course; he could never have admitted being a Socinian. But he was also right, in a

---

[127] Jörg Deventer, "Nicht in die Ferne – nicht in die Fremde? Konfessionsmigration im schlesisch-polnischen Grenzraum im 17. Jahrhundert," in Bahlcke, ed., *Glaubensflüchtlinge* (note 124), pp. 95–118.

[128] Jablonski, *Tagebuch*, quoted in Palladini, *Die Berliner Hugenotten* (note 14), p. 13.

[129] See also Günter Mühlpfordt, "Arianische Exulanten als Vorboten der Aufklärung. Zur Wirkungsgeschichte des Frührationalismus polnischer und deutscher Arianer vom 16. bis ins 18. Jahrhundert," in Johannes Irmscher, ed., *Renaissance und Humanismus in Mittel- und Osteuropa*, vol. 2, Berlin, 1962, pp. 220–246.

[130] Samuel Pufendorf to Adam Rechenberg, Berlin, no date (end of 1693 or beginning of 1694), *Gesammelte Schriften*, vol. 1: *Briefwechsel*, ed. Detlef Döring, Berlin, 1996, p. 368; see Döring, *Frühaufklärung und obrigkeitliche Zensur in Brandenburg* (note 1), p. 13.

sense, to reject the charge because he absorbed much more in Frankfurt than just the theological views of the antitrinitarians. One might say that he became a radicalized Socinian: a man who had transferred his intentions – seeing Christianity as a moral philosophy, rejection of eternal hellfire, the imperfection of the first man – into a naturalistic, no longer really Christian framework. How had it come to that?

10 Professor Becmann's Lecture

Stosch's student years again appear to provide the key. There are parallels here with the radicalization that Urban Gottfried Bucher underwent as a student in Wittenberg, a case we examined in Chapter 1. There too a student had pulled together his own worldview by drawing on the lectures he heard and what he read in the reviews. In the case of Stosch, however, it was not even necessary to flip or mirror the standard lessons, as Bucher had done, because Stosch's teacher served up various paradoxical views on a silver platter.

That teacher was Johann Christoph Becmann.[131] In his early years Becmann was a highly unconventional philosopher who took extraordinary liberties. For him "liberty of philosophizing" (*libertas philosophandi*) was a basis of his beliefs and evidently also of his actual practice. Freedom of thought, of conscience, of religion, of research, was for him a basic human right (*jus hominis, quia homo est*). Rights like this were valid for subjects over against their ruler; therefore in Becmann's hands the absolutist state became a system of reciprocal rights and duties – he argued for a constitutional state. Because Becmann proceeded from the theories of the Calvinist political theorist Johannes Althusius, he regarded the rights of

---

[131] On Becmann (1641–1717) see ADB, vol. 2, pp. 240f. For his political ideas, see Horst Dreitzel, "Hobbes-Rezeptionen. Zur politischen Philosophie der frühen Aufklärung in Deutschland," in Hans-Erich Bödeker, ed., *Strukturen der deutschen Frühaufklärung 1680–1720*, Göttingen, 2008, pp. 263–307; Wolfgang Weber, *Prudentia gubernatoria*, Tübingen, 1992, pp. 145–150; Merio Scattola, *Dalla virtu alla scienza. La fondazione e la trasformatione della disciplina politica nell'eta moderna*, Milan, 2003, pp. 454–461. On the connections among Becmann, Masius, and Pufendorf, see Frank Grunert, "Zur aufgeklärten Kritik am theokratischen Absolutismus. Der Streit zwischen Hector Gottfried Masius und Christian Thomasius über Ursprung und Begründung der summa potestas," in Friedrich Vollhardt, ed., *Christian Thomasius (1655–1728). Neue Forschungen zur Frühaufklärung*, Tübingen, 1997, pp. 51–77. A portion of Becmann's literary estate dealing mainly with his geographical works can be found in the Geheimes Staatsarchiv Preußischer Kulturbesitz, Berlin, VI. HA, "Nachlass J. C. Becmann." Printed letters to Schurtzflisch from the early period of interest to us, namely from 1671, are in Conrad Samuel Schurtzfleisch, *Epistolae nunc primum editae*, Wittenberg, 1700, pp. 17–19 and 25f. Stosch did not attend Strimesius's lectures for the simple reason that Strimesius began teaching there only in 1674, when Stosch had just left the university.

subjects as providing the possibility of legitimate resistance, if, for example, a monarch failed to live up to his duties. From this point of view, the state was the product of a balance of the needs and interests of human beings, needs and interests that led to contracts and sometimes to the transfer of individual rights to some larger entity. In this way Becmann managed to synthesize Althusius's Calvinist view of the state with that of Hobbes, who as we know proceeded from the interests of, and calculations of interest by, individuals. The Hobbesian claim of a right to protect oneself (*conservatio sui*) was aligned with claims of "protection of the state" (*conservatio status*), which played a prominent role in German political theory of that time. But Becmann also preserved a broad space for a sort of individual utilitarianism, broader perhaps than that found in any other established German theorist, even if such rights had to be balanced with those of others.

That was Becmann's theory. In the concrete context of his university and his dealings with students, he translated theory into practice by putting forward without hesitation various "paradoxes," scandalous books that ran counter to common opinion, works that he read with them or at least discussed. Stosch heard and took notes[132] on his ethics lectures in 1669–1670, and especially one that evidently impressed him deeply. When Stosch quoted Hobbes and Gassendi in his *Concordia*, as he often did, he was mining his lecture notes. According to Stosch, his Frankfurt professors were learned men, some of whom

> had read Socinian books as well as the author of the *Pre-Adamites*,[133] and had read Hobbes more carefully than I had; for such books, and especially the content of the Pre-Adamite book, are excerpted in the *Universal History* by Doctor Becmann;[134] and the *Leviathan* of Hobbes is excerpted in the ethics lectures by the same man; from his oral discourses I also learned for the first time that the soul of man consists in the flux of blood and spirits, as he refers to the nature of the soul in his published ethics as an example of learned ignorance (*doctae ignorantiae*).[135]

That last point is of special interest. It gives us some insight into the way in which a professor might make "paradoxes" (i.e., dangerous and

---

[132] See *Acta Stoschiana* (note 19), p. 674.
[133] This was the extremely controversial book by Isaac La Peyrère, *Praeadamitae*, Amsterdam, 1655. See Richard H. Popkin, *Isaac La Peyrère (1596–1676): His Life, Work and Influence*, Leiden, 1987.
[134] See Johann Christoph Becmann, *Historia orbis terrarum geographica et civilis*, Frankfurt, 1673. The work was later often reprinted. Stosch, however, probably meant the lecture that Becmann gave on universal history.
[135] *Acta Stoschiana* (note 19), pp. 671f.

unorthodox teachings) known to students. He could pass on the doctrine as normally handed down – here the immortality and immateriality of the soul – but then mention the opposite doctrine, as propounded for example by contemporary materialists and mortalists. One might then declare the opposition as irreconcilable and draw the conclusion that human beings in such cases must then exercise a learned ignorance, *docta ignorantia*, reason enough for a humble self-reflection on the limits of human nature. Like Bucher a bit later, Stosch found the naturalistic understanding of the soul to be more persuasive than the traditional, Christian one, and he adopted it in his book: "And even if the souls of men and animals differ by many degrees from each other, it is not foolish to declare that they are of the same essence . . . ."[136]

Most importantly, Gassendi's utilitarian ethics, his political Epicureanism, which we learned about in Chapter 4 of this book, as a reservoir for radical ideas, must have played a huge role in Becmann's lecture because – originating in a close engagement with Hobbes[137] – it offered a foundation for politics that inspired Becmann.[138] All of this resurfaced in Stosch's *Concordia*, especially in its passages on moral philosophy. After all, the book had promised in its title to deal with moral philosophy. According to Stosch, the good is whatever is useful for the mental and bodily health of men.[139] He described happiness along the same lines: "Happy are those who aside from mental gifts and [earthly] possessions have received a sort of bodily constitution that allows them the opportunity to live free of pain and a mind (*anima*) that rejoices in striving for wisdom."[140] But Stosch was not lucky in this way. He had been a sickly child and had problems with his health all his life, so that after just ten years in service, in 1686, he had to give up his position as a court official and withdraw to his home. So he added:

> But happy too are they who, although they have a body that tends to sickness, nonetheless rule it with so much care, keeping it within bounds with such moderation, that even if they cannot avoid pains entirely, they at

---

[136] Stosch, *Concordia* (note 2), p. 78. See also Annemaie Nooijen, *"Unserm grossen Bekker ein Denkmal?" Balthasar Bekkers "Betoverde Weereld" in den deutschen Landen zwischen Orthodoxie und Aufklärung*, Münster, 2009, pp. 202–211.

[137] Gianni Paganini, "Hobbes, Gassendi et le De cive," in Miguel Benítez et al., eds., *Materia actuosa. Antiquité. Age Classique. Lumières. Mélanges en l'honneur d'Olivier Bloch*, Paris, 2000, pp. 183–206.

[138] On Gassendi see also Silvie Taussig, *Pierre Gassendi (1592–1655). Introduction à la vie savante*, Turnhout, 2003.

[139] Stosch, *Concordia* (note 2), pp. 38ff

[140] Ibid., p. 44. German in Stiehler, *Materialisten* (note 3), p. 50.

least make them smaller and tolerable, so that they do not too much hinder their spirit from enjoying life's pleasures.[141]

That was a more realistic image of Stosch's way of life. Epicureanism meant for him an educated, refined pleasure in life, which Gassendi had resurrected and defended in opposition to the blanket condemnations of Epicurus as an atheist and voluptuary. So Stosch noted in this regard:

> See Gassendi, *Remarks on the Philosophy of Epicurus*, Volume 2, p. 25, where he says, "The wise man believes that the highest happiness is that of God alone; while man [is happy only to the extent that he] receives some portion of it." Ibid., p. 19: "The wise man will steel himself against fortune." Ibid., p. 113.[142]

At the place where Stosch took up questions of law and considered Pufendorf's talk of "moral entities," he posed the question – as an example of his way of thinking – whether a person is obliged by natural law to have children. That gave him a chance to ask whether justice should orient itself to nature or to God. "If one understands the law as a natural rule and a natural instinct, then it's clear that one is obliged by it, that is to follow the constitution of one's body or to bring it in accord with nature to beget similar beings. To that extent it would be right to do that and wrong to hinder it." As for himself, Stosch had had several children, and thought of himself as a "fertile father" (*foecundus genitor*).[143] "If, however, one understands the law as the command of God, then I say no." For a natural law conceived as divinely given, begetting children could not be a command. "The 'light of nature' does not recognize any commandment in the true sense; and whoever's body is not suited for procreation or is not so inclined will not be under any divine or natural duty to do so." Natural law understood as divine, therefore, had no force to prevail against one's natural tendencies. "He will be regarded as wiser if he suppresses his sexual drive and prefers celibacy to marriage. For that reason this whole business of the body should be measured according to the constitution and instinct

---

[141] Stosch, *Concordia* (note 2): "Felices et illi, quibus cum obnoxium morbis corpus obtigerit, ea tamen providentia id regunt, ea temperantia corrigunt, ut nisi dolores penitus devitent, illos saltem leves tolerabilesque sic reddant, ut non valde obstent, quo minus animo suis frui voluptatibus concedatur."

[142] Ibid., p. 45: "Vide Gassendi Animad. In Epicuri Philosophiam Tom. 2 p. 25, ubi docet Sapientem existimaturum Felicitatem Soli Deo summam competere; Homini eam tantum quae magis ac minus recipiat; item pag. 19. Sapientem adversus Fortunam se comparaturam, item pag. 113." See Gassendi, *Animadversiones in decimum librum Diogenis Laertii qui est de vita, moribus, placitisque Epicuri*, Lyon, 1649. Gassendi's "Ethics" can be found in vol. 3. Therefore it can be assumed that Stosch was using the two-volume edition of Lyon, 1675.

[143] In his autobiographical sketch, printed in Küster, *Marchiae litteratae* (note 123), p. 2.

of the body rather than by reason and law."[144] Again he cited Gassendi. Natural law, the reader must conclude, even if it was formulated using Pufendorf's concepts, had a basis that was only naturalistic and utilitarian. So we have reached those minimal positions that Budde opposed in 1698, five years after the Stosch scandal, as we saw in the previous chapter.

11   Becmann's Literary Round Table

How closely was the young Stosch involved with Becmann? And how closely was he connected to the Socinians? This much is clear: Stosch was deeply disappointed that Becmann, from whom he had learned so much, had now, twenty years later when Stosch published his *Concordia*, become a theologian representing the other side, Orthodoxy; indeed he had become Stosch's chief opponent. He must have been disappointed in the same way that later Lau was disillusioned by Thomasius. Stosch in fact complained

> that Herr Professor Becmann, who at the beginning of his professorate taught me and other disciples so many paradoxes, as I can and will prove from my lecture and reading notes, [changed and] after he became a professor of theology formulated maxims that asserted the more rigid opinions of the [Protestant] Reformers; so now if you do not sing his tune exactly, you'll be branded heterodox . . . .[145]

This was a common occurrence: with the switch over to the higher faculty of theology came a change in roles. Stosch suspected that Becmann undertook this volte-face intentionally because in his younger years he had brought himself under suspicion with his Hobbesianism and his knowledge of heterodox writings – and probably also because of his consorting with Socinian students. He wanted, in Stosch's words, to "repair" his Orthodox reputation, which "at the beginning he had almost lost because of teachings that savored of libertinism (*libertinismum olentia*

---

[144] Stosch, *Concordia* (note 2), pp. 68f.: "Si legem pro dictamine et instinctu naturali capias, statuendum esse, eum ad id teneri, hoc est, ex constitutione corporis ipsius sequi, vel eum naturaliter ferri ad procreationem sui similium, ac proinde recte id facere et male impediri. Si vero legem pro Jussu divino capias, respondeo negando. Lumen enim naturae Jussum proprie dictum ignorat, et cuius corporis ad generandum vel non aptum vel non proclive est, cum nulla obligatione divina vel naturali ad id teneri et Sapientiorem haberi qui libidinis affectu suppresso coelibatum matrimonio praefert. Vid. Gassend. A in Ph. E. t.2, p. ac properea totum hoc negotium corporis constitutione et instinctu potius metiendum esse, quam ratione et lege."

[145] *Acta Stoschiana* (note 19), p. 663.

dogmata) ...."[146] So now he persecuted others and especially the Socinians.

When Johann Friedrich Mayer was corresponding with Becmann in 1687 about the book *De tribus impostoribus*, he was dealing with a man who, though Calvinist, was regarded as a solid and Orthodox theologian. The embittered Stosch could see this change only as corruption inspired by ambition: "Freedom, high office, dignity, bread, and temporal welfare" were to follow, and that supposedly provided sufficient grounds for Becmann to renounce his real views.[147] In 1677 Samuel Strimesius had attacked Becmann for his Hobbesianism in a work entitled *Praxiologia apodictica seu Philosophia moralis demonstrativa, pithanologiae Hobbesianae opposita* ("An Incontestable Theory of Action or A Conclusive Moral Philosophy, As Opposed to the Specious Arguments of the Hobbesians"),[148] but Becmann returned the favor by accusing Strimesius of Socinianism and Arminianism.

In his early years Becmann regarded the Bible as a text that one might handle with complete freedom. He taught his students the theory of accommodation, the idea that the biblical text spoke in florid metaphors aimed at simple people even if behind the words lay a complicated scientific and theological doctrine, one that was not suitable for the ears of simple folk. Thus Stosch claimed that

> with Herr Becmann he had only maintained this: that whatever Scripture said about the motion of the sun was expressed so as to accommodate the imagination and understanding of the vulgar [*ad Phantasiam & captum vulgi*]. See his *Dissertations* and *Corollaries*; and in addition he held that anyone would all too easily fall into error if he took everything literally and interpreted whatever was spoken parabolically and figuratively and improperly as if it was to be understood as proper and simple ....[149]

Along with the method of "learned ignorance," the theory of accommodation was the second strategy for bridging the ever-growing gap between physical and scientific descriptions and the literal text of the Bible.

---

[146] Ibid., p. 664.
[147] Ibid. On Mayer and Becmannn, see also Mulsow, *Enlightenment Underground* (note 60), chapter 3.
[148] Samuel Strimesius, *Praxiologia apodictica seu Philosophia moralis demonstrativa, pithanologiae Hobbesianae opposita*, Frankfurt a.O., 1677; see also Strimesius, *Origines morales, seu Dissertationes aliquot selectiores, vera moralium fundamenta complexae*, Frankfurt a.O., 1679.
[149] *Acta Stoschiana* (note 19), p. 683.

Especially in England Latitudinarian scholars used this strategy when they tried to combat atheism by using the new physics apologetically.[150]

Stosch's suspicion that Becmann's theology was a sort of Nicodemism that concealed his philosophical views should not be dismissed out of hand.[151] Of course Becmann's surprisingly two-faced approach could also be interpreted the other way around: precisely because he was confessionally a Calvinist and an opponent of church unification, even though that was the official policy at the Hohenzollern court, perhaps he was drawn politically to support absolutism and noble domination over the peasants.[152] Admittedly, this interpretation, in which Becmann's Hobbesianism was the supposed Nicodemism as opposed to his supposed Calvinism, does not take the stages of his university career as a professor into account. His theological writings only began after he attained his doctorate in theology in 1672, and then, much later, with his shift to a professorship in theology.

In any event, Stosch cast aspersions at Becmann and turned the suspicions of Socinianism, which he had endured, back at his teacher:

> I have never read such forms of speech in Socinian books and never consorted with Socinians or their authors; but it appears that the Frankfurt theologians know them better than I do, and especially Herr Dr. Becmann, who back in my day dined with a Socinian named Felbinger and other Hungarian Socinians.[153]

Becmann had indeed, like most professors, taken in a series of students who either lived with him or at least dined at his table. That was a recognized method for augmenting one's meager salary. At the dinner table of the young professor the latest philosophical theories must have been discussed, but also – even if in coded language – Socinian topics. Stosch noted during his trial:

> If anything back then had smacked of Socinianism or Hobbesian ideas, they were probably the above-quoted words that Herr Dr. Becmann inculcated

---

[150] See Margaret C. Jacob, *The Newtonians and the English Revolution, 1689–1720*, London, 1976. See e.g., Thomas Burnet's use of the theory of accommodation for his notion of the Flood. On that, see Paolo Rossi, *The Dark Abyss of Time: The History of the Earth and the History of Nations from Hooke to Vico*, Chicago, 1987.

[151] One could actually test this suspicion only by making a careful examination of Becmann's correspondence.

[152] See Günter Mühlpfordt, "Die Oder-Universität," in Günther Haase and Joachim Winkler, eds., *Die Oder-Universität Frankfurt. Beiträge zu ihrer Geschichte*, Weimar, 1983, pp. 19–72, here at pp. 50f.

[153] *Acta Stoschiana* (note 19), p. 668. [Translator's note: Stosch used the word "Ungern" ("unwilling") but evidently meant "Ungarn" or Hungarians.]

in me and in others so energetically, both in speech in in writing; and now he wishes to tarnish his disciple, who explains himself better than he does, using arguments from Scripture and Orthodoxy, by accusing him of Socinianism. It is shameful for a scholar, if he should deflect guilt but then discover his own spears turned against himself.[154]

What was this student getting at when he said that something in the lessons of his professor had "smacked" of Socinianism. The issue had clearly triggered the highly sensitive memory of a student who was trying to isolate from certain expressions used by his teacher whatever might tend toward secret, radical, Socinian conclusions. That presumes that intellectuals might set forth their ideas on controversial topics by using certain patterns or tactics of expression that could then be decoded by attentive students. Stosch had decoded his teacher's words – rightly or wrongly – to conclude that Becmann was really a follower of Hobbes and Sozzini and that he was practicing Nicodemism by teaching officially as a good Calvinist at the university.

But had Stosch observed all of this from afar rather than at close range? A dedicatory poem sheds some light on that question, a poem that Stosch contributed to a dissertation by his professor in 1669 – the year of Becmann's ethics lecture:

> O friend / how greatly may the stars increase your fame
> By shielding this my verse from God's reproof /
> No further witness is needed, nor any further teaching /
> For every mouth resounds in praise of you.
> I place your fame beside your friendship /
> And thus with double favor am I highly pleased.
>   – Placed here in honor of his specially valued friend
>   by F. W. Stoschius.[155]

Unless this poem was intended for the respondent, Johannes Steinheuser from Spandau (which seems most unlikely), we must conclude that Stosch was on very good terms with the young Professor Johann Christoph Becmann, who was, after all, only seven years older. Furthermore, he spoke emphatically, after all, of friendship. We do not know for sure, however, that he himself belonged to Becmann's literary table group. But we do know some of the names who did take part in this

---

[154] Ibid., p. 676. There the text erroneously prints "rela" instead of "tela."
[155] I found the dedicatory poem in Johann Christoph Becmann (Praes.) / Johannes Steinheuser (Resp.), *I. N. D. E. D. N. J. C. Dissertatio historico-politica de iudiciis Dei*, Frankfurt a.O., June 16, 1669, last page. In the later editions of 1673 and 1682 the poem is absent.

little society. For example, in 1667 Friedrich Lucä met Jeremias Felbinger from Brieg in Frankfurt, a man who "was my table companion at Herr Becmann's."[156] At the time Felbinger was already 51 years old, surely an unusual presence among the others, who were all in their twenties. He was a well-known antitrinitarian, the author of a book entitled *Politicae Christianae* ("Christian Politics"), among other things, and a translation of the New Testament using the Greek edition of Étienne de Courcelles.[157] Felbinger had lived in many places and been expelled from many, always living on the barest margins of existence. He was not a pure Socinian but tended, like Christoph Sand, toward Arian notions. In an anecdote Lucä reported that Felbinger had once offered him his translation of the New Testament in exchange for another book. "I agreed to the exchange out of curiosity, but I found in this translation, which had been printed in Amsterdam, so many prevarications pointing to Socinianism that my hair stood on end at this scandalous pollution of Holy Scripture."[158]

Who took such people into his circle? Becmann? Lucä speaks elsewhere of Friedrich Becmann, not of Johann Christoph. This was his half-brother, who also taught as a professor of logic and as an associate professor of theology at the University of Frankfurt on the Oder. On the other hand we possess the testimony of Stosch, who claimed that Johann Christoph Becmann "back in my time" had had "a Socinian by the name of Felbinger" as his table companion.[159] This puzzle can be solved only if we assume that the two Becmann brothers lived together and therefore shared a common dinner table. It was the table of a historian and a theologian, a society enamored of "paradoxical" ideas, a community that included several Transylvanian antitrinitarians as well as one Arian, who repeatedly took pains to distance himself from the Socinian confession. Was Friedrich Becmann trying in this way to gain insight into the world of his religious opponents?

---

[156] Friedrich Lucä, *Der Chronist Friedrich Lucä*, Frankfurt, 1854, p. 149. Lucä speaks of a theologian's household headed by Friedrich Becmann; he says that he was the son of Christian Becmann from Zerbst. Friedrich Becmann, the son of a first marriage, was a professor of logic and an associate professor of theology at the University of Frankfurt a.O. while Johann Christoph Becmann was the child of a second marriage.

[157] Jeremias Felbinger, *Politicae Christianae compendium*, Breslau, ca. 1648; *Das Neue Testament, aus dem Griechischen ins Teutsche übersetzet*, Amsterdam, 1660.

[158] Lucä, *Der Chronist Friedrich Lucä* (note 156), pp. 149f.   [159] See note 143.

12   Michael Servetus's *De Christianismi restitutio* in Frankfurt on the Oder

In 1668, when Jeremias Felbinger was a member of the table society in the Becmann house and Friedrich Wilhelm Stosch was in contact with Johann Christoph Becmann, Felbinger had an amazing stroke of luck. He was present when the Socinian theologian Johannes Preuß received one of the future patriarchs of the Transylvanian Socinians, Daniel Markos from Szent-Iván, who later became the rector of the Unitarian College in Kolozvár (Cluj) and superintendent of Transylvania. Markos was returning from England, where he had established connections and been a part of the exiled Socinian communities who had sought refuge there after being banished from Poland in 1658. We have already seen in the case of Samuel Crell how close the connections were between Continental Unitarians and England. In the year 1668 when Markos left England, the *Bibliotheca fratrum Polonorum* ("Library of the Polish Brethren") was printed in Amsterdam, a collection of classic Socinian writings.[160] In Transylvania Markos intended to found new congregations.[161]

While in Frankfurt, Markos surely met the resident Socinians from Hungary, who dined with the Becmann brothers and socialized with Felbinger. He was also carrying with him a secret treasure: one of the three copies of Michael Servetus's notorious *De Christianismi Restitutio* ("Restitution of Christianity") that had not been burned by the authorities.[162] All the other exemplars of the print run of a 1,000 copies had been destroyed by the magistracy of Geneva in conjunction with the burning of Servetus himself in 1553. For antitrinitarians therefore, the book that Markos had in his possession was virtually a holy relic, and he must have had weighty reasons to carry it with him on such a long and unsafe journey.[163] The *Restitutio* could be called the founding document of antitrinitarianism, the book that set the whole movement in motion.

---

[160] See Herbert J. McLachlan, *Socinianism in Seventeenth-Century England*, Oxford, 1951, p. 139. On the *Bibliotheca*, see Jerome Vercruysse, "Bibliotheca fratrum Polonorum. Histoire et Bibliographie," *Odrodzenie i Reformacja w Polsce* 21 (1975), pp. 197–212.

[161] On the Socinians who migrated to Transylvania after being driven out of Poland, see Janusz Tazbir, *Bracia Polscy w Siedmiogrodzie, 1660–1784*, Warsaw, 1964.

[162] This was the so-called Vienna exemplar that resides now in the Austrian National Library. On it, see Herbert Hunger, "Michael Servet und das Exemplar seiner *Christianismi restitutio* in der Österreichischen Nationalbibliothek," *Biblos* 1 (1952), pp. 61–78.

[163] For 1665 Markos's possession of the book is proven; see Erich F. Podach, "Die Geschichte der *Christianismi restitutio* im Lichte ihrer Abschriften," in Bruno Becker, ed., *Autour de Michel Servet et de Sebastien Castellion*, Haarlem, 1953, pp. 47–61, here at p. 48.

But it was also a witness to Calvin's inhumane harshness against the new doubts about the Trinity.[164]

Anyway, Markos had it with him when he took a break from his travels, resting at Preuß's house in Żelechów near Lagow in the Neumark and permitting his host to make a copy of it for himself. Preuß did so with the help of Jeremias Felbinger and another of his protégés.[165] We see here the tight connections between Żelechów – the social group around Preuß and the Schlichting family – and Frankfurt on the Oder, where Felbinger was living in the social circle around Friedrich Becmann. At the time Felbinger was leading a sort of double life: in Żelechów he was helping the genuine antitrinitarians in their activities, but in Frankfurt he played the part of a penitent, who was copying the writings of the Socinian Johann Crell supposedly for the benefit of Reformed theologians. We know this because Lucä provided the odd information that Felbinger in Frankfurt at the time "had the task of copying for the faculty the manuscripts that the theologian Crell had left behind for the faculty and was preparing them for publication."[166] Crell's writings were rarities, and so it was a clever move on the part of the Frankfurt theologians to use a supposedly former Socinian in order to get hold of them. Felbinger clearly had Crell's works in his possession. But whether the copies were really intended for publication is extremely doubtful. Lucä in fact reported on the sad end of this story: "Later the university itself noticed what was going on with this ravening wolf in the sheep's clothing of humility, for he gave in to his desires and tried to lead the youth into error through secret meetings but also to hoodwink their elders." That was a horrible situation for university administrators: clandestine student groups in which hopeful young academics were turned into Socinians. "In the copying of Crell's writings he was discovered to have committed many forgeries and was then driven out of the city and the territory, uprooted like a poisonous plant."[167] Felbinger had mimicked the remorseful reconvert and had fobbed off the theologians with false Crell texts.

It was copying programs like that of Felbinger in these years that led to the volumes published as the *Bibliotheca fratrum Polonorum*, as organized by Frans Kuyper, in which such authors as Fausto Sozzini, Johann Crell, or

---

[164] See Roland H. Bainton, *Hunted Heretic: The Life and Death of Michael Servetus 1511–1553*, Boston, 1953; Lawrence and Nancy Goldstone, *Out of the Flames: The Remarkable Story of a Fearless Scholar, a Fatal Heresy, and One of the Rarest Books in the World*, New York, 2003.

[165] Today this copy resides in the Bibliothèque Nationale in Paris; see Podach, "Die Geschichte der *Christianismi restitutio* im Lichte ihrer Abschriften" (note 163), p. 31.

[166] Lucä, *Der Chronist Friedrich Lucä* (note 156), pp. 149f.   [167] Ibid., p. 150.

Samuel Przypkowski were collected and printed.[168] Here again there was a transfer between Brandenburg and the Netherlands. As far as the Servetus copy from 1668 went, it exerted an important influence (along with one other copy prepared for Christoph Crell by Andreas Lachowski) on the historical understanding of the case of Servetus. After all it was Samuel Crell – whose father-in-law was Preuß – who made Preuß's copy available for research. In connection with the manuscript of the *Judaeus Lusitanus*, we *know* that Crell was responsible for the large-scale distribution and marketing of Servetus copies in Amsterdam from the 1720s to the 1740s. At this point, however, we are pursuing only the immediate fate of the Preuß copy; as scholars all the way down to Johann Lorenz Mosheim took account of it, we can observe the ambivalent impact of radical texts during the early Enlightenment.[169]

Let us again leave aside the case of Stosch. In 1717 scholarly engagement with the case of Servetus was reaching a crisis. Under the influence of Bayle and Naudé, a whole generation of Huguenots had begun demanding a revisionist version of Reformed history; one of them was Michel de La Roche, a historian who collected some archival information from Geneva and published a new *Histoire de Michel Servet* in the journal *Mémoires Littéraires*.[170] Even though La Roche's study represented a huge advance over previous depictions of the case, which had not really succeeded in freeing themselves from historiographic legends and slanders, it nonetheless suffered from one major deficit. It had naturally been written in ignorance of the central text by Servetus, because the *Resititutio Christianismi* was nowhere to be found.

But then an anonymous writer reviewed La Roche's work as well as a recently published study of Servetus by Peter Adolph Boysen, an article published in the fifth fascicle of the first volume of the Bremen journal, *Bibliotheca Historico-Philologico-Theologica*. This unidentified writer was astonishingly well-informed: readers must have been amazed that he quoted verbatim from the *Restitutio*. The publisher of the journal, the Reformed theologian Theodor Hase, who had himself written works to salvage the reputations of unjustly persecuted "atheists," introduced these

---

[168] See Vercruysse, "Bibliotheca fratrum Polonorum" (note 160); Simonutti, "Resistance, Obedience and Toleration" (note 47).

[169] For the distribution of Servetus, see Mulsow, *Enlightenment Underground* (note 60), chapter 2; and see Mulsow, "Einleitung," in Johann Lorenz Mosheim, *Versuch einer unparteiischen und gründlichen Ketzergeschichte*, vol. 2, Hildesheim, 1999, pp. 5–13.

[170] See Margaret D. Thomas, "Michel de la Roche: A Huguenot Critic of Calvin," *Studies on Voltaire and the Eighteenth Century* 238 (1985), pp. 97–196.

excerpts with much fanfare: "This book is the rarest of all; I know of no mortal who claims to have seen a printed copy of it with his own eyes, except for Christoph Sand and the eminent [Peter von] Mastricht."[171]

How had this submission found its way to the Bremen journal? We know that the anonymous author was Samuel Crell. And it was La Croze, a friend of Crell's, who had taken on the task of transmitting Crell's text to his friend Hase. But to ensure the Socinian's safety he did not reveal Crell's name to Hase.

In those years a young man had established contact with La Croze, who was one of the most enthusiastic readers of La Roche's study and also of the anonymous review of it because he himself had been gathering material about Servetus ever since 1715. This was none other than Johann Lorenz Mosheim, who was then trying to compile a *Bibliotheca vulcani*, a history of book burnings.[172] Mosheim's contact with La Croze paid off for him because La Croze had been permitted to have a copy made of the Servetus text from Crell's copy when he transmitted Crell's review to Hase.[173] So then, when Mosheim was besieging La Croze with questions about Servetus, La Croze could exercise his customary generosity by lending Mosheim his copy. That placed Mosheim in the position of being the first scholar to be able to write an analysis of the Servetus case on the basis of a knowledge of the *Restitutio*. His first work on the subject was *Historia Michaelis Serveti*, published in 1727, a book that concealed its authorship under the name of a 'respondent'; but he showed his continuing fascination with the case more fully in 1748, in the second volume of his history of heretics, the "Alternative Attempt at an Impartial History of Heretics," and its supplementary volume.[174] Later La Croze gave the manuscript to Zacharias Conrad von Uffenbach, but then, shortly thereafter came to regret his gift.[175]

[171] *Bibliotheca Historico-Philologico-Theologica*, Classis 1, Fasc. 5 (1718), pp. 739f.

[172] Martin Mulsow, "Eine "Rettung" des Michael Servet? Der junge Mosheim und die heterodoxe Tradition," in Martin Mulsow et al., eds., *Johann Lorenz Mosheim 1693–1755*, Wiesbaden, 1997, pp. 45–92.

[173] This copy is today in the Staats- and Universitätsbibliothek Göttingen, Ms. theol. 259. Concerning La Croze and Mosheim, see Martin Mulsow, *Die drei Ringe. Toleranz und clandestine Gelehrsamkeit bei Mathurin Veyssière La Croze*, Tübingen, 2001.

[174] Mosheim, *Versuch einer unparteiischen und gründlichen Ketzergeschichte*, vol. 2 (note 169); Mosheim [sometimes listed under the name of Heinrich von Allwoerden], *Historia Michelis Serveti*, Helmstedt, 1727.

[175] See Mulsow, *Die drei Ringe* (note 173), pp. 88f.

13   Stosch's *Concordia rationis et fidei*

With this excursus on the history of the reception of *Christianismi restitutio* we have plunged far into the eighteenth century, and I hope it has been instructive to see an example of the long-term consequences that the "double-milieu" of the Brandenburg Socinians and the Frankfurt academics had. If the circulation of the *Restitutio* was one such consequence, then the creation of the *Concordia rationis et fidei* was surely another.

Earlier we left Samuel Crell standing at the door of Friedrich Wilhelm Stosch in 1702. We recall that Crell was looking for the papers left behind by Johann Bergius, and like Philipp van Limborch he harbored the hope that they might be found among the papers of Bartholomäus Stosch. We have no evidence concerning how the conversation between Crell and Stosch may have gone. And yet we now know the biographical background that connected the aging Stosch – who died in 1704 – to Socinian activities and freethinking conversations around the year 1670. Crell would have been well-informed about them through Preuß, Strimesius, and other friends. So he might have understood how this man's intellectual development had progressed.

And that is been the point of this chapter. I have tried to interpret the *Concordia rationis et fidei* as a radicalization emerging from a Remonstrant and Socinian milieu. We have seen that in Frankfurt on the Oder dissimulation was commonplace, as was dealing with radical writings. Felbinger played the role of a remorseful ex-Socinian; Becmann provided provocative ideas and texts from England and Holland to his students as stimulants of thought, but he also incorporated them in judiciously into his writings. Stosch absorbed from this milieu the stimulation that he needed to cobble his notes and reading excerpts together into his own little philosophical book. In a passage tucked away in one of his manuscripts, Peter Friedrich Arpe even described the product as a small jewel.[176]

How did things develop in the 1670s and 1680s so that the stimulations to be found in Frankfurt finally matured into the book that Stosch finished in 1692? There was after all a span of twenty years between his first inklings and his fully formed doctrines. In that period much happened

---

[176] Staats- and Universitätsbibliothek Hamburg, Ms. theol. 1222, p. 72: "De Concordia rationis et fidei non pauci multa praedare monuerunt. ... Huc venit Frid. Guiluelmi Stossii Concordia rationis et fidei; atro notata lapillo, quae inter libros rariores locum invenit cum Amstelod. 1692. 8. prodiisset." Arpe described Stosch's book in this footnote to his richly expanded personal copy of his *Apologia pro Vanino* as a "small jewel that has been labeled disastrous/dark."

in intellectual history. If one started with the influences conveyed by Becmann, could one say that the core of Stosch's views encompassed the teachings of Gassendi and Hobbes, but also the biblical criticism of La Peyrère and Socinian doctrines (a critique of the Trinity, the divinity of Christ, original sin, the creation *ex nihilo*, the immortality of the soul, and the eternity of the fires of hell)? With this core Stosch had become, as it were, a "Socinian Gassendist."[177] That means that he proceeded from a fundamental assumption that the world had an atomistic structure and from a theory of morality grounded in utility. This foundation served as a basis for criticisms of religious and political doctrines and for his Socinian inclinations. That means, of course, that Stosch was not really a Gassendist or a Socinian in any strict sense because he did not follow Gassendi in all matters nor did he subscribe to the biblical foundations cited by the Socinians.

Here we encounter what we noted at the beginning: that Stosch's opponents accused him of representing a "new Socinianism," the very concept to which Stosch had paid so much attention. His "Socinian Gassendism" was of exactly the diffuse type of neo-Socinianism that developed in the last decades of the seventeenth century and could transition seamlessly into deism or even atheism. Anyway, starting from this core over the next few decades he added further material from his reading that fitted, at least halfway, into his basic assumptions and also provided a critique of religion. Take, for example, the doctrines of Pufendorf on natural law that rose to dominance in the 1670s: it is not surprising that in the *Concordia* Gassendi's naturalistic and utilitarian moral positions were supplemented with Pufendorf's notions of natural law.[178] That was, however, not always logical, as we have seen, just as other "addenda" were not logical, but they may have served as camouflage even as they pervaded the legal passages of the *Concordia*. They tried to join legal doctrine with an ethics that was mainly drawn from Spinoza, who himself had borrowed from the Epicureanism of Gassendi. It seems quite possible that after 1677 Spinoza could certainly have had an influence on Stosch, perhaps as early as the 1680s.

---

[177] This agrees fundamentally with the judgment of Winfried Schröder, who, in his book, *Spinoza in der deutschen Frühaufklärung* (note 2), was of course mainly interested in Stosch's part in the reception of Spinoza, but who came to the conclusion, pp. 49f., "daß die Selektivität der Rezeption der Metaphysik Spinozas in Stoschs 'Concordia' auf der primär atomistisch-materialistischen Orientierung seines Denkens beruht . . . ."

[178] See esp. Stosch, *Concordia* (note 2), pp. 56–71.

Starting in 1687 Theodor van Craanen, the Cartesian doctor, was active at the court of the electors of Brandenburg.[179] Stosch finally had a conversational partner with whom he could expand his knowledge of natural science and discuss physical and physiological problems. Thus the book Stosch was writing gained a stronger dose of natural science.

And then there was the strong influence of Jean Le Clerc, the Arminian who in 1701 had worked so zealously to write a refutation of George Bull for timely inclusion in Limborch's *Historia vitae episcopii*. In the *Concordia* Le Clerc is present at many points: for one, he was the author of the *Logica, ontologia et pneumatologia* of 1692, a book deeply influenced by John Locke's empiricism that served to transmit his ideas.[180] But he had also written the *Epistolae theologicae* under the pseudonym of Liberius de Sancto Amore. Stosch may not have realized that these two works were by the same author. It is clear enough that the *Epistolae* of 1679 shaped his thinking earlier than did the philosophical works, which belonged to the last layer of works he read before finishing the final draft of the *Concordia*; but they were so important that they created the framework and also provided the basic tenor of the "Prooemium" with its definition of what faith and reason were.[181]

Le Clerc's Lockean philosophy fitted well with Gassendi's empiricism because Locke had already – partially – adopted some of his suggestions.[182] Le Clerc's theology in the *Epistolae* transmitted just that mixture of Socinianism and Arminianism that we have described earlier. It was well suited to provide Stosch with a license to experiment with theological and philosophical views. When Crell spoke with Stosch – if he did actually gain admission to him – he would have been able to agree with him about Le Clerc and much of what he stood for because both of them regarded the Amsterdam Remonstrant as a central point of reference. We do not know, however, if they ever had that conversation.

In any event, Stosch ended his *Concordia* on a decidedly antischolastic note: against dogmatic speculations, teachings that defied reason, and topics like "tritheism." He favored a simple Christianity:

> In matters of faith it seems equally dangerous to me to believe too much and too little, and it is proper to say so. The safest way has always seemed to

---

[179] See Schröder, *Spinoza in der deutschen Frühaufklärung* (note 2), p. 33.
[180] Jean Le Clerc, *Logica, ontologia et pneumatologia*, London, 1692.
[181] Stosch, *Concordia* (note 2), Prooemium, unpaginated first page.
[182] See Richard W. F. Kroll, "The Question of Locke's Relation to Gassendi," *Journal of the History of Ideas* 45 (1984), pp. 339–359; Rolf W. Puster, *Britische Gassendi-Rezeption am Beispiel John Lockes*, Stuttgart, 1991.

me to be to follow nothing but what the Bible says and also use only those things that are clearer and more believable than other things. Indeed, a simple and rational faith that remains within the limits of the words and phrases of Holy Scripture is the truest faith.[183]

This was the Christianity that Detlef Döring has made central to his interpretation. But what kind of Christianity was that? If only those biblical passages are acceptable that are "clear" – that is, conformable to reason – then that created a minimalism in which the Bible no longer possessed its own authority but was only an expression of a sensible morality; one which could only be cited if reason had already ratified the result. Everything else must yield to criticism and skepticism, as Stosch formulated it, or they might be reformulated using the doctrine of accommodation. The "Harmony of Reason and Faith," a harmony that Pierre-Daniel Huet had still been able to interpret as favoring faith,[184] had clearly become for Stosch a harmony that favored reason.

14   A Short Summary of a Complex Situation

In *Enlightenment Underground* I emphasized the central importance of Berlin and Brandenburg but now it can be stressed again with a view to Crell and Stosch: Berlin and Brandenburg had a special importance for the early Enlightenment in Germany. Because of the Brandenburg policy of religious toleration and the resulting influx of Huguenots, on the one hand, and the tacit toleration of Socinians, on the other, we find here, as in no other German territory, a heavy importation of Arminian, Socinian, and even Jewish ideas. The contact of these ideas with German traditions in political theory, as taught in Frankfurt on the Oder, led almost necessarily to results of the sort we see in Stosch's *Concordia*.

Let us look again at the concept of "intellectual field" that we introduced at the beginning of this chapter. The field that we have been observing here can be described as having at least three components. Geographically, it was a transnational field that connected Remonstrants and Socinians in the Netherlands with those of Brandenburg, and they had contacts also in England, Poland, and Transylvania. These connections provided a constant flow of travelers, migrants, study journeys, foreign postings to new jobs, but also international mailings of manuscripts and books. In terms of intellectual content, the field revealed a tense balance

---

[183] Stosch, *Concordia* (note 2), Praefatio ad lectorem, unpaginated page 4:
[184] Pierre-Daniel Huet, *Alnetanae quaestiones de concordia rationis et fidei*, Paris, 1693.

between Reformed and Socinian doctrines; tactically each side had to distance itself from each other, but in content there were many connections, and many Remonstrants cannot be easily distinguished from Socinians, while some Socinians such as Samuel Crell were close to the Remonstrants. In this field, scholars aimed for tactical advantages, for example claiming authorities like Johann Bergius for one side or the other. The theories deriving from Locke, Pufendorf, or Spinoza were also up for grabs. Third and finally, the field had its institutional aspect, inasmuch as academics had to position themselves carefully between Orthodox and heterodox, tradition and innovation, with careers that might advance (as Becmann did when he became a theologian) or crash (as in the case of Felbinger, who was exiled). The movements in this dimension occasionally demanded shrewd maneuvering as Becmann showed, who moved from being rather radical in his views to a place in the middle of Orthodoxy.

Does such a three-dimensional picture actually help us to understand Friedrich Wilhelm Stosch and his *Concordia*? Maybe yes. For we can now see that the question is no longer whether Stosch was really an atheist or a Reformed Christian; instead the whole scandal and Stosch's book itself can appear as an expression of a field of forces in which Stosch – as a forerunner of many later freethinkers – was not isolated even if his position was radical. Stosch developed his own standpoint in relative isolation, only occasionally speaking with others like van Craanen or Wagner; and he expanded it when, for reasons of health, he had to withdraw from professional activities in 1686. He was thrilled to put his thoughts into book form, and yet he wanted his book to circulate only within private circles and not to be sold openly.[185] Let us recall the denunciation from the woman in Dorotheenstadt that mentioned an "extremely wicked book filled with the most dangerous opinions"; she reported that the book "was discussed at secret conventicles in her house."[186] That must have been another book entirely, but possibly Stosch imagined that meetings like this might provide for a controlled circulation of his ideas. When the distribution of his book spun out of control, however, Stosch was shocked. In this sort of situation, Theodor Ludwig Lau was not the only one driven to the edge of suicide when he was arrested and jailed because of his "atheist" writings.[187] Stosch felt the same way. While in jail, he too was tempted to

---

[185] *Acta Stoschiana* (note 19), p. 671.   [186] See note 14.
[187] See Martin Mulsow, *Knowledge Lost: A New View of Early Modern Intellectual History*, Princeton, 2022, chapter 1.

take his own life. He wrote a commentary on his fateful year 1693, which he set down in a little, hand-written autobiographical sketch that read as follows: "From my forty-sixth year onward because of my love of truth and peace I have been kicked by asses and wickedly bad-mouthed, so that I came close to sacrificing myself to the fame of martyrdom."[188]

---

[188] These were the words in his manuscript autobiographical sketch, which came through Christian Goetz to Georg Gottfried Küster: *Marchiae litteratae specimen tertium* (note 123), p. 2

CHAPTER 6

The Founders of Religion as Human Beings
Moses and Jesus between Inflation and Deflation

1 Inflating and Deflating Moses

The bedroom of King James II of England had a staircase that led down to a laboratory that housed the royal alchemist Edmund Dickinson.[1] When he was not experimenting, Dickinson worked on a large book that he wanted to call *Physica vetus et vera* ("The Old and True Physics"). There he planned to describe the philosophy of Moses in such a way that it could finally be rightly understood and scientifically explained. When the king could not sleep, he went downstairs to Dickinson, where they discussed alchemy, philosophy, and politics, but probably also Moses.

Alchemy, philosophy, and politics? As we know, the early modern period saw a variety of debates about Moses. In *Enlightenment Underground*, chapter 3, I touched on the accommodationist theories concerning Moses that John Spencer and others defended, according to which Moses behaved toward his people like a scheming politician or clever teacher; chapter 5 pursued this theme further. *Enlightenment Underground* also showed how such theories could be transformed into a denunciation of Moses as a deceiver. The discussions of other founders of the great religions, and especially Jesus and Mohammed, were exactly parallel in their ambivalence and complexity. Here we will try to get to the bottom of this pendular process: between a representation that inflated or glorified its subject and another that deflated or at least represented the

---

[1] On Dickinson (1624–1707) see William N. Blomberg, *An Account of the Life and Writings of Edmund Dickinson, M.D.*, London, 1737, expanded 2nd edn., 1739; the article on "Dickinson" in *Dictionary of National Biography*, vol. 15, London, 1888, pp. 33f. The current biographies of James II do not notice Dickinson. This chapter is based on two essays of mine that are here reworked and combined: Martin Mulsow, "Moses omniscius oder Moses politicus? Moses-Deutungen des 17. Jahrhunderts zwischen sakraler Enzyklopädik und libertinistischer Kritik," in Andreas B. Kilcher and Philipp Theisohn, eds., *Die Enzyklopädik der Esoterik. Allwissenheitsmythen und universalwissenschaftliche Modelle in der Esoterik der Neuzeit*, Munich, 2010, pp. 177-202; and Muslow, "Joseph als natürlicher Vater Christi. Ein unbekanntes clandestines Manuskript des frühen 18. Jahrhunderts," *Aufklärung* 25 (2013), pp. 73-112.

subject in naturalizing terms. How far did the prophet Moses fall when he became just a politician? How far did Jesus fall when he went from being the Son of God to a mere man? How were such understandings changed and desacralized? And what was the connection between this development and the more general reception of Hellenistic and late ancient sources?

Let us start with Moses. There were early modern discussions of Moses the Egyptian, Moses the politician and lawgiver, Moses as an expert on nature or as chemist, and others as well. How did these discussions interact? A small episode from the reign of James II may illuminate this question. If Dickenson and James could switch back and forth in their considerations of chemistry and politics, what happened when they discussed Moses? Or, to put the question differently, how did Moses look from these two perspectives? And how did his image change during the transitional period of the late seventeenth and early eighteenth centuries in which these two late-night conversationalists lived?

These are huge questions. I will treat them by looking at a few treatises on Moses from the seventeenth century and a few selected topics concerning Moses. But first let us note that one cannot speak of the "Moses complex" without taking into account the way in which writers in Hellenistic antiquity either raised or lowered the figure of Moses. As Arthur Droge has shown,[2] many Mediterranean cultures created national heroes for themselves, even before they had contact with Greek civilization. But the practice of creating such heroes became far more common in the cultural competitions characteristic of Hellenism. According to Gabrielle Oberhänsli-Widmer,

> The spread of the figure of Moses ran ... from the differentiated images in the Bible to a polarization in the post-biblical world. The complex protagonist of the books of Exodus to Deuteronomy split into a figure, on the one hand, of universal knowledge, a serene, superhuman and commanding hero, versus a corrupt demagogue on the other.[3]

The parallel reception of both these images was, I would argue, characteristic of the seventeenth century. To illustrate this point, just look at the transformation of the elevated Moses image into two different figures: on

---

[2] Arthur J. Droge, *Homer or Moses? Early Christian Interpretations of the History of Culture*, Tübingen, 1989. Further: Moses Hadas, *Hellenistische Kultur*, Vienna, 1981, passim; Arnaldo Momigliano, *Hochkulturen im Hellenismus. Die Begegnung der Griechen mit Kelten, Römern, Juden und Persern*, Munich, 1979, passim; David Winston, "Moses in Hellenistic Literature," *Encyclopedia Judaica* 12 (1971), pp. 388–393. See also the generally informative article by Gabrielle Oberhänsli-Widmer, "Moses/Moseslied/Mosesegen/Moseschriften," in TRE, vol. 23, Berlin, 1994, pp. 330–357.

[3] Oberhänsli-Widmer, "Moses [...]" (note 2), p. 355.

the one hand an early modern figure that stood for absolute (i.e., sacralized) claims of knowledge, but also its opposite. I would argue that toward the middle of the seventeenth century the revived tradition of a deflated Moses as demagogue began to affect that first, inflated image, using ideas of accommodation and leading to new complexities. In a third step, in an excursus we will look at how the Hellenistic anti-Moses literature was deployed and expanded, and that will allow us to clarify the relations between knowledge and politics. And finally we will examine the choices that a more complex interpretation of Moses now permitted in the late seventeenth century: (1) abandoning Moses as a legitimating figure altogether as a result of historical criticism and a preference for the new over the old; or (2) recasting the discussion of Moses so thoroughly that one could transform the omniscient hero into a pantheist and the demagogic politician into a republican.

2   Omniscient Moses: An All-Knowing Hero?

But first we must look at the efforts to elevate or inflate Moses, and that takes us back into antiquity. With Philo of Alexandria the image of Moses was already that of an all-knowing hero playing the roles of king, prophet, priest, and lawgiver.[4] Of course the fundamental omniscience of Moses was hardly isolated from his other qualities. His legislative abilities as a wise lawgiver were based on his knowledge of the whole world. If one understood the world, one could also obey its laws. Using these ideas, Philo interpreted matters according to the stoic ideal of conforming the norms of one's life to the laws of nature. Philo says at the beginning of his treatise *De opificio mundi*:

> Many legislators simply took what they thought to be right and established laws in simple and unadorned fashion to accord with their preferences; others wrapped their thoughts in a pompous cloak that impressed the masses by cloaking the truth in mythical images. But Moses avoided both of these, the first because it was unconsidered, unphilosophical, and all too comfortable, but the other because it was full of lies and deceit . . . .[5]

[4] Philo Alexandrinus, *De vita Mosis. Les oeuvres de Philon d'Alexandrie*, vol. 22, ed. Roger Arnaldez et al., Paris, 1967. On that, see Giovanni Reale and Roberto Radice, *La filosofia mosaica. Filone di Alexandria*, Milan, 1987. However, see the tendencies that predate Philo: Richard Goulet, *La philosophie de Moïse. Essai de reconstruction d'un commentaire philosophique préphilonien du Pentateuque*, Paris, 1987.
[5] *Die Werke Philos von Alexandria in deutscher Übersetzung*, vol. 1, ed. Leopold Cohn, Breslau, 1909: "Ueber die Weltschöpfung nach Moses," p. 28.

In contrast Moses chose a more exalted way of beginning in order to show the harmony of law and nature.

In Clement of Alexandria we read that Moses was highly learned in arithmetic and geometry, in harmony and medicine.[6] Other ancients found different ways to praise his knowledge. For Eupolemon, Moses was the first to give writing to the Jews.[7] Justin had also praised him.[8] Eusebius esteemed his wisdom and logic so highly that he regarded Plato as merely a Greek-speaking Moses.[9] Rabbinic literature added further ideas, for example, that Moses had established thirteen rules for hermeneutics.[10]

This constructed memory of Moses as a philosopher and polyhistor had its origin in the supposed opposition of Jews to Greeks.[11] For us the most interesting point is that this origin was updated in the late sixteenth and in the seventeenth century. This was a modernization with two roots: strengthened religious emphases during the age of confessionalism but, second, various encyclopedic efforts during the same period. The religious confessionalizing efforts made from the mid-sixteenth century onward produced a more systematically "sacralized" scholarship than that of the Middle Ages – that is, a scholarship that drew its criterion for knowledge from the books of revelation, against which the book of nature had to demonstrate its agreement. In this sense both the Catholic Francisco Vallés and the Calvinist Lambert Daneau were practicing *physica sacra* ("sacred

---

[6] Clemens Alexandrinus, *Stromata* I, 343 and passim.

[7] Eupolemos-Fragment according to Alexander Polyhistor, in Albert-Marie Denis, ed., *Fragmenta pseudepigraphorum quae supersunt graeca una cum historicum et auctorum judaeorum hellenistarum fragmentis*, Leiden, 1970. On Eupolemos and Pseudo-Eupolemos, see Droge, *Homer or Moses?* (note 2), pp. 13ff.

[8] Justinus Martyr, *Dialogus*, Apol. I, 54 and passim; Pseudo-Justin, *Cohortatio ad Graecos*.

[9] Eusebius, *Praeparatio Evangelica* XI, 6.

[10] See Johann Heinrich Zedler, *Großes und vollständiges [. . .] Lexicon*, vol. 21, Leipzig, 1739, article on "Moses Vielwissenheit," cols. 1888–1897, here at col. 1889, following Daniel Wilhelm Moller (praes.) / Georg Schwindel (resp.), *Dissertatio inauguralis, quam de Mose philosopho [. . .] submittet [. . .]*, Altdorf, Juni 1707, which in turn depends on the collections of Rabbi Ismael: "1) Leve & grave. 2) Comma aequale. 3) Constitutio Principii ex uno Scripturae loco, & constitutio principii ex duobus locis. 4) Generale & speciale. 5) Speciale & generale. 6) Generale & speciale, iterumque generale. 7) Generale egens speciali, & speciale egens generali. 8) Cum aliquid sub generali contentum excipitur a generali ad docendum aliquid de isto generali. 9) Cum aliquid sub generali contentum excipitur, ad imponendum aliud onus, quod convenit cum ipsius ratione. 10) Quando excipitur, ad imponendum aliud onus, quod cum ipsius ratione non convenit. 11) Quando excipitur ad arguendum de re plane nova. 12) Res quae discitur ex sua ipsius significatione & res quae dicitur ex fine suo. 13) Duo loca Scripturae sibi invicem repugnantia." For the early modern period, therefore, the fact that Moses had a specific logic was taken as proven. See, e.g., Johann Julius Struve, *Rudimenta Logicae Ebraeorum*, Jena, 1697.

[11] Zedler's article (note 10) led to disciplines that Moses supposedly had mastered: philosophy, logic, metaphysics, physics, ethics, politics, history, geography, music and poetry, mathematics, astronomy, structural engineering, magic, kabbalah, chemistry, and the art of writing.

physics").[12] But we might take note of such common titles as *Ethica Moysaica* ("Mosaic Ethics") by Kort Aslaksson[13] or *Biblische Policey* ("Biblical Politics") by Dietrich Reinkingk.[14] At the same time, however, the burgeoning encyclopedism of the day was an effect of the pluralization of knowledge, of the printing of books, and of efforts to cope with an exploding multiplicity.[15] Combining the two, it is no wonder that from the middle or late sixteenth century there was a sort of "sacred historical encyclopedism." The omniscience of Moses in such discussions was, however, just one possibility: that idea had to compete with the omniscience of Adam, Noah, or Solomon,[16] or even with the whole "philosophy of the patriarchs."[17]

---

[12] Francisco Vallés, *De iis quae scripta sunt phisice in libris sacris seu de sacra philosophia*, Turin, 1587; Lambert Daneau, *Physica Christiana*, Geneva, 1588. There is no comprehensive study of the early modern "philosophia Mosaica." But see Ann Blair, "Mosaic Physics and the Search for a Pious Natural Philosophy in the Late Renaissance," *Isis* 91 (2000), pp. 32–58. See also Hans Ahrbeck, "Einige Bemerkungen über 'Mosaische Philosophen' des 17. Jahrhunderts," *Wissenschaftliche Zeitschrift der Martin-Luther-Universität Halle-Wittenberg* 7(5) (1958), pp. 1047–1050, and the comprehensive work of Wilhelm Schmidt-Biggemann, *Geschichte der christlichen Kabbala*, 4 vols., Stuttgart, 2012–2014.

[13] Conradus Aslacius, *Ethica Moysaica*, Hanau, 1613. The Norwegian Aslacius (Kort Aslaksson) was a professor in Copenhagen. Dietrich Reinkingk, *Biblische Policey, Das ist: Gewisse, auß Heiliger, Göttlicher Schrifft zusammengebrachte [...] Axiomata und Schlußreden*, Frankfurt, 1653.

[14] See the sections on "Philosophia sacra" or "Philosophia Moysaica" in Daniel Georg Morhof, *Polyhistor in tres tomos, literarium, philosophicum et practicum*, ed. Johannes Möller, Lübeck, 1708, vol. II, Book II, cap. III, pp. 164–175: "De Physica Mosaica, ejusque interpretibus, veteribus et recentioribus"; Jakob Brucker, *Historia critica philosophiae*, Leipzig, 1743, vol. 4(1), pp. 610–643: "De Philosophis Mosaicis et Christianis." There was even a sacral, Mosaic jurisprudence: see, e.g., Pierre Pithou, *Collatio legum Mosaicorum et Romanorum*, London, 1660; or Conrad Heresbach, *Epitome jurisprudentiae Christianae*, Neustadt, 1586; as well as the natural law of John Selden.

[15] See, e.g., Elisabeth Eisenstein, *The Printing Press as an Agent of Change*, 2 vols., Cambridge, 1979; on the concept of pluralization, see Martin Mulsow, "Pluralisierung," in Anette Völker-Rasor, *Oldenbourg Lehrbuch Geschichte: Frühe Neuzeit*, Munich, 2000, pp. 303–307.

[16] As examples, see on Adam the references mentioned in Johann Wilhelm Feuerlein (praes.) / V. H. Regenfus (resp.), *Dissertatio philosophica de philosophia Adami putativa*, Altdorf, 1715; as well as *De Adami logica, metaphysica, mathesi, philosophia practica, et libris*, Altdorf, 1717. For Noah see the references in Brucker (note 14), vol. 1, Leipzig 1742, pp. 66f. On Solomon, see esp. Juan de Pineda, *Ad suos in Salomonem commentarios / Salomon Praevius, sive De rebus Salomonis Regis libri octo quibus ipsa vitae eius auspicia, regnum, sapientia, opulentia, domus regia, corporis animique bona, morum depravatio, ac mors denique execrandae vindex impietatis non minus luculenter quam solide proponuntur, ac summa tandem operis universi chronologica illustrantur*. (I am citing the first printed Italian edition: Venice, 1611, esp. Lib. III, pp. 83–155: "De sapientia illi divinitus infusa.")

[17] See the critical and summary statement at the end of the argument in Christoph August Heumann, "Von der Philosophie der Patriarchen," in *Acta Philosophorum, das ist: Gründl. Nachrichten aus der Historia Philosophica, Nebst beygefügten Urtheilen von denen dahin gehörigen alten und neuen Büchern*, Issue 5, Halle, 1716, pp. 755–809, and Issue 6, Halle, 1716, pp. 925–943. One side aspect along with confessionalization and encyclopedism is doubtless the effort to reconstruct the so-called *prisca theologia*, which began with Ficino at the end of the fifteenth century. This effort

The discourse on Moses (or Adam, Solomon, et al.) as a philosopher or the idea of the *Omniscience of Moses* was simultaneously a quasi-encyclopedic metadiscourse, which subsumed various areas of special competence that were supposedly documented by specific biblical passages. It worked like this: Moses introduced writing, and therefore he was a grammarian; he burned the golden calf and then reduced it to powder, and therefore he had mastered chemistry; he described Noah's ark precisely, and so he was a mathematician. Or one might say that Solomon knew all the plants from hyssop to cedar, and so he was a botanist.[18] The theology of creation depended on viewing the past as perfect, and fascinatingly that implied that all knowledge had been revealed at the very beginning of things.[19] No wonder the early Enlightenment tossed out the philosophy of the patriarchs as a "pious fairy fable."[20]

We now arrive at our two main questions: Within the metadiscourse in which Moses stood for a figure of absolute knowledge, how did the various individual topics relating to Moses interact with one another? And, second, how was this whole topic cast into confusion as the philological basis for such attributions began to crumble toward the end of the seventeenth century? As a first step we need to recognize that we can follow this metadiscourse over more than 100 years, all the way down to the entry on "Moses's Omniscience" (*Vielwisserheit*) in Zedler's *Universal-Lexicon* (from 1739)[21] and the article entitled "Mosaic or Christian Philosophy" in Diderot's *Encyclopedia*, which drew heavily on Brucker,[22] in which Diderot disparagingly remarked that this hybrid product was neither good philosophy nor good religion.[23]

This sort of "Christian Philosophy" had certain academic citadels. Many of them were Calvinist strongholds, such as the Reformed University in Herborn at the beginning of the seventeenth century. There one might

was oriented to universal truths and could be transformed into encyclopedism, but it was also set up to harmonize Christians and pagans, and could therefore (e.g., with Athanasius Kircher) continue to exist as a sacred discipline under the primacy of Christianity.

[18] Heumann, "Von der Philosophie der Patriarchen" (note 17), pp. 931f. describes this conclusion as a typical projection of scholars in their clouded perceptions, warped by their *déformation professionelle*. [Translator's note: for the omniscience of Solomon, see 1 Kings 4:33–34.]

[19] See Wilhelm Schmidt-Biggemann, *Philosopha perennis. Historische Umrisse abendländischer Spiritualität in Antike, Mittelalter und Früher Neuzeit*, Frankfurt, 1998. See also my review of it: *Philosophische Rundschau* 46 (1999), pp. 344–350.

[20] See Hans-Robert Jauß on fairy tales: "Das Vollkommene als Faszinosum des Imaginären," in *Ästhethische Erfahrung und literarische Hermeneutik*, Frankfurt, 1982, pp. 303–323.

[21] Zedler, *Lexicon* (note 10), col. 1888.

[22] Jakob Brucker, *Historia* (note 14); see there also vol. 1, Leipzig, 1742, pp. 78–85 on Moses and his philosophy. On Brucker, see Wilhelm Schmidt-Biggemann and Theo Stammen, eds., *Jacob Brucker (1696–1770). Philosoph und Historiker der europäischen Aufklärung*, Berlin, 1998.

[23] "Mosaïque ou Chrétienne Philosophie," in *Encyclopédie*, Neuchâtel, 1765, vol. 10, pp. 741–745.

find the leading professors Johann Heinrich Alsted and Johannes Piscator, along with a variety of less well-known teachers, who worked all the harder to live up to the expectations of these great men. One of them was Zacharias Rosenbach. He composed a work with the title *Moses omniscius, sive Omniscientia Mosaica*,[24] ("Moses the Omniscient, or The All-Knowingness of Moses"), which was based on Alsted's *Triumphus biblicus*[25] but amazingly also on Benito Arias Montano,[26] the chaplain of King Philip II of Spain and the editor of the Antwerp Polyglot Bible.[27] Arias Montano was a highly learned Erasmian biblical scholar, conversant in ten languages, who in his *Phaleg* of 1572[28] had endeavored to show that the Bible contained all the treasures of the sciences, and especially those of geography.[29] In making this claim he was a true forerunner of Alsted's in believing that the Bible was really "the only" book, in the sense that it

[24] Zacharias Rosenbach, *Moses omniscius, sive Omniscientia Mosaica: Sectionibus VI. quam brevissime exhibens supra septies mille veteris testamenti voces, secundum Rerum Locos Communes Novos ita dispositas, ut quis inde [...] omnium autorum scripta accurate resolvere [...] cupit, expedite admodum componere possit. Opus, quale hucusque visum non est: omnibus iis, qui rerum varietate delectantur, maxime vero pietati student, jucundissimum, utilissimum, ac summe necessarium*, Frankfurt a.M., 1632. Rosenbach was a physician and professor of physics and languages at the university of Herborn. On Herborn generally, see Gerhard Menk, *Die Hohe Schule Herborn in ihrer Frühzeit (1584–1660). Ein Beitrag zum Hochschulwesen des deutschen Kalvinismus im Zeitalter der Gegenreformation*, Wiesbaden, 1981; for the medical faculty especially, see Dieter Wessinghage, *Die Hohe Schule Herborn und ihre medizinische Fakultät*, Stuttgart and New York, 1984. Sacred jurisprudence was taught in Herborn by Wilhelm Zepper, *De legibus Mosaicis forensibus*, Herborn, 1614.

[25] Johann Heinrich Alsted, *Triumphus biblicus, sive Encyclopaedia Biblica, exhibens triumphum philosophiae, iurisprudentiae et medicinae sacrae itemque sacrae theologiae, quantum illarum fundamenta ex scriptoribus sacris veteris et novi testamenti colliguntur*, Frankfurt, 1625; on Alsted, see Howard Hotson, *Johann Heinrich Alsted 1588–1638: Between Renaissance, Reformation and Universal Reform*, Oxford, 2000; and Thomas Leinkauf, "Systema mnemonicum und circulus encyclopaediae. Johann Heinrich Alsteds Versuch einer Fundierung des universalen Wissens in der ars memorativa," in Jörg Jochen Berns and Wolfgang Neuber, eds., *Seelenmaschinen. Gattungstraditionen, Funktionen und Leistungsgrenzen der Mnemotechniken vom späten Mittelalter bis zum Beginn der Moderne*, Vienna, 2000, pp. 279–308. Rosenbach had contributed the medical and natural-scientific sections in Alsted's *Compendium lexici philosophici*, Herborn, 1626.

[26] Benedictus Arias Montanus, *Phaleg, sive De gentium sedibus primis*, Antwerp, 1572, Praefatio. Quoted in Rosenbach according to the table of contents, unpag., fol. c2v. On Montano and his involvement in the circle around Plantin, see Alastair Hamilton, *The Family of Love*, Cambridge, 1981; Leon Voet, *The Golden Compasses*, 2 vols., Amsterdam, 1969; Theodor Dunkelgrün, *The Multiplicity of Scripture: The Confluence of Textual Traditions in the Making of the Antwerp Polyglot Bible (1568–1573)*, Dissertation, Chicago, 2012.

[27] On the various polyglot Bibles, see Jacques Lelong, *Discours historique sur les principales éditions des Bibles Polyglottes*, Paris, 1713; Peter N. Miller, "Les origines de la Bible Polyglotte de Paris: philologia sacra, Contre-Reforme et raison d'état," *XVIIe siècle* 194 (1997), pp. 57–66.

[28] Montanus, *Phaleg, sive De gentium sedibus primis* (note 26).

[29] See Arno Borst, *Der Turmbau von Babel. Geschichte der Meinungen über Ursprung und Vielfalt der Sprachen und Völker*, Stuttgart, 1957–1963, vol. 3(1), p. 1152; for a thorough treatment, Giuliano Gliozzi, *Adamo e il nuovo mondo. La nascita dell' anthropologia come ideologia coloniale: dalle genealogie bibliche alle teorie razziali (1500–1700)*, Florence, 1976, pp. 150ff.

contained everything and therefore provided an adequate foundation for all the sacred disciplines. *Non est liber nisi scriptura*, as Alsted said ("There is no book but Scripture"). One hundred years later Samuel Bochart produced his own *Phaleg*, with a *geographia sacra* that was based on Arias Montano but he had the problem of dealing with the tremendous expansion of scholarship over the intervening years.[30]

In any event Rosenbach quoted Arias Montano's claim that from the careful study of Holy Scripture he had obtained a knowledge that would fill many volumes and was superior to profane compendia of knowledge. Indeed, in the *Moses omniscius* of the Herborn professor Moses's knowledge was condensed into a dictionary. Rosenbach disaggregated the omniscience of Moses and represented its topics in tables in the style of Ramus. Following the ontology taught in Herborn, this analysis of Mosaic knowledge began with entries on *aliquid* and *nihil* ("something" and "nothing").[31] Rosenbach regarded this topical dictionary as an Old Testament complement to a New Testament work on the "Omniscience of Christ" and presented itself as a linguistic tool for the disciplines of sacred history. Rosenbach's own interest was in natural science, and especially botany, which he pursued both empirically and sacrally in the manner of a "modern" *botanica sacra*. When the court preacher and ecclesiastical superintendent in Kassel (Hesse), Theophil Neuberger, gave a copy of Rosenbach's book to his master, the Landgrave of Hesse, he may not have been thinking only about Rosenbach's natural scientific interests, however, but also about the interests of this son of the learned Moritz of Hesse, which he hoped he could place in the safe harbor of *physica sacra*.[32]

[30] Samuel Bochart, *Geographia sacra, cujus pars prior PHALEG de dispersione gentium & terrarum divisione facta in aedificatione turris Babel; pars posterior CHANAAN de coloniis et sermone Phoenicum agit [...]*, Caen, 1646. I am using the Frankfurt a.M., 1681 edition. See Praefatio, unpag., fol. **3. And see Zur Shalev, *Sacred Words and Worlds: Geography, Religion, and Scholarship, 1550–1700*, Leiden, 2011.

[31] See generally Wolfgang Hübener, "Scientia de aliquo et nihilo. Die historischen Voraussetzungen von Leibniz' Ontologiebegriff," in *Zum Geist der Prämoderne*, Würzburg, 1985; further Wilhelm Schmidt-Biggemann, *Topica universalis. Eine Modellgeschichte humanistischer und barocker Wissenschaft*, Hamburg, 1983.

[32] See the entry in the copy: 4 Exeg. 728 in the Bayerische Staatsbibliothek Munich: "Sum Hermanni Hassiae Landgravii ex dono Dn. Theoph. Neubergeri Super. 1637. 3. Aprilis." Neuberger (1593-1656) was a Calvinist who had studied under David Paraeus in Heidelberg. On him, see ADB, vol. 23, pp. 477f.; Christian Gottlieb Jöcher, *Allgemeines Gelehrten-Lexicon*, 4 vols., Leipzig, 1750-1751 (7 supplementary vols., Hildesheim, 1960–1998); Hermann Landgrave of Hesse had composed works on astronomy and meteorology: *Teutsche Astrologia oder Teutscher Discurss von allerhand astrologischen Spekulationen*, Grebenstein, 1637; and *Historia Meteorologica. Das ist Vier und zwanzig Jährige eigentliche und treußeissige Observation [...] durch Uranophilum Cyriandrum*, Kassel, 1651. See Bruce T. Moran, *The Alchemical World of the German Court: Occult Philosophy and Chemical Medicine in the Circle of Moritz of Hessen (1572–1632)*, Stuttgart, 1991, p. 172.

And yet the development of the Herborn *Philosophia Mosaica* should give us pause. Was the figure of Moses in this encyclopedic metadiscourse still that of a real person? Probably not, for the collective memory had been diluted into an attenuated artificial memory; Moses in his omniscience was only a lexicographical or rhetorical constellation. He was like a hollow body that concealed tables, systems, and archives. The individual topics were, to be sure, distinguished in a philosophically responsible way, but they had no living connection to one another. Our question, concerning how the various subjects such as politics and knowledge related to one another, cannot even be asked in this sort of metadiscourse.

And the hollow body of Moses already had a long prior history. At the end of the seventeenth century it was still possible for the Orthodox Lutheran August Pfeiffer of Leipzig to compose a work, *Pansophia Mosaica*, which explicitly derived from Alsted.[33] For Pfeiffer the only difference was first that he outdid the project of the Herborn Reformed professor by locating all knowledge and all the world's arts not just in the Old Testament, but in the very first book of Moses, Genesis.[34] Pfeiffer may have been inspired by the aging Luther's Commentary on Genesis. But examined more closely, the hollow body of the omniscient Moses had an entirely different function: toward the end of the century apologetic interests outweighed all others. So Moses was no longer really a reservoir for sacralized disciplines but a bulwark against "atheists, pagans, Jews, Turks, and all heretics."[35] But the topoi remained, and also their lack of communication with each other. And so Moses did not become a real person who could act and embody this knowledge.

3   The Influence of the Libertine Tradition and the Abyss of Accommodation Theory

In the further developments of the separate sacralized disciplines, and especially in "Mosaic physics," this situation changed but

---

[33] August Pfeiffer, *Pansophia Mosaica e Genesi delineata, Das ist / Der Grund-Riß aller Weisheit / Darinnen auß dem Ersten Buch Mosis Alle Glaubens-Articul; die Widerlegung der Atheisten / Heyden / Jüden / Türcken und aller Ketzer; alle Disciplinen in allen Facultäten; der Ursprung aller Sprachen; der Extract von allen Historien / Antiquitäten und Curiositäten; alle Professiones, Handwercke und Handthierungen; alle Tugenden und Laster; aller Trost / kurtz und deutlich gewiesen worden von D. Augusto Pfeiffern*, Leipzig, 1685. In the history of reading, the context for reducing all matters to the Bible or even to Genesis alone can of course be found in the priority for simple people of reading the Bible (*sola scriptura*). With a reference to Alsted, Pfeiffer speaks on p. 3 of the Bible as a "Bibliotheca portatilis."

[34] See Pfeiffer, *Pansophia Mosaica e Genesi delineata* (note 33), pp. 28f.

[35] See also the reference of Pfeiffer to the aplogetics of Mersenne, Parker, and Voetius: ibid., p. 131.

little.[36] From the middle of the seventeenth century onward there was a Cartesian variant, which we can find, for example, in Amerpoel's *Cartesius Mosaizans* ("Descartes Thinking Like Moses"), Beaufort's *Cosmopoeia divina* ("The Divine Construction of the Cosmos"), or, in a more exotic vein, in Henry More's *Conjectura cabalistica* ("Kabbalistic Conjectures").[37] To explore only More's work, he set up Moses the politician as a figure with whom he could argue. He seemed to think that he was obliged to do so in 1653, in his defense of the *Conjectures*, for by then libertine voices were to be heard that claimed Moses had behaved tactically just like other politicians.[38] More shaped his argument as a defense of the similar thesis of Diodorus Siculus, who based himself, as we know, on the historical work of Hecataeus of Abdera.[39] But it could have just as easily have been borrowed from Machiavelli or Naudé.[40]

The libertine interpretation of Moses had, in fact, become unavoidable by the mid-seventeenth century. Just as the updated version of *pansophia Mosaica* had roots in both confessionalism and encyclopedism, so in like manner the boom in this libertine interpretation originated in early modern political thinking about reason of state.[41] The chapter on Moses in the *Theophrastus redivivus* from around 1650 was typical – it was a summary of libertine criticism of religion by a still unknown author. In it the author combined a secular conception of politics with a debunking of

---

[36] I cannot here go into the "philosophia Moysaica" of the hermetic-Paracelsists, such as Fludd, Comenius, or Johannes Bayer et al. On Comenius, see Jaromir Cervenka, *Die Naturphilosophie des Johann Amos Comenius*, Prague, 1970.

[37] Johannes Amerpoel, *Cartesius Mosaizans*, Leeuwarden, 1669; Louis de Beaufort, *Cosmopoeia divina sive fabrica mundi explicata*, Leiden, 1656; Henry More, *Conjectura cabalistica*, London, 1653.

[38] Henry More, "Defence of the Threefold Cabala," in *Conjectura cabalistica* (note 37), pp. 94–98. See also Richard H. Popkin, *The Third Force in Seventeeth-Century Thought*, Leiden, 1992, pp. 113f.

[39] See Diodorus Siculus, *Bibliotheca historica*, esp. XL, 3; *Diodorus of Sicily*, ed. and tr. F. R. Walton, Loeb Classical Library, Cambridge, MA, 1967, p. 281. I quote here from Henry More's later Latin version: *Triplicis Cabbalae Defensio*, in *Opera omnia*, vol. 2(2), London, 1679; repr. Hildesheim, 1966, p. 505. On More and his relationship with tradition, see Joseph M. Levine, "Latitudinarians, Neoplatonists, and the Ancient Wisdom," in Richard Kroll, Richard Ashcraft, and Perez Zagorin, eds., *Philosophy, Science, and Religion in England 1640–1700*, Cambridge, 1992, pp. 85–108.

[40] See the treatments of Moses as lawgiver and politician by many, including Machiavelli: *Il Principe*, cap. 6; *Discorsi*, Lib. 1, cap. 9; Gabriel Naudé, *Apologie pour tous les grands personnages qui ont esté faussement soupçonnez de magie*, Paris, 1625. On Naudé: Lorenzo Bianchi, *Rinascimento e libertinismo. Studi su Gabriel Naudé*, Naples, 1996.

[41] In addition there was the naturalism of Renaissance science, which grew out of "Averroistic" Aristotelianism. This naturalism strengthened the "profane" understanding of Moses as a politician and offered natural explanations for the supposed miracles depicted in Exodus. For this tendency, see, e.g., Pietro Pomponazzi, *De naturalium effectuum causis sive De incantationibus*, composed ca. 1520, published in Basel, 1567 in his *Opera*. See the critical new edition by Vittoria Perrone Compagni, Florence, 2011.

all supposed miracles in favor of natural explanations.[42] What survived was a Moses who, as the later *Moïsade* by Voltaire's rival, put it, presented to the credulous people "the most cunning fiction disguised in the sacred garment of religion."[43]

[42] *Theophrastus redivivus*, ed. Guido Canziani and Gianni Paganini, 2 vols., Florence, 1981 and 1982, vol. 2, pp. 430–457, e.g., p. 431. The mainly ancient sources for the *Theophrastus redivivus* include Josephus, *Contra Apionem* (note 63) (the story of Manetho concerning Osarseph is also used at p. 435); Tacitus, *Historiae*; Marcus Junianus Justinus, *Epitoma*; and Pliny, *Naturalis historia*. See on this Gianni Paganini, "La critica della civiltà nel Theophrastus redivivus. I. Natura e cultura," in Tullio Gregory et al., eds., *Ricerche su letteratura libertina e letteratura clandestina nel Seicento*, Florence, 1981, pp. 49–82; Guido Canziani, "La critica della civiltà nel Theophrasus redivivus. II. Ordine naturale e legalità civile," ibid., pp. 83–118. Lorenzo Bianchi, *Tradizione libertina e critica storica*, Milan, 1988, pp. 107–139. In addition libertine interpretations offered the titillating story that Moses was the son-in-law of the Midianite priest Jethro, who had advised him in forming his conspiracy against the Egyptians. The story was tantalizing if one considers Ernst Axel Knauf's speculation that Yahweh may have been a Midianite god, who was transposed into the Exodus event, an event that had been initiated by a Syrian treasurer in Egypt by the name of by/'r'sw in about 1187 BCE, during the critical juncture when an attempted usurpation was collapsing. The transfer occurred through the "Hymn of Jahweh's Victory at the Sea of Reeds." When *by* and his group arrived in Palestine alive, they were able to mobilize the common fervor against the Egyptians and to pass along the Yahweh god to the peasant tribes that were just then forming in central Palestine. See Ernst Axel Knauf, *Midian. Untersuchungen zur Geschichte Palästinas und Nordarabiens am Ende des 2. Jahrtausends v. Chr.*, Wiesbaden, 1988, esp. pp. 125–149.

[43] I will quote here from the manuscript copy of the text by Jakob Friedrich Reimmann in his collection, *Systema systematum atheisticorum*, Ms. WB 1789 in the City Archive of Hildesheim. The contemporary attribution to Jean-Baptiste Rousseau is not entirely certain. Sometimes the name Lourdet is given for this. For literature on Rousseau see Alexandre Cioranescu, *Bibliografie de la littérature française du 18e siècle*, vol. 3, Paris, 1969, pp. 1512–1516. "Le vulgaire en aveugle à l'erreur s'abandonne / Et la plus froide fiction / Masquee au coin sacré de la Religion / Des sots admirateurs dont la terre foisonne / Frape l'imagination. // Ces Visions melancholiques / Des Peuples arrogans soumettent la fierté / Et prodvisent en eux cette docilité / Qui dans les sages Republiques / Entretient la tranquillité / Les hommes vains et fanatiques / Recoivent sans difficulté / Les fables les plus chimeriques / Un petit mot d'Eternité / Les rend benins et pacifiques / Et l'on reduit ainsi le Public hebeté, / A baiser les biens dont il est garotté. // Moyse le premier par semblables pratiques / Scut fixer des Hebreux l'esprit inquieté / Et surprit leur credulité / En rengeant ses loix-politiques / Sous l'etendant de la divinité. // Il faignit d'avoir vu sur un mort écarté / Des visions beatifiques / Il fit entendre à ces hommes rustiques / Que Dieu dans son eclat, et dans sa Majesté / A ses yeux eblouis s'etoit manifesté. // Il leur montra Fables authentiques / Qui contenoient sa volont. / Il appuya par des tons patetiques / un conte si bien inventé / Tout le monde fut enchanté. / De ces fadaises magnifiques / Ce mensonge subtil passant pour verité / De ce legislateur fonda l'authorité / Et donna cours aux creances publiques, / Dont le peuple fut infecté." (I adopt the spelling in the manuscript, which seldom employs accents.) This very aggressive text also existed in a more cautious version (which Reimmann also copied), in which "Moses" was replaced with "Numa," and the Jews with the Romans. The text was typical of the continuing libertine and anti-Christian interpretations of Moses in the eighteenth century, which found expression in numerous clandestine manuscripts. See, e.g., the *Dissertation sur Moïse où l'on fait voir qu'il est un fourbe et un imposteur*, Bibliothèque Mazarine, Paris, 1194, piece no. 7, pp. 59–110. See also Baron d'Holbach, *Le Christianisme devoilé*, "Londres," 1767, part 2. For a general introduction, see Bertram Schwarzbach, "Les adversaires de la Bible," in Yvon Belaval, ed., *Le Siècle des Lumieres et la Bible*, Paris, 1986.

My argument is that the libertine tradition with its all-too-human Moses, now represented as a politician, had the effect of slowly moving the sacral-encyclopedic discourse toward a restored image of Moses as a concrete, human figure rather than just a conceptual hollow body. Of course in the sacral political literature of the early modern period Moses had remained an actual person, but that starting point did not necessarily affect other areas of scholarship. In the context of literature criticizing Moses, things were different.

At least in the case of John Spencer, by the 1680s in Cambridge the idea of Moses as a politician had grown so strong that he could be presented as the political instrument of God, whose mission was to subject the barbarous and primitive Jews to an anti-idolatrous "withdrawal treatment,"[44] to wean them from the Egyptian religion. Spencer believed that God could work only as a "remote cause," and that conviction drew him to see Moses as a "profane" politician.[45] Later discussion of the divine mission of Moses had its origins in this option.[46] The fact that contemporary libertines such as Charles Blount and John Toland used Spencer's argument is a rather different matter.

And yet there was, I think, another factor that contributed to bringing together *physica sacra* and libertine-political interpretations of Moses. That was the theory of accommodation, the argument that Moses had remained silent about (or had disguised) certain facts in order to make difficult or less palatable realities more acceptable to simple people. The argument was old, but it gained increasing recognition in Old Testament commentaries of the sixteenth century, for example that of Jean Le Mercier.[47] The

---

[44] The term comes from Jan Assmann, *Moses the Egyptian*, Cambridge, MA, 1998, p. 78. See John Spencer, *De legibus Hebraeorum ritualibus, et earum rationibus, libri tres*, Cambridge, 1686. See Martin Mulsow, *Enlightenment Underground: Radical Germany 1680–1720*, tr. H. C. Erik Midelfort, Charlottesville, 2015, chapter 2.

[45] See on that John Gascoigne, "The Wisdom of the Egyptians and the Secularisation of History in the Age of Newton," in Stephen Gaukroger, ed., *The Uses of Antiquity. The Scientific Revolution and the Classical Tradition*, Dordrecht, 1991, pp. 171–212; and Mulsow, *Enlightenment Underground* (note 44), chapter 2.

[46] See William Warburton, *The Divine Legation of Moses Demonstrated on the Principles of a Religious Deist, from the Omission of the Doctrine of a Future State of Reward and Punishment in the Jewish Dispensation*, London 1738–1741; 2nd edn, London, 1778; on this, in addition to Assmann, *Moses the Egyptian* (note 44), see Wolfgang Hartwich, *Die Sendung Moses*, Munich, 1997.

[47] Jean Le Mercier, *In Genesin commentarius*, Geneva, 1598, e.g., p. 11. See Arnold Williams, *The Common Expositor: An Account of the Commentaries on Genesis 1527–1633*, Chapel Hill, 1948, pp. 176ff. See the debate at that time within the Catholic Church concerning the strategy of accommodation used by missionaries confronting foreign cultures: Johannes Betray, *Die Akkommodationstheorie des P. Matteo Ricci S. J. in China*, Analecta Gregoriana 76, Rome, 1955; David E. Mungello, *Curious Land: Jesuit Accommodation and the Origins of Sinology*, Honolulu,

pressure during the confessional age toward making Aristotelian, but then also Copernican or Cartesian physics compatible with the biblical text, pushed this interpretation into even greater visibility.[48] The argument burst into prominence especially when critics like Spencer came to view the ancient Hebrews as a primitive people. Edmund Dickinson, therefore, provided a literal interpretation of the Creation story that emphatically defended the Hebrews at the time of Moses as a superior culture probably in order to refute certain libertine followers of Spencer.[49] He did not want to take the easy route that some of his colleagues took, who simply assumed that the accommodation thesis was a warrant for one's own speculations, and instead insisted on a philologically sensible but difficult reconstruction of Mosaic physics on the basis of the text of Genesis. The fact that Dickinson nonetheless derived a quasi-modern idea of the world that was not much different from Boyle's corpuscular theory probably did not derive from mere physicalist prejudices but instead from a philological hypothesis common in the seventeenth century. This was the hypothesis that Moschus the Phoenician, the early if not the first atomist mentioned by Diogenes Laertius, Strabo, and some other ancient sources, could have been identical with the biblical Moses. As early as 1598 the Frisian philologist Johannes Arcerius Theodoretus had daringly launched this

1989. Further, Amos Funkenstein, *Theology and the Scientific Imagination from the Middle Ages to the Seventeenth Century*, Princeton, 1986.

[48] See the harmonizations of Aristotelianism and Mosaic teachings in Hieronymus Zanchius, *De operibus Dei intra spacium sex dierum creatis opus*, Neustadt, 1591, or in Daneau, *Physica Christiana* (note 12). On the later harmonizations with Cartesian philosophy and Copernicanism, see Klaus Scholder, *Ursprünge und Probleme der Bibelkritik im 17. Jahrhundert. Ein Beitrag zur Entstehung der historisch-kritischen Theologie*, Munich, 1966; Hans Frei, *The Eclipse of Biblical Narrative: A Study in Eighteenth and Nineteenth Century Hermeneutics*, New Haven, 1974.

[49] Edmund Dickinson, *Physica vetus & vera: sive Tractatus de naturali veritate hexaemeri Mosaici. Per quem probatur in historia Creationis, tum generationis universae methodum atque modum, tum verae philosophiae principia, strictim atque breviter a Mose tradi*, London, 1702, chapter 19, pp. 270–312: "De Israelitis Aegyptiacis." E.g., p. 312: with his harsh words against the "atheus" Dickinson surely did not mean Spencer; but he probably did intend freethinkers, who went further along the track that Spencer had opened. On antisemitism among the English deists, see Leon Poliakov, *Geschichte des Antisemitismus*, vol. 5, Worms, 1983, pp. 70–81. Dickinson himself followed rather the traditional strategy of interpreting the *translatio sapientiae* in such a way that after the Flood Ham brought not only idolatry to Egypt but also the original wisdom, and from there that wisdom passed over to Moses and to the culturally advanced Israelites. Dickinson does not explicitly mention Spencer, but Heumann, "Von der Philosophie der Patriarchen" (note 17), p. 792, suspected that the chapter was directed against Spencer. Dickinson appears to me to have understood *physica sacra* more literally than his colleague Thomas Burnet. See Burnet's *Archaeologiae philosophicae sive Doctrina antiqua de rerum originibus*, London, 1692, esp. pp. 43–71: "De Hebraeis, eorumque Cabala." On the debates around Burnet (and especially his preparatory work toward an aesthetic of the sublime), see also Marjorie Hope Nicolson, *Mountain Gloom and Mountain Glory: The Development of the Aesthetics of the Infinite*, Ithaca, N.Y., 1959.

suspicion in his Latin translation of Iamblichus's *De vita Pythagorae*, and they became a broadly discussed topic – even though by the eighteenth century they were no longer defensible.[50] Authors who were attracted to *physica sacra* or to early modern corpuscular theory, such as Daniel Sennert, were naturally eager to support this suggestion.[51] And not the least of those inspired by Arcerius's argument was Ralph Cudworth, whose impressive effort to oppose the godless atomism of Hobbes by proving a more original and uncorrupted atomism was proved, as he thought, by sacred history as well as by the rational consensus of ancient sages.[52] According to Cudworth, this was an atomism that was enlivened by spirit. So in the first years of the eighteenth century, Dickinson was only spelling out logically what had been secretly suggested for a century. In accordance with the Hebrew text of Genesis, he was describing how the world arose from tiny particles (*globuli*) and little rods (*longulae*) or fine bits, like flakes of metal (*bracteae*).[53]

The theory of accommodation offered space not only for the new science but also a taste of secrecy and esotericism – if one wanted to judge what Moses had *not* told the simple people to be a secret. Paradoxically, such esoteric elements could also point to the need for reason and

---

[50] Iamblichus, ["ΙΑΜΒΛΙΧΟΥ ΧΑΛΚΙΔΕΩΣ"], [...] *De vita Pythagorae & protrepticae orationes ad philosophiam libri II*, ed. Johannes Arcerius Theodoretus Frisius, [Heidelberg], 1598. See Danton B. Sailor, "Moses and Atomism," *Journal of the History of Ideas* 25 (1964), pp. 3–16.

[51] See Daniel Sennert, *Hypomnemata physica*, Frankfurt, 1636; Boyle too appealed to this thesis. See, e.g., his *Sceptical Chymist*, in *The Works*, 6 vols., London, 1772, vol. 1, p. 498; or also vol. 4, p. 48 in his work, "The Excellency of Theology." On Sennert and Boyle, see William R. Newman, *Atoms and Alchemy: Chymistry and the Experimental Origins of the Scientific Revolution*, Chicago, 2006.

[52] See Ralph Cudworth, *The True Intellectual System of the Universe: The First Part; wherein, All the Reason and Philosophy of Atheism Is Confuted; and Its Impossibility Demonstrated*, London, 1678, esp. chapter III; there, e.g., p. 105. On Moschus, see pp. 12f. In his opposing commentary on Cudworth's book, Mosheim admittedly energetically rejected the identification of Moschus with Moses. On Mosheim's commentary, see Sarah Hutton, "Classicism and Baroque: A Note on Mosheim's Footnotes to Cudworth's *The True Intellectual System of the Universe*," in Martin Mulsow et al., eds., *Johann Lorenz Mosheim (1693–1755). Theologie im Spannungsfeld von Philosophie, Philologie und Geschichte*, Wiesbaden, 1997, pp. 211–228; Marialuisa Baldi, "Confutazione e conferma: l'origenismo nella traduzione latina del Trie Intellectual System (1733)," in Baldi, ed., *Mind Senior to the World. Stoicismo e origenismo nella filosofia platonica del Seicento inglese*, Milan, 1996, pp. 163–204. Behind the chaos of atomistic matter was always the problem of the preexistence of this matter. See Harry A. Wolfson, "Plato's Preexistent Matter in Patristic Philosophy," in Luitpold Wallach, ed., *The Classical Tradition: Literary and Historical Studies in Honor of Harry Caplan*, Ithaca, N.Y., 1966, pp. 409–420; Wolfson, *The Philosophy of the Church Fathers*, Cambridge, MA, 1956. On Cudworth generally see Martin Mulsow's article on "Cudworth" in Franco Volpi, ed., *Großes Werklexikon Philosophie*, Stuttgart, 1999, vol. 1, pp. 345–347.

[53] Dickinson, *Physica vetus & vera* (note 49), pp. 35ff. See Katherine Brownell Collier, *Cosmogonies of Our Fathers: Some Theories of the 17th and 18th Centuries*, New York, 1934; repr. New York, 1968, pp. 149–165. See Nikolaus Hieronymus Gundling's depiction in *Historia philosophiae moralis*, Halle, 1706, p. 66.

philosophy, which were not easily reconciled with esotericism. Cudworth had understood this when he spoke of the "arcane theology" of the Egyptians,[54] but less reliable thinkers hit upon the idea of taking the topos of Moses as an educated Egyptian and combining it with the theory of accommodation and Egyptian hieroglyphics, and then harnessing them all for their own purposes. In this way a space opened up not just for natural science but also for the emerging scholarly field of comparative religions. The law student from Leiden, Adrian Beverland, did not spare the sacred text of Genesis with its myth of the fall into sin, but instead enlisted it for his own cultural comparisons: Moses had supposedly learned a hiero-glyphic code, so that he could tell simple folk a fable of the fall into sin as if it involved only a tree and its fruit, whereas the story really referred to the phallus and sexual intercourse. He proved these contentions with a comparison of Hebrew culture with other Eastern and Roman cultures and their symbols.[55] Occult secrets could now include not just holy matters but sexuality or rulership. Certain kinds of knowledge had long been forbidden; and the apostle Paul had enjoined Christians, "Do not seek to know high things," a saying that had a strong resonance throughout the early modern period.[56]

Beverland's Moses was on the one hand the product of the learnedly obscene philological tradition that had started in the Renaissance,[57] but it was also the result of a surprisingly modern text-critical and comparative history of religions. These qualities made his book deeply offensive to Beverland's contemporaries and revealed the dangerous abyss opened up by theories of accommodation. That abyss grew even deeper as sacred history was declared compatible with profane history. This interpretation impinged not only on theories of the flood or on the uses to which the books of Thomas Burnet and Spencer were put by English freethinkers,[58]

---

[54] Cudworth (note 52), p. 316; see Assmann, *Moses the Egyptian* (note 44), pp. 118–130.

[55] I cite the improved version from the year 1679: *Peccatum originale κατ' ἐξοχήν sic nuncupatum, philologice προβληματικός elucubratum a Themidis Alumno. Vera redit facies, dissimulata perit.* [...]. On Beverland see R. de Smet, *Hadrianus Beverlandus (1650–1716). Non unus e multis peccator. Studie over het leven en werk van Hadriaan Beverland*, Brussels, 1988; Martin Mulsow, "Unanständigkeit. Zur Mißachtung und Verteidigung des Decorum in der Gelehrtenrepublik der Frühen Neuzeit," *Historische Anthropologie* 8 (2000), pp. 98–118.

[56] Carlo Ginzburg, "High and Low: The Theme of Forbidden Knowledge in the Sixteenth and Seventeenth Centuries," *Past and Present* (1976), pp. 28–41. For the passage from Romans 11:20: KJV = "Be not highminded, but fear." RSV = "Do not become proud but stand in awe."

[57] David O. Frantz, *Festum Voluptatis: A Study of Renaissance Erotica*, Columbus, Ohio 1989, esp. chapter 1: "In Praise of Apples, Figs, and Keys: The Learned Tradition."

[58] See Manlio Iofrida, "La presenza della cultura libertina in Inghilterra alla fine del '600: Charles Blount, Thomas Burnet e William Coward," in Tullio Gregory et al., eds., *Ricerche su letteratura*

but also and especially on the symbolism involved in the fall into sin, which affected the very center of Christian doctrine.

4 Power Politics and Deceptive Knowledge: The Uses of Hellenistic Literature Opposed to Moses

At this point we can no longer overlook the fact that, over the course of the seventeenth century, sacred history, *philosophia Mosaica*, could be transformed into rationalism and libertinage. The rhetorical hollow body of the omniscient Moses took on flesh and blood more quickly than many desired. So in this context it is interesting to see how the libertine tradition handled the Hellenistic legacy. What we are calling *philosophica Mosaica* had absorbed the exaltations of Moses common from Philo to Eusebius and yet we note that they carried with them a centrifugal encyclopedic impulse that inflated Moses into a heroic but impersonal body of knowledge. The libertine tradition with its all-too-human Moses, a man who used deceit and tricks, set up a centripetal force opposing the inflated Moses, one that deflated him.[59] It did so, we should not be surprised to learn, by using the anti-Moses literature of the Hellenistic age, the disparagements, to the extent that they could be recovered. It is important to notice that certain aspects of Moses's knowledge survived intact. True, his knowledge was now subordinated to his politics, but as the Jewish lawgiver he was still credited with a high degree of understanding. Even the infamous *Traité des trois imposteurs* that dealt with the three "impostors," Moses, Jesus, and Mohammed, explicitly cited the passage in the book of Acts (7:22) in which Moses was described as "learned in all the wisdom of the Egyptians."[60] Indeed, it even added, "Moses is presented to us as the greatest politician, the most learned naturalist, and the most famous

---

libertina e letteratura clandestina nel Seicento, Florence, 1981, pp. 387–394; Paolo Rossi, *The Dark Abyss of Time: The History of the Earth and the History of Nations from Hooke to Vico*, Chicago, 1984; Nicola Badaloni, *Introduzione a G. B. Vico*, Milan, 1961.

[59] There was a comparable dynamic in the discussions of Solomon during the seventeenth century. The inflation into a hyperdiscourse about the omniscient patriarch Solomon (see one representative example: Juan de Pineda, *De rebus Salomonis* (note 16), Lib. III) was opposed by a critical tradition that emphasized the fallible Solomon (his polygamy, superstition, etc.) and in its libertine variant even made him into a Pyrrhonist skeptic and thus a figure who served to legitimate *libertinage érudit*. These conflicting images survived into the eighteenth century. See Martin Mulsow, "Eclecticism or Scepticism? A Problem of the Early Enlightenment," *Journal of the History of Ideas* (1997), pp. 465–477.

[60] *Traité des trois imposteurs*, critical edition, ed. and tr. Winfried Schröder, *Traktat über die drei Betrüger*, Hamburg, 1992, p. 60: "En un mot en disant *qu'il fut élevé dans toutes les sciences des Egyptiens*, c'est tout dire . . . ."

magician of his age."[61] Of course it is clear that in this deflationary context his omniscience was now different. He was no longer a figure of glorious and fundamental knowledge but of political power and the ability to deceive. Thus the *Traité* stated: "He knew how to use all the knowledge he'd acquired, I mean his supposed magic, against Egypt, and in doing this he was subtler and more clever than the other magicians at the court of the pharaoh."[62]

So how was the ancient anti-Moses literature used? From Flavius Josephus's *Contra Apionem* scholars knew the story of the Egyptian priest Manetho, according to which the ancestors of the Jews had been Egyptian lepers.[63] They had been isolated from society and turned over to the priest Osarseph, who had a deep knowledge of nature. But the lepers allied themselves with the neighboring Jerusalemites against the Egyptians and pushed back into Egypt with Osarseph, who later took the name of Moses. It took thirteen years before they were finally driven out by King Amenophis, who pursued them to the borders of Palestine.

In this telling, Moses was an Egyptian priest. But Moses also appears in the Latin treatise *On the Three Impostors* (which was written by Johann Joachim Müller in 1688, as we have seen, a book that was completely different from the French version with a similar title); here the topos from the book of Acts appears again, claiming that Moses was "educated in all the occult arts of the Egyptians"; this text asserted that Moses used his knowledge "to make himself a great military leader (*dux magnus*) and to make his brother a high priest."[64] The story of Manetho, however, was first added in a manuscript comment on the Latin treatise on the impostors, one that had also been inspired by a reading of the French *Traité*, which alluded to this episode.[65] Winfried Schröder discovered this added comment and identified its author as Johann Christian Edelmann. There we find the Manetho story, one that Edelmann had already elaborated and

---

[61] Ibid. Justin Champion suspects that Toland's interest in Moses influenced editions of the *Traité* published after ca. 1709.

[62] *Traité des trois imposteurs* (note 60), pp. 62–64.

[63] Flavius Josephus, *Contra Apionem* I, 26; English tr. in H. St. J. Thackeray, *Josephus: The Life, Against Apion*, Loeb Classical Library, Cambridge, MA, 1926, pp. 255–265; see Funkenstein, *Theology and the Scientific Imagination* (note 47), pp. 273f.; and Assmann, *Moses the Egyptian* (note 44), pp. 54ff.

[64] Anonymus [Johann Joachim Müller], *De imposturis religionum (De tribus impostoribus). Von den Betrügereyen der Religionen. Dokumente*, critical edition, ed. and commentary Winfried Schröder, Stuttgart, 1999, p. 116. The free translation I quote from Edelmann is on p. 207.

[65] At least in the printed version of 1719, *La vie et l'esprit de Mr. Benoit de Spinosa*, pp. 89f. See Schröder's commentary (note 64), p. 208.

interpreted in his manuscript "Fifth View," entitled "Moses' Face Uncovered,"[66] that was itself based on a work by Pierre-Daniel Huet.[67]

We have now arrived at the period of biblical criticism after Spinoza and Richard Simon. Agreeing with Spinoza, Edelmann regarded Ezra as the editor of the Pentateuch (a view that recent research by Richard Friedman has revived).[68] Edelmann tried to explain who the historical Moses actually was and what the hidden background for Ezra's story of the Exodus was. With his expanded version of Manetho's story, Edelmann hoped to clarify a circumstance that was otherwise difficult to understand: that during the persecution of the lepers as depicted, Osarseph-Moses succeeded in reaching Palestine only after forty years. He did so by first claiming that the lepers had been swineherds, afflicted with some contagious scabies or leprosy from the consumption of too much pork. He also imagined that after the exodus from Egypt the Jerusalemites had again separated themselves from the lepers. Only the latter had moved directly to Palestine, while the Jerusalemites along with their leader Moses had had to wait a full generation, "for an entire race had to die out before his (i.e., Moses's) 'cure' could be effective on their successors. He therefore forbade them to eat the foods that had been partly responsible for starting or spreading their leprosy."[69] The "cure" of which he spoke was the laws that Moses gave his group. Part of Moses's laws was therefore a normative inversion of Egyptian laws, because they were intended to combat the causes for the leprosy that had supposedly been fostered by the eating of swine flesh.

Edelmann had learned of the idea of normative inversion from Johann Georg Wachter's *Spinozism within Judaism*, the work that opposed the "Judaizing" of Johann Peter Späth by downgrading the Old Testament. The Jewish Torah with its ceremonial laws – according to Wachter and John Spencer – was nothing more than the reversal of Egyptian laws. Edelmann quoted Wachter in the "Fifth View" of his *Moses*: "The learned Herr Wachter has really clobbered this proud race in his above-mentioned,

---

[66] Johann Christian Edelmann, "Moses mit aufgedecktem Angesichte, 5. Anblick," in *Gesammelte Schriften*, vol. 7(2), ed. Monika Ammermann-Estermann (general ed. Walter Grossmann), Stuttgart, 1987, pp. 67ff, here at p. 68.

[67] Pierre-Daniel Huet, *Demonstratio evangelica*, Paris, 1679. I am using the Amsterdam edition, 1680, pp. 87, 105, 113.

[68] Richard Elliott Friedman, *Who Wrote the Bible*, New York, 1987.

[69] [Johann Christian Edelmann], *Extract aus einer von Euander übersetzten und mit Anmerkungen herausgegebenen Handschrift unter dem Titel Von den Betrügereyen der Religionen*, Berlin, 1761, Ms. 6728 in the University Library of Breslau (Wrocław), ed. and commentary by Winfried Schröder in the volume noted above (note 64), here at p. 210.

most valuable treatise called 'Spinozism within Judaism,' which appeared in Amsterdam in 1699 in octavo."[70] Edelmann especially stressed those passages of Wachter in which the latter refuted the first response of Johann Peter Späth (alias Moses Germanus) to Wachter's reply, in which Späth had argued that the pagans had adopted their ceremonies from the Jews. In so doing, the Judaizing Späth had relied not only on Huet but also, especially, on Edmund Dickinson, who in his early work *Delphi Phoenizizantes* from 1655 had put forth the Hebraizing thesis that the religious rituals of the pagans merely "aped" those of the Jews, taking as his prize example the ceremonies at Delphi. In contrast, Wachter said, "You are relying on Dickinson, but in vain. For I could in turn simply cite other authorities."[71] He seemed to be implying that he had authors such as Spencer up his sleeve, and so he inverted things and argued that "The greater part of your Torah is a pagan-Egyptian law."[72] Notably with the episode of the Golden Calf he aimed to show that the Jewish ceremonial law was just an inversion of the Egyptian.[73] But of course Wachter argued for this inversion in his own way: "Such a sudden change in the human view of the immutable God could have had no other cause than the idolatrous mind of the people, for whom the existing ceremonies were too simple and crude and who therefore required a more elaborate system of ceremonies." That brought him to his general thesis, that Judaism had a tendency to "deify the world," which was most visible in the Kabbalah, which, with its notions of emanation, was ultimately a forerunner of Spinozism.[74]

---

[70] Edelmann, "Moses, 5. Anblick" (note 66), pp. 35ff.

[71] Johann Georg Wachter, *Der Spinozismus im Jüdenthumb, oder Die von dem heutigen Jüdenthumb und dessen Geheimen Kabbala vergötterte Welt*, Amsterdam, 1699; repr. ed. Winfried Schröder, Stuttgart, 1994, p. 57. On the relationship between Späth and Wachter see Martin Mulsow, *Spinozism, Arianism, and Kabbalah: Unexpected Conjunctions in German Intellectual History of the Late Seventeenth Century. With the edition of an unknown attempt at rewriting Spinoza's Ethics by Johann Georg Wachter (1704)* (forthcoming).

[72] Wachter, *Der Spinozismus* (note 71), p. 65.

[73] Ibid., pp. 40f. Wachter does not name Spencer, but see John Spencer, *De legibus Hebreorum ritualibus et earum rationibus*, Cambridge, 1685 (I am using the edition printed in The Hague, 1686), Lib. II, cap. V, pp. 249ff: "De lege altare terreum statuente," as well as cap. VII, pp. 259ff: "Praeceptum, quo cautum est, ne ad altare gradibus ascenderetur."

[74] Wachter, *Der Spinozismus* (note 71). We have noted that a few years later Wachter made a volte-face and turned his initially negative evaluations into positive ones. For his view of tradition, that meant that Egyptian–Jewish connections were now viewed as the transfer of an esoteric religion of reason. Wachter now constructed a succession from Egyptian wisdom to Jewish Kabbalah to the Essenes to Jesus to the logos doctrine of the early Church Fathers and all the way to Spinoza. See Martin Mulsow, "A German Spinozistic Reader of Cudworth, Bull and Spencer: Johann Georg Wachter and his Theologia Martyrum," in Christopher Ligota and Jean-Lous Quantin, eds., *History of Scholarship*, Oxford, 2006, pp. 357–383.

Here Edelmann could insert his argument. His understanding of the inversion, however, was different from Spencer's. For Manetho "leprosy" was originally a surrogate for an undescribed trauma that had generated xenophobia – Jan Assmann speaks of a memory of the trauma of the Amarna religion[75] that survived in Manetho's story – in which the identification of Osarseph with Moses was a later addition. Edelmann, in contrast, understood this leprosy in entirely rational terms, as a real disease. The laws of Moses were for him not, as Spencer had thought, inversions of Egyptian idolatry but inversions of the preferences shown by a group of swineherds and political rebels. Edelmann's argument – which quite possibly had an impact on Hermann Samuel Reimarus in the mid-eighteenth century[76] – thus shows the peculiar dynamic of anti-Moses histories, ranging from Hellenism through the libertine tradition and on to the sober rationalism of serious biblical criticism.

5 Destruction or Reorganization? Moses in the "Quarrel between the Ancients and the Moderns"

The real problem upsetting the relations between knowledge and politics was probably that the omniscient Moses was more completely destroyed than Moses the politician. This was the age of historical criticism. In 1702 when Dickinson chose the title *Physica vetus et vera* ("Physics both Old and True") for his book, he revealed, whether he wanted to or not, that he found himself on the defensive in the controversy between the "ancients and the moderns," for he was defending the ancient as true.[77] The Quarrel signified not only a sluffing off of older feelings of illegitimacy and inferiority over against Greco-Roman antiquity but also, tangentially, the end of dependence on an original sacred history. This was nowhere clearer than in Nikolaus Hieronymus Gundling's history of philosophy, *Historia philosophiae moralis* of 1706.[78] Even though the pressure of

[75] See Assmann, *Moses the Egyptian* (note 44), pp. 26–29. On the Amarna religion see now also Kent Weeks, *The Lost Tomb*, London, 1998.
[76] See Martin Mulsow, *Monadenlehre, Hermetik und Deismus. Georg Schades geheime Aufklärungsgesellschaft 1747–1760*, Hamburg, 1998, pp. 177–187.
[77] On the "Quarrel," mainly in England, see Joseph M. Levine, *Battle of the Books*, Ithaca, N.Y. 1991.
[78] Gundling, *Historia philosophiae moralis* (note 53). See Mulsow, *Enlightenment Underground* (note 44), chapter 6; in addition: Helmut Zedelmaier, *Der Anfang der Geschichte. Studien zur Ursprungsdebatte im 18. Jahrhundert*, Hamburg, 2003, pp. 77–95. In a lecture Gundling made it clear that he read Dickinson in connection with the "Quarrel." Posthumously printed in *Vollständige Historie der Gelahrtheit*, vol. 1, Frankfurt and Leipzig, 1734, pp. 34ff.; repr. in Peter K. Kapitza, *Ein bürgerlicher Krieg in der gelehrten Welt. Zur Geschichte der Querelle des Anciens et des Modernes in Deutschland*, Munich, 1981, pp. 168f.

historical criticism made the problem of Moses more and more problematic, Gundling's theological colleagues at other universities continued to describe the philosophical Moses or the omniscient Moses either affirming that tradition or, at most, declaring themselves undecided about it. The learned Pietist Johann Heinrich May from Gießen and the Altdorf student of Wagenseil, Daniel Wilhelm Moller,[79] treated the topic in dissertations: at the end of his work Moller had gone so far as to notice the treatise *De tribus impostoribus*, illustrating the new centripetal historicizing tendency, but he did not actually react to it. Even Gundling's colleague in Halle, Johann Franz Budde, agreed with scholars such as Ole Borch in claiming Moses to be the founding father or at least an early representative of chemistry.[80] Attacking Conring's critique (stimulated by Casaubon) of Mosaism and Hermeticism in medicine, Borch defended the expertise of Moses by emphasizing biblical passages like those that described Moses melting and grinding the Golden Calf to powder and then dissolving it.[81] All the opponents of such a chemically expert Moses felt forced to explain his procedure mechanically.[82]

---

[79] Moller (praes.) / Schwindel (resp.), *Dissertatio inauguralis, quam de Mose philosopho [...] submittet [...]* (note 10). ... For evidence that Moller was a student of Wagenseil, see there, p. 6 and Johann Heinrich Majus, *Dissertatio de Mose philosopho*, in *Theses selectae ex antiqua et recentiore philosophia deprompta*, Gießen, 1707.

[80] Johann Franz Budde, *Introductio ad historiam philosophiae Ebraeorum. Accedit dissertatio de haeresi Valentiniana*, Halle, 1702.

[81] Exodus 32:20: Moses "took the calf which they had made, and burnt it in the fire, and ground it to powder, and strawed it upon the water, and made the children of Israel drink of it." Olaus Borrichius (Ole Borch), *De ortu, et progressu chemiae, dissertatio*, Copenhagen, 1668, pp. 41ff., on Moses. Dickinson, *Physica vetus & vera* (note 49), pp. 317ff. Borch argues along with Kircher (*Oedipus aegyptiacus*, 3 vols., Rome, 1652–1654) and against Conring (*De Hermetica Aegyptiorum vetere et Paracelsorum nova medicina, liber unus, quo simul in Hermetis Trismegisti omnia, ac universum cum Aegyptiorum tum Chemicorum doctrinam animadvertitur*, Helmstedt, 1648), for the origins of Moses's medical knowledge in Egypt. For a discussion of the Egyptian origins of medicine, see Nancy G. Siraisi, "Hermes among the Physicians," in Martin Mulsow, ed., *Das Ende des Hermetismus*, Tübingen, 2002, pp. 189–212. In Germany one finds the "chemical" tradition of the *philosophia Mosaica* connected to the unorthodox thinking, based on experience and experiment, of the probably anonymous work by "Arnoldus Bachimius Denston" ("Cosmosophus"), *Pansophia enchiretica, seu philosophia experimentalis in Academia Mosis primum per sex prima capita Geneseos tradita, demum per ignem examinata & probata*, Nuremberg, 1682. I have been unable to determine whether the work was related to the experimental physics in Altdorf and of Johann Christoph Sturm. See the foreword after the mention of Moses and his knowledge: "Hunc Praeceptorem ego secutus, alios neglexi, & quidquid ratio, & experientia suggessit, boni publici causa huc contuli."

[82] That can be found also in Gundling, *Historia philosophiae moralis* (note 53), and Bayle, who wrote about dissolving the golden calf in his *Dictionnaire*, 2nd edn., Rotterdam, 1701, his article on "Aaron," Rem. B (note that there is no article on Moses at all): "L'Ecriture dit expressement, que ce fut un Veau de fonte; & si elle dit ensuite, que Moïse le brûla & le réduisit en poudre, cela ne doit pas nécessairement s'entendre comme si cette Idole avoit été faite d'une Matiere combustible: cela

Gundling, who had studied theology under Wagenseil in Altdorf but had then renounced that field to become a philosopher and jurist in Halle, was one such opponent; he ruthlessly radicalized Hermann Conring's historical skepticism and conducted a general attack on all myths of origin, whether they were biblical, Hermetic, or some other. As we have seen, he gathered together an unprecedented collection of arguments from various defenders of the moderns, such as John Spencer, Jean Le Clerc, John Locke, Hermann von der Hardt, and Christian Thomasius, and used them as an effective team.[83] Even though he showed genuine respect for scholars like Dickinson, he wondered if his theory of vortices of *globuli* and *bracteae* had perhaps more genuine origins in Descartes than in Moses.[84] He went on to show that the pluralization of *Philosophia Moysaica* into Aristotelian, Cartesian, and atomistic versions actually discredited all sacral interpretations; mutual destruction was the necessary consequence.[85]

To be sure there were also defenders of the "modern" who recognized the danger of throwing the baby out with the bathwater: the baby of the pantheistic politician along with the bathwater of historical criticism. Gundling's rampaging attack on the *praeiudicium antiquitatis* ("prejudice in favor of antiquity") was at first nothing more than a slogan, a polemical

peut signifier que Moïse réfondit cet Or, & qu'il le divisa en parties très-menuës, qui, étant jettées dans l'eau, y devinrent imperceptibles, comme celles qu'on dit que le Tage & le Pactole charrient." The explanation of this passage had become, as the treatment in Zedler's *Lexicon* (note 11) suggests, a touchstone for "Enlightened" biblical exegesis that no longer involved itself in the model of the earlier sacralized disciplines. For the intensity of the topic for the Mosaic-alchemical side, see, e.g., Lambert Alard's text, published in 1723: *Moses güldenes Kalb nebst dem magischen-astralischen-philosophischen absonderlich dem cabalistischen Feuer, vermittelst welchen Moses, der Mann Gottes, dieses güldene Kalb zu Pulver zermalmt, auffs Wasser gestäubet, und den Kindern Israel zu trinken gegeben*, Frankfurt, 1723.

[83] See Mulsow, *Enlightenment Underground* (note 44), chapter 6.

[84] Gundling, *Historia philosophiae moralis* (note 53), p. 67. The histories of philosophy by Heumann were influenced by Gundling; see Heumann, "Von der Philosophie der Patriarchen" (note 17) and Brucker, *Historia critica philosophiae* (note 14).

[85] Gundling, *Historia philosophiae moralis* (note 53), p. 67: "Certent nunc inter se Philosophi, an Moses Aristotelicus fuerit, an Platonicus, Stoicus, an Cartesianus denique, aut Gassendista." There appears to have been here a similar dynamic to what Alan Charles Kors has described for the origin of French atheism in the "fratricide" in the pluralized apologetics within a centralized culture. Aristotelian and Cartesian apologists accused each other of drawing atheistic consequences; anyone who took both sides seriously could draw the conclusion that atheism was unavoidable and therefore true. See Alan Charles Kors, *Atheism in France 1650–1728*, vol. 1: *The Orthodox Sources of Disbelief*, Princeton, 1990. The pluralization of apologetics produced tragic results in that its inherent impulse toward concordance prompted it to harmonize the biblical text with recent scientific currents, and so it was drawn into the competition of contemporary movements. Because its discourse was partially "parasitic" on scholarly discourse, this could not be avoided. In the competition, however, sacral claims had to be discredited over the long term. But an Aristotelian Moses and a Cartesian Moses both damaged the image of Moses. On pluralization, see also note 15.

term with which he could reject all appeals to mythical origins. But in 1706, when Gundling published his *Historia philosophiae moralis*, a complex thinker like John Toland could have taught Gundling that such boundless destruction was not necessarily the most reasonable way to deal with foundational memories. Those were the years when Toland was composing his *Origines Judaicae* ("Jewish Origins"), which appeared in 1709 and contained Toland's dispute with Huet. Pierre Daniel Huet was one of the prophets who helped to make Moses the central starting point for all ancient traditions.[86] In his *Demonstratio evangelica* ("Demonstration of the Gospel") of 1679 he tried to list all the ancient references to Moses and to claim them as proof that Mosaic culture came first.[87] Toland emphatically disagreed with this claim, especially with respect to the testimony of Strabo.[88] According to him, Strabo had seen Moses as a pantheist, or a sort of Spinozist before his time,[89] and for Toland this was a crucial indication that even the political contents of the Mosaic tradition could be treated favorably and adapted for his own purposes. That was the foundation of Toland's comprehensive Moses project, which he intended to call the *Respublica Mosaica* ("Mosaic Republic"), but which he never finished.[90]

---

[86] Edward Stillingfleet pursued a different strategy to the same goal in his *Origines sacrae* of 1662. There a historical skepticism had begun to confront the established sacred history of the Jews with the "uncertain" histories of other nations. Instead of dependence like that of Huet, Stillingfleet insisted on uniqueness. But this of course gave up the concordance-oriented view that united Greece and Israel. See Sarah Hutton, "Edward Stillingfleet, Henry More, and the Decline of Moses Atticus: A Note on Seventeenth-Century Anglican Apologetics," in *Philosophy, Science and Religion in England 1640–1700*, Cambridge, 1992, pp. 68–84.

[87] Pierre Daniel Huet, *Demonstratio evangelica ad serenissimum Delphinum*, Paris, 1679. I am again citing the Amsterdam edition of 1680. See there, esp. Propositio IV, cap. II, pp. 73–99. On Strabo, p. 93. On Huet, see generally Christopher Ligota, "Der apologetische Rahmen der Mythendeutung im Frankreich des 17. Jahrhunderts (P. D. Huet)," in Walther Killy, ed., *Mythographie der frühen Neuzeit. Ihre Anwendung in den Künsten*, Wiesbaden, 1984, pp. 149–161, as well as April G. Shelford, *Transforming the Republic of Letters: Pierre-Daniel Huet and European Intellectual Life 1650–1720*, Rochester, NY, 2007.

[88] See John Toland, *Origines Judaicae*, The Hague, 1709. On that, see the introduction by Alfredo Sabetti to the Italian translation, Naples, 1984, pp. 7–54: "Un difficile messaggio di liberazione: l'Adeisidaemon e le Origines Judaicae di John Toland." See also Huet's reaction to Toland's attack in a letter, which Huet pretended was a missive by a certain Mr. Morin to him, but which he had actually written himself: "Lettre de Mr. Morin de l'Academie des Inscriptions à Mr. Huet, ancien Evêque d'Avranches, touchant le livre de Mr. Tollandus Anglois, intitulé 'Adeisidaemon et Origines Judaicae,'" *Memoires pour l'Histoire des Sciences et des beaux Arts* 34 (1709), p. 1601.

[89] See Assmann's exciting but complex verification of this interpretation of Moses in *Moses the Egyptian* (note 44), namely by study of the history of the memory of the Amarna religion, which left traces both in the discourse on Moses-Egypt and the early modern adoption of the late-Egyptian hermetic religion.

[90] John Toland, *Nazarenus, or, Jewish, Gentile, and Mahometan Christianity*, London, 1718, appendix; Toland, *Hodegus, or the Pillar of Cloud and Fire*, London, 1720; Toland, *Origines Judaicae*, London, 1709.

He discussed the matter in 1708 in a manuscript that circulated in Baron von Hohendorf's social circle: "You know that I have already promised the public a work entitled LA REPUBLIQUE DE MOYSE, concerning all the forms of government that I judge to have been the most excellent and perfect."[91] During the early modern period, if one hoped to see Moses as a strong legislator – as did Petrus Cunaeus[92] – one might appeal to authors such as Flavius Josephus (along with the Bible); but in so doing one was using sources that tended, of course, to inflate the figure of Moses. As we know, Toland was shaped by the republicanism of James Harrington,[93] but just as he interpreted Moses as a Spinozist, he embraced the politics of sacral discourse, and transformed it. His ideal was a Mosaic state, which he saw as a state with a civil religion but without superstition. For him, a crucial source was Simone Luzzato[94] along with John Spencer's amplification of

---

[91] Austrian National Library, Vienna, Ms. 10325: *Projet d'une dissertation sur la colonne de feu et de nuee des Israelites: dans une lettre à Megalonymus*. See Justin Champion, "Respublica Mosaica: Toland and the *Traité des trois imposteurs*," unpublished lecture. I quote the manuscript according to this work, which shows the careful differentiations Toland made in his thinking about Moses. The lecture was later included in shortened form in chapter 7 of Champion, *Republican Learning: John Toland and the Crisis of Christian Culture, 1696–1722*, Manchester, 2003, pp. 167–189. Toland's text was later published in slightly modified form as *Hodegus*. See also Champion, "Legislators, Impostors, and the Politic Origins of Religion: English Theories of Imposture from Stubbe to Toland," in Silvia Berti, Françoise Charles-Daubert, and Richard H. Popkin, eds., *Heterodoxy, Spinozism, and Free Thought in Early-Eighteenth-Century Europe: Studies on the "Traité des trois imposteurs,"* Dordrecht, 1996, pp. 333–356

[92] Petrus Cunaeus, *De republica Hebraeorum libri III*, Leiden, 1617, pp. 2ff. See Flavius Josephus, *Contra Apionem*, in *Opera*, ed. B. Niese, 5 vols., 2nd edn., Berlin, 1955. The allusion there to the *Cymbalum Mundi* refers to the legendary (because it is untraceable) book ascribed to Bonaventure des Perières *Cymbalum mundi en francoys, Contenant quatre Dialogues Poetiques, fort antiques, ioyeux, & facetieux* (1537), which was regarded as extremely irreligious.

[93] See Toland's copy of Harrington, an edition from 1700; on that, John G. A. Pocock, *The Machiavellian Moment*, Princeton, 1975, chapter XIII. Although Harrington was a neo-Machiavellian, his *Oceana* preserved elements of the sacral tradition. Here *Oceana* is quoted according to the edition of 1771: James Harrington, *The Oceana and Other Works of James Harrington, with an Account of His Life by John Toland*, London, 1771, pp. 74–75: "And such was the art whereby my Lord Archon (taking council of the Commonwealth of Israel, as of Moses; and the rest of the commonwealths, as of Jethro) framed the model of the Commonwealth of Oceana." Harrington attached his "pagan" interpretation of the Mosaic tradition to a text (Exodus 18:13–26) that probably represents an expanded layer of the Yahwist text. But whereas the Yahwist was concerned to deny the Midianite origin of the belief in Yahweh, here there was an insertion by an author who was free of such bias. Knauf, *Midian* (note 42), pp. 157f., claimed that this textually expanded layer "derives the introduction of civil government from Jethro – and so, from the gentiles – and bracketed it off from the realm of the sacral. That was for ancient Near Eastern conditions a breathtakingly modern text, intellectually proving that the community of persons called Israel could exist within the framework of a state that was not established by Yahweh at all."

[94] Toland was deeply indebted to Spencer but to Simone Luzzatto as well, who likewise quoted Maimonides; see Luzzatto, *Discorso circa il stato de gl'Hebrei*, Venice, 1638. See Champion, "Respublica Mosaica" (note 91); on Luzzatto, see Benjamin Ravid, *Economics and Toleration in Sixteenth Century Venice: The Background and Context of the Discorso of Simone Luzatto*, Jerusalem,

Maimonides's view that the Mosaic laws attacked idolatry with a "withdrawal treatment."[95] But for him the withdrawal treatment was now a repudiation not just of *idolatry* but of all *superstition* more generally.

It was characteristic of Gundling and the early German Enlightenment that they were content to destroy the image of *Moses the Philosopher* but did not move on to the more complicated project of totally transforming the discourse on Moses. For that they would have needed both a German republican tradition and an openness to Spinozism. And so they could not follow Toland in combining Moses's knowledge and politics in a new way; they could not see the legislative actions of Moses operating with an autonomous knowledge independent of supernatural connections to sacrifices and ceremonies. That imposed serious limits because only a full transformation could have transformed the barren scholarly fascination with late-ancient efforts to elevate or to denigrate Moses and cleared the way for the new interpretations of Moses that we find in the eighteenth and nineteenth centuries.[96] That transformation was much easier in England.

So let us return again to the bedchamber of the English king with its alchemical foundation, its downstairs laboratory. Edmund Dickinson held the theory – probably inspired by rabbinic sources[97] – that Moses the chemist was so burdened by his political tasks that he employed Bezaleel and Ahaliab as laboratory assistants.[98] Perhaps this picture of the politician with his scientific collaborators enables us to draw a conclusion out of the perplexing centrifugal and centripetal tendencies of the various Moses discourses in the seventeenth century. Perhaps one could say that the Omniscient Moses was tired of bearing all his knowledge alone, so that he delegated his science? And was not such an act of delegation an allegory for the metadiscourse on *Moses the Omniscient* as it wore itself out? It was only through this act of delegation that Moses regained his freedom to act politically, and only through the collapse of the encyclopedic Moses that

1978; B. Septimus, "Biblical Religion and Political Rationality in Simone Luzzatto, Maimonides and Spinoza," in Isadore Twersky, ed., *Studies in Medieval Jewish History and Literature*, vol. 2, Cambridge, MA, 1984, pp. 143–170; Abraham Melamed, "English Travellers and Venetian Jewish Scholars. The Case of Simone Luzzatto and James Harrington," in Gaetano Cozzi, ed., *Gli Ebrei e Venezia. Secoli XIV-XVIII*, Milan, 1987, pp. 507–526.

95 See again Assmann, *Moses the Egyptian* (note 44), p. 78.

96 The only scholar in early eighteenth-century Germany who could have done that was probably Johann Georg Wachter. See note 74 concerning his volte-face, which made it possible for him to take a positive view of both Spinozism and Judaism.

97 See Johann Christoph Wolf, *Bibliotheca Hebraea*, 4 vols., Hamburg, 1715–1733, vol. 1, § 414, p. 264.

98 See Exodus 30:2; and Dickinson, *Physica vetus & vera* (note 49), pp. 319ff.

space was cleared for the fresh thinking about the divine mission of Moses during the eighteenth century.

6   Mohammed

In the early modern period the great founders of monotheistic religions were thought of as a triad: Moses, Mohammed, and Jesus. Other figures, such as Zoroaster, were considered too problematic to be included in this canon. But if by the late seventeenth century Moses had in at least some circles been made into an all-too-human figure, one who acted with political cunning like contemporary rulers, what happened to Mohammed? Was he, too, subjected to a discussion that either inflated or then later deflated him? From the Islamic side the answer is yes. The glorified founder of this religion, who – according to tradition – received the surahs of the Koran personally from the archangel Gabriel, was cut down to size rather early by some Arab and Persian thinkers.[99] Granted, their treatises have mostly been lost, but from the refutations they provoked they can be partially reconstructed. The medieval topos of the "three impostors" probably depended on these lost sources.[100]

If Christians wanted to deflate Mohammed and deny him the status of prophet, they did not have to rely on such Islamic sources alone; on the contrary, there were other polemical traditions they could use.[101] And so in the West it was normal rather than exceptional to disqualify Mohammed as nothing more than a fraud and to picture him as a skillful politician and devious soldier. What would have been sacrilege in the cases of Moses or Jesus was actually routine in the case of Mohammed – just look at the example of Humphrey Prideaux and his book, *The True Nature of Imposture Fully Displayed in the Life of Mahomet*.[102]

---

[99] See Paul Kraus, "Beiträge zur islamischen Ketzergeschichte. Das Kitāb az-Zummurrud des Ibn ar-Rāwandī" (1933/34), repr. in Kraus, *Alchemie, Ketzerei, Apokryphen im frühen Islam. Gesammelte Aufsätze*, Wiesbaden, 1994, pp. 109–190; Sarah Stroumsa, *Freethinkers in Medieval Islam: Ibn al-Rāwandī, Abu Bakr al-Rāzī, and Their Impact on Islamic Thought*, Leiden, 1999; Dominique Urvoy, *Les penseurs libres dans l'Islam classique*, Paris, 1996; Muhammad Abū al-fadl Badran, "'... denn die Vernunft ist ein Prophet.' Zweifel bei Abū l-Alā al-Ma'arri," in Friedrich Niewöhner and Olaf Pluta, eds., *Atheismus im Mittelalter und in der Renaissance*, Wiesbaden, 1999, pp. 61–84; on Rāwandī see also Josef van Ess, *Theologie und Gesellschaft im 2. und 3. Jahrhundert Hidschra. Eine Geschichte des religiösen Denkens im frühen Islam*, vol. 4, Berlin, 1997, pp. 295–349.

[100] Friedrich Niewöhner, *Veritas sive Varietas*, Heidelberg, 1988.

[101] To cite only one work, see Thomas E. Burman, *Reading the Qur'ān in Latin Christendom, 1140–1560*, Philadelphia, 2007; see, e.g., Mulsow, *Enlightenment Underground* (note 44), chapter 2.

[102] Humphrey Prideaux, *The True Nature of Imposture Fully Displayed in the Life of Mahomet*, London, 1697.

It therefore should not surprise us that radical Enlighteners here again pushed for the opposite conclusion and tried to build up Mohammed as the hero of a pure monotheism and of reliable ethics, as we saw in the case of Henry Stubbe. Several Enlighteners joined in this effort.[103] The relationship between inflating and deflating Mohammed was just the opposite of what happened with Moses.

Scholarly concern about the person of Jesus in the context of Christian culture presents us with another contrast. To deny Jesus's divinity or even to making any argument that tended in that direction was of course a highly sensitive matter. The fact that Socinians did so was deeply offensive and, as we will see, it took a long time before researchers began serious research on the "historical Jesus."[104] But in this case too there were indications that inflating and deflating interpretations were interacting with each other. As in the case of Moses, early modern authors could take off from the polarized views of late antiquity. That is what the next sections deal with.

7   A "Natural" Jesus

The process of downgrading Jesus can be described from various perspectives. One was the growing emphasis in the seventeenth century on the natural. "Nature" and "naturalness" became the basis of legitimacy for many subjects, in contrast to metaphysics, transcendence, and the "supernatural."[105] Theologically this tendency found expression not only in

[103] For Stubbe see Mulsow, *Enlightenment Underground* (note 44), chapter 3; Jonathan Israel, "Rethinking Islam: Philosophy and the 'Other,'" in *Enlightenment Contested: Philosophy, Modernity, and the Emancipation of Man 1670–1752*, Oxford, 2006, pp. 615–639; Martin Mulsow, "Socinianism, Islam and the Radical Uses of Arabic Scholarship," *Al-Qantara* 31 (2010), pp. 549–586.

[104] Cristiana Facchini is currently researching Jewish forerunners of the Life-of-Jesus studies. Judaism, with its distance from Christianity, naturally had an easier time seeing Jesus as just a man, and indeed had strong motives for doing so.

[105] Wolfgang Proß, "'Natur,' Naturrecht und Geschichte. Zur Entwicklung der Naturwissenschaften und der sozialen Selbstinterpretation im Zeitalter des Naturrechts (1600–1800)," *Internationales Archiv für Sozialgeschichte der deutschen Literatur* 3(1), 1978, pp. 38–67; Simone de Angelis, Florian Gelzer, and Lucas Gisi, eds., *"Natur," Naturrecht und Geschichte. Aspekte eines fundamentalen Begründungsdiskurses der Neuzeit (1600–1900)*, Heidelberg, 2010; Jean Ehrard, *L'idée de la nature en France dans la première moitié du 18.me siècle*, Paris, 1963; Ronald W. Harris, *Reason and Nature in 18th Century Thought*, London, 1968; Paul Hazard, *Die Herrschaft der Vernunft. Das europäische Denken im 18. Jahrhundert*, Hamburg, 1949, pp. 173–250; Panajotis Kondylis, *Die Aufklärung im Rahmen des neuzeitlichen Rationalismus*, Stuttgart, 1981; Lorenzo Bianchi, ed., *Natura e storia*, Naples, 2005; Lorraine Daston and Gianna Pomata, eds., *The Faces of Nature in Enlightenment Europe*, Berlin, 2003. One should not forget the remarkably influential interpretation (concentrating on the seventeenth century) of

"naturalism" – that is, in a propagation of "natural religion," which developed as religion without revelation – but also in a "natural" understanding of Jesus Christ, who was viewed as a simple man, but not as God. What result did that have for the understanding of the birth of Jesus? Should one go so far as to deny the virgin birth and conception by the Holy Spirit?[106] Should one simply assume a "natural birth"? But then who was the father? Joseph? Or maybe some other man?

In the polemics of late antiquity against Christianity the last suggestion was defended by Celsus in the second century in a dialogue with a Jew, in which the Jew says, "when she [Mary] was pregnant she was turned out of doors by the carpenter to whom she had been betrothed, as having been guilty of adultery, and ... she bore a child to a certain soldier named Panthera."[107]

Among the Jews a current of polemic claimed that Jesus was the *natural* son not of Joseph but of Panthera, after an act of infidelity by an adulterous Mary. That found expression later in the Talmud (Shab 104b), in a passage that discussed whether Jesus was the son of a man named Stada or of "Pandera."[108] In the Middle Ages these legends were carried over in the *Toledot Jeschu*, a manuscript full of polemics that Christoph Wagenseil was the first to publish in 1681 as *Tela ignea Satanae* ("The Fiery Darts of Satan").[109] The basic focus of this anti-Christian tradition was not on the naturalness of the sonship of

Wilhelm Dilthey, which he developed in the late nineteenth century: "Das natürliche System der Geisteswissenschaften im siebzehnten Jahrhundert," *Archiv für Geschichte der Philosophie* 5 and 6, 1892/93, repr. in *Gesammelte Schriften* II, Stuttgart and Göttingen, 1957, pp. 90–245. See on that, Martin Mulsow, "Diltheys Deutung der Geisteswissenschaften des 17. Jahrhunderts. Revisionen, Aktualisierungen, Transformationen," in Thomas Leinkauf, ed., *Dilthey und Cassirer. Die Deutung der Neuzeit als Muster von Geistes- und Kulturgeschichte*, Hamburg, 2003, pp. 53–68.

[106] Theological literature on the virgin birth is vast. Here I will mention only a few titles: Hans von Campenhausen, *Die Jungfrauengeburt in der Theologie der alten Kirche*, Heidelberg, 1962; Giovanni Miegge, *Die Jungfrau Maria. Studie zur Geschichte der Marienlehre*, Göttingen, 1962; article on "Maria/ Marienfrömmigkeit," in TRE, vol. 22, Berlin, 1992; Josef Brosch, ed., *Jungfrauengeburt gestern und heute*, Essen, 1969. For a polemic: Gerd Lüdemann, *Jungfrauengeburt? Die Geschichte von Maria und ihrem Sohn Jesus*, Springe, 2008.

[107] Celsus according to Origen: *Contra Celsum* I, 28. The translation here is that of Frederick Crombie, *The Ante-Nicene Fathers*, vol. 4, ed. Alexander Roberts et al., Buffalo, 1885. On Celsus and his anti-Christian polemic, see Winfried Schröder, *Athen und Jerusalem. Die philosophische Kritik am Christentum in Spätantike und Neuzeit*, Stuttgart, 2011.

[108] See Peter Schäfer, *Jesus in the Talmud*, Princeton, 2007, pp. 15–24.

[109] *Liber Toldos Jeschu*, in Christoph Wagenseil, ed., *Tela ignea Satanae, Hoc est: arcani & horribiles Judaeorum adversus Christum Deum & Christianam religionem libri anekdotoi. Joh. Christophorus Wagenseilius ex Europae Africaeq; latebris erutos, in lucem protrusit. Additae sunt Latinae interpretationes, et duplex confutatio. Accedit Mantissa de LXX. hebdomadibus Danielis*, Altdorf, 1681, with its own pagination, pp. 1–24.

Christ – that was implicit of course – but on the blasphemous denunciation of Jesus as a bastard.

The arguments within early Christianity were different. The Jewish-Christian Ebionites had no interest in seeing Jesus as God; but Jewish-Christian Gnostics like Cerinthus and Carpocrates impugned the virgin birth as well.[110] Moreover, there were those who opposed the veneration of Mary, the so-called Antidicomarionites, whom Epiphanius of Salamis in 370 called a Christian sect in Arabia, known for denying the perpetual virginity of Mary.[111] That did not necessarily require assertions about the natural conception of Jesus, but it did present the danger of trivializing the position of Mary. What such arguments were about became apparent in the late fourth century with Helvidius, who in the course of combatting celibacy and asceticism in Christianity (in a work that no longer survives) asserted that after Jesus was born, Mary lived as Joseph's wife, conceiving and bearing several more children with him.[112]

Only in the early modern period did a more radical thesis become a real threat: that Jesus himself had been born of the natural intercourse between Mary and Joseph. This argument came at the moment when the antitrinitarian movement beginning in the mid-sixteenth century prompted a rise in skepticism about the divinity of Christ.[113] Surprisingly, most antitrinitarians including Fausto Sozzini refrained from asserting the natural procreation of Jesus. Sozzini thought that Jesus was conceived by means of the miraculous agency of the Holy Spirit (*sine viri ope* – i.e., "without the help of a man"); that was the reason the man Jesus was also called the "Son of God."[114] But there were also some antitrinitarians who

---

[110] On Cerinthus and Carpocrates, see Kurt Rudolf, *Die Gnosis*, Leipzig, 1977; Christoph Markschies, "Kerinth: Wer war er und was lehrte er?," *Jahrbuch für Antike und Christentum* 41 (1998), pp. 48–76; Clemens Scholten, "Karpokrates (Karpokratianer)," in *Reallexikon für Antike und Christentum*, vol. 20, Stuttgart, 2004, pp. 173–186.

[111] Epiphanius, *Panarion*, Book III, cap. 78 (Adversus Haereses), tr. Frank Williams, *Nag Hammadi and Manichaean Studies* 79, 2nd edn., Leiden, 2013, p. 616.

[112] On him, see Georges Jouassard, "La personalité d'*Helvidius*," in *Mélanges Saunier*, Lyon, 1944, pp. 139–156; Thomas R. Karmann, "'Er erkannte sie aber nicht, …' Maria, das Virginitätsideal und Mt. 1,18–25 im späten 4. Jahrhundert," in Hans-Ulrich Weidemann, ed., *Asceticism and Exegesis in Early Christianity: The Reception of New Testament Texts in Ancient Ascetic Discourses*, Göttingen, 2013, pp. 118–147, esp. pp. 127ff; Stefan Rebenich, *Hieronymus und sein Kreis*, Stuttgart, 1992, pp. 176f.

[113] This skepticism affected especially the doctrines of the two natures of Christ and of the preexistence of Christ as the Logos. See Otto Fock, *Der Socinianismus: nach seiner Stellung in der Gesammtentwickelung des Christlichen Geistes, nach seinem historischen Verlauf und nach seinem Lehrbegriff dargestellt*, Kiel, 1847, pp. 510–551.

[114] See, e.g., Fausto Sozzini, *Opera*, in *Bibliotheca Fratrum Polonorum*, vol. 1, Amsterdam, 1668, p. 654a. The Socinians were trying to show that Jesus was indeed a man, but not a normal one;

were more extreme on this point. For example Szymon Budny, a Polish-Belarusan humanist, saw Joseph as the natural father of Jesus. For that reason other Unitarians, and especially Marcin Czechowic, vilified Budny and excommunicated him as a "Josephite."[115]

Naturally within the voluminous anti-Socinian polemics of the seventeenth century one can find evidence of how the Orthodox defended themselves against such assertions. Yet, for the most part, theologians who dealt with the problem of the virgin birth did not, on the surface, consider the current debates of their day and concentrated only on the ancient heresies. Thus, for example, in 1678 when he took up this topic, the Altdorf theologian Johann Saubert, in his *Palaestra theologico-philologica* ("Theologically Philological Wrestling School"), placed Helvidius and the Antidicomarianites in the center of his discussion.[116] He also treated the objections of Jewish authors, who had pointed out that Joseph and Mary were not only engaged to be married but were married, meant that they had engaged in sexual relations.[117] Here we approach the tradition which challenged Lutheran Orthodoxy most directly in that period. Another work pointing in this direction was the little treatise of Johann Crause in Jena, who in 1667 published a disputation *De Josepho et Maria savatoris parentibus* ("On Joseph and Mary, the Parents of the Savior"), because he felt that the "parents of the Messiah" raised a question "which is surrounded and defiled by many fables."[118] Crause did not exactly specify which fables were in circulation. But he did name as his model Richard Montagu, the bishop of Norwich who had fought against the "Puritan Anglicans" with their profane tendencies. Almost fifty years earlier, in 1622 in his *Analecta ecclesiasticarum exercitionum* ("Fragments of Ecclesiastical Exercises"), Montagu had said:

---

rather, he was a special sort of man. Therefore they supported the dogma of the supernatural birth, but in an unorthodox way. Christ's body was not made from the blood of the Virgin Mary through the power of the Holy Spirit, but God added "what the man otherwise usually adds, by creating the male seed at the place of conception." Fock, *Der Socinianismus* (note 113), p. 534. See Abraham Calov, *Scripta antisociniana*, vol. 3, Ulm, 1684, p. 168.

[115] See Kestutis Daugirdas, *Andreas Volanus und die Reformation im Großfürstentum Litauen*, Mainz, 2009, pp. 223–230, esp. pp. 226f. I am grateful to Kestutis Daugirdas for the reference to Budny. See also Stefan Fleischmann, *Szymon Budny*, Cologne, 2006.

[116] Johann Saubert, *Palaestra theologico-philologica*, Nuremberg, 1678, pp. 218ff: "Haeresis Ebionis et Cerinthi: Error Helvidianorum et Antidicomarianitarum."

[117] Ibid., pp. 222f.

[118] Johann Crause (praes.) / Georg Erdmann Voigt (resp.), *Exercitium academicum de Josepho et Maria salvatoris parentibus*, Jena, 1667, A2r.

> They destroy and detest all holidays and do not allow that Christians should
> preserve anything that, so to speak, still savors of Judaism; and similarly
> they discard the "shreds of Papism," as they call them, and banish them to a
> plague-land, and then for this same reason they use the natural light of the
> Savior to pull their plows, manure their fields, pursue their amusements,
> conduct their business, and in this way transform everything, as if with their
> industry they wish to profane this light.[119]

For Montagu the great "purification" that the Puritans were aiming for
was an absurd undertaking, one that dramatically overshot its mark,
because it meant in fact a desacralization of the Church and of life.
Lutherans in Germany fought such a desacralization even though there
were no Puritans there (and not yet even any Pietism). So whom were
they really fighting?

They were mainly combatting Jewish anti-Christian polemics. Such
polemics played a role that we must not underestimate, for they introduced dangerous arguments that initiated Europe-wide debates and
could later move over into radical Enlightenment.[120] Accordingly, during the seventeenth century the Orthodox responded to critiques of
Christian dogmas stemming from attacks on ritual that treated the sacred
as profane. Crause quoted the *Sefer ha-nizzachon* of Rabbi Yom-Tov
Lipmann of Mühlhausen from around 1400, whose work Theodor
Hackspan stole from a Jewish correspondent and published against his
will in 1644.[121] Hackspan had stolen it because he wanted to use

[119] Crause (praes.) / Voigt (resp.), *Exercitium academicum* (note 118), A2r; Richard Montagu, *Analecta
ecclesiaticarum exercitationum*, London, 1622, p. 369. Crause had his quotation at second hand. He
copied it from Johann Sebastian Mitternacht's work, *De nativitatis Dominicae anno*, Leipzig, 1659;
see p. 80.

[120] We saw that in some detail in Mulsow, *Enlightenment Underground* (note 44), chapter 1. On the
impact of anti-Christian polemics in advance of the Enlightenment, see Richard H. Popkin, "Some
Unresolved Questions in the History of Scepticism: The Role of Jewish Anti-Christian Arguments
in the Rise of Scepticism in Regard to Religion," in *The Third Force in Seventeenth-Century
Thought*, Leiden, 1992, pp. 222–235; Popkin, "Jewish Anti-Christian Arguments as a Source of
Irreligion from the Seventeenth to the Early Nineteenth Century," in Michael Hunter and David
Wootton, eds., *Atheism from the Reformation to the Enlightenment*, Oxford, 1992, pp. 159–181;
Popkin, "The Image of the Jew in Clandestine Literature circa 1700," in Guido Canziani, ed.,
Filosofia e religione nella letteratura clandestina secoli XVII e XVIII, Milan, 1994, pp. 13–34; Silvia
Berti, "At the Roots of Unbelief," *Journal of the History of Ideas* 56 (1995), pp. 555–575; Adam
Sutcliffe, *Judaism and Enlightenment*, Cambridge, 2003; as well as Mulsow, *Enlightenment
Underground* (note 44), chapter 1.

[121] *Liber Nizachon Rabbi Lipmanni: Conscriptus anno a Christo nato M.CCC.XCIX. diuque desideratus.
Accessit tractatus de usu librorum Rabbinicorum, prodromus apologiae pro Christianis adversus
Lipmannum triumphantem*, Nuremberg, 1644. See Ora Limor and Israel Jacob Yuval,
"Scepticism and Conversion: Jews, Christians and Doubt in Sefer ha-Nizzahon," in Allison
Coudert and Jeffrey S. Shoulson, eds., *Hebraica veritas? Christian Hebraists and the Study of
Judaism in early Modern Europe*, Philadelphia, 2004, pp. 159–179.

Lipmann's critique of Karaite-Sadducee Judaism for the benefit of Christianity.[122] But in publishing he also unleashed arguments against Christianity, among them Lipmann's powerful case against the supposedly miraculous birth of Jesus.[123] Hackspan's colleague at the University of Altdorf, Sebald Schnell, translated parts of the *Sefer ha-nizzachon* into Latin even before his friend had published it and added a refutation of Lipmann's attack on the virgin birth to the translation.[124] In doing so, he was treating the most threatening arguments in the text with the seriousness they deserved. And indeed the problems highlighted by Lipmann were quoted not just by Crause but also by Saubert,[125] who was a follower of Hackspan and Schnell in Altdorf and knew the arguments raised by Lipmann all too well.

The crucial point revolved around the complicated legal relations in Joseph's family tree because Christ's legitimacy depended on Joseph's genealogy. So far as Mary was concerned, Crause mentioned Socinians such as Valentin Schmalz, Johann Crell, and Jonas Schlichting, who had already noted problems in that area.[126] Socinianism and Judaism: these were obviously the sources from which threats to the virgin birth were flowing. But were these threats as seen by alert theologians really transposed into radical Enlightenment works? Were the Orthodox right to be so worried? Was there a book in which the announced arguments – from Lipmann to Budny – were gathered together and brought to a crisis?

8   A Clandestine Manuscript

Yes, there was indeed such a work. A treatise asserting that Jesus was only the natural son of Joseph did circulate as a clandestine manuscript in the early eighteenth-century in Germany,[127] but so far scholars have completely ignored this manuscript and the copies of it. Even the

---

[122] See Dietrich Klein, *Hermann Samuel Reimarus. Das theologische Werk*, Tübingen, 2009, pp. 139ff; and Klein, "Inventing Islam in Support of Christian Truth: Theodore Hackspan's Arabic Studies in Altdorf, 1642–6," *History of Universities* 25 (2010), pp. 26–55.

[123] See *Liber Nizachon Rabbi Lipmanni* (note 121), § 8.

[124] Sebald Schnell, *Setira al-Ledat Yeshu we-alsbe-ba'u kulam le-Gehinnom Hoc Est Numerus IIX Spectans cap. 2 Genes. vs. 17 Arcani libri Nitzachon*, Typis Academicis nuper exscripti, Quo Rabbi Lipman Fidem Christianam de Jesu Salvatoris nostri secundam carnem nativitate [. . .] quem Pontificii appellant, limbum Patrum; Sub annum [. . .] Judaicum 5159 Christianum vero 1399 impugnavit, Altdorf, 1643.

[125] Saubert, *Palaestra* (note 116), p. 224. See Crause, *Exercitium academicum* (note 118).

[126] Crause, *Exercitium academicum* (note 118), fol. B5v.

[127] On the phenomenon of clandestine literature, see Gianni Paganini, *Introduzione alle filosofie clandestine*, Bari, 2008, as well as the literature cited in the Introduction.

otherwise extremely complete list of radical underground writings by Miguel Benítez takes no notice of it.[128] But, as we will see, the text enjoyed a small, even if limited, circulation.

"The devil wrote this down on March 13, 1743." That sentence came at the end of a carefully decorated manuscript, which resides today in the Duke August Library in Wolfenbüttel.[129] The text was entitled *De Josepho parente naturali meditatio* ("A Meditation on Joseph the Natural Father of Christ") (see Figure 7). This was a clandestine work, one that circulated only in the underground; one guesses that immediately from the fact that a second copy of the text of the manuscript exists in Wolfenbüttel, bound together with the *Meditationes de Deo, mundo, homine* by the freethinker Theodor Ludwig Lau.[130] At several points in this book we have repeatedly met Lau, who caused a furor with his religiously critical works in 1717 and 1719.[131] Works like this were collected, copied, and often bound with other radical writings. Sometimes such volumes were then given titles like "Anti-Christian Works," or "Atheist Writings," or something similar.[132] As we will see the State and University Library in Dresden also possesses a variant of this manuscript.

In going through the prehistory of this idea, we have already seen the heterodox nature of its thesis, which it announced in its title: that Joseph was the natural father of Christ, and therefore the notion of a virgin birth could be dismissed. The content of the manuscript can be summarized briefly. The story of the conception of Christ was reconstructed from the gospels of Matthew and Luke in such a way that after Mary had been informed of her pregnancy by the angel, her betrothed at first regarded her as unfaithful or suspected that she was merely fantasizing. For his part, Joseph dreamt that the angel had admonished him to sleep with Mary so that the Holy Spirit might purify his seed, which then would save all of mankind. Joseph followed this admonition, not from sexual desire, but *ex praecepto coelestis nuncii* ("at the instruction of the heavenly

---

[128] Miguel Benítez, *La face cachée des lumières. Recherches sur les manuscrits philosophiques clandestins de l'âge classique*, Paris, 1996; the latest expanded version is in Benítez, *La cara oculta de las luces*, Valencia, 2003.

[129] HAB Cod. Extrav. 265.14. "Diabolus descr[ipsit] d. XIII. Martii 1743." A critical edition of the text based on the various manuscripts can be found in Martin Mulsow, "Joseph als natürlicher Vater Christi" (note 1), pp. 101–110.

[130] HAB Cod. Extrav. 157.11.

[131] See Mulsow, *Enlightenment Underground* (note 44), Introduction and chapters 4 and 7. On him, see also Mulsow, *Knowledge Lost: A New View of Early Modern Intellectual History*, Princeton, 2022, chapters 1–3.

[132] See Martin Mulsow, "Die Transmission verbotenen Wissens," in Ulrich Johannes Schneider, ed., *Kulturen des Wissens im 18. Jahrhundert*, Berlin, 2008, pp. 61–80.

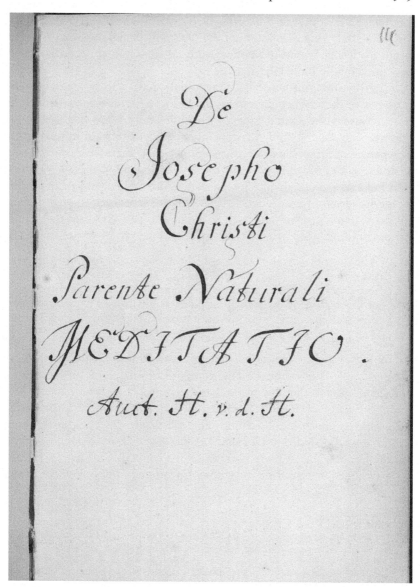

Figure 7   *De Josepho Christi parente naturali meditatio*, Herzog August Bibliothek Wolfenbüttel Ms. Extrav. 265.14

messenger").[133] Afterward he brought Mary as his wife (*suam uxorem*) to his house following the custom of the Jews, but he did not sleep with her again so that he would not pollute with his own human seed the womb sanctified by the Holy Ghost.

After disarming certain objections philologically and by citing parallel passages,[134] the author comes to his main reason for his reconstruction: "If Joseph was not the natural father of Christ, it would follow that he was not the true Messiah."[135] But this conclusion was put forward to prevent its acceptance. "If Joseph was not the natural father, then I ask why was the genealogy of Christ derived from the line of Joseph? Why did Matthew and Luke so anxiously name Joseph's ancestors?"[136] For indeed these two evangelists had provided a detailed genealogy of Jesus back through Joseph all the way to Abraham and even to Adam.[137] The author of the manuscript continues:

> If he [Joseph] was not the father of Christ, they would have had to present the genealogy of Mary. Consider please, who would ever try to prove reasonably that I am from the ducal house of Braunschweig if the Duke of Braunschweig were only my step-father? Especially if my mother never slept with this man? Away with such jokes.[138]

The fact that here the Duke of Braunschweig was adduced as an example was a clear indication that this text came from the territory of Braunschweig-Wolfenbüttel. The tone was casual and provocative – indeed, similar to the tone of the Latin version of *De tribus impostoribus*, from the hand of Johann Joachim Müller; but it was also somewhat scholastic, arranged by objections and replies, like one finds in the final part that was appended to *De tribus impostoribus*.[139] But we should be clear on the fact that this text was not written with an anti-Christian intention. It was aimed at ensuring that Joseph's attested royal genealogy was

---

[133] HAB Cod. Extrav. 265.14, p. 6.

[134] The objections concerned, e.g., translations that read: "This one virgin is pregnant." For, in contrast, the text on pp. 25f. claimed, "1.) Gal. 4. V. 4. heisset es: Da die Zeit erfüllet war sandte Gott seinen Sohn gebohren von einem Weibe ἐκ γυναικός non vero ἐκ παρθένου. 2. עלמה ['alm.] Es: 7:V:14. denotat juvenculam nulla habita status ratione, Eine junge Frau. 3.) Dicimus Die Jungfrau ist schwanger, quae nondum nupta est marito. Judaei probant ex Proverb: 30:V:9. עלמה denotare virginem corruptam. 4.) Locus ille plane ad Christum non spectat, sed ad mulierem, quae tempore Esaiae vixit. forte Esaiae concubinam. Es: c.7."

[135] Ibid., p. 27.   [136] Ibid., p. 32.   [137] Matthew 1:1–17; Luke 3:23–38.

[138] HAB Cod. Extrav. 265.14, pp. 32ff.

[139] Anonymus [Johann Joachim Müller], *De imposturis religionum (De tribus impostoribus); Von den Betrügereyen der Religionen; Dokumente*, critical edition, ed. and commentary Winfried Schröder, Stuttgart, 1999.

connected to the figure of Jesus as Messiah, and that his claim to be the Christ was justified. For Fausto Sozzini and his followers, therefore, at least Christ's legal title to the position of Messiah was certain.[140]

The text went on to base the natural conception of Christ in Christology as well, as the logical implication of the [orthodox] doctrine concerning his two natures: "If he was true man, he must have been conceived in a natural manner."[141] But the author also argued that his argument allowed one to minimize the recourse to miracles:

> Because God does not usually perform miracles when he can act through natural causes. Tell me, why was such a great miracle necessary if [the goal was] to form not some imaginary man but a truly natural man who could eat and drink? Was Joseph really not able to engender such a man? I believe that I know what oppresses and stresses you: You imagine that Christ in this way could not have remained immune from Original Sin. But your anxiety is useless and foolish, because there simply is no Original Sin. And even if there were, couldn't the Holy Ghost then sanctify and purify the seed of Joseph?[142]

From this passage, if not earlier, it becomes obvious that the author, despite his Christian foundations, was a radical thinker. He did not believe in the doctrine of original sin.[143] And therefore it followed for him that Jesus did not have to be some "pure" being, the product of a virgin birth, who because of this quality could save mankind from their sin. The doctrine of original sin had come under special attack from the Socinians, because it was contrary to their premises of human freedom and the human capacity for reason, but it was also superfluous if one also rejected, as Socinians did, the doctrine of satisfaction, the idea of justification and salvation through the sacrifice of Christ on the cross.[144] The author of *De Josepho* appears to have shared this rejection. We will see that not all the copyists who circulated this text went that far – they omitted that extreme sentence. The author, however, had kept both options open, either the truly radical denial of original sin or the weakened one ("and even if there were"), in which original sin still existed but, even so, not the virgin birth because the a [divine] "purification" of the seed made its theological function superfluous.

---

[140] See Fock, *Der Socinianismus* (note 113). [141] HAB Cod. Extrav. 265.14, p. 36.

[142] Ibid., pp. 38ff.

[143] The critique of the doctrine of original sin had become rather widespread in late-seventeenth-century Germany, especially under the influence of Arminianism; see Anselm Schubert, *Das Ende der Sünde. Anthropologie und Erbsünde zwischen Reformation und Aufklärung*, Göttingen, 2002.

[144] See Fausto Sozzini, "De statu primi hominis ante lapsum disputatio," in *Bibliotheca fratrum Polonorum*, vol. 2, Amsterdam, 1668. See Fock, *Der Socinianismus* (note 113), pp. 655ff.

The tone of the work had now become almost that of a polemical pamphlet. The assumption that the Messiah was without a father could not be found anywhere in the Prophets and was termed *insipida* (i.e., foolish). The Fathers of the Church might have come up with this along with dozens of other little songs (*cum sexcentis aliis naeniis effinxerunt*) and thrust them (*obstruserunt*) at the credulous people as articles of faith.[145] Our anonymous writer had clearly run out of patience with Christianity. He regarded its doctrines as corrupt and the result of priestly deceit. This tone reminds us again of the Latin *De tribus impostoribus*, whose author viewed the founders of religion as impostors and who used a precise knowledge of Jewish traditions to express his contempt for Christianity. The very first sentence of *De Josepho* reads: "Fabulas multas de Christo Messia nostro circumferri, non solum credo; sed ex plurimis rerum documentis compertum habeo" ("Many fables about Christ the Messiah are in circulation. After consulting many documents I not only believe that but am certain of it"). This seems to me to echo the first sentence of *De tribus impostoribus*, which begins similarly with an accusative and infinitive: "Deum esse, eumque colendum esse, multi disputant . . . ."[146] Here was criticism of unbelievable fables: here was Enlightenment.

9   The Professor and His Collector

The title page names the author as "H.v.d.H." This abbreviation is easy to decode as "Hermann von der Hardt," which the Dresden manuscript confirms. That manuscript says explicitly: "Herr Herm. Van der Hardt." We will have to consider whether "the devil" who supposedly wrote the manuscript was Hardt himself, or whether "the devil wrote this down" should perhaps be more precisely translated as "The devil copied this." We do know that Hermann von der Hardt was a contentious, unpleasant professor of Oriental languages at the University of Helmstedt.[147] In his day

---

[145] HAB Cod. Extrav. 265.14, pp. 43ff.   [146] *De imposturis religionum* (note 139), p. 99.

[147] On Hermann von der Hardt (1660–1746) see the thorough study by Hans Möller, *Hermann von der Hardt als Alttestamentler*, typewritten habilitation thesis, Leipzig, 1962; see in addition A. G. Hoffmann, article on "Hardt" in *Allgemeine Encyclopädie der Wissenschaften und Künste*, Sect. II, Part 2, Leipzig, 1828, cols. 388–395; Ferdinand Lamey, *Hermann von der Hardt in seinen Briefen und seinen Beziehungen zum Braunschweiger Hofe, zu Spener, Franke und dem Pietismus. Beilage I zu den Hss. der Großherzoglichen Badischen Hof- und Landesbibliothek Karlsruhe*, Karlsruhe, 1891; Dieter Merzbacher, "Die 'Herwiederbringung der herrlichen Schriften, so fast verloren gewesen,' Das 'concilium Constantiense,' ein Editionsprojekt Hermann von der Hardts und des Herzogs Rudolf August von Braunschweig-Lüneburg," in Dorothea Klein et al., eds., *Vom Mittelalter zur Neuzeit. Festschrift für Horst Brunner*, Wiesbaden, 2000, pp. 569–592; Ralph Häfner, "Tempelritus und Textkommentar. Hermann von der Hardts, 'Morgenröte über der Stad

he was famous, regarded as the shining light of his university and for many years the rector, even though he has been forgotten today. That is because Hardt's theories and his behavior were embarrassing to later generations of theologians. Emerging from a Pietist background, he transformed himself into a rationalist exegete of the Bible and fired off wild speculations about the origin of the books of the Bible, their authors, and the times of their composition. In his view many ancient texts and especially the biblical books had been written in an enigmatic style. They were encrypted because their histories and myths actually contained political and historical accounts of wars, treaties, the founding of cities, and invasions, which turned such texts into *arcana* that could not be simply broadcast to everyone. Even back then, according to Hardt, instruction was a "political" art, which meant that lessons were formulated *pro indulgentia erga traditiones vulgi* – that is, with consideration for the traditions of the people, intending that the simple people *should not* understand the meaning of a story and should not become discontent.[148] "In this way," the Helmstedt professor explained,

> this long symbolic story, containing a three-fold riddle, became the required model for the enigmatic style of the ancients for depicting the fates of great kings. They painted a historical picture of a single great hero by portraying a different famous deed by a different king, so that a three-fold image created a three-fold riddle using the same symbolic words.[149]

Chebron.' Zur Eigenart des literaturkritischen Kommentars im frühen 18. Jahrhundert," *Scientia Poetica* 3 (1999), pp. 47–71; Hardts, "'Denn wie das buch ist, muß der leser seyn' – Allegorese und Mythopoesis in den 'Hohen und hellen Sinnbildern Jonae' des Helmstedter Gelehrten Hermann von der Hardt," in Herbert Jaumann, ed., *Die europäische Gelehrtenrepublik im Zeitalter des Konfessionalismus*, Wiesbaden, 2001, pp. 183–202; Martin Mulsow, "Sintflut und Gedächtnis. Hermann von der Hardt und Nicolas- Antoine Boulanger," in Martin Mulsow and Jan Assmann, eds., *Sintflut und Gedächtnis. Erinnern und Vergessen des Ursprungs*, Munich, 2006, 131–161; Mulsow "Religionsgeschichte in Helmstedt," in Jens Bruning and Ulrike Gleixner, eds., *Das Athen der Welfen. Die Reformuniversität Helmstedt 1576–1810*, Wolfenbüttel, 2010, pp. 182–189; Asaph Ben Tov, "Helmstedter Hebraisten," ibid., pp. 224–231; Martin Mulsow, "Harpocratism: Gestures of Retreat in early Modern Germany," *Common Knowledge* 16 (2010), pp. 110–127; Mulsow, "Der Silen von Helmstedt," in Franke Berndt and Daniel Fulda, eds., *Die Sachen der Aufklärung*, Hamburg, 2012, pp. 300–313; Mulsow, "Politische Bukolik. Hermann von der Hardts Geheimbotschaften," *Zeitschrift für Ideengeschichte* 7(4) (2013), pp. 103–116; Mulsow, "The Bible as Secular Story: The Northern War and King Josias as Interpreted by Hermann von der Hardt (1660–1746)," in Dirk van Miert et al., eds., *Scriptural Authority and Biblical Criticism in the Dutch Golden Age: God's Word Questioned*, Oxford, 2017, pp. 351–373.

[148] On this separation of an elite from the people, see Gianni Paganini, "Wie aus Gesetzgebern Betrüger werden. Eine philosophische Archäologie des 'radikalen' Libertinismus," in Jonathan I. Israel and Martin Mulsow, eds., *Radikalaufklärung*, Berlin, 2014, pp. 49–91. On "political" thinking in general, see Gotthard Frühsorge, *Der politische Körper. Zum Begriff des politischen Körpers im 17. Jahrhundert und in den Romanen Christian Weises*, Stuttgart, 1974.

[149] Hermann von der Hardt, Aenigmata prisci orbis. Jonas in luce in Historia Manassis et Josiae, ex eleganti veterum Hebraeorum stilo solutum aenigma, Helmstedt, 1723, p. 32.

This amounted to a complicated hermeneutic of decoding, in which the Bible was reduced to a secular, political text. That was the reason Hardt was repeatedly disciplined by the princely court in Wolfenbüttel, notably after 1704, when Duke Rudolf August died and Hardt lost the close protection he had enjoyed. From 1713 onward he stood under constant censorship, his most important books were confiscated, he was forbidden to interpret the Bible, and finally in 1727 he lost his teaching position.[150] Right up to his death in 1746, however, the old man continued to compose and publish his daring and – by current standards – mistaken decodings (even though sometimes he did hit the bull's eye), books that appeared in small print runs, using various pretexts.

Can we imagine that Hardt could have written a text like *De Josepho?* To approach an answer we will have to make some distinctions. Hardt dealt almost exclusively with the Old Testament, steering clear of New Testament topics. One cannot openly declare that he was an Enlightener or just a Deist because his work as an exegete and his enthusiasm for the biblical tradition were still far too dominant; he seems at least to have retained his faith in the Providence of God. To be sure, there were points on which he agreed with the author of *De Josepho*. As a student of Esdras Edzardus, Hardt was a great connoisseur of rabbinic literature, and he drew many suggestions from this literature for his euhemerist exegesis. It is easy to believe that he followed certain Lutheran and Calvinist authors[151] in criticizing the Church Fathers for their credulity; and he certainly may not have really believed the doctrine of original sin – as an author who regarded the story of Adam and Eve in paradise as nothing more than a city legend concerning Miletus, this seems entirely possible. But on dogmatic matters, of course, Hardt hid his own thoughts all his life.

Even so, it is hard to believe that this professor, who painstakingly held himself to academic rules and to high standards, could have composed a work that attacked a central Christian dogma frontally and repeatedly engaged in polemics of a verbally abusive sort. So how can we square this skepticism with the obvious manuscript attribution of the text to Hermann von der Hardt as the author? Perhaps we should regard the text as only indirectly prompted or inspired by Hardt? From the tone of the work we can conclude that we may actually be dealing with someone from

---

[150] See Möller, *Hermann von der Hardt als Alttestamentler* (note 147), pp. 87ff
[151] See Wilhelm Schmidt-Biggemann, "Die Entstehung der unitarischen Exegese und die philologische Destruktion des Trinitätsdogmas," in *Apokalypse und Philologie. Wissensgeschichten und Weltentwürfe der Frühen Neuzeit*, Göttingen, 2007, pp. 79–122.

the circle around Hardt, who may have spread radicalized reports of suggestions that he may have uttered orally, and that may have been adopted by his students or auditors.

To substantiate this suspicion we might take a look back at episodes in which something similar had occurred. In the case of the *Histoire de Bileam* from 1706, it is true that a work was fabricated from oral remarks of Hardt's.[152] The ghostwriter for this was a remarkably prominent man, namely Gottfried Wilhelm Leibniz. Hardt had conversed with him and with Queen Sophie Charlotte of Prussia about the passage in Numbers 22:28, about Balaam's ass, who began to speak.[153] Hardt voiced his idea that one could explain this episode as a dream-event. Together they considered whether Balaam might have been the sort of dreamer who might sometimes have had such visions while on a journey. Leibniz was the one who without further ado wrote down the suggestion, in French so that the queen could read it without trouble. Shortly after Hardt had the text printed, which Leibniz then corrected for a later edition.[154] They continued to correspond about it for a time. For Hardt the work was part of a small series of biblical interpretations, which were all written in French (for the queen) and were all published anonymously; they all interpreted biblical passages in a rationalistic or euhemerist manner.[155]

When the Jesuit *Journal de Trévoux* received a notice from Trier in June of 1710, containing a warning about Hardt, it concerned just these works. It claimed:

> Germany has not been immune to a certain sort of audacious critique that is always ready to favor incredulity, despite the happy inclination for religion that a naturally strong mind gives to its peoples. Three or four ungodly writers have scandalized her [Germany] for some time with their conjectures, which they have dared to spew forth. These writers include the Messrs. Thomasius, Gundling, van der Hard [sic], etc.[156]

These observers were clearly alert to the dangers of rationalist Bible exegesis. Such rumors also circulated in Helmstedt. A traveler, Gottlieb Stolle, reported as early as 1703 on what he heard:

---

[152] See Wilhelm Brambach, *Gottfied Wilhelm Leibniz: Verfasser der Histoire de Bileam: mit Vollständigem Abdruck der Histoire de Bileam in der von Leibniz gebilligten Form*, Leipzig, 1887.

[153] On the exegetical problem of this passage and the history of its interpretation, see Bernd Roling, *Physica sacra. Wunder, Naturwissenschaft und historischer Schriftsinn zwischen Mittelalter und Früher Neuzeit*, Leiden, 2013, pp. 9–64.

[154] Badische Landesbibliothek Karlsruhe Ms. 320, p. 4.

[155] *Histoire de Bileam; Renards de Samon; Machoire d'Ane; Corbeus d'Elie; L'antichrist*, [Helmstedt], 1707.

[156] *Journal de Trévoux*, June, 1710.

Although he had more courage in expressing his opinions openly than Lord Abbot [Johann Andreas] Schmidt [of Marienthal], he did behave like a wise man who took circumstances into account regarding persons and other conditions, and requested his listeners to keep his paradoxes to themselves, so that he would not be defamed at the Chancery as a heretic. In general he is thought to be a Socinian, and they say he became one in Holland because he associated so eagerly with the Unitarians there.[157]

So we can expect certain "paradoxes" from Hardt. It seems important to me, however, that at this point it was often other persons who took down the hesitant Hardt's remarks without further ado. That is true for another short text in the little series of works: the *Renards de Samson* ("Samson's Foxes"). Here it was suggested that the 300 foxes that Samson hunted in Judges 15:4 were nothing more than hay stacks. This thesis, set forth again with the intention of removing miracles from the Bible, had been disclosed in 1704, in the *Observationes selectae* in Halle, shortly before the printing of Hardt's work (in 1707); its title was *Metamorphosis vulpecularum Samsonis in straminis manipulos* ("The Transformation of Samson's Foxes into Bundles of Straw"). This time it was quite possibly the young and ambitious Jakob Friedrich Reimmann from Halberstadt, who had heard Hardt's orally presented ideas and had transformed them into a text.[158] Reimmann was also later an energetic collector of the writings of Hardt.[159]

Let us have a look at Reimmann, the rector of St. Martin's School in Halberstadt. Had he read the heterodox manuscript *De Josepho Christi parente naturali meditatio*? Yes, he knew that text and he gives us valuable information about its origins. In Reimmann's *Catalogus bibliothecae theologicae systematico-criticus*, a comprehensive listing of theological works on the basis of his own reading, we find – directly after the entry of the *Esprit de Spinosa* and the *Cymbalum mundi/Symbolum sapientiae* (i.e., two of the most important and infamous atheist texts of the early radical

---

[157] Gottlieb Stolle, *Reisejournal* (partly written with Hallmann), Biblioteka Uniwersytecka, Wrocław, R 766, pp. 4f. On this travel report, see Martin Mulsow, "Eine Reise durch die Gelehrtenrepublik. Soziales Wissen, Wahrnehmungen und Wertungen in Gottlieb Stolles Reisejournal von 1703/4," in Ulrich J. Schneider, ed., *Kultur der Kommunikation. Die europäische Gelehrtenrepublik im Zeitalter von Leibniz und Lessing*, Wiesbaden, 2005, pp. 185–202.

[158] *Observationes selectae ad rem litterariam spectantes* vol. 8, Obv. XIV, Halle, 1704. On the *Observationes* und Reimmann's participation, see Martin Mulsow, "Ein kontroverses Journal der Frühaufklärung: Die Observationes selectae, Halle 1700–1705," *Aufklärung* 17 (2005), pp. 79–99. On Reimmann see Martin Mulsow and Helmut Zedelmaier, eds., *Skepsis, Providenz, Polyhistorie. Jakob Friedrich Reimmann 1668–1743*, Tübingen, 1998.

[159] See the many copies of Hardt's writings in the State and University Library Göttingen.

Enlightenment)[160] – a section on *De Josepho*.[161] Reimmann describes the manuscript, ascribes it to Hermann von der Hardt, and adds, "I obtained [this work] from a certain friend, who added that it had been secretly stolen by some student from this scholar and for this reason and against the will of its owner it had been passed on to others and had come into the library of the famous Prince . . . ."[162] Who was the friend that had given Reimmann the manuscript? It is possible that this was Leibniz, because Reimmann kept up a vigorous correspondence with him; indeed, Leibniz sometimes visited the Halberstadt school rector in his home.[163] Leibniz also maintained good relations with Hermann von der Hardt, so that he could certainly have learned from Hardt himself details such as those concerning a theft. Still, there were other intermediaries that come to mind, some directly from Helmstedt: for example, Johann Andreas Schmidt or Johann Fabricius.[164] In any event the "library of the famous Prince" was, with some certainty, the prince of Braunschweig-Wolfenbüttel's library, which was under Leibniz's supervision and where the text ultimately landed.

And yet even the information from the friend seems to be cloaked in some uncertainty: Reimmann admitted, "I cannot say with certainty that everything happened just this way." But he did not remain indifferent to the text itself, because he added, "Here is our opinion: that this *Meditatio* is unspeakable, horrifying, and scandalous."[165]

10 The Circle Around Hardt

For an Orthodox theologian the text must indeed have been horrifying. At least for the aging Reimmann, who in 1731 when he published his *Catalogus* was no longer the brash young man who, in his middle-thirties had himself perhaps adopted certain of Hardt's ideas. But we must ask

---

[160] *Esprit de Spinosa*, s.l., 1719; edition in the *Traktat über die drei Betrüger*, ed. Winfried Schroder, Hamburg, 1992, *Cymbalum mundi sive Symbolum sapientiae*, ed. Guido Canziani, Winfried Schröder and Francesco Socas, Milan, 2000.

[161] Jakob Friedrich Reimmann, *Catalogus bibliothecae theologicae systematico-criticus*, Hildesheim, 1731, pp. 1030f.

[162] Ibid.

[163] On Leibniz's visits, see Kurt Müller, *Leben and Werk von G. W. Leibniz – Eine Chronik*, Frankfurt, 1984. A first perusal of the partly still unpublished correspondence between Leibniz and Reimmann from the period before 1711, kindly undertaken for me by Nora Gädeke, has not answered this question.

[164] On them see, e.g., Horst-Rüdiger Jarck et al., eds., *Braunschweigisches Biographisches Lexikon: 8. bis 18. Jahrhundert*, Braunschweig, 2006.

[165] Reimmann, *Catalogus bibliothecae theologicae* (note 161), pp. 1030f.

again if it was really possible that Hermann von der Hardt had written such a radical text as *De Josepho*. Even though he may have had Socinian tendencies, as rumors suggested, we know that as a professor he was careful when anything became public. I have already suggested that someone could have seized upon an oral remark and then fabricated a text from it, as happened in the cases of *The Story of Balaam* and the *Transformation of Samson's Foxes*. Did someone take detailed notes on a conversation with Hardt within a small, intimate circle? Or could the text reflect a private disputation exercise that may have formulated an extraordinarily provocative thesis? It did sometimes happen that radical positions were played out internally in a form that impressed some participants in the exercise as being more radical than anyone intended.[166] In the previous chapter we saw that happen with Bucher. In this context the rumor of a secret theft (*clanculum surreptam*), a rumor that Reimmann transmitted, would obtain a more concrete sense: Hardt could have been the originator of the ideas, but his arguments might have been stolen from him in a sense, and then misused in a text that had radical implications and a provocative tone.

In case Hardt cannot be seen as the direct author of the text, therefore, who would it have been who "stole" his ideas, wrote them down, and perhaps radicalized them further? In this quest, we come back again to the "devil," who – according to the note in the Wolfenbüttel manuscript – either wrote or copied the work. If the "devil" is to be understood literally and not simply as the prince of hell, a figure of evil incarnate, could the designation have been a personal name? Someone named Teufel? Someone from the circle around Hardt, who could have transformed his thoughts into pamphlets? When we look, we discover that there was indeed a "Teufel," a student of Hardt. And not just a normal, well-behaved student, but rather a man who pursued and propagated his more radical thoughts. In 1706 this Christian Teufel published under the pseudonym "Christianus Theophilus" an extremely daring work entitled *Delicatissimum Salomoneum epithalamium* ("The Most Pleasant Nuptial Song for Solomon").[167] Intended specifically as a wedding poem for the Prussian crown prince, the work argued that Psalm 45 was not a theological text but simply a wedding poem from ancient Israel, one that came

---

[166] See Martin Mulsow, "Der ausgescherte Opponent. Akademische Unfälle und Radikalisierung," in *Die unanständige Gelehrtenrepublik. Wissen, Libertinage und Kommunikation in der Frühen Neuzeit*, Stuttgart, 2007, pp. 191–216.

[167] *Delicatissimum Salomoneum Epithalamium in gratiam tanti Israelitar. regis ante tot secula cantatum, nunc in gratiam gloriamque serenissimi principis ac domini D. Frederici Wilhelmi et Don. Sophiae Dorotheae [...] cum auspiciatissimum inirent matrimonium*, s.l., 1706. See fols. A4r f.

directly from the context of the wedding to King Solomon with the daughter of the king of Tyre.

Again the reactions of the Orthodox displayed their absolute revulsion. Löscher's *Unschuldige Nachrichten* ("Innocent Reports") printed this reaction:

> Oh, God, look into this and trample Satan under our feet! Oh, may the unfortunate author and those who have used him in this matter [meaning probably Hardt and his friend Johann Fabricius] recognize [their error] and repent before a millstone is hung around their necks or even more severe judgments be imposed for such offenses.[168]

That was a realistic threat because being drowned with a millstone around one's neck was used as a punishment for the worst criminals.

We do not know much about the life of Christian Teufel. One note conveys the rumor that Teufel had once been protected by Hardt with respect to a different heresy concerning the naming of the animals by Adam.[169] That was probably in 1705 when a little epistolary treatise was published under the title *Ad Paulum Martinum Noltenium [. . .] de vocatis ab Adamo animalibus epistola* ("A Letter to Paul Martin Noltenius [. . .] Concerning the Animals Given Names by Adam").[170] In an argument with Samuel Bochart the author claimed that the scene described in Genesis 2:18–20 was not a naming of the animals that might justify any number of metaphysical conclusions about Adam's wisdom and language; instead, it should be understood more as a command to the Israelites not to seek contact with the spirits of the dead but to be satisfied with animals. Enlighteners such as Gundling quickly and eagerly accepted this interpretation as part of their rejection of theological and metaphysical constructions.

Because this epistolary treatise appeared under the name of Hermann von der Hardt and not Teufel, there may well have been an earlier part to

---

[168] *Unschuldige Nachrichten von alten und neuen theologischen Sachen auf das Jahr 1707*, Leipzig, 1707, pp. 265, 270–71, with thanks to Elke Matthes for the reference. Johann Fabricius was regarded as much too liberal and conciliatory toward the Catholics. For the polemics from the Lutheran Orthodox side against him, especially those of Sebastian Edzardi, see Ulrich Groetsch, "Adversus Hereticos: Sebastian Edzard's Epic Battle for Souls," in Johann Anselm Steiger, ed., *Das akademische Gymnasium zu Hamburg im Kontext frühneuzeitlicher Wissenschafts- und Bildungsgeschichte*, Berlin, 2017, pp. 137–162.

[169] Johann G. Heinsius and Johann M. Schröckh, *Unpartheyische Kirchen-Historie Alten und Neuen Testaments [. . .], Dritter Theil, in welchem die Geschichte vom Jahr 1730 bis 1750 enthalten sind*, Jena 1754, p. 1044.

[170] Hermann von der Hardt, *Ad Paulum Martinum Noltenium [. . .] de vocatis ab Adamo animalibus epistola*, Helmstedt, 1705.

this story, an oral disputation of Teufel's, who may have presented Hardt's theses in a more provocative form and may then have been attacked by the Orthodox in Helmstedt – whereupon his teacher may have moved to protect him. Another rumor concerning Teufel, one that Johann Bernhard Hassel the superior court preacher in Wolfenbüttel transmitted to Johann Vogt, claimed that he was said "ultimately to have become ... a Jew."[171] That sheds an interesting but also highly ambiguous light on him, especially with a view to *De Josepho Christi parente naturali meditatio*. If that work actually did have something to do with Teufel, could its contents have led someone to conclude that the author had converted to Judaism? That might not have been complete nonsense. The author was, like Hardt himself, well-informed about Jewish customs and took them as a standard for his interpretation. "You don't know the customs of the Jews, my friend," he said condescendingly in the manuscript. "Between betrothal and marriage there was almost no difference, except for the solemn journey to the groom's house (*deductionem in domum*). It was no crime to have slept with one's betrothed."[172] He referred to scholarly literature, Buxtorf, Selden, Lightfoot, and "old manuscripts" – by which he may well have meant Jewish (i.e. rabbinic) manuscripts.[173] It is not impossible that such knowledge of rabbinic works and Judaica occasionally led to Judaizing by a Christian or even to conversion. Hardt himself spoke of theologians who had supposedly converted to Judaism.[174] This particular report dealt with three persons of the Reformed faith, who were therefore probably not his students.

11 Löscher's Review of *De Josepho*

If we wish to speculate further about the possible author of *De Josepho*, it would be vital first to establish when the manuscript was written. From the start there is a difficulty because of the date of the copy we began with: 1743. If the text was actually written in that year, there would be a huge gap between 1743 and the documented activities of Teufel (around 1706). Teufel would have been almost forty years older by then: around 60 instead

[171] Adam Rudolph Solger, *Bibliotheca sive supellex librorum impressorum in omni genere scientiarum maximam partem rarissimorum*, vol. 3, Nuremberg, 1763, p. 310, Nr. 2035 under the rubric "Libri paradoxi et suspecti."

[172] HAB Cod. Extrav. 265.14, pp. 48f.

[173] Ibid., p. 48: "Vid. Buxtorf. Seldenus Ligtfoot et MS. Antiquit. tit. sponsa."

[174] As Gottlieb Stolle reported (note 157), pp. 10f. On such conversions, see Martin Mulsow and Richard H. Popkin, eds., *Secret Conversions to Judaism in Early Modern Europe*, Leiden, 2004.

of around 20. That seems most unlikely. If the work is really that of Teufel, it must have been written well before 1743.

And indeed it can be shown to be much older. Johann Christoph Wolf referred to the manuscript as early as 1725 in the first volume of his comprehensive *Curae philologicae et criticae* ("Philological and Critical Efforts"), in which he summarized the recent research on the books of the New Testament.[175] He reported that "there has been an attempt, as unfortunate as it was foolish," to prove that Joseph was the natural father of Christ. Wolf had not personally seen the text, but he referred to a review in the *Unschuldige Nachrichten* for 1711. This journal, the "Innocent Reports of Old and New Theological Matters," which had appeared from 1701 on, edited by Valentin Ernst Löscher, can be regarded as the official publication of Lutheran Orthodoxy.[176] That puts us at a date well before 1743 and well into the period when we know Teufel was active. Obviously Löscher or one of his collaborators received a leaked copy of *De Josepho*, and he reacted to it in his journal:

> A manuscript – an irregular tract – has reached one of us concerning Joseph as the natural father of Christ, written in a pernicious style and including malicious and mordant remarks that corrupt good morals, so that it merits a notice here. We appeal to the author, whoever he may be, to repent, so that he might be relieved of his mental disorder and learn to think in the light of grace and to distance himself from his fantastical stories (to say nothing worse about them), which are stuffed with indecency.[177]

That was the official and anxious tone of the ecclesiastical establishment.

The Saxon State Library in Dresden possesses a copy of *De Josepho*, which was probably the very copy reviewed in the *Unschuldige Nachrichten*.[178] It is a text that deviates in many details (but not in its general thrust) from the Wolfenbüttel copy from 1743 that we have been discussing. The Dresden copy seems like a revision that makes the text more fluent and more readable.[179] It leaves out some sentences (and the

---

[175] Johann Christoph Wolf, *Curae philologicae et criticae*, vol. 1, Hamburg 1725, p. 15.

[176] See Martin Greschat, *Zwischen Tradition und neuem Anfang. Valentin Ernst Löscher und der Ausgang der lutherischen Orthodoxie*, Witten, 1971; Klaus Petzoldt, *Der unterlegene Sieger: Valentin Ernst Löscher im absolutistischen Sachsen*, Leipzig, 2001.

[177] *Unschuldige Nachrichten von alten und neuen theologischen Sachen auf das Jahr 1711*, Leipzig, 1711, p. 622.

[178] Mscr. Dresd. A. 189. C.

[179] It is difficult to determine which text came first. Even if the Wolfenbüttel manuscript Ms. 265.14 extrav. originated as late as 1743 and therefore probably later than the Dresden manuscript, I am assuming that it was copied from an original manuscript, one that probably came from Wolfenbüttel or Helmstedt, and may represent an earlier stage of the text than the Dresden

final section of the text, a last *objectio*, is missing), but it also adds a few sentences. It might derive from the author himself, or from an editor, who took liberties with the text – and perhaps shrank back from the explicit denial of original sin, for that is one sentence he omits. We can prove that this is the version of the text that the *Unschuldige Nachrichten* used from the fact, for instance, that it referred on page 626 to "Prolepsis vel Hysterosis," which were the terms (for linguistic inversions) used in the Dresden variant. In the Wolfenbüttel variant, however, these terms were given as ὕστερα πρώτερα. It seems highly likely that the Dresden manuscript, therefore, is the very exemplar that sat on Löscher's desk, for starting in 1709 he was living in Dresden as the pastor of the Church of the Cross and as an assessor in the Superior Consistory.

12 Early Circulation

We need to start with the assumption, then, that this text was completed in 1711 or even earlier. It is fairly clear that the work originated in the territory of Braunschweig-Wolfenbüttel, probably from the circle around Hermann von der Hardt, and possibly – as we suspect – written by one of the professor's students, a younger man who adopted certain of his teacher's ideas and transformed them into a text, which then circulated at least a little. It wound up in the Ducal Library in Wolfenbüttel, and then from there – or maybe by other routes – was sent on by a concerned contemporary to the "guardians" of Lutheran Orthodoxy in Dresden. But from early on it appears that there were at least two variants of the text, one that was probably a reworking of the other.

At first the text appears to have circulated very little. One copy went to Jakob Friedrich Reimmann, most likely sent by friends that Hardt and Reimmann had in common. Probably a few other scholars in Helmstedt also had copies. But it failed to attain the widespread distribution enjoyed by *De tribus impostoribus* (which was both more attractive and more radical). For two decades no one seems to have noticed the text. Perhaps

manuscript. On the other hand, the possibility that the Dresden variant is primary cannot be completely dismissed. In one detail there is a small textual shift: "It is ignoble to say that Christ was born of an irregular marriage: You call Christ a bastard. But what would be wrong with concluding that [Mary's] intercourse with Joseph, if he was the one, occurred on a different day than the wedding." (p. 46 in the Wolfenbüttel text). Here the scribe placed a remark in the margin that appears only later in the Wolfenbüttel text: "Therefore Mary performed no public penance, even though she gave birth too soon." In contrast, the second Wolfenbüttel manuscript (Cod. Extr. 157.11) is quite close to the first (from 1743), because there are only a few insignificant changes.

it was the appearance of Reimmann's *Catalogus bibliothecae theologicae systematico-criticus* in 1731 that reawakened interest because collectors and admirers of forbidden and heterodox writings used such lists of clandestine works as a way of informing themselves about the black market.[180] Especially during the years around 1743, when the Wolfenbüttel manuscript was finished, responses to *De Josepho* begin to surface. Johann Christian Edelmann, known throughout the Holy Roman Empire as a freethinker, and one well-informed about the German clandestine literature scene,[181] wrote in his *Confession of Faith* in 1746:

> Those who know what the famous man, the good Herr Reimmann in his *Catalogo Syst. Crit.* Vol. 1, page 1030, decided the initials listed as H.v.d. mean ... but who have actually seen and read his learned work on this subject (which is still circulating as a clandestine manuscript among scholars), will not so easily subscribe in all places to the judgment of Herr Reimmann, when he declares these modest thoughts to be a shameless, cursed, and noxious work, worthy of [being consigned to] eternal darkness, especially if they consider that outside our Fatherland, namely in England, this same claim, namely that Joseph was the natural father of Lord Jesus, is offered publicly for sale, indeed, in London, not only with the name of the author (who is now reported to be dead) but with that of the publisher, for 6 *Stüber* [i.e., a small coin of little value].[182]

Edelmann here called *De Josepho* a secret work, one that "is still circulating as a clandestine manuscript among scholars." Had he read the Wolfenbüttel copy of 1743 when he wrote his *Confession of Faith*? Or a similar copy? If it was the Wolfenbüttel copy, was he able to understand the note: "Diabolus adscripsit"? And yet another question: If the copyist was referring to Christian Teufel with the word *Diabolus*, "devil," why was the work then ascribed to "H.v.D. H."? And so many years after the composition of the work, how did this scribe learn of "Teufel's" role in it? We must recognize that there is much here that is still unclear; notably, our suggestion that Teufel "appropriated" the text or perhaps just copied it remains pure speculation so long as no better proof turns up. All the same we can now pursue a bit of the trail of evidence for the reception of the

---

[180] Mulsow, "Die Transmission" (note 132).
[181] See Johann Christian Edelmann, *Sechs Briefe an Georg Christoph Kreyssig*, ed. Philipp Strauch, Halle, 1918; on Edelmann in general, see Annegret Schaper, *Ein langer Abschied vom Christentum. Johann Christian Edelmann (1698–1767) und die deutsche Frühaufklärung*, Marburg, 1995.
[182] Johann Christian Edelmann, *Abgenötigtes, jedoch andern nicht wiederaufgenötigtes Glaubens-Bekenntnis*, s.l., 1746 (repr. Stuttgart, 1969), pp. 96f. I am grateful to Elke Matthes for the reference.

text, or at least the way the notion that Jesus was the natural son of Joseph percolated through the eighteenth century.

13   The Road to the Enlightenment

On that last question Edelmann made another useful observation. What book was he talking about when he said that in England it was "offered publicly for sale"? It was doubtless the little forty-eight-page booklet entitled *The Supernatural Incarnation of J. Christ Proved to be False*, which did indeed appear in 1742 under the authorship of Edward Elwall,[183] a draper and merchant, in other words, a simple man. His work opposing the "supernatural incarnation" was also rather simple. For example, he stated: "And that Joseph was the real Father of Jesus, appears plainly, from his natural Affection to him ... ."[184] Elwall was a Unitarian and a Sabbatarian Baptist, and therefore by no means an "Enlightener." Instead, he was a Dissenter or Nonconformist (a member of what would later be called the "free church.") But his position was not so simple as Edelmann implies. Denying the Trinity was punishable by law, and Elwall therefore was formally accused in 1726. He got lucky and won his trial, which he and many other heterodox Englishman down to Joseph Priestley took as a sign of hope.[185] It is of course most unlikely that when Elwall was writing his little book he knew of the *De Josepho* manuscript that was circulating underground in Germany. The cloth merchant gave no hint that he had read this much more learned text.

Even so, Elwall's book was a symptom of the dwindling acceptance of a miraculous virgin birth in the age of the Enlightenment. Increasingly a Unitarian attitude became common, and Jesus was ever more commonly

---

[183] Edward Elwall, *The Supernatural Incarnation of Jesus Christ Proved to be False: having No Foundation in the Prophets, nor in all the Old Testament; and utterly inconsistent with his being the Son of David. But the main Prop and Support of all the absurd Doctrines, both of Papists and Protestants; to the great Scandal and Reproach of the true Christian Religion. And that our Lord Jesus Christ, was the real son of Joseph and Mary*, London, 1742; 2nd edn., London, 1743. On Elwall (1676–1744), see *Oxford Dictionary of National Biography*, Oxford, 2004, s.v.

[184] Elwall, *Supernatural Incarnation* (Note 183), p. 6. See also pp. 8f. We have come full circle back to the earliest skeptics concerning the virgin birth, the Jewish Christians. The "Nazarenes" had again become popular among Dissenters through the work of John Toland. See Toland, *Nazarenus, Or, Jewish, Gentile, and Mahometan Christianity*, London, 1718; new edn., Justin Champion, Oxford, 1999.

[185] See *The Triumph of Truth; being an account of the trial of E[dward] E[lwall] for Heresy and Blasphemy at Stafford Assizes. [Written by himself.] [...] To which are added extracts from some other pieces of Mr. E.'s, concerning the Unity of God [...] By the author of an appeal to the [...] professors of Christianity* [i.e. Joseph Priestley], Leeds, 1771.

regarded only as a moral teacher.[186] In this process Edelmann was a transitional figure: he knew, at least at secondhand, the old, scholarly clandestine tradition, but he also stood for a newer, "naturalistic" world-view that had begun to break with revealed truths. After Edelmann, however, the direct stream of reception for *De Josepho* seems to have dried up; or at least we have not yet found any evidence of its later influence. That does not mean that its general attitude did not find followers in the later eighteenth century. To the contrary, in 1796 a work appeared under the title, "Report that Jesus was born of the Holy Spirit and a Virgin – explained by ideas of the time," which struck a series of skeptical notes. To be sure, even some years after the French Revolution, the author did not yet dare to sign his name; he used the abbreviation "Br." The essay found a place in Johann Ernst Christian Schmidt's *Bibliothek für Kritik und Exegese des Neuen Testaments* and drew on rabbinic literature.[187] The author cautiously said that he believed that he "was entitled to explain the report of a conception by the Holy Spirit, of a birth by a Virgin – using Jewish categories of understanding."[188] In its review, the *Allgemeine Literatur-Zeitung* of Jena summarized the declared position of its author this way: that "ever since Semler first blazed a trail in exegesis," notions like the virgin birth could be understood "according to Jewish ideas of the time" – that is, within the context of their own time and culture. During the late eighteenth century, that was a typical but by no means correct view for such statements did not acknowledge the clandestine advances made in the first half of that century. They had been forgotten. That is true not only for discussions of the virgin birth but also for criticism of the Canon of the New Testament, which began well before Semler but were not set forth in published works.[189]

Contextualizing the virgin birth by referring to Jewish concepts had more than just positive connotations, of course, considering the anti-Jewish desire of many Enlighteners to distance themselves from "primi-tive" traditions. It is easy to find such judgments as this: if we do not make "a very sharp distinction between Jewish prejudices and the noble and pure

---

[186] Jonathan Sheehan, *The Enlightenment Bible: Translation, Scholarship, Culture*, Princeton, 2005, pp. 118–147.

[187] *Bibliothek für Kritik und Exegese des Neuen Testaments*, vol. 1, part 1 (1796), essay no. 4,, pp. 101–110. Schmidt himself, the editor, was a theological rationalist.

[188] Ibid., p. 103.

[189] Martin Mulsow, "Paalzow, Lessing und die *Historische Einleitung in die Offenbarung Johannis*," in Christoph Bultmann and Friedrich Vollhardt, ed., *Lessings Religionsphilosophie im Kontext. Hamburger Fragmente und Wolfenbütteler Axiomata*, Berlin, 2011, pp. 337–347.

ideas of Christianity, we will make no progress in the advance of the only desirable and truly moral religious Enlightenment."[190] That was the view of Carl Venturini in 1800, who had been born in 1768 in Braunschweig and was a historian and a theological rationalist. He too omitted to put his name on the title page of his "Natural History of the Great Prophet of Nazareth," and he did not list Copenhagen, where he was then living and teaching, as the place of publication, claiming "Bethlehem" instead.

Over against an "inherited inclination toward the miraculous and the supernatural,"[191] he joined many of his generation by invoking the "natural," with the help of which the life of Jesus could be not only reconstructed but embellished like a novel. These were the years when research into the "life of Jesus (*Leben-Jesu-Forschung*) was germinating and growing, until finally in the 1830s David Friedrich Strauß, in a nonsacral, purely biographical reconstruction of the life of Jesus, created the decisive standard work and summa of these efforts.[192] For Strauß the virgin birth was just one myth among others, invented by the early Christians in order to express their ideas.[193] He recapitulated many of the arguments that had been presented ever since the Jewish polemics and the Socinian interpretations down to the rationalistic exegeses in favor of the natural sonship of Jesus; these were points that the clandestine *De Josepho* had also made. By 1836 the naturalization of the Son of God appeared to have reached its goal. Along with many other exposures of supernatural "myths," it had resulted in research into the life of Jesus, which soon became a surrogate for theological treatments of the figure of Christ.

So what kind of naturalizing process have we described when we concentrate on Joseph's fatherhood? Did God become man? Was this a

---

[190] *Natürliche Geschichte des großen Propheten von Nazaret*, "Bethlehem" [Copenhagen] 1800, p. 4.

[191] Ibid., 13.

[192] David Friedrich Strauß, *Das Leben Jesu, kritisch bearbeitet*, Erlangen, 1836, pp. 105–197.

[193] See Heinrich M. Köster, "Die Jungfrauengeburt als theologisches Problem seit David Friedrich Strauss," in Brosch, ed., *Jungfrauengeburt gestern und heute* (note 106), pp. 35–88, esp. pp. 38f. Strauß listed certain exegetical objections including – for example, that the lists of Jesus's ancestors were constructed, irreconcilable, and made sense only if they were meant to prove that Jesus was descended from David, and that Joseph therefore had to be his father; that Matthew and Luke would have retrospectively fitted these details into the story they made up of the virgin birth; that the various announcements of Jesus's birth were also irreconcilable and therefore without any historical value; that Luke 1:32 prophesies only a mighty king, the son of David as described in 2 Samuel 7:14 and Psalm 2:7; that the birth of Jesus from a virgin as announced in Luke 1:34f. was added later; and Matthew 1:21 describes Jesus's mission as messianic, so that the reception of the Holy Spirit (Matthew 1:18) and the quotation from the verse of Isaiah 7:14, following the words of the LXX, had to originate with the evangelist, who applied it to Jesus in defiance of the context. On Strauss, see Friedrich Wilhelm Graf, *Kritik und Pseudo-Spekulation. David Friedrich Strauß als Dogmatiker im Kontext der positionellen Theologie seiner Zeit*, Munich, 1982.

process of secularization? And was this part of a unique and linear process? No, it does not seem so. The argument for the "natural" sonship of Jesus was, as we have seen, a thesis that could be used for various purposes. In *De Josepho Christi parente naturali meditatio* the doctrine that Jesus was the Messiah was not abandoned; to the contrary, it was necessary for logical and argumentative reasons: Jesus had to be the natural son of Joseph because otherwise the genealogy of the Messiah would have been scrambled. Moreover, there was an effort to cleanse the "pure" Christian religion, removing fables and "false miracles."[194] That was certainly a different argument from that of those who assumed they had to eliminate all supernatural events and were prepared to forfeit even the Messiahship of Christ. But over the course of the eighteenth century the growing emphasis on the natural sonship of Jesus ultimately merged with other kinds of naturalization, such as natural law, natural theology, and the new natural sciences. And then the notion came to prevail that Jesus was a man, who taught a natural morality, in tune with natural law, and that this was just what natural theology already regarded as right.

---

[194] HAB Cod. Extrav. 265.14, pp. 1f.

Conclusion

This book, along with its companion volume *Enlightenment Underground* and some of my other earlier works, draws a new picture of the origins of the German Enlightenment. It has mainly highlighted moments of radical Enlightenment, but it has also illuminated the conditions under which such moments took shape and shows that long-acknowledged scholarly discussions were deeply entangled with clandestine dissenters, and that the moderate Enlightenment, like that of Halle, was bound up with the Enlightened underground. The big picture that emerges is multifaceted and no longer focuses on Halle alone as the center and no longer emphasizes Pufendorf and Thomasius as the only protagonists but discovers a multitude of less well-known thinkers from various and unexpected locations in Germany.

Of course Crell and Wachter, Lau and Fischer, Stosch and Bucher, Heber and Hardt do not by themselves represent an alternative origin for the German Enlightenment; they do not displace Thomasius and his school. But they are valuable and rare indicators of other factors, theories, schools, and milieus that also played a role in the huge intellectual shift that occurred between 1680 and 1720. The lens labeled Bucher, for example, allows us to see how the mortality of the soul, a topic that agitated Italian scholars in the early sixteenth century and later many of the currents of the radical Reformation and the English Revolution, became a newly and acutely vexed question in early eighteenth-century Germany. Claiming that the soul was mortal undermined traditional views of rewards and punishments in heaven or hell for souls after death, which in turn threatened the social system of morals supported by early modern states; that explains why theologians and magistrates reacted with such fierce hostility. Typically this transition from an immortal to a mortal soul has been interpreted as an aspect of secularization and as a central part of the semantic conversion of traditional into modern social systems. But the case of Bucher shows just how complicated that process could be – we need to give up all notions of an intentional move toward secularization. Instead we have to interpret a book like *The Confidential Correspondence of Two Good Friends Concerning the Essence of Souls* as a form of "relational authorship," which highlights the interaction of a student's doubts, the interests of his professor, the encouragement of a patron, and the arbitrary power of an early Enlightenment publisher, who brought an originally private academic argument into the harsh light of public attention.

The spatial dimension is also noteworthy in this case: that dispute about the soul broke out in Lutheran Wittenberg, emerging from dissatisfaction with an inflated Orthodox thesis – in this case the thesis that even the souls of animals were immortal or at least immaterial. As happened repeatedly in the genesis of the radical Enlightenment, an overreaching theology generated a counter-theory. And the reception of "influences" from Western Europe, which have often been trotted out to explain the German Enlightenment, played a distinctly minor role in this story. Much more important was the shift from Saxon Wittenberg to Prussian Halle, with the concomitant support of a patron, Tschirnhaus, who came from the socially elevated layer of the court nobility. The history of the *Correspondence's* publication then played itself out in various other places, for example in Jena and Leipzig. Thus it was not just authorship that was "relational" here, but the process of publication also occurred within a relational network: a network of central German cities. In this way the whole process combined diverse strata and milieus ranging from simple students to publishers and on to the major intellectuals at a princely court. Such patterns recur in other detailed case histories: almost always what was later described as "radicalism" emerged from the collaboration of various persons, places, and social groups.

In this way once an extreme position – like that of the mortality or insubstantiality of the soul – was born, it could unfold its ongoing impact over the course of the whole eighteenth century. At first a flood of outraged refutations might criminalize the "radical" text, marginalizing and forbidding it, and removing it from circulation. But then a counter-dynamic of clandestinity might set in: collectors often deliberately searched for forbidden and therefore rare works, and thus helped such texts to survive; later, less dogmatic minds could learn of forbidden theses from the attacks on them and were often stimulated to push a forbidden idea even further. New scholarly contexts permitted a thesis to appear in a new light and to seem more acceptable, at least to some. All that happened with Bucher's *Correspondence*. By the 1740s and 1750s – often within the new context of Wolffianism – we can detect a true surge of publications on the soul and its immortality, which is a sure sign of just how threatened the Orthodox thesis now appeared. In looking over the whole century, we can see the *Correspondence* as a prelude, a forerunner of the later materialistic theories of Denis Diderot, the Baron d'Holbach, or – in Germany – of Karl von Knoblauch and Johann Gottlieb Karl Spazier. But what do we mean by a "forerunner"? It is a concept that has often misled us into overemphasizing certain isolated sentences from earlier works like those of Bucher to show that they "prepared the way" or "set the stage" for some later movement. Yet such analyses do not actually help at all; indeed they distort our view of the real and complex origins of early radical positions. That is why this book takes such pains to pursue a series of exemplary case histories that display their true origins.

Providing an alternative account of the early German Enlightenment requires not just proof of relationality and the involvement of highly diverse places and milieus within the splintered landscape of the German territorial states; we have also had to broaden our view of the whole panoply of the disciplines involved. In the past the "early Enlightenment" has been seen only in the fraught relations of philosophy and natural law. But the palette of relevant academic fields was clearly much broader than that, back then as well as today. It would be odd indeed if the shock waves of new thinking within the little world of the university were felt only in philosophy and jurisprudence without affecting the fields of theology, physics, history, literary history, and Oriental studies (to say nothing of nonacademic fields like literature). But the converse was also true: why should not shock waves originating in theology, physics, history, literary history, and Oriental studies have reached philosophers and jurists?

This book, therefore, has paid attention to disciplines that are usually neglected in such studies. As we can see already with the case of Bucher, doctrines concerning the soul took up a notoriously ambiguous position between theology, philosophy, and medicine, with connections to still other fields. Chapter 2 aims directly at the heart of physics in the years around 1700 (i.e., at the concept of nature). This notion had become more controversial than ever because "progressive" experimental physicists, beginning especially with Robert Boyle, were advocating a nature that contained no intrinsic forces. The reason for their contention was not just natural scientific but also religious: these thinkers hoped to prevent any tendency to deify nature, as did happen with certain spiritualists, esoterics, and even with certain traditionalists among the natural philosophers. Here again, as with the discussion of the soul, a concern for social stability also played a role. Spiritualist currents could, according to these scholars, endanger the institutionalized and confessionalized Christian church and thus the solidarity of state and society. The word of the day was "idolatry," but idolatry was not just that of pagans or primitive peoples. Rather, as the chapter shows, scholars were eager to repudiate idolatrous threats within their own ranks. The trouble was that around 1700 there were various discourses concerning idolatry, not just those of a "conservative" bent aimed at stabilizing the institutional church, but others as well that used the concept subversively to criticize religion in general, including Christianity. The chapter pursues two cases, that of Andreas Rüdiger and that of Christian Gabriel Fischer. They were both natural philosophers and physicists who felt compelled to join in the controversies over "nature" and sought, each in his own way, to find a path between the threat of too much atheism and that of too much religion. For Rüdiger in Leipzig, that occurred, as it had earlier with Bayle, with the help of reflections on the origins of idolatry in the early civilizations of the ancient Middle East. Rüdiger thought he could see that Egyptian rulers and priests had failed in an attempt to convey abstract truths to simple people, an attempt that had continued almost down to the present day and had produced a situation that demanded an epistemological and semiotic reformation. He pursued that goal with the philosophy of Thomasius. In contrast, Fischer in Königsberg based himself on the philosophy of Wolff and hoped from that foundation to develop a position that was, on the one hand, monistic rather like that of Spinoza, but, on the other hand, not completely monistic, because a creator outside the world was supposed to guarantee that "intermediate causes" would not be idolatrously regarded as divine. As with Boyle and Rüdiger, he oriented himself to the findings of recent Oriental scholarship that had recovered the most ancient teachings of the East.

This is also a story that can be pursued down through the eighteenth century, all the way to the "modern" physics that declared its independence from theology. But again we must insist that it is not helpful to celebrate Fischer as a martyr of the modern, a "forerunner" of a "secularized" physics. His motives ran contrary to that because they were themselves partly theological in nature. It is no wonder that it is hard to categorize the works of contemporary critics of Rüdiger and Fischer. They fired away with accusations of "atheism" and "Spinozism," attacks that were hopelessly inaccurate and did not capture the contorted maneuvers that accompanied the problem of idolatry. Even modern categories like "radical Enlightenment" and "moderate Enlightenment" have difficulties here. For me the most interesting aspect of Rüdiger and Fischer is that they reveal the limits of such efforts to categorize. We can understand their positions only if we see such Enlightenment classifications in action, as part of a description of certain tactics and deliberate interventions in the discourse of that period. Pierre Bourdieu sometimes used the word *illusio* for such a process, for it conveys both the mistaken illusion an observer succumbs to if he believes that he's dealing with a Spinozist or a non-Spinozist and the playful illusion than characterizes an actor who uses such tactics, even if for men like Fischer – who lost their livelihoods – this was a bitter and dangerous game.

Whereas Chapter 2 deals with physics, Chapter 3 takes up the doctrine of temperaments and medical theorizing, which I have investigated closely for their tendencies to become radical. It quickly emerges that there is another paradox here. It was obviously the venerable old Hippocratic doctrine of the four temperaments that suddenly seemed so promising to the progressive early Enlightenment intellectuals of Halle. Why? And then a second paradox perfects our confusion: while Gundling was, on the one hand, one of the figures who made Hippocrates so prominent, he was, on the other hand, precisely the one who accused the ancient physician of atheism. Was not the Enlightenment in Halle thereby pulling the rug out from under its own feet just after putting it in place? We have to recognize once again that only an analysis that is both interdisciplinary and dynamic can resolve the paradoxes of these intellectual processes and positionings: interdisciplinary because we must see that the doctrine of the temperaments was so attractive to the early Enlighteners of Halle precisely because its integrative power could be deployed across all the disciplines. This early Enlightenment regarded itself as an ensemble of critiques: a critique of prejudices, of superstitions, of tradition, and of politics. To accomplish such a critique, however, its practitioners needed standards of analysis, and the doctrine of temperaments offered a seductively simple toolkit with which to assess intellectual, social, or political processes. If, for example, Spanish history was understood as the result of the choleric-melancholic national temperament of the Spaniards, such an analysis provided apparent insights into Spanish national literature, diplomacy, ecclesiastical history, and the colonial expansion. The "art of recognizing different tempers of men" was the legacy of a sort of typical courtly expertise but it stood explicitly and directly behind the critical scholarship of the Halle intellectuals. No wonder psychology – in the form it took around 1700 as a blend of medicine and philosophy – attained such prominence.

At the same time, men like Gundling tried to liberate medicine from the grip of theology. The suspicions leveled at paganism and idolatry that were so virulent at the time shaped perceptions in this field as well: if an ancient authority, such as Hippocrates, was not a Christian, the logic of many contemporaries drove them to conclude that, like all pagans, he was ultimately an atheist. But if a person was an atheist, he could not serve as a guarantor for the discipline he supposedly authorized. Medicine could not be permitted to be an atheistic endeavor for then it could not be curative. The result was that many scholars were driven to see ancient thinkers like Hippocrates as "theologians." They created a "Theologia Hippocratis" that would harmonize with Christian doctrine. This was a typical set of conclusions forced by confessionalization with its overburdening of nontheological disciplines and topics with theological content. If like Gundling one recognized this wretched development and hoped to rectify it, then one might be driven to peculiar role reversals that, for example, the Enlightener Gundling, who otherwise opposed the branding of others as heretics, might himself now play a role as a "manufacturer of heretics" (*Ketzermacher*) by diagnosing Hippocrates along with many other ancient authorities as atheists. He did so, as the chapter shows, in order to follow Bayle in advocating a proper separation of disciplines: a physician could follow the "atheist" Hippocrates and still be a good doctor.

But in this case too contemporaries were irritated by the *illusio*: they often had a hard time understanding why Gundling was behaving as he did. And the subsequent history of medicine had an even harder time. From a purely historical or philological point of view near the end of the eighteenth century it had become simply incomprehensible why the generation around 1700 had wasted time on such irrelevant quibbles as the supposed atheism of the ancient physician from Cos.

With these topics my book has arrived, finally, in Halle, and of course natural law remains a central element of the early Enlightenment in Halle; but now this element gets decentered as well. The doctrine of modern natural law starting with Grotius and Pufendorf (which has often been conceived as the *secularization* of law) was unquestionably the very backbone of this early Enlightenment. In *Enlightenment Underground* that can be felt in essentially every chapter, but in that book I dispensed with the chance to deal directly with natural law in detail because other scholars were already doing great work on the subject and I wanted to concentrate on the more neglected aspects of the age. But in the long run that was unsatisfactory. And so Chapter 4 seizes on Richard Tuck's interpretation of antiskepticism as the essential characteristic of modern natural law in order to tell the story of this antiskepticism in a new manner and relate it to the clandestine literature of the underground. This gives an entirely new tone to the account.

As soon as we adjust our perspective just a little, moving from the reception of Pufendorf to that of Grotius and Selden, from establishment works to those of the clandestine world, entirely different places (such as Wittenberg and Frankfurt on the Oder) come into view and new dynamics emerge that are wholly different from what we have recognized earlier. The chapter concentrates on the intellectual development of Johann Franz Budde as a guide and indicator, for he reveals a sequence of reactions to certain concerns: first his concern about how to harmonize the rules of natural law with those of the Bible (a problem that had vexed John Selden earlier); but then his attempt to oppose moral demands rooted in skepticism or utilitarian considerations by constructing a comprehensive moral foundation. Skeptical attacks on conventional wisdom had found expression not only in clandestine works like the *Symbolum sapientiae* but also in projects in natural law that competed with those of Pufendorf by constructing the boogeyman of a "pagan" Grotius. Once again we can detect an "anxiety of influence," a worry about drawing too much from an idolatrous pagan antiquity, here focused on jurisprudence. Ultimately it emerges that two processes were woven together in a complicated manner: building up the antiskeptical ammunition of moral philosophy and natural law, on the one hand, and the detachment of ethics and law from their tight connection to the biblical framework (from what Schneewind has called the "Pythagoras Story.") But with Budde, antiskepticism strengthened the Pythagoras Story, so that once again there can be no thought of drawing some straight line toward secularization.

Chapter 5 and my forthcoming book *Spinozism, Arianism, and Kabbalah* seize upon the insight sketched earlier in *Enlightenment Underground* that debates about the Trinity provided decisive catalysts for Orthodox positions but also for heterodox and radical thinking, results that went far beyond purely theological questions. Thus, as I argued in my earlier book, the Socinians and their various coalitions with Jewish, Arminian, and deist positions had a much greater importance than their relatively small numbers and marginal social position around 1700 would lead us to suppose. Chapter 5 treats Friedrich Wilhelm Stosch, who represents a prominent case of radical Enlightenment, a man who stood in direct contact with this antitrinitarian milieu; and *Spinozism, Arianism, and Kabbalah* on Johann Georg Wachter shows, surprisingly, that even an emphatic advocacy of the Trinity (though one inflected by Arianism and subordinationism) could lead to radical conclusions.

The case of Stosch – one of the most famous instances of censorship and accusation within the history of the German radical Enlightenment – was a sort of background study, from which we can see how a dangerous brew developed in Berlin and Frankfurt on the Oder, combining a mixture of Socinianism and Arminianism along with the foreign ingredients of Hobbes, Gassendi, and Spinoza, all eventually dished up through the lectures of the headstrong Professor Johann Christoph Becmann. It is only through our detailed reconstruction, unraveled as in a detective story, of the correspondence between Philipp van Limborch and Samuel Crell that we gain a sense of how strongly contested certain citations and sources were within the tense field of theological controversy. It was precisely because these positions flowed all too easily into each other that they had to be kept officially – and especially with a view to the court of the elector in Potsdam – strictly separate from each other. The fact that the court preacher's own son with his amateur philosophical sketch fundamentally repudiated the precarious balance between the Reformed and the Lutherans, and between Remonstrants and Socinians, presented an accident that should not have happened. This was an accident that cast a harsh light on the many lazy compromises that underlay the famous Brandenburg "tolerance." I have unfurled the concept of "intellectual field" in order to describe the tactics, initiatives, and dynamics that enveloped Stosch, Crell, Becmann, and many others. In contrast, the simple accusation of atheism and even the confirmation of their "radicalism" are fairly useless because they tell us almost nothing. In brief, one could say that Stosch developed an intellectual *habitus* from his early connections with Socinians and Remonstrants, onto which during the 1670s and 1680s philosophical elements taken from Gassendi, Spinoza, Le Clerc, and others were attached, so that in the end he could produce an eclectic text that positively shocked his contemporaries.

The history related in *Spinozism, Arianism, and Kabbalah* is entirely different. It is also a sort of background study, but an extended one, for it describes not one specific religious-political milieu like that of Brandenburg, but rather what I would call, using Dieter Henrich's terms, a "constellation": the common space for thought and for problems shared by a loose group of theorists in Amsterdam, Berlin, Hamburg, and Magdeburg, who all proceeded from a certain common base and often in conversation with one another, but then developed in different directions. That common base included the simultaneous reading of Böhme, Cudworth, Spinoza, and the *Kabbala denudata* ("The Kabbalah Unveiled"), which all appeared on the book market around 1680. The generation of theologizing thinkers included so-called radical Pietists, Spinozists, Socinians, and converts to Judaism, for whom – if we take at face value these labels and slogans – it would seem most unlikely that they had anything to say to one another. And yet we find the Kabbalist Franciscus van Helmont sitting together with the "Jewish" Johannn Peter Späth, and the Pietist Johann Wilhelm Petersen in dialogue with the Socinian Samuel Crell. This book takes as its task the reconstruction of such discussions, thus extending and making more concrete many of the motifs that were announced earlier in *Enlightenment Underground* (such as the doctrine of the Logos, of the First Born of all Creatures, and subordinationism). The debates in Leipzig and Hamburg over the dangers (or the harmlessness) of the spiritualists combined to produce a huge intellectual force that inspired young scholars like Wachter. The generation who worried about the integrative aspects of the Trinity sometimes argued that their doctrine showed the concurrence of the Kabbalah with the Logos theology of the ancient Church Fathers and with Spinozan rationality but, over the long term, these considerations were just an episode; and from the viewpoint of modern scholarship many of their fundamental assumptions today seem mistaken. But from those discussions came results whose impact was felt far into the eighteenth century: the hypothesis concerning the importance of the Essenes for Christ, a notion that was rekindled by later freethinkers such as Carl Friedrich Barth; or the notion of a historical succession of "esoteric" currents or arcane systems of philosophy, an idea that appealed to the Freemasons and the Illuminati during the second half of the eighteenth century; or the quest for a theologically acceptable, "pantheistic," Spinoza, which developed an overwhelming power during the fight over Spinoza after 1785 and became one of the origins of German idealism. Seen in this way, the "radicalism" of these early thinkers, which is so hard to classify or describe, became a crucial factor in the origins of the German Enlightenment that we must not ignore.

Finally Chapter 6 turns even more directly to religion than did the previous chapter on the Trinity. Here I focus on the founders of the great monotheistic religions: Moses, Mohammed (though only briefly), and Jesus. As we saw in *Enlightenment Underground*, these founders were all accused of fraud in infamous underground works such as *De tribus impostoribus* and the *Traité des trois imposteurs*.[1] They had all deceived mankind in pretending to offer direct contact with divinity for political

---

[1] See Martin Mulsow, *Enlightenment Underground: Radical Germany 1680–1720*, tr. H. C. Erik Midelfort, Charlottesville, 2015, chapter 3.

reasons, in order to rule over ordinary people; God seemed to provide legitimacy for their religious laws. And popular credulity had made their fraud possible.

This last chapter places the thesis about fraud into different contexts and connects it with the argument that Hellenistic and late ancient backgrounds provided a crucial template for dealing with the founders of the three great Religions of the Book around 1700. The first context concerns Moses: there were obviously more than just efforts to demote Moses, like those we found in the treatises alleging fraud. Those deflations were actually preceded by a whole age of unbridled efforts to inflate Moses. As with the debate about the soul or in the theological disputes over Hippocrates, this was an effect of confessionalization with its theological overreach. In the case of Moses all knowledge could ultimately be derived from the perfect knowledge of Moses (or of Adam or Solomon). The model for such excessive claims lay in the exaltations of Moses that Jewish-Hellenistic thinkers invented in their competition with other Near Eastern and Greek traditions. During the age of confessionalism these seeds flourished luxuriantly. So this chapter argues that the deflations of Moses at the hands of libertines and radical Enlighteners were at least partly a reaction to the immoderate exaggerations of those who had venerated Moses. They focused instead on Moses as an "all-too-human" politician, even if that meant adopting many aspects of the too-perfect Moses. It is interesting to notice the national variations; in England Moses was recast as a republican by freethinkers like Toland; but, in Germany, Enlighteners like Gundling were content to dethrone the philosophy of Moses. Meanwhile, radicals went much further and turned Moses into a complete scoundrel. Once again it becomes crucial to recognize the *illusio* and the dynamism that characterized such seemingly paradoxical shifts of position.

That is no less true for the debates about Mohammed, which ranged from idealizations among certain freethinkers (for example, Henry Stubbe or Voltaire) to condemnations among the Orthodox, but actually also among some freethinkers. Here too it was possible either to present Islam in a positive light in contrast to Christianity or to besmirch the religion as an especially egregious example of how a religion could deceive and politically manipulate people. And then in addition we find the usual interweavings of these arguments with other polemics, like those directed against the Socinians, who resembled Muslims in worshiping just one unitary God (without the Trinity). Such references – often unspoken – complicated these discussions and repeatedly led scholars, and especially Orthodox theologians, into unexpected alliances and positions.

So far as Jesus Christ was concerned, scholars had to be more cautious; even though criticism of Mohammed was welcome, and a critique of Moses was permissible within limits, a depiction of Jesus as just a human being or, more radically, as a deceiver was perceived as a frontal attack on Christianity and therefore as suicidal for any thinker within the Holy Roman Empire. The few underground writings that dared to do so, such as the anonymous *De tribus impostoribus*, are well-known. But much less known until now has been a minor contribution to the "humanization" of Christ, the Son of God, a work that asserted that he was the natural son of Joseph. That claim implied that he was not the Son of God, not the product of some sort of procreation between God and the Virgin Mary. On closer analysis this clandestine work, which I ascribe to the circle of those around Hermann von der Hardt, is like many of other "radical" texts studied in this book in that it cannot easily be enrolled in some simple thesis about secularization. Instead, the author seems to have been concerned to show that Jesus descended from the line of David (and even further back) down to Joseph, and these considerations led him to argue against the virgin birth. The relevant context therefore was the Jewish critique of Jesus as the Son of God and – once again – the Socinian emphasis on the same point. Any broad line of influence down to the late eighteenth century and to the naturalizing that we find in the quest for the "historical Jesus" – which seem so seductive – cannot be taken at face value. So here again, no real "forerunners."

Taken together this book, along with *Enlightenment Underground* and *Knowledge Lost*, presents a new history of the beginnings of the German Enlightenment. It is clearly no longer limited to the world of Halle and it has gained in depth by adding motifs, contexts, and Europe-wide entanglements; it cannot be pigeon-holed as only a precursor of such later developments as "secularization," "materialism," or "emancipation," and it resists any static description of simple oppositions between "Radical Enlightenment" and "Moderate Enlightenment" or "Orthodoxy." What we discover in place of these abstractions is that we must painstakingly reconstruct the dynamism of contested positions as they arose. Often they led to paradoxical utterances that contemporaries around 1700 found obscure or mystifying, even if they lent themselves to accusations of apparent atheism and Spinozism.

My choice to concentrate methodologically on "lesser" and ignored thinkers at the radical fringes of intellectual society does not, however, imply an effort to write a new history of heroes or to enthrone these thinkers on pedestals they do not deserve.[2] No, my focus is meant only to use the analysis of details emerging from these microhistories to obtain a corrective to current master narratives and to fashion from these details the fragmentary elements of an alternative view. Many more fragments could still be added. So far as clandestine literature is concerned, collectors and historians in the eighteenth century were especially interested in works that evaluated and criticized religion. For them these were the most prominent items, but the underground of anonymous and socially radical works extended further. We should also pay attention to politically and socially radical arguments, and beyond them there were also economic, scientific, and other sorts of heterodoxy.[3] Future studies of such underground writings should follow the precept that secret extremist works have to be understood in their interaction with the discourse that was established and openly public.

From all these case histories it is not hard to generate further questions. As I suggested in *Knowledge Lost,* paying attention to the fragility or precariousness of knowledge energizes two long-term investigations: one the history of security and the other the history of freedom. And the same is true here. Paying attention to the dynamism within apparently opposed positions, between radicals and nonradicals, of course makes it hard to discern broad lines of development. The whole tenor of this book has been directed against master narratives of the sort we are accustomed to. And yet the changes in perspective that come from concentrating on the ways that knowledge can be lost and on the tactics that marginalized thinkers used in resisting such losses, make it possible for us now to replace the older narratives with several new but cautious generalizations, lines of practice, expectations, fears, and fascinations. And from these new perspectives it should now be easier to write an alternative history of the origins of the German Enlightenment.

---

[2] I say this in response to the critique of Caspar Hirschi (published in the Frankfurter *Allgemeine Zeitung* on February 1, 2019, p. 10). Hirschi thinks I must now be committed to such a "heroic story," even though I have repeatedly shown explicitly that I do not intend any such account. Instead I am aiming at showing a multiplicity of factors and to emphasize completely unintended processes.

[3] I have tried to survey the full breadth of the underground in an edited collection of essays: Martin Mulsow, ed., *Kriminelle – Freidenker – Alchemisten. Räume des Untergrunds in der Frühen Neuzeit,* Cologne, 2014.

Bibliography

Manuscript Sources

Amsterdam, Universiteitsbibliotheek

Ms. III D 17 fol. 166r.: Draft of letter Limborch to Crell, November 26, 1701
Ms. III D 17 fol. 167r.: Draft of letter Limborch to Crell, September 24, 1702
Ms. J 21a/b: Samuel Crell to Philipp van Limborch
Ms. 95 Cc2: Wartensleben to Cocceji, February 19, 1707

Berlin, Staatsarchiv Preußischer Kulturbesitz

I. HA, Rep. 47, Tit 20a, Paket 15725: Denunciation of Stosch
I. HA, Rep. 13, Nr. 24, Fasz. 22: Judgment of the Court Preachers
VI. HA, Literary estate of J. C. Becmann

Danzig, Technische Universität

Herrn Nathanael Jacob Gerlachs [. . .] Reise [. . .] in einem akkuraten Journal beschrieben [. . .] durch Christian Gabriel Fischern aus Königsberg. Anno 1727–1731, 12 vols. (3533 S.), folio.

Dessau, Landesarchiv Sachsen-Anhalt

Z 44, B 2e Nr. 18a: "Die in Dessau geschehene Arrestierung des Doktors und Professors Graetz von Zerbst," 1730.

Dresden, Sächsische Landesbibliothek

Mscr. Dresd. A. 189. C: *De Josepho Christi parente naturali meditatio*

Dresden, Sächsisches Landeshauptarchiv

Loc. 9571: Kellner to Tschirnhaus, Oct. 1704

Dresden, Stadtarchiv

Kirchliche Wochenzettel der Kreuzkirche, July 23, 1724

Erfurt, Universitätsbibliothek

UB Erfurt 03 - R. 8° 00221ac: Selden, *De jure naturali* (possession of Boineburg)
UB Erfurt 03 - R. 4° 01455g: Selden, *De jure naturali* (possession of Boineburg)

Göttingen, Staats- und Universitätsbibliothek

Ms. theol. 259: Servetus, *Restitutio Christianismi*

Hamburg, Staats- und Universitätsbibliothek

Cod. geogr. 68: Klumpf Diary of his journey; pp. 85–145: Text on Späth; pp. 254–344: Copies of Späth letters.
Cod. theol. 1222: Arpe, *Apologia pro Vanino*, author's annotated copy.
Sup. ep. Uffenbach
Sup. ep. 76, 251–302: Planer to Valentin Ernst Löscher
Sup. ep. 82, fol. 32r.: Heber to Johann Friedrich Mayer, May 9, 1692
Sup. ep. 117, 181: Hocheisen to Wolf, 1703

Hildesheim, Stadtarchiv

Ms. WB 1789: Jakob Friedrich Reimmann, *Systema systematum atheisticorum*

Karlsruhe, Landesbibliothek

Ms. 320,4, Hardt, *Histoire de Bileam*

Paris, Bibliothèque Mazarine

1194, pièce 7, 59–110: *Dissertation sur Moïse où l'on fait voir qu'il est un fourbe et un imposteur*

Rome, Bibliotheca Apostolica Vaticana

Ms. Barb. lat. 2188, fols. 57f.: Vossius to Holstenius, October 8, 1650

Vienna, Österreichische Nationalbibliothek

Ms. 10325: Toland, *Projet d'une dissertation sur la colonne de feu et de nuee des Israelites: dans une lettre à Megalonymus*

Wolfenbüttel

Cod. Extrav. 265.14: *De Josepho Christi parente naturali meditatio*
Cod. Extrav. 157.11: *De Josepho Christi parente naturali meditatio*

Wrocław, Universitätsbibliothek

Cod. IV. oct 49: Stolle, Travel journal 1703/1704
R 766: Gottlieb Stolle, Travel journal

Zurich, Zentralbibliothek

Ms. F 200–206: Estate of Johann Jakob Zimmermann, *Apologia virorum illustrium falso atheismi suspectorum*

Printed Primary Sources

Abano, Pietro d', *Conciliator controversiarum, quae inter philosophos et medicos versantur*, Venice, 1565.
Abbadie, Jacques, *La vérité de la religion chrétienne*, Rotterdam, 1684.
Abū Maʿšar, *Abū Maʿšar on Historical Astrology. The Book of Religions and Dynasties (On the Great Conjunctions)*, ed. and tr. Keji Yamamoto and Charles Burnett, 2 vols., Leiden, 2000.
Adami, Johann Gottlieb, *Gebührende Antwort auf [. . .] U. G. Buchers in seiner Sachsen-Landes Natur-Historie beygefügten Beschuldigung Even Elisabeth Hennigin [. . .]*, Waldenburg, 1724.
Alard, Lambert, *Moses güldenes Kalb nebst dem magischen-astralischen-philoso-phischen absonderlich dem cabalistischen Feuer, vermittelst welchen Moses, der Mann Gottes, dieses güldene Kalb zu Pulver zermalmet, auffs Wasser gestäubet, und den Kindern Israel zu trinken gegeben*, s.l., 1722.
Alberti, Michael (praes.) / Friedrich Brösike (resp.), *De religione medici*, Halle, 1722.
Alsted, Johann Heinrich, *Triumphus biblicus, sive Encyclopaedia Biblica, exhibens triumphum philosophiae, iurisprudentiae et medicinae sacrae itemque sacrae theologiae, quantum illarum fundamenta ex scriptoribus sacris veteris et novi testamenti colliguntur*, Frankfurt, 1625.
    Compendium lexici philosophici, Herborn, 1626.
Amerpoel, Johannes, *Cartesius Mosaizans*, Leeuwarden, 1669.
[Arnauld, Antoine], *Extraict de quelques erreurs et impiétez contenues dans un livre intitulé: "La deffence de la vertu," par le Père Antoine Sirmond, de la Compagnie de Jésus*, s. l., 1641.
[Arpe, Peter Friedrich] *Apologia pro Vanino*, "Cosmopoli" [Rotterdam], 1712.
Arpe, Peter Friedrich, *Feriae aestivales*, Hamburg, 1726.

Aslacius, Conradus, *Ethica Moysaica*, Hanau, 1613.

["Bachimius Denston, Arnoldus," ("Cosmosophus")], *Pansophia enchiretica, seu philosophia experimentali in Academia Mosis primum per sex prima capita Geneseos tradita, demum per ignem examinata & probata*, Nuremberg, 1682.

Baillet, Adrien, *Jugement des savants sur les principaux ouvrages des auteurs*, Paris, 1685–86.

Barbeyrac, Jean, "Preface du Traducteur," in Samuel Pufendorf, *Le droit de la nature et des gens*, Amsterdam, 1706, i–xcii.

Baumgarten, Siegmund Jacob, *Untersuchung theologischer Streitigkeiten [. . .]*, vol. 1, ed. Johann Salomo Semler, Halle, 1762.

Bayle, Pierre, *Pensées diverses sur la comète*, Rotterdam, 1683.

  Dictionnaire historique et critique, Rotterdam, 1697, 2nd edn., 1701.

  Continuation des pensées diverses écrites à un docteur de Sorbonne, à l'occasion de la comete qui parut au mois de Decembre, 1680 [. . .], Rotterdam, 1704.

  Réponse au questions d'un provincial, Rotterdam, 1704.

  Oeuvres diverses, The Hague, 1727; repr. Hildesheim, 1964–1968.

Beaufort, Louis de, *Cosmopoeia divina sive fabrica mundi explicata*, Leiden, 1656.

Becher, Johann Joachim, *Aphorismi ex institutionibus medicis Sennerti*, Frankfurt, 1663.

  Actorum laboratorii chymici Monacensis seu physicae subterraneae libri duo, Frankfurt, 1681.

Becmann, Johann Christoph (praes.) / Johannes SteinhZeuser (resp.), *I. N.D. E. D. N. J. C. Dissertatio Historico-Politica de Iudiciis Dei*, Frankfurt/Oder, June 16, 1669.

  Meditationes politicae, Frankfurt/Oder, 1672.

  Historia orbis terrarum geographica et civilis, Frankfurt, 1673.

  Meditationes politicae XXIV, Frankfurt/Oder, 1679.

  Dissertationum academicarum [. . .] volumen unum, Frankfurt/Oder, 1684.

Bekker, Balthasar, *De betoverde Weereld*, Amsterdam, 1691.

  Die Bezauberte Welt: Oder Eine gründliche Untersuchung Des Allgemeinen Aberglaubens / Betreffend / die Arth und das Vermögen / Gewalt und Wirckung Des Satans und der bösen Geister über den Menschen / Und was diese durch derselben Krafft und Gemeinschafft thun, Amsterdam, 1693; repr. and ed. Wiep van Bunge, Stuttgart, 1997.

Berg, Johann, *Apostolische Regul / Wie man in Religions-Sachen recht Richten solle / Erkläret durch D. Johannem Bergium, Weiland Churfürstl. Brandenburg. Consistorial- Raht und Hoff-Prediger*, Cölln an der Spree, 1695.

Berg, Konrad, *Praxis catholica divini canonis contra quasvis haereses et schismata*, Bremen, 1639.

Beyer, Andreas, *Siclus sacer et regius*, Leipzig, 1667.

  Bibliotheca Historico-Philologico-Theologica, 8 classes in 16 vols., Bremen, 1718–1723

Bibliothek für Kritik und Exegese des Neuen Testaments, vol. 1, part 1 (1796).

Bierling, Friedrich Wilhelm (praes.) / Johann H. Prashuhn (resp.), *De superstitione adhibita tamquam arcano dominationis*, Rinteln, September 20, 1701.

Blasius, Gerard, *Anatome animalium*, Amsterdam, 1681.

Blomberg, William N., *An Account of the Life and Writings of Edmund Dickinson, M. D.*, London, 1737; expanded 2nd edn., 1739.

Blumenbach, Johann F., "Über den Bildungs-Trieb und das Zeugungsgeschäft," *Göttinger Magazin* 1(5) (1780), 247–266.

Bochart, Samuel, *Geographia sacra, in duas partes divisa*, vol. 1: *Phaleg, inscripta, seu de dispersione gentium et terrarum divisione facta in aedificatione turris Babel*; vol. 2: *Chanaan, seu de coloniis et sermone Phoenicium, cum tabulis chronographicis*, Caen, 1646; also Frankfurt, 1681.

Bocrisius, Johann Heinrich, "Apologetica pro subsistentia, immaterialitate et immortalitate animae rationalis" in *Miscellanea Lipsiensia*, vol. 8, Leipzig, 1719.

Boecler, Johann Heinrich, *In Hugonis Grotii Juris belli ac pacis ad illustrissimum Baronem Boineburgium commentatio*, Strasbourg, 1664.

Borrichius, Olaus, *De ortu, et progressu Chemiae, dissertatio*, Copenhagen, 1668.
Hermetis Aegyptiorum et chemicorum sapientia, Copenhagen, 1674.

[Bouhours, Dominique], *Sentiment des Jesuites touchant le peché philosophique*, Paris, 1690.

Boyle, Robert, *The Works of the Honourable Robert Boyle*, 6 vols., ed. Thomas Birch, London, 1772.
A Free Enquiry into the Vulgarly Received Notion of Nature, ed. Edward B. Davis and Michael Hunter, Cambridge, 1996.

Browne, Thomas, *Religio medici*, London, 1642; Latin edn., Leiden, 1644.

Brucker, Jakob, *Historia critica philosophiae*, Leipzig, 1742–1744.

Bucher, Urban Gottfried, *Der Ursprung der Donau in der Landgraffschafft Fürstenberg*, Nuremberg, 1720.
Das Muster eines nützlichen Gelehrten in der Person Herrn Dr. J. J. Becher's, Nuremberg, 1722.
Sachsen-Landes Natur Historie, Pirna 1722.

[Bucher, Urban Gottfried and Johann Baptist Roeschel], *Zweyer Guten Freunde vertrauter Brief-Wechsel vom Wesen der Seelen / Si licet aliis quod lubet dicere, nobis quid lubeat liceat credere. / Sammt eines Anonymi lustigen Vorrede* / The Hague / bey Peter von der Aa, /Anno 1713.

[Bucher, Urban Gottfried and Johann Baptist Roeschel], *Zweyer Guten Freunde vertrauter Brief-Wechsel vom Wesen der Seele. Sammt des Editoris Vorrede und des Autoris näheren Erklärung, wie auch anderweitigen Untersuchung des Wesens der Seele u. des Geiste*, Amsterdam, 1723.

Budde, Johann Franz, *Prudentiae civilis rabbinicae specimen sive R. Isaaci Abarbanelis dissertatio de principatu Abimelechi observationibus illustrate*, Jena, 1693.
De eo, quod abominabilis Deo est, ceu charactere legis moralis, Halle, 1694.
Pineas Zelotes sive De iure Zelotarum in gente Hebraea, Halle, 1694.
Historia juris naturalis and *Synopsis juris naturalis et gentium juxta disciplina ebraeorum*, in Philipp Reinhard Vitriarius, *Institutiones juris naturae et gentium*, Halle, 1695.
Elementa philosophiae practicae, Halle, 1697.

Budde, Johann Franz, (praes.) / Joachim Heinrich Engelbrecht (resp.), *Exercitatio historico-critica de scepticismo morali*, Halle, 1698.

(praes.) / Clamor Johannes Busch (resp.), *Ethicam Chilonis Lacedaemonii*, Halle, 1699.

(praes.) / Clamor Johannes Busch (resp.), *Ethicam Solonis Salaminii [. . .]*, Halle, 1699.

(praes.) / Philipp Wilhelm Busch (resp.), *Ethicam Cleoboli Lindii [. . .]*, Halle, 1699.

(praes.) / Philipp Wilhelm Busch (resp.), *Ethicam Pittaci Mitylenaei*, Halle, 1699.

(praes.) / Carl Gottlob Goldstein (resp.), *Ethicam Thaletis Milesii [. . .]*, Halle, 1699.

(praes.) / Carl Gottlob Goldstein (praes.) / Carl Gottlob Goldstein (resp.), *Leges Solonis cum Mosaicis dissertatione morali conferent atque contendent [. . .]*, Halle, 1699.

(praes.) / Johann Ludwig Stösser (resp.), *Ethicam Periandri Corinthii [. . .]*, Halle, 1699.

Sapientia Veterum, hoc est dicta illustriora septem Graeciae Sapientum, Halle, 1699.

De Spinozismo ante Spinozam, Halle, 1701.

Introductio ad historiam philosophiae Ebraeorum. Accedit dissertatio de haeresi Valentiniana, Halle, 1702.

De Arabicorum Haeresi commentatio, Jena, 1713.

Theses theologicae de atheismo et superstitione, Jena, 1716; also Jena, 1717.

Bull, George, *Opera omnia quibus duo praecipui Catholicae fidei articuli, de S. Trinitate & justificatione. Orthodoxè, perspicuè, ac solidè explanantur, illustrantur, confirmantur; Nunc demum in unum volumen collecta, ac mult. correctius quàm antè, unà cum generalibus Indicibus edita. Contra Danielem Zuickerum, Ejusq; nuperos in Anglia sectatores; Annotata Joannis Ernesti Grabe*, London, 1703.

Burnet, Thomas, *Archaeologiae philosophicae sive Doctrina antiqua de rerum originibus*, London, 1692.

Calov, Abraham, *Scripta anti-Sociniana, quibus haeresis illa pestilentissima non tantum ex ipsis Socinistarum scriptis bona fide detegitur, sed etiam e Scripturis Sacris, haud neglectis antiquitatis ecclesiasticae testimoniis, solide profligatur [. . .]*, Ulm, 1684.

Cämmerer, August Friedrich, *Untersuchung über die Seele*, Leipzig, 1714.

Camus, Jean-Pierre, *Animadversions sur la preface d'un livre intitulé, Deffence de la vertu*, Paris, 1642.

Canz, Israel Gottlieb, *Meditationes philosophiae*, Tübingen, 1750.

Cellarius, Christoph, *Sciagraphia philologiae sacrae*, Jena, 1678.

Chauvin, Pierre, *De naturali religione liber, in tres partes divisus. Ubi falsa candidè refelluntur, vera probantur vel deteguntur, ac Orthodoxarum Ecclesiarum fratres ad concordiam vocantur*, Rotterdam, 1693.

Clarke, Samuel, *A Letter to Mr. Dodwell*, London, 1731.

Cocceji, Heinrich von, *Vita viri perillustris [. . .] Henrici de Cocceji in qua fata ejusdem succinte enarrantur, motae controversiae ordine recensentur, singulaque scripta exacta enumerantur*, Quedlinburg, 1721.

Cocceji, Samuel von, *Introductio ad Henrici De Cocceji Grotivm illustratum: continens dissertationes proeminales XII in quibus principia Grotiana circa jus naturae per totum opus dispersa, ad justam methodum revocantur [. . .]*, Halle, 1748.

Conring, Hermann, *De origine formarum secundum Aristotelem disputatio*, Leiden, 1630.

Introductio in naturalem philosophiam et naturalium institutionum Liber I. Quibus praecipue vera ac Aristotelica, cum philosophandi ratio, tum doctrina de Ortu rerum ex materia, illustratur, Helmstedt, 1638.

De Hermetica Aegyptiorum vetere et Paracelsorum nova medicina, liber unus, quo simul in Hermetis Trismegisti omnia, ac universum cum Aegyptiorum tum Chemicorum doctrinam animadvertitur, Helmstedt, 1648.

Corpus Hermeticum XIII; English tr., intro., and ed. Brian Copenhaver, *Hermetica: The Greek Corpus Hermeticum and the Latin Asclepius in a New English Translation, with Notes and Introduction*, Cambridge, 1995,

Courcelles, Étienne de, *Diatriba de esu sanguinis inter Christianos*, Amsterdam, 1659.

Coward, William, *Second Thoughts concerning Human Soul, 2nd Ed., corrected and Enlarg'd*, London, 1704.

Crause, Johann (praes.) / Georg Erdmann Voigt (resp.), *Exercitium academicum de Josepho et Maria salvatoris parentibus*, Jena, 1667.

[Crell, Samuel], *Tractatus tres; quorum qui prior Ante-Nicenismus dicitur; is exhibet testimonia patrum Ante-Nicenorum: In quibus elucet sensus Ecclesiae Primaevo-catholicae, quoad articulum de Trinitate. In secundo brevis responsio ordinatur, ad D. G. Bulli defensionem Synodi Niccenae. Auctore Gilberto Clerke, Anglo. Argumentum postremi: Vera et antiqua fides de divinitate Christi, explicata et asserta, contra D. Bulli Iudicium Ecclesiae Catholicae etc. Per Anonymum*, s.l., 1695.

Cogitationum novarum de Primo & Secundo Adamo [. . .] compendium, s.l., 1700.

Kurtze and einfältige Untersuchung, ob and warum die Reformierte Evangelische Kirche die also genannten Sozinianer mit gutem Gewissen dulden oder auch in ihre Gemeinschaft aufnehmen könne oder solle, s.l., 1700.

[Crell, Samuel, "Lucas Mellier"], *Fides primorum christianorum ex Barnaba, Herme, et Clemente Romano demonstrata*, London, 1697.

Crinto, Pietro, *De honesta disciplina libri XXV*, Florence, 1504.

Cudworth, Ralph, *The True Intellectual System of the Universe*, London, 1678; repr. Hildesheim, 1977.

Cunaeus, Petrus, *De republica Hebraeorum libri III*, Leiden, 1617.

Cymbalum mundi sive Symbolum Sapientiae, critical edition, ed. Guido Canziani, Winfried Schröder, and Francisco Socas, Milan, 2000.

Daillé, Jean, *La Foy fondée sur les Saintes Escritures, Contre les nouvelles methodistes*, 2nd edn., Charenton, 1661.

Daneau, Lambert, *Physica Christiana*, Geneva, 1588.

Dickinson, Edmund, *Delphi phoenicizantes*, Oxford, 1655.

Physica vetus & vera, sive tractatus de naturali veritate hexaemeri Mosaici, London 1702.

[Diderot, Denis], "Mosaïque ou Chrétienne Philosophie," in *Encyclopédie*, vol. 10, Neuchâtel, 1765, 741–745.

Dietrich, Johann Gottlob (praes.) / Gottfried Klemm (resp.), *Dissertatio physica de anima brutorum*, Wittenberg, 1704.

Diodorus Siculus, *Bibliotheca historica; Diodorus of Sicily*, ed. and tr. F. R. Walton, Loeb Classical Library, Cambridge, MA, 1967.

Diogenes Laertius, *Lives of Eminent Philosophers*, ed. and tr. C. D. Yonge, London, 1905.

Lives of the Eminent Philosophers, ed. and tr. Robert Drew Hicks, Cambridge, MA, 1925.

Edelmann, Johann Christian, *Abgenötigtes, jedoch andern nicht wiederaufgenötigtes Glaubens-Bekenntnis*, s.l., 1746; repr. Stuttgart, 1969.

Sechs Briefe an Georg Christoph Kreyssig, ed. Philipp Strauch, Halle, 1918.

"Moses mit aufgedecktem Angesichte, 5. Anblick," in *Sämtliche Schriften*, vol. 7(2), ed. Monika Ammermann-Estermann (general ed. Walter Grossmann), Stuttgart, 1987.

[Edelmann, Johann Christian], *Extract aus einer von Euander übersetzten und mit Anmerkungen herausgegebenen Handschrift unter dem Titel Von den Betrügereyen der Religionen*, Berlin *1761*, Ms. 6728 of the University Library Wrocław, in [Johann Joachim Müller], *De imposturis religionum (De tribus impostoribus). Von den Betrügereyen der Religionen. Dokumente*, critical edition, ed. and commentary Winfried Schröder, Stuttgart, 1999.

Elswich, Johann Hermann von (praes.) / Johann Sigismund Buchwald (resp.), *Controversiae de atheismo recentiores*, Wittenberg, 1716.

Recentiores de anima controversae, Wittenberg, 1717.

Elwall, Edward, *The supernatural incarnation of Jesus Christ proved to be false [. . .]. And that our Lord Jesus Christ, was the real son of Joseph and Mary*, London, 1742.

Engelschall, Christian Gottfried, *De praejudiciis vitae*, Dresden, 1724.

Epiphanius, *Panarion*, Book III, cap. 78, (Adversus Haereses) tr. Frank Williams, Nag Hammadi and Manichaean Studies 79, 2nd edn., Leiden, 2013.

Erbauliche Gedancken über D. Nicol. Hieron. Gundlings Otia / So Von einem Liebhaber der Warheit wohlmeinend Dem Leser und sonderlich dem Herrn Doctori hiermit eröffnet werden, Nuremberg, 1706.

Esprit de Spinosa, s.l., *1719*; ed. in the *Traktat über die drei Betrüger*, ed. Winfried Schröder, Hamburg, 1992.

Fabricius, Johann Albert, *Bibliotheca graeca*, 14 vols., Hamburg, 1705–1728.

Felbinger, Jeremias, *Politicae Christianae compendium*, Wrocław, [ca. 1648].

Das Neue Testament, aus dem Griechischen ins Teutsche übersetzet, Amsterdam, 1660.

Feuerlein, Jakob Wilhelm (praes.) / V. H. Regenfus (resp.), *Dissertatio philosophica de philosophia Adami putativa*, Altdorf 1715.

(praes.) / V. H. Regenfus (resp.), *De Adami logica, metaphysica, mathesi, philosophia practica, et libris*, Altdorf, 1717.

Filesac, Jean, *De idololatria magica, dissertatio*, Paris, 1609.

De idolatria politica et legitimo principis cultu commentarius, Paris, 1615.

Fischer, Christian Gabriel, *Quaestio philosophica, an spiritus sint in loco? Ex principiis rationis scientificiae resoluta*, Königsberg 1723; repr. Königsberg, 1740.

[Fischer, Christian Gabriel], *Vernünftige Gedanken von der Natur, was sie sey: daß sie ohne Gott und seine allweise Beschränkung unmächtig sey, und wie die einige unmittelbare göttliche kraft in und durch die Mittelursachen, nach dem Maaß ihrer verliehenen Wirkbarkeit oder Tüchtigkeit, hie in der Welt alles allein thätig wirke; durch fleißiges Nachsinnen, Ueberlegen und Schließen gefasset, und zur Verherrlichung göttlicher Majestät, auch Förderung wichtiger Wahrheiten, herausgegeben von einem Christlichen [i.e., Christian] Gottes [Gabriel] Freunde [Fischer]*, s.l., 1743.

Fludd, Robert, *De utriusque cosmi [. . .] historia*, Oppenheim, 1617.

Fortgesetzte Sammlung von alten und neuen theologischen Sachen, Leipzig, 1720–1750.

Fragmenta pseudepigraphorum quae supersunt graeca una cum historicum et auctorum judaeorum hellenistarum fragmentis, ed. Albert-Marie Denis, Leiden 1970.

Galenus, Claudius, "Quod animi mores corporis temperamentum sequantur," in *Opera omnia*, vol. 4, ed. Karl Gottlob Kühn, Leipzig, 1821–1833, 767–822.

Garcia, Carlos, *Anthipathia Gallorum et Hispanorum, Das ist Angebohrne Wider-Artigkeit der Frantzosen und Spannier gegen einander. Nachsinnig beschrieben in Spannischer Sprach von Herrn Dr. Carlo Garzia. In das Italianische versetzt von Clodio Vilopoggio. Auß disem der eyferigen Teutschen Nation zur Nachricht so lustig als nützlich zulesen ins Teutsch gantz neu verfertigt und gedruckt*, Regensburg, 1701.

Gassendi, Pierre, *Exercitationes paradoxicae adversus Aristoteleos*, Grenoble, 1624.

Animadversiones in decimum librum Diogenis Laertii qui est de vita, moribus, placitisque Epicuri, Lyon, 1649.

Opera omnia, Lyon, 1658.

Gerhard, Johann Ernst (praes.) / Johann Vogelhaupt (resp), *Ritus foederum gentis Ebreae*, Wittenberg, 1650.

Glauber, Johann Rudolf, *De auri tictura sive auro potabile vero*, Amsterdam, 1646.

Goelicke, Andreas Ottomar, *Hippocrates ab atheismi crimine nuper ipsi imputato absolvitur*, Halle, 1713.

Defensio pro Hippocrate entheo opposite declaratione sententiae de atheismo Hippocratis Nic. Hier. Gundling denuo suscepta, Duisburg, 1714.

Historia medicinae universalis, vol. 5, Frankfurt, 1719.

Goetten, Gabriel W., *Das jetzt lebende Europa*, vol. 3, Braunschweig, 1737.

Grotius, Hugo, *De jure belli ac pacis*, Paris, 1625; ed. Johann F. Gronovius, Amsterdam, 1702.

Gruber, Daniel, ed., *Commercii epistolici Leibnitiani prodromus*, 2 vols., Hanover and Göttingen 1745.

Guenther, Gotthard, *Schediasma historico dogmaticum de anima*, Leipzig, ca. 1706.

Gundling, Nikolaus Hieronymus, *Historia philosophiae moralis*, Halle, 1706.

Otia, 3 parts, Halle, 1705–1707.

"Hobbesius ab Atheismo liberatus," in *Observationum selectarum ad rem litterariam spectantium*, vol. 1, Halle, 1707, 37–77.

"Plato atheos," *Neue Bibliothec* 31 (1713), 1–31.

"Declaratio suae de atheismo Hippocratis sententiae," *Neue Bibliothec* 29 (1713), 802–818.

Via ad Veritatem, Halle, 1713.

Gundlingiana, Halle, 1715–1728.

Ausführlicher Discours über den jetzigen Zustand der europäischen Staaten, Frankfurt and Leipzig, 1733.

Vollständige Historie der Gelahrtheit, 5 vols., Frankfurt and Leipzig, 1734–1736.

"Brief an . . .Heumann," in *Satyrische Schriften*, Jena and Leipzig, 1738.

Philosophischer Discourse anderer und dritter als letzter Theil, oder Academische Vorlesungen über seine Viam ad Veritatem moralem und Kulpisii Collegium Grotianum nebst nöthigen kurzen Anmerckungen und zulänglichen Registern, Frankfurt and Leipzig, 1740.

Ausführlicher Discours über das Natur- und Völkerrecht, Frankfurt and Leipzig, 1747.

Hardt, Hermann von der, *Epistola ad Paulum Martinum Noltenium de vocatis ab Adamo animalibus*, s.l., 1705.

Histoire de Bileam; Renards de Samon; Machoire d'Ane; Corbeus d'Elie; L'antichrist, [Helmstedt], 1707.

Aenigmata prisci orbis. Jonas in luce in Historia Manassis et Josiae, ex eleganti veterum Hebraeorum stilo solutum aenigma, 1723.

Harrington, Thomas, *The Commonwealth of Oceana*, London, 1656; 1771; repr. and ed. J. G. Pocock, Cambridge, 1992.

Hase, Theodor (preas.) / Rudolph W. Boclo (resp.), *De gentilium philosophis atheismi falso suspectis*, Bremen, 1716.

Heber, Georg Michael, *In ambiguarum legum interpretatione criterium veritatis non dari*, Wittenberg, 1700.

Heidanus, Abraham, *De origine erroris libri VIII*, Amsterdam, 1678.

Helmont, Franciscus Mercurius van, *Seder olam sive Ordo saeculorum, historia enarratio doctrinae*, s.l., 1693.

Hempel, Christian Friedrich, "Umständliches Leben und Schrifften, Collegia, Studia, Inventa und eigene Meinungen," in Nikolaus Hieronymus Gundling, *Vollständige Historie der Gelahrtheit*, vol. 5, Frankfurt and Leipzig, 1736.

Hennig, Georg Ernst Sigmund, "Leben des Professors Fischer in Königsberg," *Preußisches Archiv* 1 (1790), pp. 312–333.

Heresbach, Conrad, *Epitome jurisprudentiae Christianae*, Neustadt, 1586.

Hering, Daniel Heinrich, *Beiträge zur Geschichte der Evangelisch-Reformierten Kirche in den Preußisch-Brandenburgischen Ländern*, vol. 2, Wrocław, 1785.

Hermann Landgraf von Hessen, *Teutsche Astrologia oder Teutscher Discurss von allerhand astrologischen Spekulationen*, Grebenstein, 1637.

Historia Meteorologica. Das ist Vier und zwanzig Jährige eigentliche und trewfleissige Observation [. . .] durch Uranophilum Cyriandrum, Kassel, 1651.

Herrn von Hofmannswaldau und andrer Deutschen auserlesene und bißher ungedruckte Gedichte, vol. 4, Glückstadt, 1704.

Herzog, Johann Chr., *Sciagraphia philosophiae practicae Apollonii Thyanei*, Leipzig, 1709.

Heumann, Christoph August, *Der Politische Philosophus*, Frankfurt and Leipzig, 1714.

"Von der Philosophie der Patriarchen," in *Acta Philosophorum, das ist: Gründl. Nachrichten aus der Historia Philosophica, Nebst beygefügten Urtheilen von denen dahin gehörigen alten und neuen Büchern*, Issue 5, Halle, 1716, 755–809; Issue 6, Halle, 1716, 925–943.

Hobbes, Thomas, *Elementorum Philosophiae sectio tertia, De cive*, Paris, 1642.

Leviathan, London, 1651; ed. C. B. Macpherson, London, 1968.

Hocheisen, Johann Georg, *Dissertationum physicarum quibus elementicolae Comte de Gabalis examinantur, dissertatio prior, dissertatio posterior*, Wittenberg, 1705.

Hochstetter, Andreas Adam, *Collegium Puffendorfianum super libris duobus de officio hominis et civis*, Tübingen, 1710.

Hoffmann, Friedrich, *De officio boni theologi ex idea boni medici*, Halle, 1702.

Oratio de Atheo convincendo ex artificiosissima machinae humanae structura, Halle, 1705.

(praes.) / Thomas Kennedy (resp.), *Dissertatio inauguralis physico-moralis de temperamento fundamento morum et morborum in gentibus*, Halle, 1705.

(praes.) / Urban Gottfried Bucher (resp. et auctor), *Leges naturae in corporum productione et conservatione*, Halle, 1707.

Hoffmann, Johannes, *Deorum gentilium praecipuorum origines [. . .]*, Jena, 1674.

Holbach, Paul-Henri Thiry, Baron d', *Le Christianisme devoilé*, "Londres" [Nancy], 1761; Amsterdam, 1767.

Hollmann, Samuel Christian (praes.) / Adrian Gottlieb Söhner (resp.), *Dissertatio prior de stupendo mysterio anima humana sibi ipsi ignota*, Greifswald, 1722; expanded Wittenberg 1724; Göttingen, 1750.

Hottinger, Johann Heinrich, *Historia orientalis quae ex variis orientalium monumentis collecta*, Zurich, 1651.

Huet, Pierre-Daniel, *Demonstratio evangelica*, Paris, 1679.

Alnetanae quaestiones de concordia rationis et fidei, Paris, 1693.

"Lettre de Mr. Morin de l'Academie des Inscriptions à Mr. Huet, ancien Evèque d'Avranches, touchant le livre de Mr. Tollandus Anglois, intitulé 'Adeisidaemon et Origines Judaicae,'" *Memoires pour l'Histoire des Sciences et des beaux Arts* 34 (1709), p. 1601.

Iamblichus, *De vita Pythagorae & protrepticae orationes ad philosophiam libri II*, ed. Johannes Arcerius Theodoretus Frisius, [Heidelberg], 1598.

Jöcher, Christian Gottlieb, *Allgemeines Gelehrten-Lexicon*, Leipzig, 1750.

Josephus, Flavius, *Contra Apionem*; in *Flavii Josephi opera*, vol. 7, ed. Benedikt Niese, Berlin 1892.

Against Apion, tr. and ed. John M. G. Bardlay, Leiden, 2013.

Journal des Savans [Sçavans, Savants], Paris, 1665–1792.

Journal de Trévoux, Trévoux (Dombes), 1701–1782.

[Kayser, Johann Friedrich], *De eo, quod θεῖον est in disciplinis*, Halle, 1715.

Kircher, Athanasius, *Oedipus Aegyptiacus*, 3 vols., Rome, 1652–1654.

Kirchmaier, Georg Kaspar, *De imperio antediluvianorum*, Wittenberg, 1660.

Knorr von Rosenroth, Christian, ed., *Kabbala denudata*, Sulzbach, 1677–1684; repr. Hildesheim, 1974.

Küster, Georg Gottfried, *Marchiae litteratae specimen tertium*, Berlin, 1743.

L'âme matérielle, ed. Alain Niderst, Paris, 1973.

La Croze, Mathurin Veyssière de, *Thesaurus epistolicus Lacrozianus*, ed. Ludwig Uhl, Leipzig, 1742–1744.

La Mothe le Vayer, François de, *Discours de la contrarieté d'humeurs qui se trouve entre de certaines nations, et singulierement entre la Francoise et l'Espagnole: traduit de l'Italien de Fabricio Campolini Veronois*, Paris, 1636.

De la vertu des païens, Paris, 1642; also in Jacques Prévot, ed., *Libertins du XVIIe siècle*, vol. 2, Paris, 2004.

De la vertu des payens, seconde édition augmentée, Paris, 1647.

Oeuvres, Paris, 1650.

Cinq dialogues faits a limitation des Anciens, ed. Ludwig Martin Kahle, Berlin, 1747.

[La Peyrère, Isaac], *Praeadamitae sive Exercitatio super versibus duodecimo, decimo tertio et decimo quarto capitis quinti Epistolae D. Pauli ad Romanos, quibus inducuntur Primi Homines ante Adamum conditi*, s.l., 1655.

Lactantius Firmianus, Coelius, *Divinae institutiones*, in *Opera omnia quae extant*, ed. Servatius Gallaeus, Leiden, 1660.

Lafitau, Joseph François, *Moeurs des sauvages amériquains comparées aux moeurs des premiers temps*, Paris, 1724.

Lamy, Guillaume, *Discours anatomiques de M. Lamy [. . .] Avec des Reflexions sur les Objections qu'on luy a faites contre la maniere de raisonner de la nature de l'Homme & de l'usage des parties qui le composent, et cinq Lettres du mesme Autheur, sur le sujet de son Livre*, Rouen, 1675.

Le Clerc, Daniel, *Histoire de la Médecine*, Geneva, 1696, Amsterdam, 1702.

Le Clerc, Jean, ["Liberius de Sancto Amore"], *Epistolae theologicae, in quibus Varii Scholasticorum errores castigantur*, s.l., 1679.

Logica, ontologia et pneumatologia, London, 1692.

Ars critica, Amsterdam, 1697.

Le Mercier, Jean, *In Genesin commentarius*, Geneva, 1598.

Leeuwenhoek, Antonius van, *Arcana naturae detecta*, Delft, 1695.

Lefebvre, Tanneguy, *Tanaquilli Fabri epistolae*, Saumur, 1665; 2nd edn., Rome, 1674.

Leibniz, Gottfried Wilhelm, *Die philosophischen Schriften*, ed. Carl Gerhardt, Berlin, 1875–1890; repr. Hildesheim, 1978.

Lelong, Jacques, *Discours historique sur les principales éditions des Bibles Polyglottes*, Paris 1713.

Liber Toldos Jeschu, in Christoph Wagenseil, ed., *Tela ignea Satanae*, Altdorf, 1681, separate pagination: 1–24.

Limborch, Philipp van, *Theologia christiana ad praxin pietatis ac promotionem pacis Christianae unice directa*, Amsterdam, 1686.

De veritate religionis christianae amica collatio cum erudito Judaeo, Gouda, 1687.

Historia vitae Simonis Episcopii scripta a Philippo a Limborch e Belgico in Latinum sermonem versa, et ab auctore aliquot in locis aucta, Amsterdam, 1701.

Lipmann Mühlhausen, Yom-Tov, *Liber Nizachon Rabbi Lipmanni: Conscriptus anno a Christo nato M.CCC.XCIX. diuque desideratus. Accessit tractatus de usu librorum Rabbinicorum, prodromus apologiae pro Christianis adversus Lipmannum triumphantem*, Nuremberg, 1644.

[Lloyd, David], *Wonders No Miracles*, London, 1666.

Locke, John, *Le Gouvernement Civil, Oder die Kunst Wohl zu Regieren Durch den berühmten Engelländer Jean Lock Beschrieben (translator anon.)*, s.l., 1691.

An Essay concerning Human Understanding, Oxford, 1975.

Loen, Johann Michael von, "Ausbildung des Professor G.," in *Gesammlete kleine Schriften*, 1st part, 4th edn., Frankfurt and Leipzig, 1753, p. 218.

Loescher, Valentin E. (praes.) / G. E. Habbius (resp.), *Deismus fanaticorum aliquot praenotationibus theologicis expensus*, Wittenberg, February 1, 1708.

Praenotationes theologicae contra naturalistarum et fanaticorum omne genus [. . .] custodiendae, Wittenberg, 1708; Wittenberg, 1713.

Ludovici, Carl Günther, *Ausführlicher Entwurf einer vollständigen Historie der Wolffischen Philosophie*, Leipzig, 1737/1738.

Luzzatto, Simone, *Discorso circa il stato de gl'Hebrei*, Venice, 1638.

Machiavelli, Nicolo, *Discorsi sopra la prima deca di Tito Livio*, Rome, 1531; English tr., Harvey C. Mansfield and Nathan Tarcov, *Discourses on Livy*, Chicago, 1996.

Il Principe, 1st edn., Rome, 1532; English tr., William J. Connell, The Prince with Related Documents, Boston, 2005; 2nd edn., 2016.

Magirus, Johannes, *Anthropologia*, Frankfurt, 1603.

Maier, Michael, *Atalanta fugiens, hoc est, Emblemata nova de secretis naturae chymica*, Oppenheim, 1618.

Maimonides, Moses, *More nebuchim, sive Liber Doctor perplexorum*, Basel, 1629.

De idololatria, Amsterdam, 1641.

Guide for the Perplexed, tr. M. Friedländer, 4th edn., New York and London, 1904.

Majus, Johann Heinrich, *Dissertatio de Mose philosopho*, in *Theses selectae ex antiqua et recentiore philosophia deprompta*, Gießen, 1707.

Menage, Gilles, *Amoenitates juris civilis*, Frankfurt and Leipzig, 1680; first published in 1668.

Menagiana, ou les bons mots, les pensées critiques, historiques, morales et d'Erudition de Monsieur Ménage, recueillies par ses amies, 4 vols., Paris, 1715.

Menasseh Ben Israel, *Conciliator*, Amsterdam, 1633.

De creatione problemata XXX, Amsterdam, 1635.

Mitternacht, Johann Sebastian, *De nativitatis Dominicae anno*, Leipzig, 1659.

Moller, Daniel Wilhelm (praes.) / Georg Schwindel (resp.), *Dissertatio inauguralis, quam de Mose philosopho [. . .] submittet [. . .]*, Altdorf, 1707.

Montagu, Richard, *Analecta ecclesiaticarum exercitationum*, London, 1622.

Montanus, Benedictus Arias, *Phaleg, sive De gentium sedibus primis*, Antwerp, 1572.

[Montfaucon, Nicolas-P. Villars de], *Le Comte de Gabalis, ou entretiens sur les sciences secretes*, Amsterdam, 1670.

More, Henry, *Conjectura cabalistica*, London, 1653.

Triplicis Cabbalae Defensio, in *Opera omnia*, London, 1679, vol. 2(2); repr. Hildesheim 1966.

Morhof, Daniel Georg, *Theologia gentium politica*, Rostock, 1661.

Polyhistor, in tres tomos literarium, philosophicum et practicum, divisus. Opus posthumum, ut multorum Votis satisfieret, accurate revisum, emendatum [. . .] a Johanne Möllero, Lübeck, 1708.

[Mosheim, Johann Lorenz and Allvoerden, Heinrich von] *Historia Michelis Serveti*, Helmstedt, 1727.

Müller, Gottfried Polycarp, *Dissertatio pro loco gemina de mente substantia, a corpore essentialiter diversa*, Leipzig, 1714.

[Müller, Johann Joachim] *De imposturis religionum (De tribus impostoribus). Von den Betrügereyen der Religionen. Dokumente*, critical edition, ed. and commentary Winfried Schröder, Stuttgart, 1999.

Nachrichten von den neuesten theologischen Büchern, vol. 3 (1743).

Naudé, Gabriel, *Apologie pour tout les personnages qui sont esté faussement soupçonnez de Magie*, Paris, 1625.

Neumann, Johann G. (praes.) / Johann G. Hocheisen (resp. et auctor), *Disputatio theologica qua Deismum in Theosophia deprehensum [. . .] publice sistit [. . .]*, Wittenberg, March 8, 1709.

Nitsche, Georg, *Beantwortung der Frage: Ob die heilige Schrifft GOtt sey?*, Gotha, 1714.

Observationes selectae, Halle, 1700–1705.

[Oelven, Christoph Heinrich], *Monatliche Curieuse Natur- Kunst- Staats- und Sitten-Praesenten*, Berlin, 1708.

Overton, Richard, *Man Wholly Mortal,* London, 1655.

Purité de la vie et de la mort. La "Réponse" du médicin Gaultier, ed. Olivier Bloch, Oxford, 1993.

Pasch, Georg, *De novis inventis*, Leipzig, 1700.

Patrizi, Francesco, *Zoroaster et eius CCCXX oracula chaldaica*, Ferrara, 1591 (separately published in Patrizi's *Nova de universis philosophia*, Ferrara, 1591).

[Perières, Bonaventure des], *Cymbalum mundi en francoys, Contenant quatre Dialogues Poetiques, fort antiques, ioyeux, & facetieux*, Paris, 1537.

Pfanner, Tobias, *Systema theologiae gentilis*, Basel, 1679.

Pfeiffer, August, *Pansophia Mosaica e Genesi delineata*, Leipzig, 1685.

Philo Alexandrinus, *Ueber die Weltschöpfung nach Moses*, in *Die Werke Philos von Alexandria in deutscher Übersetzung*, vol. 1, ed. Leopold Cohn, Wrocław, 1909.

De vita Mosis, in *Les oeuvres de Philon d'Alexandrie*, vol. 22, ed. Roger Arnaldez et al., Paris, 1967.

Photios, "Contra Manichaeos," in Johann Christoph Wolf, ed., *Anecdota Graeca sacra et profana*, 4 vols., Hamburg, 1722–1724, vol. 1, 1–298 and vol. 2, 1–283.

Pineda, Juan de, *Ad suos in Salomonem commentarios / Salomon Praevius, sive De rebus Salomonis Regis libri octo*, Venice, 1611.

Pithou, Pierre, *Collatio legum Mosaicorum et Romanorum*, London, 1660.

Planer, Johann A. (praes.) / M. E. Wendius (resp.), *Novam de animae humanae propagatione sententiam [. . .] publice tuebitur [. . .]*, Wittenberg, 1712.

Catalogus Bibliothecae J. B. Roeschelii, Wittenberg, 1713.

Plato, *The Works of Plato*, tr. Benjamin Jowett, 4 vols., Oxford, 1871; rev. edn. New York, 1937.

Poiret, Pierre, *De eruditione solida, superficiaria et falsa*, Amsterdam, 1692.

Pomponazzi, Pietro, *De naturalium effectuum causis, sive de incantationibus*, Basel, 1567; critical edition, ed. Vittoria Perrone Compagni, Florence, 2011.

Abhandlung über die Unsterblichkeit der Seele, Hamburg, 1990.

Porphyrios, *De abstinentia*, in Arthur A. Long and David N. Sedley, *Die hellenistischen Philosophen: Texte und Kommentare*, Stuttgart, 2000.

[Preuß, Johann and Bartholomäus Stosch?], *Duae considerationes vocum, terminorum ac phrasium, quae in doctrinâ trinitatis a theologis usurpantur, & quâ ratione lis circa doctrinam de trinitate mitigari possit ac debeat. conscripta a veritatis et pacis studioso, ut doctoribus occasio detur planiora et pleniora in eandem sententiam commentandi*, "Cosmopolis," s.d.

Prideaux, Humphrey, *The True Nature of Imposture Fully Displayed in the Life of Mahomet*, London, 1697.

[Priestley, Joseph], *The Triumph of Truth; being an account of the trial of E[dward] E[lwall] for Heresy and Blasphemy at Stafford Assizes. [Written by himself.] [. . .] To which are added extracts from some other pieces of Mr. E.'s, concerning the Unity of God [. . .] By the author of an appeal to the [. . .] professors of Christianity*, Leeds, 1771.

Przypkowski, Samuel, *Cogitationes sacrae ad initium Evangelii Mathaei et omnes epistolas apostolicas nec non tractatus varii argumenti praecipue de iure Christiani Magistratus [. . .]*, "Eleutheropolis" [Amsterdam], 1692.

Pufendorf, Samuel, *Elementorum jurisprudentiae universalis libri II*, Cambridge, 1672.

Specimen controversiarum circa ius naturale ipsi nuper notarum, Uppsala, 1677.

Briefwechsel, ed. Detlef Döring (*Gesammelte Werke* vol. 1), Berlin, 1996.

Rachel, Samuel, *In universam Aristotelis philosophiam moralem introductio*, Helmstedt, 1660.

"Prolegomena, in M. Tullii Ciceronis De officiis libros tres, quibus natura honesti, aliaque ad jus natura," in Cicero, *De officiis libri III*, Frankfurt and Kiel, 1668.

De jure naturae at gentium dissertationes, Kiel, 1676.

De jure naturae et gentium dissertationes, ed. Ludwig von Bar, tr. John Pawley Bate, 2 vols., Washington, D.C., 1916.

Reimmann, Jakob Friedrich, *Historia universalis atheismi et atheorum falso et merito suspectorum*, Hildesheim, 1725; repr. ed. Winfried Schröder, Stuttgart, 1992.

Catalogus Bibliothecae Theologicae Systematico-Criticus, Hildesheim, 1731.

[Reimmann, Jakob Friedrich], "Nescire animalia rationalia quid sit anima rationalis," in *Observationes selectae*, Additimentum (1705), Obs. XIV, 354–389.

Reinkingk, Dietrich, *Biblische Policey, Das ist: Gewisse, auß Heiliger, Göttlicher Schrifft zusammengebrachte [. . .] Axiomata und Schlußreden*, Frankfurt, 1653.

Rosenbach, Zacharias, *Moses omniscius, sive Omniscientia Mosaica*, Frankfurt a. M., 1632.

Roth-Scholz, Friedrich, ed., *Deutsches Theatrum Chemicum*, Part 1, Nuremberg, 1728.

Rüdiger, Andreas, *De usu et abusu terminorum technicorum in philosophia*, Leipzig, 1700.

Philosophia synthetica methodo mathematicae aemula comprehensa, Leipzig 1707.

Physica divina, recta via, eademque inter superstitionem et atheismum media ad utramque hominis felicitatem, naturalem atque moralem ducens, Frankfurt, 1716.

Ryssel, Johann Jacob, *De historia et prudentia historica tractatus criticus ubi ea, quae ad rem spectant historicam, succincte declarantur*, Leipzig, 1690.

Saint-Evremont, Charles de, *Oevres meslées*, Paris, 1695.

Sand, Christoph, *Nucleus historiae ecclesiasticae exhibitus in historia Arianorum*, [Amsterdam], 1668; 1776.

Tractatus de origine animae, "Cosmopoli," 1671.

Saubert, Johann, *De sacrificiis veterum*, Jena, 1659.

Palaestra theologico-philologica, Nuremberg, 1678.

[Scaliger, Joseph Justus], *Prima Scaligeriana, nusquam antehac edita, cum praefatione T. Fabri*, Utrecht, 1670.

Schacher, Polycarp Gottlieb (pares.) / R. A. Behrens (resp.), *Dissertatio de consideratione animae rationalis medica*, Leipzig, 1720.

Schede, Elias, *De diis Germanis, sive Veteri Germanorum, Gallorum, Britannorum, Vandalorum religione, syngrammata quatuor*, Amsterdam, 1648.

Schellhammer, Günter Christoph, *De natura libri tres*, Kiel, 1697.

Natura sibi et medicis vindicata sive de natura liber bipartitus, Kiel, 1697.

Naturae vindicatae vindicatio, Kiel, 1702.

Scherzer, Johann Adam, *Trifolium orientale: continens commentarios R. Abarbenelis in Haggaeum, R. Sal. Jarchi in Parsch. I. Geneseos, et R. mos. Majemonidae theologiam [. . .]*, Leipzig, 1663.

Schnell, Sebald, *Setira al-Ledat Yeshu we-alsbe-ba'u kulam le-Gehinnom Hoc Est Numerus IIX Spectans cap. 2 Genes. vs. 17 Arcani libri Nitzachon*, Altdorf, 1643.

Schurtzfleisch, Conrad Samuel, *Epistolae nunc primum editae*, Wittenberg, 1700.

Seidel, Christoph Matthäus, *Ausspruch der alten jüdischen Kirche wider die Unitarier, in dem Streite von der Dreyeinigkeit und Gottheit unsers Erlösers*, Berlin, 1707.

Selden, John, *De diis Syris syntagma*, London, 1617; 1621.

    De jure naturali et gentium iuxta disciplinam Ebraeorum libri VII, London 1640.

    De jure naturali et gentium, Strasbourg, 1665.

    De diis Syris syntagmata II, Leipzig, 1672; Amsterdam, 1680.

    De successionibus ad leges Ebraeorum in bona functorum, Frankfurt/Oder, 1673.

    De successione in pontificatum, Frankfurt/Oder, 1673.

    Uxor Ebraica, Frankfurt/Oder, 1673; new edn., 1695; Wittenberg, 1712.

    De jure naturali, Frankfurt/Oder, 1695; repr. Wittenberg, 1712.

Sennert, Daniel, *Hypomnemata physica*, Frankfurt, 1636.

Simon, Richard, *Histoire critique du texte du Nouveau Testament*, Rotterdam, 1689.

Simonis Simonii Lucensis, primum Romani, tum Calviniani, deinde Lutherani, denuo Romani, semper autem Athei summa religio, Kraków, 1588.

Sirmond, Antoine, *La deffense de la vertu*, Paris, 1641.

Solger, Adam Rudolph, *Bibliotheca sive supellex librorum impressorum in omni genere scientiarum maximam partem rarissimorum*, vol. 3, Nuremberg, 1763.

Souverain, Jacques, *Le platonisme dévoilé ou Essai touchant le verbe platonicien*, "Cologne," 1700; modern edn., ed. Sylvain Matton, Paris, 2004.

[Souverain, Jacques], *Platonism unveil'd*, London, 1700.

    Lettre à Mr*** touchant l'apostasie, edité par Sylvain Matton et présentée par Élisabeth Labrousse avec une étude de Martin Mulsow, Paris and Milan, 2000.

Sozzini, Fausto, *Opera. Bibliotheca Fratrum Polonorum*, vol. 1, Amsterdam, 1668.

Spencer, John, *De legibus Hebraeorum ritualibus, et earum rationibus*, Cambridge, 1685; The Hague, 1686; Leipzig, 1705; Tübingen, 1728.

Spener, Philipp Jakob, *Vertheidigung des Zeugnisses von der Ewigen Gottheit Unsers HErrn JESU CHRISTI, als des Eingebohrnen Sohns vom Vater [. . .] Sowohl Gegen den Angriff seiner hievon gehaltenen Predigten / welche hier mit beygedruckt sind / als auch am meisten gegen Enjedinum, Freyherrn von Wollzogen / Jer. Felbinger / Jo. Preussen / u. a. In den letzten Jahren seines Lebens verfasset und kurtz vor seinem seel. Ende geschlossen / so nun an das öffentliche Licht gestellet wird / Sampt einer Vorrede Pauli Antonii*, Frankfurt a. M., 1706.

Spinoza, Baruch de, *Tractatus theologico-politicus*, "Hamburg," 1670; German: *Theologisch-politischer Traktat*, ed. Günter Gawlick, Hamburg, 1984.

    Ethica, in *Opera posthuma*, s.l., 1677.

    The Chief Works of Benedict de Spinoza, tr. and intro. R. H. M. Elwes, London, 1883.

    Die Ethik, German tr. von Jakob Stern, Stuttgart, 1977.

Spinoza, Benedict de, *Theological-Political Treatise*, tr. and ed. Jonathan Israel and Michael Siverthorne, Cambridge, 2007.

Sprengel, Kurt, *Apologie des Hippokrates und seiner Grundsätze*, Leipzig, 1789.

Stahl, Georg Ernst (praes.) / Johann Andreas Wendt (resp.), *De mutatione temperamenti*, Halle, 1712.

[Stahl, Georg Ernst], "Aristotelis error circa definitionem naturae," in *Observationes selectae* 3 (1701).

Stanley, Thomas, *Historia philosophiae orientalis*, Leipzig, 1711.

Stigel, Johann, *De anima, commentarii clarissimi atque doctissimi viri, D. Philippi Melanchthonis, explicata*, Wittenberg, 1581.

Stolle, Gottlieb (praes.), Laurentius Hagemann (resp.), *Quaestio historico-philosophica, an Homerus fuerit philosophus moralis*, Jena, 1712.

Anleitung zur Historie der Gelahrheit, Jena, 1736.

Tagebuch, ed. Gottschalk E. Guhrauer, in *Allgemeine Zeitschrift für Geschichte* 7 (1847).

Eine Reise durch die Gelehrtenrepublik. Gottlieb Stolles Journal der Jahre 1703/4, ed. Martin Mulsow, Wiesbaden, 2018.

Stosch, Friedrich Wilhelm, *Concordia Rationis et Fidei, Sive Harmonia Philosophiae Moralis & Religionis Christianae*, "Amstelodami," 1692; repr. ed. Winfried Schröder, Stuttgart, 1992.

Stosch, Melchior Friedrich von, *Genealogia des Hoch-Gräflich Freyherrlich- und Hoch-Adelichen Geschlechts derer von Stosch*, Leipzig/Wrocław, 1736.

Strimesius, Samuel, *Praxiologia apodictica seu Philosophia moralis demonstrativa, Pithanologiae Hobbesianae opposita*, Frankfurt/Oder, 1677.

Origines morales, seu Dissertationes aliquot selectiores, vera moralium fundamenta complexae, Frankfurt/Oder, 1679.

Strodtmann, Johann Christoph, ed., *Beiträge zur Historie der Gelahrtheit*, vol. 1, Hamburg, 1748.

Stubbe, Henry, *The Miraculous Conformist*, Oxford, 1666.

[Stübel, Andreas], *Aufgefangene Brieffe, welche zwischen etzlichen curieusen Personen über den jetzigen Zustand der Staats- und gelehrten Welt gewechselt worden*, Wahrenberg, 1699–1703.

Der neubestellte Agent von Haus aus, mit allerhand curieusen Missiven, Brieffen, Memorialien, Staffeten, Correspondencen und Commissionen, nach Erforderung der heutigen Staats- und gelehrten Welt, "Wahrmund" [i.e., Groschuff in Leipzig], 1704–1709.

Der mit allerhand Staats- Friedens- Kriegs- Hof- Literatur- und Religions- wie auch Privat-Affairen beschäfftigte Secretarius und dessen der heutigen curiösen Welt zur galanten Wissenschafft ertheilete ... Expedition, 1710–1719.

Sturm, Johann Christoph (praes.) / Leonhard Christoph Riederer (resp.), *De ipsa natura*, Altdorf, 1682.

Physica electiva, hoc est, exercitationes academicae, Altdorf, 1685.

Philosophia eclectica, Altdorf, 1686.

Idolum naturae, similiumque nominum vanorum ex hominum Christianorum animis deturbandi conatus philosophicus sive de naturae agentis, tum universalis, tum particularis aliorumque cognatorum quasi numinum superstitiosis erronicisque conceptibus dissertatio, Altdorf, 1692.

Swift, Jonathan, *A Tale of a Tub and Other Works*, ed. Marcus Walsh, Cambridge, 2010.

Symbolum sapientiae, see *Cymbalum mundi*.

Telesio, Bernardino, *De rerum natura iuxta propria principia*, Rome, 1586; critical edition, ed. Luigi de Franco, *De rerum natura libri VII–VIII–IX*, Florence, 1976.

[Teufel, Christian], *Delicatissimum Salomoneum Epithalamium in gratiam tanti Israelitar. regis ante tot secula cantatum, nunc in gratiam gloriamque serenissimi principis ac domini D. Frederici Wilhelmi et Don. Sophiae Dorotheae [. . .] cum auspiciatissimum inirent matrimonium*, s.l., 1706.

The judgment of the Fathers touching the Doctrine of the Trinity, London, 1695.

Theodoret of Cyrus, *Operum tomus*, Paris, 1684.

    Theophrastus redivivus, ed. Guido Canziani and Gianni Paganini, 2 vols., Florence, 1981–1982.

Thilo, Johann Ludolf, *Gedanken über die Frage, ob die Seelen in der triumphierenden Kirche auch besonders für die hinterlassenen Angehörigen beten*, Gotha, 1714.

Thomasius, Christian, *Schediasma historicum, quo occasione definitionibus vetustae, qua philosophia dicitur Γνῶσις τῶν ὄντων varia discutiuntur ad historiam tum philosophicam tum ecclesiasticam pertinentia*, Leipzig, 1665.

    Introductio ad philosophiam aulicam, Leipzig, 1688.

    Institutiones jurisprudentiae divinae, Frankfurt and Leipzig, 1688.

    Lustiger und Ernsthaffter Monats-Gespräche Erster Theil: in sich begreifend Die sechs ersten Monate des 1688, Saalfeld, 1688

    Ausübung der Vernunftlehre, Halle, 1691

    Einleitung zur Vernunftlehre, Halle, 1691.

    Weitere Erleuterung durch unterschiedene Exempel [. . .] das Wesen aus der Menschen Gemüther zu erkennen, Halle, 1692.

    Historia sapientiae et stultitiae, 2 parts, Halle, 1693.

    De naevis jurisprudentiae romanae antejustinianeae libri duo, Halle, 1695.

    Außübung der Sitten-Lehre, Halle, 1696.

    Versuch vom Wesen des Geistes, Halle 1699.

    Fundamenta juris naturae et gentium, Halle, 1705.

    Briefwechsel. Historisch-kritischen Edition, vol. 1: 1679–1692, ed. Frank Grunert, Matthias Hambrock, and Martin Kühnel with the collaboration of Andrea Thiele, Berlin and Boston, 2017.

    Briefwechsel. Historisch-kritischen Edition, vol. 2: 1693–1698, ed. Frank Grunert, Matthias Hambrock, and Martin Kühnel, Berlin and Boston, 2020.

[Thomasius, Christian], "De scholis antediluvianis," in *Observationes selectae*, vol. 1, Halle, 1700, Obs. IXX.

    Summarischer Nachrichten [. . .] Ein und zwanzigstes Stück, Halle and Leipzig, 1717.

Thomasius, Jakob (praes.) / Johann Vake (resp.), *Disputatio physica de origine animae humanae*, Leipzig, 1669.

    (praes.) / J. F. Hekel (resp.), *Theses philosophicae, quas de quaestione: An Deus sit materia prima?*, Leipzig, 1672.

Thumm, Theodor (praes.) / Bernhard Wildersin (resp.), *Controversia de traduce sive de ortu animae rationalis*, Tübingen, 1622.

Toland, John, *Letters to Serena*, London, 1704; German tr. Günter Wichmann, *Briefe an Serena*, Berlin, 1959.

Origines Judaicae, The Hague, 1709; Italian edn., ed. and tr. Alfredo Sabetti, *Adeisidaemon e origines judaicae*, Naples, 1984, with an introduction: "Un difficile messaggio di liberazione: l'Adeisidaemon e le Origines Judaicae di John Toland," pp. 7–54.

Nazarenus, Or, Jewish, Gentile, and Mahometan Christianity, London, 1718; new edn., ed. Justin Champion, Oxford, 1999.

"Clidophorus, Or of the Exoteric and Esoteric Philosophy," in *Tetradymus*, London, 1720.

Hodegus, or the Pillar of Cloud and Fire, London, 1720.

Traité des trois imposteurs, French and German edn., ed. and tr. Winfried Schröder, *Traktat über die drei Betrüger*, Hamburg, 1992.

Triller, Daniel Wilhelm, *Diss. inaug. med. (praes. Fr. Hoffmanno) de pinguedine seu succo nutritio superfluo*, Halle, 1718.

Hippocrates atheismi falso accusatus contra virum ampl. D. Nicol. Hieron. Gundlingium, Rudolstadt, 1719; repr. in *Opuscula medica ac medico philologica*, vol. 2, Frankfurt and Leipzig, 1766.

Tschirnhaus, Ehrenfried Walter von, *Medicina mentis*, Leipzig, 1695.

Unschuldige Nachrichten von alten und neuen theologischen Sachen, Leipzig, 1707–1719.

Vallés, Francisco, *De iis quae scripta sunt phisice in libris sacris seu de sacra philosophia*, Turin, 1587.

Vanini, Lucilio [Giulio Cesare], *De admirandis naturae reginae deaeque mortalium arcanis, libri quatuor*, Paris, 1616.

Venturini, Carl, *Natürliche Geschichte des großen Propheten von Nazaret*, "Bethlehem" [Copenhagen], 1800.

Verdries, Johann Melchior, *De aequilibrio mentis et corporis commentatio*, Frankfurt, 1726.

Vico, Giambattista, *Principi di una scienzia nuova intorno alla natura delle nazioni*, Naples, 1744.

La Scienza Nuova, ed. Fausto Nicolini, Bari, 1913.

Villemandy, Pierre de, *Scepticismus debellatus seu humanae cognitionis ratio: ab imis redicibus explicata; eiusdem certitudo adversus Scepticos quosque veteres ac novos invicte asserta; facilis ac tuta certitudinis jujus obtinendae methodus praemonstrata*, Leiden, 1697.

Voetius, Gisbert, *Selectarum disputationum theologicarum*, Utrecht, 1648.

Voltaire, *Dictionnaire philosophique*, Geneva, 1764.

Dictionnaire philosophique, ed. Bertram Schwarzbach, Oxford, 1995.

Vossius, Gerhard Johannes, *De theologia gentili et physiologia christiana, sive De origine et progressu idololatriae*, Amsterdam, 1641; complete edn., Amsterdam, 1668.

Wachter, Johann Georg, *Der Spinozismus im Jüdenthumb, oder Die von dem heutigen Jüdenthumb und dessen Geheimen Kabbala vergötterte Welt*, Amsterdam, 1699; repr. ed. Winfried Schröder, Stuttgart, 1994.

"Leben Johann George Wachters," *Bibliothek der schönen Wissenschaften und der freyen Künste* 9 (1763), 160–171.

Wagenseil, Johann Christoph, ed., *Tela ignea Satanae. Hoc est: Arcani, & horribiles Judaeorum adversus Christum Deum, & Christianam religionem libri anekdotoi,* Altdorf, 1681.

[Wagner, Gabriel], Realis de Vienna, *Prüfung des Versuchs Vom Wesen des Geistes / den Christian Thomas / Prof. in Halle / 1699. An Tag Gegeben,* s.l., 1707.

Walch, Johann Georg, *Philosophisches Lexicon,* Leipzig, 1726.

Warburton, William, *The Divine Legation of Moses Demonstrated on the Principles of a Religious Deist, from the Omission of the Doctrine of a Future State of Reward and Punishment in the Jewish Dispensation,* London, 1738–1741; 2nd edn., London, 1778.

Weitere Fortsetzung der Erbaulichen Gedancken über D. Nicol. Hieron. Gundlings Otia / Worinne desselben seltsame Aufführung und schlechte Beantwortung der Einwürffe / so wider den 1. Theil der Otiorum gemachet worden / denen Liebhabern der Wahrheit aufrichtig gezeiget werden, s.l., 1709.

Wolf, Christian, *Disputatio zoologica de lupo et lycanthropia,* Wittenberg, 1666.

Wolf, Johann Christoph (praes) / Peter Adolph Boysen (resp.), *De atheismi falso suspectis,* Wittenberg, 1717.

   Curae philologicae et criticae, vol. 1, Hamburg, 1725.

   Bibliotheca Hebraea, 4 vols., Hamburg, 1715–1733.

Wolff, Christian, *Christian Wolffs eigene Lebensbeschreibung,* ed. (with an essay on Wolff) Heinrich Wuttke, Leipzig, 1841.

Wolzogen, Johann Ludwig von, *Christliche Unterweisung, wie diejenige Oerter der Schrift, welche die heutigen Christen insgemein zu Behauptung der Drey-Persöhnlichkeit des einigen und allein wahren Gottes mißbrauchen, schriftmäßig zu verstehen seyn,* s.l., 1684.

Zanchius, Hieronymus, *De operibus Dei intra spacium sex dierum creatis opus,* Neustadt, 1591.

Zedler, Johann Heinrich, *Großes vollständiges Universal-Lexicon aller Wissenschafften und Künste,* Leipzig, 1732–1754.

Zentgraff [or Zentgrav], Johannes Joachim, *De origine, veritate et immutabili rectitudine juris naturalis secundum disciplinam Christianorum,* Strasbourg, 1678.

Zepper, Wilhelm, *De legibus Mosaicis forensibus,* Herborn, 1614.

Ziegler, Caspar, *In Hugonis Grotii De jure belli ac pacis libros, quibus naturae et gentium jus explicavit, notae et animadversiones subitariae,* Wittenberg, 1666.

   Notae et animadversiones subitariae [. . .] in Hugonis Grotii De jure belli ac pacis, Wittenberg, 1666.

Secondary Sources

Ahnert, Thomas, *Religion and the Origins of the German Enlightenment: Faith and the Reform of Learning in the Thought of Christian Thomasius,* Rochester, 2006.

Ahrbeck, Hans, "Einige Bemerkungen über 'Mosaische Philosophen' des 17. Jahrhunderts," *Wissenschaftliche Zeitschrift der Martin-Luther-Universität Halle-Wittenberg* 7(5) (1958), 1047–1050.

Aichele, Alexander, "Von der Fiktion zur Abstraktion. Nikolaus HieronymusGundling über mögliche Urteilssubjekte anhand seiner Auseinandersetzung mit Dadino Alteserras Begriff der persona ficta," *Archiv für Rechts- und Sozialphilosophie* 96 (2010), 516–541.

"Was kann die Philosophie für die Jurisprudenz tun? Eine Antwort am Beispiel des Problems der Zurechnungs- und Schuldf.higkeit von Gesellschaften zwischen Immanuel Kant, Nikolaus Hieronymus Gundling und Samuel Stryk," in Kristian Kühl, ed., *Zur Kompetenz der Rechtsphilosophie in Rechtsfragen. Akten der IVR-Tagung 2008*, Wiesbaden, 2010, 31–51.

Albrecht, Michael, *Eklektik. Eine Begriffsgeschichte mit Hinweisen auf die Philosophie- und Wissenschaftsgeschichte*, Stuttgart, 1994.

Almond, Philipp C., *Heaven and Hell in Enlightenment England*, Cambridge, 1994.

Anastassiou, Anargyros, review of Robert Joly: *Hippocrate*, vol. XIII, Paris, 1978, *Gnomon* 52 (1980), 309–311.

Angelis, Simone de, *Anthropologien. Genese und Konfiguration einer "Wissenschaft vom Menschen" in der Frühen Neuzeit*, Berlin, 2010.

Araujo, Marcelo de, "Hugo Grotius, Moral Scepticism and the Use of Arguments in Utramque Partem," *Veritas: Revista de Filosofia da PUCRS* 56 (2011), 145–166.

Arndt, Johannes, *Herschaftskontrolle durch Öffentlichkeit. Die publizistische Darstellung politischer Konflikte im Heiligen Römischen Reich (1648–1750)*, Göttingen, 2013.

Arnswaldt, Albrecht von, *De Vicariatus controversia. Beiträge Hermann Conrings in der Diskussion um die Reichsverfassung des 17. Jahrhunderts*, Berlin, 2004.

Asselt, Willem, *The Federal Theology of Johannes Coccejus (1603–1669)*, Leiden, 2001.

Assmann, Aleida and Jan Assmann, eds., *Hieroglyphen*, Munich, 2003.

Assmann, Jan, *Moses the Egyptian: The Memory of Egypt in Western Monotheism*, Cambridge, MA, 1988.

Tod und Jenseits im Alten Ägypten, Munich, 2001.

Religio duplex. Ägyptische Mysterien und europäische Aufklärung, Berlin, 2010.

Badaloni, Nicola, *Introduzione a G. B. Vico*, Milan, 1961.

Introduzione a Vico, Bari, 1984; 1999.

Badran, Muhammad Abū al-fadl, "... denn die Vernunft ist ein Prophet. Zweifel bei Abū l-Alā al-Ma'arri," in Friedrich Niewöhner and Olaf Pluta, eds., *Atheismus im Mittelalter und in der Renaissance*, Wiesbaden, 1999, 61–84.

Bainton, Roland H., *Hunted Heretic: The Life and Death of Michael Servetus, 1511–1553*, Boston, 1953.

Baku, Georg, "Der Streit um den Naturbegriff am Ende des 17. Jahrhunderts," *Zeitschrift für Philosophie und philosophische Kritik* 98 (1891), 162–190.

Baldi, Marialuisa, ed., *"Mind Senior to the World."* *Stoicismo e origenismo nella filosofia platonica del Seicento inglese*, Milan, 1996.

Ball, Brian, *The Soul Sleepers: Christian Mortalism from Wycliffe to Priestley*, Cambridge 2008.

Bareau, Michel, ed., *Carlos Garcia, La oposición y conjunción de los dos grandes luminares de la tierra; O la Antipatia de los Franceses y los Españoles (1617)*, Edmonton, Alberta, 1979.

Barnes, Annie, *Jean Le Clerc (1657–1736) et la République des Lettres*, Paris, 1938.

Barth, Hans Martin, *Atheismus und Orthodoxie. Analysen und Modelle christlicher Apologetik im 17. Jahrhundert*, Göttingen, 1971.

Bartuschat, Wolfgang, *Spinozas Theorie des Menschen*, Hamburg, 1992.

Battafarano, Italo Michele, "Epitaphia ioco-seria. Loredano und Hallmann," in Alberto Martino, ed., *Beiträge zur Aufnahme der italienischen und spanischen Literatur in Deutschland im 16. und 17. Jahrhundert*, Amsterdam and Atlanta, 1990, 133–150.

"(Scherz-) Grabschriften bei Opitz," in Barbara Becker-Cantarino and Jörg-Ulrich Fechner, eds., *Opitz und seine Welt*, Amsterdam, 1990, 21–36.

Bauer, Barbara, "Der Fortschritt in der deutschen Physik. Jakob Friedrich Reimmann, ein Vorläufer der Hypothese von Frances Yates," in Martin Mulsow and Helmut Zedelmaier, eds., *Skepsis, Providenz, Polyhistorie. Jakob Friedrich Reimmann (1668–1743)*, Tübingen, 1998, 148–174.

Baur, Jörg, *Die Vernunft zwischen Ontologie und Evangelium. Eine Untersuchung zur Theologie Johann Andreas Quenstedts*, Gütersloh, 1962.

Beaude, Joseph, "Amplifier le dixième trope, ou la différence culturelle comme argument sceptique," *Recherches sur le XVIIe siècle* 5 (1982), 21–29.

Bell, Rudolph M., *How to Do It: Guides to Good Living for Renaissance Italians*, Chicago and London, 1999.

Beller, Manfred, *Eingebildete Nationalcharaktere*, Göttingen, 2006.

Bellingradt, Daniel and Bernd-Christian Otto, *Magical Manuscripts in Early Modern Europe: The Clandestine Trade in Illegal Book Collections*, London, 2017.

Ben-Tov, Asaph, "Helmstedter Hebraisten," in Jens Bruning and Ulrike Gleixner, eds., *Das Athen der Welfen. Die Reformuniversität Helmstedt, 1576–1810*, Wolfenbüttel, 2010, 224–231.

"Pagan Gods in Late Seventeenth- and Eighteenth-Century German Universities: A Sketch," in Ben-Tov, Yaakov Deutsch, and Tamar Herzig, eds., *Knowledge and Religion in Early Modern Europe: Studies in Honor of Michael Heyd*, Leiden, 2012, 153–178.

Benítez, Miguel, *La face cachée des lumières*, Paris, 1994.

La cara oculta de las luces: investigaciones sobre los manuscritos filosóficos clandestinos de los siglos XVII y XVIII, Valencia, 2003.

Benz, Ernst, *Emanuel Swedenborg: Naturforscher und Seher*, Munich, 1948; 2nd edn., Zurich, 1969.

Berkowitz, David Sandler, *John Selden's Formative Years: Politics and Society in Early Seventeenth-Century England*, London, 1988.

Berman, David, "Die Debatte über die Seele," in Jean-Pierre Schobinger, ed., *Die Philosophie des 17. Jahrhunderts: 3 England*, Basel, 1988, 759–781.

Berti, Silvia, "At the Roots of Unbelief," *Journal of the History of Ideas* 56 (1995), 555–575.

Betray, Johannes, *Die Akkommodationstheorie des P. Matteo Ricci S. J. in China*, Analecta Gregoriana 76, Rome, 1955.

Beutel, Albrecht "Causa Wolffiana. Die Vertreibung Christian Wolffs aus Preußen 1723 als Kulminationspunkt des theologisch-politischen Konflikts zwischen Pietismus und Aufklärungsphilosophie," in Ulrich Köpf, ed., *Wissenschaftliche Theologie und Kirchenleitung*, Tübingen, 2001, 159–202.

Bianchi, Lorenzo, *Tradizione libertina e critica storica. Da Naudé a Bayle*, Milan, 1988.

Rinascimento e libertinismo. Studi su Gabriel Naudé, Naples, 1996.

Bienias, Lukasz, "Über Schmiegelisten. Schmiegel und Meseritz als Wirkungsorte polnischer und deutscher Antitrinitarier am westlichen Rande der Adelsrepublik Polen-Litauen im 16. und 17. Jahrhundert," in Martin Mulsow, ed., *Kriminelle – Freidenker – Alchemisten. Räume des Untergrunds in der Frühen Neuzeit*, Cologne, 2014, 61–80.

Blair, Ann, "Mosaic Physics and the Search for a Pious Natural Philosophy in the Late Renaissance," *Isis* 91 (2000), 32–58.

Bloch, Marc, *Les rois thaumaturges*, Paris, 1924; English tr., J. E. Anderson, *The Royal Touch: Sacred Monarchy and Scrofula in England and France*, London, 1973.

Bloch, Olivier, *La philosophie de Gassendi. Nominalisme, matérialisme et métaphysique*, The Hague, 1971.

Blom, Hans, "Sociability and Hugo Grotius," *History of European Ideas* 41 (2015), 589–604.

Blom, Hans and Laurens Winkel, eds., *Grotius and the Stoa*, Assen, 2004.

Bloom, Harold, *The Anxiety of Influence: A Theory of Poetry*, New York, 1973.

Bömelburg, Hans-Jürgen, "Konfession und Migration zwischen Brandenburg-Preußen und Polen-Litauen, 1640–1722. Eine Neubewertung," in Joachim Bahlcke, ed., *Glaubensflüchtlinge. Ursachen, Formen und Auswirkungen frühneuzeitlicher Konfessionsmigranten in Europa*, Berlin, 2008, 119–144.

Bonanate, Ugo, *Charles Blount. Libertinismo e deismo nel Seicento inglese*, Florence, 1972.

Bondì, Roberto, *L'onnipresenza di Dio. Saggio su Henry More*, Soveria Mannelli, 2001.

Borghero, Carlo, "Scepticism and Analysis: Villemandy as a Critic of Descartes," in Gianni Paganini, ed., *The Return of Scepticism: From Hobbes and Descartes to Bayle*, Dordrecht, 2003, 213–229.

Borinski, Karl, *Balthasar Gracian und die Hofliteratur in Deutschland*, Halle, 1894.

Borst, Arno, *Der Turmbau von Babel. Geschichte der Meinungen über Ursprung und Vielfalt der Sprachen und Völker*, Stuttgart, 1957–1963.

Bourdieu, Pierre, *Homo academicus*, Frankfurt, 1988.

Bowersock, Glen W., *Hellenism in Late Antiquity*, Ann Arbor, 1990.

Brambach, Wilhelm, *Gottfied Wilhelm Leibniz: Verfasser der Histoire de Bileam: mit Vollständigem Abdruck der Histoire de Bileam in der von Leibniz gebilligten Form*, Leipzig, 1887.

Bremmer, Jan N., "Atheism in Antiquity," in Michael Martin, ed., *The Cambridge Companion to Atheism*, Cambridge, 2006, 11–26.

Breymayer, Reinhard, "Pietistische Rhetorik als eloquentia nov-antiqua. Mit besonderer Berücksichtigung Gottfried Polycarp Müllers (1684–1747)," in Berd Jaspert and Rudolf Mohr, eds., *Traditio – Krisis – Renovatio aus theologischer Sicht*, Marburg, 1976, 258–272.

Briggs, Eric R., "Les manuscrits de Charles Le Cène (1647?–1703) dans la Bibliothèque de la Huguenot Society of London," *Tijdschrift voor de studie van de verlichting* 5 (1977), 358–378.

Brooke, Christopher, *Philosophic Pride. Stoicism and Political Thought from Lipsius to Rousseau*, Princeton, 2012.

Brosch, Josef, ed., *Jungfrauengeburt gestern und heute*, Essen, 1969.

Brown, Harcourt, "Un cosmopolite du grand siècle: Henri Justel," *Bulletin de la Société de l'histoire du protestantisme français: études, documents, chronique littéraire* (1933), 187–201.

Buck, August, ed., *Die okkulten Wissenschaften in der Renaissance*, Wiesbaden, 1992.

Bugaj, Roman, *Michał Sędziwój (1566–1636): Życie i Pisma*, Wrocław, 1968.

Buhr, Manfred and Otto Finger, "Zweyer guten Freunde vertrauter Brief-Wechsel vom Wesen der Seelen," in Gottfried Stiehler, ed., *Beiträge zur Geschichte des vormarxischen Materialismus*, Berlin (East), 1961, 124–138.

Burke, Peter, *Kultureller Austausch*, Frankfurt, 2000.

The Fabrication of Louis XIV, New Haven, 1992.

Burman, Thomas E., *Reading the Qur'ān in Latin Christendom, 1140–1560*, Philadelphia, 2007.

Burnett, Stephen G., *From Christian Hebraism to Jewish Studies: Johannes Buxtorf (1564–1629) and Hebrew Learning in the Seventeenth Century*, Leiden, 1996.

Burns, Norman T., *Christian Mortalism from Tyndale to Milton*, Cambridge, MA, 1972.

Caminiti Pennarola, Lea, "La correspondance Ménage-Huet, un dialogue à distance," in Suzanne Guellouz, ed., *Pierre Daniel Huet (1630–1721). Actes du colloque de Caen (12–13 nov., 1993)*, Seattle, Tübingen, PFSCL 94 (= *Biblio* 17, n°. 83), 141–154.

Campenhausen, Hans von, *Die Jungfrauengeburt in der Theologie der alten Kirche*, Heidelberg, 1962.

Canziani, Guido, "La critica della civiltà nel Theophrasus redivivus. II. Ordine naturale e legalità civile," in Tullio Gregory et al., eds., *Ricerche su letteratura libertina e letteratura clandestina nel Seicento*, Florence, 1981, 83–118.

Capéran, Louis, *Le problème du salut des Infidèles. Essai historique*, Paris, 1912.

Capitani, Pietro, *Erudizione e scetticismo in François de La Mothe le Vayer*, Florence, 2009.

Cariou, Pierre, *Pascal et la casuistique*, Paris, 1993.

Caruso, Sergio, *La miglior legge di regno. Consuetudine, diritto naturale e contratto nel pensiero e nell'epoca di John Selden (1584–1654)*, 2 vols., Milan, 2001.

Cataldi Madonna, Luigi, "Wissenschafts- und Wahrscheinlichkeitsauffassung bei Thomasius," in Werner Schneiders, ed., *Christian Thomasius*, Hamburg, 1989, 115–136.

Cavaillé, Jean-Pierre, *Dis/simulations. Jules-César Vanini, François La Mothe le Vayer, Gabriel Naudé, Louis Machon et Torquato Accetto. Religion, morale et politique au XVIe siècle*, Paris, 2002.

"The Italian Atheist Academics: A Myth of the French pre- Enlightenment?, in Friedrich Vollhardt, ed., *Religiöser Nonkonformismus und frühneuzeitliche Gelehrtenkultur*, Berlin, 2013, 39–50.

Ceglia, Francesco Paolo de, "Hoffmann and Stahl: Documents and Reflections on the Dispute," *History of Universities* 22 (2007), 115–168.

Cervenka, Jaromir, *Die Naturphilosophie des Johann Amos Comenius*, Prague, 1970.

Champion, Justin A. I., *"The Pillars of Priestcraft Shaken": The Church of England and its Enemies, 1660–1730*, Cambridge, 1992.

"Legislators, impostors, and the politic origins of religion: English theories of imposture from Stubbe to Toland," in Silvia Berti, Françoise Charles-Daubert and Richard H. Popkin, eds., *Heterodoxy, Spinozism, and Free Thought in Early-Eighteenth-Century Europe*, Dordrecht, 1996, 333–356.

Republican Learning: John Toland and the Crisis of Christian Culture, 1696–1722, Manchester, 2003.

Choulant, Johann Ludwig, *Bibliotheca medico-historica*, Leipzig, 1842.

Chwolson, Daniil W., *Die Ssabier und der Ssabismus*, St. Petersburg, 1856; repr. Cambridge, 2011.

Cioranescu, Alexandre, *Bibliografie de la littérature française du 18e siècle*, vol. 3, Paris, 1969.

Cohen Rosenfield, Leonora, *From Beast-Machine to Man-Machine. The Theme of Animal Soul in French Letters from Descartes to La Mettrie*, Oxford, 1940.

Collier, Katherine Brownell, *Cosmogonies of Our Fathers. Some Theories of the 17th and 18th Centuries,* New York, 1934.

Cooper, Alix, *Inventing the Indigenous. Local Knowledge and Natural History in Early Modern Europe*, Cambridge, 2007.

Coors, Michael, *Scriptura efficax. Die biblisch-dogmatische Grundlegung des theologischen Systems bei Johann Andreas Quenstedt. Ein dogmatischer Beitrag zu Theorie und Auslegung des biblischen Kanons als Heiliger Schrift*, Göttingen, 2009.

Corbin, Alain, *The Foul and the Fragrant. Odor and the French Social Imagination*, tr. Miriam Kochan, Roy Porter, and Christopher Prendergast, Cambridge, MA, 1986.

Coudert, Allison P., *The Impact of the Kabbalah in the Seventeenth Century. The Life and Thought of Francis Mercury van Helmont (1614–1698)*, Leiden, 1999.

Coudert, Allison P., and Jeffrey S. Shoulsen, ed., *Hebraica Veritas? Christian Hebraists and the Study of Judaism in Early Modern Europe*, Philadelphia, 2004.

Crombie, Alistair C., *Styles of Scientific Thinking in the European Tradition*, London 1994.

Czelinski-Uesbeck, Michael, *Der tugendhafte Atheist. Studien zur Vorgeschichte der Spinoza-Renaissance*, Würzburg, 2007.

Daniélou, Jean, *Philon d'Alexandrie*, Paris, 1958.

Message évangelique et culture hellénistique aux 2e et 3e siècles, Paris, 1961.

"Les traditions secrèts des apôtres," *Eranos Jahrbuch* 31 (1962), 199–215.

Darmstaedter, Ernst, "Zur Geschichte des Aurum potabile," *Chemiker-Zeitung* 48 (1924), 653–655 and 678–680.

Daugirdas, Kestutis, *Andreas Volanus und die Reformation im Großfürstentum Litauen*, Mainz, 2009.

Die Anfänge des Sozinianismus. Genese und Eindringen des historisch-ethischen Religionsmodells in den universitären Diskurs der Evangelischen in Europa, Göttingen, 2016.

Daxelmüller, Christoph, *Disputationes curiosae. Zum "volkskundlichen" Polyhistorismus an den Universitäten des 17. und 18. Jahrhunderts*, Würzburg, 1979.

Der kleine Pauly, Munich, 1979.

Deventer, Jörg, "Nicht in die Ferne – nicht in die Fremde? Konfessionsmigration im schlesisch-polnischen Grenzraum im 17. Jahrhundert," in Joachim Bahlcke, ed., *Glaubensflüchtlinge. Ursachen, Formen und Auswirkungen frühneuzeitlicher Konfessionsmigranten in Europa*, Berlin, 2008, 95–118.

Döhring, Erich, "Cocceji, Heinrich Freiherr von," *Neue Deutsche Biographie* 3 (1957), 300f.

Döring, Detlef, *Pufendorf-Studien. Beiträge zur Biographie Samuel von Pufendorfs und zu seiner Entwicklung als Historiker und theologischer Schriftsteller*, Berlin, 1992.

Frühaufklärung und obrigkeitliche Zensur in Brandenburg: Friedrich Wilhelm Stosch und das Verfahren gegen sein Buch "Concordia rationis et fidei," Berlin, 1995.

Die Philosophie Gottfried Wilhelm Leibniz' und die Leipziger Aufklärung in der ersten Hälfte des 18. Jahrhunderts, Stuttgart, 1999.

Dreitzel, Horst, *Politischer Aristotelismus und absoluter Staat. Die "Politica" des Henning Arnisaeus*, Wiesbaden, 1970.

"Zur Entwicklung und Eigenart der eklektischen Philosophie," *Zeitschrift für historische Forschung* 18 (1991), 281–343.

"A Strange Marriage: Pufendorf's Natural Jurisprudence and Protestant Moral Philosophy in Early Enlightenment," Lecture given in Scotland on October 19, 1996.

"Hobbes-Rezeptionen. Zur politischen Philosophie der frühen Aufklärung in Deutschland," in Hans-Erich Bödeker, ed., *Strukturen der deutschen Frühaufklärung 1680–1720*, Göttingen, 2008, 263–308.

"Von Melanchthon zu Pufendorf: Versuch über Typen und Entwicklung der philosophischen Ethik im protestantischen Deutschland zwischen Reformation und Aufklärung," in Martin Mulsow, ed., *Spätrenaissance-Philosophie in Deutschland, 1570–1650. Entwürfe zwischen Humanismus und*

Konfessionalisierung, okkulten Traditionen und Schulmetaphysik, Tübingen, 2009, 321–398.

Droge, Arthur J., *Homer or Moses? Early Christian Interpretations of the History of Culture*, Tübingen, 1989.

Dunkelgrün, Theodor, *The Multiplicity of Scripture: The confluence of textual traditions in the making of the Antwerp Polyglot Bible (1568–1573)*, Dissertation, Chicago, 2012.

Eamon, William, *Science and the Secrets of Nature*, Princeton, 1994.

Eijk, Philip van der, "The theology of the Hippocratic treatise On the Sacred Disease," in *Medicine and Philosophy in Classical Antiquity. Doctors and Philosophers on Nature, Soul, Health and Disease*, Cambridge, 2005, 45–73.

Eisenstein, Elisabeth, *The Printing Press as an Agent of Change: Communications and Cultural Transformations in Early Modern Europe*, Cambridge, 1979.

Ellis, Mark A., *Simon Episcopius' Doctrine of Original Sin*, New York, 2005.

Encyclopaedia Judaica. Das Judentum in Geschichte und Gegenwart, vol. 9, Berlin, 1932.

Ersch, Johann Samuel and Johann Gottfried Gruber, *Allgemeine Encyclopädie der Wissenschaften und Künste*, Leipzig, 1850.

Ess, Josef van, *Theologie und Gesellschaft im 2. und 3. Jahrhundert Hidschra. Eine Geschichte des religiösen Denkens im frühen Islam*, vol. 4, Berlin, 1997.

Feil, Ernst, *Religio. Die Geschichte eines neuzeitlichen Grundbegriffs*, vol. 1, Göttingen, 1986; vol. 2, Göttingen, 1997; vol. 3. Göttingen, 2001; vol. 4, Göttingen, 2007.

Ferreyrolles, Gérard, *Les Provinciales de Pascal*, Paris, 1984.

Findlen, Paula, ed., *Athanasius Kircher – the Last Man who knew Everything*, New York, 2004.

Fiorillo, Vanda and Frank Grunert, eds., *Das Naturrecht der Geselligkeit. Anthropologie, Recht und Politik im 18. Jahrhundert*, Berlin, 2009.

Fischer, Ernst, "Patrioten und Ketzermacher. Zum Verhältnis von Aufklärung und lutherischer Orthodoxie in Hamburg am Beginn des 18. Jahrhunderts," in Wolfgang Frühwald and Alberto Martino, eds., *Zwischen Aufklärung und Restauration. Sozialer Wandel in der deutschen Literatur (1700–1848). Festschrift für Wolfgang Martens*, Tübingen, 1989, 17–47.

Fix, Andrew, *Prophecy and Reason. The Dutch Collegiants in the Early Enlightenment*, Princeton, 1991.

Fleischmann, Stefan, *Szymon Budny*, Cologne, 2006.

Florack, Ruth, *Tiefsinnige Deutsche, frivole Franzosen. Nationale Stereotype in deutscher und französischer Literatur*, Stuttgart, 2001.

Fock, Otto, *Der Socinianismus nach seiner Stellung in der Gesamtentwicklung des christlichen Geistes, nach seinem historischen Verlauf und nach seinem Lehrbegriff*, Kiel, 1847.

Frank, Günter, *Die theologische Philosophie Philipp Melanchthons*, Hildesheim, 1995.
   "Philipp Melanchthons Liber de anima und die Etablierung der frühnuzeitlichen Anthropologie," in Michael Beyer and Günther Wartenberg, eds., *Humanismus und Wittenberger Reformation*, Leipzig, 1996, 313–327.

Fränkel, Hermann, *Dichtung und Philosophie des frühen Griechentums*, Munich, 1962.

Frantz, David O., *Festum Voluptatis. A Study of Renaissance Erotica*, Columbus, OH, 1989.

Frei, Hans, *The Eclipse of Biblical Narrative. A Study in Eighteenth and Nineteenth Century Hermeneutics*, New Haven, 1974.

Friedensburg, Walter, *Geschichte der Universität Wittenberg*, Halle, 1917.

Friedman, Richard Elliott, *Who wrote the Bible?* New York, 1987.

Friedrich, Markus, "Das Verhältnis von Leib und Seele als theologisch-philosophisches Grenzproblem vor Descartes. Lutherische Einwände gegen eine dualistische Anthropologie," in Martin Mulsow, ed., *Spätrenaissance-Philosophie in Deutschland, 1570–1650*, Tübingen, 2009, 211–249.

Frühsorge, Gotthard, *Der politische Körper. Zum Begriff des Politischen im 17. Jahrhundert und in den Romanen Christian Weises*, Stuttgart, 1974.

Fuchs, Thomas, *Die Mechanisierung des Herzens. Harvey und Descartes – Der vitale und der mechanistische Aspekt des Kreislaufs*, Frankfurt, 1992.

Funkenstein, Amos, *Theology and the Scientific Imagination from the Middle Ages to the Seventeenth Century*, Princeton, 1986.

Füssel, Marian "Intellektuelle Felder. Zu den Differenzen zwischen Pierre Bourdieus Wissenssoziologie und der Konstellationsforschung," in Martin Mulsow and Marcello Stamm, eds., *Konstellationsforschung*, Frankfurt, 2005, 188–206.

Gelehrtenkultur als symbolische Praxis. Rang, Ritual und Konflikt an der Universität der Frühen Neuzeit, Darmstadt, 2006.

Garin, Eugenio, *Astrology in the Renaissance: The Zodiac of Life*, tr. Carolyn Jackson and June Allen, revised Clare Robertson, London and Boston, 1983.

Garrett, Aaron, "Spinoza as natural lawyer," *Cardozo Law Review* 25 (2003–2004), 627–642.

Garrett, Don, "Spinoza's ethical theory," in Don Garrett, ed., *The Cambridge Companion to Spinoza*, Cambridge, 1996, 267–314.

Gascoigne, John, "The Wisdom of the Egyptians and the Secularisation of History in the Age of Newton," in Stephen Gaukroger, ed., *The Uses of Antiquity. The Scientific Revolution and the Classical Tradition*, Dordrecht, 1991, 171–212.

Gawlick, Günter, "Thomasius und die Denkfreiheit," in Werner Schneiders, ed., *Christian Thomasius, 1655–1728*, Hamburg, 1989, 256–274.

Geitner, Ursula, *Die Sprache der Verstellung. Studien zum rhetorischen und anthropologischen Wissen im 17. und 18. Jahrhundert*, Tübingen, 1992.

Geyer-Kordesch, Johanna, *Pietismus, Medizin und Aufklärung in Preußen im 18. Jahrhundert. Das Leben und Werk Georg Ernst Stahls*, Tübingen, 2000.

Giannotti, Timothy J., *Al-Ghazali's unspeakable doctrine of the Soul*, Leiden, 2001.

Gierl, Martin, *Pietismus und Aufklärung. Theologische Polemik und die Kommunikationsreform der Wissenschaft am Ende des 17. Jahrhunderts*, Göttingen, 1997.

Gieryn, Thomas F., "Boundary-work and the Demarcation of Science from Nonscience: Strains and Interests in Professional Ideologies of Scientists," *American Sociological Review* 48/6 (1983), 781–795.

Giglioni, Guido, "Automata Compared: Boyle, Leibniz, and the Debate on the Notion of Life and Mind," *British Journal for the History of Philosophy* 3 (1995), 249–278.

Gilson, Etienne, "Autour de Pomponazzi. Problématique de l'immortalité de l'Âme en Italie au début du XVIe siècle," *Archives d'histoire doctrinale et littéraire du moyen âge* 28 (1961), 163–279.

Gindhart, Marion and Ursula Kundert, eds., *Disputatio 1200–1800. Form, Funktion und Wirkung eines Leitmediums universitärer Wissenskultur*, Berlin, 2010.

Ginzburg, Carlo and Carlo Poni, "High and Low. The Theme of Forbidden Knowledge in the Sixteenth and Seventeenth Centuries," *Past and Present* (1976), 28–41.

"Was ist Mikrogeschichte?," *Geschichtswerkstatt* 6 (1985), 48–52.

Glawe, Walter, *Die Hellenisierung des Christentums in der Geschichte der Theologie von Luther bis auf die Gegenwart*, Berlin, 1912; repr. Aalen, 1973.

Gliozzi, Giuliano, *Adamo e il nuovo mondo. La nascita dell' anthropologia come ideologia coloniale: dalle genealogie bibliche alle teorie razziali (1500–1700)*, Florence, 1977.

Goldenbaum, Ursula, "A Materialistic Rationalist? Urban Gottfried Bucher's Defense of Innate Ideas and Mechanism, added by his Denial of Free Will," *Quaestio. Journal of the History of Metaphysics* 16 (2016), 47–73.

Golder, Werner, *Hippokrates und das Corpus Hippocraticum. Eine Einführung für Philologen und Mediziner*, Würzburg, 2007.

Goldgar, Anne, *Impolite Learning. Conduct and Community in the Republic of Letters 1680–1750*, New Haven, 1995.

Goldish, Matt, "The Battle for 'True' Jewish Christianity: Peter Allix's Polemics Against the Unitarians and Millenarians," in James E. Force and David S. Katz, eds., *Everything connects. In Conference with Richard H. Popkin*, Leiden, 1998, 143–162.

Goldschmidt, Victor, *La doctrine d'Epicure et le droit*, Paris, 1977.

Goldstone, Lawrence and Nancy, *Out of the Flames: The Remarkable Story of a Fearless Scholar, a Fatal Heresy, and One of the Rarest Books in the World*, New York, 2003.

Görler, Woldemar, "Karneades," in Hellmut Flashar, ed., *Grundriss der Geschichte der Philosophie. Die Philosophie der Antike*, vol. 4/2: *Die hellenistische Philosophie*, Basel, 1994, 849–897.

Goulet, Richard, *La philosophie de Moïse. Essai de reconstruction d'un commentaire philosophique préphilonien du Pentateuque*, Paris, 1987.

Graf, Friedrich Wilhelm, *Kritik und Pseudo-Spekulation. David Friedrich Strauß als Dogmatiker im Kontext der positionellen Theologie seiner Zeit*, Munich, 1982.

Grafton, Anthony, "The Jewish Book in Christian Europe: Material Texts and Religious Encounters," in Andrea Sterk and Nina Caputo, eds., *Faithful*

Narratives. Historians, Religion, and the Challenge of Objectivity, Ithaca, 2014, 96–114.

Grafton, Anthony and Joanna Weinberg, *"I have always loved the Holy Tongue": Isaac Casaubon, the Jews, and a Forgotten Chapter in Renaissance Scholarship*, Cambridge, MA, 2011.

Greene, Robert A., "Henry More and Robert Boyle on the Spirit of Nature," *Journal of the History of Ideas* 23 (1962), 451–474.

"Instinct of Nature: Natural Law, Synderesis, and the Moral Sense," *Journal of the History of Ideas* 58 (1997), 173–198.

Gregory, Tullio, *Scetticismo ed empirismo. Studio su Gassendi*, Bari, 1961.

Gregory, Tullio, Guido Canziani, Gianni Paganini et al., eds., *Ricerche su letteratura libertina e letteratura clandestina nel Seicento*, Florence, 1981.

Greschat, Martin, *Zwischen Tradition und neuem Anfang. Valentin Ernst Löscher und der Ausgang der lutherischen Orthodoxie*, Witten, 1971.

Groetsch, Ulrich, "Adversus Hereticos. Sebastian Edzard's Epic Battle for Souls," in Johann Anselm Steiger, ed., *Das akademische Gymnasium zu Hamburg im Kontext frühneuzeitlicher Wissenschafts- und Bildungsgeschichte*, Berlin, 2017, 137–162.

Grote, Simon, *The Emergence of Modern Aesthetic Theory: Religion and Morality in Enlightenment Germany and Scotland*, Cambridge, 2017.

Grünberg, Reinhold, *Sächsisches Pfarrerbuch*, Freiberg, 1939/40.

Grunert, Frank "Zur aufgeklärten Kritik am theokratischen Absolutismus. Der Streit zwischen Hector Gottfried Masius und Christian Thomasius über Ursprung und Begründung der summa potestas," in Friedrich Vollhardt, ed., *Christian Thomasius (1655–1728). Neue Forschungen zur Frühaufklärung*, Tübingen, 1997, 51–77.

Normbegründung und politische Legitimität: Zur Rechts- und Staatsphilosophie der deutschen Frühaufklärung, Tübingen, 2000.

Haakonssen, Knud, *Natural Law and Moral Philosophy. From Grotius to the Scottish Enlightenment*, Cambridge, 1996.

"The moral conservatism of natural rights," in Ian Hunter and David Saunders, eds., *Natural Law and Civil Sovereignty*, New York, 2002, 27–42.

"Morality without Dignity. Samuel Pufendorf's Concept of Personhood" (in press).

Haakonssen, Knud, ed., *Grotius, Pufendorf and Modern Natural Law*, Aldershot, 1999.

Hacking, Ian, "Styles of Scientific Reasoning," in John Raijchmann and Cornel West, eds., *Post-Analytic Philosophy*, New York, 1985, 145–165.

Hadas, Moses, *Hellenistische Kultur*, Vienna, 1981.

Hadot, Pierre, *La voile d'Isis*, Paris, 2004.

Häfner, Ralph, "Jacob Thomasius und die Geschichte der Häresien," in Friedrich Vollhardt, ed., *Christian Thomasius. Neue Forschungen im Kontext der Frühaufklärung*, Tübingen, 1997, 142–164.

"Tempelritus und Textkommentar. Hermann von der Hardts *Morgenröte über die Stad Chebron* und die Eigenart des literaturkritischen Kommentars im frühen 18. Jahrhundert," *Scientia Poetica* 3 (1999), 47–71.

"'Denn wie das buch ist, muß der leser seyn.' – Allegorese und Mythopoesis in den 'Hohen und hellen Sinnbildern Jonae' des Helmstedter Gelehrten Hermann von der Hardt," in Herbert Jaumann, ed., *Die europäische Gelehrtenrepublik im Zeitalter des Konfessionalismus*, Wiesbaden, 2001, 183–202.

Götter im Exil. Frühneuzeitliches Dichtungsverständnis im Spannungsfeld christlicher Apologetik und philologischer Kritik (ca. 1590–1736), Tübingen, 2003.

Hamilton, Alastair, *The Family of Love*, Cambridge, 1981.

Hammerstein, Notker, *Jus und Historie. Ein Beitrag zur Geschichte des historischen Denkens an deutschen Universitäten im späten 17. und 18. Jahrhundert*, Göttingen, 1972.

Hartbecke, Karin, *Metaphysik und Naturphilosophie im 17. Jahrhundert: Francis Glissons Substanztheorie in ihrem ideengeschichtlichen Kontext*, Tübingen, 2006.

Hartung, Gerald, *Die Naturrechtsdebatte. Geschichte der Obligatio vom 17. bis 20. Jahrhundert*, Freiburg, 1998.

"Gesetz und Obligation. Die Spätscholastische Gesetzestheologie und ihr Einfluß auf die Naturrechtsdebatte der Frühen Neuzeit," in Frank Grunert, ed., *Die Ordnung der Praxis: Neue Studien zur spanischen Spätscholastik*, Tübingen, 2001, 381–402.

Hartwich, Wolfgang, *Die Sendung Moses*, Munich, 1997.

Heer, Friedrich, *Die dritte Kraft. Der europäische Humanismus zwischen den Fronten des konfessionellen Zeitalters*, Frankfurt, 1959.

Heiduk, Franz, *Die Dichter der galanten Lyrik. Studien zur Neukirchschen Sammlung*, Bern and Munich, 1971.

Heller, Marvin J., *Printing the Talmud. A History of the Individual Treatises Printed from 1700 to 1750*, Leiden, 1999.

"A Tale of Two Cities: Leipzig, Hamburg, and Don Isaac Abrabanel," in *Further Studies in the Making of the early Hebrew Book*, Leiden, 2013, 153–168.

Helm, Jürgen, "Die Galenrezeption in Philipp Melanchthons De anima (1540–1552)," *Medizinhistorisches Journal* 31 (1996), 298–321.

"Zwischen Aristotelismus, Protestantismus und zeitgenössischer Medizin. Philipp Melanchthons Lehrbuch De anima," in Jürgen Leonhardt, ed., *Melanchthon und das Lehrbuch des 16. Jahrhunderts*, Rostock, 1997, 175–194.

Hempfer, Klaus W., "Lektüren von Dialogen," in Klaus W. Hempfer, ed., *Möglichkeiten des Dialogs. Struktur und Funktion einer literarischen Gattung zwischen Mittelalter und Renaissance in Italien*, Stuttgart, 2002, 1–38.

Hengel, Martin, *Die Zeloten*, 2nd edn., Leiden, 1976.

Henrich, Dieter, *Fichtes ursprüngliche Einsicht*, Frankfurt, 1967.

Grundlegung aus dem Ich. Untersuchungen zur Vorgeschichte des Idealismus. Tübingen – Jena 1790–1794, 2 vols. Frankfurt, 2004.

Herberger, Maximilian, *Dogmatik. Zur Geschichte von Begriff und Methode in Medizin und Jurisprudenz*, Frankfurt, 1981.

Hill, Christopher, *The World Turned Upside Down. Radical Ideas during the English Revolution*, London, 1972.

Hinske, Norbert, "Die tragenden Grundideen der deutschen Aufklärung. Versuch einer Typologie," in Raffaele Ciafardone, ed., *Die Philosophie der deutschen Aufklärung. Texte und Darstellung*, Stuttgart, 1990, 407–458.

Hochstrasser, Tim J., *Natural Law Theories in the Early Enlightenment*, Cambridge, 2000.

Hochstrasser, Tim J., and Peter Schröder, eds., *Early Modern Natural Law Theories. Context and Strategies in the Early Enlightenment*, Dordrecht, 2003.

Höfele, Andreas and Werner von Koppenfels, eds., *Renaissance Go-Betweens. Cultural Exchange in Early Modern Europe*, Berlin, 2005.

Hoffmann, A. G., article "Hardt" in *Allgemeine Encyclopädie der Wissenschaften und Künste*, Leipzig, 1828, Sect. II, Part 2, cols. 388–395.

Hoffmann, Klaus, *Johann Friedrich Böttger: Vom Alchemistengold zum weißen Porzellan*, Berlin, 1985.

Holzhey, Helmut and Vilem Mudroch, eds., *Grundriss der Geschichte der Philosophie*: vol 5: *Heiliges Römisches Reich Deutscher Nation. Schweiz. Nord- und Ostmitteleuropa*, Basel, 2014.

Hotson, Howard, *Johann Heinrich Alsted 1588–1638. Between Renaissance, Reformation and Universal Reform*, Oxford, 2000.

Hübener, Wolfgang, "Scientia de aliquo et nihilo. Die historischen Voraussetzungen von Leibniz' Ontologiebegriff', in *Vom Geist der Prämoderne*, Würzburg, 1985, 84–104.

Hülsenberg, Dagmar, ed., *Kolloquium aus Anlass des 350. Geburtstags von Tschirnhaus am 10.4.2001 in Dresden*, Leipzig, 2003.

Hunger, Herbert, "Michael Servet und das Exemplar seiner *Christianismi restitutio* in der Österreichischen Nationalbibliothek," *Biblos* 1 (1952), 61–78.

Hüning, Dieter, *Naturrecht und Staatstheorie bei Samuel Pufendorf*, Baden Baden 2009.

Hunter, Ian, *Rival Enlightenments. Civil and Metaphysical Philosophy in Early Modern Germany*, Cambridge, 2001.

"The History of Philosophy and the Persona of the Philosopher," *Modern Intellectual History* 4 (2007), 571–600.

The Secularisation of the Confessional State: The Political Thought of Christian Thomasius, Cambridge, 2007.

Hunter, Michael and Edward B. Davis, "The Making of Robert Boyle's *Free Enquiry into the Vulgarly Received Notion of Nature* (1686)" *Early Science and Medicine* 1 (1996), 204–271.

Robert Boyle (1627–91): Scrupulosity and Science, Woodbridge, 2000.

Boyle: Between God and Science, New Haven, 2009.

Hutchinson, Keith, "Supernaturalism and the Mechanical Philosophy," *History of Science* 21 (1983), 297–333.

Hutchison, Ross, *Locke in France 1688–1734*, Oxford, 1991.

Hutin, Serge, *Henry More. Essai sur les doctrines théosophiques chez les Platoniciens de Cambridge*, Hildesheim, 1966.

Hutton, Sarah, "Henry More, Edward Stillingfleet and the Decline of Moses Atticus," in Richard Kroll et al., eds., *Philosophy, Science and Religion in England, 1640–1700*, Cambridge, 1992, 3–84.

"Classicism and Baroque. A note on Mosheim's footnotes to Cudworth's *The True Intellectual System of the Universe*," in Martin Mulsow, Ralph Häfner, Florian Neumann and Helmut Zedelmaier, eds., *Johann Lorenz Mosheim (1693–1755). Theologie im Spannungsfeld von Philosophie, Philologie und Geschichte*, Wiesbaden, 1997, pp. 211–228.

Idel, Moshe, *Messianic Mystics*, New Haven, 1998.

Iofrida, Manlio, "La presenza della cultura libertina in Ingliterra alla fine del '600: Charles Blount, Thomas Burnet e William Coward," in Tullio Gregory et al., eds., *Ricerche su letteratura libertina e letteratura clandestina nel Seicento*, Florence, 1981, 387–394.

Israel, Jonathan I., *Radical Enlightenment. Philosophy and the Making of Modernity 1650–1750*, Oxford, 2001.

   Enlightenment Contested. Philosophy, Modernity, and the Emancipation of Man 1670–1752, Oxford, 2006.

   Democratic Enlightenment: Philosophy, Revolution, and Human Rights 1750–1790, Oxford 2011.

Jacob, James R., *Henry Stubbe, Radical Protestantism and the Early Enlightenment*, Cambridge, 1983.

Jacob, Margaret C., "John Toland and the Newtonian Ideology," *Journal of the Warburg and Courtauld Institutes*, 32 (1969), 307–331.

   The Newtonians and the English Revolution, 1689–1720, Ithaca, 1976.

Jarck, Horst-Rüdiger et al., eds., *Braunschweigisches Biographisches Lexikon: 8. bis 18. Jahrhundert*, Braunschweig, 2006.

Jaumann, Herbert, *Critica. Untersuchungen zur Geschichte der Literaturkritik zwischen Quintilian und Thomasius*, Leiden, 1995.

Jauß, Hans-Robert, "Das Vollkommene als Faszinosum des Imaginären," in *Ästhethische Erfahrung und literarische Hermeneutik*, Frankfurt, 1982, 303–323.

Jorink, Eric, *Reading the Book of Nature in the Dutch Golden Age, 1575–1715*, Leiden, 2010.

Jouanna, Jacques, *Hippocrates*, Baltimore and London, 1999.

Jouassard, Georges, "La personalité d'Helvidius," *Mélanges Saunier*, Lyon, 1944, 139–156.

Jouslin, Olivier, *La campagne des Provinciales de Pascal: étude d'un dialogue polémique*, Clermont-Ferrand, 2007.

Juntke, Fritz, ed., *Album Academiae Vitebergensis*, Jüngere Reihe, Part 2 (1660–1710), Halle, 1952.

   Matrikel der Martin-Luther-Universität Halle-Wittenberg, vol. 1 (1690–1730), Halle, 1960.

Kahn, Didier, *Alchimie et Paracelsisme en France (1567–1625)*, Geneva, 2007.

Kapitza, Peter K., *Ein bürgerlicher Krieg in der gelehrten Welt. Zur Geschichte der Querelle des Anciens et des Modernes in Deutschland*, Munich, 1981.

Karmann, Thomas R., "'Er erkannte sie aber nicht. . .' Maria, das Virginitätsideal und Mt. 1, 18–25 im späten 4. Jahrhundert," in Hans-Ulrich Weidemann, ed., *Asceticism and Exegesis in Early Christianity. The Reception of New Testament Texts in Ancient Ascetic Discourses*, Göttingen, 2013, 118–147.

Katchen, Aaron L., *Christian Hebraists and Dutch Rabbis: Seventeenth Century Apologetics and the Study of Maimonides' Misneh Torah*, Cambridge, MA, 1984.

Keller, Vera, *Knowledge and the Public Interest, 1575–1725*, Cambridge, 2015.

Kemper, Hans-Georg, *Deutsche Lyrik der frühen Neuzeit*, vol. 5/I: *Aufklärung und Pietismus*, Tübingen, 1991.

Deutsche Lyrik der frühen Neuzeit: Frühaufklärung, vol. 5/2, Tübingen, 1991.

Kisser, Thomas, *Selbstbewußtsein und Interaktion. Spinozas Theorie der Individualität*, Würzburg, 1998.

Kittsteiner, Heinz Dieter, *Die Entstehung des modernen Gewissens*, Frankfurt, 1991.

Klein, Dietrich, *Hermann Samuel Reimarus. Das theologische Werk*, Tübingen, 2009.

"Inventing Islam in Support of Christian Truth: Theodore Hackspan's Arabic Studies in Altdorf 1642–6," *History of Universities* 25 (2010), 26–55.

Klibansky, Raymond, Erwin Panofsky, and Fritz Saxl, *Saturn and Melancholy: Studies in the History of Natural Philosophy, Religion and Art*, New York, 1964.

Klippel, Diethelm, *Politische Freiheit und Freiheitsrechte im deutschen Naturrecht des 18. Jahrhunderts*, Paderborn, 1976.

Knauf, Ernst Axel, *Midian. Untersuchungen zur Geschichte Palästinas und Nordarabiens am Ende des 2. Jahrtausends v. Chr.*, Wiesbaden, 1988.

Kobuch, Agatha, *Zensur und Aufklärung in Kursachsen. Ideologische Strömungen und politische Meinungen zur Zeit der sächsisch-polnischen Union (1697–1763)*, Weimar, 1988.

Koch, Hans-Theodor, "Bartholomäus Schönborn (1530–1585). Melanchthons De anima als medizinisches Lehrbuch," in Heinz Scheible, ed., *Melanchthon in seinen Schülern*, Wiesbaden, 1997, 323–340.

Konschel, Paul, "Christian Gabriel Fischer, ein Gesinnungs- und Leidensgenosse Christian Wolffs in Königsberg," *Altpreußische Monatsschrift* 53 (1916), 416–444.

Kors, Alan Charles, *Atheism in France. 1650–1729*, vol. 1: *The Orthodox Sources of Disbelief*, Princeton, 1990.

Köster, Heinrich M., "Die Jungfrauengeburt als theologisches Problem seit David Friedrich Strauss," in Hermann Josef Brosch, ed., *Jungfrauengeburt gestern und heute*, Essen, 1969, 35–88.

Krämer, Fabian, *Ein Zentaur in London. Lektüre und Beobachtung in der frühneuzeitlichen Naturforschung*, Affalterbach, 2014.

Kraus, Paul, "Beiträge zur islamischen Ketzergeschichte. Das Kitāb az-Zummurrud des Ibn ar- Rāwandī" [1933/34]; repr. in *Alchemie, Ketzerei, Apokryphen im frühen Islam. Gesammelte Aufsätze*, Wiesbaden, 1994, 109–190.

Krebs, Johann Philipp, *Antibarbarus der lateinischen Sprache*, Frankfurt, 1843.

Kristeller, Paul Oskar, "The Myth of Renaissance Atheism and the French Tradition of Free Thought," in *Studies in Renaissance Thought and Letters*, vol. 3, Rome, 1993, 541–554.

Kroll, Richard W. F., "The Question of Locke's Relation to Gassendi," *Journal of the History of Ideas* 45 (1984), 339–359.

Kudlien, Friedrich, *Der Beginn des medizinischen Denkens bei den Griechen von Homer bis Hippokrates*, Zurich, 1967.

Kühlmann, Wilhelm, "Geschichte als Gegenwart. Formen der politischen Reflexion im deutschen 'Tacitismus' des 17. Jahrhunderts," in Kühlmann and Walter E. Schäfer, eds., *Literatur im Elsaß von Fischart bis Moscherosch*, Tübingen, 2001, 41–60.

Kuhn, Heinrich C., *Venetischer Aristotelismus im Ende der aristotelischen Welt: Aspekte der Welt und des Denkens des Cesare Cremonini (1550–1631)*, Frankfurt and Bern, 1996.

Kühn, Manfred, *Kant. Eine Biographie*, Munich, 2003.

Kühn, Sebastian, *Wissen, Arbeit, Freundschaft - Ökonomien und soziale Beziehungen an den Akademien in London, Paris and Berlin um 1700*, Göttingen, 2011.

Kühnel, Martin, *Das politische Denken von Christian Thomasius: Staat, Gesellschaft, Bürger*, Berlin, 2001

Kurz, August, *Über Christian Gabriel Fischers Vernünftige Gedanken von der Natur*, Halle, 1908.

Kusukawa, Sachiko, *The Transformation of Natural Philosophy: The Case of Philip Melanchthon*, Cambridge, 1995.

Lackner, Martin, *Die Kirchenpolitik des Großen Kurfürsten*, Witten, 1973.

Lamey, Ferdinand, *Hermann von der Hardt in seinen Briefen und seinen Beziehungen zum Braunschweiger Hofe, zu Spener, Franke und dem Pietismus. Beilage I zu den Hss. der Großherzoglichen Badischen Hof- und Landesbibliothek Karlsruhe*, Karlsruhe, 1891.

Lammel, Hans-Uwe, "Kurt Sprengel und die deutschsprachige Medizingeschichtsschreibung," in Andreas Frewer and Volker Roelke, eds., *Die Institutionalisierung der Medizinhistoriographie*, Stuttgart, 2001, 27–38.

Klio und Hippokrates: Eine Liaison littéraire des 18. Jahrhunderts und die Folgen für die Wissenschaftskultur bis 1850 in Deutschland, Stuttgart, 2005.

Lange, Friedrich A., *History of Materialism and Criticism of its Present Importance*, tr. Ernest Chester Thomas, 3 vols., London, 1892.

Laver, A. Bryan, "Miracles No Wonder! The Mesmeric Phenomena and Organic Cures of Valentine Greatrakes," *Journal of the History of Medicine and Allied Sciences* 33 (1978), 35–46.

Lehmann Brauns, Sicco, *Weisheit in der Weltgeschichte. Philosophiegeschichte zwischen Barock und Aufklärung*, Tübingen, 2004.

"Die Sintflut als Zäsur der politischen Institutionengeschichte," in Martin Mulsow and Jan Assmann, eds., *Sintflut und Gedächtnis. Erinnern und Vergesen des Ursprungs*, Munich, 2006, 265–287.

Lehmann, Hartmut, ed., *Säkularisierung, Dechristianisierung, Rechristianisierung im neuzeitlichen Europa*, Göttingen, 1997.

Leicht, Reimund, "Daniel Ernst Jablonski und die Drucklegungen des Babylonischen Talmud in Frankfurt/Oder and Berlin," in Joachim Bahlcke and Werner Korthaase, eds., *Daniel Ernst Jablonski. Religion, Wissenschaft und Politik um 1700*, Stuttgart, 2008, 491–516.

Leinkauf, Thomas, "Systema mnemonicum und circulus encyclopaediae. Johann Heinrich Alsteds Versuch einer Fundierung des universalen Wissens in der ars memorativa," in Jörg Jochen Berns and Wolfgang Neuber, eds., *Seelenmaschinen. Gattungstraditionen, Funktionen und Leistungsgrenzen der Mnemotechniken vom späten Mittelalter bis zum Beginn der Moderne*, Vienna, 2000, 279–308.

Leinkauf, Thomas and Karin Hartbecke, eds., *Der Naturbegriff in der Frühen Neuzeit, Semantische Perspektiven zwischen 1500 und 1700*, Tübingen, 2005.

Levine, Joseph M., *The Battle of the Books: History and Literature in the Augustan Age*, Ithaca, 1991.

"Latitudinarians, Neoplatonists, and the Ancient Wisdom," in Richard Kroll, Richard Ashcraft and Perez Zagorin, eds., *Philosophy, Science, and Religion in England 1640–1700*, Cambridge, 1992, 85–108.

Levitin, Dimitri, "John Spencer's *De Legibus Hebraeorum* (1683–85) and 'Enlightened' Sacred History: A New Interpretation," *Journal of the Warburg and Courtauld Institutes* 76 (2013), 49–92.

Lichtenstein, Ernst, "Bildung 4/5, " in *Historisches Wörterbuch der Philosophie*, vol. 1, Basel, 1971, cols. 923–925.

Liebrenz, Boris, "Orientalistik," in Detlef Döring et al., eds., *Die Erleuchtung der Welt. Sachsen und der Beginn der modernen Wissenschaften*, Dresden, 2009, vol. 1 (the essay volume), 202–209.

Ligota, Christopher, "Der apologetische Rahmen der Mythendeutung im Frankreich des 17. Jahrhunderts (P. D. Huet)," in Walther Killy, ed., *Mythographie der frühen Neuzeit. Ihre Anwendung in den Künsten*, Wiesbaden, 1984, 149–161.

Limor, Ora and Israel Jacob Yuval, "Scepticism and Conversion: Jews, Christians and Doubt in Sefer ha-Nizzahon," in Allison Coudert and Jeffrey S. Shoulson, eds., *Hebraica Veritas? Christian Hebraists and the Study of Judaism in early Modern Europe*, Philadelphia, 2004, 159–179.

Loetz, Francisca, *Mit Gott handeln. Von den Zürcher Gotteslästerern der Frühen Neuzeit zu einer Kulturgeschichte des Religiösen*, Göttingen, 2002.

Lohmeyer, Ernst, "Vom göttlichen Wohlgeruch," *Sitzungsberichte der Heidelberger Akademie der Wissenschaften. Philologisch-historische Klasse* 9 (1919).

Lomonaco, Fabrizio, *Jean Barbeyrac Editor of Gerard Noodt*, Berlin, 2012.

Loop, Jan, "Johann Heinrich Hottinger (1620–1667) and the Historia Orientalis," *Church History and Religious Culture* 88 (2008), 169–203.

Johann Heinrich Hottinger: Arabic and Islamic Studies in the Seventeenth Century, Oxford, 2013.

Lorentzen, Rüdiger, *Daniel Wilhelm Triller und seine "wahrhaft hippokratischen" Freunde*, typewritten Dissertation, Göttingen, 1964.

Lucä, Friedrich, *Der Chronist Friedrich Lucä. Ein Zeit- und Sittenbild aus der 2. Hälfte d. 17. Jahrh. nach einer von ihm selbst hinterlassenen Handschrift*, Frankfurt, 1854.

Lüdemann, Gerd, *Jungfrauengeburt? Die Geschichte von Maria und ihrem Sohn Jesus*, Springe, 2008.

Ludwig, Bernd, *Die Wiederentdeckung des Epikureischen Naturrechts: Zu Thomas Hobbes' philosophischer Entwicklung von De cive zum Leviathan im Pariser Exil 1640–1651*, Frankfurt, 1998.

Luh, Jürgen, "Zur Konfessionspolitik der Kurfürsten von Brandenburg und Könige in Preußen 1640 bis 1740," in Horst Lademacher et al., eds., *Ablehnung, Duldung, Anerkennung. Toleranz in den Niederlanden und in Deutschland. Ein historischer und aktueller Vergleich*, Münster et al., 2004, 306–324.

Luhmann, Niklas, *Gesellschaftsstruktur und Semantik. Studien zur Wissenssoziologie der modernen Gesellschaft*, 4 vols., Frankfurt and Berlin, 1980–1999.

Lupher, David, "The *De armis Romanis* and the Exemplum of Roman Imperialism," in Benedict Kingsbury and Benjamin Straumann, eds., *The Roman Foundations of the Law of Nations: Alberico Gentili and the Justice of Empire*, Oxford, 2010, 85–100.

Lutterbeck, Klaus-Gert, *Staat und Gesellschaft bei Christian Thomasius*, Stuttgart, 2002.

Mager, Inge, "Hermann Conring als theologischer Schriftsteller – insbesondere in seinem Verhältnis zu Georg Calixt," in Michael Stolleis, ed., *Hermann Conring (1606–1681). Beiträge zu Leben und Werk*, Berlin, 1983, 55–84.

Malcolm, Noel, *Aspects of Hobbes*, Oxford, 2002.

Manea, Ioana, "L'Espagne chez La Mothe le Vayer ou comment utiliser les stéréotypes de la littérature politique pour exprimer des opinions libertines," *Loxias* 26 (2009). Online at: http://revel.unice.fr/loxias/index.html?id=2993.

Manuel, Frank E., *The Eighteenth Century Confronts the Gods*, Cambridge, MA, 1959.

Marcialis, Maria Teresa, "L'âme matérielle tra libertinismo e clandestinité," in Tullio Gregory et al., eds., *Ricerche su letteratura libertina e letteratura clandestina nel Seicento*, Florence, 1981, 353–363.

Markschies, Christoph, "Kerinth: Wer war er und was lehrte er?," *Jahrbuch für Antike und Christentum* 41 (1998), 48–76.

Marquardt, Anton, *Kant und Crusius*, Kiel, 1885.

Marti, Hanspeter, "Grenzen der Denkfreiheit in Dissertationen des frühen 18. Jahrhunderts. Theodor Ludwig Laus Scheitern an der juristischen Fakultät der Universität Königsberg," in Helmut Zedelmaier and Martin Mulsow, eds., *Die Praktik der Gelehrsamkeit in der Frühen Neuzeit*, Tübingen, 2001, 295–306.

Martus, Steffen, *Aufklärung: Das deutsche 18. Jahrhundert – ein Epochenbild*, Hamburg, 2015.

Matheus, Ricarda, "Zwischen Rom und Mainz. Konversionsagenten und soziale Netze in der Mitte des 17. Jahrhunderts," in Daniel Bauerfeld and Lukas Clemens, eds., *Gesellschaftliche Umbrüche und religiöse Netzwerke. Analysen von der Antike bis zur Gegenwart*, Bielefeld, 2014, 227–252.

Mazzotta, Giuseppe, *The New Map of the World. The Poetic Philosophy of Giambattista Vico*, Princeton, 1999.

McGuire, John, "Boyle's Conception of Nature," *Journal of the History of Ideas* 33 (1972), 523–542.

McKenna, Anthony and Alain Mothu, eds., *La philosophie clandestine à l'âge classique*, Oxford and Paris, 1997

McLachlan, Herbert J., *Socinianism in Seventeenth-Century England*, Oxford, 1951.

Melamed, Abraham, "English Travellers and Venetian Jewish Scholars. The Case of Simone Luzzatto and James Harrington," in Gaetano Cozzi, ed., *Gli Ebrei e Venezia. Secoli XIV–XVIII*, Milan, 1987, 507–526.

Mendelsohn, Everett, *Heat and Life: The Development of the Theory of Animal Heat*, Cambridge, MA, 1964.

Menk, Gerhard, *Die Hohe Schule Herborn in ihrer Frühzeit (1584–1660). Ein Beitrag zum Hochschulwesen des deutschen Kalvinismus im Zeitalter der Gegenreformation*, Wiesbaden, 1981.

Mercer, Christia, *Leibniz's Metaphysics: Its Origins and Development,* Cambridge, 2001.

Merzbacher, Dieter, "Die 'Herwiederbringung der herrlichen Schriften, so fast verloren gewesen.' Das 'concilium Constantiense,' ein Editionsprojekt Hermann von der Hardts und des Herzogs Rudolf August von Braunschweig-Lüneburg," in Dorothea Klein et al., eds., *Vom Mittelalter zur Neuzeit. Festschrift für Horst Brunner*, Wiesbaden, 2000, 569–592.

Michelis Pintacuda, Fiorella De, *Socinianesimo e tolleranza nell'età del razionalismo*, Florence, 1975.

Miegge, Giovanni, *Die Jungfrau Maria. Studie zur Geschichte der Marienlehre*, Göttingen, 1962.

Miller, Peter N., "Les origines de la Bible Polyglotte de Paris: philologia sacra, Contre-Reforme et raison d'état," *XVIIe siècle* 194 (1997), 57–66.

"Taking Paganism Seriously: Anthropology and Antiquarianism in Early Seventeenth-Century Histories of Religion," *Archiv für Religionsgeschichte* 3 (2001), 183–209.

"The Antiquarianization of Biblical Scholarship and the London Polyglot Bible (1653–57)," *Journal of the History of Ideas* 62 (2001), 463–482.

Möller, Hans, *Hermann von der Hardt als Alttestamentler*, typewritten habilitation thesis, Leipzig, 1962.

Momigliano, Arnaldo, *Hochkulturen im Hellenismus. Die Begegnung der Griechen mit Kelten, Römern, Juden und Persern*, Munich, 1979.

Moran, Bruce T., *The Alchemical World of the German Court: Occult Philosophy and Chemical Medicine in the Circle of Moritz of Hessen (1572–1632)*, Stuttgart, 1991.

Moreau, Isabelle, *"Guérir du sot." Les stratégies d'écriture des libertins à l'âge classique*, Paris, 2007.

"Pierre Bayle et La Mothe le Vayer: de la liberté de conscience à l'indifférence des religions," in Philippe Fréchet, ed., *Pierre Bayle et la liberté de conscience*, Toulouse, 2012, 135–150.

Moriarty, Michael, *Disguised Vices: Theories of Virtue in Early Modern French Thought*, Oxford, 2011.

Motsch, Andreas, *Lafitau e l'emergence du discours ethnographique*, Sillery, 2001.

Mühlpfordt, Günter, "Arianische Exulanten als Vorboten der Aufklärung. Zur Wirkungsgeschichte des Frührationalismus polnischer und deutscher Arianer vom 16. bis ins 18. Jahrhundert," in Johannes Irmscher, ed., *Renaissance und Humanismus in Mittel- und Osteuropa*, vol. 2, Berlin, 1962, 220–246.

"Die Oder-Universität 1506–1811. Eine deutsche Hochschule in der Geschichte Brandenburg-Preußens und der europäischen Wissenschaft," in Günther Haase and Joachim Winkler, eds., *Die Oder-Universität Frankfurt. Beiträge zu ihrer Geschichte*, Weimar, 1983, 19–72.

"Radikaler Wolffianismus. Zur Differenzierung und Wirkung der Wolffschen Schule ab 1735," in Werner Schneiders, ed., *Christian Wolff*, 2nd edn., Hamburg, 1986, 237–253.

Müller, Ingo W., *Iatromechanische Theorie und ärztliche Praxis im Vergleich zur galenistischen Medizin: (Friedrich Hoffmann – Pieter van Foreest, Jan van Heurne)*, Stuttgart, 1991.

Müller, Klaus, *Tora für die Völker. Die noachidischen Gebote und Ansätze zu ihrer Rezeption im Christentum*, Berlin, 1998.

Müller, Kurt, *Leben und Werk von G. W. Leibniz – Eine Chronik*, Frankfurt, 1984.

Müller, Reimar, *Die epikureische Gesellschaftstheorie*, Berlin, 1972.

Mulsow, Martin, "Asophia philosophorum. Skeptizismus und Frühaufklärung in Deutschland," in *Transactions of the 9th International Congress on the Enlightenment (Studies on Voltaire and the Eighteenth Century)*, Oxford, 1997, vol. 1, 203–207.

"Eclecticism or Skepticism? A Problem of the Early Enlightenment," *Journal of the History of Ideas* (1997), 465–477.

"Eine 'Rettung' des Michael Servet? Der junge Mosheim und die heterodoxe Tradition," in Mulsow et al., eds., *Johann Lorenz Mosheim, 1693–1755*, Wiesbaden, 1997, 45–92.

"Eine 'Rettung' des Servet und der Ophiten? Der junge Mosheim und die häretische Tradition," in Martin Mulsow et al., eds., *Johann Lorenz Mosheim 1693–1755. Theologie im Spannungsfeld von Philosophie, Philologie und Historie*, Wiesbaden, 1997, 45–92.

"Einleitung," in Johann Lorenz Mosheim, *Versuch einer unparteiischen und gründlichen Ketzergeschichte*, vol. 1, repr. Hildesheim, 1998.

Frühneuzeitliche Selbsterhaltung. Telesio und die Naturphilosophie der Renaissance, Tübingen, 1998.

Monadenlehre, Hermetik und Deismus. Georg Schades geheime Aufklärungsgesellschaft 1747–1760, Hamburg, 1998.

"Einleitung," in Johann Lorenz Mosheim, *Versuch einer unparteiischen und gründlichen Ketzergeschichte*, vol. 2, repr. Hildesheim, 1999.

"Vernünftige Metempsychosis. Über Monadenlehre, Esoterik und geheime Aufklärungsgesellschaften," in Monika Neugebauer-Wölk, ed., *Aufklärung und Esoterik*, Hamburg, 1999, 211–273.

"Ignorabat Deum: scetticismo, libertinismo ed ermetismo nell' interpretazione arpiana del concetto vaniniano di Dio," in Francesco Paolo Raimondi, ed., *Giulio Cesare Vanini e il libertinismo*, Galatina (Lecce), 2000, 171–182.

"Jacques Souverain, Samuel Crell et les cryptosociniens de Londres," in Jacques Souverain, *Lettre à Mr*** touchant l'apostasie*, ed. Sylvain Matton, Paris and Milan, 2000, 49–63.

"Pluralisierung," in Anette Völker-Rasor, *Oldenbourg Lehrbuch Geschichte: Frühe Neuzeit*, Munich, 2000, 303–307.

"Unanständigkeit. Zur Mißachtung und Verteidigung des Decorum in der Gelehrtenrepublik," *Historische Anthropologie* 8 (2000), 98–118.

Die drei Ringe. Toleranz und clandestine Gelehrsamkeit bei Mathurin Veyssière La Croze (1661–1739), Tübingen, 2001.

"John Seldens *De diis Syris*. Idolatriekritik und vergleichende Religionsgeschichte im 17. Jahrhundert," *Archiv für Religionsgeschichte* 3 (2001), 1–24.

Review of Merio Scattola, "Das Naturrecht vor dem Naturrecht," *Ius Commune. Zeitschrift für Europäische Rechtsgeschichte* 28 (2001), 440–444.

"Pythagoreer und Wolffianer: Zu den Formationsbedingungen von vernünftiger Hermetik und gelehrter 'Esoterik' im Deutschland des 18. Jahrhunderts," in Anne-Charlott Trepp and Hartmut Lehmann, eds., *Antike Weisheit und kulturelle Praxis. Hermetismus in der Frühen Neuzeit*, Göttingen, 2001, 337–396.

"Säkularisierung der Seelenlehre? Biblizismus und Materialismus in Urban Gottlieb Buchers Briefwechsel vom Wesen der Seelen (1713)," in Lutz Danneberg et al., eds., *Säkularisierung der Wissenschaften seit der frühen Neuzeit, Band 2: Zwischen christlicher Apologetik und methodologischem Atheismus*, Berlin, 2002, 145–173.

"Der vollkommene Mensch. Zur Prähistorie des Posthumanen," *Deutsche Zeitschrift für Philosophie* 51 (2003), 739–760.

"Literarisches und Philosophisches Feld im Thomasius-Kreis. Einsätze, Umbesetzungen, Strategien," in Manfred Beetz and Herbert Jaumann, eds., *Thomasius im literarischen Feld*, Tübingen, 2003, 103–116.

"Views of the Berlin Refuge: Scholarly Projects, Literary Interests, Marginal Fields," in Sandra Pott, Lutz Danneberg, and Martin Mulsow, eds., *The Berlin Refuge 1680–1780: Learning and Science in European Context*, Leiden, 2003, 25–46.

"Antiquarianism and Idolatry. The 'Historia' of Religions in the Seventeenth Century," in Gianna Pomata and Nancy G. Siraisi, eds., *Historia. Empiricism and Erudition in Early Modern Europe*, Cambridge, MA, 2005, 181–210.

"Arcana naturae. Verborgene Eigenschaften und universelle Methode von Fernel bis Gemma und Bodin," in Thomas Leinkauf and Karin Hartbecke, eds., *Der Naturbegriff in der Frühen Neuzeit, Semantische Perspektiven zwischen 1500 und 1700*, Tübingen, 2005, 31–68.

"Eine Reise durch die Gelehrtenrepublik. Soziales Wissen, Wahrnehmungen und Wertungen in Gottlieb Stolles Reisejournal von 1703/4," in Ulrich J. Schneider, ed., *Kultur der Kommunikation. Die europäische Gelehrtenrepublik im Zeitalter von Leibniz und Lessing*, Wiesbaden, 2005, 185–202.

"Ein kontroverses Journal der Frühaufklärung: Die *Observationes selectae*, Halle 1700–1705," *Aufklärung* 17 (2005), 79–99.

"Johann Christoph Wolf (1683–1739) und die Geschichte der verbotenen Bücher in Hamburg," in Johann Anselm Steiger, ed., *500 Jahre Theologie in Hamburg. Hamburg als Zentrum christlicher Theologie und Kultur zwischen Tradition und Zukunft*, Berlin, 2005, 81–112.

"Samuel Crell: An Intellectual Profile," in Lech Szczucki, ed., *Faustus Socinus and his Heritage*, Kraków, 2005, 477–494.

"The 'New Socinians': Intertextuality and Cultural Exchange in Late Socinianism," in Martin Mulsow and Jan Rohls, eds., *Socinianism and Arminianism*, Leiden, 2005, 49–78.

"Zum Methodenprofil der Konstellationsforschung," in Martin Mulsow and Marcello Stamm, eds., *Konstellationsforschung*, Frankfurt, 2005, 74–97.

"A German Spinozistic Reader of Cudworth, Bull and Spencer: Johann Georg Wachter and his Theologia Martyrum (1712)," in Christopher Ligota und Jean-Louis Quantin, eds., *History of Scholarship*, Oxford, 2006, 357–383.

"Idolatry and Science. Against Nature Worship from Boyle to Rüdiger, 1680–1720," *Journal of the History of Ideas* 67 (2006), 697–711.

"Sintflut und Gedächtnis. Hermann von der Hardt und Nicolas-Antoine Boulanger," in Martin Mulsow and Jan Assmann, eds., *Sintflut und Gedächtnis. Erinnern und Vergessen des Ursprungs*, Munich, 2006, 131–161.

"Den 'Heydnischen Saurteig' mit den 'Israelitischen Süßteig' vermengt: Kabbala, Hellenisierungsthese und Pietismusstreit bei Abraham Hinckelmann und Johann Peter Späth," *Scientia Poetica* 11 (2007), 1–50.

Die unanständige Gelehrtenrepublik. Wissen, Libertinage und Kommunikation in der Frühen Neuzeit, Stuttgart, 2007.

"Die Transmission verbotenen Wissens," in Ulrich Johannes Schneider, ed., *Kulturen des Wissens im 18. Jahrhundert*, Berlin, 2008, 61–80.

"Esoterik versus Aufklärung? Vermessung des intellektuellen Feldes anhand einer Kabale zwischen Weißmüller, den Gottscheds und Ludovici," in Monika Neugebauer-Wölk, ed., *Aufklärung und Esoterik. Rezeption – Integration – Konfrontation*, Berlin, 2009, 331–376.

"Das Vollkommene als Faszinosum des Sozialimaginären," in Aleida Assmann and Jan Assmann, eds., *Vollkommenheit. Archäologie der literarischen Kommunikation X*, Munich, 2010, 185–200.

"Der Wolffianer Christian Gabriel Fischer und seine Vernünftigen Gedanken über die Natur," in Jürgen Stolzenberg and Oliver-Pierre Rudolph eds.,

Christian Wolff und die europäische Aufklärung, Part 5, Hildesheim, 2010, 145–162.

"Exil, Kulturkontakt und Ideenmigration in der Frühen Neuzeit," in Herbert Jaumann, ed., *Diskurse der Frühen Neuzeit*, Berlin, 2010, 441–464.

"Harpocratism. Gestures of Retreat in Early Modern Germany," *Common Knowledge* 16 (2010), 110–127.

"Mikrogramme des Orients. Johann Christoph Wolfs Notizhefte und seine Cudworth-Lektüre," in Denis Thouard, ed., *Philologie als Wissensmodell*, Berlin, 2010, 345–396.

"Moses omniscius oder Moses politicus? Moses-Deutungen des 17. Jahrhunderts zwischen sakraler Enzyklopädik und libertinistischer Kritik," in Andreas B. Kilcher and Philipp Theisohn, eds., *Die Enzyklopädik der Esoterik. Allwissenheitsmythen und universalwissenschaftliche Modelle in der Esoterik der Neuzeit*, Munich, 2010, 177–202.

"Religionsgeschichte in Helmstedt," in Jens Bruning and Ulrike Gleixner, eds., *Das Athen der Welfen. Die Reformuniversität Helmstedt 1576–1810*, Wolfenbüttel, 2010, 182–189.

"Socinianism, Islam and the Radical Uses of Arabic Scholarship," *Al-Qantara* 31 (2010), 549–586.

"Paalzow, Lessing und die *Historische Einleitung in die Offenbarung Johannis*," in Christoph Bultmann and Friedrich Vollhardt, ed., *Lessings Religionsphilosophie im Kontext. Hamburger Fragmente und Wolfenbütteler Axiomata*, Berlin, 2011, 337–347.

"Der Silen von Helmstedt," in Franke Berndt and Daniel Fulda, eds., *Die Sachen der Aufklärung*, Hamburg, 2012, 300–313.

"Henry Stubbe, Robert Boyle and the Idolatry of Nature," in Sarah Mortimer and John Robertson, eds., *The Intellectual Consequences of Religious Heterodoxy 1600–1750*, Leiden, 2012, 121–134.

"Josephe.-F. Lafitau und die Entdeckung der Religions- und Kulturvergleiche," in Maria Effinger, Ulrich Pfisterer and Cornelia Logemann, eds., *Götterbilder und Götzendiener in der Frühen Neuzeit*, Heidelberg, 2012, 37–48.

"Eine unwahrscheinliche Begegnung. Siegmund Ferdinand Weißmüller trifft Christian Wolff in Marburg," in Monika Neugebauer-Wölk et al., eds., *Aufklärung und Esoterik. Wege in die Moderne*, Berlin, 2013, 183–207.

"Joseph als natürlicher Vater Christi. Ein unbekanntes clandestines Manuskript des frühen 18. Jahrhunderts," *Aufklärung* 25 (2013), 73–112.

"Politische Bukolik. Hermann von der Hardts Geheimbotschaften," *Zeitschrift für Ideengeschichte* 7(4) (2013), 103–116.

"Nikolaus Hieronymus Gundling," in Helmut Holzhey and Vilem Mudroch, eds., *Grundriss der Geschichte der Philosophie – Die Philosophie des 18. Jahrhunderts*, vol. 5(1), Basel, 2014, 67–71.

"Radikalaufklärung, moderate Aufklärung und die Dynamik der Moderne," in Jonathan Israel and Martin Mulsow, eds., *Radikalaufklärung*, Berlin, 2014, 203–233.

"Tempel, Münzen und der Transfer von Bildern: Zur Rolle der numismatischen Illustration im religionsgeschichtlichen Antiquarianismus," in Sabine Frommel and Eckhard Leuschner, eds., *Architektur- und Ornamentgraphik der Frühen Neuzeit: Migrationsprozesse in Europa / Gravures d'architecture et d'ornement au début de l'époque moderne: processus de migration en Europe*, Rome, 2014, 295–312.

"Impartiality, Individualisation, and the Historiography of Religion: Tobias Pfanner on the Rituals of the Ancient Church," in Bernd-Christian Otto, Susanne Rau and Jörg Rüpke, eds., *History and Religion: Narrating a Religious Past*, Berlin, 2015, 257–268.

Moderne aus dem Untergrund. Radikale Frühaufklärung in Deutschland, 1680–1720, Hamburg, 2003; tr. H. C. Erik Midelfort, *Enlightenment Underground: Radical Germany, 1680–1720*, Charlottesville, 2015.

"Vor Adam. Ideengeschichte jenseits der Eurozentrik," *Zeitschrift für Ideengeschichte* 9 (2015), 47–66.

"John Selden in Germany. Religion and Natural Law from Boecler to Buddeus (1665–1695)," in Ann Blair and Anja-Silvia Goeing, eds., *For the Sake of Learning: Essays in Honor of Anthony Grafton*, Leiden, 2016, 286–308.

"Heumanns Eisenacher Naturrechts-Kolleg von 1713. Eine vorläufige Skizze," in Mulsow, Kasper Risbjerg Eskildsen, and Helmut Zedelmaier, eds., *Christoph August Heumann (1681–1764). Gelehrte Praxis zwischen christlichem Humanismus und Aufklärung*, Stuttgart, 2017, 127–137.

"The Bible as Secular Story: The Northern War and King Josias as Interpreted by Hermann von der Hardt (1660–1746)," in Dirk van Miert et al., eds., *Scriptural Authority and Biblical Criticism in the Dutch Golden Age. God's Word Questioned*, Oxford, 2017, 351–373.

"Transnational Dissidence. Samuel Crell's Socinian Exile," in Yosef Kaplan, ed., *Early Modern Ethnic and Religious Communities in Exile*, Cambridge, 2017, 94–116.

"The Seventeenth-Century Confronts the Gods: Bishop Huet, Moses, and the Pagans," in Martin Mulsow and Asaph Ben-Tov, eds., *Knowledge and Profanation. Transgressing the Boundaries of Religion in Premodern Scholarship*, Leiden 2019, 159–196.

Prekäres Wissen. Eine andere Ideengeschichte der Frühen Neuzeit, Berlin, 2012. English tr., *Knowledge Lost: A New View on Early Modern Intellectual History*, tr. H. C. Erik Midelfort, Princeton, 2022.

Mulsow, Martin and Claudia Schmitz, "Eigennutz, Statuserhaltung und Naturzustand. Tradierungen des ethisch-politischen Epikureismus vom 15. bis zum 17. Jahrhundert," in Gianni Paganini and Edoardo Tortarolo, eds., *Der Garten und die Moderne. Epikureiche Moral und Politik vom Humanismus bis zur Aufklärung*, Stuttgart, 2004, 47–86.

Mulsow, Martin, ed., *Kriminelle – Freidenker – Alchemisten. Räume des Untergrunds in der Frühen Neuzeit*, Cologne, 2014

Mulsow, Martin and Frank Rexrodt, eds., *Was als wissenschaftlich gelten darf. Praktiken der Grenzziehung in Gelehrtenmilieus der Vormoderne*, Frankfurt, 2014.

Mulsow, Martin and Marcelo Stamm, eds., *Konstellationsforschung*, Frankfurt, 2005.

Mulsow, Martin, Kasper Ribjerg Eskilsen, and Helmut Zedelmaier, eds., *Christoph August Heumann (1681–1764). Gelehrte Praxis zwischen christlichem Humanismus und Aufklärung*, Stuttgart, 2017.

Mulsow, Martin and Richard H. Popkin, eds., *Secret Conversions to Judaism in Early Modern Europe*, Leiden, 2004.

Mungello, David E., *Curious Land. Jesuit Accommodation and the Origins of Sinology*, Honolulu, 1989.

Napoli, Giovanni di, *L'immortalità dell' anima nel Rinascimento*, Torino, 1963.

Nardi, Bruno, *Studi su P. Pomponazzi*, Florence, 1965.

Negt, Oskar, *Geschichte und Eigensinn*, Frankfurt, 1993.

Nellen, Henk, *Hugo Grotius: A Lifelong Struggle for Peace in Church and State, 1583–1645*, Leiden, 2014.

Nelson, Eric, *The Hebrew Republic: Jewish Sources and the Transformation of European Political Thought*, Cambridge, MA, 2010.

Netanyahu, Benzion, *Don Isaac Abravanel, Statesman & Philosopher*, Philadelphia, 1953.

Newman, William R., *Atoms and Alchemy: Chymistry and the Experimental Origins of the Scientific Revolution*, Chicago, 2006.

Nicolson, Marjorie Hope, *Mountain Gloom and Mountain Glory: The Development of the Aesthetics of the Infinite*, Ithaca, N.Y., 1959.

Niewöhner, Friedrich, *Veritas sive varietas. Lessings Toleranzparabel und das Buch von den drei Betrügern*, Heidelberg, 1988.

Niewöhner, Friedrich, ed., *Die Seele der Tiere*, Wiesbaden, 2001.

Nikitinski, Oleg, *Gian Vincenzo Gravina nel contesto dell' umanesimo europeo*, Naples, 2013.

Nischan, Bodo, "John Bergius: Irenicism and the Beginnings of Official Religious Toleration in Brandenburg-Prussia," *Church History* 51 (1982), 389–406.

   Prince, People, and Confession. The Second Reformation in Brandenburg, Philadelphia, 1994.

Noack, Lothar and Jürgen Splett, *Bio-Bibliographien – Brandenburgische Gelehrte der Frühen Neuzeit. Berlin-Cölln, 1640–1688*, Berlin, 2001.

Nobis, Heribert M., "Die Bedeutung der Leibnizschrift 'De ipsa natura' im Lichte ihrer begriffsgeschichtlichen Voraussetzungen," *Zeitschrift für philosophische Forschung* 20 (1966), 525–538.

Nolde, Dorothea, *Grenzüberschreitende Familienbeziehungen: Akteure und Medien des Kulturtransfers in der frühen Neuzeit*, Cologne, Weimar, and Vienna, 2008.

Nooijen, Annemarie, *"Unserm grossen Bekker ein Denkmal"? Balthasar Bekkers Betoverde Weereld in den deutschen Landen zwischen Orthodoxie und Aufklärung*, Münster, 2009.

Nüssel, Friederike, *Bund und Versöhnung. Zur Begründung der Dogmatik bei Johann Franz Buddeus. Forschungen zur systematischen und ökumenischen Theologie*, Göttingen, 1996.

Nutton, Vivian, "Wittenberg Anatomy," in Peter Ole Gell and Andrew Cunningham, eds., *Medicine and Reformation*, London, 1993, 11–32.

Obdrzalek, Suzanne, "Living in Doubt: Carneades' Pithanon Reconsidered," *Oxford Studies in Ancient Philosophy* 31 (2006), 243–279.

Oberhänsli-Widmer, Gabrielle, "Moses/Moseslied/Mosesegen/Moseschriften," in TRE, vol. 23, Berlin, 1994, 330–357.

Othmer, Sieglinde C., *Berlin und die Verbreitung des Naturrechts in Europa*, Berlin, 1970.

Paasch, Kathrin, "La critica della civiltà nel Theophrastus redivivus. I. Natura e cultura," in Tullio Gregory et al., eds., *Ricerche su letteratura libertina e letteratura clandestina nel Seicento*, Florence, 1981, 49–82.

"Épicurisme et Philosophie au XVIIe siècle. Convention, utilité et droit selon Gassendi," *Studi filosofici* 12/13 (1989–90), 5–45.

"Hobbes, Gassendi et le De cive," in Miguel Benitez et al., eds., *Materia actuosa. Antiquité. Age Classique. Lumières. Mélanges en l'honneur d'Olivier Bloch*, Paris, 2000, 183–206.

Die Bibliothek des Johann Christian von Boineburg (1622–1672): ein Beitrag zur Bibliotheksgeschichte des Polyhistorismus, Berlin, 2005.

"Wie aus Gesetzgebern Betrüger werden. Eine philosophische Archäologie des 'radikalen' Libertinismus," in Jonahan I. Israel and Martin Mulsow, eds., *Radikalaufklärung*, Berlin, 2014, 49–91.

Paganini, Gianni *Introduzione alle filosofie clandestine*, Bari, 2008.

Palladini, Fiametta, *Samuel Pufendorf discepolo di Hobbes: per una reinterpretazione del giusnaturalismo moderno*, Bologna, 1990.

"Un nemico di Samuel Pufendorf: Johann Heinrich Boecler," *Jus Commune* 24 (1997), 133–152.

Die Berliner Hugenotten und der Fall Barbeyrac. Orthodoxe und "Sozianier" im Refuge (1685–1720), Leiden, 2011.

Park, Katherine, "The Organic Soul," in Charles B. Schmitt et al., eds., *The Cambridge History of Renaissance Philosophy*, Cambridge, 1992, 464–484.

Paschetto, Eugenia, *Pietro d'Abano, medico e filosofo*, Florence, 1984.

Pelletier, Arnaud, "Substances défendues: l'accès à la substance selon Christian Thomasius et l'enjeu métaphysique des échanges entre Leibniz et Gabriel Wagner," in Herbert Breger and Sven Erdner, ed., *Natur und Subjekt, IX. Internationaler Leibniz-Kongress*, vol. 3, Hanover, 2011, 821–830.

Petersen, Erik, *Johann Albert Fabricius. En Humanist i Europa*, 2 vols. Copenhagen, 1998.

Petzoldt, Klaus, *Der unterlegene Sieger: Valentin Ernst Löscher im absolutistischen Sachsen*, Leipzig, 2001.

Pietsch, Andreas, *Isaac La Peyrère. Bibelkritik, Philosemitismus und Patronage in der Gelehrtenrepublik des 17. Jahrhunderts*, Berlin, 2012.

Pingree, David, *The Thousands of Abū Ma'shar*, London, 1968.

Pintard, René, *Le libertinage érudit dans la première moitié du XVIIe siècle*, Paris, 1943.

Pitassi, Maria Cristina, *Entre croir et savoir. Le problème de la méthode critique chez Jean Le Clerc*, Leiden, 1987.

Pitt, Leonard, *A Small Moment of Great Illumination: Searching for Valentine Greatrakes, the Master Healer*, Washington, DC, 2006.

Plassmeyer, Peter and Sabine Siebel, eds., *Experimente mit dem Sonnenfeuer – Ehrenfried Walther von Tschirnhaus*, Dresden, 2001.

Pocock, John G. A., "Time, History and Eschatology in the Thought of Thomas Hobbes," in John H. Elliott and Helmut G. Koenigsberger, eds., *The Diversity of History*, Ithaca, N.Y., 1970, 149–198.

The Machiavellian Moment, Princeton, 1975.

Podach, Erich F., "Die Geschichte der *Christianismi restitutio* im Lichte ihrer Abschriften," in Bruno Becker, ed., *Autour de Michel Servet et de Sebastien Castellion*, Haarlem, 1953, 47–61.

Poliakov, Leon, *Geschichte des Antisemitismus*, vol. 5, Worms, 1983.

Popkin, Richard H., *The History of Scepticism from Erasmus to Spinoza*, Berkeley, 1979.

"Jewish Anti-Christian Arguments as a Source of Irreligion from the Seventeenth to the Early Nineteenth Century," in Michael Hunter and David Wootton, eds., *Atheism from the Reformation to the Enlightenment*, Oxford, 1992, 159–181.

"Some Unresolved Questions in the History of Scepticism: The Role of Jewish Anti-Christian Arguments in the Rise of Scepticism in Regard to Religion," in *The Third Force in Seventeenth-Century Thought*, Leiden, 1992, 222–235.

The Third Force in Seventeeth-Century Thought, Leiden, 1992.

"The Image of the Jew in Clandestine Literature circa 1700," in Guido Canziani, ed., *Filosofia e religione nella letteratura clandestina secoli XVII e XVIII*, Milan, 1994, 13–34.

The History of Scepticism from Savonarola to Bayle, Oxford, 2003.

Popkin, Richard H., ed., *Isaac La Peyrère (1596–1676): His Life, Work and Influence*, Leiden, 1987.

Pott, Martin, *Aufklärung und Aberglaube. Die deutsche Frühaufklärung im Spiegel ihrer Aberglaubenskritik*, Tübingen, 1992.

Pott [now: Richter], Sandra, *Medizin, Medizinethik und schöne Literatur*, Berlin, 2002 (*Säkularisierung in den Wissenschaften seit der Frühen Neuzeit*, vol. 1).

"'Le Bayle de l'Allemagne': Christian Thomasius und der europäische Refuge. Konfessionstoleranz in der wechselseitigen Rezeption für ein kritisches Bewahren von Tradition(en)," in Manfred Beetz and Herbert Jaumann, eds., *Thomasius im literarischen Feld*, Tübingen, 2003, 131–158.

Reformierte Morallehren und deutsche Literatur von Jean Barbeyrac bis Christoph Martin Wieland, Tübingen, 2003.

Predeek, Albert, "Ein verschollener Reorganisationsplan für die Universität Königsberg," *Altpreußische Forschungen* 4(2) (1927), 66–107.

"Ein vergessener Freund Gottscheds," *Mitteilungen der deutschen Gesellschaft für vaterländische Sprache und Alterenermer* 12 (1937), 109–123.

Primavesi, Oliver, "Medicine between Natural Philosophy and Physician's Practice: A Debate around 400 BC," in Susanna Elm et al., eds., *Quo Vadis Medical Healing: Past Concepts and New Apporaches*, Berlin, 2009, 29–40.

Proietti, Omero and Giovanni Licata, eds., *Il carteggio Van Gent-Tschirnhaus (1679–1690): Storia, cronistoria, contesto del "editio posthuma" spinoziana*, Macerata, 2013.

Prosperi, Adrano, *L'eresia del Libro Grande. Storia di Giorgio Siculo e della sua setta*, Milan, 2000.

Proß, Wolfgang, "Natur, Naturrecht und Geschichte. Zur Entwicklung der Naturwissenschaften und der sozialen Selbstinterpretation im Zeitalter des Naturrechts (1600–1800)," *Internationales Archiv für Geschichte der Literatur* 3 (1978), 38–67.

Ptaszyński, Maciej, "Das Ringen um Sicherheit der Protestanten in Polen-Litauen im 17. Jahrhundert," in Christoph Kampmann and Ulrich Niggemann, eds., *Sicherheit in der Frühen Neuzeit*, Cologne, 2013, 57–75.

Puster, Rolf W., *Britische Gassendi-Rezeption am Beispiel John Lockes*, Stuttgart, 1991.

Rademaker, Cornelis S. M., *Gerardus Joannes Vossius*, Zwolle, 1967.
Life and Work of Gerardus Joannes Vossius, Assen, 1981.

Rauschenbach, Sina, *Judentum für Christen. Vermittlung und Selbstbehauptung Menasseh Ben Israels in den gelehrten Debatten des 17. Jahrhunderts*, Berlin, 2012.

Ravid, Benjamin, *Economics and Toleration in Sixteenth Century Venice: The Background and Context of the Discorso of Simone Luzatto*, Jerusalem, 1978.

Reale, Giovanni and Roberto Radice, *La filosofia mosaica. Filone di Alessandria*, Milan, 1987.

Rebenich, Stefan, *Hieronymus und sein Kreis*, Stuttgart, 1992.

Rhein, Stephan, ed., *Melanchthon und die Naturwissenschaften*, Pforzheim, 1997.

Ricuperati, Giuseppe, "Il problema della corporeità dell' anima dai libertini ai deisti," in Sergio Bertelli, ed., *Il libertinismo in Europa*, Milan and Naples, 1980, 369–415.

Riedesel, Erich, *Pietismus und Orthodoxie in Ostpreußen*, Königsberg, 1937.

Robertson, Lesley et al., eds., *Antoni van Leeuwenhoek: Master of the Minuscule*, Leiden, 2016.

Rodríguez-Noriega Guillén, Lucia, ed., *Epicarmo de Siracusa. Testimonios y Fragmentos*, Oviedo, 1996.

Roling, Bernd, *Drachen und Sirenen. Die Rationalisierung und Abwicklung der Mythologie an den europäischen Universitäten*, Leiden, 2010.
Physica sacra. Wunder, Naturwissenschaft und historischer Schriftsinn zwischen Mittelalter und Früher Neuzeit, Leiden, 2013.

Rosenblatt, Jason P., *Renaissance England's Chief Rabbi: John Selden*, Oxford, 2006.

Rossi, Paolo, *The Dark Abyss of Time: The History of the Earth and the History of Nations from Hooke to Vico*, Chicago, 1984.

Roth, Cecil, *A Life of Menasseh ben Israel,* Philadelphia, 1934.
"The Mystery of the Resettlement," in *Essays and Portraits,* Philadelphia, 1962, 86–107 and 306–308.
Rubiés, Joan-Pau, "Theology, Ethnography, and the Historicization of Idolatry," *Journal of the History of Ideas* 67 (2006), 571–596.
Rudolf, Kurt, *Die Gnosis,* Leipzig, 1977.
Ruestow, Edward G., *The Microscope in the Dutch Republic: The Shaping of Discovery,* New York, 1996.
Rump, Johannes, *Melanchthons Psychologie in ihrer Abhängigkeit von Aristoteles und Galen,* Dissertation, Jena, 1897.
Rüping, Hinrich, *Die Naturrechtslehre des Christian Thomasius und ihre Fortbildung in der Thomasius-Schule,* Bonn, 1968.
Sailor, Danton B., "Moses and Atomism," *Journal of the History of Ideas* 25 (1964), 3–16.
Salatowsky, Sascha, *De anima. Die Rezeption der aristotelischen Psychologie im 16. und 17. Jahrhundert,* Amsterdam, 2006.
"Debatten um den Ursprung der Seele. Der Arianer Christoph Sand und sein lutherischer Kritiker Balthasar Bebel," *Morgen-Glantz* 24 (2014), 111–132.
Die Philosophie der Sozinianer. Transformationen zwischen Renaissance-Aristotelismus und Frühaufklärung, Stuttgart, 2015.
Salatowsky, Sascha and Winfried Schröder, eds., *Duldung religiöser Vielfalt – Sorge um die wahre Religion. Toleranzdebatten in der Frühen Neuzeit,* Stuttgart, 2016.
Samfiresco, Elvire, *Ménage polémiste, philologue, poète,* Paris, 1902.
Sangmeister, Dirk, *Vertrieben vom Feld der Literatur. Verbreitung und Unterdrückung der Werke von Friedrich Christian Laukhard,* Bremen, 2017.
Sargent, Rose-Mary, *The Diffident Naturalist: Robert Boyle and the Philosophy of Experiment,* Chicago, 1995.
Sauder, Gerhard, "Bayle-Rezeption in der deutschen Aufklärung (Mit einem Anhang: In Deutschland verlegte französische Bayle-Ausgaben und deutsche Übersetzungen Baylescher Werke)," *Deutsche Vierteljahresschrift für Literaturwissenschaft und Geistesgeschichte* 49 (1975), Sonderheft, 83*–104*.
Scattola, Merio, *Das Naturrecht vor dem Naturrecht. Zur Geschichte des "ius naturae" im 16. Jahrhundert,* Tübingen, 1999.
Dalla virtu alla Scienza. La fondazione e la trasformatione della disciplina politica nell'eta moderna, Milan, 2003.
"Geschichte aus dem Negativen. Christian Thomasius und die Historiographie des Fehlers und Vorurteils," in Martin Espenhorst, ed., *Unwissen und Missverständnisse im vormodernen Friedensprozeß,* Göttingen, 2013, 145–166.
Schäfer, Peter, *Jesus in the Talmud,* Princeton 2007.
Schaper, Annegret, *Ein langer Abschied vom Christentum. Johann Christian Edelmann (1698–1767) und die deutsche Frühaufklärung,* Marburg, 1996.
Scheller, Immanuel, *Lateinisch-Deutsches Wörterbuch,* 3rd edn., Leipzig, 1804.
Schepers, Heinrich, *Andreas Rüdigers Methodologie und ihre Voraussetzungen. Ein Beitrag zur deutschen Schulphilosophie im 18. Jahrhundert,* Cologne, 1959.

Schindler, Norbert, *Widerspenstige Leute. Studien zur Volkskultur in der frühen Neuzeit*, Frankfurt, 1992; English tr., Pamela Selwyn, *Rebellion, Community and Custom in Early Modern Germany*, Cambridge, 2002.

Schmale, Wolfgang, *Kulturtransfer. Kulturelle Praxis im 16. Jahrhundert*, Vienna, 2003.

Schmidt, Francis, "La discussion sur l'origine de l'idolatrie aux XVIIe et XVIIIe siècles," *L'idolatrie. Rencontres de l'École du Louvre*, Paris, 1990, 53–68.

Schmidt-Biggemann, Wilhelm, *Topica universalis. Eine Modellgeschichte humanistischer und barocker Wissenschaft*, Hamburg, 1983.

Philosophia perennis. Historische Umrisse abendländischer Spiritualität in Antike, Mittelalter und Früher Neuzeit, Frankfurt, 1998.

"Pietismus, Platonismus und Aufklärung. Christian Thomasius' Versuch vom Wesen des Geistes," in Frank Grunert and Friedrich Vollhardt, eds., *Aufklärung als praktische Philosophie. Werner Schneiders zum 65. Geburtstag*, Tübingen, 1998, 83–98.

"Die Historisierung der Philosophia Hebraeorum im frühen 18. Jahrhundert. Eine philosophisch-philologische Demontage," *Aporemata. Kritische Studien zur Philologiegeschichte* 5 (2001), 103–128.

"Hermes Trismegistos, Isis und Osiris in Athanasius Kirchers Oedipus Aegyptiacus," *Archiv für Religionsgeschichte* 3 (2001), 67–88.

"Die Entstehung der unitarischen Exegese und die philologische Destruktion des Trinitätsdogmas," in *Apokalypse und Philologie. Wissensgeschichten und Weltentwürfe der Frühen Neuzeit*, Göttingen, 2007, 79–122.

Geschichte der christlichen Kabbala, 4 vols. Stuttgart, 2012–2014.

Schmidt-Biggemann, Wilhelm, ed., *Christliche Kabbala. Johann Reuchlins Wirkung*, Siegmaringen, 2003.

Schmidt-Biggemann, Wilhelm and Theo Stammen, eds., *Jacob Brucker (1696–1770). Philosoph und Historiker der europäischen Aufklärung*, Berlin, 1998.

Schneewind, Jerome B., "No Discipline, No History: The Case of Moral Philosophy," in Donald R. Kelley, ed., *History and the Disciplines: The Reclassification of Knowledge in Early Modern Europe*, Rochester, 1997, 127–142.

The Invention of Autonomy: A History of Modern Moral Philosophy, Cambridge, 1998.

Schneider, Hans-Peter, *Justitia universalis. Quellenstudien zur Geschichte des "christlichen Naturrechts" bei Gottfried Wilhelm Leibniz*, Frankfurt, 1967.

Schneiders, Werner, *Naturrecht und Liebesethik. Zur Geschichte der praktischen Philosophie im Hinblick auf Christian Thomasius*, Hildesheim, 1971.

Aufklärung und Vorurteilskritik. Studien zur Geschichte der Vorurteilstheorie, Stuttgart, 1983.

Hoffnung auf Vernunft. Aufklärungsphilosophie in Deutschland, Hamburg, 1990.

Scholder, Klaus, *Ursprünge und Probleme der Bibelkritik im 17. Jahrhundert. Ein Beitrag zur Entstehung der historisch-kritischen Theologie*, Munich, 1966.

Scholten, Clemens, "Karpokrates (Karpokratianer)," *Reallexikon für Antike und Christentum* vol. 20, Stuttgart, 2004, 173–186.

Schöpflin, Karin, "Seele. II. Altes Testament," in TRE, vol. 30, Berlin, 1999, 737–740.

Schrenk, Gottlob, *Gottesreich und Bund im älteren Protestantismus vornehmlich bei Johannes Coccejus. Ein Beitrag zur Geschichte des Pietismus und der heilsgeschichtlichen Theologie*, Gütersloh, 1923; repr. Gießen and Basel, 1985.

Schröder, Peter, *Christian Thomasius*, Hamburg, 1999.

Schröder, Winfried, "Einleitung," in Johann Georg Wachter, *Der Spinozismus im Jüdenthumb* [originally Amsterdam, 1699], with an intro. by Winfried Schröder, Stuttgart, 1994, 14f.

Spinoza in der deutschen Frühaufklärung, Würzburg, 1987.

"Einleitung," in Johann Georg Wachter, *De Primordiis Christianae Religionis (1703/1717) – Origines Juris Naturalis (1704) – Elucidarius Cabalisticus (1706) (Freidenker Der Europaischen Aufklarung)*, ed. Winfried Schröder, Stuttgart, 1995.

Ursprünge des Atheismus. Untersuchungen zur Metaphysik- und Religionskritik des 17. und 18. Jahrhunderts, Stuttgart, 1999.

"Il contesto storico, la datazione, gli autori e l'influenza su pensiero dell' epoca," in *Cymbalum mundi sive Symbolum sapientiae*, critical edition, ed. Guido Canziani, Winfried Schröder, and Francisco Socas, Milan, 2000, 9–35.

Athen und Jerusalem. Die philosophische Kritik am Christentum in Spätantike und Neuzeit, Stuttgart, 2011.

Schubert, Anselm, *Das Ende der Sünde. Anthropologie und Erbsünde zwischen Reformation und Aufklärung*, Göttingen, 2002.

Schulze, Hans-Joachim, "Texte und Textdichter" in *Die Welt der Bach-Kantaten*, vol. 3, ed. Christoph Wolff, Stuttgart, 1998/1999, chapter 6.

Schulze, Winfried, "Die Entstehung des nationalen Vorurteils. Zur Kultur der Wahrnehmung fremder Nationen in der europäischen Frühen Neuzeit," in Wolfgang Schmale, ed., *Menschen und Grenzen in der Frühen Neuzeit*, Berlin, 1998, 23–49.

Schunka, Alexander, "Konfession und Migrationsregime in der Frühen Neuzeit," in Ute Frevert and Jochen Oltmer, eds., *Europäische Migrationsregime* (*Geschichte und Gesellschaft*, 35(1) (2009)), Göttingen, 2009, 28–63.

Schwarzbach, Bertram, "Les adversaires de la Bible," in Yvon Belaval, ed., *Le siècle des Lumières et la Bible*, Paris, 1986.

Schwerhoff, Gerd, *Zungen wie Schwerter. Blasphemie in alteuropäischen Gesellschaften 1200–1650*, Konstanz, 2005.

Scribano, Maria Emmanuela, *Da Descartes a Spinoza. Percorsi della teologia razionale nel Seicento*, Milan, 1988.

Seifert, Arno, "Staatenkunde. Eine neue Disziplin und ihr wissenschaftstheoretischer Ort," in Mohammed Rassem and Justin Stagl, eds., *Statistik und Staatsbeschreibung in der Neuzeit, vornehmlich im 16.–18. Jahrhundert*, Paderborn, 1980, 217–248.

Septimus, Bernard, "Biblical Religion and Political Rationality in Simone Luzzatto, Maimonides and Spinoza," in Isadore Twersky, ed., *Studies in Medieval Jewish History and Literature*, vol. 2, Cambridge, MA, 1984, 143–170.

Shalev, Zur, *Sacred Words and Worlds: Geography, Religion, and Scholarship, 1550–1700*, Leiden, 2011.

Shapin, Stephen, *A Social History of Truth: Civility and Science in Seventeenth-Century England*, Chicago, 1994.

Shapiro, Barbara J., *Probability and Certainty in Seventeenth-Century England: A Study of the Relationships between Natural Science, Religion, History, Law and Literature*, Princeton, 1983.

Shaver, Robert, "Grotius on Scepticism and Self-Interest," *Archiv für Geschichte der Philosophie* 78 (1996), 27–47.

Sheehan, Jonathan, *The Enlightenment Bible. Translation, Scholarship, Culture*, Princeton, 2005.

"The Altars of the Idols: Religion, Sacrifice, and the Early Modern Polity," *Journal of the History of Ideas* 67 (2006), 648–674.

Shelford, April G., "François de La Mothe le Vayer and the Defence of Pagan Virtue," *The Seventeenth Century* 15 (2000), 67–89.

Transforming the Republic of Letters: Pierre-Daniel. Huet and European Intellectual Life 1650–1720, Rochester, NY, 2007.

Simon, József, *Die Religionsphilosophie Christian Franckens (1522–1610?): Atheismus und radikale Reformation im frühneuzeitlichen Ostmitteleuropa*, Wiesbaden, 2008.

Simons, Olaf, "Von der Respublica Literaria zum Literaturstaat? Überlegungen zur Konstitution des Literarischen," *Aufklärung* 26 (2014), 291–330.

Simonutti, Luisa, *Arminianesimo e tolleranza nel Seicento olandese. Il carteggio Ph. Van Limborch – J. Le Clerc*, Florence, 1984.

"Resistance, Obedience and Toleration: Przypkowski and Limborch," in Martin Mulsow and Jan Rohls, eds., *Socinianism and Arminianism*, Leiden, 2005, 187–206.

Siraisi, Nancy G., "Hermes among the Physicians," in Martin Mulsow, ed., *Das Ende des Hermetismus*, Tübingen, 2002, pp. 189–212.

Smith, Pamela H., *The Business of Alchemy: Science and Culture in the Holy Roman Empire*, Princeton, 1994.

Spalding, Paul, "Der rätselhafte Tutor bei Hermann Samuel Reimarus. Begegnung zweier radikaler Aufklärer in Hamburg," *Zeitschrift des Vereins für Hamburgische Geschichte* 87 (2001), 49–64.

Sparn, Walter, "Omnis nostra fides pendet ab Historia. Erste Beobachtungen zum theologischen Profil des Hildesheimer Superintendenten Jakob Friedrich Reimmann," in Martin Mulsow and Helmut Zedelmaier, eds., *Skepsis, Providenz, Polyhistorie. Jakob Friedrich Reimmann (1668–1743)*, Tübingen, 1998, 76–94.

Spink, John S., *French Free-Thought from Gassendi to Voltaire*, London, 1960.

Splett, Jürgen, "Becmann," in Lothar Noack and Jürgen Splett, eds., *Bio-Bibliographien Brandenburgischer Gelehrter der Frühen Neuzeit. Mark Brandenburg 1640–1713*, vol. 3, Berlin, 2001, 36–60.

Spoerhase, Carlos and Kai Bremer, eds., *Gelehrte Polemik: Intellektuelle Konfliktverschärfungen um 1700*, Frankfurt, 2011.

"Theologisch-polemisch-poetische Sachen": *Gelehrte Polemik im 18. Jahrhundert*, Frankfurt, 2015.

Stamm, Marcelo, "Konstellationsforschung – Ein Methodenprofil: Motive und Perspektiven," in Martin Mulsow and Marcelo Stamm, eds., *Konstellationsforschung*, Frankfurt, 2005, 31–73.

Starkloff, Carl F., *Common Testimony. Ethnology and Theology in the "Customs" of Joseph Lafitau*, St. Louis, 2002.

Stausberg, Michael, *Faszination Zarathushtra. Zoroaster und die Europäische Religionsgeschichte der Frühen Neuzeit*, Berlin and New York, 1998.

Steiger, Johann Anselm, "Die Rezeption der rabbinischen Tradition im Luthertum (Johann Gerhard, Salomo Glassius u. a.) und im Theologiestudium des 17. Jahrhunderts. Mit einer Edition des universitären Studienplanes von Glassius und einer Bibliographie der von ihm konzipierten Studentenbibliothek," in Christiane Caemmerer et al., eds., *Das Berliner Modell der Mittleren Deutschen Literatur. Beiträge zur Tagung Kloster Zinna 29.9.–01.10.1997 (= Chloe 33)*, Amsterdam, 2000, 191–252.

Steiner, Uwe, *Poetische Theodizee. Philosophie und Poesie in der lehrhaften Dichtung im achtzehnten Jahrhundert*, Munich, 2000.

Steneck, Nicholas H., "Greatrakes the Stroker: The Interpretations of Historians," *Isis* 73 (1982), 161–177.

Stiehler, Gottfried, *Materialisten der Leibniz-Zeit. Ausgewählte Texte*, East Berlin, 1966.

Stiehler, Gottfried, ed., *Beiträge zur Geschichte des vormarxistischen Materialismus*, East Berlin, 1961.

Stiening, Gideon, "Deus vult aliquas esse certas noticias. Philipp Melanchthon, Rudolph Goclenius und das Konzept der notitiae naturales in der Psychologie des 16. Jahrhunderts," in Barbara Bauer, ed., *Melanchthon und die Marburger Professoren (1527–1627)*, Marburg, 1999, vol. 2, 757–787.

Stolberg, Michael, "Die Lehre vom 'calor innatus' im lateinischen Canon medicinae des Avicenna," *Sudhoffs Archiv* 77 (1993), 33–53.

"Lykanthropie," *Der Neue Pauly*, vol. 15(1): *Wissenschafts- und Rezeptionsgeschichte*, ed. Manfred Landfester, Stuttgart and Weimar, 2001, cols. 243–246.

"Particles of the soul. The medical and Lutheran context of Daniel Sennert's atomism," *Medicina nei secoli* 15 (2003), 177–203.

Stolleis, Michael, *Geschichte des öffentlichen Rechts in Deutschland*, vol. 1: *Reichspublizistik und Policeywissenschaft 1600–1800*, Munich, 1988.

Stolzenberg, Daniel, *Egyptian Oedipus: Athanasius Kircher and the Secrets of Antiquity*, Chicago, 2013.

Stolzenburg, Arnold F., *Die Theologie des J. F. Buddeus und des Ch. M. Pfaff. Ein Beitrag zur Geschichte der Aufklärung in Deutschland*, Berlin, 1926; repr. Aalen, 1979.

Straumann, Benjamin, *Hugo Grotius und die Antike*, Baden-Baden, 2007.

Roman Law in the State of Nature: The Classical Foundations of Hugo Grotius' Natural Law, Cambridge, 2015.

Strauß, David Friedrich, *Das Leben Jesu, kritisch bearbeitet*, Erlangen, 1836.

Strauss, Leo, *Persecution and the Art of Writing*, Glencoe, 1952.

Stroumsa, Guy G., *A New Science: The Discovery of Religion in the Age of Reason*, Cambridge, MA, 2010.

Stroumsa, Sarah, *Freethinkers in Medieval Islam: Ibn al-Rāwandī, Abū Baks al-Rāzī, and Their Impact on Islamic Thought*, Leiden, 1999.

Suitner, Riccarda, "Jus naturae und natura humana in August Friedrich Müllers handschriftlichem Kommentar zu Andreas Rüdigers Institutiones eruditionis," *Aufklärung* 25 (2013), 113–132.

Sutcliffe, Adam, *Judaism and Enlightenment*, Cambridge, 2003.

Szydlo, Zbigniew, *Water which Does Not Wet Hands: The Alchemy of Michael Sendivogius*, London and Warsaw, 1994.

Taatz-Jacobi, Marianne, *Erwünschte Harmonie. Die Gründung der Friedrichs-Universität Halle als Instrument Brandenburg-Preußischer Konfessionspolitik – Motive, Verfahren, Mythos (1680–1713)*, Berlin, 2014.

Tardieu, Michel, "Sabiens Coraniques et 'Sabiens' de Harran," *Journal Asiatique* 274 (1986), 1–44.

Taussig, Silvie, *Pierre Gassendi (1592–1655). Instroduction à la vie savante*, Turnhout, 2003.

Taylor, Charles, *Sources of the Self: The Making of the Modern Identity*, Cambridge, MA, 1989.

Tazbir, Janusz, *Bracia Polscy w Siedmiogrodzie, 1660–1784*, Warsaw, 1964.

Thadden, Rudolf von, *Die brandenburgisch-preussischen Hofprediger im 17. und 18. Jahrhundert. Ein Beitrag zur Geschichte der absolutistischen Staatsgesellschaft in Brandenburg-Preußen*, Berlin, 1959.

Thomas, Margaret D., "Michel de la Roche: A Huguenot Critic of Calvin," *Studies on Voltaire and the Eighteenth Century* 238 (1985), 97–196.

Thomson, Ann, *Bodies of Thought: Science, Religion, and the Soul in the Early Enlightenment*, Oxford, 2008.

Tilton, Hereward, *The Quest for the Phoenix: Spiritual Alchemy and Rosicrucianism in the Work of Count Michael Maier (1569–1622)*, Berlin, 2003.

Tomasoni, Francesco, *Christian Thomasius. Geist und kulturelle Identität an der Schwelle zur europäischen Aufklärung*, tr. Gunnhild Schneider, Münster, 2009.

Toomer, Gerald, *John Selden: A Life in Scholarship*, Oxford, 2009.

Traninger, Anita, *Disputation, Deklamation, Dialog. Medien und Gattungen europäischer Wissensverhandlungen zwischen Scholastik und Humanismus*, Stuttgart, 2012.

Treske, Erika, *Der Rosenkreuzerroman Le Comte de Gabalis und die geistigen Strömungen des 17. und 18. Jahrhunderts*, Greifswald, 1933.

Trombley, Frank R., *Hellenic Religion and Christianization c. 370–529*, 2 vols. Leiden, 1993 and 1994.

Tuck, Richard, *Natural Right Theories*, Cambridge, 1979.

"Grotius, Carneades, and Hobbes," *Grotiana* n.s. 4 (1983), 43–62.

"The Modern Theory of Natural Law," in Anthony Pagden, ed., *The Languages of Political Theory in Early Modern Europe*, Cambridge, 1988, 235–263.

Hobbes, Oxford, 1989.

Tutino, Stefania, *Shadows of Doubt: Language and Truth in Post-Reformation Catholic Culture*, Oxford, 2014.

Urvoy, Dominique, *Ibn Rushd*, London, 1991.

Les penseurs libres dans l'Islam classique, Paris, 1996.

Valente, Luisa, "Le principe de l'approche contextuelle et sa genèse," in Joel Biard and Irène Rosier-Catach, eds., *La tradition médiévale des catégories (XIIe–XVe siècles)*, Louvain, 2003, 288–311.

Vandenbosche, Hubert and Jeroom Vercruysse, "Charles Le Cène: un Traducteur peu commun," in Andreas Wissowatius, *Religio rationalis*, ed. Zbigniew Ogonowski, Wiesbaden, 1982, 63–66.

Vasoli, Cesare, "Riflessioni sul 'problema' Vanini," in Sergio Bertelli, ed., *Il libertinismo in Europa*, Milan and Naples, 1980, 125–168.

Vercruysse, Jerome, "Crellius, Le Cène, Naigeon ou les chemins de la tolérance socinienne," *Tijdschrift voor de Studie van de Verlichting* 1 (1973), 244–320.

"Bibliotheca Fratrum Polonorum. Histoire et Bibliographie," *Odrodzenie i Reformacja w Polsce* 21 (1975), 197–212.

Verdigi, Mariano, *Simone Simoni. Filosofo e medico del '500*, Lucca, 1997.

Vermeulen, Corinna L., "Strategies and Slander in the Protestant Part of the Republic of Letters, Image, Friendship and Patronage in Etienne de Courcelles' Correspondence," in Toon van Haal et al. eds., *Self-Presentation and Social Identification: The Rhetoric and Pragmatics of Letter Writing in Early Modern Times*, Leuven, 2002, 247–280.

Voet, Leon, *The Golden Compasses. The History of the House Plantin-Moretus*, 2 vols., Amsterdam, 1969.

Vollhardt, Friedrich, "Die Grundregel des Naturrechts. Definitionen und Konzepte in der Unterrichts- und Kommentarliteratur der deutschen Aufklärung," in Frank Grunert and Friedrich Vollhardt, eds., *Aufklärung als praktische Philosophie. Werner Schneiders zum 65. Geburtstag*, Tübingen, 1998, 129–147.

Christian Thomasius (1655–1728). Neue Forschungen im Kontext der Frühaufklärung, Tübingen, 1997.

Selbstliebe und Geselligkeit. Untersuchungen zum Verhältnis von naturrechtlichem Denken und moraldidaktischer Literatur im 17. und 18. Jahrhundert, Tübingen, 2001.

Wade, Ira O., *The Clandestine Organization and Diffusion of Philosophic Ideas in France from 1700 to 1750*, Princeton, 1938.

Walker, Daniel P., *The Decline of Hell: Seventeenth-Century Discussions of Eternal Torment*, London, 1964.

Wallmann, Johannes, "Pietismus und Sozinianismus. Zu Philipp Jakob Speners antisozinianischen Schriften," in *Theologie und Frömmigkeit im Zeitalter des Barock. Gesammelte Aufsätze*, Tübingen, 1995, 282–294.

"Philipp Jakob Spener und György Enyedi," in *Pietismus und Orthodoxie. Gesammelte Aufsätze III*, Tübingen, 2010, 277–290.

Waquet, Françoise, ed., *Mapping the World of Learning: The "Polyhistor" of Daniel Georg Morhof*, Wiesbaden, 2000.

Watkins, Eric, "The Development of Physical Influx in Early Eighteenth-Century Germany: Gottsched, Knutzen, and Crusius," *The Review of Metaphysics* 49 (1995), 295–340.

Weber, Wolfgang, *Prudentia gubernatoria. Studien zur Herrschaftslehre in der deutschen politischen Wissenschaft des 17. Jahrhunderts*, Tübingen, 1992.

Weeks, Kent, *The lost Tomb*, London, 1998.

Weigl, Engelhard, *Schauplätze der deutschen Aufklärung*, Hamburg, 1997.

Wessinghage, Dieter, *Die Hohe Schule Herborn und ihre medizinische Fakultät*, Stuttgart and New York, 1984.

Whaley, Joachim, *Germany and the Holy Roman Empire 1493–1806*, 2 vols., Oxford, 2012.

Whelan, Ruth, "The Wisdom of Simonides: Bayle and La Mothe le Vayer," in Richard H. Popkin and Arjo Vanderjagt, eds., *Scepticism and Irreligion in the Seventeenth and Eighteenth Centuries*, Leiden, 1993, 230–253.

Wilbur, Earl M., *A History of Unitarianism: Socinianism and its Antecedents*, Cambridge, MA, 1945.

A History of Unitarianism in Transylvania, England, and America to 1900, Cambridge, MA, 1952.

Wilde, Manfred, "Korrespondenten von G. W. Leibniz: Johann Caspar Westphal, geb. 28. November 1649 in Rügenwalde/Pommern – gest. 24. März 1722 in Delitzsch/Sachsen," *Studia leibnitiana* 38/39 (2008), 219–234.

Wille, Dagmar von, "Apologie häretischen Denkens. Johann Jakob Zimmermanns Rehabilitierung der 'Atheisten' Pomponazzi und Vanini," in Friedrich Niewöhner and Olaf Pluta, eds., *Atheismus im Mittelalter und in der Renaissance*, Wiesbaden, 1999, 29–44.

Williams, Arnold, *The Common Expositor: An Account of the Commentaries on Genesis 1527–1633*, Chapel Hill 1948.

Wilson, Catherine, "De ipsa natura: Leibniz on Substance, Force and Activity," *Studia leibnitiana* 19 (1987), 148–172.

Winiarczyk, Marek, "Der erste Atheistenkatalog des Kleitomachos," *Philologus* 120 (1976), 32–46.

Winston, David, "Moses in Hellenistic Literature," *Encyclopedia Judaica* 12 (1971), 388–393.

Winter, Eduard, *E. W. Tschirnhaus und die Frühaufklärung in Mittel- und Osteuropa*, Berlin, 1960.

Frühaufklärung. Der Kampf gegen den Konfessionalismus in Mittel- und Osteuropa und die deutsch-slawische Begegnung, East Berlin, 1966.

Wolff, Hans Walter, *Anthropologie des Alten Testaments*, ed. Bernd Janowski, Gütersloh, 2010.

Wolfson, Harry A., *The Philosophy of the Church Fathers*, vol. 1: *Faith, Trinity, Incarnation*, 2nd edn., Cambridge, MA, 1964.

"Plato's Preexistent Matter in Patristic Philosophy," in Luitpold Wallach, ed., *The Classical Tradition: Literary and Historical Studies in Honor of Harry Caplan*, New York, 1966, 409–420.

Wollgast, Siegfried, *Philosophie in Deutschland zwischen Reformation und Aufklärung 1550–1650*, 2nd edn., Berlin, 1993.

"Einleitung," in Gabriel Wagner, *Ausgewählte Schriften und Dokumente*, ed. Siegfried Wollgast, Stuttgart, 1997, 11f.

Wootton, David, "New Histories of Atheism," in Michael Hunter and David Wootton, eds., *Atheism from the Reformation to the Enlightenment*, Oxford, 1992, 13–53.

Wotschke, Theodor, "Die unitarische Gemeinde in Meseritz-Bobelwitz," *Zeitschrift der Historischen Gesellschaft für die Provinz Posen* 26 (1911), 161–223.

"Zur Geschichte der Unitarier in der Mark," *Jahrbuch für brandenburgische Kirchengeschichte* 7/8 (1911), 227–242.

Wrzecionko, Paul, ed., *Reformation und Frühaufklärung in Polen. Studien über den Sozinianismus und seinen Einfluß auf das westeuropäische Denken im 17. Jahrhundert*, Göttingen, 1977.

Zacharasiewics, Waldemar, *Die Klimatheorie in der englischen Literatur und Literaturkritik: Von der Mitte des 16. bis zum frühen 18. Jahrhundert*, Vienna, 1977.

Zagorin, Perez, "Hobbes without Grotius," *History of Political Thought* 21 (2000), 16–40.

Zambelli, Paola, "Pietro Pomponazzi's *De immortalitate* and his clandestine *De incantationibus*: Aristotelianism, eclecticism or libertinism?," *Bochumer Philosophisches Jahrbuch für Antike und Mittelalter* 6 (2001), 87–115.

White Magic, Black Magic in the European Renaissance, Leiden, 2007.

Zanier, Giancalo, *Ricerche sulla diffusione e fortuna del "De incantationibus" di Pomponazzi*, Florence, 1975.

Zedelmaier, Helmut, "Aporien frühaufgeklärter Gelehrsamkeit. Jakob Friedrich Reimmann und das Problem des Ursprungs der Wissenschaften," in Martin Mulsow and Helmut Zedelmaier, eds., *Skepsis, Providenz, Polyhistorie. Jakob Friedrich Reimmann (1668–1743)*, Tübingen, 1998, 97–129.

Der Anfang der Geschichte. Studien zur Ursprungsdebatte im 18. Jahrhundert, Hamburg, 2003.

Zenker, Kay, *Denkfreiheit. Libertas philosophandi in der deutschen Aufklärung*, Hamburg, 2012.

Ziskind, Jonathan R., "Petrus Cunaeus on Theocracy, Jubilee and the Latifundia," *The Jewish Quarterly Review*, New Ser. 68 (1978), 235–254.

Zurbuchen, Simone, *Naturrecht und natürliche Religion. Zur Geschichte des Toleranzbegriffs von Samuel Pufendorf bis Jean-Jacques Rousseau*, Würzburg, 1991.

Index

Abbadie, Jacques, 238
Abravanel, Isaak, 176, 180
Abū Ma'šar, 99
accommodation, theory of, 287, 289–290
Acoluthus, Andreas, 176
*Ad Paulum Martinum Noltenium [. . .] de vocatis
ab Adamo animalibus epistola*, 319
Alberti, Michael, 154
alchemy, 38, 276
Alexander of Aphrodisias, 19
Allix, Pierre, 239
Alsted, Johann Heinrich, 282, 284
Altdorf, University of, 127, 296–297, 307
Althusius, Johannes, 257
Âme matérielle, 24
Amerpoel. Johannes, 285
Amsterdam, 11, 248
  as fictitious location, 75
  as publishing and intellectual center, 14,
    221, 236, 241, 245, 252–253, 265–266,
    268
Anaximenes, 147
antitrinitarianism, 266
antitrinitarians, 304
Apologia pro Vanino, 77
Arianism, 334
  origins of radical thinking in, 227
Arias Montano, Benito, 282–283
Arminianism, 335
Arminians, 11, 236, 273
Arnoldi, Johann Conrad, 170
Arpe, Peter Friedrich, 12, 77, 270
Aslaksson, Kort, 280
Assmann, Jan, 295
atheism
  accusations of the ancients, 153
  in antiquity, 144
  as confusion of God and the world, 144
  danger of, 59, 333
  debates on, 73
  fear of, 76, 155

atomism. *See* corpuscularism
  Hobbes, 289
  origins, 288
August Pfeiffer, 176

Barbeyrac, Jean, 159–160, 217–218
Barnes, Annie, 233
Barth, Carl Friedrich, 336
Basson, Sebastien, 203
Bayle, Pierre, 127, 133–134, 161
  Continuation des pensées diverses (1680), 143
  idolatry, 104
Beaufort, Louis de, 285
Becher, Johann Joachim, 36, 58
Becmann, Friedrich, 265
Becmann, Johann Christoph, 178, 221, 242,
    257, 270, 335
  changing religious views, 261–264
Bekker, Balthasar, 76, 222
Bergius, Conrad, 240
Bergius, Georg Conrad, 241, 244
Bergius, Johann, 228, 241, 244, 249, 252, 270,
    274
Berigard, Claude, 203
Berlin, 11
  early Enlightenment, 273
Berlin, Consistory of, 225–226, 241, 244
Beverland, Adrian, 290
Beyer, Andreas, 176
Bible as a political text, 314
Bibliotheca Fratrum Polonorum, 230, 266–267
Blasius, Gerhard, Anatome animalium, 93
Blount, Charles, 22, 124, 287
Blumenbach, Johann, 117
Bochart, Samuel, 283, 319
Boecler, Johann Heinrich, 166, 174
Boineburg, Johann Christian von, 166–170
book burnings, 2, 8, 23, 223, 266–267, 269
Borch, Ole, 296
boundary work, directed against the theology
    faculty, 156